Te Ao o Meri

Tu tonu au i te taku tai
o te awa e rere nei ko Whanganui
kia whakarongo ake ki nga ia
e haruru mai nei
mehe wharauroa e tangi haere ana
tuparara te maru o te tangata

THE STORY OF

Suzanne

AUBERT

Jessie Munro

AUCKLAND UNIVERSITY PRESS

BRIDGET WILLIAMS BOOKS

First published in 1996 by Auckland University Press with Bridget Williams Books,
University of Auckland, Private Bag 92019, Auckland.

Reprinted 1997 (August, September), 1998

ISBN 1 86940 155 7

This book has been commissioned by the Daughters of Our Lady of Compassion
(the Sisters of Compassion), and published with the assistance of the
Historical Branch of the Department of Internal Affairs.

The author wishes to acknowledge the support of a Claude McCarthy Fellowship,
and residency at the Stout Research Centre for the study of New Zealand history,
society and culture, at Victoria University of Wellington.

Internal design by Afineline, Wellington
Typeset by Archetype, Wellington
Printed by GP Print, Wellington

To Kirsten and Ruth
and the memory of my father

And in memory of
Sister Philippine Dunne, Joan Akapita, Ruth Ross
Te Manihera Keremeneta, John McMahon, Antoine Séon

I have known only two of these people; one, Father Séon, died long ago.
They represent all the different people who have contributed
and carry on contributing to the story of Suzanne Aubert
through their love, knowledge, inspiration or strength.

Contents

Prologue

Of the church : O te whare karakia*
The bells begin to ring : Ka timata te tangi o te pere [1]

From high on Morikau sheep station up the Whanganui River valley there is a clear sightline down to Hiruharama. But at six in the morning, at the first sound of the angelus, it could still be dark. Or a white mist could be blanketing the whole settlement – the wharepuni, the cluster of houses, the church with its little shingled spire, the low, twin-gabled presbytery facing its verandah downstream, the convent standing a little aside, two-storeyed, added on. The banks of the river would still be bedded down. No line of waka, no mission boat tied up, no eel weirs, nothing seen, only the sound of the bell coming up the sheep-runnelled hills. At twelve, when it rang the second time, even though the mist had risen, the work day would be in full swing and dinner-time waiting, so noon down on the marae very likely went unnoticed by the Morikau stockmen.

But on a golden summer evening with the sun starting to lower over Taranaki there was time and enough light, when the bell rang for the third time, to look down and to listen. Eric Fisher used to do this when he worked up on Morikau:

> One of the most entrancing moments after the day's work, was to walk after tea from the Cook-house to a point adjacent to the Homestead, where you were hundreds of feet above the River and looked North West down on to the River where Hiruharama Pa (Jerusalem) nestled across the Mangoihe Stream. At 6 p.m. you would hear the Angelus ringing out, the sound of the bells from the Church drifting up to where you stood gazing at the Maoris who had been roaming round the Marae, and see them remain still with bowed head in prayer.[2]

When Eric Fisher came to Morikau and first watched the prayers down at the marae, it was 1915 and he was fifteen years old. By then the bell, punctuating the day with its call, had been heard for a long time at Hiruharama. Lots of people would have rung it. Rure Te Manihera Keremeneta rang it often. Even when he worked on the heights as a bullocky, he heard the morning bell and walked down the steep hillside and across the gully of the Mangoihe creek to the church. He hardly ever missed half-past-six Mass. And then he walked all the way back up again.[3] His voice in harmony with the priest's would be heard going along at the back of the church, 'not that loud and not that soft, it just sort of fits in with the flow of the Mass', putting 'the Maori on top of the Latin. The feeling was Maori'.[4] The bell was rung by other catechists, or by one of the sisters from the convent in the early morning, by the kids from the school at midday, or by the priest.

From the spire above the marae, the bell rang out clear enough to be heard on still days far away across the river in the Waitotara Valley. And it was heard four miles down the river in Ranana, depending on the way the wind was blowing. Three strokes of the bell, each followed by a pause for the Hail Mary, then nine more strokes to finish saying the prayer. The sound of the Jerusalem bell was stronger than the little, low Ranana bell. But around both places many people would stop and pray, wherever they were. In Jerusalem Weheora Wanihi, granddaughter of Taiwhati, said: 'There was six o'clock angelus. Prayers before church, prayers before dancing in the pa. . . . A prayer at seven p.m. And twelve o'clock, the angelus. We had to kneel, even on the tennis court,' she laughed, 'even if we were working in the garden.' The Ratana bell would go too, for choice, when Wehe was young. Many went to both Katorika prayers and Ratana prayers. Wehe's father used to ring the Ratana bell. She said that, wherever they could hear the bell, they somehow kept the angelus tradition. They even said it to themselves way up on the farm where she and her husband looked after the cherry orchard. 'We carried it in our own heart, in our own way.'[5]

It was the same in Ranana. Ani Haami, who inherited her Catholic faith from her parents, Taho Miriama Metera and Neri Metera, handed on the prayers to her mokopuna. Erina Scanlon remembered:

> She made sure that we all went to the church to say our prayers. And at six o'clock in the morning we all had to stand up and say the angelus, regardless of where you were. Standing beside our bed, she made sure we got used to it. It sort of became a habit. Six o'clock in the morning, twelve o'clock at lunchtime, six o'clock at night, angelus. Even when we were doing potatoes,

working in the garden, because we used to have big vegetable gardens and we had to work. Quite often, we'd cook up something out in the open, and forget that the embers are still hot, and kneel down and – 'Ow! the old knees!' No matter what we were doing, playing, stop! the angelus, and somebody will start it off and everybody will answer it, no matter where you are, everybody, stop.[6]

This book is the story of a woman who, like the priests, brought her Catholic faith from France. She had her turn in ringing the angelus bell. To Maori she was known as Meri, the 'none kuia', 'te whaea tapu', a 'wahine tino whakapono', a very holy lady. Pakeha called her a succession of names – Sister Mary Joseph, Sister Joseph, then Mother Mary Joseph, Mother Joseph, Mother Mary Aubert – before they finally settled on Mother Aubert as they stuck her into the albums of their history.

Old people like Neri Poutini, and Tamakehu who brought up Wehe, used to say Meri was a 'wahine kaha ki te mahi', a great worker. Hapai and Puke used to tell Ivan Emia about her riding around on a horse with her medicines: 'They said, "E tino pai, te kuia nei. Kei a ia te matauranga, te aroha me te tumanako." In her heart were kindness and love. She always wanted to help, ki te awhina, ki te manaki nga whanau o te awa. She was always very strong, no matter how far she went, and she was always loved by the people, by nga kuia up there and nga kaumatua. They said she was a pretty smart lady.' The old people talked about her 'moving around the people, getting to know the people and understanding. She wasn't afraid, so I believe, just listening to my great-grandmother. They used to say she used to mix a lot with the people, communicate with people, and I don't think she had much problem with that, just from what I used to hear.'

Meri was Suzanne Aubert and the people were right about her. She was a pretty smart lady and not afraid of much. She never did have much problem either with moving around, mixing and communicating with people. Long after she died Rure used to line the kids up, Erina among them, and talk about her. 'You more or less got it for breakfast, dinner and tea. Because when we used to be up at Jerusalem for Mass, for Benediction, he used to come out with: "Why don't some of you kids, tamariki, be like her, set an example?"'

A sense of example was what Joan Akapita, granddaughter of Te Huinga Mareikura, gained from the memories. 'As I grew up, I looked around and thought what a wonderful woman Mother Mary Aubert was because prayer was a regular part of life. She cared for them all. You didn't have to be a Katorika, a Ratana or whatever. It's by her actions and deeds that she showed her faith in God. She didn't save ten apples for Katorika, five for Mihinare, two for Ringatu, Presbyterians etc. She didn't push her Gospel down people's throats; she lived her Gospel.'[7]

The angelus bell had rung over the hills around Hiruharama before Suzanne ever went there. French priests and brothers had canoed up the river, climbed the steep tracks, dug gardens, built flour mills and chapels, and baptised Maori. For years, too, the angelus had been ringing in many other places in New Zealand. In 1860, when twenty-five-year-old Suzanne arrived in New Zealand, she walked into the ongoing action of a drama which had started the year after she was born.

CHAPTER ONE

France – the mission
1838-1859

Are you disposed to enter on my service? :
E pai ranei koe kia mahi maku?[1]

Jean-Baptiste François Pompallier, Catholic Bishop of Auckland, set sail for Europe in June 1859. It was almost twenty years since the tall, handsome, purple-clad Frenchman had been so noticeable at the signing of the Treaty of Waitangi. Now, as the French whaler *Général d'Hautpoul* took him on the chill wintry breeze past Rangitoto and out of the harbour, the people waving goodbye had mixed feelings. The Sisters of Mercy and their pupils were sad to see him go. Others, both lay and clergy, had their doubts that he would even come back.[2] The bishop had been gone almost four years the previous time he had returned to Europe.

Pompallier was on his way to Rome because every five years or so all bishops, even from the furthest missions in the world, were supposed to report in to the Pope. Pompallier also had to see Cardinal Barnabò. He was the cardinal at the head of the Vatican congregation, known by its Latin name of Propaganda Fide, which governed most Catholic foreign mission affairs. The visit was routine, of course, but all through the time of Pompallier's leadership there had been undercurrents of complaint from his clergy. As captain of the mission barque, an image he often used, Pompallier needed to justify the course he had charted for it.

The bishop was also leaving New Zealand because he needed to recruit more priests, brothers and nuns. And he needed more funding. He was travelling cheaply on a whaler not from choice but necessity. He had more chance of obtaining both people and money if he was there in person. He always had a magnetic presence. Suzanne Aubert would be one of a large band of people to respond to his devout and romantic portrayal of life out in the New Zealand mission field.

Le Général d'Hautpoul landed at Le Havre in September, after a speedy passage. Down in Lyon the Marists heard of his arrival. Their congregation, the Society of Mary, handled the Catholic mission for most of the South Pacific and their headquarters were in Lyon. Father Rocher, a priest who had recently returned from Sydney, wrote back there: 'Yesterday's newspaper announced that Bishop Pompallier had arrived at Le Havre.'[3]

Rocher was writing regularly to Father Poupinel in Sydney. From the Marist base there, Poupinel travelled around their mission stations, so had his finger on the pulse of the whole Pacific mission. Poupinel in turn wrote often to Father Yardin, in Lyon, who helped plan and supply the mission projects. One of the topics the three men were corresponding on at that time was the women's congregation which the Marists had started to set up in 1857 for the Island mission stations.[4] Poupinel and Yardin were going to be important in Suzanne's story.

Bishop Pompallier had once led the Marist mission out in the Pacific. But the relationship between Pompallier and the Marists would always be sceptical now, cool and guarded. In Lyon on 17 November, Pompallier dined with them on his way to Rome. Rocher's pen had a slightly satirical touch in its deference: 'His Lordship is looking wonderfully well. His Lordship is leaving for Rome this week.'[5]

By February 1860, Rocher too had visited Rome. He could see how Pompallier was getting on there with the cardinal at Propaganda Fide: 'I happened to see Bishop Pompallier several times. I don't know what he's doing in Rome but according to him, he's as busy as can be. From Cardinal Barnabò, I found out that he can't find any subjects for his Diocese.'[6] Rocher added a piece of news that the cardinal had passed on to him. Barnabò had refused Pompallier's request to approach the Marists again for people to staff his Auckland diocese. Because of past incompatibility, he said, Pompallier was going to have to look elsewhere.

So Pompallier had to negotiate and gather people from several different sources. In Rome, at the Ara Coeli community of Franciscan Friars Minor, he found eight priests and brothers who were willing to come to New Zealand to set up a Franciscan mission. In April he wrote to Barnabò from Lyon to confirm these and another eight candidates. A French seminarian, a priest in training, had enrolled in Rome.[7] Cardinal de Bonald of Lyon had released for him two men from the Lyon seminary – one was his own nephew, Antoine Pompallier. In March he had stopped at Valence on his way back from Rome, and from the novices at the old-established, prestigious Convent of the Sisters of the Holy Trinity he had recruited Antoine's sister, Lucie Pompallier.[8] By April 1860 he had found three other young women willing to go. He had only two teaching brothers still to find, to teach at the boys' school in Auckland and to set up a planned religious training institute for Maori. These men would come at the last minute, from the Clercs de Saint Viateur, a Lyon congregation whose founder he knew from long ago. Rocher's May 1860 bulletin to Sydney acknowledged this success and reported that Pompallier's new contingent was meant to be leaving from Le Havre in a couple of months' time, again on a whaler.

In the same letter, Rocher mentioned Pompallier's return visit to Lyon and said he had been preaching in the cathedral there: 'I've been told he was rather longwinded.'[9] Irish Father Walter McDonald did not think so. He had come from Auckland with Pompallier, as his secretary. In his diary he did not write his bishop down as 'longwinded'. Instead, he was enthusiastic: 'His Lordship's labours here effected much good not only for the Mission of New Zealand, but also for the Salvation of Souls in this city.'[10]

It was quite normal for a returning missionary bishop to be asked by the Lyon-based Society for the Propagation of the Faith 'to animate the zeal of the members in every district that he would visit'. A missionary bishop's preaching would benefit the society, which was by now the major funding organisation, effectively a lifeline, for Catholic missions worldwide. In 1857 Pompallier's former pioneer colleague, now Bishop Bataillon, had signed up six thousand new members from his preaching back in France.[11] It would help Pompallier, too. He had already applied to the Council of the Propagation of the Faith for additional grants to take his numerous passengers to New Zealand.

For over two months Walter McDonald's diary followed Pompallier as he spoke to packed congregations in Lyon's large churches. The bishop was eloquent on the two spiritual topics closest to his heart. One was the benefits of Christian mission to *les naturels* of Oceania, the 'noble savage' he idealised and genuinely respected. The other was his ever-present devotion to Mary. Lyon was Pompallier's home city. It saw itself as the city of Mary and the city of mission, and it took both his messages to heart.[12]

In April, on the Feast of the Good Shepherd, a huge congregation listened to Pompallier. It was in the church of Saint-Nizier in the heart of Lyon near the banks of the Saône River. In his little notebook, McDonald was stumbling over his words to convey the atmosphere: 'The attendance was immense,' he wrote, 'about 5 thousand persons.' Pompallier took for his text *'Ego vobiscum sum omnibus diebus'* – I am with you always. 'The manner in which he dealt with the text selected surpassed all expectation', McDonald continued, 'for without the least exageration no subject could be better or more handsomely treated, it really was another proof of his Lordship's profound knowledge, extensive mind and apostolic Zeal. He also dwelt for some time on that most laudable work of the Society of the Propagation of the Faith, … [and in] conclusion also he gave a very interesting account of his Mission which had some good effects as was afterwards seemly reason of many persons coming to offer his Lordship certain sums of money for his interesting Mission.'[13]

Though large and loftily Gothic, Saint-Nizier would still have been hard-stretched to accommodate a loaves-and-fishes figure of five thousand. But it must have been thronged with people. Suzanne Aubert could be imagined there, a young woman of twenty-four coming through the doorway of her own parish church with all the others of the 'five thousand' filing in, taking the holy water, making the sign of the cross and moving down the aisle. Crammed among the rest, stock-still, little, square-shouldered, listening to the tall bishop in the pulpit yet not about to approach him with others who might be offering gifts for his 'interesting Mission' because, if her mother or another family member were with her, she needed to be careful not to signal any personal call to mission. But she might have stood thinking for a while on the stone flags as the church emptied in the drawing-in of the late afternoon. She would not feel alone, not with Pompallier's text fresh in her ears. And as she walked home on the paving stones of her Lyon streets, in her mind she could have already been striding out on the hard-packed, tide-sucked sand of a missionary's shore.

Days gone by : Tua o rangi[14]

Suzanne, like the others responding to Pompallier, was hearing from him stirring stories which harked back to his early days as pioneer bishop, twenty years before. He told about events which, as Father McDonald wrote, showed the 'gratitude, affection and devotion of the native catholics for their first Shepherd'.[15] He told them, for instance, of a life-threatening time in 1839 when he had been protected by Maori converts.

They had sworn that only over their corpses could threatening attackers reach their bishop.[16] The new missionaries of 1860 were presented with heroic imagery like this, intended more for the men. Of the four women, however, Suzanne for one did not realise that they were coming mainly to teach French and embroidery, along with faith, to merchant daughters of Auckland. She saw a future of proud indigenous mission. As Bishop Pompallier in Europe wove his idealistic, exhilarating tales of southern shores and apostolic fervour from the pulpit and the dinner table, his recruits did not foresee how disillusioned they could become in a war-anxious, impoverished settler diocese.

The Marists in Lyon could have told them a little more of what New Zealand would really be like, but Pompallier and the Society of Mary were no longer working together. At the beginning they had been the only congregation to provide missionaries for his enormous original mission field in Oceania. They already had over twenty years of hard-won experience in the south-west Pacific. They knew something of the world of indigenous people, unscrupulous Pacific traders and difficult lines of communication. They understood sectarian missionary rivalry and the English-speaking colonising suspicion of the French. They were still full of zeal and still sent out missionaries dazzled with shining faith, but by now they had their infrastructure and support systems better in place and they knew about financial and emotional costs.

One cost already had been the loss of all the first mission stations built up among the Maori. The Marist fathers whose names are now associated mainly with southern regions in the history of New Zealand – Moreau in Otago, Pezant and Lampila in the Whanganui area, Petitjean in Wellington, Garin in Nelson, Forest and Reignier in Hawke's Bay – these and many others had begun in the north. All mission work had started there, so to spread south was to be expected. But instead the Marists had been told to leave the north, and they pointed the finger at one person, Bishop Pompallier. They did not, of course, lay blame at the feet of their own leader back in France, their first superior general, Father Colin.

Two constant traits of Pompallier's personality would bear on the story of Suzanne. One was inspirational: the way he viewed Maori culture with intelligent awareness, the way he dealt respectfully with cultural and spiritual difference. The other was the way he related to the people who worked with him, which made most of them over the years become disillusioned, not with their work, but with him. Pompallier's rift with

Colin was the first indication. The gulf between the two leaders had formed in the very early years of the mission. The job had been too big and the brief too wide for both of them, in their inexperience. Only their own steadiness of faith and the ascetic will and devotion of their men carried the early Catholic mission through – that and the generous funding from the Society for the Propagation of the Faith, as well as the compromises settled on by the Sacred Congregation of Propaganda Fide in Rome.[17]

Propaganda Fide had caused some of the difficulties at the outset. Rome had been distracted from foreign mission during the trauma of the Napoleonic years. It then became aware of the flotilla of Protestants out in the Pacific, catching the wind of mission strong in their sails. Cardinal Fransoni of Propaganda and Pope Gregory XVI in 1835 started looking to the missionary spirit of Lyon in France to find Catholic missionaries to counter this. By May 1836 they had handed over a vast area of the Pacific, which they named Western Oceania, to their newest congregation, the Society of Mary, whose only previous mission experience had been post-revolutionary revivalist missions in mainly rural areas around Lyon.[18]

The Marists had not at first been looking for mission work in the Pacific. But Rome set a condition. It would recognise the Society of Mary as a separate congregation only if it agreed to take on this foreign mission. The Marists were being asked to win for Catholicism the islands of the whole of the south-west Pacific Ocean. They accepted, and were recognised by the Pope as a new congregation of priests independent of diocesan control. In September 1836 they elected Father Jean-Claude Colin as their capable but untested first superior general. The Marist priests then took their three vows of poverty, celibacy and obedience, and by December of the same year the first batch of missionaries had set sail for a Pacific of their untutored imagination.

As members of the Society of Mary they were obedient to Colin back in Lyon. Propaganda Fide had charged him with 'everything pertaining to the religious rule and interior life' of the 'subjects supplied' to the mission.[19] He was to train them, and to look after their souls and overall well-being. But it was Pompallier who would lead them in their active missionary lives on the other side of the world. His brief was to convert the natives and he was responsible for the men while they were doing this. Pompallier was then a priest in his mid-thirties, also from Lyon. He was thought to have impressive potential but in fact had very little experience in real leadership beyond local parish or community level. He had worked closely with the men who were setting up the Society of Mary. He had intended to be Marist but being appointed to the status of bishop, as Vicar Apostolic of Western Oceania, changed his mind, 'since', as he explained to Cardinal Fransoni, 'according to Your Eminence's opinion, and Cardinal Sala's, I mustn't take vows [of obedience] to a mere priest, which would be inappropriate, especially after swearing direct obedience to His Holy Father the Pope'.[20]

So the two leaders, Colin and Pompallier, were taking stock of each other. And both directed the Marist mission. The vast distances of geography brought spans of silence to frustrate them. They were both conscious of their new positions and anxious to perform well. They clashed over their zones of leadership. They disagreed, for instance, over the bishop's right to read all the correspondence of his priests. They differed over their respective rights to handle the money provided by the Propagation of the Faith.

Once settled, with New Zealand as his base, Pompallier made liberal gifts to Maori chiefs, including fine French woollen cloaks 'of every shade of striking colour', as William Colenso noted.[21] This display might seem showy largesse to Colin, when Marist endeavour was meant, in the spirit of Mary, to be unobtrusive and discreet, not claiming attention. Their very motto, *Ignotus et quasi occultus*, called for the Marists to be 'unknown even to the extent of being hidden', the focus not on themselves but on others. Out in New Zealand, however, Pompallier sensed the need for a form of barter as a conversion tactic among the different Maori hapu and iwi. He felt that, to catch up at all on the twenty-four-year start of the Protestant missions, he and his church needed instant recognition, instant mana. Meanwhile his money disappeared. He probably underrated how much Catholicism might be attractive and novel to the Maori anyway, as an alternative to the older Protestant missions which were increasingly dislocating their traditional society.

Pompallier established a high profile, not only to win mana for Catholicism with Maori chiefs, but also to claim a more secure status for himself, his men and his mission at the changeover to a British colony. Being French and 'Papist' was often seen as alien, hostile and suspicious. In 1841 Father Comte explained this approach to Colin, listing Pompallier's 'position as bishop which gave him standing in the eyes of all, his role as superior which made him distributor of items sent from

France, his objectivity which earned him the respect of the whites, his gestures of generosity to everyone, his love for the New Zealanders'.[22] All this went into a 'politic of prestige' which not only his own men but later historians have recognised.[23]

The Maori word for a Protestant was a generic *mihinare*, from missionary. But the word for a Catholic was personified in Pompallier himself: *pikopo*, from the Latin word for bishop, *episcopus*. To be 'pikopo' was to have the chiefly image of bishop prominent. Pompallier was the only bishop then. Anglican Bishop George Selwyn did not arrive until 1842, and he in his turn would alarm his plain, evangelical English missionaries with his more high church, 'Puseyite' view of episcopal position. Meanwhile Pompallier was unchallenged in any hierarchical image-making. Anti-Catholic Colenso saw this happening quite clearly at the signing of the Treaty of Waitangi in 1840. He recorded Maori comment that Pompallier was the only chiefly, fit companion for the governor: 'Ko ia ana te tino rangatira! Ko Pikopo anake te hoa mo te kawana.'[24]

At Waitangi the Anglican missionary, Rev. Richard Taylor, had to admit Pompallier's achievement. 'I feel assured he came either as a spy', he wrote in his diary, 'or to get himself acknowledged as an important personage before the natives, which I think he succeeded in doing.'[25] Pompallier's was an intelligent and gentlemanly presence in the treaty discussions. His main purpose was to make sure that legal discrimination against Catholics, which had only recently been stopped in England, in 1829, would not emerge in the new colony. Because of this, he wanted 'free toleration' in 'matters of faith' to be written into the treaty. As a counterbalance to any concession to Catholicism, Anglican William Colenso pushed for Maori ritenga or custom also to be included. So in the final agreed wording was the right for Catholic and Maori to have their own form of Christian or traditional religion.[26] More than once, the tall, good-looking Pompallier in his bishop's robes, his religious conviction balanced by tolerant demeanour and articulate diplomacy, had negotiated a way out of difficulties. Father Colin, the man at the desk back in France, had little chance of understanding this.

Pompallier certainly squandered money, though not so much directly on himself. As a result, he left his missionaries penniless in ones and twos in isolated stations where they were seen begging ship's biscuit from passing traders. But he was not responsible for all the hardship. Even getting to New Zealand had been costly. The new missionaries under

Pompallier headed for the Pacific via Valparaiso in South America, to confer there with the Picpus missionaries for Eastern Oceania. He was not sure then that New Zealand would be the base. It proved a long and expensive route, whereas ships were now plying regularly from Europe via the Cape of Good Hope to Australia. In all, the voyage from France to New Zealand took over a year before they crossed the bar of the Hokianga harbour and sailed upriver on 10 January 1838. On the way four men were left at Wallis and Futuna Islands near New Caledonia. There were only three men, at first, to set up the New Zealand head-quarters for the Catholic mission to Western Oceania.

By July 1840 Pompallier had bought his own schooner, which he renamed the *Sancta Maria*. He paid too high a price for it, and its copper sheathing and upkeep continued to drain mission resources. Pompallier's defence was his need to visit the scattered mission stations in the Pacific. After all, New Zealand was not his only responsibility. The killing of Father Pierre Chanel at Futuna in April 1841 would be caused in part by the lack of back-up visits. New Zealand itself relied on sea travel around its long coastline, and mission stations then were mostly on the coast. Colin was not convinced. He saw self-aggrandisement in Pompallier's schooner floating in the bay with its flag flying the stars of the Immaculate Conception of Mary.[27]

Pompallier's image was less of a problem than its corollary, the diversion of the money which Colin's men desperately needed. Colin had taken conscientiously his role of provider of missionaries. By 1842, forty-one men had been sent to the Pacific mission, thirty-four coming to New Zealand. Of these, nineteen were priests – almost a third of all Marist priests at the time.[28] As their poverty became more obvious, the Catholic mission lost mana in Maori eyes, regardless of Pompallier's prestige. The weakness in personification was that, whenever Pompallier was not present, there was only the powerless memory of a figurehead. Father Garin noted: 'In the beginning, the mission had the finest reputation for being well-off. We were thought rich, but what a turn-around there is just now!'[29]

In December 1842 Ensign Best came across Father Pezant. 'I never remember seeing a more miserable figure,' he noted. In his journal he described Pezant: 'Travel worn unshaven & unwashed he wore the tricornered hat of his order, his long coat & a kind of black petticoat were tucked up with the Skirts under the waistband and a pair of Old

Wellington boots were drawn over his Trousers. From his neck hung a large crucifix and on his back was a kind of sack containing in all probability all he possessed in the world.'[30] Even if many a missionary travelled through the swamps and bracken and around tide-threatened headlands dressed in rough and dirty clothes, what Best took from this was destitution. That was the image of the Catholic missionary in 1842.

At the same time Father Forest recounted to Father Epalle in France a drawn-out trip he had had to take from Auckland to the Bay of Islands. It was on the poorest, cheapest coastal trader he could find. He was wedged tightly below deck with drunken shipmates who hoicked and spat, urinated and defecated around him. He described how everyone stumbled among the dogs and their droppings, how they passed around and shared the dirty billy of tea sweetened with brown sugar. The men took advantage of a Maori girl passenger who had boarded the boat with her basket of washing. 'If I had had a bit of money', he said, 'I would not have taken this ship; there were others, really comfortable ones, which were coming to the Bay of Islands.'[31] It was not usual for him to write so negatively or graphically of his experience. He was not doing so on his own account: 'I'll stop now. It is two o'clock in the morning. His Lordship asked me last night to tell you this to show you, and Rev. Father Superior as well as the gentlemen of the Propagation of the Faith, what our situation is.'[32] If Epalle had not already been in Lyon raising money with the Propagation of the Faith, Pompallier would not have commissioned this less than glamorous report.

Pompallier's nature leant to the cerebral and spiritual side, not to the practical, with a distaste for what he saw as the spirit of commerce among the Protestants. He did not intend to deviate from active mission work into running farms. There was some wisdom in this. The Catholic mission would never be accused of land-grabbing opportunism, as several Protestant missionaries were. The reverse of this medal was the total vulnerability of his men. They were well schooled spiritually for privation in the cause of their own sanctity. They were less equipped to survive physically.

Chiefly mana in those years rose if there was a resident missionary. As Father Petitjean explained to Colin, 'It is a question of honour for the New Zealanders to have foreigners living with them, especially a priest. It is also a temporal resource.'[33] But in many cases the missionaries had to rely instead on the hospitality of the hapu which had 'adopted' them. It was an embarrassment to the Maori if their priest became too visibly poor and isolated. He was no longer seen as either a temporal or spiritual resource for his hosts and was dispensable. He could be spurned and sometimes starved. This may have been Father Séon's experience at Matamata in 1842.

Comte, Tripe, Petitjean, Forest, Servant, Epalle – the list continues of priests who were writing letters home to Marist headquarters in Lyon. Their theme was the jeopardy the mission was in rather than their own personal hardships, though these also could be glimpsed. Petitjean's previous loyal reticence gave way in May 1842. He wrote in detail to Colin an analysis which, as a summary of Pompallier's nature and behaviour, would remain true for the rest of the bishop's life:

> Our bishop has many talents for attracting the natives; he has, it seems to me, the qualities of the accomplished missioner. He had from afar a brilliant reputation for ability, confidence, a fortune and even noble blood. But he does not appear to be reliable in his words, promising too much, quite rash in business, banking on his future and eating up loans, laying little which is of solid foundation, easy to charm, flatter and catch unawares or at least yielding to everybody because he wished to make use of everything and win all. . . . We are like an army that has consumed part of its munitions in fireworks. . . . The debt is crushing. We negotiate bills of exchange on France at a great loss. We pay interest at 15% together with the interest for the interest every three months.[34]

Colin and Pompallier's correspondence had been politely acrimonious and self-righteous for some time, but finally Propaganda Fide had to step in. Epalle went back to France in 1842 and with Colin negotiated an unusual and very generous advance from the Propagation of the Faith. It was an extraordinary allocation intended specifically to save the mission from ruin. The Propagation of the Faith's Lyon loyalty had rallied to their local mission congregation and its leader, also from Lyon. The amounts voted to Western Oceania in 1842 and 1843 were the highest ever given to any French mission.[35] The Council of the Propagation of the Faith was conscious of all the extenuating factors and sent only the most courteous of recommendations to Pompallier, delicately suggesting that after selling the schooner he never again overreach his resources. In the rescue of the mission, Pompallier too had been rescued handsomely. The irony was that he would expect it as his due.

In the years to come, he did not greatly change his controlling style. He did not easily delegate, share decision-making or take suggestions from his priests out in the stations. In 1845, Father Forest wrote to Epalle, now in Sydney:

> If the manner of administration of Bishop Pompallier does not change, no subject will remain here, French or English. . . . As long as Bishop Pompallier directs by himself the temporal affairs of the mission, everyone will suffer. Enormous expenses are made without any or almost any good result. . . . As long as Bishop Pompallier wants to do everything alone or by himself without heeding either his vicars general or the other administrators of his mission, the Catholic religion will make little progress here.
>
> P.S. Please make no mention of this letter to Bishop Pompallier.[36]

Pompallier left for France in April 1846. Less than a decade after arriving in New Zealand, he wrote a letter of resignation to Rome and recommended an English-speaking replacement for the English colony. His own English, nevertheless, was good.[37] Colin backgrounded the continuing difficulties for Rome and said of his missionaries that 'not one of them hesitates to see in this worthy bishop two men: one of a great zeal and a large heart; the other of a narrow judgement that makes indescribably difficult mutual relations of administration and dependence'.[38]

Pompallier would have liked to leave mission problems behind him, but Rome did not accept his resignation. Instead, from 1848, he was to be bishop of a northern diocese based at Auckland, with his own clergy who would be largely diocesan and therefore under his control, not members of an independent religious congregation. He would have to obtain them himself from mainly French and Irish seminaries. He no longer had a guaranteed supply sent from the Society of Mary. The Marists were to go south to a base at Port Nicholson. A separate diocese would be set up, with their colleague, Philippe Viard, as its bishop.[39] The Marists would also continue work in the Pacific Islands, which were no longer under Pompallier's jurisdiction. When the Marists withdrew from the original stations in the north, these stayed largely abandoned until, a decade later, the Franciscans arrived at the same time as Suzanne Aubert.

When Pompallier returned in 1850, he brought the new group of subjects he had had to scout around for. Among them were French, Irish, English and Germans, and nearly all were still in training to be priests. Seven months on the voyage out provided time for learning Maori and English and for the swiftest of ecclesiastical study. Pompallier felt this was enough time and ordained most of his clergy to the priesthood within two months of landing.[40] The Marists were leaving soon and he needed a full quota of priests for his new diocese straight away. Not only were they hastily ordained, they were then speedily assigned to their posts. Alone, though usually with a Maori helper, they went to Opotiki, Tauranga, Hokianga, Waikato, the Bay of Islands.

In comparison with the destitution of the early 1840s, these men were better off in the more comfortable years of the 1850s. But this relative improvement was meaningless to them. They were mostly foreign, isolated, new to the country, and raw as both priests and missionaries. Their only line of communication was to Pompallier. Unlike the Marists, they had no support from any religious congregation beyond his borders. In the nineteenth century, a bishop's independence and power were great, and distance reinforced this.[41]

At first Pompallier wrote from Auckland sheaf after sheaf of letters of spiritual and cultural guidance to these apprentice priests. They were kindly letters, advising them how to relate to Maori and how to accept and submit to their divinely appointed situation. But he began to be lulled into complacency in the round of religious and social duties of the capital, and he did not visit his outlying priests nor run any spiritual retreats for them.[42] He saw himself as the pastor of his flock, the captain of his mission barque – the two conventional images that illustrate his writing – but his shepherds tending the flock, his sailors trimming the sail, were only learning. He was pastor and captain, but also quartermaster, handling accounts, dispensing supplies. The men were tethered firmly, even at a distance, to this one man, their bishop. When they offered opinions, his answers reminded them of their subordination: 'Fulfil the will of God better in future by fulfilling your Bishop's, for your own salvation and the good of the diocese.'[43]

For many of them, the tether rope frayed and gave way. As early as October 1852, allegations against Pompallier were sent to the Pope.[44] By December of that year seven priests wrote to the Propagation of the Faith requesting passage money to go back to Europe. In 1853, Propaganda Fide asked Bishop Viard to investigate the complaints. There were no differences over doctrine, ritual or observances, such as the more fundamentalist English missionaries had with Bishop Selwyn. In fact in spiritual matters there was general accord. But to the usual accusation of mismanagement of finances were added drunkenness and incautious closeness to the Sisters of Mercy. These three categories of complaint were not unusual as channels of discontent. Pompallier was not alone as a bishop in being targeted in this way. Viard's report settled each accusation and advised Pompallier to take care. As a result, however, Pompallier's letters to the priests seem to have stopped and they were more alone than ever.[45]

In this affair, the mission had cracked and shown the faultline. The diocese of Auckland was now in effect the town of Auckland, the capital of New Zealand, the centre of provincial government, a new trading settlement with outlying settler districts, growing apace. From the north and the south prospering Maori chiefs, farmers and traders brought their boats or canoes into port with their produce. They were received regularly by the bishop. From the 1850s he is recorded only twice as travelling out of Auckland to see his often-mentioned 'flock', his *hipi*, in their own homes. He wrote and spoke of his Maori mission but was no longer really in touch.

The wasted years of the 1850s laid up little in store to help Suzanne and her companions weather the wars of the 1860s. Pompallier was also beginning to age. Administration and the immediacy of the town's needs kept him comfortably anchored in the Pakeha capital. His talents were safe there. The fine preacher excelled in the new little cathedral completed by Viard during his four-year absence, the caring pastor handled the confessional, the urbane diplomat relaxed in the capital's political and social scene, the mellow host responded to the constant stream of Maori visitors, the avuncular director benevolently controlled the hard-working, appreciative Sisters of Mercy whose work was the visible success story he needed.

On the ship back to New Zealand in 1850 had come eight Sisters of Mercy from Carlow in Ireland. More arrived through the following years. They contributed what the young colony then lacked. They brought all their optimism as the first female congregation. To the Maori and settlers they brought schooling, education in the faith, visiting the sick and those in prison. They had the womanly and marketable skills of sewing and embroidery, the social and marketable skills of languages and music. For themselves, they also brought tuberculosis from the tough years of the Irish famine. Letter after letter back to Ireland told of the women who died. From the very beginning, the settlers loved and respected them. They needed the calm order and routine the sisters gave. 'I think we have selected a suitable place for the teaching of our Holy Religion as there are a number of Irish soldiers in the regiment quartered here and some of their wives and daughters come to us for instructions.'[46]

The sisters' description of their first temporary convent gives a sense of settled, clean order. 'We are living in a small wooden building as neatly furnished as any brick one. The walls are papered with a pretty and neat pattern; the doors are of painted oak; and the windows rise on pulleys. Our little dwelling is indeed very comfortable.' They also had the warm glow of their bishop's regard and support. Most gave him unstinting loyalty in return, the recognition he always craved for. The pattern was evident even on board ship. Mother Cecilia Maher described in a letter a typical evening after the Litany of the Blessed Virgin Mary.

> The Bishop then says a short fervent prayer, he then sits down in the midst of his 'dear daughters' & tells some of his adventures, which under existing circumstances are deeply interesting. Fancy us seated around him, with a beautiful sky spangled with stars above, the splendid sea rolling beneath, the fine ship with its sails unfurled, the Irish priests Garnett, Clery and O'Rourke, sitting behind us, & the Bishop relating the miraculous escapes, wonderful adventures, scenes in the Holy Land, in Rome & &, and in the Southern Ocean. He is loved & respected; nothing can exceed his kindness & he is so polite & sweet in his attentions to all; he expresses such gratitude to Carlow, & said that in no place he visited was he more charmed than at the College & by the clergy.[47]

They gave him, after his years of itinerant mission work in a rough and ready society, the missing feeling of community and comfort that partly lay behind his resignation proffered in France in 1846. With them Pompallier was more in his element.

> He is extremely kind & a true Father. He never recognizes any one if you will, in the Com'y [community] but the Superioress. He would not send the smallest thing even to be repaired but it must pass through the Mother's hands. He frequently comes to our recreations, no other person ever. He is exceedingly cheerful & has most interesting histories to relate. His information is great & his experience I believe unparalleled.
>
> I never knelt to such a confessor. Before your first confession is concluded he knows you thouroughly. One feels in his guidance as if your vessel was in the hands of a Pilot so skillful that it cannot, 'with God's blessing', be lost.[48]

Mother Cecilia excelled in planning and budgeting. From her the bishop received possibly his only praise for bookkeeping:

> You cannot think how pleasantly money matters are arranged. We have 4 schools; every school pays all repairs & expenses for itself & every farthing over is handed to the Bishop quarterly. He then signs all the books & he gives me quarterly what supplies us well & always tells me to ask for more if I require it. . . . . He is most exact in business and always keeps his accounts in excellent order.[49]

The Sisters of Mercy were answerable to him, they were his diocesan congregation and he basked in their success. But his priests, dotted in outlying stations, were not invited 'to ask for more' if they required it and did not feel God's blessing quite so surely on the 'vessel' piloted by Pompallier. They saw money going to the settler area of the sisters and accused Pompallier of unfair distribution. From the viewpoint of their uncosseted lives they also saw the bishop enjoying the sisters' hospitality and, in predictable retaliation, accused him of impropriety.

The diocese of Auckland limped on unbalanced to the end of the 1850s. There were now only seven priests in all, hardly any to cover the huge districts beyond the Auckland area itself. Father Garavel's successful Rangiaowhia mission was the only strong exception to lacklustre if not abandoned stations, and this even before the wars of the 1860s. Within the town, four priests were not enough for the influx of settlers. The sisters, too, could do with more women religious to help staff and fund the schools. So they suggested French sisters to Pompallier, for needlework and the teaching of their language. This was what was waiting for Suzanne.[50]

Pompallier's return to Europe in 1859 had to fill these gaps in the ranks of clergy and religious. When he enrolled Suzanne Aubert and all her companions, he did not do so with balance sheets and plans in hand. Instead he used his gift of arousing people's fervour and tapping zeal to gather in behind him expectant missionaries. Even with more experienced congregations, like the Franciscan Friars Minor, he told them just what was needed to win them over. He would return once more with a keen but ill-prepared band and, through the turmoil of the 1860s, an ageing and rheumatic bishop would again run into troubles with his missionaries.

CHAPTER TWO

France – childhood and family
1835-1860

Where do you live? : Keiwhea to ḳainga tuturu?
Who are your parents? : Kowai ou matua?[1]

The parish church of Saint-Nizier in Lyon is a fitting place to have Suzanne step into her own story. It was her home territory. She lived around the corner, one street down nearer the banks of the Saône River. Saint-Nizier was her church, and had been since she was about five and arrived in Lyon with her family. Its two spires rose above the offices, shops and apartments around. It was a confident church, proud of its history of Roman martyrdom. She grew up in this parish and was instructed for her First Holy Communion by the local parish Sisters of Saint Charles.[2]

It suits also as the setting where she linked herself for ever with a land so far away. A mission atmosphere was all around.[3] Many lay women of Saint-Nizier worked for the missions. Pauline Jaricot was one who was well known. She had started up the networks of supporters who funded the work of the Propagation of the Faith. Clusters of people kept enrolling others in an effective pyramid system. They each gave just a little bit of money but every single coin, every *sou*, rattled in and multiplied for the Catholic mission. Their prayers for the missionaries multiplied in the same way.

Suzanne read the *Annales de la Propagation de la Foi* (Annals of the Propagation of the Faith) printed in Lyon. This was a little blue bi-monthly magazine of mission reports and letters from around the world – '*Missions d'Asie, Missions d'Afrique, Missions d'Amérique, Missions de l'Océanie . . .*' The letters were regularly edited to keep the 'edifying' bits foremost. Even so, they still brought to the fireside missionaries at home vicarious adventure, foreignness, excitement, commitment. When Suzanne was twenty, she may have read Father Reignier's 1855 letter written from Hawke's Bay, describing how he narrowly escaped being ambushed, walking through the bush alone and serenely saying his rosary.[4] She would have had no idea that much later an older Reignier would be her mission companion for years.

Like thousands of other readers, she would have recently been reading a long account by Father Poupinel, written 'on board the *Joanie-Dove*'. Among his descriptions was a hard trudge up the Horowhenua coastline in 1858 with Father Séon. Poupinel was enjoying the firm sand of low tide with the seabirds alongside, wheeling and diving for fish. Then the tide turned. He had to struggle through the chaos of driftwood and loose dry sand above high-water mark. He realised that he, the Sydney adminis-trator, the Marist Visitor, a desk man for much of his time, was not as fit as his frontier colleague. 'I was far from being a real bloke', he admitted.[5] They got lost among the sand dunes, swamps and tall clumps of flax as they cut inland to track down the river fords. On they trekked to Wanganui. Séon was going to be a mission hero for Suzanne and she would nurse him as he died.

And Suzanne, the young woman reading late by candlelight in Lyon, would also have met up with Ngati Hau at Hiruharama. Poupinel went on up the Whanganui River by waka and described Father Lampila's mission. He told Catholic Europe how the church bell there called the rhythm of the day. He was struck by the spirituality of these people. Not all were Christian, yet they observed the prayers with dignity and constancy. 'Every day, morning and evening', he wrote, 'the bell calls the Maoris to the church to pray together; if the missionary is away on Sunday, they gather together regardless, and a catechist recites the prayers of the Mass. The way they sing Vespers, in their language, is just the same.'[6]

One lay woman from Saint-Nizier had figured in the Annals. In 1845, Françoise Perroton, already forty-nine years old, had gone out to the Pacific to Futuna – on her own and in defiance of her family. She lived for twelve years isolated from other European women until the first of the Marist lay sisters arrived to join her.[7] From among Saint-Nizier's parishioners also came founders of some of France's multiplying new religious congregations. Claudine Thévenet took her Sisters of Jesus and Mary out to India in 1842. Louis Querbes' Clerics of Saint Viator were out in North America as well as working at home in France. There were Saint-Nizier people among the Marist missionaries, including Bishop Viard of Wellington.

Saint-Nizier provided not only the exotic appeal of mission but also the local and daily routine of social welfare work. Frédéric Ozanam, who started the lay St Vincent de Paul movement, was married in the church. The French Revolution in 1789 had dismantled abruptly the country's centuries-old church-directed welfare infrastructure. The upheaval had been traumatic. After the revolution, devout people set about rebuilding the networks.[8] Along with priests and nuns, the parishioners of Saint-Nizier ran charitable works: hospices, dispensaries, soup kitchens, factory workshops, homes for the incurably handicapped or ill, foundling children, old people, homes for the poor, or sick, or young girls 'at risk'.[9] The Dames de Saint-Nizier sewed, held committee meetings, kept their minutes, organised fundraising and sallied forth with their collecting boxes.[10] The parish was busy in both mission work and social work.

Saint-Nizier looked across the Saône River up to the heights above the cliffs where the chapel of Fourvière, Lyon's sanctuary dedicated to the Virgin Mary, watched over the city below. Action and reflection seemed to be facing each other across the river. Suzanne lived in between the two churches and her character was formed by both. It stayed that way throughout her life and she wrote the combination down for her novices:

— What ought to be the life of a Sister of Compassion?
— It should be a long act of faith, hope and charity; it should combine the life of Martha and Mary, walking arm in arm together, and never separate.[11]

Bishop Pompallier had preached his mission message to a packed Saint-Nizier in the afternoon of the Feast of the Good Shepherd. He went up to Fourvière in the springtime evening to preach again, this time of his devotion to the Virgin Mary. Perhaps Suzanne walked across the bridge, climbed the long, steep flight of steps to the shrine she often visited, and joined the listeners there. Whether she did or not, Pompallier had his next recruit. She had made up her mind before the end of April, because Pompallier's 23 April letter to Barnabò indicated he had everyone except the two brothers.

Suzanne was keeping in touch with Father Yardin about her plans. She said in later years that at this time in Lyon he was her spiritual director, a regular confessor and counsellor, so he would be privy to the hard choice she was making. He was responsible for setting up the Marist women's congregation for the Pacific mission, a group of women Suzanne would have liked to join.[12] For years, she had been wanting to become a nun. Neither her mother nor her father would agree. They had two sons living, but she was the only daughter.

So her family did not know that she was now planning to leave, and they were not meant to know. She said that she told her parents she would wait until she was twenty-five and then take matters into her own hands, regardless. She implied that they were monitoring her movements more closely as she reached that age in June 1860, so she avoided openly meeting Pompallier to keep her family from suspecting. Her negotiation was done through Yardin. She may never have been among the Saint-Nizier 'five thousand' in body, though definitely in spirit. The first steps in recruiting Suzanne Aubert may even have been taken discreetly by Pompallier and Yardin over the Marist dinner-table back in November 1859.

In August 1860, Yardin referred to Suzanne and to her family's opposition in a letter to Sydney: 'Bishop Pompallier is embarking at Le Havre on the *Général Teste* to return to his Diocese', he told Poupinel. 'He is taking with him some Franciscans, seminarians and four religious, among whom is his niece. There are two of them that I know well; they wanted to go to our missions. The idea of the Novitiate frightened them off because of certain family reasons. One of them will perhaps write to you. She is Mlle Aubert . . .' The Marists were no longer sending out women who, like their first *pionnières*, had no formation as religious sisters. Suzanne could not easily enter the novitiate they were setting up in Lyon if her family strongly objected. And if she went to New Caledonia, a French convict colony since 1853, she could also be recalled through French law. For these two reasons Suzanne had to let go of her hopes for the Lyon-based Marist mission. Bishop Pompallier's appeal came at the right moment. He was accepting lay women without religious formation as his plan was to provide this in the novitiate of the Sisters of Mercy in Auckland. And Pompallier's foreign diocese in New Zealand seemed safely beyond her parents' reach.

Yardin's mention of Suzanne carried on with a personal comment, a quick pen sketch of her: 'She is Mlle Aubert, who looks towards Spain to see if England is burning.'[13] In a saying which is a metaphor of Counter-Reformation unsubtlety, Yardin was classifying her as cross-eyed. Suzanne had a cast in one eye which was more noticeable when she was tired. She said she had not been born that way. The damage to her eye came from an accident when she was two, along with an early crippled childhood which now lay behind her, overcome. But the crooked eye remained and this 'deformity', she said, meant that she would not be accepted as a nursing sister with the Sisters of St Vincent de Paul, France's active Sisters of Charity.[14] Perhaps her parents' opposition was partly defensive, in reaction. They may have been protecting their child. Throughout her life she was sensitive to people who were marginalised through disability. Yardin's comment confirms that her 'handicap' was likely to go with her wherever vocation was discussed. It is the first known reference to her in her New Zealand story, and she enters the record labelled.

For her first two years Suzanne had stared straight from her little square-jawed, dark-brown-eyed, determined face. Life seemed very secure. Her family was bourgeois – middle class, stable and respectable. They lived in the town of St-Symphorien-de-Lay in the region of the upper Loire River, about a hundred kilometres north-west of Lyon on the then main road to Paris. St-Symphorien was where her father had been born and grown up, where her grandfather had held the comfortable minor legal position of *huissier*. *Huissiers* were a type of bailiff, responsible for service of process, execution of judgements and maintenance of order at hearings.[15] The profession was run as a closed state monopoly. It could be passed on within a family, and in fact Suzanne's father, Louis Aubert, continued his father's practice. Her father's family was large and owned property.[16] Her grandmother was documented as 'Dame Suzanne Lambert, épouse Aubert'; the 'Dame' indicated her secure middle-class status. Suzanne was named after her and was her godchild.

This grandmother had been born in Tarare, a bigger town to the south-east, just over forty kilometres from Lyon. Mountainous country lay between Tarare and St-Symphorien-de-Lay. Her son Louis, Suzanne's father, found his own bride back in Tarare. More likely she was chosen for him. She was Clarice Périer, a distant cousin. Louis was twenty-seven and Clarice twenty-four when they were married in Tarare on 26 November 1832. It was a good middle-class match. Louis was already launched on his acceptable career and had completed all the requirements to practise as a *huissier* on his own account. He brought to the marriage the value of ten thousand francs, 'including the value of his position as huissier'. His father was described on the marriage documents as a man of private means and a property owner, no longer a *huissier*, so Louis must have bought the practice or been helped into it by the time of his wedding. In fact, Etienne Aubert, Louis's father, lived only one month more after his son was married.

Clarice Périer was the eldest in a family of four children. Her mother was a widow: 'Dame Joséphine Rodde, veuve Périer'. The family was comfortably off. Suzanne said her mother was beautiful. Her photograph shows her, even as an older woman, standing straight and alert. She looks taller than Suzanne would be. Her daughter-in-law, remembering back in 1921, described her as exceptionally intelligent, a woman of refinement and culture, but sometimes difficult in temperament.[17] Clarice brought proudly to the marriage her eventual equal share in her father's estate, a gold watch and a goodly trousseau.[18] Some of this, the marriage contract carefully noted, was an advance from her mother on her inheritance. It included a four-poster bed, with its red-tasselled curtains, bolsters and all the bedding listed in precise detail. In addition to her own trousseau, she had a generous gift from an unmarried aunt who was in business as *fabricante en broderie*.[19] This brought her more household items, such as a gold-framed mirror and the usual two and three dozen of this and that.

The marriage was fittingly endowed and the relatives were all there signing the documents. The prospects were good for the newly-weds. The bed crossed the rugged range of hills to St-Symphorien where Alphonse, the first son, was born one year later. The new father registered the birth, with the young schoolteacher and the notary's clerk as witnesses. A daughter followed on 19 June 1835, born in midsummer at six o'clock just in time for the evening angelus. The feast of Corpus Christi separated her birth and her baptism two days later in the parish church. She was named Marie Henriette Suzanne Aubert.

When she was very little – she thought two and a half years old – Suzanne's life nearly ended. This was the story she passed on of an event she was too young to remember. She could not have heard it from her St-Symphorien grandmother, as the older Suzanne Aubert had died at the beginning of 1836. From her mother and her father she must have heard the tale told again and again. Beyond the bottom gate of the garden there was a pond, 'as wide as a lake at this season of the year'. It was iced over thinly in the cold of winter. Suzanne and Alphonse chased a piglet out across the ice, which cracked. Suzanne fell through and struck rocks. She was taken unconscious from the water by her father. The narrative recounts feverish efforts to save her life.[20]

As a result of the accident, her arms and legs were crippled and she could not see. Her mother took her to shrines for a hoped-for miracle, and to spas for therapeutic treatment. The way Suzanne told it, Clarice seemed never to have given up. But she also implied that the travelling, the pilgrimages and the spas gave interest to her mother. Suzanne recovered eventually. There are no letters, no diaries, no doctor's report to confirm this story. Other accounts have blurred edges of reality, and this may be among them. But it was real for her. Once, in her old age, in defence of the disabled, she rounded on a eugenics meeting in Wellington. She told her stunned listeners that, if those principles had been in force when she was little, she would not be there then. As a child, she had been *un monstre*, a 'freak'.

By 1840 Louis, Clarice, Alphonse, Suzanne and a second son, born in 1837 and also called Louis, had moved into the city of Lyon. A third son, Camille, was born at this time and the family was complete. Many people from outlying towns were feeling the pull to the city as Lyon expanded and industrialised in the mid-nineteenth century. Both of Louis's parents were now dead, and Suzanne would say that her accident cast a shadow over St-Symphorien. Most probably it was a career move for Louis, to establish himself in the legal world of the large city with its higher courts, and he would need to do this while still relatively young. In 1841, newly arrived, he was listed way down as forty-fifth out of forty-eight on the ladder of *huissiers*, but by 1853 he had risen to secretary of the Chambre de Discipline des Huissiers, their own professional organisation. By then he was senior, a *huissier audiencier*, and worked at the Cour d'Assises, the higher court dealing with criminal cases. By 1860, the year Suzanne left for New Zealand, he was up to tenth out of the forty-nine.[21]

While he was first building up his practice, he worked from the family's apartment on the middle floor of 5 rue Trois Carreaux, a narrow building of five floors. Suzanne indicated that her father was a generous but not very wealthy man. The costs of buying into a city practice may have set the family back, and the first apartment seems modest. There was a customs office on the ground floor, Villard the hatmaker on the first and the Aubert family on the second.[22] In 1840 and 1841 only three children were listed as living in this apartment. According to Suzanne, the youngest, Camille, was in foster care with a wet-nurse out in the country, where he stayed for up to four years because Clarice was ill. By 1845 four children are recorded, so Camille was back home with them.

As he rose in his career, Louis Aubert took offices at 11 Quai St-Antoine, a street running along the Saône. The building, with its Louis XVI façade, looked across the river up to Fourvière. Old passageways called *traboules* cut through many Lyon buildings to connect streets. Some ran through from the quay to the parallel street back from the river, rue Grande Mercière. This was where the family lived from 1846. Eventually Louis was employing eight clerks and, matching his rise in the hierarchy of *huissiers*, this second apartment at 2 rue Grande Mercière was much bigger, with the highest domestic rental value in the building. His office was closely linked to their home by one of these *traboules*. The children could run messages back and forth, and be familiar with his legal work environment.

They lived on the second floor above a mercer, a wholesale stocking manufacturer, and Monsieur Alphonse Payant, who worked for customs. In the apartment building was a cross-section of plain society from ground-floor commerce through the second- and third-floor relative prosperity to the six tiny, attic apartments at the top. Here lived the widowed, the single, and the fabric workers whose livelihood was only seasonal. Among them was Chalandon, the silk worker, his wife and child; two widows who were both dressmakers, each with a child; and a widower with two children. Suzanne Aubert would be meeting some of these every day on the stairs. She did not grow up cocooned from other people's struggle to survive and make their way.

Over the years there were usually seven people in the apartment – Louis and Clarice, three children, one maid and sometimes another worker or boarder. Only three children were listed because Camille was away at first, then Alphonse at his Jesuit school; or Suzanne for three years, from 1847 or 1848, boarding at the nearby Benedictine school. Or the listing was made after Suzanne's brother, Louis, died at the age of about twelve.[23] Suzanne instinctively protected people with disability not just because of religious belief or her own experience, but because of Louis. He was born 'with a slightly abnormal head – he was hydrocephalic. . . . Later, he showed remarkable skill in anything of a mechanical nature, but could not learn anything abstract.' She remembered him sitting there, skilfully reassembling watch parts. He was sweet-natured and serene in his childhood faith.

Law as well as faith surrounded Suzanne on both sides of her family. If her paternal grandfather was a *huissier*, and her father also, her grandfather on her mother's side was a *greffier*, or court registrar, and his father before him a *notaire*, akin to a family lawyer. Written law was becoming even stronger in nineteenth-century France, after a codified system was begun by Napoleon in 1806. Less attention was given than in British law to trial by jury, to cross-questioning of witnesses in court. Instead, more emphasis was put on the careful preliminary preparation of documents to be submitted to the court for deliberation by a panel of judges. No verbatim record was kept of questions asked and answers given by witnesses. Evidence was only summarised by the *greffier*. The men who worked at the documentation stage were in a responsible if undramatic profession. French law also tended to document most transactions, even at the simplest community level. From within the archives of French law practices emerge profiles from the smallest of hamlets to the largest of cities. The *notaires* and *greffiers* recorded the life of France.[24]

Suzanne's maternal grandfather, Jean-Baptiste Périer, was registrar or secretary of the court in Tarare for the judge of the Justice de Paix, which dispensed justice at the local level. He kept the rolls and registers and was responsible for writing up the documents. At this level he dealt with people's emotions, human interactions that came before the judge. Even plain cases of fisticuffs, like that of Vivier Merle, a muslin worker who was taking a track through a meadow on 15 February 1819. He was set upon and beaten up by the two Chavenot brothers, who had a grievance against him. Suzanne's grandfather recorded the evidence and the judgement.[25]

He worked a lot with family welfare, especially when children were orphaned. The wider family would be called together in a family council required by law, the children's future arrangements were discussed and the results recorded.[26] Sheaf after sheaf of his signed handwritten records documented children at their time of loss. He sometimes went with the deputy of the Juge de Paix to the home of newly orphaned children to make an inventory of all family possessions on the death of the parent, to protect the children's rights. On 20 January 1818, on a wintry morning, he had gone out to a farm at a hamlet near Tarare. The father had died on the evening of 18 January, leaving five children under age. The mother had died some years previously. The girl who helped in the house and who had nursed the dying father was there; all the relatives were away at the funeral. The timing was relevant.

He wrote down everything, starting with the focal point of the household, the hearth: skimming ladles, copper spoon, two old cast-iron stewpots with lids, an old axe for the firewood; then moved around the room: an oak wardrobe over the keyhole of which they placed the seal of the office of the Justice de Paix. He as registrar kept the key. The listing continued through the house (including lantern, ladder, cauldron, bread baskets), up in the loft, out in the stable (cow, goat) and the barn, not forgetting to list 'a little fodder to feed the cow'. The girl, Marie Sarcey, took an oath that she had taken nothing, then the deputy of the Juge de Paix and Suzanne's grandfather left.[27] In this way the orphaned children's patrimony was protected as far as possible.

Jean-Baptiste Périer carried on doing this sort of work through the early 1820s. But his own children would quite soon be fatherless. He too died in winter, on 1 February 1826 at the age of forty-nine. He was still listed as the registrar up to his death, so it was not an illness that would have stopped him working long before. He signed his will on 17 January from his sickbed in his home in rue Montagny. Suzanne never knew this grandfather who worked for orphaned children long before she did. Her mother, Clarice, was only seventeen when her father died. As the eldest of the four children, she found family duty and responsibility coming on her shoulders early. Perhaps this was, unconsciously, another reason why she did not want Suzanne to leave the family for religious life.

Suzanne's grandmother, Joséphine Rodde, Madame Périer, was in her forties when her husband died, perhaps unexpectedly early. She was left to carry on bringing up her four children alone. She had a comfortable house in Tarare at 6 rue Montagny, on the hillside, looking out across the valley of the town to the matching line of hills rising high on the other side. The house had 'adjoining land and garden' under separate titles.[28] As an old woman, Suzanne remembered it in a letter as 'full of so many souvenirs'. She meant memories. It was 'Montagni, built by my mother's father a few years after his marriage; where he and his wife lived and died, where they reared their family, where we spent so many happy days'.[29]

Joséphine Rodde lived in a prospering town and she was not poor. But she had insight into the sudden reversals of life. Suzanne spoke of her as being very active in parish welfare, teaching her grandchildren always to be respectful towards the poor, in fact to see in them the figures of Joseph, Mary or Jesus. Joséphine's baptism entry shows a parish priest, who was a paternal uncle, as godfather and the superior of a convent as godmother. Religion was strong in her background, and people in Tarare had a steady tradition of a practising faith.[30] The name Périer figures in the parish records of women's charitable works there. This grandmother had a big influence on Suzanne as she grew up. She seems to have had depth of character and independent judgement. She was Suzanne's only surviving grandparent, in any case, so would have reigned unchallenged in influence and affection.

Suzanne was on the other side of the world when her grandmother died on 20 November 1863. She recorded it in her little 'Aide-mémoire': '26 January, 1864: I receive the news of the death of my beloved grandmother who died on 20 November at the age of 80.'[31] Suzanne got her age wrong: she was seventy-eight. In 1896, after her mother died, Suzanne inherited the house and part of the adjoining property in Tarare. Through her later career in New Zealand, her French inheritances, handed down from her grandmother and mother, as well as from her father, brother and cousin, would continually help to finance her projects, buy land and bolster her independence and ideas.

Tarare was a boom town in the first half of the nineteenth century. Its prosperity came from the textile industry. Lyon's specialisation was silk but Tarare's was muslin. The silken gowns of pre-revolution days gave way to the soft, wafted fashions of muslin, popularised by Josephine, the wife of Napoleon. Tarare was profiting from this shift in style but also from its own initiative. The whole process of weaving cotton muslin was perfected there. Napoleon had visited the town more than once and praised it for its commercial enterprise. Tarare was full of people in the industry at various levels; between 1818 and 1827 the industry employed forty thousand people.[32] In the records of the Périer family there are '*négociants en mousseline*', and sometimes a woman figures in the textile industry, such as Clarice's aunt who ran her embroidery business. Tarare was a stable, welcoming focus for much of Suzanne's childhood memories.

Suzanne's whole family at this time was relatively educated, aspiring, and secure, although nothing could be taken for granted in nineteenth-century *laissez-faire* France. The Lyon area was one where, at least in some quarters, *bourgeois* would have fewer derogatory overtones than in other parts of France. For centuries Lyon had been the 'city of fairs, of jingling coin and credit, of financiers from over the Alps, across the Rhine and from Switzerland. Lyon was the meeting point for business.'[33] Long before, the merchant and banking town-fathers had effectively taken control of the city from the old nobility, and the silk merchants and other wealthy trading people traditionally had established status.[34]

Suzanne Aubert's family also had the relatively stable tenure of a government profession. Her confident dealing with all levels of hierarchy and with any sector in New Zealand was ingrained from her family and Lyon background, as well as being inborn. She had little previous experience of being subservient.

Yet in Lyon there was also a sharp division between the prosperity, even if relative, of some and the hardships of the workers in the mainly textile and clothing industries. Lyon's was 'an economy dominated by a capricious silk market and social relations shaped by abiding antagonism between silk merchants and their labour force meant constant social tension'.[35] Economic rewards were very unevenly distributed and seasonal unemployment or under-employment common. Half of the silkworkers were women, and the care of their children was a dilemma. From the 1820s onwards, Lyon was a leading centre of working-class radicalism. *Bourgeois* would still be a negative term to these people and there was a long history of confrontation which culminated in the 1848 revolution. Suzanne was at her Benedictine boarding-school at the time, in the silk-worker area of La Rochette. She said her father had been in the National Guard. Both sides of the issue were discussed in the household.

In this context, the system of charitable workshops which was one of the church's responses to hardship was considered to be unjust and repressive, and these workshops, or *providences*, were targeted in the 1848 revolution. Orphaned children sometimes worked years of unpaid long hours in them, and this tended to keep overall wages depressed. Other charitable measures could seem merely palliative to radical thinkers. Through her life Suzanne might respond mainly to the immediate needs of social welfare, yet what she said and did shows she was aware from a young age of underlying questions of social justice, especially for women and children.

CHAPTER THREE

France – women and faith
1789-1860

It is time to go away : Ko te taima tenei ki te haere[1]

At this point in her story Suzanne Aubert could easily pack up and leave with Bishop Pompallier for Auckland. There are no known documents for her years as a girl and young woman in France, only the brief note, 'Left for the missions', alongside her name in the roll of the Benedictine boarding-school at La Rochette in Lyon.[2] There is no marriage contract, no trousseau list like her mother's to help pin her down. She did not enter a French congregation, so there is no profile of her in religious archives. Two fruitful sources for documenting women's experience in France are straight away eliminated. She said she had done lay nursing for the Sisters of Charity, but there is no record of this in their archives.

There is evidence that in New Zealand she was writing and receiving family letters regularly for many years but there are only scraps of this correspondence left. In July 1913 she had gone back up the Whanganui River to Jerusalem just before leaving for Rome. The rough walk of four miles down to Ranana for Mass was too hard for her at the age of seventy-eight. Or rather staying back while the others were away gave her the sorting time she needed. Only one other sister was there, in the kitchen. She realised Mother Aubert was destroying her papers when she tracked down the smell of burning wool to the Community Room. In front of the fire was Suzanne: 'She had dropped a paper on the hearth which had ignited and set fire to her skirt.'[3] Suzanne Aubert left Jerusalem the next day with a whole new panel hurriedly sewn into her habit and the ashes of her family record left behind.

It would be simpler, therefore, just to imagine her filling a trunk with items from the list Father Yardin had on hand for the Marist lay sisters in Oceania. It recommended, she remembered, sensible 'loosefitting and light' garments including 'three dozen grey twill britches for riding horses'.[4] Into other trunks would go devotional books, manuals of botany, chemistry and medicine, writing materials, perhaps the little red notebook for her 'Aide-mémoire'. She said two carriers helped her lug these heavy trunks down the stairs in rue Grande Mercière one day when nobody was around. Then she could be on her way to Le Havre and briskly out to New Zealand, where she would get down to work, the old world behind her. But make this mental leap across those missing years and there would be a blank where she had been, and only a flat cut-out figure would go across the Pacific. It would also mean a cowardly skirting around all the memories that she shared with people and that one sister gathered into a collection of reminiscences. This is a full and valuable resource but has often been accepted unquestioningly. With these memories, a legend began to girdle itself around her story and as the years went by tightened into a firm knot.[5]

Mother Aubert in her seventies and eighties was a very popular public figure in Wellington. Her French background over the years somehow filled up with an impressive list of notable people she had met and achievements she had made that would have stretched the capacities of most contemporary French girls of the bourgeoisie. First, in the field of social Catholicism, she was meant to have known Sister Rosalie, the French Sister of Charity who defended the welfare and integrity of the poor and working classes;[6] Pauline Jaricot, who, as well as her mission interest with the Propagation of the Faith, worked in support of Lyon girl silkworkers;[7] and Frédéric Ozanam, founder of the St Vincent de Paul movement. In nursing she indicated she had trained (at one stage briefly at the same time as Florence Nightingale) with the Sisters of Charity and then worked with them in nursing Crimea casualties and cholera victims. In medicine, she said that she had met Ricqlès, from the Lyon Jewish community, who patented medicines. She also said she had studied medicine extensively in Lyon.

Then, in the domain of sanctity, the roll-call was even more notable: Jean Vianney, Catherine Labouré, Philippine Duchesne, Madeleine-Sophie Barat, Giovanni Bosco, Giuseppe Cottolengo, Julien Eymard, Pius IX are all names that carry a lot of spiritual value in nineteenth-century Catholicism. In the mission world were again Pauline Jaricot and Philippine Duchesne, Lavigerie, and the early Marists, among whom were named Cholleton, Champagnat, Jean-Claude and Pierre Colin.

Then there were Jewish converts Ratisbonne and Herman Cohen. More names, and 'others too numerous to mention'.[8]

In the lay world of social strata, there were a few classes in piano from Liszt; this would be unlikely by the 1850s.[9] And there was just a whisper of a family connection with de la Rochejacquelein, the counter-revolutionary aristocratic family from the Vendée, and a line through to Prime Minister Casimir Périer. Suzanne's sister-in-law lends support to the latter claim in a 1921 letter, yet genealogical records show that any connection was not close. The Wellington undertaker notched her father up to 'Judge of the Supreme Court of France' on her death certificate. And an aristocratic *de* slipped into her name: Aubert de Lay. Add for good measure a Périer château, Vizille, and she had a spiritual, professional and social *curriculum vitae* that covered the range of her activities and would inspire devout Catholics, medical laypeople and the fashionable charitable oligarchy of Wellington.

But all this, drawn from the 'Reminiscences', leaves historians sceptical about many points and questioning what psychological or creative need drove Suzanne to embroider, change and invent.[10] It is not too hard to see in the warm public relations glow surrounding Mother Aubert the origins of legend. Was she pumped with leading questions: 'Mother, surely you knew so-and-so'? She was a good publicist and an interesting – even sparkling – raconteur. Constant, invited retelling can imprint a 'real' personal memory of an unexperienced event.[11] She lived till very old, when memory time starts a-gathering and there were people waiting to wrest legend from the grasp of oral history. But she herself was offering legend. Her listeners got a fertile blend of provable fact, possible fact, inflated fact and also fiction-that-*thought*-it-was-fact, fiction-that-*wished*-it-were-fact. The last aspect is important, as anyone or anything she mentioned would be relevant either to her projects or to the spiritual growth of her sisters. Her anecdotes, like parables, most often had a purpose, whether it was to instruct, edify or entertain.

Much was undoubtedly true. Everything that Suzanne Aubert did in her long years in New Zealand points to her potential to move through many challenging situations with energy and aplomb. What the roll-call of the true-or-not legend does is reinforce the importance her religious vocation held for her. All the names she kept producing represent some actual mentors and other, more distant role models for an active young woman with a streak of drama and plenty of faith in her make-up.

To gain an idea of the three-dimensional, twenty-five-year-old woman who arrived in New Zealand, the icon-like image that emerges from the 'Reminiscences of Mary Joseph Aubert, Foundress of the Sisters of Compassion' could be rounded out in the context of what had been happening in France, and specifically in her region, to men and women, their families and their relationship with religion.[12] Her family all stood in their places as typical of their period and location, and their collective experience went into her luggage along with everything else. The intangibles of her background constantly influenced her attitudes and actions in New Zealand. They were going to be updated by the events and people filling her life with the immediacy of a new society. But the old influences were always firmly there.

The rivers Saône and Rhône meet at Lyon. Floodwaters sometimes threatened the streets near the river quays, where Suzanne's family lived. Figuratively, her family also experienced the often stormy confluence of church and state. The headwaters for this can be traced back to before the revolution.[13] Nevertheless, the receding waves of the revolution were still being felt across France through the nineteenth century, as both simple citizens at parish level and sophisticated theorists and politicians came to terms with what had happened.

Before the revolution, six to ten percent of the total land area of France had been owned by religious orders. Much of this was later confiscated by the state and resold. Through the century after it would not be in the interests of the buyers to be too conciliatory to the church. At the height of the turmoil, priests and nuns were massacred, in some instances caged on barges which were sunk in the estuary of the Loire. An estimated two to three thousand priests were killed and 32,500 left the country, the involuntary beginnings of the great French nineteenth-century missionary wave.[14] The clergy were expelled from the ancient enclosures of their abbeys and convents and many were persuaded or forced to marry. The Christian godhead was rejected and replaced by the figure of reason.

In the upheaval that accompanied the revolution, French families suffered extreme hardship. Women were often the ones left to fend for their dependants. For their own economic, social and spiritual reasons, many women supported the stable institution which they knew best and which responded to their immediate and basic needs – the local parish church, with its routine of communal worship, its school, its traditional network of welfare activities. Their standpoint could therefore seem counter-revolutionary. As the revolution was analysed and reviewed through the nineteenth century, the stance taken by many, though not all, women became the standard representation of women's influence on its course. Women in general came to be scapegoated by republican politicians and historians and labelled as one of the major conservative forces, in collusion with the church, that had undermined the revolution.[15]

A clear indication of women's action had come in 1791, when priests were required to acknowledge the new regime by taking an oath of allegiance to the Civil Constitution of the Clergy.[16] France divided into 'juring' priests, those who took the oath, and 'non-jurors', who held out – at risk. Women often spurned priests who took the oath.[17] Underground networks supported 'non-juring' priests and nuns in hiding. Again, women took an active part in helping them to continue administering the forbidden sacraments or to continue teaching and nursing. The diocese of Lyon, with its *culte caché*, a 'hidden worship' movement, ran the best-organised of these networks.[18]

Both Suzanne's grandmothers had lived in Tarare through these years when to be religious held its own drama and danger. Tarare was in the hills and forty-three kilometres from Lyon, just far enough away from the atrocities of the city to act as a refuge for persecuted religious. Some members of disbanded congregations from Lyon, like the Benedictine Sisters and the Sisters of Saint Charles, were sheltered there. Dispersed, without religious costume, they carried on working as individuals. To take two school classes, Sister Chavard walked long distances every day for years from the village of Ancy in the morning to the hamlet of Maillard in the afternoon.[19]

The revolution had polarised and heightened religious and secular elements in French society. One of the most influential figures in Suzanne Aubert's youth, and in the whole of nineteenth-century Catholic France, was Jean-Marie-Baptiste Vianney, the parish priest or *curé* of Ars, near Lyon. He had grown up on a peasant farm which harboured priests on the run. The years of persecution helped make people like Jean Vianney ascetically extreme in their piety and reactionary in their fervent reforming. But others, once the church was so thoroughly challenged in the revolution, began to see clay feet on the statuary of established religion or simply no longer believed, and they became secular and anticlerical (the word in common currency in nineteenth-century France to describe the rising hostility to the church, the sceptical questioning of its hierarchy and the periodic political dismantling of its institutions). For many, especially after the restoration of a conservative Catholic monarchy, the church was tainted with the aftertaste of the rejected *ancien régime*.

It was as if the seismic upthrust of the revolution had emptied the water of religion from the estuary only to have it race back more strongly in the aftermath. For some, like Suzanne's grandmothers, this would be reassuring and invigorating, whereas others had seen the mud, weeds and stones of the bare bed, and would never view the refilled estuary in the same accepting light again. All through the nineteenth century and beyond, this tension in France of pious zeal versus indifference or active opposition was there like a tide, ebbing and flowing according to social pressures, or whichever monarchy, republic or empire was governing at the time.

After the revolution, Napoleon rescued the church yet aimed to reduce it at the same time. To him, religion was a sensible means of re-establishing and maintaining social control, if it were controlled itself.[20] He saw the church's usefulness in rebuilding the collapsed social structures, restaffing the abandoned schools. After the 1801 Concordat with Rome, religious congregations were gradually allowed to re-form but only in an active sphere, out in the community, in works of charity, teaching, and later in nursing. They were not yet permitted to go back into the old enclosed, contemplative monasteries. In Lyon, the Sisters of Saint Charles, traditionally an active congregation whose sisters, like others of its type, took only simple, yearly vows, were allowed to reassemble to teach before the old, prestigious, enclosed Benedictines were. The Sisters of Charity openly took up their nursing tasks again. In this climate, new male congregations around Lyon, like the Society of Mary and the Clerics of Saint Viator, began to form, and they too went out into active service. The emphasis in French religious experience of the nineteenth century went on action and mission.

The first surge of mission was to rescue the 'lost generation'. In so many areas, no catechism had been taught, no sacraments observed, churches had been destroyed, the bells melted for cannon, the priests gone. In the 1820s people like the early Marists swung into evangelical mission work out in the hills around Lyon and set up schools to re-establish Catholic education.[21] The urgency of the task often channelled priests into what seems an almost excessive and reactionary piety. The gentle-faced parish priest who became St Jean Vianney had been sent to the parish of Ars, in the countryside about thirty kilometres north of Lyon, to revive its moribund religious spirit. He set extreme ascetic standards for both his parishioners and himself. He banned the young people from dancing in an attempt to rein in sexual looseness; he tried to keep the men from drinking in the *cabarets*. He regularly scourged himself with chains and went without food and sleep. His aims in this were to win back the people and to keep his soul pure and humble.

Suzanne Aubert, like so many others, venerated him. 'Strength of zeal' was holy. His habit of doling out for himself daily rations of cold potatoes from the one weekly cooking, until he was eating green mould by the end of the week, found its counterpart in New Zealand. Father Séon, an early Marist missionary, at one stage of poverty went beyond the known culinary desert of the pioneer man-on-his-own into this spiritual world of stark physical deprivation, living on meagre rations of nothing but cold beans.[22] Suzanne nursed Séon in the 1870s as he was dying and in her letters this ascetic old man, along with the Curé d'Ars, was clothed in sanctity.

Sometimes she would apply these exacting standards to herself and her companions. The Sisters of Compassion might often have to cook up and eat a relentless succession of sparse servings of donated seasonal vegetables. Celery followed celery followed celery. Suzanne's self-denying toughness had instilled itself long before, in France. It was also there in her younger brother, a parish priest in France. When he was dying, he asked to lie on the hard floor rather than in the undeserved comfort of a bed.[23] She herself refused any pain relief when she was dying; she cut the cloth of her own death out of the same pattern of rigorous and devout self-denial. A good many of France's clergy, in the years that formed Suzanne, were no longer the well-off, well-born people who once had entered the old monasteries and convents. They now tended to come from middle-class and poorer origins. The way they could define and practise asceticism was to push their already familiar economy of lifestyle right out to the limits of pared-down hardship.

Behind such dedication was often intense mysticism. The 'other world' was always present to the Curé d'Ars. On the bright side, he attributed the miracles happening at Ars to the intercession of St Philomena, the girl martyr of the Roman catacombs whose presumed tomb had been discovered in Rome in 1802. Pauline Jaricot had sent him a portion of a relic. On the dark side, he reportedly fought off through the night constant attacks by the devil, whom he vividly called, in French peasant tradition, the *grappin*, the grappling hook.

Historians of French religion identify a strong thread of mysticism weaving through the orthodox, rational and positively minded faith of Lyon.[24] It was a well-tempered mix. Suzanne admired the great mystic, Teresa d'Avila. She said she taught herself Spanish as a young woman in Lyon in order to read Teresa's writings in the original. Yet Suzanne herself was not a mystic in the usual sense. She interpreted faith in a framework attainable by ordinary people, not just by rigorous and intellectual souls. In practical effect if not in style, Suzanne Aubert contributed to Christianity what Thérèse de Lisieux also did, a pattern of faith which was unthreatening, understandable and achievable, and which emphasised love above retribution. She wrote in her *Directory*: 'Let us not try to tread any extraordinary mystical pathway. Let us go to God in a loving, simple way, leaning only on Him.'[25]

She stood at a nineteenth-century divide in Catholic theology. Lyon had theologians from both sides.[26] Behind her were the steep scarps of the stricter elements of Tridentine tradition, dating from the Council of Trent and the Catholic Reformation, still very much present. In front was the gentler, more accommodating slope of what became known as Liguorian theology, offering, as did her own positive intuition, a more tolerant perspective.[27] An open perspective would also be fruitful in New Zealand in the bicultural (at least for her), multi-denominational yet close-knit new society of the lower North Island.

The mystical vision of the Curé d'Ars extended to prediction and prophecy. The village of Ars became the centre for a constant stream of pilgrims. In just two years, from 1857 to 1859, eighty thousand pilgrims from all social strata went to Ars.[28] Suzanne was among those queueing for days and nights to make their confession and to receive his direction for their future lives. The archives of French congregations record 1840s and 1850s examples of people who decided to enter religious life as the result of a simple phrase of the curé – though he did tell others to marry instead.[29] Congregations as much as 'registered' themselves with the curé. Abbé Richard, helping Marist Bishop Bataillon to find vocations for his Pacific mission, wrote to him in 1858: 'Fortunately the Curé d'Ars, whom I saw recently, consoled me by assuring me that the Lord was pleased with our venture and He would send us subjects and material assistance.'[30]

Suzanne's parish church of Saint-Nizier, Lyon, as it is today. Even in Suzanne's time it was surrounded by apartments, shops and offices.

Pauline Jaricot, Saint-Nizier
parishioner, active in supporting
foreign mission, social welfare and
social justice.   OPM

Suzanne's devotional card:
'Our Lady of Fourvière, pray for us'.

The sanctuary to Our Lady
of Fourvière, as it was just
after Suzanne left for New
Zealand. Votive paintings
and plaques can be seen
on the walls.
COMMISSION DE FOURVIÈRE

St-Symphorien-de-Lay.

Suzanne's own album photographs of her family, probably sent to her in Auckland in the 1860s.
Far left: Her father, Louis Aubert, who wrote on the back: 'To my daughter'.
Left: Her younger brother, Camille, probably at his ordination.

Suzanne's elder brother, Alphonse.

Most likely Suzanne's mother, Clarice Aubert.

RAVERAT, c.1860, ARCHIVES DE LA MAIRIE DE TARARE

Tarare in 1860. The Périer home was not far from the viewpoint of the artist.

Pilgrims cluster around the Curé d'Ars. Suzanne would be one of many young bourgeois women like the one on the curé's left.

The Sisters of Charity dispense remedies, visit the poor in their homes, take soup to the sick, teach, help women in trouble, visit prisoners.

This 1865 votive painting from Fourvière appears to show the Aubert family: from left, Louis Aubert with Camille, Suzanne, possibly her mother's sister Zoé in the foreground, Clarice Aubert rising from her sickbed, Louis kneeling beside Alphonse, on the far right perhaps Suzanne's grandmother, Joséphine Périer.

A Sister of Charity escorts an
orphan child to a Providence.
BIBLIOTHÈQUE NATIONALE,
PARIS

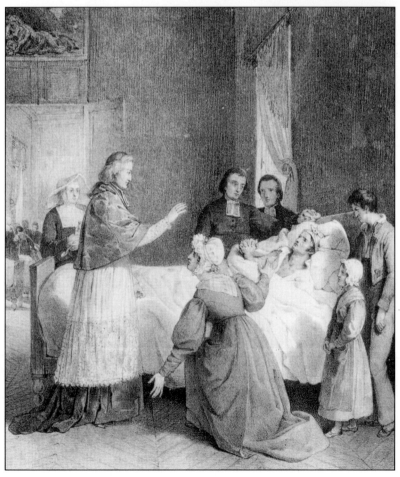

A Sister of Charity waits with medicine bottle and spoon at the foot of the sickbed as the
last rites are administered.   BIBLIOTHÈQUE NATIONALE, PARIS

The curé's advice was instant and unpredictable; he seemed to have uncanny insight and divined people's inner natures. Those who lived too far away to make the pilgrimage often wrote him letters. These came mainly from women and, poignant, sometimes obsessive and desperate, they remain as a record of many women's feelings and experiences.[31] But Suzanne did not live far away. She travelled the short distance to Ars several times, she said, to join the long lines. She took two directions for her life from her undoubted visits to the Curé d'Ars. One was to reject the marriage she said had been planned for her. Her parents had promised her to Jean Verrières, the motherless son of a friend, while she and Jean were still young children. In nineteenth-century France, middle-class and upper-class families still very often arranged their sons' and daughters' marriages.[32] The curé upheld what Suzanne wanted, rather than her mother. Then, on a trip in 1858, which was the peak year of pilgrimages before he died in 1859, he gave her a series of predictions about her future life. As she grew older, she allotted these to various events in the course of her career.[33]

Jean Vianney's words had a third, much later and documented, effect. It occurred in Rome at a time when the cause for his canonisation was being strongly advanced. Suzanne's claim as a Lyonnaise of the 1850s to have known and received guidance from the Curé d'Ars must have given an extra boost to her chances of gaining the Decree of Praise for her congregation. In July 1914 she wrote to her friend Isa Outhwaite that she had gone to a papal audience for Lyon people, in honour of the Archbishop of Lyon's elevation to cardinal. She said that Pope Pius X told her: 'Place your affairs in the hands of the Holy Curé of Ars. He is beginning again to work miracles just now.'[34] In Rome among the cardinals, the little old nun 'from the Antipodes' most probably polished the fine points of any memories of the curé and most certainly and humanly basked in the respect the hierarchy gave her as a veteran pilgrim. Back in New Zealand in 1922, she recommended the curé to many people. Once – and out of character – she ventured into politics, in this case the politics of her friend Nancy Johnston, who was married to political candidate John Rolleston. Vianney 'foretold to me before I left home all that happened to me since I landed', she wrote. 'I send you some of his photos that I got printed, and I feel confident that if you beg of him to help in the electoral crusade, you will feel the effects of his powerful intercession.'[35]

Rome gave the Curé d'Ars an important role in Suzanne's congregation. Even before he was finally canonised, he was placed among the patron saints of the Sisters of Compassion. The announcement that he had been made a saint came in 1925, before her death. In the regard of the Cardinal Protector and the general Catholic public in New Zealand, it certainly gave extra strength to the pedigree of the Sisters of Compassion. The *Tablet* interviewed her at the time:

> This and other incidents the aged Mother Aubert told in quick succession. It was evident that the approaching canonisation filled her mind, and that May 31 will be among the greatest in the history of her Institute. The Curé, who was her adviser, is also the father and protector of her religious family.[36]

Around the marble behind the basilica altar in Ars is engraved the recognition of the curé's role in the formation of the congregation.

These massive pilgrimages to Ars when the young Suzanne lived nearby were only one indication of a renewed interest in pilgrimages, shrines, relics and visions in nineteenth-century France. The veneration of Mary increased enormously. Ordinary people saw her in visions. There was Catherine Labouré, a Sister of Charity, in 1830; then two children out shepherding at La Salette in 1846, and Bernadette Soubirous at Lourdes in 1858. In 1854 Pius IX proclaimed the Dogma of the Immaculate Conception of Mary. This meant that Mary herself was now considered to have been born with the gift of grace, not needing baptism. Pilgrimages to Marian shrines became very popular and miracle cures were widely reported.

Marianism had resurged partly as a result of revolution conditions. Saying the rosary, for instance, could be a relatively safe, home-based expression of faith: 'The rosary was the perfect expression of a fortress faith. It offered the one means whereby the simple and illiterate, stripped of a priesthood and the familiar rituals of church ceremony, could maintain contact with their deity and could do so collectively.'[37] Perhaps, also, the major role women played in sustaining faith through these years lay behind the greater emphasis the early Marists gave to Mary as an active disciple, rather than as the mother at Nazareth. In founding the Society of Mary, they aimed to live out a spirit of support and compassion, of involvement and identification with others which for them came from Mary's presence among the disciples at Pentecost. It was a spirit which attempted to acknowledge the changed times, and quietly heal divisions and unite people.[38]

It was this strong awareness of Mary, then, that propelled the first

French missionaries to New Zealand. In 1846 Father Garin described Maori reaction to a newly arrived statuette of Mary: 'Just at this time', he wrote to his parents, 'I heard that someone in France had sent me a statue of the Blessed Virgin. I was waiting for this statue to be able to establish the devotion [of the rosary] with more solemnity.' After the rosary was recited, the worshippers clustered around the altar to look closely at the statue of Mary: 'a hundred times I heard them saying: – How beautiful Mary is! Kapai a Maria!'[39]

Nowhere in France was more ready for this renewed Marianism than Lyon, with its traditional motto '*Lyon à Marie*' (Lyon belongs to Mary) and its sanctuary to Mary, Our Lady of Fourvière. Lyon held to the doctrine of the Immaculate Conception long before it became dogma. So did Lyon-born Pompallier out in the Pacific, with the stars of the Immaculate Conception flying from his schooner masthead.

The importance of Marian shrines to the devout in nineteenth-century France was incontestable. Suzanne's family had its own story to tell. She said her mother was ill when her brother Camille was born in 1840, and he was placed in foster care with a wet-nurse. Her mother's health continued to worsen. In August 1845, when Suzanne was ten, Clarice was thought to be dying of cancer. She was bedridden. During Assumption, as a last resort and against her husband's wishes, she was helped by a group of military conscripts who carried her stretcher up the steep hill to Fourvière. Inside the sanctuary, as the Mass progressed, she was cured; able to get up, go to the altar rails and receive communion. Suzanne was there. Following normal procedure after a claim for a miraculous cure, a doctor attested Clarice's instant recovery. In 1921 the parish priest of Chatte, where Suzanne's sister-in-law then lived, wrote that he had in front of him Clarice's account of her cure and copied out the wording of the doctor's report.[40] No actual doctor's certificate survives.

In the museum at Fourvière there is a votive painting dated twenty years later, 18 August 1865, in thanksgiving for what seems to be this incident. Suzanne had spoken of seeing the painting in 1919 on her way back from Rome. It shows a woman stepping down from her sick bed in front of the altar with its huge and vivid background framing the Virgin of Fourvière. Her family are grouped in a semi-circle around her, the colours of mid-nineteenth-century dresses and shawls contrasting with sober bourgeois suits. The picture is large and the figures are clearly shown. They fit what is known of Suzanne's family. She said her father had not actually been there but he is painted into the picture, standing with his hand on the shoulder of Camille, the youngest boy. Half-way between them and Clarice is Suzanne herself, a black-haired girl of ten in a bonnet, bright pink dress and white pantaloons. She looks poised to dart forward. Kneeling to the right of the bed is Louis, the disabled brother who died not long after. His head is noticeably bigger than his older brother's, for alongside him stands Alphonse, slim and slightly dapper. Three other women are confident, main figures in the fore-ground. One holds herself very erect and appears to be a widow. She is probably Suzanne's grandmother, Joséphine Périer. The central figure may be her aunt Zoé.

Clarice's recovery came in the middle of a wave of reported miracles at Fourvière. One very similar to hers was recounted by a pilgrim to Ars, telling what he had heard the curé say in a sermon on 28 October 1845: 'See, my children, what has just happened recently at Fourvière! A poor woman despaired of by doctors and everyone, wished to be carried to the church. Her relations were unwilling so she had herself carried by four soldiers. . . . Her sister followed her. At Mass, she kept repeating 'Remember me, remember me' again and again. After Mass she insisted on staying. She said to the Holy Virgin: You have granted graces to all those who asked them of you; you would not want me to be the only one to receive nothing, and suddenly she felt cured and off she went with the others . . .'[41]

Because the three boys and the girl shown in the painting correspond so aptly to Suzanne and her brothers at the time, the painting really does seem to be Clarice Aubert's thanks to Mary for what was, for her, a miraculous cure. It was painted after a lapse of twenty years, which would confirm a long-lasting recovery of health. Or, if Suzanne's father was still less than enthusiastic about expressions of piety, by 1865 Clarice might have been able to use her own money, inherited after the death of her mother in 1863, to commission her handsome votive painting.

Louis Aubert's reticence about his wife's religious devotion was referred to several times by Suzanne. It was not unusual for the time. There was a perceived rivalry between men and the church over the role of women. Both sides had a similar aim, however: women were to live out their life of family duty quietly and with decorum.[42] Even the reaffirma-tion of Mary emphasised this. Through the centuries, the concept of Mary and her role in Christianity had been changing.[43] The nineteenth-century phase accentuated her 'hidden life' and this spilled over to the church's view of woman as retiring and ultimately submissive. By mid-century, the Society of Mary was widening its emphasis from Mary the disciple to include Mary living quietly at Nazareth. Out in the Pacific, for instance, Françoise Perroton was pleased to learn that she had been affiliated to the Third Order of Mary in 1846. But she wrote back, puzzled, to Father Eymard: '[My sisters] try, you tell me, to imitate the hidden life of the Blessed Virgin. Father, what am I to do to become like them; my life is not really a hidden one. I realise that with the stir I have caused, I can never hope to come near to a model as perfect as Mary.'[44] Françoise was voicing the dilemma of women faced with a model of 'unattainable virtue'.

Women's relationship with the church continued to be debated through the nineteenth century. The Civil Code had since 1806 handed women a role with no civil status. Children were under the authority of their father alone, a wife under the authority of her husband.[45] Laymen might grumble about interfering priests, yet they valued religion's custodial influence on their wives and daughters. But 'their' became the operative word. Anticlerical thinking entered the domestic sphere when men felt the church was claiming the greater allegiance of women.[46] An anticlerical book on the purported 'priest-woman-husband' triangle was written by the historian Jules Michelet in 1845 and reprinted at least eight times by 1875.[47] It was a heated topic. Devout women could be pulled both ways in a tug of war.[48]

The tensions seemed all the greater because, at least outwardly, religion was becoming more of a women's preserve in France.[49] Although the pattern varied considerably according to region and period, many ordinary men of France, more than in any other European country of the time, stopped going regularly to church and receiving the sacraments.[50] This did not necessarily mean a loss of faith, but the revolutionary questioning of the church had had its effect. Men often observed only the great feasts of Easter and Christmas and the community-reinforcing processions such as Corpus Christi.

Suzanne indicated that her father was fairly typical. Those in minor legal positions such as *notaire*, *greffier* and *huissier* tended, like teachers, to be anticlerical.[51] Her father would have many anticlerical colleagues. In 1921 the parish priest of Chatte wrote what Suzanne's sister-in-law had told him about Louis Aubert: 'In spite of his charitable nature, M. Aubert, like most of his contemporaries at the time, while publicising the excellence of religion, did not practise it.'[52] Suzanne said that her father was not an active churchman, even though he had sisters who were Benedictine nuns.[53] He did, however, go to Mass at Easter and Christmas and he did take part in the annual Corpus Christi procession. She said she had constantly prayed for him to be reconciled with the church, and this happened just before he died.

The forces contributing to anticlericalism were complex. Enlightenment thinking and the revolution had reinforced people's secular worth, for instance. A man no longer philosophically needed the church in order to feel an upright citizen. This *honnête homme* could stand alongside the saint. The loss of vast land holdings also reduced the church's temporal power. The recording of births, marriages and deaths was now done by the state and this meant a loosening of legal ties with the church. The church's objection to lending money at interest was out of step with growing capitalism. The rise of papal influence, peaking with the proclamation of papal infallibility, was another thorn. The remnants of Gallicanism, whereby the church in France had been linked more to the state and less to Rome, were overcome by Ultramontanism, with its focus across the Alps on Rome. This did not suit the veterans of Napoleon and their heirs. At a very local level, men disliked the attacks by zealous priests on dancing and drinking in *cabarets*.[54] And, not least, many disapproved of what they saw as church interference over birth control in marriage.[55]

The birth rate had been declining in France before the end of the eighteenth century, but the process speeded up in the first half of the new century. France was unique in Europe for this early decline.[56] For the Auberts, Clarice's illness could have curtailed more family. Nevertheless, with four children she was already above the national average. She had no more after the age of thirty-two, like her mother before her. The equal division of inheritance was undoubtedly one reason for limiting the size of a family: the patrimony had more chance of staying intact. Personal attention to individual children was also becoming more valued in middle-class French families.

Abstention, the not infrequent taking of a mistress, and abortion were factors. But coitus interruptus as birth control became a major arguing point. This *onanisme conjugal* was a sin to be confessed. Liguorian theology absolved women, but not men, from the responsibility of this method of contraception. Women's access to the sacraments was safeguarded.

If you did not confess, however, you could not take communion, and men increasingly refused to go to confession, and to church in the first place, rather than be denied absolution and the sacraments.[57]

It made no difference whether it was the local curé in the confessional or the middle-class, individual *directeur de conscience* or spiritual director coming to the family home, husbands could see the priest as a rival in influence.[58] There was some of this tension in Suzanne's family. The 'Reminiscences' record a visit she made with her mother to see Dupont, the 'Holy Man of Tours'. He was not a priest but, as promoter of the devotion to the Holy Face of Our Lord, was receiving pilgrims and giving spiritual guidance. Sister Angela wrote:

> Madame Aubert thought a great deal of him, but, somehow, Suzanne was not enthusiastic at all . . . What tended to prevent her from ever caring very much for M. Dupont, was that a letter he wrote to her mother, after the visit to him . . . , was delivered to M. Aubert's office by mistake. He opened and read it, and was very displeased indeed. The subject matter was a very delicate one, in which he was himself concerned. Madame Aubert was annoyed that her husband had read a letter not meant for him – he had never done such a thing before, it was accidental at first, and, seeing his own name, he read to the end without reflecting further. He was much too honourable a man to do such a thing unless he were taken unawares. Suzanne's sympathies went to her father in this affair – already there was a strong sympathy between them.[59]

Mother Aubert liked and was comfortable with men and understood the forces and strains that controlled them as well. She preferred to bridge gaps between laypeople and clergy, between men and women. In Lyon there was more co-operation than in many other dioceses. There was also more tolerance, and a tendency to separate religion from politics. These were her attitudes too in New Zealand.[60] For her, St Joseph was a reassuringly essential figure in the Holy Family. With the overwhelming ratio of 'blokes' to women in settler New Zealand, this was a warm and constructive philosophy. Perhaps some of it came from a wistful nostalgia for her father and a desire for harmony.

The socialising among women of the bourgeoisie was very often within the church, not just at Mass but in societies which dealt with particular areas of social welfare, mission or prayer. There were many available at Saint-Nizier.[61] Suzanne said that her mother was actively working, like her grandmother, in church welfare organisations, especially helping with pregnant girls and their babies. She said that she herself helped nurse with an organisation caring for girls who had sexually transmitted

diseases. This traditional social Catholicism, which gave needed support
to the poor, was increasingly being questioned, however, by those who
felt it was time to make society more equal rather than just assuage
the results of social inequality.[62] Suzanne and her family lived through
the 1848 revolution in Lyon, surrounded by silkworkers and other
working-class people, aware of these forces for change. In New Zealand
she would protest against the harsh laundry work imposed on unmarried
mothers. Yet, like many of the women in the earlier revolution, her
grandmother's, her mother's and her own response, both in France and
in New Zealand, was to meet identifiable immediate needs rather than
seek wider solutions. If nothing else, Christian charity was an integral part
of her belief, and was a more attainable sphere of activity for women of
her background.

There were also many women's mission groups around Lyon.
Wherever there was a French priest in a New Zealand parish, there were
very likely women stitching back in France. In the Wellington diocese, the
church linen which clothed the altars and the celebrants in the little
wooden hinterland churches of the Maori mission was stitched in the
main by these sewing circles. Father Soulas and Father Cognet would
write requests and letters of thanks from Jerusalem. In 1860, Father
Rocher contentedly reported to Poupinel out in Sydney how things were
going with the ladies. The Ladies of Saint-Chamond had run a good
lottery for them. They suggested, too, he might prepare for them a kava
ceremony after Easter. When he visited the Ladies of the Third Order in
Lyon, twelve of them were busy sewing mission smocks. They proudly
showed him a chest full of vestments almost ready to go. The Ladies of
the Council of Nicaea had almost finished a whole lot of chasubles.[63]

This bustling lay work seldom extended to lay governance. Pauline
Jaricot, one of the most active pioneers in women's lay work, was still
made to feel the curb of her lay status.[64] Minutes of the Saint-Nizier
women's groups show the priest guiding the meetings:

> Tuesday, 21 December 1858, the lady members of the Charity of the Poor
> Incurables of the parish of St Nizier held their annual general meeting.
> Monsieur le Curé presided and opened it with the prayer, followed by the
> reading of the minutes of the preceding meeting and the roll call. Monsieur le
> Curé read the accounts of receipts and expenses of the Charity during the year
> ending. He then urged us to go and see ladies who are thinking of becoming
> members. It is for all ladies to work at extending membership as this will be a
> way of relieving a greater number of poor. Mesdames, said Monsieur le Curé,

you have had a retreat. I was sorry to see there were not enough of you there, there is a lot to gain from these exercises, when you come to them in a spirit of simplicity and the desire to know your duties better. But if you seek man you lose God: let this thought govern you. It will be a means of sanctification for you.[65]

On he went, faithfully reported by Madame la secrétaire, for another page and a half.

This was the realm of the laywoman. But the work of religious sisters was of great importance. Women were entering religious life in unprecedented numbers. Although many older female orders and congregations were reconstituted after the revolution, it was the multiplication of new female congregations that was possibly the greatest phenomenon in nineteenth-century French Catholicism. These continued to rebuild the church-run health, education and welfare systems.

By 1850 there were more female religious than priests, brothers and monks combined. Between 1800 and 1880, two hundred thousand women entered noviciates of four hundred congregations. Recruiting was at a peak between 1855 and 1859 with five thousand novices each year, eighty percent of whom stayed on. By comparison, only thirteen hundred priests were ordained each year at this time. The 1861 census showed that France had ninety thousand women in religious congregations, three quarters of them in teaching for the new literate age. The actual total was probably higher.[66]

Many women found in religious life the independence and action that bourgeois family life was likely to deny them. From 1806 onwards, the civil code had legally confined women in a subordinate role.[67] The previous religious definition of the perfect life for women was cloistered, but the revolution had changed that abruptly when ninety percent of nuns were secularised. Napoleon obliged the new communities to be active. The women were not to be behind walls. They went out. The *bonne soeur* became a byword in French village homes and schools for support that was always on hand. Teaching was first on the agenda. The Sisters of Saint Charles ran local schools all around the area Suzanne grew up in.

From 1840, women increasingly moved into nursing, and after 1852 new congregations specialising in nursing rocketed in number. The women nursed in both homes and hospitals. The Little Sisters of the Poor, in nursing the incurable aged, were also seeking to save the same 'lost generation' the priests had tried to reach forty years before. Suzanne

Aubert's work with the derelict old in Wellington was to be in a similar mould. In the French equivalent of the Crimean war break-through in nursing, it was the Sisters of Charity who were 'ladies of the lamp'.

Lyon, of course, was a good example. Hospitals, hospices, pharmacies were run by female congregations, including the Sisters of Charity, the Sisters of Saint Charles and the Sisters of Saint Joseph. Lots of building was going on. In the prosperous 1850s more schools and hospitals were built than in the preceding twenty-five years. The germ of Mother Aubert's later 'bricks and mortar' phase is there. The women ran or were active in huge enterprises which perhaps gave them more scope than marriage. They had stability, respectability and finally security for their old age within their communities. The widow's lot was not so reliable. Overall, quite apart from intangible spiritual gifts from a religious calling, there could be earthly advantages: 'although the male clergy did not always take kindly to uppity females, there is no doubt that the *congrégations* were the best, indeed the only, chance of a real professional career that an able woman in nineteenth-century France had'.[68]

There was the authority of the diocesan bishops as a heavy canopy over both male and female congregations.[69] Intended by Napoleon to act like 'Prefects in purple', bishops between 1830 and 1860 had almost absolute power over clergy in France, especially diocesan clergy. This lay behind much of Pompallier's attitude. Just as the lay woman was subject to her husband and the curé, so was the religious to the bishop. But an energetic woman might 'manage' her bishop successfully, as Mother Cecilia Maher presumably did with Pompallier in Auckland. Or she could benefit from a perceptive, more benign bishop, as Suzanne Aubert did later with Bishop Redwood. As a last resort, when there was disagreement in interpreting the work that an institute was called to do, she could bypass the bishop and go straight to the Vatican for resolution. This usually took the form of a Decree of Praise, which began the process of granting independent governance to the congregation, putting it largely outside diocesan control. This is what strong women sometimes did, women like Mary Potter, Mary MacKillop, Euphrasie Barbier and, in her own turn, Suzanne Aubert.

Suzanne was among the throngs of young women of her time wanting to enter religious life. The 'Reminiscences' and her later letters record that for years she wanted desperately to join the Sisters of Charity and did a considerable amount of volunteer nursing with them, looking after both

Crimea veterans and cholera victims. This is quite possible. Somewhere she certainly learnt nursing skills. It could not have been purely by reading the many French medical volumes she owned and studied in New Zealand, where she marked relevant pages with scraps of Hawke's Bay newspapers or little devotional cards.

She said she had given her parents until she was twenty-five before she would independently join a congregation. While she was waiting out the years she must have acquired these medical skills. She was known as a good bone-setter, a useful attribute in accident-rife pioneer New Zealand. She was interested in pharmacy and knowledgeable in chemistry and botany. She was already experimenting with medicines in the 1860s. Perhaps she helped at the Quatre-Chapeaux pharmacy run by the Sisters of Saint Charles, or at the pharmacy at Tarare, where the same sisters welcomed herbs and plants grown or gathered by the local women to make into remedies for their hospital.[70]

For whatever reason, her parents opposed her wish to join religious life. They had one son in the lay world on the jurist path of the family men, another training as a priest. Their bonding with their only daughter, intelligent, articulate, practical and capable, was evidently a very strong factor in the family dynamic. It may have helped the two parents, tugged by the strains on nineteenth-century bourgeois marriage, to find common ground. Suzanne was blocked from stepping into this world of active sisters until Bishop Pompallier appeared on the scene and she saw her chance to go.

In Suzanne's trunks were packed all these invisible people and influences. The Sisters of Charity and the world of nursing were there; the Benedictine nuns with their structured spiritual life and the intelligent teaching they gave her; the laywomen of Lyon and Tarare with their many charitable *oeuvres*; the Curé d'Ars – his stoic, ascetic piety and his vision for her; the mission strand of the Propagation of the Faith, the Pacific tradition of the local Marists and Françoise Perroton; the merchants of her Tarare and Lyon background with their practical, property-owning acumen; her father and his less pious world of the aspiring professional *honnête homme* – which would fuel her respect for honourable even if creedless settlers; Camille, her seminarian brother with his foster-child experience; Louis, her dead brother, born disabled; her mother and her grandmother in the mould of the middle-class, devout laywoman. All this and more went with her to New Zealand.

When Suzanne finally left for New Zealand, it had to be in defiance of her family and without their knowledge. She 'ran away'. In 1868, her brother wrote to Father Poupinel in Sydney: 'My father has thought he should write to my sister and give her a formal order to come back to France and take up again in the fold of her family the place that she had abandoned without any notice or prior permission.'[71] Suzanne left for Paris and from there went to Le Havre, letting her family think she was going to Ars for the first anniversary commemorations of the death of the curé on 4 August. Her father left before her on business. As if just for a few days, they kissed goodbye at the apartment building door. 'I was stiff, frozen stiff', she remembered. 'My teeth were chattering in my head. I was glad it was dark on [those] stairs or he would have seen something . . . I knew I would never see him again. It was like death – it was *worse* than death!'[72] Suzanne was experiencing not just the commonplace of most of the people about to go away to New Zealand – an aching grief at realising, as a young person, you would never see your parents again. With her the pain was sharper still. She did not even have their blessing and farewell.

CHAPTER FOUR

From France to New Zealand
1860

Unfurl the sails : Koķirihia nga tera[1]

Two of Pompallier's other mission recruits for New Zealand described their departure in a letter. 'We left Paris on 3 September', they wrote to the superior of their congregation, 'and off we were on the road to Le Havre where we arrived the next day at 5 o'clock in the morning. There all twenty-three of us assembled: to give you an idea, our Bishop, an Irish priest and an Irish seminarian, nine Franciscans from Italy of whom six are priests, two seminarians from Lyon, finally both of us. I was forgetting one seminarian from Bordeaux and one from Nancy.'[2] Somehow they overlooked mentioning the four women who came into their overall tally. Lucie Pompallier, Péroline Droguet, Antoinette Deloncle and Suzanne Aubert were unobtrusively boarding too.

Several of the men listed by the letter-writers would feature in Suzanne's story over the next decade. Their impressions and reactions, even from their male perspective, would sometimes parallel her own experiences, at other times contrast with them or throw them into relief. First on the list was Bishop Pompallier. He had his complement of missionaries safely garnered now and could put behind him the anxious times assembling his subjects. He could also put off their reaction to realities he had not prepared them for. Le Havre gave him a heart-warming send-off: 'By midday we were on the ship, we were leaving the harbourside where almost the whole town had gathered to receive the benediction of the Bishop and wish us good fortune for our voyage.'[3]

The Irish priest mentioned next was Pompallier's secretary, Father Walter McDonald. He had packed the bishop's gear to go on the *Général Teste*, listing fourteen assorted boxes of vestments, clothes, rosaries, relics, a large portrait of the Blessed Virgin Mary, copies of Pompallier's just printed background summary in French of the Catholic Mission in New Zealand, Maori histories of the Old and New Testament, other books, blotting paper in bulk, and two 'rools of Portraits of the Bishop'.[4] One of the photographs from these two rolls was already hanging in the reception room of the Franciscan superior general in Rome, left behind by a relieved and appreciative Pompallier. McDonald and Pompallier were the only ones returning to Auckland. All the others were new.

The only other English-speaker was James Hoyne, a student training to be a priest. Pompallier would have liked more men from All Hallows Missionary College just outside Dublin. Back in 1848 he had already said that he saw the new All Hallows training ground as heaven-sent. It prepared its missionaries mainly for the Irish emigrants dispersed around the English-speaking world. They would be secular priests under the sole authority of the bishop, not members of an independent religious congregation.[5] On this latest trip he had written to the director and set forth his needs: 'I want many Missionaries, Resources to convey them to Auckland, and helps of all kinds, good prayers, holy Sacrifices and communions: all celestial things that I have already, I hope, in your holy Seminary for foreign Missions. May God reward you more and more, your Respectable codirectors and the beloved Students of your Apostolic Nursery!'[6]

When Pompallier was in Ireland in May 1860, he enrolled at All Hallows two other young men he had met there, but he could not leave any money then for their training. He had to put off paying. He asked: could All Hallows 'do the favour to expect the funds in this manner for a year?'[7] All Hallows was at a low point in its development in the early 1860s and the men emerging from it did not always have the depth of training or understanding necessary for far-off missions or raw new countries. Pompallier already knew that James Hoyne on his own, only a seminarian anyway and not a mature priest, would not be enough to meet the demand in Auckland, with its Irish fencible settlers and rising immigrant wave. But he could not have foreseen that other Irish would soon pour into Auckland province – thousands of soldiers, followed by government-assisted settlers on confiscated land, and gold-diggers for the booming Thames goldfields.

From the Ara Coeli community of Friars Minor in Rome came eight Franciscans.[8] These were well-trained priests and brothers, comparatively well equipped. The three names which would crop up most often in the years to come were Ottavio Barsanti, Domenico Galosi and Nivardo Jourdan. The Franciscans had a written agreement between their order and Pompallier, who saw the future relationship as reassuringly simple: 'As religious, they are all in the hands of the religious Superior', he explained to the head of the Clercs de Saint Viateur, 'and as members of the Mission [of the Diocese of Auckland], they are in the hands of the Bishop through the local Superior, who is at the head of the Religious and appointed by the religious authority of their institute.'[9] Not so simple in fact. Pompallier had had no experience with members of an independent congregation since his failed beginnings with the Marists. Back then, as local head of mission, he had clashed with the Marist superior general over this sharing of responsibilities. How would he handle the matter of authority with the Italian Franciscans?

Money must surely be another bone of contention, again. The Society for the Propagation of the Faith had already given Pompallier his year's allocation, which would be taken up entirely by travel expenses. It was not enough, as he wrote to Propaganda Fide in Rome. If Cardinal Barnabò could not provide the shortfall, Pompallier would send his Franciscan missionaries 'a letter of credit for two to three thousand francs, to enable them to make the trip from Rome to Lyon to Le Havre'. The cardinal was to do what he could, please, and God would do the rest.[10] What would happen when the letters of credit fell due?

Next were five French priests in training: Emmanuel Royer, Laurent Vinay, Hugues d'Akermann and, released from Lyon by the cardinal, François Boibieux and Pompallier's own nephew, Antoine Pompallier. They were young and eager and in only the early stages of their seminary studies.

Last were the 'both of us' penning the letter, the two teaching brothers Pompallier had recruited to run a planned college for Maori teachers. Brothers Jean-Marie Grange and Pierre Archirel were from the Clercs de Saint Viateur, a congregation originally from the parish of Saint-Nizier. Their letters document very vividly and fully the events of the trip to New Zealand. As chroniclers, they become significant in Suzanne's story because, in this discrete segment of her life, her oral account passed down the years has been corroborated by their contemporary record. Many details of her 'Reminiscences' might be wrong, but in the essentials they probably contain more that is 'true' than is historically provable.

The headquarters of the Clercs de Saint Viateur were at Vourles, outside Lyon, where Pompallier had spent much of his childhood. He had worked as a curate to their founder, Louis Querbes, so there was a friendly association going back for years. At Easter he had been trying to persuade them to release some men, but their limited resources and manpower as a new congregation were fully stretched in France and Canada. After two abortive mission attempts elsewhere, they were shying off ill-equipped ventures and refused Pompallier's requests. They did offer to reconsider at a later date. On his return from Rome, he renewed his persuasive efforts.

Grange was in his mid-thirties and Archirel in his mid-forties. They ran two neighbouring schools and were very well-regarded and dependable members of the congregation.[11] Pompallier's call to mission had its effect: 'Yesterday morning', wrote Grange, 'Monsieur Archirel and I were with Bishop Pompallier, who won us both over to him and his work. Embarkation has to be within three weeks, so we need a prompt reply from the Father Superior.'[12] When the superior was away, Pompallier had approached the two men directly. Favre was a little unsure still as superior, having just taken over in 1860 after the death of the founder. But there is a wry awareness in his commentary:

> His Lordship returned to the charge with renewed pleas not to let him go away without taking with him some of the children of his friend M. Querbes who had, he said, promised this to him previously and who would not have failed to honour this promise, if he were still alive.
>
> Providence allowed the Prelate to have a discussion with two local confrères and he was so convincing that he won them over and he quite made up their minds to follow him. All this was going on while I was away . . .[13]

Favre urgently but responsibly sampled opinion among seventeen local superiors of the congregation. They sent back requests for the practical details that Pompallier had been short on: was there more information available on the planned institute, what did His Lordship exactly have as his aim for it, would the two men be guaranteed not to be separated, what sort of pupils would be taught, what languages needed, where would they be based, what about the customs of the country about which they knew nothing? Surely long friendship with Pompallier was not enough reason to send two of the best men seven thousand leagues away? One community leader in the Loire sent a pithy no: 'I have consulted God and common sense and the response I received was that it would be pure stupidity to send off to get lost in the forests of Oceania two confrères who are dear and useful to us. If we have to trim branches from our little tree, let them be rotten ones!'[14]

But the speed and urgency had their own momentum and, in a bewilderingly short time, the two men were in Paris waiting for word from Pompallier to proceed to Le Havre. 'We've just learnt by hearsay that the Bishop is working at reducing his costs, arranging a load of supplies, which will mean another delay. We don't know yet the departure date.'[15] Pompallier finally summoned them and they travelled overnight to board ship and sail straight away. Their families were not told. Archirel's brother and sister-in-law found out by chance when they brought butter and cheese on a routine visit and were told why he was gone. They were very upset and told Archirel's sister, who went to Vourles at daybreak the next day to demand an explanation. They were consoled with the argument that Providence had intervened.

In fact, the Clercs de Saint Viateur themselves were bewildered by the turn of events and were not at all sure what might be the work of Providence, which one did not question, and what just might be manipulation. Grange unwittingly voiced their unease: Pompallier won the men over 'to him and his work' in that order. He reassured the superior that the brothers' status would be like the Franciscans' and a copy of that agreement would give them 'an idea of the harmony and the union which exists between the Regulars [members of an order] in my Diocese and the bishop himself'.[16] But actually there was no independent religious congregation then in the diocese. Pompallier worded the letter so that what applied to the (equally new) Franciscan missionaries made it seem as though there were well-proven working relations with an established congregation in Auckland. The Sisters of Mercy, despite their origins in and association with Carlow in Ireland, were still diocesan communities under the complete authority of the local bishop. He continued: 'Don't be afraid on any account, my dear friend; all measures are well in hand in advance so that a religious institute may grow, flourish and bear fruit in its own nature and independent sphere in my diocese.' All around him were men and women trusting in promised measures. Without those measures, Providence was all they had.

Up the gangplank on 4 September 1860 went Pompallier's newest consignment of missionaries for New Zealand. The ship, a three-master, pulled away from the quay as the clockface of the library at Le Havre showed midday. The houses of Le Havre were scarcely out of sight when the ship met the open sea. With the lighthouse and the cliff of La Hève still in view, the sea was doubtless starting to claim 'its accustomed tribute in seasickness'. 'From the second day out, several were off-colour, then others were lying down, dragging themselves around, vomiting; some were in a bad way right from departure to arrival.' But not them, wrote the two men. 'We, thanks be to God, were not seasick. Mr Grange is in better health even than at Rochetaillée. His Lordship often said to us that we were born sailors.'[17] Suzanne was not a born sailor. She was one of the sufferers and hated sea travel ever afterwards.

On board already was a crew of forty men, officers and sailors. The newcomers were 'squeezed in like anchovies in a barrel. Both of us shared a wretched little cabin only two metres long, where daylight came through a pane narrower and no longer than a hand. Our beds were one above the other. One of us could only get ready for bed or get up when the other was out of the cabin; so we spent almost the whole day on the deck in the open air.'[18] With the secret of sea travel under their belts, the two novice sailors could join the crew in the regular 'ten paces up and down, up and down' that was part of ship health, 'each leaning his body instinctively against the roll of the ship, taking the same number of paces as the man next to him, straightening his body against the pitch, pivoting always at the same spot and to the same side, shaking disdainfully from his head the spray from a wave that has broken over the bulwarks, . . . keeping up the conversation all the while.'[19]

The ship headed down the Atlantic. The men recorded their version of the ever-repeated and ever-fresh emigrant experience:

> [I]n the Ocean we were in absolute solitude; sea and sky, sea and sky, and never any other object on these vast depths than our ship, sometimes on an even keel and other times rolling this way or that, sometimes driven strongly by the winds and waves either in the direction we were heading or the opposite one, and at other times bestilled on this expanse of water as smooth as ice, where not a puff of wind came to imprint the lightest of wrinkles. Being becalmed like this is greatly to be feared at the equator where the sun is so fierce; we had one of these calms which lasted ten days.[20]

They also had two bad squalls which terrified them and sent the sailors scrambling over the rigging. In the first the ship heeled over on its side in roaring seas rising high above it; sails had to be cut to right it. In the second, a sailor fell from the top of the mast into water so rough that he could be glimpsed only when he came to the peak of the mountainous wave. He was rescued with difficulty and brought back to the ship 'where the captain gave him a revolting reception. Poor sailors!!!'

In the tropics, in one of the calm spells, Antoinette Deloncle gave them their third scare:

> Another day a nun fell into the sea, I don't know how, and was noticed the very moment after by a Franciscan who raised the alarm. The ship echoed with shouts and the racing feet of the sailors; boats were lowered and after a few minutes she was rescued. Poor girl! . . . If the ship had been going at the same rate as an hour earlier, she would have been drowned before the boat could get to her. And how come she wasn't eaten by the sharks that we had seen in such great numbers in these waters? Truly Providence was looking over us in a wonderful way![21]

Suzanne may not have been breezily pacing up and down deck very much. She was often seasick in a cabin she shared with Antoinette Deloncle. Antoinette must have been the other girl in Father Yardin's reference to the two young women who had wanted to join the Marist mission in the Pacific. Both families were opposed to this. Suzanne said that Antoinette was the only one she had known before leaving. She was only nineteen years old and, like Suzanne, may have run away from home to go with Pompallier. Both women were unwell. Suzanne said that Antoinette suffered heat stroke soon after they crossed the equator on 7 October,[22] and developed 'brain fever'. Suzanne nursed her day and night for a week. The cabin was kept locked, so they must have been concerned about what the sick girl might do. When Suzanne fell asleep this time, Antoinette took the key from under Suzanne's pillow, slipped out of the tiny cabin and threw herself overboard.

Suzanne said Pompallier blamed her for this but Péroline Droguet helped with the nursing from then on until Antoinette seemed to have recovered. Antoinette's suicide attempt or cry for help is a neutral entry in Suzanne's little red notebook : '14 October 1860. Sister Marie fell into the sea.'[23] What had gone so wrong? A French whaling surgeon identified shipboard depression as 'maritime spleen' and explained to his readers 'these great attacks of sadness that nothing can explain and nothing can cure'. He recognised the cause when his own mood turned to black in the listless calms of the tropics.[24] In Antoinette's case, was it the combination of seasickness in the relentless pitching and tossing, heat stroke, cramped living quarters on an unsuitable vessel, insufficient rations, the shock of changed circumstances? Was the strain of breaking from family and country just too much? Was reality already proving unbearably different from the picture painted? Or had her decision to go in the first place come from some psychological trauma? Antoinette never fully recovered, and she was the first casualty.

Look back and see the waves rising up high like the spouting of a whale :
Tahuri koutou ki muri, titiro atu, e tu ana te wai, koia ano hei
te pupuhatanga tahora, teitei noa ake te puahata[25]

There was something that Pompallier did not tell his new recruits before leaving, nor the Society for the Propagation of the Faith, nor Propaganda Fide in Rome, nor the Franciscans, nor the Clercs de Saint Viateur. He used various terms for the ship but not the word 'whaler'. Yet Pompallier, McDonald and two students destined for Rome had already come to France in 1859 on the whaler *Général d'Hautpoul*, owned like the *Général Teste* by Guillot Frères of Le Havre. The report by the captain of the former echoes almost ruefully the usual financial theme:

> Bishop Pompallier requested a passage for himself and three others, in order to take advantage of such a direct and speedy opportunity of visiting our Holy Father. Although I had already refused to take passengers, I agreed to take him, and postponed my departure for a few days to give him time to make his preparations. It was decided that he should pay me £200 sterling or 5,000 francs, for the four persons. I agreed to accept payment on arrival in France in order to spare him the difficulties he might have in procuring the necessary funds. As my ship was not fitted for carrying passengers I was obliged to prepare her for the guests and buy provisions. Everything being very expensive in the growing colony, this ran me into a considerable sum.[26]

All but one of the outward passengers came from France and Italy, so to leave from England would be an additional cost. Most shipping at that time would take them only to Melbourne or Sydney, where Pompallier would have to purchase further passage across the Tasman. The cheapest solution was a voyage direct to Auckland on the ship owned by 'my excellent Christian friends', Guillot Brothers. This much he explained in a letter to Barnabò, but he did not mention that the purpose of the voyage was whaling.[27]

Whalers were tightly fitted out for officers and men only, with seven to eight whaleboats, pulleys and tackle, the furnace on deck, *le blubber's-room* opening below – everything designed to handle and process huge whale carcasses and to store the end-products. On board this whaler went up to twenty-six extra people, many of whom would never have been at sea before. The reek of whale oil, and of rotting or burning whale flesh, was no help to Suzanne's seasickness. Three sperm whales were caught in the southern Pacific. The smoke, flame and smell of the furnace went with them across the grey, windswept stretch to Auckland.

Keeping further south would shorten the distance to be covered in the unbroken trip. Suzanne always believed that they did not call into Sydney, as she thought they would, because they went south to track whales. She was expecting to become a member of the new Marist Third Order of Mary at the Sydney headquarters before going on to Auckland. When she arrived in Auckland, she noted down what she thought was only a temporary solution: 'we are lodged with the Sisters of Mercy'. But Pompallier already knew the ship was going straight to Auckland. He had in fact requested a direct passage from Guillot Frères, and pointed this out as a financial advantage to Barnabò back in April.[28] He was not totally direct with the four French women.

To add to the difficulties, provisions ran short. Three times rations had to be cut back. The hold was searched in vain for the stores meant to be loaded at Le Havre. Suzanne's memory was that the bishop 'was inclined to blame the captain' and then he 'sadly recognised' that Guillot Frères 'had played him false'.[29] Archirel and Grange admitted to 'some periods of weakness, because we were not fed according to the agreement between His Lordship and the shipowners in Le Havre. The captain accused these gentlemen of not having loaded on board the necessary stores; but thanks be to God, we are all in good health.'[30] The Franciscans noted that before embarking they had accepted Pompallier's reassurances about provisions.[31] It could be that Guillot Frères' provisioners did not fulfil a commission depending on yet another letter of credit.

The monotony of the days with no landfall or ship contact, and the hunger, were relieved by study and talks given by the bishop. On the 1850 voyage he had done the same with great success for the Sisters of Mercy, who wrote of them with pleasure.[32] He presumably thought he had taken the eight students of 1850 a long way in their studies, as he quickly ordained them priests. He did the same with the students of 1860. As an educator, Pompallier was able to use his real strengths. Teaching had been his background before he was quickly promoted to bishop and mission leader in 1836.

With reason, Pompallier attracts the constant barbs of criticism for his disregard of practical planning, his financial mismanagement which rebounded on his people, his complacency and self-centredness, his paralysing belief in absolute episcopal authority, and his unconscious prevarication which would blindfold him as much as it did others until disillusionment cleared their vision but never his. Official archives, however, tend to emphasise the troubles of distressed missionaries at the expense of the other happy times. Families might have received the letters of contentment but such letters rarely survived. The view of Pompallier building up so far in this story is somewhat sceptical, and the balance needs to be redressed. He was 'a genuinely devout man of very consider-able talent and vision, an idealist willing to spend his life in the service of others. His vision, however right and admirable, outreached his capacity to fulfil it – and he never realised or admitted the difference.'[33] In the *conférences* he gave on the moving deck of the ship, his listing reputation rolls back towards equilibrium. Because here, with limitless sky above and ocean around, he could impart this vision and idealism far from any landlocked need for the capacity to fulfil it. Throughout her life, Suzanne gave credit to Pompallier for the vision which she had the capacity to realise and to share with others.

One of Pompallier's strengths was, paradoxically, his inability to extricate the Maori from the matrix of early mission. His memory of himself as the tall, handsome, eloquent younger man suddenly given a titular bishopric and a huge slice of the world's surface on a platter was important to cherish. With himself cast in this nostalgic role, the Maori had to remain as proud, independent hapu and iwi led by chivalrous chiefs full of prowess and worthy to be peers in a duel of faiths. He actually wrote and had published in Paris in 1860 a twenty-nine verse poem of the history of the mission called 'Memories of New Zealand'.

Mission was romantic, poetic, even epic. His views were tinted a little through the eighteenth-century optimistic 'noble savage' prism which had coloured also the approach of the early French explorers, especially Marion du Fresne.[34] The higher the valour of the Maori, the higher Pompallier's own spiritual worth would be. In Europe he had Father McDonald write on his behalf a long account of the 1845 attack on Kororareka, and this had just been printed in the 1860 issue of the Annals of the Propagation of the Faith. But the harking back to 1840s events nearly backfired on him in 1860 when one of the Clercs de Saint Viateur superiors reacted sharply: 'Why expose our confreres maybe to be

eaten by these savages? You've no doubt read the letter written by
Bishop Pompallier's secretary dated Rome, 2 February 1860. You've seen
what danger His Lordship and his companions were exposed to. It's not
all that encouraging.'[35] The irony was that just a few years into the
future their own man, Grange, would narrowly escape the same death as
Rev. Carl Völkner.

   The wars of the north which had hampered the mission, the population
decline among Maori, their new and dynamic trading patterns, were all
currents that really called for Pompallier to modify this view of himself and the mission. He could not do it. He saw Maori as both fierce
aristocratic warriors and passive corralled lambs under his spiritual
shepherding. This was the model he conveyed to the 1860s missionaries.
There was nothing negative or supercilious, nothing belittling beyond
the persistent biblical sheepfold metaphor. The mission to the Maori was
a great crusade. Respect and consideration were positive attitudes owed to
these people still on the threshold of Christianity. Through the 1860s wars
the fierce warrior theme would still be valid. But the Maori largely turned
their back on Christian shepherding.

   In his 1859 printed account of the mission to Maori, Pompallier was
firm about the importance of knowing their language. To know the
language was to understand them better: 'Knowing something of a
foreign language can sometimes give to an educated and perceptive man
certain insights into the nature of peoples, the origin of their race and their
intellectual and moral capacities.'[36] Pompallier considered himself a good
linguist and saw this as a simple prerequisite. Archirel, who had had to
give up training for the priesthood because he could not cope with Latin,
tried his hardest on board ship. 'We worked at English and Maori; His
Lordship and his secretary taught us. Mr Grange understands and already
speaks English well; as for me, I'm starting to stammer out a few words.'[37]
They had to learn two new languages at once. As Suzanne recalled it, the
Bishop taught the women a little Maori but not much English.

   Pompallier emphasised the need to learn Maori in a long letter on the
subject to All Hallows, gently reminding the Irish college that Catholic
settlers were not meant to be their only apostolate. Without knowing
the Maori language, 'a priest may remain too national and not become
apostolical'. Missionaries needed to learn the 'language with a good
amount of perfection'. The souls of the Maori were 'of the same value,
before the cross of redemption, as the souls of the Europeans'. Pompallier

was not reminiscing this time; his diagnosis of what a newly arrived
priest might feel was up to date and accurate:

> The apprehension to be changed from a place of comfort amongst emigrants;
> the defects of the aborigines not well civilised; the anticipation of a future
> extinction of their race, which perhaps will never take place, except at the end
> of the world, may be consideration which might paralyse the zeal of an
> apostolic vocation not yet well tried in the practice of the apostolic life.
>
> But what strikes me with affliction often in New Zealand, is to see only a
> small number of British Catholic priests knowing the Neo-Zelandaise
> language and English Protestant Ministers numerous and spokeing it so much
> as to exercise the functions of preachers.[38]

Pompallier would be aware that many of the English Protestant ministers
were by now the second generation, born in New Zealand and mostly
speaking Maori bilingually from childhood.

'A place of comfort amongst emigrants' was precisely what Suzanne
did not want. She followed Pompallier's advice, learning Maori and
becoming 'well tried in the practice of the apostolic life'. Here on the ship,
she must surely have been determinedly learning her Maori vocabulary
from the small book Pompallier had just had printed in France: 'Air : Hau;
Ame humaine : Wairua; Ami : Hoa; An : Tau; Ancre : Punga; Ange :
Ahere . . .'[39] – air, soul, friend, year, anchor, angel.

Respecting Maori culture went along with learning the language
in Pompallier's mission principles. How much this consideration had been
strategic in the beginning is a moot point. He was undoubtedly promoting Catholicism over Protestant 'heresy' by offering Catholic tolerance
to Maori as an attractive alternative to Anglican and Wesleyan onslaughts
on such customs as haka and tattooing. Certainly Rev. William Williams
saw Pompallier's gradualist approach as a threat.[40] But Pompallier's
awareness of the importance of cultural identity seems genuine and
intrinsic.

He consistently pointed out that expectations had to be relative to the
environment. Out in the mission field the priests were not to be inflexible.
They needed to distinguish between 'very bad things, extremely bad
things, and slightly bad things; others which are neither good nor bad
in the eyes of God, others finally which are slightly good, extremely
good and very good'.[41] A certain synthesis of traditional and Christian
customs and values was a stage on the path to the new faith. Back in
1841 Pompallier told his priests not to worry about what their Maori
parishioners were wearing to church: 'God does not require European

dress from those who want to serve Him – He wants our hearts and that is all. . . . It is better to go to Heaven after wearing your own country's clothing than go to Hell in European clothes.'[42]

His humanitarian theory and teaching remained consistently respectful of Maori identity over the years. Even if he never went outside Auckland in later life, he instilled these principles into the men who did live among the Maori. His press release on his return to Auckland in 1860 was bilingual. It contained the full text in Maori of the welcome speeches and the names of the chiefs doing the welcoming, as well as the English account of the Pakeha welcome from clergy and laypeople. It was only the newspaper editor who 'for lack of space' edited the Maori right down. Suzanne lived next door to Pompallier for eight years, working with Maori girls. She kept these values throughout her life.

Pompallier taught them on the ship how to achieve results through tolerance. Again, as often, he did not always practise what he preached but the psychology in the preaching was sound. He used the same message of appropriate response in dealing with a shipboard dispute. A missionary had rounded on the second mate, telling him off for swearing 'in real whaling style' at a sailor. The swearer's rage only redoubled. Pompallier pointed out to the priest that he was partly responsible for the escalation with his ill-timed ticking off: the man in his anger would not even know what he was saying. There was a time and a place for everything.[43] Suzanne remembered this incident and used it often with the sisters as an analogy for dealing with children. A sister had to make sure she confronted children at such a time and in such a way that they were not panicked into telling a lie. Otherwise the sister would have been responsible for that lie. She wrote the principle into her *Directory* for the sisters:

> Correction must be made with discretion and prudence, and never under the influence of passion. It must be just and in proportion to the offence. The child ought to be able to understand by the degree of the correction what is the degree of the fault.[44]

Pompallier's tolerance went beyond personal psychology to public policy. Arriving only two years before the Treaty of Waitangi, the French 'alien' bishop learnt quickly to weave a tolerant thread through prejudice in the new British colony. As Catholic bishop he also wove the same thread through the sectarian animosity of English missionaries. The earlier ones had left England when Catholicism was still legally discriminated against there. He was in fact as much against 'heresy' as they were against 'Popery' and his tolerance could be strategic. In 1840 Surveyor-General Felton Mathew wrote that Pompallier's 'conversation and manner impressed me with the conviction of his being a very good man – and he presents a striking contrast in liberality of sentiment and disinterestedness of conduct with our own missionaries . . . I have a great reverence for this man and intend to call on him.'[45]

By 1860 the bishop had proved this policy very successful for promoting harmony in Auckland. It was a way of keeping prestige and credibility in a disparate settlement with a swarm of different denominations. The Italian Barsanti, coming from a monocultural Catholic world, would initially be shocked by all these 'sects', but Pompallier's tolerance was practical and reassuring for new settlers who were, like as not, hoping to have turned their back on old world conflict.

Pompallier could publicly seek sympathy and esteem. He used tolerance and his 'good citizen' record to advance the cause of Catholicism. One instance was in February 1859, when some Bible Society members had made slighting remarks about Catholicism at a public meeting in the presence of the governor. The issue was Catholicism's withholding the whole text of the Bible from its people. Pompallier wrote a long letter to Governor Thomas Gore Browne which he had published in the *New-Zealander* along with the governor's reply. He explained and defended the Catholic position. Then he emphasised his 'devotedness to the population of New Zealand, white and Natives' and expressed his relief that Governor Browne 'could never agree with anything that would breathe fanaticism in proceedings and expressions'.[46] The moral high ground was Pompallier's, the governor was co-opted up there with him, and the bishop emerged the civilised Christian compared with the 'intolerant' members of the Bible Society.

Pompallier's example of how to foster Catholicism in New Zealand was a model for Suzanne later on. It probably also came from their joint Lyon background. A fund of positive religious opinion, banked skilfully out there in the secular world, worked wonders for the psychological security of a young nation. This was one of Pompallier's main contributions to the history of New Zealand.

Auckland on the horizon put a stop to the shipboard instruction. They nearly ran aground off the coast; they narrowly escaped striking a rock coming into the harbour. Flying from the masthead the French signal (rather than the whaler one), they announced the bishop's welcome return. It was 30 December, a fine summer afternoon with the harbour sparkling and the town in holiday mood. It was a Sunday, and the next day would be New Year's Eve. Pompallier could not have timed it better for an exuberant reception. People flocked down to the harbour to watch the passengers come in to the wharf in three boatloads. The newspaper account of the landing has echoes of Archirel and Grange's listing at Le Havre. Bringing up the rear were the nine students with Walter McDonald. In the middle was the boat with the six Franciscans and the two brothers of the Clercs de Saint Viateur. In the first boat were the bishop, his vicar general, James McDonald, and Father O'Hara, the curate of St Patrick's, who had both gone out to the ship. And this time out front with them were the four young women. With the boat rocking against the wharf piles, Suzanne Aubert took a Maori hand stretched out to help her and scrambled up to land in New Zealand.[47]

The women did not go unmentioned on their arrival. In fact, Antoinette was singled out in the shipping news in the *New-Zealander* of 2 January. In what looks like a press release from the ship or its agents, D. Nathan & Co., emphasising the care given to the voyagers, the near-drowning of 'one of the ladies' was described: 'She had gone on deck early one morning to take the air, it was blowing fresh, the sea was rough, when by some means or other she was thrown overboard. Happily the occurrence was instantly observed, a boat promptly lowered, and the poor lady providentially rescued from a watery grave, having sustained no other injury than a thorough soaking.' The captain and agents, and Pompallier too, must have known it would be talked about and might have wanted to defuse any other interpretation.

The same piece referred to the women as 'Sisters of Mercy'. Pompallier had the report of his welcome printed and later circulated. The *Southern Cross* published an edited version: 'This highly esteemed Prelate arrived in our harbour on Sunday afternoon last, Dec 30, accompanied by 17 Clergymen, and 4 Religious for the Convent, to assist the Sisters of Mercy in their good educational works.'[48] The French women's programme could not have been spelt out more clearly.

And the 'mission barque' that had brought Suzanne to New Zealand? The newspaper noted its departure. The *Général Teste*, 560 tons, sailed out again from Auckland harbour on 12 January 'for the Whaling grounds, with 20 barrels of sperm oil' on board.

CHAPTER FIVE

Auckland – new mission recruits
1861-1863

He wishes to dictate everywhere :
Ko tana e minaminatia ai ko te whakahau[1]

It was five in the afternoon when the ship came in to land. Franciscan Father Barsanti thought it a day of true paradise and marvelled at the bright clear light.[2] At least three thousand people had been down there greeting Pompallier and his new missionaries. As evening drew in, up at the little stone cathedral of St Patrick in Chapel St, off Wyndham St, a crowd squeezed in and spilled over outside. Pompallier, his vicar general, James McDonald, and Father O'Hara changed into vestments for Benediction and the official welcome began. First, in English, came the speeches of the clergy, then the laypeople to whom Pompallier 'replied at some length'. Then followed the catechist Raniera's 'address in Maori signed by a very large number of natives to which His Lordship made a suitable reply in the Native language'.[3] The French and Italians, understanding nothing so far, all finally joined in the familiar Latin of the *Te Deum*. After the Benediction of the Blessed Sacrament and Pompallier's Apostolic Blessing on all present, most of the newcomers went away to temporary billets in homes of local parishioners. It was, all in all, a very promising beginning.

The women's accommodation was not temporary and they did not have far to go. The Sisters of Mercy were based right next door to St Patrick's – the convent even shared a wall with the church.[4] Close by was the bishop's house. There would be no noise of children at the sisters' school over the next two or three days. Wyndham St and Hobson St were also quiet by day with the tradespeople closed over New Year. The saddler, the butcher, the coachbuilder, the printer, the outfitter, the bootmaker and the auctioneer were gone, and the cattle saleyards were presumably deserted. But the several hotels in the area would liven up

New Year's Eve audibly. Sheehan's hotel, the 'Governor Browne', was nearby. The weather carried on shining for the citizens of Auckland at the Ellerslie races on New Year's Day.

With their pupils gone over New Year, the Sisters of Mercy all went into retreat. The newly arrived women were back on dry land and at last with other women around. They would be craving welcome and mothering from the older women among the sisters. Instead they were left in 'utterly lonely' silence and the flatness of anticlimax.[5] The wafts of Auckland's imperfect drainage replaced the smell of whale oil. And the low wooden houses straggling down to the sea overlaid the remembered lines of apartment buildings along the rivers of Lyon.

The new postulants were to train for 'religious life and the work of education of the young people of their sex'.[6] This was the principal emphasis of the Sisters of Mercy, although they also went out to visit the sick, the hospital and the prison, and ran a large orphanage and an institute for Maori girls in Auckland. Like the priests after the years of anti-religious revolution in France who set out to save the 'lost generation' of their own people, the sisters stayed in the Auckland area, teaching mainly the children of Irish settlers. Their mission was not just education and upbringing; it was 'salvation of young people'.[7] They maintained Catholic continuity in a new generation running a bit footloose in a freer social framework than that of Ireland. The sisters were busy. Auckland's population was growing fast: nearly 8000 in 1861, it would be swelled by soldiers to nearly 12,500 by 1864. Women immigrants in New Zealand were marrying young and families were having a lot of children: nine was a typical figure.[8]

The number of sisters had increased to twenty by now, coming out mostly from Ireland. But there had already been several deaths (ten by 1863), apparently mainly from tuberculosis. The sisters were pleased to receive the four new postulants, for a specific purpose. It was not for the parish day schools – for that English speakers were needed. 'French sisters, even if they have gone to England, do not satisfy a nation so uncompromising over the pronunciation of its language', commented Bishop Viard ruefully.[9] No, it was precisely for their French language that the new sisters would be useful in Auckland. Up on Mount St Mary above Freeman's Bay, the Sisters of Mercy ran under the name of St Anne's a 'boarding school for young ladies' where teaching went 'right up to literature, music, modern languages and arts necessary for a fully-rounded education'.[10] They also gave private lessons.

This brought in much-needed money which helped fund the schooling of poorer children. It was also another form of mission – a civilising one, creating harmony and good feeling across the sectors and denominations.[11] Early hostility had settled to background, if still acid, commentary from more intransigent personalities like Rev. Henry Williams. In the 'rubbing shoulders' of these years there was a fair amount of interaction and tolerance in daily life. On 6 December 1860, Father Garavel had officiated at St Patrick's at the wedding of a young Catholic man, Phipps Macdonald, to Protestant Helen Hursthouse. Archdeacon Kissling upheld the Anglican side with another service afterwards at St Mary's in Parnell.[12] Protestants happily sang in Catholic choirs, although Rome would soon put a stop to this.[13]

Auckland was a place where there was diversity; there was 'no immigration of a distinctive character as in the case of Wellington, Canterbury and Otago'.[14] There was no planned settlement with religious preference. Franciscan Barsanti incredulously listed the number of different 'sects'.[15] There was also a significant Jewish business community with the time and place of its religious observances well signalled in *Chapman's Almanac* alongside the Christian services. Auckland was still the capital, and daughters of officials as well as of merchants needed ladies' skills. The cityfathers – and citymothers – appreciated the Sisters of Mercy for their cultural contribution.

Up till now, Sister Mary Bernard Dickson, who knew French, Italian and German,[16] and Sister Philomena Dwyer, a good musician as well as linguist, had coped. Now there was Suzanne, a native French speaker and competent in Italian, a talented pianist and singer. Lucie and Antoinette would have similar skills. Péroline is said to have come from a simpler social background and seems to have worked mainly on kitchen, garden and laundry duties. They were all practised in needlework. The Sisters of Mercy also raised money by selling embroidery such as Berlin wool work and commissions for military insignia. On paper, the prospects for the education syllabus looked good.

After six months as postulants, on 30 June, Lucie, Suzanne and Péroline were received into the Sisters of Mercy as novices. Lucie was Sister Mary Baptist, Suzanne was Sister Mary Joseph and Péroline was Sister Mary Theresa. In early June, Antoinette had gone south with Sisters Mary Bernard and Mary Augustine to transfer to Viard's diocese and rescue the Wellington school from closure. Bishop Viard was corresponding for quite some time with his fellow Marists back in Lyon about the plan to bring out their sisters to work in his diocese.[17] He was hesitant by nature, but was also thinking through the psychology, the human factor in these new ventures, far more than Pompallier. 'French Sisters', he wrote, 'would be very useful for what does not concern the principal branches of instruction. But here a new difficulty arises. Making women of two nations so opposite in character and customs live together could become the source of many problems.'[18] By the time he was writing these words, he may well have heard about troubles brewing in Auckland.

It was not just independently-minded Suzanne who had trouble adapting. In fact, she said at first she could communicate with Sister Mary Bernard, who was Mother Cecilia Maher's assistant, and enjoyed her interest and knowledge in medicine. Sister Mary Bernard was an English convert who had nursed in the Crimean war and had met Sisters of Charity there. If Suzanne also had nursed Crimean casualties, the two would have had more than a knowledge of French in common. Suzanne did not have her company for long, as she had gone to Wellington by June.

With her went Antoinette, now Sister Mary Angeline. Suzanne recorded their departure in her little notebook. But the trouble had already begun before they left. Antoinette was in distress again. She objected to Pompallier's manner in the confessional, and it was not pure altruism that had him offering her to Viard in Wellington. She seemed contented there at first and conscientiously taught French, inspected the children's sewing, and helped teach arithmetic to the Maori girls. Viard realised that her emotional stability was fragile: 'The health of Sr Mary Angeline requires a lot of good care and attention.'[19] He spoke too of how 'happiness . . . has always been eluding her'.[20]

Péroline was only eighteen years old and less educated than the others. She must have been lonely. But what about Lucie? How would she adapt to life in a little diocesan congregation of the Irish Sisters of Mercy when she had already been for a while in the grander order of the Trinitarians? And how would she manage to balance being the bishop's niece with her postulant status? Pompallier, as part of his 'politic of prestige', had in colonial New Zealand let his background ennoble itself somewhat. His relatives had to share that loftier lineage, and for Lucie this could sit ill with being a postulant in a little weatherboard convent. For all four women, homesickness, struggles with two languages, different food and different food preparation could lead to the miseries.

The reaction was not all one-sided. The Sisters of Mercy, after a decade of undivided attention and affection from their bishop, now had to adapt to four women of the same nationality, same region even, same language and tastes as him, and one of them was from his own family. Back in 1859, in his parallel Maori and French poem on the mission, Pompallier had penned his usual pastoral theme for the Sisters of Mercy and their institution up at Mount St Mary:

Me hari, e hata Maria,	O sainte Marie, soyez bénie!
I runga i tou maunga!	Sur la montagne choisie pour vous!
Na, ona Reme, ona Hipi tapu,	Là, les agneaux et les brebis spirituelles
E noho ra hei whanau mou!	Sont pour vous une légion angélique.[21]

He lauded them in the image of spiritual ewes up on the mount chosen for Mary, taking care of the lambs in an angelic fold. Now the superior, Mother Cecilia Maher, would like as not receive a kindly but short note which ended, in one instance: 'have the kindness to forward my enclosed letter to Sister Mary Baptist'.[22] How could 'they ever avoid being humanly piqued at the obvious preference of the Bishop for his niece and her companions?'[23] Equally, how could the new women prepare themselves for religious life under English speakers they could not understand yet? Pompallier stepped in. The Sisters of Mercy were under his sole direction, too, but they would have watched him at that time concentrating his energies on the French women.

How, then, were the men dealing with the Auckland of the early 1860s? Archirel and Grange noted the magnificent site Auckland had, the wildness of the landscape, its hilliness, the wide but unformed roads, the little wooden houses, the well-stocked shops with very expensive goods. They were moved by the piety and spirit of prayer of the Maori who came in deputations to greet the bishop and receive his blessing. They also gained an impression of poverty among many Maori from the state of the assorted native and European dress they wore. Three weeks after arriving, they shifted to their place of work and reported back home to France:

On 23 January, we left the presbytery of the Cathedral to go to a station which is still temporary, on the outskirts of the town near the sea on a little mountain called Mount St Mary's. There's a large diocesan property there which is still mostly not broken in and covered in large part with bracken. In the middle are a few wooden houses which serve as dwellings for the religious institutions up there, a little parish church also made of wooden planks which serves as a chapel to these institutions.

It's here that His Lordship is hoping to set up soon his little Seminary; at the moment there's an establishment for girls of white and Maori race run by the Sisters of Mercy. Near them on the outside of a board fence are a few huts that some former Maori catechists live in, and finally our temporary establishment called the Maori college.

They did not know it quite yet but would realise very quickly that their institute was doomed from the outset by the political and economic situation in the province of Auckland. Meanwhile there were clues. Their letter continued: 'A few years ago, there was just this college with up to a hundred pupils; today there are only fifteen, including the catechists who are kept here merely to guard the establishment of the nuns in case of attack, which has already happened while His Lordship was away.'[24]

From the very outset they were aware of a state of war: 'On our arrival at Auckland we were distressed to learn that the war between the Maoris and the English had not ended, and that next day there was going to be a decisive battle. The Maoris have the upper hand.' But it seemed reassuringly far away. 'The war zone is in the south of the North Island, in Bishop Viard's diocese, and it is heading up a little into the south of Bishop Pompallier's diocese. An English warship left yesterday from Auckland to assist. People in Auckland are calm. An attack is not possible; there is still one warship in the harbour and a garrison in the town. They are expecting still more troops.'[25] By March, they were less confident: 'Some tribes have been at war for more than a year against England which is mistress of the country. . . . The hostilities are three days away from Auckland, the capital of the whole of New Zealand. The Governor is right now in the war zone conducting peace talks. There's considerable concern. Let us pray and pray.'[26]

The newspapers on their arrival were full of the arguments over the causes, issues and implications of the war, arguments that Grange and Archirel would not have the knowledge of English to follow. General elections were in the offing and columns were taken up by candidates' statements on the matter. The February papers serialised Sir William Martin's pamphlet pointing at land hunger as the main impulse to war, along with the government's refutation. Wiremu Nera Te Awaitaia of Waikato was quoted: 'You must understand this: the war is not a struggle of the Maori with the Pakeha; it is not a war with the Missionary; it is not a war with the Magistrate; *it is a war of the King with the Queen.*[27] But letters to the editor pointed out the detrimental effect war would have on everyone's lives. 'One false step taken and both races are involved in the consequences; their interests are so interwoven that the state of the one cannot but affect the well being of the other.'[28]

Archirel and Grange did not realise that they were being affected along with New Zealand colonists. They had not yet made the connection between this war and their own mission prospects. Perhaps influenced by Pompallier's Frenchness in spite of his New Zealand citizenship, they seemed to see it as an issue removed from daily life in the colony, an imperial war on a different plane. They had grasped that British sovereignty was the larger issue.

Pompallier was reasonably clear on this and included it in his report to the Propagation of the Faith for 1861: 'Towards the end of 1859, war came to Taranaki in the Province of New Plymouth in New Zealand, between the natives and the English Colonial Government. The causes of this war are the rights of sovereignty and of property that the New Zealand chiefs with their King do not wish to cede to the English.'[29] The 12,000 Imperial troops in New Zealand by 1864 were there to try to impose actual English sovereignty over the Maori whereas for over twenty years it had been nominal.[30]

Pompallier recognised the reluctance of Maori to cede their autonomy to English law. He had seen this desire to maintain a balance of power in 1845, in his experience of Hone Heke and Kawiti's war. But even if he recognised early on the nationalist element in the conflict, he could not conceive of complete Maori self-determination. By the 1860s he was too bound up in the new colony's society, too implicated with Governor Grey, to be really neutral.[31] And there was no way he would be allowed, even had he wanted, to present his church as some 'alternative' party. In fact, substantive British sovereignty was being diplomatically imposed on French Pompallier as well. His correspondence with Ngati Haua leader Wiremu Tamihana was checked by Grey and the Colonial Secretary:

> The contents of the letter appear unexceptional to the Colonial Secretary, but he does not think it a becoming thing that any British subject should engage in a friendly correspondence couched in complimentary language with a Rebel who is engaged in fighting against Her Majesty's Troops and who has throughout the Rebellion stood in the prominent position of the chief leader of the movement. To sanction such a proceeding would, it appears to him, establish a precedent which might prove exceedingly inconvenient.

I am therefore directed to request you to abstain for the present, from all communication with the Rebel Natives, whether by letter, printed documents, or personal intercourse of yourself or your clergy.[32]

By 1863, as Kingite aid to the Taranaki conflict turned into war in the Waikato, Pompallier's brand-new missionaries were in the thick of it. His long-established 'politic of neutrality' did lead him to hope that his Maori mission would not be greatly affected by any war. There were some grounds for thinking this initially. For instance, Maori turned against Anglican prayers for Queen Victoria's victory over all her enemies, but they saw no political or temporal element in prayers to the Virgin Mary. Then, as the war progressed, Bishop Selwyn reaped Maori disillusionment when he became chaplain to the Imperial forces and especially when he was accused of involvement in the attack on Rangiaowhia.

Pompallier understandably hoped that Catholicism would win out with the Maori as they became disenchanted with Protestant England. His personal proselytising style was not belligerent like that of some of the 'anti-Papists', but he was more than keen to occupy a vacuum. The Maori 'fight with a daringness and tactical expertise which are amazing their adversaries. The latter have hardly won anything against them over more than a year of hostilities. Casualties are not very great. The natives hate more and more Protestantism and all of them want to embrace Catholicism.'[33] This mission optimism lay behind peacemaking letters he wrote to Wiremu Tamihana and Matutaera Tawhiao, the second Maori King. Pompallier was promoting Catholicism. But he was wrong; the Maori did not turn to Catholicism in their gradual withdrawal from other European Christian observance. They withdrew into their own interpretations of Christianity. Father Barsanti would publish a book in 1868 on the Maori Pai Marire faith and its effect on the Christian mission.

Even before 1863, the city of Auckland was affected by war. It would be harassed on its outskirts, as New Plymouth was, yet it would never be attacked because its neutrality was as vital to the Maori war economy as to the Pakeha.[34] But immigration had dropped dramatically from 1860. British merchants held back consignments and prices consequently rose in New Zealand. Maori commodity trade, especially in wheat, fell off. 'Native wheat no longer comes in, nor can any be expected to arrive at next harvest. We are entirely dependent on Australian and Californian supplies.'[35] Significantly, fewer Maori now came to the city. As Archirel noted, there were scarcely any pupils, let alone prospective Maori priests, for their institute to teach. There were no prospects for the Clercs de Saint Viateur, no money to meet their present hunger, little chance that Archirel in his forties, with a history of failure in Latin, would ever adequately learn Maori and English.

Pompallier was edging them into diocesan control. From the beginning he had them in diocesan habit, not that of their congregation, and was pushing them towards the priesthood. Grange was studying theology but Archirel, struggling with his languages, declined in the meantime. Grange was ordained and posted out to the Maori mission at Whakatane, with the older and senior Archirel now almost a laybrother manual helper. Pompallier's action was driving a wedge between the two friends.

When a desperate Archirel succeeded early in 1864 in getting his understanding congregation to recall him and, most importantly, send money to rescue him, Pompallier wrote that Archirel had failed in the mission because he had been too stubborn, 'not listening enough to the direction of the Bishop or not being sufficiently *in manu episcopi* [under control of the bishop], in works to do with my flocks in need of pasturing'.[36] Pompallier succeeded in retaining Grange in spite of the French congregation's wish to recall him as well. Suzanne knew Archirel mostly from a stage when he was helping Pompallier with accounts. She noted down his return to France.

The young students who had arrived with Suzanne were nearly all out in Maori mission stations for the early part of the Waikato war, somehow still valiantly 'pasturing' Pompallier's flocks. They had had minimal priestly training: one month with James McDonald, then another month with O'Hara – neither of whom they understood – and for an hour on some evenings with Pompallier himself.[37] They were then ordained and despatched with urgency to Whakatane, Opotiki, Rangiaowhia, Tauranga, Rotorua, Ngaruawahia. They were sent out 'among the Maoris in their districts with a few provisions consisting of coffee, sugar, tea, biscuits, a little tobacco for the Maoris, a little flour for the wafers, a few bottles of wine for the Masses, a little box of candles, and a portable altar'.[38]

Through 1863 and early 1864 they stayed on, increasingly isolated, although the presence of military would have made them less isolated from other Pakeha than their 1840s counterparts. Antoine Pompallier, just twenty-four years old, was at Ngaruawahia at a very delicate phase of the Waikato war.[39] Grey required the priests to be recalled from 'rebel' territory in April 1864. However, in December 1864, Boibieux was seen at his Rotorua station and commended by Lieutenant Meade:

> It would be difficult to conceive a life of greater devotion than his. Wifeless, childless, with no companionship save that of his little congregation of natives . . . his life is passed in his Master's work in a place where even the barest necessities of life are procured with the greatest difficulty. He spoke with affection of his native friends and hopefully of the ultimate progress of civilization and Christianity amongst them, though he confessed that under the combined influence of the war and the new fanaticism he, as well as the Protestant missionaries, had almost entirely lost the influence enjoyed in years gone by.[40]

By 1865 the missionaries were out in the field again, but were gradually all forced to withdraw, Grange in danger of being killed in the same Hauhau impetus that resulted in Rev. Carl Völkner's death. Yet, regardless of war conditions, the pattern of their missionary existence was seen as not atypical: 'This is the Mission story of every missionary in the Diocese of Auckland, each man taken one by one over twenty-five years since this Mission was founded.'[41]

The voices summing up indignantly the conditions of the missionaries were those of Franciscan Fathers Barsanti, Galosi and Jourdan. From their pens flowed the most detailed analysis of Auckland diocese in the 1860s and their reams of paper were ballast for ships returning to Europe, so weighted were they with the men's pent-up feelings, now vented freely. Their break with Pompallier was explosive. They traced the quick change from the affection they had for and from Pompallier in Europe and on board ship to the firm signs that he wanted no independent congregation of theologically assured, canonically confident, mature priests functioning alongside him. Even in Paris before departure, he wanted them to give up their distinctive Franciscan habit. The process of control over many aspects tightened from the first days after arrival, when Pompallier tried to have them live in one community on the North Shore with the secular students. Their dismay was apparent from the first month and simmered on into anger.

In October came an eruption. It was violent. It began when James McDonald, on Pompallier's orders, blocked Barsanti's entry to St Patrick's to say Mass. In the next few minutes, if not seconds, angry words led to blows, a thrown missal and a broken chalice. O'Hara, newly ordained Royer, and Boibieux were witnesses. Over the following days and weeks the affair continued. From the Franciscan viewpoint, the psychological spark for the incident was easy to understand, and Barsanti's remorse was immediate. But Pompallier seemed determined not to forgive or resolve the issue.

The whole story was treated as the stuff of grand opera, and the Italians wrote it up with dramatic care. Feelings were intensely expressed, motives were finely explored, characters were brought on stage and analysed, the scenes were set, the plot detailed and the themes identified and discussed – themes of jealousy, rivalry, tyranny, sycophancy, poverty and devotion, set against the simple background of the Catholic parishioners of Auckland and their little wooden homes. For at least two more years, the Franciscans continued to examine Pompallier and his administration and to try and explain what had gone wrong, what was still wrong. They tried, in their anger and frustration, to convey the absolute side to Pompallier's nature:

> The Bishop wants to be alone, or rather, unique, in the length and breadth of his domain, just the way the Pope is within the whole Church, just the way the Eternal Father is within the whole of creation. Even the tiniest insignificant things have to pass through his hands; hence he wants to be everything, namely Pope, Bishop, Emperor, Parish priest, Curate, Sacristan, Janitor, Keeper, Chaplain to the nuns, Chancellor, Substitute, Secretary, Bailiff. He has a Vicar General, but in name only . . . he is persuaded that he is *omniscient, omnipotent, infallible*, and nobody can manage to get these strange ideas out of his head.[42]

If the Franciscans' tale were given full justice here, they would be upstaging Suzanne Aubert, and this is her story. But it overlaps hers because the attention in their writing was slanted away from the wider conditions of New Zealand as a whole. The mission field they were given was in the Far North, away from the war zones, a mission neglected by Pompallier since the departure of the Marists at the end of the 1840s, and now an area outside the main political and social arena. Tangled in the drama of their conflict with Pompallier, they wrote with their focus very much on Auckland, whose Catholic families they described warmly as 'all Irish, good people, easy-going, sweet-natured, of a very living faith'.[43] There they were finally given, with Rome's intervention, the comfortable parish of Parnell. It would be headquarters for their wider mission.

By sifting through the detail in their writings, like an archaeologist in a midden, one finds some artefacts, glimpses of the women religious in Auckland. It is through Barsanti's unconsciously comic account of his reaction to the half-burnt, half-raw mutton chop dished up to him by Irish Sister Philomena after Mass one morning at St Anne's, and her hurt reaction when he recooked it, that the French women's difficulties in adjusting culturally can also be sensed.[44] It is the Franciscans' viewpoint on what they saw as the comfortable situation of the Sisters of Mercy, in comparison with the men out in the field, that keeps track of relativity. The bishop, they said, considered the Sisters of Mercy 'as the noblest part of his clergy'.[45] But they also pointed out that any relative advantage the women might have depended on their compliance: 'The Sisters of Mercy by running a school for the girls earn more than enough to live on. However, their earnings pass through the hands of the Bishop and go into the central administration.'[46] It was they who, with reproof in their tone, painted a vivid domestic picture of the Sisters of Mercy housekeeping for Pompallier, sweeping, dusting, bedmaking, cooking.

It was their version, too, of Antoinette's departure for Wellington that survived. They wrote that she had not wanted to confess to Pompallier and, following constitutional rights to have an occasional extraordinary confessor, she had asked for another. He said it was to be his vicar general or himself: no one else. She had to choose. She pointed out that she knew little English yet and James McDonald knew no French, but finally she gave way. 'To practise obedience', wrote Father Jourdan, 'she went to the Vicar General, began her confession, then after a while realised that he was not understanding one iota of what she was saying. So she started to laugh, and ran out laughing and kept on laughing uncontrollably for fully a three- or four-hour stretch. Soon after, the Bishop got rid of her by sending her to Wellington.'[47] The story is no doubt biased. The Franciscans were aggrieved that they were barred by Pompallier from being possible confessors even though they could speak French. Yet it rings true. It shows the poignancy of the feverishly emotional reactions of the young woman who had 'fallen into the sea'.

The differences between the French novices and the Irish sisters reached a head. 'The Bishop was fond of his niece and the Sisters felt that they were second in the Bishop's estimation.'[48] Later, in January 1863, mild Viard would use the word 'hatred' to describe some sisters' feelings against Lucie.[49] Whether Pompallier would have made the same decision if his niece had not been involved is a moot point, but he decided to separate out the French novices and to found a new diocesan congregation. In 1862 he wrote to Rome: 'On 18 May last, I also professed five

Religious under the name of the Holy Family, Sisters who will be given special responsibility for the native New Zealand girls. In a few months' time, I shall send you their Rules, to receive the approval of the Sacred Congregation.'[50] No Rule ended up in Roman archives, nor in Auckland; it may never have been sent. The congregation was under Pompallier's direction; he was their sole confessor; he was to live mainly up at Mount St Mary in a new bishop's house. Lucie Pompallier had gone straight from novice to superior. She was Mother Mary Baptist; Suzanne as Sister Mary Joseph was bursar, in charge of accounts and paperwork; Péroline Droguet continued in practical work as Sister Mary Theresa.

When Antoinette heard of the new congregation, she wanted to return from Wellington to join them. She was restless and really uncertain whether she wished to stay in religious life. Viard gave her £5, some reassuring and perceptive advice, and two letters of recommendation, one for whichever course she chose – religious or lay. She arrived back in Auckland on 20 September 1862 – after surviving the shipwreck of the *Lord Worsley* off the Taranaki coast on 1 September, followed by a few chilly nights ashore in the war zone. The travellers were given shelter by the Maori. A passenger's diary mentioned her: 'Amongst our passengers was a very interesting young French lady, a Roman Catholic, *'soeur de la Sainte Famille'*, I believe, on her way to Auckland to aid in the work of Christianity and civilization. With infinite patience she essayed to teach these savage women knitting and sewing.'[51] The shipwrecked passengers were finally given safe passage and an escort to New Plymouth by 'the principal chief of the king party' in the district, Erueti. He would later be known as the prophet Te Whiti.[52] Why is there no record of Mother Aubert, who loved a good story, ever speaking of this? Was it Antoinette's ever-sadder experience that stopped her? Certainly Antoinette could have done without this second traumatising incident at sea.

The Sisters of Mercy went on to develop their new property on eighteen acres handed over to them by Pompallier out of land at Mount St Mary bought in 1853. It was part-settlement for dowry money Pompallier had used to pay passages for other clergy. The sisters built a new convent then a chapel at St Mary's, feeling the general financial tightening in Auckland but managing carefully. 'Blessed be God we are self-supporting but after building a fine large Convent you may be sure we are now poor indeed.'[53] They carried on with their school and orphanage. They now confessed mostly to Father James McDonald. Right across the road was the new Congregation of the Holy Family, at St Anne's, next to the bishop's residence. Both sites were beautiful, looking over the harbour. Below them lay the curve of Freeman's Bay with its little jetty and sawmill. In 1862, Antoine Pompallier was up there too, as curate at the local church. Lucie had her own brother, close in age, and her uncle nearby. There was a cosy French family atmosphere. This was emphasised by the new habit the sisters wore: full, blue, gathered skirt, short cape, goffered coif beneath the veil. It was typically French from the Lyon area. The Sisters of Mercy recognised that the 1860s would be different from the 1850s: 'The Bishop's interest was with them [the French women]; he was never the same to the Sisters of Mercy.'[54]

The Maori girls had already been living up at St Anne's since 1854. By 1857, the institute had three Sisters of Mercy and twenty-six pupils. At the time the Congregation of the Holy Family took it over, there were twenty. Suzanne always said she had not wanted to work with daughters of Pakeha colonists or temporary British military. Her idea of mission work in New Zealand was bringing Catholicism to the indigenous people. This was the way the Annals of the Propagation of the Faith had depicted mission. The pages did not fall open at descriptions of embroidery, piano, singing, French or Italian lessons. Refinements were in fact taught to some Maori girls. Father Barsanti demurred at the impractical salon skills the Sisters of Mercy were teaching their Maori pupils. He was not the only one to worry that this might lead them not back to their kainga but into prostitution.

Suzanne was ready for anything that was culturally different, new, exciting and testing. In her red notebook she made this entry for 18 May:

> We receive the habit and make our profession in the Congregation of the Holy Family. The ceremony takes place at five in the evening in the Church of the Immaculate Conception, Bishop Pompallier officiating and Revd Fathers James McDonald and Anthony Pompallier assisting. There are five of us in all, three French and two Maori, Peata and Ateraita. We break our fast at eight in the evening, the feast consisting of a sheep's head that we hack into with a tomahawk.[55]

That had more the ring of active missionary rigour and prowess. Sister Mary Joseph could now get on with being a 'proper' missionary at last.

CHAPTER SIX

Auckland – the Nazareth Institute
1863-1869

I will not let it go : E ḳore e tuḳua e au[1]

When the five women prostrated themselves before the altar as newly professed Sisters of the Holy Family, the brand-new boots of the two Maori women, shiny, copper-soled and creaking, were what fascinated little Nelly Boylan watching with her mother. The sight of them stayed fixed in her memory.[2] Peata was one of these women, and would be Suzanne's only companion who stayed right through the triumphs and trials of her remaining nine years in Auckland. Peata was forty-one when she was professed along with Suzanne, but seemed already old to the younger woman.

Peata may not have seen much of the ceremony herself, as she was going blind by the 1860s, but she must have felt it deeply. For her, the evening ceremony in the Church of the Immaculate Conception and the new habit and boots were the culmination of twenty-two years of dedication to the Catholic faith. As a missionary to Maori, Suzanne could not have found a better mentor than Peata. It was she who helped Suzanne feel a real missionary at last. In her past she had everything that fired Pompallier's – and Suzanne's – romantic and zealous concept of conversion. Her background was noble and heroic, her mana high, her Catholic devotion constant and fervent. All the old religious vocabulary could be applied to her. She was devoted to the Blessed Sacrament, Suzanne said, and would spend a good part of the night praying in the chapel.

'E Peata, e taku tamahine tapu, aroha. Kia Wakapainga Koe e Hehu Kerito to tatou Atua', wrote Pompallier from Auckland in January 1851.[3] That was how he started a letter to Peata when she was in Wellington, calling her his 'beloved holy daughter' on whom he wished the blessing of Jesus Christ our God. For Pompallier the 'tamahine tapu' in this case had the sense of 'wahine tapu', or nun. When he spoke to the eager Sisters of Mercy back at Carlow in Ireland in 1849, Mother Cecilia Maher wrote then how he had told them of 'the young [Maori] girls who have begged of him to let them consecrate themselves to God. See what an inspiration, without having heard of religious life. In some instances he has permitted them to make annual vows.'[4] If any Maori woman had made simple annual vows before the arrival of the Sisters of Mercy, it would have been Peata. In this sense she could be considered the first, not just the first Maori, religious sister in New Zealand.

Bishop Ullathorne visited the infant New Zealand mission in 1840 from Australia and mentioned Pompallier telling him of a convert woman he called 'Hoke'. In an 1840 letter Pompallier described baptising Nga Puhi chief Rewa's niece, already a widow at the age of nineteen, and her child. He gave her the name Beata, or Blessed, and her little daughter became Avotia.[5] Peata's next appearance in documentation comes in 1850 when she had gone down with Bishop Viard to found the new diocese of Wellington.[6] Her daughter had disappeared from the record by then.

Pompallier had been away from New Zealand for nearly four years, so it was natural for Peata to carry on helping Viard at the time the Marists shifted south. In Viard's register for St Mary's, Wellington, 'Peata of the Bay of Islands' stood godmother on 14 July 1850 at the first female baptism, of a ten-month-old girl from Otaki. But by January 1851 Pompallier was writing to Viard: 'Beata writes to me that she wants to come back and asks me to obtain a passage for her on the *Victoria*. I cannot refuse anything to this dear convert; she is one of the first daughters of Jesus Christ at the Bay of Islands. The Sisters of Mercy will keep her in their convent which is well established now.'[7]

He enclosed a separate letter to Peata herself, ending it reassuringly:

E nui toku aroha tapu me to nga wahine tapu, noku ki a koe. Na ka tae mai koe ki Akarana, ka noho koe ki a ratou hei hoa aroha. Naku i tuhituhi ki te Epikopo Wiari kia tupato ia a koe mo tau taenga mai ki a ahau i Akarana. Heoi e tatari ana ahau ki a koe e tamahine aroha.[8]

'I send you much holy love, and the sisters do too', he told her. 'When you get to Auckland, you will now stay with them as loving companions. I have written to Bishop Viard to take care of you for your journey back to me in Auckland. In conclusion, I am waiting for you to come, loving daughter.' The care in this personal letter shows Pompallier at his best.

In April he was able to report back to Viard that 'Beata is happy living with my nuns'.[9]

It was not just that Peata was one of the first converts which counted for Pompallier. Nor that she was continuing so faithfully in her religious life. Peata provided him with his perfect prototype Maori Christian. She was a proud young woman of high chiefly birth risking all for her new faith. Both the Sisters of Mercy and Suzanne ruefully recorded that, in Pompallier's reckoning, Peata could do no wrong. As others of his personal converts faded away or died as the years went by, Peata was a nostalgic reminder of early 1840s glory. And her story served, in 1849 and again in 1860, to fire the dedication of mission candidates and supporters. Even as late as November 1869, when Pompallier was planning a history of his mission, he wrote to Auckland from France asking for three photos of Peata to be taken and sent over.[10] Peata, and not Suzanne or the girls, was really the central figure in the two surviving photos from that time.

Only his account of her origins and deeds remains. Her name was Hoki and he wrote that she was a niece of Rewa. If she was a niece in the strict sense, she could have been a daughter of Moka (Kainga Mataa), who was an associate of the Catholic mission at Kororareka, or of Te Wharerahi (Wharenui), both important chiefs. Te Wharerahi married Tamati Waaka Nene's sister, Tari, extending influence into Hokianga. Or Hoki could have been the daughter of unrecorded sisters.

Pompallier emphasised her high standing. This was important to him, with his strong and often-expressed belief in the divinely ordained status of ruler and leader. The conversion of someone of chiefly rank also usually meant that others would follow, although less so with women. Hoki was baptised by Pompallier in 1840 at a high point of his popularity among Maori, just a month before the signing of the Treaty of Waitangi. Rewa's stand against signing is often linked to Pompallier's influence.[11] He was the last to sign and did so reluctantly. In 1840 he was associated with the Catholic mission and strengthened Pompallier's position when he arrived at Waitangi in the bishop's company.[12]

Hoki came to Catholicism from an Anglican Church Missionary Society background. This, in the militant tone of the time, was a coup for the bishop. He described how she then confronted the Protestant missionaries and passionately defended the worth of his little booklets explaining the Apostles' Creed, the Ten Commandments and the Lord's Prayer against their argument for the integral text of the Bible. This was a defence that Catholic missionaries had to use countless times. The printed word had come to have huge prestige for Maori. Size and volume mattered, and the Protestant New Testament literally carried more weight.[13] Back in 1840, Hoki was out in the forefront of the great religious debates to come.

Hoki, now Peata, also defended her Catholic faith and her bishop in 1845. She 'starred' as a soldier of Christ in Pompallier's version of what happened after the destruction of Kororareka. Three weeks after the fire the ash of the burnt wooden houses had blown away. All that remained were the iron nails strewn on the ground and the brick chimneys 'like a forest of dead tree trunks, a scene of desolation and ruin'. Only about fifteen houses and the Catholic mission establishment were still standing. So were the Church Missionary Society house and church, but Pompallier omitted this. Both Pakeha and Maori had gone. Pompallier commented: 'The place of the sheepfold remained and the sheep were no longer there.'[14] Then six war canoes of an unnamed great chief came back to finish the destruction, in revenge for chiefs killed.

But there was Peata, aged twenty-four, striding up and down along the water's edge, defying the men who halted their canoes fifty yards away to discuss her challenge, vaunting her mana, with its clear implication of reprisal, to stall their advance. The canoes veered away to land further along the bay. The local party, probably Rewa's, who had been alerted in the night, arrived and the affair ended peacefully. Gifts were exchanged with the bishop and they all shared a meal.

This was Pompallier's story published fifteen years after the event – and there is no supporting documentation – but it was doing the rounds of the Catholic world. And now here Suzanne was, working and learning with Peata. Suzanne said Pompallier allowed them to go out to local pa with Peata to learn language and customs and to listen to whakapapa.[15] This would be unusual for religious sisters. But the tiny congregation had probably just the barest guidelines for their Constitutions and was totally concentrated on Maori mission, so it is quite possible. Pompallier was indulgent both to the congregation and to Peata personally. If Peata had the wide kinship network of a paramount Nga Puhi chief, she had entrée to many marae. For instance, Tupanapana, first wife of the most influential Orakei chief, Paora Tuhaere, was a granddaughter of Te Wharerahi, Rewa's brother, while his second wife, Harata, was a daughter of Rawiri Tarapata Moka and granddaughter of Moka.[16] Tuhaere, despite his Anglican church connections, later offered land and accommodation to Suzanne and Peata.

As for the Kororareka story, Kawiti and Hone Heke's handling of the northern war was so impressive that if it were known, even just through Pompallier, that Peata had withstood singlehanded any warrior force associated with them, her prestige and the congregation's would be enhanced in the eyes of both Maori and informed Pakeha.[17] *If* it happened as Pompallier told it, Peata stands for courage alongside women like Heni Te Kiri-Karamu, the wahine toa of Gate Pa.[18] Peata stands at the top of a list Suzanne wrote of Maori people whose faith had inspired her.

Ateraita was professed along with Peata but has never vied for the title of 'first Maori nun', so strong has been the Peata story. Her own Maori name is not recorded. Her baptismal name of Ateraita was after the French princess Adélaïde, daughter of Louis Philippe, who had supported Pompallier's mission. Ateraita came from the Whakatane area and had been converted by the Maori wife of the Danish settler Hans Falk, usually known as Phillip Tapsell. She must have been with the sisters in Auckland long enough to be professed with the new congregation, not just admitted as a postulant or novice. By 18 September 1862 there were already two Maori novices, Erahia from Whangaroa and Rupina from Rotorua. Erahia left in December. Suzanne recorded that on 17 June 1865 Sister Ateraita left but returned again one week later. Whatever crisis happened three years after her profession, it was when the wars had spread through her own district.

In 1862 and 1863 Suzanne Aubert, now Sister Mary Joseph or Meri Hohepa,[19] must have been enjoying life. There was still the raw edge of the rift with her father, but she seems to have been in regular contact with her family. The boarding institute and school for Maori girls which the Sisters of the Holy Family took over was renamed the Nazareth Institute early in 1863. It had had seventeen pupils on the roll in 1862 and passed muster academically with the inspectors in January and April before the transfer. They had complimented the Sisters of Mercy on the management (a 'model of neatness and regularity'), on manual work (the 'forte of this school'), on discipline and 'remarkably neat and well-behaved' girls.[20]

Pompallier now had the former buildings demolished and started an ambitious new building programme. The Sisters of Mercy were building their convent on the other side of New St, and on the bishop's side construction of the institute buildings and then the bishop's new house went ahead on a glebe of three and a half acres which was registered in his name as diocesan bishop. The Franciscans worried over the concentration of expenditure up at Mount St Mary, which in their eyes was the bishop's *villegiatura*, his country estate. The government was giving a pound-for-pound subsidy for the Maori school buildings, so half the costs had to be met from diocesan funds.[21]

The French sisters' first attempts at teaching were fairly haphazard. Crammed temporarily into the bishop's residence with a new intake of pupils, the school got a mediocre report in 1863 from Henry Taylor, the inspector. He summed up: 'The pupils seem healthy, happy, and very submissive to orders. The teaching is either defective in kind or deficient in quality.'[22] The sisters were slapped on the wrist for marking the roll in advance, a criticism made also of other institutions. They were funded by a capitation grant, so the numbers were important. Mother Mary Baptist as manager wrote a well-reasoned explanation in reply. The hand of her uncle, with his fluent command of English, lies behind this letter.[23]

The sisters shifted into the new convent on 14 August 1863. The finished institution was 'spacious', simple but beautiful behind its 'substantial sawn kauri fence, 6 feet high'. There were five buildings: the two-storeyed convent with nine rooms including the chapel; the school with its dormitory above; the dining-room, kitchen (with 'a Leamington cooking-range') and refectories for the teachers and pupils; a gate-house with provision stores; a washhouse and bathroom. There was also a 'cow-house' and a 'store for hay'. Through 1863 and 1864 they laid out paths, a garden and a large recreation area for the children. It was planted with eighteen weeping willows and had 'brick pathways and scoria laid for the play-ground'.[24]

Recreation was not just stick-games and skipping on the scoria: 'during recreation time they are trained in the practice of horticulture'. Viard sent word that he was sorry he could not send them the promised gooseberry slips as the shrubs in his garden were now too old.[25] They developed a large vegetable garden with expert horticultural advice from a Presbyterian Scot, and Sister Mary Joseph became a keen gardener. By 1866, they had constructed an oratory with a statue of Mary at the far end of the garden in the interior courtyard.

The sisters renewed their simple vows each year and after the ceremony took tea with the bishop in the dining-room of his new residence. Antoinette left, again, but Maori women were entering. Arieta received the white veil of a novice and another young Maori woman became a postulant. Among their pupils were two daughters of French men who had married Maori women: Mary Ann Borel and Adelaide Bidois.[26] Another girl, Sally Page, had figured in government reports as the centre of a kidnapping dispute between her Pakeha father and the previous owner of her enslaved Maori mother, now dead.[27]

Beyond the fence, the rolling hills behind Freeman's Bay beckoned, and so did the water below. When the warm wind blew and the pupils grew restless, Peata would say it was not the time to be cooped up inside, and out they went. At the back of the grounds were fifty acres at Cox's Creek, part of a government donation in trust for educational purposes. They probably still had the run of this even after it was leased out in 1866. Down at the harbour edge of Freeman's Bay was another trust property of five acres in the name of the bishop. Suzanne remembered lots of excursions, doubling as nature lessons and religious education. She took her pupils into the garden of friends, the Outhwaite family, and there they would eat pipi cooked in an old frying-pan. She would 'hunt mushrooms on the Auckland hills in the early morning with the lovely brise [breeze] so pure and refreshing'.[28]

In school there was plenty of singing, some as mnemonics to assist geography and number work.[29] This was successful in geography, as the 1866 inspection by William Rolleston noted: 'The children went through some exercises in singing and geography in a pleasing and satisfactory manner.'[30] In arithmetic, the girls may have remembered the tunes rather than their tables: 'their knowledge of the multiplication table and the simple rules of arithmetic is not such as I should have expected, as the teaching appears to be well and systematically conducted'. The girls read and wrote moderately well, but Rolleston was puzzled that the same English sentences he had given for dictation at the Wesleyan Three Kings school were 'attempted without success'.[31] It would not have occurred to him that his English was without the strong French accent they were used to hearing.

Who exactly taught what is uncertain. Peata handled much of the care and discipline. Again, she would have been invaluable. The teacher of the Wesleyan school remarked that 'parents will only trust their children to us if they have some friend among the monitors or teachers . . . we rely much on the opinion of this monitor'.[32] Taylor's 1863 comment that the girls seemed healthy and happy is relevant. In 1866 Rolleston too was 'on the whole favourably impressed with the general tone and character of the school and with the order and neatness which prevailed'. Having a playground, garden and trees made for attractive surroundings rather than institutional bleakness. By comparison, Father Poupinel, in New Zealand in 1866 on a routine visit to the Wellington diocese, was concerned about the Maori girls in Wellington, left 'without entertainment, without fun, without life', whereas they needed 'open air, lots of movement, outdoors work'. He noted in his report:

> When I got back from Dunedin, I stayed five whole days in Wellington and nearly always busy writing away. My room was no more than thirty metres from the house and yard where these girls are: my window was usually open; their yard was only enclosed by bare boards. In these five days I heard not a single word, no voices calling out from their midst.[33]

There came the time, though, when it no longer mattered what idyllic surroundings there were, what experienced and respected Maori kuia was on hand, what care came from a young and enthusiastic teacher busy learning her pupils' culture. Gradually the little iron bedsteads began to empty and the two sheets, two blankets and one quilt for each pupil were all too often folded away in linen presses. The Nazareth Institute became a predictable casualty of war, along with the other Maori schools in Auckland: Roman Catholic St Mary's College for men and boys on the North Shore, the Wesleyan Three Kings' Institution and the Anglican St Stephen's School in Parnell. Maori pupils stopped coming to the Pakeha capital for education. For the three denominations charged with 'Native education' this was doubly distressing, since education was a major channel for their mission. Many Maori were literate in their own language by the 1850s, but almost all works printed in Maori were religious.[34] Literacy in Maori had in effect meant knowledge of Christianity.

The growing colony's education system lacked cohesiveness. By 1852 responsibility for settler education had been delegated to the six separate provinces, all of them different in funding, philosophy and quality. Auckland province was not generous to education; its system was inefficient and administered in practice mainly through the various religious denominations.[35] But assistance for Maori education continued to come directly from the governor and the central colonial government. A scheme set up by Governor Grey in 1857 gave control and proportional funding to the three traditional missionary denominations: the

Anglicans, the Roman Catholics and the Wesleyans. Grey was almost totally in control and his allocations could be arbitrary. Initially quite generous funding was provided in limited areas to set up institutions but lacked follow-up for maintenance. There was no government school for Maori north of Auckland yet several in Auckland with never many pupils. The preference was for boarding, to take pupils away from their kainga. Teaching English was a requirement along with religious and 'industrial' or manual training. The aim was assimilation.[36]

The Nazareth Institute's ambitious new buildings in 1863, replacing accommodation considered 'ample and comfortable' in 1860 and 'small but very neat' in 1862, came at a buoyant phase in Auckland's development. Pompallier was friendly with Grey, who handled the Maori education vote and who had just arrived back for a second term as governor. Military expenditure created an atmosphere of free spending and generous credit.[37] But Pompallier's expansive building programme was ill timed: not only did the economy slip back, but the 'Native Schools' system, the reason for the building, was breaking down. The French sisters could not have guessed this. With the wars, pupils faded away from the mission schools of all three denominations, which struggled on with only a handful of pupils, now mainly 'half-caste', as children of mixed parentage were also covered under the system.

The mission schools cared temporarily for Pakeha children sent to Auckland for safety during the war. Then came destitute children in the severe depression which set in after the troops left and after the capital shifted to Wellington in 1865.[38] These settler children were subsidised by provincial money, but when the subsidies were cut back in 1868, then eliminated, the native institutions were penniless. In 1868, William Fox reported that the Anglican St Stephen's had 'degenerated into something between a hospital, a nursery, and an almshouse for the decrepit and the destitute'.[39] Finally, on 31 December 1868, the capitation allowance for the Maori denominational boarding-schools also ended. The 1867 Native Schools Act had directed that government funding was now to go to a system of village day schools which would be controlled and administered by the Department of Native Affairs instead of the governor. The Nazareth Institute as a government school for Maori girls was finished.

The institute had fared better than some, however, as girls continued to stay longer during the war years than boys or men. Many of its pupils, also, came from the North, which stayed neutral through the 1860s wars, or from the Rotorua area where Arawa largely stayed aloof or provided soldiers for the Imperial side. Yet, whereas the Sisters of Mercy could cope with the strains on their orphanages with income from select school pupils, private pupils and 'judicious management',[40] the Sisters of the Holy Family had no recognised income other than the government capitation grant and the Propagation of the Faith allowance, both channelled through the bishop.

They were ultimately dependent on Pompallier, and he was as badly indebted as ever. In fact, along with many other Aucklanders, he was going under.[41] Promissory notes were everywhere and he was raising loans to pay the interest on loans. Diocesan properties had been mortgaged in 1866, including St Anne's, where the Nazareth Institute was.[42] Money from the Propagation of the Faith was not getting through to several priests. Neither, it seems, was some of the government capitation money. Father Vinay, whose school down in Rangiaowhia received a good report, indicated to the inspector that he was receiving no government subsidy from Pompallier. The latter denied this, pointing to bills paid. Rolleston advised that 'the grant in future should be paid directly to the local manager of each school'.[43] Whereas the Wesleyans had a superintendent responsible to a district meeting and the Anglicans had an education board, Pompallier handled everything. Sister Mary Joseph found it was her turn to suffer from his 'obscure financial practices'.[44]

Why was Sister Mary Joseph the casualty? Why not also Mother Mary Baptist? It was because Lucie Pompallier went back to France before the worst of the hardship began. She left on 18 February 1868 with her uncle. Pompallier had decided once more to raise funds to rescue the diocese. Bankruptcy was a scandal; people were publicly observed being marched off to gaol.[45] A bishop would never suffer this humiliation but to some extent, and almost understandably, he was running away. He was not quite giving up, but was falling back on a tried and true solution, to project the appeal of distant mission and the magnetism of his personality in order to raise money in Europe.

But at sixty-seven Pompallier was old, tired and probably housebound with rheumatism. He had spent more than half his life tallying his antipodean sheep and now was losing count. Bishop Selwyn at this same time was being given honourable 'retirement', at least from foreign mission, with the bishopric of Lichfield in England, and Pompallier, after establishing in Auckland the framework of worthwhile parishes and pastorates, would have liked something similar. Later, when the French government was anxiously enquiring into the financial scandal, this description of him at the time was reported back to France. Still 'a tall, large, robust old man of a fine presence and with a face both gentle and commanding', he nevertheless was no longer active. 'The problem was that he became old, portly, and ended up no longer being able to leave his armchair. He therefore ceased being in a fit state, not only to manage, but even to oversee, his interests.'[46]

Lucie slipped on board the French naval transport, *Chevert*, so the story goes, without her uncle or others, including Suzanne, being aware of her plans. Certainly, none of the newspapers reporting the farewell to the bishop or his boarding the ship mentioned that his niece was travelling with him.[47] The Sisters of the Holy Family were described as farewelling him, not one of their own as well. Lucie had had little time to reach her decision, as Pompallier was leaving at short notice, taking the opportunity of the French government vessel to negotiate a passage which he could not otherwise pay for. He had had free passages from French naval ships much earlier in his career.

Once her mind was made up, Lucie had speedily prepared. One of Pompallier's creditors later trying to get payment was the National Mart run by S. and J. Vaile, who finally in desperation sent a polite letter and an itemised copy of the account to Propaganda Fide in Rome. They had supplied 'goods and cash to the Convent of the Holy Family' going back to 1867. The very last 'purchase' on the list was dated 15 February 1868, three days before Pompallier was due to leave. It was the only time cash was listed: £7 10s. On 8 February they had listed: '1 Holland dress & jacket, altering ditto, making 1 dress, making 1 jacket, making dress & jacket . . .'[48] These appear to be the clothes that transformed Mother Mary Baptist back to Mademoiselle Lucie Pompallier. In Tahiti, 'His Lordship was accompanied by his niece, who, it seems, used to wear the habit of a religious in Auckland and carried out the functions of Superior of a community. She had put aside the habit before her arrival in Tahiti, and was included in the invitations extended to society ladies in Papeete.'[49]

Pompallier very likely knew she would be coming with him, if he had issued the promissory notes. All documents indicate that Lucie stayed with him, taking care of him on the voyage, in France and in Rome. It would be unusual for a bishop of his age, slowed by rheumatism, to travel alone without secretary or companion. Who can blame Lucie for leaving?

Her brother Antoine had already left, her uncle was going and, even though he had mentioned a speedy return, this was unlikely.[50] Neither the Sisters of Mercy, nor Father Poupinel, nor Suzanne thought that Lucie had a real vocation. Once Pompallier was gone, Lucie would have been marooned and penniless in Auckland with singlemindedly dedicated and undoubtedly disapproving Suzanne, and equally disapproving sisters over the road.

Pompallier had no money. This became clear in Tahiti, where an understanding French Commissaire Impérial reimbursed the captain of the *Chevert*, gave Pompallier and Lucie free hospitality, and lent them passage money from Callao to France. He too later joined the list of embarrassed creditors seeking payment. Letters would go back and forth between the ministries of Cultes and Colonies untangling Pompallier's liabilities.[51] After a long, eventful and taxing voyage, the tired and ill bishop reached France. Once there, he was within the Marists' sights. In August: 'Bishop Pompallier is in Paris with his niece, staying at a hotel . . . they say that Bishop Pompallier will get a bad reception in Rome.'[52] And again in December: 'Bishop Pompallier is in hiding. They said he had come to Lyon and asked to borrow one thousand francs, but we haven't seen him. I don't think he'll want to be in a hurry to go to Rome. He's afraid of what will happen to him.'[53]

He tried to raise money, and for a while was hopeful. An audience with Napoleon III and his empress gained him exemption from repaying his passage money.[54] He had a *Notice* printed and circulated for subscriptions to the mission.[55] He carried on collecting until February 1869 and managed to pay £700 off his debts. But the old charisma was gone, and subscriptions on behalf of the Pope, in political strife in Italy, and for the Vatican Council were absorbing the resources of the faithful. He resigned on 23 March 1869 his 'bishopric of thirty-three years', half his life.[56] After that it would be difficult to raise money for Auckland. In November 1869 he wrote to James McDonald, saying that McDonald must now manage locally, 'if necessary with the sale of some properties of the Diocese, *in positivis* necessity finds in itself its own approbation, and the approbation of reasonable minds'.[57] There was a certain dignity and pathos in this wistful plea to finish with the long-drawn-out mess.

From Pompallier's perspective, there had been a lack of 'approbation of reasonable minds' in Auckland since his departure. Father James McDonald, the vicar general and apostolic administrator after

Pompallier's resignation, and his brother Father Walter McDonald loyally struggled to cope with the mounting resentment among the laity. This peaked in a much-publicised Memorial, outlining the problems and financial situation, which was sent to Rome in August 1869.[58] The lay Catholics were incensed as much by the ignorance they had been kept in, the lack of consultation, as by the financial scandal itself. The Catholic community of Auckland felt humiliated, and righteous judgement welled up as a natural reaction. The promissory notes were dishonoured; the mortgages fell due. People rallied, including a Protestant shipwright William Swanson, who bought the controversial North Shore St Mary's school property to safeguard it and later sell it back to the Catholic diocese at no interest.

In fact, the crumbling mess of Auckland education in general, fuelling newspaper columns, only compounded the Catholics' embarrassment and added to the publicity.[59] In front of a Commission of Enquiry, McDonald had had to confess that even he, the vicar general, was ignorant of Pompallier's mode of business: 'There was no ledger kept [for the native institutions, specifically St Mary's, North Shore], nor accounts to which I have access, in which the capital account of the College was entered as distinct from the annual current revenue and expenditure. The Bishop, no doubt, possesses such.'[60]

The bishop possessed very little by then. A public auction on 21 September 1868, advertised in the newspapers since 12 September, sold up his furniture and effects to settle a dishonoured promissory note. The 'Harmonium, Hair-seated Chairs, Cheval Glass, Hat Stand . . .' went out the door of his residences at St Anne's and St Patrick's, along with 'Brussels Carpets, Druggets' and everything else. Pompallier in Paris, still bishop at this stage, was stunned by the 'deplorable' news but resigned himself to the clear will of God.[61]

Meanwhile, the clergy were suffering. The diocesan coffers were bare and James McDonald was obviously trying to pay debts out in the lay world rather than fund his own men and women. It was a simple case of 'officers and captain last', but the 'officers' had not been consulted. The Franciscans wrote directly to the Propagation of the Faith. Since 1867, they said, they had had from Pompallier only £100 and a promissory note which had been dishonoured.[62] Boibieux and Grange had received nothing; their creditors were waiting, and the two priests threatened also to report overseas: 'if your answer does not come to us before Sunday night we shall take your silence as refusal to our request & then the European mail goes on Monday'.[63]

Sister Mary Joseph too had nothing. Pompallier had written to McDonald from Tahiti: 'I hope, you will be able likewise to send to me the two thirds of my parochial funds from St Patrick's Cathedral, the other third being for Sister Mary Joseph and the community of the Holy Family.'[64] And from Lyon, perhaps with a hometown prick to his conscience, he upped this intention: 'as for Sister Mary Joseph, instead of giving to her a third part of my parochial funds, give the half part'.[65] Did he suspect this money would never get through? Was he making a grand but empty gesture? Suzanne said that she received £1 and a denial that Pompallier had said anything about parochial funds.[66]

The evidence also suggests this: McDonald was not handing on to Sister Mary Joseph the last instalments from the government capitation grant, including the December 1867 quarter, £26 13s 7d, which arrived after Pompallier's departure.[67] And someone, somehow, was blocking her outward mail: 'Last month, March 1869, having an important letter for France, and having previously noticed that they are the very ones that are stopped . . .' runs Suzanne's first surviving letter in English, where she laid out her concerns to Daniel Pollen, agent of the general government in Auckland.[68]

It would be wrong to see Suzanne only as endlessly long-suffering during this time and passively enduring hardship in a trial of asceticism. Her letter to Pollen casts light on what was happening to her now that she, with Peata's help, was in charge of what she still saw as the Nazareth Institute. She was stepping into planning and management, into lobbying, into public relations; she was enjoying her new-found independence, testing her skills, even flexing her muscle. Behind and beside the thirty-three-year-old woman is the double-exposure outline of the future Mother Aubert. Along with Auckland's Catholic laity, she was becoming more visible, more vocal, more strategic. She used indirect action and later, instead of writing to Governor Bowen about the capitation grant, on 22 September 1868 she wrote to his wife, whom she had met before.[69] Suzanne, not McDonald, was writing directly to the Native Affairs office about school business. She sent reports to the newspapers about activities at Nazareth.[70] Later she would publish in the newspapers thanks and acknowledgements for support and donations.[71]

There is a tone of equal dealing with equal when Robert Eyton inspected the institution in May 1868. She enjoyed giving her views and being heard and heeded. He and 'the lady in charge of this school' discussed not only how to ensure that pupils avoided prostitution on leaving school, but also the threatened closure of the school, its debts, alternative plans and possible government subsidies. The ability of Suzanne Aubert to sense the occasion, to be flexible where it would serve to further her cause, comes through. By 1867, for instance, the government had turned against the large city-based boarding institutions. She knew this and discussed an alternative with Eyton: 'Sr Marie Joseph informs me that [if the institute closed] she will endeavour to establish a day school for both sexes in some district more thickly inhabited by Natives, probably near Whangarei.'[72]

This confidence and enjoyment were nowhere more evident than in the newspaper account of the welcome to the new governor, Sir George Bowen, and his wife in May 1868. What also comes out of the report is a respect for Maori protocol. The school was not merely a carbon copy of a Pakeha orphanage and the governor's party was in effect being welcomed on to a marae:

> On arriving in front of his Lordship Bishop Pompallier's residence, native girls under the direction of the Sister in charge of the Institution came out and welcomed the party with their usual salutations, 'Haere mai, haere mai' (Welcome, welcome). His Excellency and Lady Bowen acknowledged the compliment in a very cordial manner. The party were conducted into the school room of the pupils, which was neatly prepared for the occasion. Addresses in English and Maori were read by two pupils of the Institution. The singing of the children was remarkable for the accord and beautiful effect. There was also a dialogue in the Maori style, which created much merriment.
>
> In addition to the pupils present, we noticed the two Arawa chiefs named Ringori te Ao and Pereme Rotoehu, and a half-caste named William Whitaker from Whangaroa.
>
> During their stay his Excellency and Lady Bowen frequently gave expression to approving remarks on the happiness of the children, and the appearance which they presented of being so much at home.[73]

Suzanne's bubble of optimism was quickly going to be burst, however, even if her determination was never quashed. She had been under the impression that the small glebe where the Nazareth buildings stood belonged to the congregation of the Sisters of the Holy Family, that it had been made over to them at the same time as the eighteen acres were transferred to the Sisters of Mercy. Viard, in Auckland in 1863 officially investigating the diocese following the Franciscans' complaint, recorded Pompallier's intention: 'after also giving six of these acres to the Sisters of the Holy Family where they are going to educate native girls with Government funds, His Lordship is going to sell the remaining twenty acres'.[74]

The intention never became a reality. The property was diocesan and, once Pompallier resigned, the tiny congregation he had founded, with only its simple annual vows, no longer officially existed. In the same letter to McDonald which acknowledged that property would have to be sold, Pompallier, now with no income, was laying his own claim: 'The property of St Anne on Mount St Mary owes to the Bishop £1000 one thousand pounds . . . because that money was employed for the purchase of it in the beginning from the patrimonial funds of the Bishop.'[75] This property included his residence, the Church of the Immaculate Conception and the buildings of the institute. But somewhere in all the financial tangle Suzanne had for many years thought they were paying off debt on a property which would be theirs. She recollected that, in addition to all the work with the Maori girls, for a long time she had been raising extra money by laundering, teaching French and music privately, and by staying up through the night sewing for private commissions.

To meet the mortgage and arrears of interest, the property was sold by the mortgagee to Joseph Bennett on 2 October 1869. He in turn sold three of its buildings for removal in mid-1870.[76] The large convent building, with its little chapel inside, was rolled to the front of the section and 'thoroughly renovated, at a large expense' into a private dwelling, as yet unoccupied. It was now 'a very fine double storey house, with verandah running around it, and fitted up with French windows, English grates, marble chimney-pieces and other fixtures of an equally first-class character'.[77] Suzanne judged the whole affair to be close to sacrilege. It seemed to her 'like a haunted house' and when it burnt down in a sudden fire on a wet July night, while she watched, it was 'as though she had witnessed the visible judgement of God'.[78] The fire was reported as the handiwork of an 'incendiary'.[79]

Meanwhile she, Peata and the remaining girls had moved out, probably first to two little cottages on the same site. In late October 1869 they left St Anne's, and went into temporary accommodation in a disused bakery on Outhwaite property, then again in April 1870 to the Shelly Beach house of John Campbell, a surveyor and property developer, while he was away in Europe.[80] In all this time, they were living at subsistence level. Along with the other poor, they gathered bones from carcasses and sold them. Freeman's Bay by 1870 had its own bone mills, run by J. and J. Soppet. And like others they were the recipients of charity.

All this time, Sister Mary Joseph kept on building up support with the public for her venture of continuing a Maori school. People rallied behind her: John King, Edouard Cafler, John Campbell, the Outhwaite family, William Hurst, William Swanson, Paora Tuhaere, Donald McLean and the Bowens.[81] 'Mr King represents my interests very enthusiastically with the Government. Several of my friends have just been named members of the Council.'[82] She probably exaggerated a good deal of this backing, but clearly she was convincing the clergy that she had considerable support. And the further she moved into the public arena along with the lay-people, the more she was unsettling many of the clergy with her resilience and unorthodox readiness to use initiative.

Meanwhile, like so many now, she had finally become disillusioned with Pompallier. This would not have been fully formulated or expressed until the arrival of Bishop Goold from Melbourne on 25 October 1869, when his visitation closed the book on Pompallier's long era. He had been sent by Rome to investigate and report on Pompallier's administration and the sorry affairs of Auckland, and to set things right. He came with an agenda essentially pre-set. He was to be a catalyst and, in three weeks, energetically sluiced out the diocesan drains. There was to be no question of exonerating Pompallier; rather, a quick and merciful sentence was required.[83]

Whereas Viard's previous visitations in 1853 and 1863 had preferred positive viewpoints and had given positive interpretation wherever possible, Goold's neat cast-list had four main roles which, if simplistically identified, would be: Pompallier as 'the villain', the two McDonald brothers as 'culpable ineffectual henchmen', the Sisters of Mercy as 'accomplices', and Sister Mary Joseph as 'informant'.[84] Father Poupinel, still Marist Visitor in Sydney, had spoken positively of her to Goold before he crossed the Tasman. Goold would have arrived with Suzanne cast as a credible witness.[85]

In a sense they were all scapegoated. James McDonald, for instance, was summarily relieved of his long-held position of vicar general and posted to Drury, where he took up again his mission to the Maori. He had been, especially after Garavel's departure, the main priest going around the various Maori settlements and he would do this for the rest of his life,

the only priest in the Auckland diocese until the arrival in 1886 of
the St Joseph's Missionary Society to keep Maori mission alive – just as
Suzanne would do in the Wellington diocese. But now, ironically, these
two future Maori missioners were in opposition. Like others, Suzanne
turned against McDonald when he was down and wrote a derisory pen-
portrait of him to Father Poupinel, describing how the 'ex-Grand-Vicar
has not set foot in Auckland since the departure of Bishop Gould' and
painting him in his poverty ineffectually darning, 'cobbling with white
thread the bottom of his, so he claims, one and only pair of pants'.[86]

Likewise scapegoated were the Sisters of Mercy, who more than anyone
else represented Pompallier's camp. Ageing Mary Cecilia and Mary Paula
were confronted and questioned. They continued to defend Pompallier
loyally and resented Goold's directive to remove, as Suzanne put it, 'the
pictures of this Holy Bishop!! of this Apostle of New Zealand!! of this
Father beyond all compare!! of this martyr to calumny and illwill etc!!!'[87]
This is the only instance of Suzanne Aubert succumbing to the
nineteenth-century habit of studding writing with exclamation marks.
She does not match the Franciscans for accumulated emotiveness about
Pompallier, but the level of scorn is high.

More than once Suzanne, as the *Sororem Mariam Josepham* of Goold's
report to Rome, has been branded as a bell-wether or Judas figure. Two
letters she wrote to Marists in 1869 have passages which are pettily
sarcastic about Pompallier, Lucie, James McDonald and the Sisters of
Mercy. But Goold consulted others as well, and other evidence besides
hers was sent to Rome. She does not deserve to be simplistically singled
out. The saga of the 1860s – Pompallier, the priests, the sisters, the wars,
the economic collapse, the schooling troubles – is complex, and Suzanne's
position and action become clearly understandable once the story is told.

Neither did Pompallier deserve the instant blacklisting he got.[88] Rome
had known for years the manner of man he was and the nature of his
diocese. Plenty of other nineteenth-century bishops, struggling with the
isolation of their considerable local power, had their problems and
failures. Propaganda Fide's files were already bursting with complaints
about Pompallier, dating back to 1842. The testimony of Suzanne Aubert,
however direct and articulate, only added to others. Goold even noted
in his diary: 'Father Fynes called to give information about the
Diocese and the Bishop. . . . Had to ask Father Fynes to put his statements
in writing.'[89]

Even the Sisters of Mercy were not a solid phalanx protecting their bishop. They had their disaffected members, two of whom had opposed Pompallier in 1863. Correspondence from Sister Philomena Dwyer was also filed in Rome.[90] There could have been a kinder way for Rome to reconcile the laity and clergy to the reality of the diocese, and to one another, than to encourage highly critical judgement of Pompallier at this stage.

It was not Goold's fault. He had been instructed to do this, and had been envisaging the cleansing effects of catharsis. The Jesuit Father Dalton, who came with him, gave retreats which were welcomed by emotionally exhausted and spiritually starved people. Both Suzanne and the Sisters of Mercy wrote of him with gratitude; he 'gave sermons which would melt hearts of stone'.[91] Goold, too, preached warmly and well. He boosted the confidence of the people 'who were delighted with him'. But then 'the Bishop and Father Dalton, much pleased with their trip and with the kind-hearted, homely people whom they met' went away.[92] In Rome for the Vatican Council, Goold declined to remain apostolic administrator and in doing this denied Auckland the benefit of continuity. Propaganda Fide let the Propagation of the Faith's grant of 55,000 francs wait for the new bishop while the clergy of Auckland struggled on.[93]

All this time Suzanne was not well. From Tahiti, Pompallier had asked James McDonald to give his greetings and blessing to the clergy, to the Sisters of Mercy and to Sister Mary Joseph: 'Encourage them all and specially the poor last one, who is subject to bad health and is too much alone under the charge of assistant and office of teacher at Nazareth.'[94] If she had had any *new* evidence for Goold, it might have been what lay behind her ill health. In 1866 'something' had happened which threw the Sisters of the Holy Family into disarray. At the same time, while preparing, she said, a remedy for Pompallier's rheumatism, she had an accident which seriously damaged her health, and left long-term effects. Goold alluded in his report to her 'deplorable story already sent to you'.

In February 1866 Poupinel had passed through Auckland on his way back to Sydney after his regular visit to the Marist missions in Wellington. Nothing Pompallier did could impress Poupinel. He considered that Pompallier lived 'much too close to his community of the Holy Family', that 'if it succeeded in doing any good, you might as well say that miracles are happening in Auckland greater than when

Our Lord used mud to open the eyes of the man born blind':

> There has been a great upheaval in this house in the last three months; the
> third woman from Lyon has been sent away, so have Maori Sisters or
> postulants, in all about six or seven. I've been told that the Lyonnaise was in
> Wellington but I didn't see anything of her when I passed through. . . . You've
> got what I've said about Suzanne Auber[t] in a letter to Mr Bessy; it's all true.
> I'll add what follows just for you, you mustn't tell her mother. About a
> fortnight ago, she was pulling the cork out of a flask of ammonia; this acid
> shot out like champagne and burnt her lips; unfortunately some drops got into
> her mouth and burnt her tongue and stomach. Luckily the doctor was there
> and treatment was prompt. Nevertheless this poor child, always so full of
> energy, spirit and courage, could no longer take any nourishment without her
> system rejecting it. However, we hope her internal injuries will heal just as the
> external ones have. I said a Mass for her on the first of March.
>
> I think she is a sensible person with a love of goodness; I realise she can't
> actually be happy about it all; but seeing she has lots of character, as they say,
> she seems to be taking it in good part and saying: what's done is done.[95]

This is a good contemporary summing-up of Suzanne's personality.
Without more evidence, what lay behind the upheaval and Suzanne's
accident is only conjecture. Certainly the Marists described graphically
Lucie lording it in the Church of the Immaculate Conception; certainly
Péroline left suddenly and was found by Father Bucas walking to
Onehunga to catch a boat to Wellington;[96] certainly Father Paul Sarda,
who was rumoured to have become attached to Lucie, was dismissed
abruptly by Pompallier and despatched on his way, to die tragically in the
wreck of the *General Grant*.[97] Not least, Pompallier had a major rupture
with his own nephew, Antoine, over the Sarda affair and told Poupinel he
had decided to dismiss him.[98] Pompallier reported to Propaganda that
Paul Sarda and Antoine returned to France because their 'nerves were
under strain in this climate' and his nephew needed treatment for short
sight.[99] Within two days Poupinel had whisked Antoine away from 'this
wasp's nest' and back with him to Sydney.

Yet from this incident comes the clearest indication that Suzanne did
not criticise Pompallier easily. Even in the middle of all this distress, she
refused to turn against him. Her criterion for loyalty was his support for
the Maori mission. Poupinel's letter had continued:

> She told me: please say to Father Yardin that I can't write to him, because
> *it's impossible*; but I'll never stop being grateful to him; I'll always be sorry that
> family difficulties prevented me from being a Marist. She added: If we were
> to lose Bishop Pompallier in one way or another, our institution would

collapse, we've definitely been warned about that. I love our work, and I'm grateful to His Lordship who has been good to me; I want to keep faith with our Maori girls and the bishop; but if this community were to collapse, would you, Father, care to receive me?

In the final collapse of Pompallier's mission, Suzanne's priorities continued to lie with the Maori mission: 'I'm determined, with God's grace, to die on the job rather than give up.'[100] Gould had taken to Rome a petition she got up 'in support of the Maoris', asking for the mission to be handed into Marist care.[101] Where other denominations were sending away their pupils, she clung to her few remaining girls in their temporary housing. She raised money, drew up plans for building a new school on land donated to her by John Campbell 'of Campbellville'. She was corresponding about it with Father Dalton in Australia. This land she now fiercely determined would be inalienable. 'I'm still in a state of open warfare with the *Gentlemen* of the *Diocesan Commission*. I front up to them politely but I have a lot of trouble overcoming the difficulties they are creating for me. They can't manage to forgive me for making the new establishment inalienable and this has led to endless nitpicking and wrangling.'[102]

There was a touch of dramatic obstinacy in her independence. She was playing her cards too tightly to her chest and, if she felt herself to be still a religious sister, this was puzzling and unacceptable to the six priests appointed by Goold to run the diocese: 'Since the visitation of the Rt Rev Bishop Goold she has energetically laboured to advance her views, with which however the D[iocesan]. Commission had not been made acquainted: no correspondence either oral or written, having taken place between her and the D. Commission upon her proceedings.'[103] They questioned her about how she saw her religious status. She answered that according to the letter she was no longer a religious, but in her spirit she was a member of whatever society the new bishop would appoint to care for the Maori, and that Goold had urged her to carry on caring for the institute as previously.[104] Father Dalton was encouraging her by letter but in Auckland she felt that only Father Grange among the clergy supported her. 'I think that the Commission would have already excommunicated me were it not for good Father Grange whose integrity and virtue scared them off.'[105]

As Suzanne, with the rest of Catholic Auckland, waited for the new Irish bishop who would replace Pompallier, she and Peata were indeed alone. None of her three companions of 1860 was still with her. Lucie had married in France, and as Madame Aunier would continue caring for Pompallier. He died in her home in Puteaux on 21 December 1871. She would have three children.[106] Péroline joined the Wellington convent of the Sisters of Mercy on 21 November 1867 and was professed on 29 April 1871. Already dying of tuberculosis, she was sent to the newly arrived French Sisters of the Mission in Nelson for sunshine and French companionship. There, as Sister Mary Stanislaus Joseph, she died on 17 August 1871.[107]

And Antoinette? In October 1865 she was still in Auckland as Mademoiselle Deloncle, advertising evening French lessons in the newspaper.[108] With probably just enough money to get as far as Sydney on her way back to France, as happened with several priests over the years, she was stranded there. Suzanne must have anxiously enquired back home whether Antoinette had arrived because, in the one torn scrap remaining from her mother's letters, Clarice seems to be replying: 'I do not know what has become of Antoinette. Her mother was counting very much on her return when we left Lyon.'

Antoinette instead stayed in a Sydney boarding-house, first teaching and sewing, then increasingly living in her own world of delusions, spiralling inwards in a darkened room, her days and nights turned upside down. She visualised people invading her head, Father Poupinel and the Chief Justice and French Consul, Sir Alfred Stephen, threatening her. Her landlady finally had to commit her to a mental institution in April 1869. From then until her death thirty-five years later, she passed from one Sydney mental home to another, her file continuing to describe with compassion an emaciated woman obligingly sewing and living lost in her mind's circling script.[109] If talkative Mother Aubert never spoke much of Antoinette, it may have been as much from sadness as from discretion.

Pompallier, too, had disappeared from Suzanne's life, but one part of his influence stayed with her. As she had pointed out in 1866, it was his understanding and support for Maori mission, his respect for Maori. The guidance he wrote for his priests in 1841, 'Instructions for the Work of the Mission', was unusually perceptive and culturally sensitive for the time.[110] Suzanne is never recorded as speaking ill of Pompallier to her sisters; rather, she is recorded as recommending his viewpoints. She probably read his 1859 published guidelines, *Instruction on Christian Wisdom*, printed for his new 1860s missionaries to learn in Maori. As Pompallier leaves this story, his enlightened hopes, not his fallible example, can speak for him:

Ako Tuawa:

Ko te Atua pono te tino matua, te matua kaha rawa o nga iwi katoa o te ao, na, o te hunga katoa katoa: a te hunga katoa ko tana whanau aroha. Koia nga tangata katoa ko nga tuakana, ko nga teina ranei te tahi ki te tahi. Mo reira e tino tika kei mahi kino ratou tetahi ki tetahi; na, kaua te hangareka, ma te manawapa, me te korero teka, me te tahae, me te tutu, me te wawai, ara, kaua nga kino katoa. Engari kia pai te tangata ki te tangata, kia tika ratou tetahi ki tetahi, ara, kia aroha pono tetahi ki tetahi.

Fourth lesson of wisdom:

God is the first father, the all-powerful father of all the nations of the world; and all the peoples and men of each country whatever, are the beloved family of God. Men are therefore all brothers of one another. Hence it follows that they must not harm one another; far from them therefore deception, jealousy, fraud, theft, quarrelling, ructions and all that can harm one's neighbour; but on the contrary, let them do good to one another, observing goodness and justice to one another; it is by all these lessons carried out in practice, that they will truly love one another.[111]

Auckland in 1859, with the barracks in the centre background and rows of wooden houses and hotels leading down to the harbour.   A. ROBERTSON, AUCKLAND CITY ART GALLERY

Antoine Pompallier, Lucie's brother.

Lucie Pompallier, Mother Mary Baptist, Superior of the Sisters of the Holy Family.

Bishop Thomas Croke. ACDA

Pompallier in 1848, aged 45.
ACDA

Bishop Jean-Baptiste
François Pompallier as
Suzanne knew him.

Freeman's Bay, Auckland, in 1863.

J. EASTWOOD, F1092761/2 ATL

The Nazareth Institute, c.1866. Centre left, the spire of the chapel of the Sisters of Mercy across the road; on the right the church of the Immaculate Conception. It is probably Lucie standing on the path; Suzanne or Péroline in the doorway.

Peata, Suzanne (seated right) and their pupils, taken probably in 1869.

Suzanne, unusually for a nineteenth-century nun, is shown sitting on the ground with her pupils.

2536 CANTERBURY MUSEUM

Top left: Father Victor Poupinel. MAW
Top right: Father Euloge Reignier. MAW
Lower left: Father Antoine Séon.
Lower right: Father François Yardin.

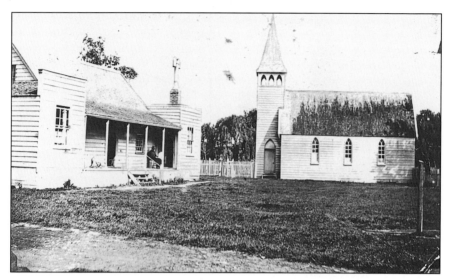

The presbytery and church at Meanee in the 1870s. Father Séon is sitting on the verandah.
Suzanne used the end nearest the church as a dispensary.   MAW

The new presbytery, c.1880. In the foreground is the newly arrived missioner for the Maori,
Father Christophe Soulas. Father Reignier stands withdrawn on the verandah. Brother Joachim
Gatta wheels the barrow. Suzanne's dispensary, 'the red shed', is alongside.   MAW

Brother Basile
Montchalin. MAW

The grape harvest, Meanee,
in the 1880s.   MAW

Suzanne's tiny devotional
books, carried in her pocket.

Francis Redwood, Bishop of
Wellington from 1874.

The church at Pakipaki, opened in 1880.   493991/2 ATL

Urupene Puhara, son of
Puhara Hawaiikirangi.
    P. PARSONS

Marata, his wife.   P. PARSONS

CHAPTER SEVEN

From Auckland to Meanee
1869-1872

She has gone to Napier : Kua riro ia ki Nepia[1]

Sister Mary Joseph and her new Auckland project were very vulnerable. She may have lost sight of this as she bustled about in the semi-euphoria of her community support, minding her girls, making ends meet, raising money, publicising. She was stalling the Auckland diocese's attempts to gain ownership of the land donated by Campbell because she was hoping it would go instead to a Maori mission unified across the dioceses, and under the charge of the Society of Mary. This was the reason she gave for sending the petition to Rome with Bishop Goold. When she told the priests of the Diocesan Commission that she considered herself in spirit a member of whatever society the new bishop would appoint to run the Maori mission, she was guardedly speaking the truth. She hoped it would be the Marists, and she had already aligned herself with them.

After she had met Poupinel at the time of her illness in 1866, the Marists were more aware of her. And, once Pompallier had resigned, she was freer to correspond with them. Poupinel and Yardin were either in Sydney or in Lyon, but not too far away in Hawke's Bay was Father Euloge Reignier. She met him in 1869, when he stayed twice in Auckland, waiting first for a ship to Sydney, then for another back to Napier. Reignier wrote to Yardin in July that he had heard details of the problems in Auckland from the Franciscan fathers, another priest and 'Mlle Aubert (Soeur Marie Joséphine)'. He also said that she had asked about joining a new French congregation in Napier, initially linked to the Marists. They told her, however, that all novices had to go to Lyon for their formation; 'but she cannot go to Lyon; she is too afraid of the sea'.[2] Seasickness would set her vomiting blood from her still damaged digestive system.

It was not just this fear that held her back. Other factors steered her away from these sisters, who had been working in Napier since 1865. They had recently broken away from the Marists to form an independent congregation called the Sisters of Our Lady of the Missions.[3] They led a semi-enclosed lifestyle, which would not suit the active, outgoing, fresh-air-loving Suzanne. She said she was not keen on grilles.

What also kept her from joining them was knowing that, if she went back to Lyon, she might never come back to the missions. Her parents were still urging her to return to the family fold. They now knew about the failure of the mission, and something about her 'health already so endangered'. Late in 1868, her brother had written on their behalf to the Marists' Pacific headquarters in Sydney. They wanted to know whether Father Forest in Napier or Father Petitjean in Wellington could be authorised to buy her passage as soon as she agreed to return. The cost would be immediately reimbursed by the Aubert family. They knew their daughter well. 'My father . . . does not want to send directly to my sister a sum of money which she would possibly use according to her own wishes for staying on in Auckland.'[4]

It was the Society of Mary to which Suzanne affiliated herself. She welcomed the support expressed in their letters. Her letters to Father Poupinel spilled out a wistful homesickness for Lyon and Fourvière, her love for her family, her worries about the war hanging over France, her gratitude and regard for Goold and Dalton, and her hopes for the Maori mission. She was pouring out to friends her feelings about the situation in Auckland, and taking their counsel. Poupinel detected in these letters her exhausted hyperactivity, and damped down her flares of anger with kindness: 'for pity's sake rid your memory as much as possible of all these heart-rending, deplorable experiences. So avoid any opportunity of mentioning them. Most of all, put out of your heart all your bitter feelings of resentment against people whom God made use of to try you so severely.'[5]

Jesuit Father Dalton had encouraged her to join the Third Order of Mary. It is not clear from the records whether she was joining as a 'private', isolated novice the group of French women now working in the Pacific Islands, who were in 'a sort of half-way house between the laity and fully-fledged religious' and who would later be called the Third Order Regular of Mary, or another Third Order of Mary, which was a lay group allied to the Society of Mary and whose members were called tertiaries.[6] Whichever it was, by November 1869 Yardin had asked

Reignier to receive her into the Third Order. In a year's time she was to go down to Napier for her profession. Reignier admired her determination to guarantee a school for her girls: she was a 'courageous Christian'.[7] He was also establishing a *Providence* for Maori girls and planning a school for younger Maori boys. They were like partners in the venture of retrieving mission-based education for Maori.

What would make her vulnerable in this? The Marists were not implicated in Pompallier's downfall in any way, and Bishop Goold had reported favourably of her to Rome. It was the nature of the new bishop which weakened her chances of continuing her work in Auckland. From the outset Bishop Thomas Croke was prejudiced against anyone who was not Irish, anyone associated with the French Marists in New Zealand, and anyone who criticised the Sisters of Mercy. Sister Mary Joseph was a bull's-eye target on all three counts.

Throughout Croke's career he was known for his active support of the Irish nationalist cause. One famous instance of this came later, in 1883, when as Archbishop of Cashel he was summoned to Rome and censured by the Pope for supporting Parnell.[8] But in 1871 he was just one of several Irish diocesan bishops in Australia, and now in New Zealand, whose aim was not only to safeguard the emigrants' Catholic faith but also their Irish ethnicity and nationality. They were all disciples of Archbishop (later Cardinal) Paul Cullen of Dublin, who taught 'rigid episcopal authority at all levels to his students'.[9] In Australia in the 1860s these men were beginning to supersede the early English Benedictines and establish secular and Irish diocesan power.[10] To have Irish priests and bishops to minister to mainly Irish Catholics made sense and they did what they felt was best for the church, but their agenda was strongly ethnic Irish, not Australian. They would not have seen merit in reconciling their settler parishioners to a largely non-Irish future and helping them invest in 'the growth of a shared identity, shared with all comers, reasonably and by choice'.[11]

Through these same years, Mary MacKillop was working to consolidate Australia's own female congregation, the Sisters of St Joseph. Her Australian colonial birth and Scottish background did not count in her favour with several bishops. Neither did her vision of sisters working together across the Australian colonies rather than separately in cellular, diocesan Irish outposts. One of her opponents, Matthew Quinn, was pleased that an Irish bishop was going to Auckland. He wrote to the rector of the Irish College in Rome: 'Croke's appointment to Auckland is consoling news for that much and long afflicted church. By all accounts it is and has been in a frightful condition. Croke is just the man for the occasion.'[12]

This Irish network already had its first link in New Zealand. Croke came to Auckland at the end of 1870 but Bishop Patrick Moran had been in Dunedin since the beginning of the year, when he took over the southern portion of Viard's previously huge diocese of Wellington. Moran was the first non-French bishop in New Zealand and had come straight from thirteen years in a largely Calvinistic environment in southern Africa as Bishop of the Eastern Province of Cape Colony. In countering the Presbyterian establishment in Otago, he adopted a militantly separate, Irish nationalist stance.[13]

Moran's target became not merely Protestants but also his fellow Catholics, the Society of Mary. It did not matter that the Marists now had a seminary in Ireland and were enrolling Irish men; they were still an independent, non-Irish order. Nothing that Marist Father Moreau had done in the difficult terrain of the goldfields was acceptable to Moran. He blamed Moreau for the raw outpost he found instead of the well-appointed establishment he had somehow been expecting to inherit.[14] To be fair to Moran, it should be added that Bishop Viard had been hard-pressed to staff the diocese effectively during the goldrush years. And as this gentle but increasingly dithery bishop aged, he was becoming ineffectual. Poupinel, as Marist Visitor, was writing concerned letters back to Lyon. And, of course, Irish-born parishioners were sometimes exasperated by priests who had French as their first language, Maori as their second, and English as a poor third. French priests in fact continued to outnumber English-speaking priests in New Zealand until the mid-1880s.[15]

Bishop Croke came to Auckland determined to 'Irish' the diocese. He too wrote back to the Irish College rector in Rome: 'An Irish bishop was not sent here a day too soon. Had there been much more of a delay, I fear that the faith would have died out here altogether.'[16] He was already informed by Moran's attitudes. The two were colleagues and fellow patriots. They preached what Suzanne once referred to as 'the faith of Patrick and the Gospel of Erin'.[17] Later Moran would visit Croke when he was back at Cashel in Ireland, where he 'told an audience that there were two Irelands, one at Home and one abroad, separate but not different'.[18] In the early 1870s it could seem to less than objective French observers that Moran from the south and Croke from the north, both secular and Irish, would have liked to close in on the beleaguered, largely Marist-staffed Wellington diocese in the middle.

The last thing Croke would have wanted was an energetic, free-wheeling, somewhat unclassifiable ex-diocesan nun, a sort of female religious 'forest ranger', French, Marist, already standing up to diocesan authority and on record as speaking against the Irish Sisters of Mercy. Bishop Croke's own sister was superior of the Bathurst Sisters of Mercy in Australia. Sister Mary Joseph, in spite of her enlisted supporters, had little chance. Croke was a man in a hurry, set on restoring diocesan control, diocesan finances and diocesan property.[19] The Franciscans found his opposition to their order too strong, and withdrew in 1873. Meanwhile, little Sister Mary Joseph's talk of inalienable, non-diocesan property would be quite beyond the pale.

It was lucky for her, as she waited for the new bishop, that she actually had three options in mind. The first was to build on the land in Auckland; the second was to go up north, as she had discussed with Inspector Eyton back in 1868; the third was to go to Hawke's Bay, where the French sisters were. On 13 November 1870, Father Reignier advised her:

> You tell me in your letter how you feel compelled to take up work soon, either at Mongonui or Meanee Flat.[20] Bravo! I told you when I was staying in Auckland that I was ready right then to take you off to our part of the country. In spite of your extraordinary courage, it's hard for you to overcome so many obstacles in your path. It's like being of the order of Melchesidech – without father, mother or family. In fact, look what's become of your Father Founder and his useless Reverend Mother! . . . On your side you've got the Government, Mr Campbell, a few priests. Perhaps Father Garavel, whom I've spoken to about you, will help you; perhaps the new Bishop too; but unless you found a new Order, you haven't much chance of succeeding; unless you intend establishing the Sisters from here.
>
> Are there priests at Mongonui where you're talking of going? If not, you won't prosper there. It'll be better for you to come to the Marist Fathers at Meanee Flat. It's not such a marvellous place for someone like you – used to Auckland! But you could look after my little school for Catholic children, especially teach them Catechism and singing. You could look after the Chapel, play the harmonium on Sundays, look after the sick, and make yourself useful as far as you have strength and capacity. Here you'll have at least somewhere to live, and food and clothing. The Gospel teaches us that with these, we should be content.

As for other aspects, we can work something out. If you decide to, you can come just when you are ready – tomorrow if you like. Let me know what you think. You'd better not noise abroad too soon what you want to do. I haven't said anything to the Sisters of Napier, only to Father Michel, the resident priest at the Mission.[21]

Reignier was clear-sighted in pressing her to the third option, to come south. Her first two options were within the Auckland diocese. Croke, when he arrived one month later, would be interested in neither. The resolution of her situation, when it came, was predictable and soon over. From the moment of his arrival, she hounded Croke almost daily for his approval to build. She was ill and had almost lost her sight, so perhaps subconsciously she was pushing him into a corner, unintentionally forcing him to a decision which would let her take respite and refuge in Reignier's warm offer, without feeling that she had lost the good faith of the community or her missionary integrity. With a theatrical flourish, Suzanne wrote up in a long letter to Yardin the dialogue of her final Auckland scenes with the 'visibly annoyed' bishop. It ended:

– You must go back to France, go a long way away from here, away from New Zealand.
– My Lord, by taking away my veil and my pupils, you give me back my freedom. I'm going to use this to advantage and do what I think best. . . . I came here for the Maoris; I'll die here among them. Nobody can stop me doing that; I'll do what I please . . . [22]

Erin prevailed in Auckland and Suzanne settled her affairs. She remembered tramping around the town stubbornly returning title deeds and donation money to the people who had given them specifically for her Maori school.[23] Croke was not expecting this loss of finances as a parting shot.[24] Her pupils were farewelled back to their kainga. On 7 January she left Shelly Beach. She stopped wearing the habit that had distinguished her since 1862 and, as Mademoiselle Aubert, in simple grey, went to stay with the Outhwaite family in Park Rd.

As the loose ends of the Nazareth Institute and Pompallier's era were tied off and snipped, what was happening to the other woman in the distinctive French blue habit? Peata had become blind. She did not go to Hawke's Bay with Suzanne, who also had very poor eyesight. 'Sensible' solutions prevailed. Suzanne said that Croke sent Peata back to the Sisters of Mercy, where she had lived in the 1850s. (Suzanne, though, would have been quite capable of sidestepping Croke's instructions.) There, the memories say, Peata walked the corridor by night, holding and stroking a grey silky gown that Lady Bowen had once owned. Peata loved the feel of the material, the swish of the skirt.[25] In these sounds in the dark, Celtic ghosties and other imaginings crept out to disturb the sisters. Perhaps Peata gleaned the emotional leavings of the bad harvest the Sisters of the Holy Family and the Sisters of Mercy had both reaped in the 1860s, because some months later she either went, or was sent, back up North. She wandered into the bush and her body was found eight days later.[26] In both Suzanne's and the Sisters of Mercy's recollections of all this, there is a certain defensiveness. Their consciences were not easy. To look forward, though, Peata would always be there, way out front for the rest of Suzanne's life, heading the list of Maori people she counted as role models.

The Outhwaite home gave Suzanne a warm family haven and she would ever afterwards write to Marie Louise Outhwaite as 'Dear Mrs Outhwaite, my very dear mother' or 'My very dear friend'. Marie Louise was the French wife of lawyer Thomas Outhwaite, who had come to New Zealand in 1841 as registrar of the new colony's Supreme Court in the company of William Martin as Chief Justice and William Swainson as Attorney-General.[27] They had four children. Isa (Louisa) Outhwaite, seven years younger than Suzanne, was born in Auckland in 1842. She remained Suzanne's friend for life. Here in this circle of early and educated colonists like the Martins, who shared Pompallier's and her vision of Maori mission, Suzanne was cared for during her last month in Auckland while she waited for a passage on the *Lord Ashley* to Napier.

She finally sailed on 15 February 1871, with Father Grange's company as far as his mission station at Tauranga. The *Daily Southern Cross* passenger listings recorded her '2 cases pianos, 6 packages luggage'.[28] Father Reignier would have liked more books for the school projects: 'She was really big-hearted to leave five hundred of her books and so many things with Dr Croke. She would have done as well to have brought them here. She brought her pianos and a harmonium.'[29] And so at the age of thirty-five she settled into life at the Marist Mission at Meanee (as it was then spelt), out from the new and growing village of Taradale.

Suzanne was not strong enough to pitch straight into school teaching. But, as Reignier wrote, she did her best to compensate:

> I'm sorry to say that Sister Mary Joseph because of her lack of strength and her eyesight can't yet run a school. She has extraordinary courage and willingness and the most sunny nature. She really held the fort in Auckland, dealing

superbly with so many things. She takes the church choir here and sings beautifully and makes herself extremely useful. She's a most fortunate addition to the place. She has really deserved God's help. She has deserved finding a happier place of refuge, away from storms.[30]

Reignier realised she needed rest in order to save her sight. She kept apologising for her brief little letters. The doctors advised against any close work and Father Reignier 'growls immediately he sees me look at anything'. She mentioned this in a letter to Victorine Outhwaite in April, and also showed that it was a real home she was gradually settling into:

> I wrote also to Lady Bowen, to apologise for not sending the music I promised her, but the fact is the crate was damaged and the music all torn. I will have to copy it out again, and I can't possibly do this just right now. I hope Lady Bowen will understand and not be disappointed. I would be really upset if I couldn't oblige her after all the kindness she has shown me.
>
> My dear friend, I wish you could be here for a while. We'd be able to go for lovely horse rides along some excellent tracks. The Fathers are so good. They let me do anything I want to except make use of my eyes.
>
> The countryside is pretty, but we are surrounded by tall trees and we live in a kind of solitude which makes you think of the Grande Chartreuse. I miss you more than I can tell you. I often talk about you to Father Michel who can't move around much and is interested in all my doings.
>
> My chickens arrived safe and sound. If Marie comes, I'd like her, if she can, to bring me two [Mu]Scovy ducks. Mrs Soppet kindly promised to let me have some. If she can't just at the moment, two of my own big old white ones would be lovely to have, because the ones we have at the farm here belong to a breed which is so little and ugly that they are hardly worth raising. If Marie came she could ask for my two ducks from Mrs Cousin.[31]

She missed Auckland and its wide views, but coming to Meanee was a godsend. Being French, she would have termed it *providence*: 'The good fathers are so good to me they spoil me too much and I'm really happy here with them. I'm infinitely grateful to Mgr Crooke for sending me packing, however rough and ready the manner of it.' The Meanee mission, with its wooden church alongside, was active and outgoing in spite of its ageing priests. It was the right place for her at this time: a French household, which gave her a familiar background, and a busy and by now well-established pioneer farm, grounding her securely in a New Zealand future.

The mission was situated on the flats by the Tutaekuri River. It had been located on the main road from the south to Napier, though soon this would be a side road from Taradale. It did not take long to gauge the main drawback to this position. The Meanee side was flooded more and more as the years went by. In April, Suzanne was writing to the Outhwaites during 'a week of torrential rains. The rivers are beginning to overflow their banks and we'll have to use stilts to walk round the house, there's so much mud and water all around. Meanee is just a great big swamp the whole of winter.'[32]

The brothers ran a well-respected, innovative farm doing its bit for the district.[33] They advertised the services of the stud stallion and farmers all around, Maori and Pakeha, Catholic and Protestant, used it to breed their draught-horses. With her hens and ducks, and her ever-growing medicinal herb garden, Sister Mary Joseph slipped into the farm routine. She was not the only woman. As Reignier was careful to point out to Poupinel, the sister had for companions the housekeeper and the part-Maori woman who helped, and her quarters were well removed from the main household.

There were two older priests, Reignier and Michel, as well as lay brothers. Jean Florentin Françon had been the main farm manager before transferring to Sydney in 1869. Basile Montchalin was the expert stockman. Laurent Cyprien Huchet, who came at the same time as Suzanne, was an experienced orchardist and wine-grower from the Loire. His lines of grapevines stretched out at the mission, flanked by orchards and paddocks of lucerne and marigold, oats and maize. What has been written about the Marist clergy tramping the rough West Coast applies also to these Hawke's Bay men; they 'exuded a quality of matter of fact acceptance of, and commitment to, the rough primitive land. That won them enduring local affection and deep respect.'[34]

These men were all straightforward and kind father figures. They kept Suzanne buoyed up through the lingering illness and death of her own father. The only surviving communication from her parents (besides the piece of Clarice's letter talking about Antoinette) was a short undated note from her father. He tells her he can hear the nightingales singing in the summer evenings. And he adds a postscript: 'I write with great difficulty.' Before he died he became reconciled with the church, and sent word to Suzanne that she had done the right thing in following her own calling. He gave her his blessing.

In the French household at Meanee, they all shared the letters and newspapers from France telling of the aftermath of the Commune. 'For two months I've had no news from my family. Oh, where is France heading to? It makes me tremble. I haven't got the courage to read the papers.'[35] Later, the backlash from the fall of Napoleon III's empire reanimated anticlerical opposition to religious orders, including the Society of Mary. Father Forest over in Napier was one of the very earliest Marists. Father Michel and Father Reignier in Meanee were also veterans. There was empathy and understanding over the situation in France.

Suzanne said she was a 'little ground-ivy' finding a hold once again on the familiar Marist tree of her Lyon childhood. But she did not cling to the mission for her upkeep. Reignier's daybooks show no payment to her, beyond little sums for items like coach travel to Waipawa and music manuscript paper, or one-off advances for the printing of her prayer-book and travel to Wellington for medical treatment.[36] In fact, she even brought in small contributions from bazaars and 'fancy fairs'. After her father died, she had a little money of her own which she placed with the Bank of New Zealand. She checked up with the Outhwaites in Auckland whether this investment was advisable. Part of the money had already been lost in bank failure in France before it had been passed over to her. 'I would be very sorry for the loss of this sum since it's this little income which helps me pay for my clothing and keep up my pharmacy stocks. I've been told that the Bank of New Zealand isn't very safe, so I'm coming to you, dear Mother, to ask you if you think this is the case. Would you be able to ask Mr Outhwaite where he thinks would be the safest place to deposit this money?'[37]

Suzanne liked being in a home, in a mission, in a community, in a frontier district reaching out. She liked widening circles. From her central base she walked out to their perimeters, or beyond – even over the winding, steep Napier–Taupo road – and around their circuits. As she recovered her strength and sight (though she had several serious relapses), she walked and walked. She became a familiar figure in her odd lay grey alpaca outfit, her blue girdle of the Third Order of Mary, and her straw sunhat tied down with a grey gauze scarf. Two detachable pockets under her skirt were weighted with tiny books of devotions and a piece of bread and cheese.[38] On her back was often a rucksack with medicines; sometimes she carried a flax kit. Like as not, her little white dog, Prince, would be hopping alongside. She was recognisable. She was 'Sister Joseph', 'the Sister', 'Meri'.

The closest of her circuits was the mission itself and the Taradale area. Here she called herself a 'stop-gap' and did teach catechism, train the local choir, play the harmonium.[39] She loved preparing the church for the religious feast-days with decorations including her own embroidery. And she helped on the farm. In January 1872, she explained to Marie Louise why she was so late in writing:

> In the fortnight leading up to Christmas I was so busy with the decorations of the church that I didn't have a moment to spare. The day after the feast-day, the Sisters from Napier came with all their pupils. The cook took fright with the amount of work that meant, and went off on a week's holiday. And as soon as the Sisters left, twelve extra workmen turned up at our place for the harvest, and I had to do the work on my own.[40]

Suzanne never became a regular schoolteacher in Father Reignier's Maori schools. The Sisters of the Mission were running St Joseph's Providence for Maori girls in Napier. Reignier had lay teachers helping with St Mary's, the residential and day school for boys on the Taradale side of the Meanee mission station. She did help out when needed, minding the sisters' school sometimes when they had to be away. The sisters liked her and appreciated her worth. Mother Marie de la Rédemption asked her if she would take over '*le management*' of the Providence, with sisters doing the teaching. The letter was kind and friendly but Suzanne did not take up the offer.[41] She is said to have taught James Carroll as a boy. Certainly he was a supporter of her projects when he was Minister of Native Affairs in the Liberal government. When she lay dying, he came to Island Bay to give her a long farewell hongi.

Some influential local chiefs were turning towards non-sectarian schooling, however. The *Hawke's Bay Herald* followed the discussions. 'Connected with this education question, it is noteworthy that the leading natives are opposed to any system of public school instruction of a sectarian character.'[42] Karaitiana Tokomoana was building a public school at Pakowhai; Renata Kawepo was doing the same at Omahu. Suzanne was getting to know these chiefs, and was also discovering a more effective channel of Maori mission for her than the thorny path of schooling. Teaching in general would have been too much of a constraint for her by now. In the build-up to the Education Act of 1877, with its emphasis on free, compulsory and secular schooling, the Catholic church was drawing away into the separate system it felt was essential for safeguarding the Catholic faith. From Dunedin, Bishop Moran was always battling for this.[43] The Papal Syllabus of Errors of 1864 had condemned the exclusion of the church from education. Being restricted to Catholic schooling would not give her the outgoing mission she wanted.

Suzanne became too valuable to keep within classroom walls. And she liked it that way. She wrote to Marie Louise in 1872:

> I don't mind that you've met Bishop Croke. The good Lord has worked out everything for the best. I feel I'm able to do more good among the Maoris where I am presently than I could do in my school at Auckland. I'm now visiting fairly regularly six or seven pa, and the chiefs, who were a bit unfriendly and suspicious at first, now give me a warm welcome.[44]

Father Reignier, who covered a huge tract of country with his Maori mission, was also having to cope with the influx of settlers. It was the same old story, the mission to the Maori being diverted by settler need. So Sister Joseph, the handy 'stop-gap', stepped eagerly into her longed-for role of missioner. In effect, she and Reignier were the only Maori missioners in the Wellington diocese in these years. And Reignier handed more and more over to her as the years went by.

Here is the Doctor : Tenei ano te takuta[45]

Suzanne was identifying herself as a 'sicknurse' by now, and as a 'Sister of Charity', a French way of defining nurse.[46] When she went around the various pa, she was bringing her medical skills in her missionary baggage. The word *visite* which she used in her letter has the meaning in French also of 'medical call', and she was welcomed for this. Pompallier had not been greatly in favour of 'Christianity through medicine': 'Be prudent for the pharmacie . . . We are the surgeons of the souls but we don't come to the natives to take responsibility of their life and health.'[47] Father Garin was the only Catholic missioner to have made a mark through treating illness.[48] But Suzanne had some training and considerable experience and skill by now.

Illness cut its path again in Maori communities after the wars of the 1860s. Pakeha began to pour into Hawke's Bay in the years of Premier Julius Vogel's immigration scheme, and with them came more epidemics which brought death to the Maori. The *Hawke's Bay Herald* on 1 February 1872 reported that 'smallpox is said to have broken out among the Maoris at Omahu'. Suzanne was out vaccinating people:

> I am very grateful to Lady Martin for her kind offer [of a book Lady Martin had written in 1869 partly on Maori medicine]. I accept it with great pleasure. This book will come in very handy for me. Please tell her that when you thank

her for me. Here everybody is panicking and wants to be vaccinated. There are not many doctors about. Also it looks as if the fever is raging pretty strongly among the Maoris. It's a time of distress and suffering. . . . I am very pushed for time today, as I have to go and get some vaccine.[49]

She would be out and about at dawn, gathering leaves and herbs. Two little settler children used to look out for her in the early morning, to watch her coming back with soaked boots in the dew-wet grass, slipping through the fence wires with a flash of red flannel petticoat.[50] The early hour mattered in some of her remedies. One, for asthma, is redolent of her French background: 'Gather the snails while the dew is still on the plants in the morning; crush and put equal parts of vinegar and water; stand twenty-four hours, drain off liquid and drink.'[51]

She was countering illness, but death was also part of her mission. She needed to be there when people were dying – especially babies. If babies died without baptism, Catholic belief saw them existing in a spiritual space called limbo. Anyone, not necessarily a priest, could baptise someone *in articulo mortis* (in the grip of death). It could be a quiet action, a private action *sine ceremoniis, insciis parentibus* (without ceremony, without the parents knowing). What mattered to the devout Catholic was saving the child's soul. If the person survived, the church hoped the baptism would be formalised by a priest in church.

At a time when Maori were no longer flocking to any denomination for baptism, the Meanee registers show Suzanne as Sister Mary Joseph baptising babies around a wide circuit. Father Reignier was used to a familiar Latin formula to record which man had done the baptism. He had trouble remembering his Latin in order to adapt the formula to a woman. His pen hovered, scratched out, blotched, sometimes managing the *quae* but finally giving up and settling on: '*pro Sorore Mary Joseph* who *baptizavit* [*hunc infantem*]'. The register shows when and where she went: Waiohiki, Petane, Omahu, Te Pakipaki, Pakowhai, Te Karamu, Ohiti, Ngatahira, Matiawi, Koupatiki, Opepe (in the hills towards Taupo), Te Karaka, Ngahape, Moteo and more. She also sometimes stood godmother in regular baptisms administered by Father Reignier or Father Séon, who came to Meanee in 1872. On 19 March 1873, she was godmother to Maria Makarema, daughter of Urupene Puhara and Marata Te Here at Te Pakipaki. On 20 August, she was godmother to Nikora Nuku, son of Hemi Nuku and Kararina of Ngatahira.

Wherever she visited, she would have been bringing her medicines as well. Medical tomes marked with scraps of the local newspaper, and frill-edged devotional cards, some from the Marian shrine of La Salette, still show what she had been reading. She was following up the new-fashioned use of cocoa, among other substances. And she was experimenting with blue gum:

> I've been studying it thoroughly for three years now and I'm convinced through experimentation that it has huge potential medicinal properties. I've discovered a herb which I've used in an ointment to cure in three months a cancerous sore which had been defeating every remedy. It was an Irish woman sixty years old. She's been cured for four months now and she's not feeling any fatigue. I'm trying it out now on other people.[52]

On paralysed Father Séon, she tried electric shock treatment in 1873 and reported he was much more mobile. This experiment did not halt his illness for long.

So long as one did not claim the title or degree of doctor, anyone could in effect practise medicine in those years.[53] The Medical Practitioners Registration Act 1869 had imposed state control on the medical profession, but no medical training was available in the colony and the field was virtually open for all-comers. There were few registered doctors – only four in central Hawke's Bay – and skilled amateurs helped out in times of need. Rev. Samuel Williams from Te Aute was often consulted for his medical knowledge.

So up the drive to the mission came scores of people to consult the sister. Clusters of Maori waited on the grassed area in front of the buildings. Father Reignier was supportive of her two roles as missioner away and medicine woman at Meanee, but once or twice, beset by people wanting her help, he was exasperated with her when she was away up-country. From her red shed built with nails forged by the brothers – which may have been part of the original Pakowhai mission building shifted to Meanee in 1858 – she diagnosed and treated her patients. She also nursed the sicker Maori patients in a large room, 'part work-room and part hospital'.[54] In the red shed, she experimented with new medicines which used native plants. People saw her across the paddocks, up on the hillsides, pushing through the swamps and bush, gathering plants with a Maori woman companion. She was adding more local Maori knowledge to what Peata had given her in the 1860s.

Newspapers were full of advertisements for patent medicines, the accessible cure-all in settler households. The Hawke's Bay newspapers were no exception, the same advertisement page extolling each week the virtues of Hitchen's Blood Restorer, St Jacob's Oil, Weston's Wizard Oil, Holloway's Pills, Dinneford's Solution of Magnesia, Dr Bright's Phosphodyne, Dr Heilbron's Wormcakes – and on and on. Medicines were a simple, usually harmless, form of mild addiction for many people.[55] Again, state supervision was light. The government set no standards, and an association of pharmacists was formed only in the 1870s. Selling remedies was a sure-fire venture.

What was happening with Suzanne's medicines, however, was unusual on two counts. First, they were free. She funded them with her own money. At the outset she had a grant of £40 from the Native Affairs department for 'poor, sick natives', arranged by Donald McLean, Minister of Native Affairs from 1869.[56] Her medicines were also local, indigenous, and used Maori medicinal ingredients along with Pakeha chemistry and Pakeha wine. No recipes remain, but wine was definitely used in dispensing the medicines. Every day sick Maori came for remedies. In 1873 she treated 1353 people.[57] Both Pakeha and Maori felt at ease with her remedies – and both probably were at ease with the alcohol content.

'Everyone around used to go to her dispensary, even the Protestant Minister.' This was the distinct memory of one local family, the Lopdells, recalling her cure of one of their children after the doctor had given up.[58] She was careful always to defer to the doctors, though. The 'Protestant Minister' was probably Philip Anderson, vicar of Taradale. He and his wife, Kate, were coping with bouts of illness hitting Fanny, the home help, and Philip, their little son. Anderson's diary entries through 1876 and 1877 tell the way his family and the whole community kept turning almost automatically to 'the Sister':

Found baby ill & sent for the Sister about 8 pm. . . .
   Dr Spencer & Mrs Robinson called. Also Ansel Tiffen & Sister Maria Joseph.
. . .
   Fanny very ill again. Got Mrs Howard & fetched Tiffen who stopped the night & got the Sister at daybreak. . . .
   The Sister came before 7 and prescribed for Fanny, who seems better. . . .
   The Sister called to see her at 9 am. . . .
   Fanny very far from what I would have liked to see her. Milne called before breakfast & the Sister after dinner. . . .
   Fanny came to morning service & sat in an armchair placed for her in the Vestry, but was very ill afterwards. Kate went in Harpham's cart for the Sister. . . .

Kate took Philip to see the Sister & found her from home. . . .

Philip worse. Cissy Luke called. Sent for the Sister in the evening, who sent a powder for Philip. . . .

Very anxious about Philip. The Sister came to see him at dinner time. . . .

Sidney Anderson went for more medicines from the Sister. . . .

Fanny sat up all night with Philip. Sister Marie Joseph came in the morning & prescribed for him & encouraged us to hope that she would be able to make him well. . . .

Philip very weak but mending otherwise. . . .

Philip better.[59]

CHAPTER EIGHT

Hawke's Bay – Maori and Pakeha
1872-1879

The priest will preach tomorrow : Ko te pirihi ia e kauwhau apopo
The minister preached last night : Na te minita i kauwhau inapo[1]

The twelve extra workmen for the 1872 New Year harvest finished on 4 January. Sister Mary Joseph was holding the fort on her own because the cook had taken an unexpected holiday. She dished up dinner, cleared up afterwards, rolled down her sleeves and straight away set out for the Napier gaol. It would not be an ordinary charitable prison visit. She was going into Napier to be, metaphorically speaking, a duellist. During the night, Sister Mary Joseph, with Father Reignier and Father Forest (the Napier parish priest) as seconds, would be taking on William Williams, Anglican Bishop of Waiapu, flanked by his son, Archdeacon William Leonard Williams, and his nephew, Rev. Samuel Williams. The contest would end at dawn.

Suzanne would have been aware of the tradition of the great missionary debates of the 1840s and 1850s which oratorically-minded Maori had willingly refereed and judged. Rev. William Colenso once bested Father Séon decisively; Father Lampila trounced Rev. Richard Taylor up the Whanganui River – though Lampila tended to change the rules and persisted in challenging his Protestant ministers to trial by fire. William Williams himself had had a run-in with the 'Romish priest, M. Lampiller' at Turanga in 1849. He sidestepped the fiery challenge. The two argued the merits of their respective creeds for ten hours, from 'two small tents . . . pitched under the shade of the willow trees' with 'a table . . . placed in the midst, upon which were arranged the Scriptures in the original languages, with the Vulgate and Douay Bibles, and the Maori New Testament'.[2] But this historical phalanx of cassocked French priests and black-garbed Bible-flourishing English evangelicals would not have been marching through Suzanne's mind as she trudged off in the summer dust to catch whatever cart or coach had her in Napier by 2.40 p.m. Her purpose was too urgent for such comparison.

This confrontation was not the same as the old ones. It was informal, unstaged. But it was not far different in its aim of winning souls. This time, only one was at stake: the soul of Kereopa, the Hauhau leader who had been captured and tried, and was now waiting to be hanged, for the 1865 killing of Rev. Carl Völkner at Opotiki. Each side strongly argued that Kereopa had said he had been baptised by them many years before: as Anglican 'by the Bishop of Nukutaurua (Table Cape)', as Catholic 'by F. Reignier some 25 or 30 years ago'.

In this exchange, Bishop Williams assumed that the priest was in control and the woman was the traditional artful accomplice. 'I believe', he wrote, 'that there was a deeply laid plot on the part of Father Regn[ie]r. The Sister of Mercy was sent to prepare the way for her superior. There was no application for admission on the ground that he was a RC, but the woman was sent to prepare the way by artifice in order to get Kereopa under control.'[3] There was indignation in William of Waiapu's four-page letter to Donald McLean. Leonard Williams and Samuel Williams had been helping Kereopa prepare for death. Unexpectedly, here was 'a young French woman who had expressed a wish to see Kereopa, for that she knew him, was acquainted with many circumstances wh[ich] transpired in 1865 – & moreover that Kereopa had saved the life of the priest Father Grange at Whakatane. The woman was permitted to see Kereopa – under an order sent by Telegram'. Why on earth, he was implying, had McLean let her in?

The rules of the contest were up to date. It was fought at first through New Zealand telegraph:

Napier. 2.40 p.m. 4 Jan. 1872. To Hon. McLean. Wellington. Please will you allow me to see Kereopa. Reply. Marie Joseph Aubert.

7.14 p.m. To Hon. McLean. Kereopa requests to see Father Forrest. Reply. Marie Joseph Aubert.

To Marie Joseph. Deputy Sheriff will be instructed to admit Father Forest to see Kereopa. Donald McLean.

To Deputy Sheriff. Kereopa expresses a wish through Marie Joseph to see Father Forest. Let this be done subject to gaol regulations and presence of officers and interpreter. Donald McLean.

To Hon. Native Minister. The prisoner Kereopa is not a Roman Catholic and never was. But Father Regnier has made application to be allowed to see him. I recommend and so does Millar that he should not be admitted for I believe that mischief would be excited. This request has come about through a French woman who had permission this afternoon from you to see the prisoner. Bishop of Waiapu.

To the Bishop of Waiapu. Subject to gaol regulations I gave the permission last night and do not like to rescind it. It is simply a permission for Father Forest to see Kereopa. I do not think that can do much harm, interview taking place in presence of witnesses. Donald McLean.[4]

Round one to Marie Joseph, who had impressed McLean in Auckland.

She spent the night in the cell with Kereopa. On 11 January she wrote to McLean asking for the return of a letter to Reignier 'written with a lead pencil' partly by her with Kereopa dictating, the rest by Kereopa himself to ensure credibility. She had handed it to Miller, the gaoler. The letter had disappeared and she wanted it back 'to put through a fair publication of it, a stop to the public statements made by the Revd Mr. Williams against me'.[5] Reignier had not been admitted because Kereopa did not ask for him 'expressly for religious assistance' because, 'he said, I thought I should be obliged to confess my sins before witnesses'. Rev. Samuel Williams accompanied Kereopa to the scaffold. Round two to the Williamses?

Before Kereopa was hanged, he had requested that the chief Tareha take his body for burial. The same morning Kereopa was executed a telegram went from the prison to Wellington: 'Tareha is waiting for leave to take Kereopa's body away. Kereopa died without the slightest murmur.' In the afternoon the body went 'in a plain whitepine coffin' to be buried at Waiohiki. The newspapers put the spotlight on Kereopa. The *Hawke's Bay Herald* said he died very 'game'. The *Evening Post* of 6 January reported:

> Kereopa confessed to having ordered Mr. Volkner's murder, but denied the actual perpetration of the deed. . . . At eight o'clock yesterday morning Kereopa, accompanied by the Rev. S. Williams, ascended the scaffold, not the slightest emotion was visible, and he preserved the same stoical indifference that he exhibited when upon his trial. . . . The Rev. J.[S.?] Williams knelt in front of the prisoner, and prayed in the Maori language, for which the prisoner appeared grateful. Mr Williams was requested by the Deputy Sheriff to ask the prisoner if he had anything to say. He answered 'No'. . . . During the whole of the night previous to his execution, a Sister of Mercy attended Kereopa. He refused all refreshments and stimulants.

The *Daily Southern Cross* of 9 January 1872 was clearer still. 'The Bishop of Waiapu has been visiting the condemned man but Kereopa declines to change his creed. He desires to die a Hau Hau, true to his faith and religion.' Round three to Kereopa.

There was more to it than salvation, although that was Suzanne's priority. There was also the question of justice. Suzanne may have read Colenso's 'Fiat Justitia', a pamphlet in passionate defence of Kereopa. This used Paora Tuhaere's land problems as an example of injustice, and she knew Tuhaere from her Auckland days. She would also have known that the chiefs were asking why Kereopa was to be hanged whereas Te Ua had been pardoned. She said she had heard Father Grange's story of how Kereopa had spared him from Völkner's fate. Grange had supported Suzanne in the recent Auckland troubles; she cared about him and later would write to France on his behalf. She cared also about Kereopa, telling Marie Louise Outhwaite how he 'assured me he had never wished for the death of Mr Workner [Völkner], nor of any European and that he had only eaten Mr Workner's eyes in a moment of frenzy excited by the sight of blood'. In this letter, Suzanne saw Kereopa as *'le bon larron maori'*, identifying him with the 'good thief' who died, penitent, alongside Jesus. She hoped 'that the good God who seeks only to be merciful will have taken pity on this poor unfortunate man'.[6]

Bishop Williams, on the other hand, was strongly arguing for Kereopa's guilt.[7] He wanted Kereopa himself to admit this:

> During my interviews from day to day, I had not been satisfied with the modified acknowledgment he made of his crime. He spoke well in other respects of his hope of pardon before God, through the merits of his Saviour, but I told him he could not expect to be accepted of God if he tried to shift the guilt of the crime to the Whakatohea.[8]

The bishop was upset that the Catholics were pushing their religion through the argument of justice. 'Those Catholics tried very hard to get him over to their church, praising up their religion and insisted upon his not being near so bad as folks tried to make him out to be.'[9] But the *Daily Telegraph* of 5 January gave Kereopa the benefit of the doubt. 'He had confessed to having ordered the murder of the Rev. Mr Volkner, but denies, and there is every reason to believe that he has stated the truth, that he was the actual perpetrator of the deed.'

Nobody really won that duel. And Suzanne stepped back from religious polemics. Perhaps Kereopa's stoicism made its mark. There was also the question of her reputation, which significantly she wanted cleared of the accusation of religious meddler and stirrer. She was finding that the best way for her to channel good will and acceptance for Catholicism was to be available, helpful, medically skilful, friendly and popular. Her model for being out and about and available was Father Reignier, one of a few old missioners still on the roads. He had, she wrote to Poupinel, 'a heart like an artichoke, ready to give a leaf to everybody' and was 'here, there and everywhere, doing good'.[10] Rev. Philip Anderson, vicar of Taradale, who had known Reignier since 1865, summed him up:

> No matter how far inland he might be, no matter how rough the country, or how bad the weather, ten to one but you would meet Fr Reignier jogging along on his old roan cob. . . . He was universally respected, and every house, station, farm, or bush hut had always a welcome for him from its owner of whatever Faith . . .[11]

Tolerance and harmony were powerful in themselves. Pompallier had opposed the old sectarian duelling, which tended to happen when he was not around. As the 1859 incident with Governor Browne and the Bible Society showed, he preferred the diplomatic approach. He had told his priests that they should leave to God the care of proving the truth of their form of religion. His attitude to Protestant missionaries was: 'see them little, pray for them, refute among the people the errors and systematic calumnies they employ against the Catholic Church. Avoid, however, in any words said or letters written any kind of personal attack.'[12] The question, as mission to the Maori started up again slowly after the hiatus of the wars, was what would now be the tone? Kereopa showed with courtesy that Maori themselves largely decided.

Frostiness was still there in Archdeacon Williams' journal for 1872. He was riding up the coast and all around on roughly the same tracks as those taken by Father Reignier.

> Nov 11 Waikahua: Goldsmith informed me that the R.C. priest was to start for the Wairoa this morning. If this is correct he has got the start of me. . . .
>
> Nov. 14 Waikokopu: The R.C.P. had been at both these places not long before us, asking & obtaining subscriptions. He certainly seems to be a good beggar. . . .
>
> 30 Nov. Waikahua: The R.C.P. has been very busy dunning people for subscriptions. He got £3 from McLean & £1 from Locke. The latter only gave under great pressure, but my father [the bishop], when he heard of it told McLean that as he had done that for the R.C. church he would not let him alone until he had given a subscription to our church. After much pressing he promised us £3 & Locke very readily offered £2.

Williams was also disappointed that Maori girls were being sent to the sisters' school in Napier, when the Anglican Maori girls' school at Hukarere would not be ready before 1874.

But by 1873 there was a noticeable thaw. The 'R.C.P.' now had a name: 'May 31 Wairoa: As I came back, I met F. Reignier who stopped to speak about the Courthouse, but as I only require it for tomorrow evening he will have plenty of time for his services.'[13] What emerges from Williams' journals is that no missionary was now purely a missionary to Maori. The journal does range over his distress at how Maori were being inveigled into drinking, his continuing disapproval of women having their lips and chins tattooed, his plans for Maori education, the epidemics, illnesses and 'mate-kai', the starvation killing Maori babies. But it also breathes more and more the itinerant parish minister to settlers of varied origin and creed.

A certain rivalry with the Presbyterian Rev. W. H. Root, who also was building a church at Waikahua, began to ease out the 'R.C.' plaint in Williams' journal. There was also sickness and need among the settlers, especially in a serious typhoid epidemic in 1875, and sectarian rivalry became inappropriate. In fact, let it be recorded, a certain 'holier than thou' tolerance was creeping in. On 14 July 1875, a Michael Hannon died suddenly at Waikahua. Murphy, an 'R.C. member of the community', asked Williams to take the service. Williams agreed, and noted with some satisfaction: 'Mr Root, I hear, had been applied to bury poor Hannon, but upon learning that he was a R. Catholic he declined positively at once.'[14]

The fact was that they were all 'fellow-settlers'. The crusty Anglican William Colenso, spurned by his bishop for an extramarital liaison with a Maori woman, once offered in 1858 to minister in a non-sectarian chapel.[15] Many years before, he had had 'a not very unfriendly' debate with Reignier late one afternoon on the open beach between Petane and Tangoio. Later, Colenso summed up their association: 'Father Reignier & myself often met afterwards, in travelling etc., but not to dispute; & of him to the last I ever had a high opinion as a neighbour, a fellow-settler, & a Roman Catholic priest, but' – he had to add a proviso – 'he was an educated Frenchman.'[16]

In Hawke's Bay there seems to have been a climate of reasonable tolerance at this time. Even among the landed runholders there was a variety of backgrounds and creeds, from the prevailing Anglican to Quaker, Roman Catholic, Wesleyan and Presbyterian. 'Ministers were respected for their personal qualities rather than their doctrines.'[17] Suzanne confirmed this order of things. When Catholic Father Rolland came across from Taranaki in 1874, she wrote to Marie Louise that he was 'well liked in Napier'. He was 'blessed with a conciliatory and friendly personality'.[18] When she herself nearly died in 1878, Reignier wrote: 'For four or five weeks she has not been able to carry out her works of charity. The district, European and Maori, would really grieve to lose her. She has a lot of friends.'[19]

The huge influx of new settlers between 1872 and 1876 served to reinforce the variety and the need for an immediate *modus vivendi*. Eighteen seventy-four is the year of highest immigration ever, and these four years are recognised as a turning-point in New Zealand history. Overall, the 'period that was crucial in New Zealand's social and cultural development was the Vogel era, for in the years 1870–1885 occurred nearly thirty percent of the net immigration of 1860–1950'.[20] Suzanne found herself in the middle of all this and it suited her temperament. Immigrant ships brought into Napier, from where they spread through the province, people who were English, Irish, Scottish, Welsh, Cornish, Scandinavian, German. This meant, in religious terms, Anglican, Roman Catholic, Presbyterian, Wesleyan, Primitive Methodist, Congregationalist, Baptist, Brethren, Lutheran and more.

These people had, however, a similarity of aims and values which would pull them together, making religious divisions a lesser consideration. In this they would lend new support to the older wave of settlers, and together they would give a lead to the clergy.[21] To some extent the people were speaking and the clergy listened, as Rev. Anderson recorded over a project to set up an interdenominational cemetery in Taradale:

> I acted as mediator and spokesman for my neighbours of whatever creed, as they asked me to do. . . . Trustees of the Anglican, Scots, and R.C. Churches were appointed, lots were cast, the ground was fenced and divided amongst the three religious bodies. . . . A common road was made right through the whole ground and only harmony prevailed amongst us all.[22]

The settlers coming into New Zealand were on the whole impatient of transferred grievances. They were here to better themselves and get along. John Sheehan, the first New Zealand-born cabinet minister, who had been in Auckland when Suzanne was there, expressed this theme of forbearance:

> Let us not ask who is Irish, English or Scotch, but let us be warned by what has happened in the old country and try to build up something better. Let us endeavour to smooth all differences between Catholics and Protestants and to forget the wrongs that both these have suffered. Let us build up a new order of things.[23]

The *Daily Telegraph* of 17 July 1871 could not have agreed more. It deplored the founding of the Orange Lodge in Hawke's Bay and said that New Zealand had been considered 'neutral ground':

> This colony has been happily settled by people from all parts of the British Islands, and those who wish to stir up strife in Hawke's Bay between the two great parties who have kept Ireland in a state of agitation since the days of William of Orange, may take our word for it that the majority of settlers will not allow the peace and prosperity of the province to be interfered with for the purpose of gratifying a worn-out political feeling.

Many of the English settlers coming to Hawke's Bay were fresh from the agricultural disputes challenging the farming hierarchy in England in the early 1870s. Some had been members or supporters of the National Agricultural Labourers' Union. They were not subservient and liked the comparative egalitarianism and lack of repression they found in rural Hawke's Bay. They also came with a dream of a co-operative community. [24] Suzanne had already experienced an eclectic background in Auckland. And she had a keen awareness of where the wind of people's preference was blowing. She knew Pompallier's politic of tolerance; she knew that New Zealand had already had a staunch Catholic as Premier, Frederick Weld, with little sectarian protest; she knew the widespread opposition to any idea of a state religion. Historical opinion has confirmed this. 'Special privileges were not accorded to one denomination over another and local reaction was immediate whenever this principle of equality appeared to be under threat.' [25]

Suzanne had found that, without compromising your own beliefs, you could co-exist in friendship. Importantly for her, friendship was also a strategy for mission. Later, whenever she 'taught' this to her sisters, she would illustrate it with any of a number of incidents in her life. In Auckland, when she had been staying in Shelly Beach, she had a bigoted Protestant woman for a neighbour who resented the Catholic household arriving next door. But the woman was a keen gardener and would look over the fence with longing at a specially beautiful lily unfurling slowly, the only lovely flower in John Campbell's neglected garden. Suzanne cut the lily stem and offered it over the fence. 'And they exchanged a few words about its beauty and its rarity. Ever after that, they were the best of friends.' [26] Or she would tell of the Scottish Presbyterian who willingly helped her plan and lay out the paths that converged so beautifully at the Catholic shrine in the garden of St Anne's. She knew that neighbourly co-operation among settlers was a thin membrane barely covering a turmoil of feelings going far back in inherited history. Her approach was to protect the delicate, pulsing fontanelle of a new society until it had firmed and safely closed.

The settlers coming in were usually young. And the Vogel scheme aimed to attract families. Babies arrived prolifically in the following years. In 1877 Susan Nairn, one of the runholders, considered 'N. Zealand a dreadful place for babies everyone has an annual affair – it must be the climate'.[27] Isolated rural settlement meant that sectarian difference was often not an issue to parents when it came to baptising a child. At Ruahoru on 22 November 1872, Archdeacon Leonard Williams had noted: 'The priest has been here & christened G. Taylor's, the mother being a Pikopo. They had arranged between themselves that the first person who came should christen the child.'[28]

On the other hand, a family's choice was sometimes made decisively. Suzanne told and retold the story of the older settler Jeffares family. Thomas Jeffares was descended from an anti-Catholic Cromwell soldier; Mary Jeffares was a firm Catholic. She had the first baby baptised Catholic before her husband knew. She kept the minister and her husband at bay over the next with a brand snatched from the fire to defend the baby in the bed between her and the wall. All her nine children were baptised Catholic. Thomas Jeffares became a friend of Suzanne. In 1876 he raised money and bought her a horse and trap for her sick visiting. She refused the gift for herself, because she preferred the versatility and conspicuous simplicity of walking and riding, and donated it to the nurses of Napier hospital.[29]

From 1874 Leonard Williams' journal fills up with babies who are 'ailing', being baptised, dying. He recorded the grief of one mother at Waikahua whose baby had just died:

> Poor Mrs King seems to be thoroughly prostrated. She is not strong & the want of rest for many nights past is telling upon her. I went to see her this evening & after one or two coherent remarks she fell into a sort of insensible state, staring vacantly at nothing & when I wished her good night she took no notice whatever.[30]

Sister Mary Joseph was now tending sick babies more and more. English, Irish, Scottish and one or two Scandinavian names appear steadily on the register of the babies she was baptising. Before they had been mainly Maori names. By the end of the 1870s, at least, she was also helping at childbirth. She was often seen with Margaret Young, a local midwife, who had come from Somerset in March 1879.[31]

In all her nursing, in all her communications with a cross-section of settlers, in all the travelling around the different pa, Suzanne was still very much the Catholic missioner. Her preference for tolerance and co-operation was not a cosy abdication from mission. As she nursed the paralysed Father Séon, the two of them prayed hard for a renewal of Catholicism among Maori. The Anglican church was spreading once more among their communities. It had Maori ministers. It also, significantly, had a strong second echelon of New Zealand-born ministers, often the sons of the first generation of missionaries. These men had grown up speaking Maori and were even more fluent than their fathers. And sometimes their own sons, in turn, would follow them. The extended families had settled into the establishment of New Zealand. There was both strong continuity and a network of support.

On the other side, the Catholic flow of missioners to Maori was drying up. The old priests were gradually dying and there were none to follow. New priests arriving ended up in settler parishes, with less chance to learn Maori. James McDonald was the only Catholic missioner to Maori in Croke's Auckland. Suzanne, as the 1870s progressed, was the only one in Wellington diocese, and unofficial at that. There was no one in Moran's Otago. From 1874, when the surge of Pakeha settlers unbalanced the work of the Meanee mission, letter after letter went from Suzanne to both France and Wellington asking for a new Maori missioner to be appointed:

> There would be plenty to keep a priest busy. Father Reignier is the only one who visits them now and then, but he hasn't the time to do this often enough to be really effective. The care of the white people takes up his time, and the Maoris are either joining Protestantism which is very active, or else returning to their old superstitions to which they add European vices. It makes me really feel for them.[32]

She might acknowledge that 'the minister preached last night', but she certainly hoped 'the priest will preach tomorrow'.

Suzanne pinned her hopes for a revival of the Maori mission on the new bishop coming to replace Viard in 1874. She would always be optimistic. And the reception from Viard's successor was very different from that which she had had from Croke. In the intervening three years, Croke's and especially Moran's reservations about French clergy had been felt in the diocese. In Hawke's Bay they were all apprehensive that

Moran might want them out of New Zealand, but their pattern of life on the fringes of Wellington diocese was little altered. Croke, however, left after a brief three-year tenure in Auckland and returned to Ireland to be Archbishop of Cashel. This left Bishop Moran administering Auckland diocese during another interregnum. Before that he was also administering Wellington after the death of Viard in June 1872. For a short period, then, he was bishop to the whole of New Zealand. The Irish pincers seemed to be closing in. The question now was who would succeed Viard: another secular diocesan Irish bishop, or one acceptable to the resident Marists?

The Marists had been grooming their candidate for a while. They had their New Zealand *dauphin*, Francis Redwood, waiting in the wings. Bishop Moran was not pleased at first to hear that Rome planned to appoint Redwood Bishop of Wellington, still the largest diocese in the country. But the Society of Mary had been able to list with confidence Redwood's impressive credentials for the job:

> Father Redwood is, from all accounts, the most suitable, 1°– because he is English; 2°– because he is young and active; 3°– because he is very capable and virtuous, 4°– because he will be well received by the English who are numerous in the diocese of Wellington, 5°– because, having lived for several years in Ireland, he has been able to gain an appreciation for himself of the faith and character of the Irish and he will be able to make himself accepted by them, by devoting himself entirely to the good of all without exception.[33]

His credentials were, in fact, better still. His family had come to New Zealand in 1842 with the English Catholic group that included Clifford, Petre, Vavasour and Weld. His colonial antecedence was impeccable, and he had contacts. Clifford, who had come from a very old and aristocratic Catholic family in England, pointed out to Barnabò that the prevailing culture of the colony was English, that there were two Irish bishops already, and that Viard had been French; without specifically naming Redwood, he implied that it was time for an English candidate. Wellington diocese also included Christchurch at that time and the English slant would be useful.

Redwood was only three when his family arrived in 1842 so he had a settler upbringing, a New Zealand empathy. This was another point in his favour. He also knew and understood Lyon, France and the Marists. He had been educated by Father Garin in Nelson and had gone to France in 1854, aged only fifteen, to continue his education with the Marists at

St Chamond, Toulon and Lyon. His fluency and scholarship in French had won him prizes in competition with native French candidates. After becoming a Marist priest, ordained in Ireland, he had taught in Ireland at the Marist seminary in Dundalk, and in Dublin. Against him was only his youth. The fact that he had been away from New Zealand for twenty years and knew no Maori made him no different from any Irish candidate. Redwood seemed as near as could be got to ideal, at least for many years, for both the capital and Wellington diocese in general. His style was not confrontational; he aimed at bridging gaps. He quickly set out to mollify the Irish by having his consecration in London on St Patrick's Day. He joined the Hibernians in 1875. He was loyal to Irish interests in Catholic schooling and he named his college St Patrick's. He was supportive over the Irish political question. To Sister Mary Joseph he seemed to herald a new beginning.

Redwood arrived in Wellington in November 1874 and made his first visit to Hawke's Bay in March 1875. Suzanne found him open, likeable, responsive; 'very eloquent, very pious, and devoid of pretention, although most particular as to neatness. I like him very much. I think he will be a remarkable Bishop.'[34] He also liked and trusted her. 'He showed a lot of interest in me personally.'[35] He did not seem to see her as an uppity female. She was thirty-nine; he was thirty-five. The good rapport would last between these two for another fifty-two years. Suzanne had a bishop who gave free rein to the potential in her personality. Otago under Moran might have been another story.

She rushed in as usual to plead with Redwood for a new Maori missioner and persuaded him to visit Pakipaki the next day to meet the people there. Luckily it was harvest time and many Maori were working nearby. She went out early to tell the people so they would have time to prepare a welcome. All went well. The harvesting machines were left in the paddocks, the hangi was laid, the trestle tables were spread with food, the welcome speeches were warm and appreciated. She reported back the main outcome to Marie Louise: 'He promised them at least one priest, as soon as he can find one willing to devote himself to them.'[36]

Pakipaki (or Te Pakipaki, as it was referred to in letters of the time) was a relatively recent Maori settlement out at the edge of the Heretaunga plains where the hills begin to rise, rolling back towards Waipawa. The link between the Maori of Ahuriri–Heretaunga and the Catholic missioners went back to the early 1840s, before Pakipaki was settled.

Father Baty had been briefly at Mahia; Father Lampila used to visit from Whakatane. Then Father Reignier, with Brothers Basile and Florentin, settled at Pakowhai. It was the people from Pakowhai who would later move south-west across the plain to Pakipaki.

There had been years of upheaval among the Maori of the bay, disruption during the musket wars, exile, captivity, reoccupation. For a while the area was abandoned, but by the 1840s Ngati Kahungunu had returned. By the 1850s various settlements were stable again under several powerful rangatira, including Karaitiana Takamoana, Henare Tomoana, Renata Kawepo, Te Moananui, Tareha, Te Hapuku, Paoro Kaiwhata, Puhara Hawaiikirangi. Many of these chiefs were still alive when Suzanne arrived in Hawke's Bay, and she was in contact with several. Both Renata Kawepo at Omahu and Paora Kaiwhata at Moteo summoned her for her nursing skills. Kawepo later addressed her as 'the doctor of doctors'; Kaiwhata's courtesy was trusting and inaccurate: 'No-one can die under your care.'[37]

Karaitiana Takamoana had been host to William Colenso at the Church Missionary Society station at Awapuni (or Waitangi). Renata Kawepo had been Colenso's layreader. It was Puhara Hawaiikirangi who gave hospitality and protection to the Catholic at Pakowhai. From 1850 they built up their mission by the Ngaruroro River on Puhara's land and it became a welcome stopping-point for travellers.[38] As the years went by, many chiefs began to oppose further land sales. Te Hapuku, of Ngati Te Whatu-i-apiti, stood out from the general consensus and persisted in selling. The dispute between Te Hapuku and his main opponent, Te Moananui, turned to war in 1857. Puhara Hawaiikirangi, the rangatira of the Catholic mission, was Te Hapuku's father-in-law and was drawn into the conflict with him. They were defeated in battle and Puhara died of his wounds. Pakowhai was abandoned and the pa ceremonially burnt by its people. By 1862 they had settled permanently at the edge of the Heretaunga plains and named their new home 'Paki Paki'.

The loss of Pakowhai polarised the Catholic mission geographically. Father Reignier and the brothers shifted north to property they had already bought in Meanee. The red mission house, carted in sections, the books, church vessels and vestments, the farm implements, sheep, cattle, pigs and poultry all went across the Tutaekuri River in the opposite direction, miles away from where most of the Maori who were Catholic would end up living. This was one of the main reasons Sister Mary Joseph was so constantly itinerant. She lived at Meanee but her 'flock', in Pompallier's terms, was at Pakipaki. And she was set on retaining and 'saving' this small group of people for Catholicism.

Father Yardin had come out to New Zealand from Lyon to assist Bishop Redwood. Early in 1876 Reignier and Suzanne took her old friend and adviser out to Pakipaki for a day. They went by the railway which had been extended to Pakipaki the year before. Crossing the plain, they passed pleasant settler villages and six Maori pa. At Pakipaki she and Reignier set about their nursing, catechising and pastoring in Maori while Yardin 'started observing':

> The houses are little, low, covered with reeds, for lack of tree bark. They are quite close to each other; wooden fences form yards and provide shelter for agricultural implements and animals when needed. I noticed slotted into a piece of flax something long and black that was swaying in the air – eels being dried. When they're cooked with potatoes, they constitute their favourite treat. I tasted some. It's good but a bit oily. It needed a bit of mustard to boost the flavour of the stew.

Yardin turned his attention from culinary comparison to describe in careful detail the wharepuni. He thought the weaving was 'a work of patience and real elegance which would be held in admiration even in France'. Then he outlined what was going on inside:

> This is where religious and political discussions take place, where everyone meets to talk in the evening or work by day. When I went in there were ten or so people. Men were making nets and baskets to catch eels, others were making mats, others were talking away, an old woman was making a chief's cloak – really beautiful workmanship – with no other tools than her hands. The conversation was very merry, especially among the menfolk. The Father attacked them over liquor abuse. 'It's your fault,' immediately retorted an old, white-bearded, richly tattooed Maori man. 'We weren't like that before the arrival of the Pakeha; they've ruined us with their rum.' It's only too true.
>
> The conversation then came round to me. They wanted to know who I was. I could catch my name: Patero Yardini, and that I was staying with the Epikopo. They wanted to know if I was the priest promised by the Epikopo. We hastily answered no. In fact they had asked for a young priest who would have a soft head so he could learn their language and customs more easily. With my white hair and my old, hard head, I wasn't their man. I told him that in a year's time they would have a priest for themselves but to take care of him.
>
> 'We are poor,' they replied, 'but we will share what we have with him. He will have the best place in our houses, our best blanket and the best we have to eat. Tell him not to be difficult with us and we will become better through him.' Not all were Catholic but all were polite and friendly.

Yardin's writing was vivid and animated. He set the scene and described the landscape, the buildings and the people. He captured the activity of Sister Mary Joseph. She had stuffed his pockets with little cakes:

> The children ran up to Sr Marie Joseph. I called Oramai to them, to no avail. They didn't budge. Finally I showed one of my cakes and I was quickly surrounded by the entire little population. . . . The Sister's intention was to see an old woman who was ill. She was a Protestant married to a Catholic. The Sister sat down alongside her in the tent, next to the mat which served as a bed and got her talking. She said all manner of bad things about her husband. He was a drunk who mistreated her, a real devil, etc. He wasn't there to give her any protection. . . . When we were about to leave the husband of the sick woman arrived. The Sister took my walking stick and made a show of hitting him. He scratched his ear with a doleful look, like a schoolboy caught out in some misdeed, and started saying how sorry he was. He was such a funny sight, enough to make you burst out laughing. Finally the Sister relented and ended up making peace with him on the grounds he promised to take good care of his wife and not drink any more.[39]

Yardin had known and read of Maori for twenty years or more, but he was meeting them familiarly for the first time, and then only as a visitor. There is the incidental, uninvolved curiosity of the outsider, the onlooker, in his tone. He was angling his style for publication in the *Annales de la Propagation de la Foi*, to be entertaining and anthropologically interesting but only in a lightweight manner. In his account, there is a shade of patronising jolliness, of breezy bustle, in Sister Mary Joseph's manner. There is the suspicion that she may have been 'playing to the gallery' for the benefit of Yardin and others. But, through that screen, the signs of relaxed intimacy with the place are clear. The children ran up straight away, cakes or not. She was down on the floor beside the sick woman, getting her talking. She listened. She acted on what the woman told her as soon as the Catholic husband appeared. The outcome of her altercation with him was not grim: she had exacted a promise from him to try to improve, and the atmosphere was good-humoured. Yardin wrote that, with the whole problem of drunkenness dogging the mix of the two cultures in Hawke's Bay, the 'Sister takes the better approach – laugh and always refuse money to the Maori people she loves so much'.

Suzanne saw Croke's departure as once again giving the opportunity for a unified Maori mission throughout New Zealand. This she wanted to obtain from Rome.[40] Most Maori lived in Auckland diocese and to her it did not make sense, after the Franciscans withdrew in 1873, to let their northern Maori mission stations once more be abandoned, as they had found them in 1861. The pressing need, though, was for at least one priest for Maori people in the Wellington diocese. But she had no power in diocesan circles. She was only a lay sister, just a woman. She made this clear more than once in letters, even if she couched it in wry self-deprecation: 'When I see the way things are going', she wrote to Poupinel, 'I can't help regretting that I'm not a man. But what can a doddery old maid's regrets and prayers achieve?'[41] All she could do was 'nag' discreetly and persistently. She did this as effectively as she could from Redwood's visit in 1875 until the new priest was finally announced in 1878.

The cycle of letters began. The writers were Aubert, Redwood, Poupinel, Yardin and Reignier. By 1877, the tone of her letters was urgent:

> Now is the right moment. The leading Maori chiefs have formed a committee and are holding meetings in all the main pa to get reforms under way to protect their race. The religious question is being discussed strongly. The chiefs are working hard at making religious worship an obligation. In spite of the incredible efforts of the Protestant ministers, in spite of the way we have neglected the Maori, I was pleased to hear that these poor people have declared that 'Protestantism and Catholicism are equally good'. The chiefs are leaving the people free to choose. They have decided that a church must be built in all the main pa, that there must be native catechists for the ordinary occasions and a visiting European minister for certain set times. By this very fact, they will all definitely turn to Protestantism, unless you hurry up and send priests.[42]

Several chiefs were linked strongly to the Anglican church. But, if there was freedom of choice, here was the chance for Catholicism. It was still common, though, for a community to follow the lead of its chief. One of Suzanne's letters described a hui where, she said, she surreptitiously goaded Urupene Puhara, the son of Puhara Hawaiikirangi, until he declared publicly for Catholicism. She needed his mana to bolster Pakipaki Catholics. Urupene Puhara's wife, Marata, was a friend of Suzanne and a devout Catholic. Suzanne called her a 'holy woman'.

Redwood had had little contact with Maori in his childhood in Nelson, and his very first year as bishop coincided with the largest wave of Catholic immigrants coming into Wellington diocese. He was swamped with settler need. Poupinel had to tick him off gently from Lyon for not even referring to Maori mission in his very first pastoral. After his introduction to Pakipaki through Sister Mary Joseph, though, he was as good as his word.[43] He did try but had little joy. He tended, however, to be somewhat half-hearted in his approaches to Cardinal Franchi, now heading Propaganda Fide. He felt that the Maori were dying out, chances of conversion were slim and Hauhauism had left them 'ignorant, indifferent and blasé'.[44] Secular priests were loath to leave settler parishes, and the Society of Mary was overcommitted in North America and other areas of the Pacific. Back home in France the Marists were preoccupied with increasing anticlerical persecution which eventually, by 1880, would have them shifting seminary students across the border to Switzerland.[45] Redwood wrote to Lyon in frustration: 'It's difficult going into battle without soldiers.'[46] Poupinel finally felt that he had to come to the society's defence. He wrote firmly to Suzanne: 'Nevertheless, good Sister, allow me to tell you that you exaggerate our responsibility for the state of abandonment which has come upon the Maori in New Zealand.'[47]

By 1877 she hated the disbelief on Maori faces when she said 'the priests are coming'; she stopped saying this. There was need for more than a priest, too. There was the question of a prayer-book:

> Our poor natives have not rejected grace. They desire it, they seek it. They ask, they are knocking – open the door. Give priests, give books, as they do not even have the aid of prayer-books. The supply ran out a long time ago, and there are several villages where there would be a renewal of prayer if there were only a book to give the Catechist.[48]

Government and settler prejudice was slowly, at least outwardly, discrediting tohunga. Chiefs recognised the gulf forming in the spiritual life of the people and facilitated the revival of Christian missions. It was Maori catechists – in Suzanne's experience, Raniera, Hoani Tokotoko and Hohepa Te Toko – who kept faith alive year after year.

A total revision and publication of the Maori prayer-book as a project? One can almost imagine Redwood sighing with relief, seizing on this to salve the church's conscience, to prepare the way for any new priest, to keep Sister Mary Joseph busy and off his back, to hold out something to the faithful. She was given the task. It was two years before Dinwiddie in Napier published *Ko te Ako me te Karakia o te Hahi Katorika Romana* in 1879. She tucked the receipt for the final instalment of payment as a bookmark in one of her medical tomes.

A lot of hope, and also frustration, must have gone into the revised prayer-book. 'Bishop Redwood is doing what he can', she wrote. 'He has ordered the book of Maori prayers to be corrected, so it can be reprinted, but what can the book do without the priest?'[49] Somehow she tried to make the prayer-book do as much as it could as a counter-attraction to the Protestant literature. The Catholic prayer-book in Maori had been unchanged since its first publication at Kororareka in 1847, when Pompallier was in Europe, and was largely unavailable now. Its vocabulary included many Maori renderings of Latin words, such as *epikopo* (*episcopus*) for bishop, *rehina* (*regina*) for queen, *owheteria* (*offertorium*) for offertory. Suzanne updated these words and brought them into line with the vast Protestant stock of church literature. *Pikopo* had been used generally to mean 'Catholic', anyway, so 'bishop' in her book became *pihopa*, in line with Anglican usage. *Kuini* was 'queen'. Suzanne also used more genuinely Maori terms: *kawenga* replaced *owheteria*, *rongo pai* for 'gospel' replaced evangelist *wangeriona*.

The Protestants had the full Bible in Maori by now, with Rev. Robert Maunsell's translation of the Old Testament. Maori appreciated the epic nature of the Old Testament, with its emphasis on exploits, whakapapa and tapu. Into her prayer-book, therefore, went almost a hundred pages of Old Testament stories. She was shrewd. She offered the novelty of an abbreviated Book of Maccabees, which was not included in the Protestant Bible. If this addition was her version in Maori, the result was not overly successful: 'The Maori limps.'[50] Suzanne was also nothing if not pragmatic: the gospels she included were borrowed from the Protestant Bible Society translations.[51]

In trying to produce a prayer-book as all-encompassing as possible, she doubled the size of the original. Suzanne never needed much sleep. Her daily medical and mission routine would have stayed largely the same while candles burnt down steadily through the nights. In her enthusiasm the stack of pages grew higher and higher. Reignier quietly spelt this out to Poupinel: 'The Sister is correcting and enlarging the Maori prayer-book' and 'Sister Marie Joseph not only is busy curing the illnesses of the Maori but is getting printed a great big prayer-book'.[52] Maybe she was remembering the value Maori once placed on the impressiveness of the printed volume. The spirit of the duellist was not completely quieted.

In getting bigger, the prayer-book got dearer. The farm at Meanee advanced money for the printing. Reignier's Ledger and Memorandum Book indicates that sales and the diocese had paid off the loan by October 1881. It is quite likely that some of her own family money went into the book, as it did later into building the Pakipaki church. But its price was 6s 6d, too expensive. New Zealand was pitching into depression by the close of the 1870s. And Protestants were giving, not selling, their Bibles. The Catholic Maori mission would always be run on a shoestring and had no chance of giving the book away. A cheaper selected edition of forty-five pages, *Ko etahi Ako me etahi Karakia o te Hahi Katorika Romana*, was hastily printed in 1881.

As Suzanne was writing to Poupinel in December 1877, telling him of the prayer-book project, the scene was summery and peaceful:

> Brother Cyprien has come in and is asking who I'm writing to. He wants me to pass on his good wishes. He is not very well, though he is still on his feet. Father Séon is still alive, Father Reignier is always on the go, Father Michel stays in his corner seat on the verandah, and Brother Basile does the rounds of his sheep. Joseph from Wallis looks after the vegetables and both of them care for Father Séon in those things which call for a man's help.[53]

There was a hint of change, of time passing, though. Father Séon, her mentor and model for piety and self-denial, would soon die. She always pointed out that the day Séon was buried, another priest was being ordained in France. A year after her letter to Poupinel, he wrote to Yardin about the new priest who had offered to come to the Maori mission: 'We have been very pleased with Father Soulas, a lively faith, a generous spirit and a "Breton head" with plenty of savoir-faire.'[54] Soulas's first name was Christophe but he was going to be called Pa Hoani Papita, John the Baptist. He was seen as the forerunner, the herald, of the reborn Maori mission. What this heralded for Suzanne too was great change and an end to the tranquil scene at Meanee.

CHAPTER NINE

From Pakipaki to Hiruharama
1879-1885

How do you like our church? :
E whakapai ana ranei koe ki to matou whare karakia?
It is beautiful : E pai rawa atu[1]

Suzanne had waited so long for a missioner, had invested so much of her energy in keeping Pakipaki Catholics' hopes buoyed, that for her the new priest and the new mission were absolutely going to succeed. She liked Father Soulas already 'even though I do not know him yet'. Often in the summer days of January 1879, she went up to Séon's grave where it looked out over the sweep of the flats. She was sure that Séon was 'praying with all his heart for him'. Soulas would have Séon's room at Meanee. 'There's no doubt', she wrote to Poupinel, 'he's going to feel some suffering there, where a Saint has suffered and prayed for him already, without even knowing him.'[2]

She could have been thinking of culture shock as suffering, the trauma of settling in. Or of rebuffs from both Pakeha and Maori as the new priest struggled through language barriers and cultural mistakes. She worried that a rosy haze of outdated missionary expectation could so easily cloud over into grey disillusionment instead of clearing into a mature realisation of the situation Maori were in. She felt that apathy towards Maori was rolling like a fog over the priests' and sisters' attitudes, in Napier, Meanee and in the diocese as a whole:

> What I'm most apprehensive about for the new missioner, is that he'll be influenced by all the local anti-Maori feeling here before he gets to know our poor natives for himself. Quite simply I think I would just die of grief. I'm often told that I'm unreasonable over the Maori question . . . I can't be the judge in this case as I'm essentially an interested party.[3]

She planned ahead, getting things ready for him. The prayer-book, of course, for one thing. In January she was busy correcting the proofs. But Dinwiddie, the printer, did not know Maori and there were many mistakes. Redwood thought proofreading something as familiar to Soulas as the prayer-book would be a good way for him to learn Maori as quickly as possible.[4] The prayer-book was for his pastoral work, but Suzanne was also preparing him for his daily life. She wrote for him an exercise-book full of phrases in Maori with their French equivalents, phrases which covered ordinary activities in a Maori community. She was going to make sure that the new priest from France, with no Maori and no English, could still, for example, pick his way safely through the dogs bounding and barking around the pa at Pakipaki. 'Ka pakaru tooku potae: *Mon chapeau est déchiré* – My hat is torn', runs her text. 'My boot is also torn . . . My suit is torn . . . It was torn by the dog . . . I heard a big dog barking this morning . . . I saw Hoani hitting the white dog . . . Don't hit a good dog'. Perhaps she wrote this after he arrived. Perhaps he was the 'Hoani' who had hit out at a dog – her dog. He arrived in mid-February, at the height of the Hawke's Bay summer: 'The heat of the sun is great . . . It is very hot in the house . . . I can't stay sitting in this extreme heat'.

Sister Mary Joseph was schooling the new missioner just as Pompallier had taught his recruits on board ship. Unlike Pompallier, she was there to help him out in his new mission station. By June 1879 Soulas seemed to her 'just the missioner I was praying for'. He was, she thought, preparing himself for his work among the Maori 'with all his heart, strongly and singlemindedly depending and focusing on God'.[5]

Whose idea it was to swing straight away into building a church at Pakipaki is not clear, but by 8 June 1880 Father Yardin, the administrator of the diocese while Redwood was overseas, was blessing a newly completed church. But Yardin was not a bishop with an impressive mitre and crozier. Suzanne had to explain to disappointed Maori that she could not make a 'gold hat and staff' to order for Yardin. The 'pretty little' church was 'very well-built, in semi-Gothic style', with a little tower and a clock, and inside there was a pearly chandelier. Suzanne had banners above the windows, flowers and embroidery in wool and pearl beading decorating the altar. Her ease with Maori culture did not lead her to express it in the texture or decoration of a church. It was the same for most of the missioners. French lacework, French embroidery, French bells, French altar vessels and statuary gave Maori their environment for worship. Back in Nantes, St Etienne, St Chamond and Lyon, the *dames* were still busy sewing in their circles and proudly showing the finished articles to their *curé* before carefully folding them away into trunks for the foreign missions.

In the ceremony, however, Maori and Pakeha alternated almost in antiphony. Four priests processed in, two Irish, two French; Maori sang the 'Ave Maris Stella'; settler women of Meanee, trained by Suzanne, sang the Latin High Mass; Maori sang the motet at the offertory; finally, old Father Lampila preached the sermon in Maori. Marata, Puhara's wife, was wearing a fine cloak and huia feathers in her hair.

Suzanne's intuitions about a growing ignorance of Maori custom and etiquette were right, though. Her letter to Poupinel in France quietly suggests this even as it projects blithe happiness at the event:

> When the Mass was over, everybody went, with a good appetite by then, to have dinner. An Irishman whose house was nearby invited the Clergy and the Europeans. But the Maoris were not pleased about this, because they had killed thirty pigs. After the meal everybody mingled with good humour. Father Yardin had never eaten kumara and took one out of Brother Basile's basket. Brother Basile, remembering his young days, had begun to eat again with the Maoris, and in their fashion and very happily. Brother Claude Marie did not let himself be tempted. The Superiors of the Sisters, who had never visited a pa, were especially going into raptures over the fun and enjoyment of the Natives.[6]

Yardin's account gave some more revealing details. The Pakeha guests had returned from their settler host's table while the meal at the marae was still in progress. So Yardin was able to describe the hangi, the little flax food baskets, the way the guests seated around were offered their food. Suzanne and the brothers had opted to join the Maori:

> Brothers Basile and Cyprien, with Sister Marie Joseph, had furtively slipped out of our dining room. They had sniffed the odours of the Maori cooking, the greedy little things, and when we rejoined them, we found them sitting at the entrance of the whareangi (meeting house) with a Maori plate on their knees, chewing away with relish. I think they were right to prefer the Maori cooking to ours. I tried some from the basket. It was really delicious. We then went into the house where the Maoris were having their dinner, but they politely reminded us of the old French proverb: 'don't disturb an honest man at his meal'. We had to retrace our steps, postponing our visit until a more favourable moment.[7]

Suzanne and the two farmer brothers did not join the Maori in the important sharing of kai on the day of celebration just because of tantalising aromas wafting across an Irish porch. Yardin sensed reproof as well as etiquette in the polite manners on the marae at Pakipaki.

The big day was not over. There was a baptism ceremony in the afternoon and then the Pakeha contingent left. Suzanne stayed on:

> At half past five the clergy set off back to Napier by the train and soon there were only the Maori left, Father Soulas and your humble servant. A little after six, the bell rang for the speeches and everyone gathered in the meeting house, a large raupo building forty feet long and twenty-two feet wide. We all sat down on the mats, some still dressed in their party best, some half-dressed, and some only with the traditional blanket. All the events of the day were reported, analysed, commented on and found perfect.[8]

Not quite perfect. There were people of different creeds living in the community. Catholics were a small minority among Ngati Kahungunu. Among the people baptised that afternoon was Te Kani, aged eighteen, who had previously been baptised Protestant. His father had not been consulted and, in Suzanne's account, rose with a flourish of his best white shirt sleeves to speak in protest. Lampila had even preached on the Fourth Commandment – honour your father and mother – that very morning, he said, and where had been the honouring? Suzanne wrote up for Poupinel three long pages of the discussion that followed. Round the speakers in turn she went:

> Ratima [the father] – If he had asked me for permission, I would have said no, but if he then persisted, I would have let him be and he would have satisfied the spirit of the Fourth Commandment in giving me a mark of respect. But no, he did not say anything. . . .
>
> Another Maori – . . . It's enough to make you go out of your mind. The Catholics say they're right. The Protestants say that they are right. They preach against one another. They rebaptise in their churches at the same time as they preach that they worship the same God. Who can make sense of this? If there is only one God, let each one of us stay what we are and be strong in prayer. . . .
>
> The chief [Urupene Puhara] – . . . I did in fact tell the priest to baptise only those who had no baptismal names and not to rebaptise anyone. But he didn't take any notice of my advice. Let us hope that in a few years he will listen to me better. The Protestant minister does the same thing. Who can understand the subtle dealings of the Europeans? The population is divided. . . .
>
> The Protestant Catechist – . . . he sympathised deeply with Ratima for the sin of his son against the Fourth Commandment. But he did not blame the young man for becoming a Catholic if he found this religion the best, because each of us was free and could deal with soul and body as we thought best.

Everybody else had something to say in turn, and finally:

> Te Kani [who, in Yardin's account of what Suzanne had told him next day, also pointed out that he was married and a father by now] – . . . I have not

acted under the influence of anyone, but only by the impulse of my own free
will. . . . if the good God says to me [on the day of judgement] that I was a fool,
I'll say he's saying just the same thing as my parents did. It looks like they were
right. But if he doesn't tell me I was a fool, I will say that I was right. So I ask
you please to leave me alone . . .

Daniel [Raniera], the Catholic Catechist and 'a Judge in the district' –
According to me, these young men have changed their religion under the
influence of religious enthusiasm. It's not up to us old men to condemn them
for that. . . . If we old men have all been feeling emotional and deeply moved
today, let's not hold it against these young men. . . . If they have turned
Catholic through the inspiration of God, we mustn't make this an unhappy
time for them. If they have turned through some passing whim they will go
back of their own accord to their former way of praying. The Catholic religion
has duties which are difficult and hard to perform while the Protestant
religion is very comfortable. . . .

Ratima – . . . The thing is done, I will leave my son alone.

Everybody applauded. It was midnight and their thoughts were drifting
away in the direction of sleep. . . . This finished the day of the 8th of June,
which was for me a day of great happiness in New Zealand.[9]

It was just as well Suzanne had this day of happiness firmly embedded
in her memory, because the future could not possibly be straightforward
for Soulas, the only (and lonely) Maori missioner. He came with Celtic
Breton mysticism and rigour and hoped for mass conversions, for eager
queues at confession, for baptisms to match his name of Hoani Papita. He
did not get them in the free choice and 'laissez-faire' faith of Heretaunga
Maori. And he would be having to adapt to cultural difference. Even on
the day of the opening of the church, he was disappointed that several
people from Pakipaki could not confess to Lampila and then receive
communion because, in their eagerness to get the all-important cooking
going for the celebration, they had broken their fast. There could be no
dispensation.[10] The two values of food and fasting had overlapped.

Soulas was keen, he was proud; he was touchy, he was finicky. As
Yardin put it, Soulas easily 'forgot that truth and justice are overly harsh
virtues without charity'.[11] He could get discouraged. The people had
wanted for so long a priest for the sacraments, so where was their fervour?
He kept using the word 'lukewarm'. Because Suzanne had invested so
much dedication and so many promises in this renewed mission, she had
to throw in her lot with Soulas. She chose to. Whatever affected him
would now affect her too. She knew that to be successful he needed the
support of her knowledge and standing among Maori. At the Waiohiki

marae, near Taradale, she had taken prayers and given instruction in faith. Maori there had told her it would not happen with any other woman.

It was essential for her to smooth over the contacts between the new priest and his parishioners. From the beginning his health appeared susceptible. She may have been covering up for a certain reluctance on his part due to initial culture-shock when she wrote that he was not able actually to stay out at Pakipaki much; 'were he to spend say a month there, he would not be able to work for a long time. The way things are [with the rise of Anglicanism all around], that would be a death blow to the Maori mission'.[12] The credibility of Catholicism rested on Soulas being able to stay the course.[13]

Yardin wrote that Soulas was not there for the main discussion in the meeting-house and that at first the tone had been critical of him. But then Yardin was beginning not to like Soulas. Neither did Reignier. Suzanne had actually written in her letter to Poupinel that 'good Father Reignier, who is completely losing his short-term memory, after being invited four or five times to come to the ceremony, forgot he had been and consequently stayed home. We were all really sorry.' She would have been really sorry then; now she was being really diplomatic. Reignier had been seriously ill in 1879 but was recovering. He was getting fussier in old age but was not in the least senile, as letters from him to Redwood in May and July 1880 clearly show.[14] The veteran Maori missioner of the East Coast was simply not there at the opening. In January, Yardin, with blithe condescension to both Breton and Maori, was already pinpointing some trouble-spots:

> Will Soulas succeed? I don't yet know. He is as stubborn as a mule and has known just how to pick a quarrel with Father Reignier. He goes round and round in a little circle of ideas and clings to them like a good Breton. But I have my doubts that he's got enough breadth of understanding and light-heartedness of personality to please our Maoris who are like big children. I withhold judgement for the moment, and the only thing I'll say for definite is that he is a *queer fellow*. Sister Marie Joseph says nothing to me about it, neither for, nor against; that proves that she's none too happy.[15]

Money was always an issue, which Redwood patiently tried to sort out. It would be an obsessional theme with Father Soulas. Money-raising schemes and worry would dog him and load Suzanne with unlikely ventures. She wrote that at Meanee they called him a 'penny-pincher;

why doesn't he take care of himself, trusting in providence for the rest!' Building the Pakipaki church meant bills to pay even though the Maori contributed.[16]

Soulas also travelled around trying to 'flush out' the few Maori Catholics dotted through the diocese. He spoke openly of extending the mission, so they called him 'swell-headed; he wants to go too fast'. Suzanne did not agree:

> Alas, too fast, when everything will perish through too much slowness! Others who were full of good intentions rather more than knowledge on the subject used to give their considered opinions which were as numerous as they were contradictory and inopportune. I was afraid for only one thing above all else, that the Father, angered and disheartened not by the mission but by the circumstances in which he had to revive it, might give up completely. And in that case, you might very well have truthfully said, 'There's nothing to be done in the Maori mission'.[17]

After so many years with no colleagues in Maori mission except a lay woman, Father Reignier could see the young man taking over with his newly ordained prickly determination. Reignier did not die until 1888, but Soulas's arrival symbolically took him across the final threshold of age. His narrow escape from death in Wairoa in November 1879 would only reinforce this. Yardin thought Soulas showed no consideration for Reignier's age, experience and status as superior of the mission.[18]

But what really compounded the problems, and always would with Soulas, was the intensity of his emotions. His argument might often begin with a well-reasoned and logical development but at a certain point something would snap, 'his words and actions turning to violence'.[19] Even in letters he would wind up to such a pitch of frenzy that paranoic accusations and recriminations would push and shove past each other on the page. In one letter some years later, he gave up on words at a certain point and his pen spat out a coffin sketch with skull and crossbones to paint his feelings over what he considered a 'still-born' idea.[20]

Some such letter must have ended up with Yardin while he was administering the diocese, and he wrote to Poupinel of his concern. Poupinel replied in July 1880:

> You have not sent me Father Soulas's letter that you spoke about. But I see from yours of 22 May that you had a visit to Napier and that you have to go back there soon. You'll have been able to observe closely this young confrère and get a thorough on the spot assessment. His last letter was 23 April. It shows us, like the previous ones, a man of common sense, an active and

pious missionary and we can't draw any other conclusions. If on the other hand his head is disturbed or deranged, I shall be very sorry.[21]

Poupinel, having at long last found a priest for the elusive Maori mission, wanted Soulas to be a success, as Suzanne did. In the same letter he told how, in the escalating anticlericalism, the Jesuits had been expelled from France in June. He expected that the Dominicans and the Society of Mary would be the next to go. The personality problems of Father Soulas paled in comparison.

So it remained for four years: Soulas had to be accommodated as a lot was at stake. Redwood realised this: 'Father Soulas is zealous but over-dramatic and has a difficult nature. However he is doing good among the Maori, slowly, with difficulty. Soon we'll have to help the good father by providing him with another missioner.'[22] Suzanne kept up a balancing act. She supported the intelligent, enthusiastic, dedicated mission priest at the same time as she protected the vulnerable, hurting, deprived child within him, who could lash out so often at others, and at her. Sometimes, because she too was enthusiastic and could throw herself at projects, she almost lost her balance and had to clutch for the wire. It was the same situation as she had explained to Poupinel long ago in 1866: that she supported Pompallier, with all his faults, because he kept the mission going. This time around, though, the Maori mission survived, enlarged and multiplied.

Soulas had been travelling, both in the Wellington diocese and in the southern part of the Auckland diocese. There were many more Maori in the latter, yet war and its aftermath, the short stay of Bishop Croke, the death of his successor, Bishop Steins, and three interregnum periods had left no Catholic priest for Maori except James McDonald. For a while it seemed a combined mission could be possible, and Soulas would certainly have liked to head it.[23] But in the 1880s the new Bishop of Auckland, John Edmund Luck, who could find no secular priest willing to join McDonald in Maori mission work,[24] brought in Dutch priests from St Joseph's Foreign Missionary Society, a London-based congregation usually called the 'Mill Hills', and the dioceses ran their separate missions.

In February 1883, Soulas met a community of Maori up the Whanganui River who lived much further away from settler contact than Ngati Kahungunu did. The wildness of the landscape and the difficulties of navigating the river rapids had slowed the process of Pakeha settle-ment. Soulas saw the potential of Ngati Hau at Hiruharama when he found many Maori still remembering their Catholic prayers from the time of Father Lampila. He baptised fifty-eight people and celebrated ten marriages. He was given a petition to present to Redwood, asking for a resident priest. It was signed by 150 people who counted themselves Catholic.[25] Redwood acknowledged that in mission terms 'Pakipaki . . . can't compare with this pah.'[26]

The river had beckoned the usual file of missionaries in times past. Father Lampila had had a flamboyantly successful Catholic mission in the 1850s and early 1860s. In 1852 he had gone first to Kaiwhaiki on the gentle lower reaches of the river and had built a flour mill there. Then in 1854 he pushed up the river to Kauaeroa, a little distance downstream and across the river from Hiruharama. His mission station there was impressive: a flour mill, a school, a house for himself and the lay brother, orchards, fields of crops, grape vines and a large chapel, built by the local Maori and said to have had elaborately carved pillars and roof beams.[27] In 1865, Poupinel was there as Marist Visitor and wrote appreciatively how they had raised money for a 'chalice, ciborium and silver monstrance, fine altar candlesticks, two statues, a bell and even a harmonium'.[28] The Catholic angelus bell was already ringing strongly out across the river to Hiruharama.

Father Jean Lampila had been the most determined, the most belligerent of the old religious duellists. He was an ex-soldier and in strategy more than a match for his opponent, Rev. Richard Taylor of the Church Missionary Society. Taylor had been one of the evangelical vanguard at Waitangi and had written out the final parchment copy of the treaty there. He had disapproved of the way Pompallier 'upstaged' proceedings. By the 1850s he had a successful mission to Te Atihaunui-a-Paparangi based at Putiki, near the Whanganui River mouth, and other mission stations were dotted upriver. He had even helped rename the various kainga. Hiruharama was really Patiarero; it was Taylor who, in discussion with rangatira, called it Jerusalem (rendered in Maori as Hiruharama), along with Athens (Atene), Corinth (Koroniti) and others strung along the river banks. Lampila's encroachment upriver was anathema to him: Lampila was blatantly poaching Protestant Maori, even catechists. Taylor accused Lampila of making conversion to Catholicism the price for the flour mills the priest was erecting along the river with funding from Governor Grey.[29] Lampila is said to have encouraged Hiruharama Maori to dismantle Taylor's church and appropriate its timbers.[30]

Lampila was Marist in his zeal but un-Marist in his showmanship. His statue of the Virgin Mary reputedly wept tears. He confronted Taylor at least twice with his customary challenge to walk through fire.[31] Taylor, like William Williams and William Colenso, declined: he had a wife, family, Anglo-Saxon reputation and property. He had little to gain from such a contest, whereas Catholic Lampila would always win out, if only with the saintly crown of martyrdom. Ngati Hau appreciated this keen vying for their favours and in their oral tradition the chief Te Kere pulled Lampila back from the flames in 1862 and rewarded his dramatic display with Hiruharama's conversion to Catholicism. Taylor was disgusted and disillusioned. His loss was Hiruharama.

Wesleyan missionaries paddling upriver had already made Taylor jittery in 1848, even before Lampila came on the scene.[32] The Salvation Army would scare Soulas in the 1890s, before Ratana challenged the Catholic mission far more powerfully in the twentieth century. In the 1860s it was Pai Marire which held sway in the Taranaki and upper Whanganui River regions. Lampila survived the Battle of Moutoa in 1864, alongside kupapa Maori fighting in support of the government against the Hauhau. Old tribal issues and loyalties were involved as much as religion and land sales. The little shingle island of Moutoa, a couple of miles down from Hiruharama, gave its name to this battle in which five Maori catechists and Brother Euloge were among those killed. They were buried in graves at Kauaeroa. By the time of Poupinel's visit in mid-1865 the mission was already in decline. The Maori of the middle reaches of the river had 'agonised over where to put their loyalty'.[33] Like the Anglicans Selwyn and Maunsell, whom Maori could no longer view objectively once they were chaplains to Imperial troops, Lampila must have lost a lot of trust after he had taken part in this engagement. By 1867 he retreated, ill and disappointed, to the town parish of Wanganui and the angelus bell fell silent upriver.

After the scares of the Hauhau years, Wanganui for a long time 'turned its back on the river; the city was scared of its river'.[34] Wanganui was more a seaport than a riverport, and so the communities up the river were not as disrupted as Heretaunga Maori by the interaction of the two cultures. Time had not stood still, of course, but there was an old-time romanticised challenge of adventure and hardship waiting for any missioner who wanted once more to test Providence upriver. The memory of Lampila's dynamic, colourful, dramatic mission flared as a beacon. There was still the chance, in mission terms, of reaping fields ready for the harvest.[35] Sister Mary Joseph could be tempted. And it was Soulas's opening for success. Hawke's Bay communities were too open to Protestant and secular influences. The isolation of the river was in its favour.

Maori from the river sometimes came across to Hawke's Bay to trade in sheep and mats. They heard of the new missioner, and they knew of Meri. In 1882, on one of these trips, Taiwhati is said to have asked Redwood at Palmerston North for a priest at Hiruharama. Werahiko and Poma, chiefs from the pa at Kauaeroa, also invited Soulas to come. He may have solicited an approach. From the late 1870s, Christian mission activity, linked to schooling, was creeping back into the hinterlands, and Hiruharama was no exception. Soulas and Sister Mary Joseph would need to move quickly to stake their claim for Catholicism.

There was a government Native Schools schoolhouse on land owned by Te Keepa above the pa at Hiruharama. This had been built in 1873 and staffed by a succession of teachers.[36] In 1878 the school closed. In 1879 Father Pertuis, with two young lay women teachers, tried to revive the Catholic mission but the isolation proved too much. By 1881, George Milson was competing for the Presbyterian church with the Anglican Rev. Erueti Te Ngara, who would later be based at Pipiriki, to run the school. The Native Schools Iruharama file has Presbyterian letters from the Waverley manse supporting Milson's bid. It was matched by a July 1881 petition in favour of Rev. Te Ngara signed by thirty-four matua, or parents, including Te Keepa, Materoa, Tamatea, Reone, Poutini and others who would feature strongly in the story of Mother Aubert.[37] Many also undoubtedly signed the petition to Soulas two years later. The decision went to the Presbyterians, new challengers in the religious championship of the river. Te Keepa sought and gained the wheelbarrow and other sundry items before Milson moved in, without the 'horse, saddle and bridle' essential for hill country mission work.[38]

The Anglican church was fairly strong at Koriniti, about ten miles further down, and was strengthening at Pipiriki, six miles upriver. Within two years, Milson withdrew down the river to Koroniti, and Soulas was just in time to bag Hiruharama for Catholicism, later adding Ranana. There was a hint that the competition between communities in the 1840s and 1850s might be replayed. Ngati Hau were always open to different and differing ideas, and had a tradition of discussion and independent thinking. There was a whare wananga, a house of learning, on the

Peterehema (Bethlehem) marae within the Hiruharama settlement. 'The main korero of the river was at Hiruharama; that was the arena where people came to korero.'[39] Jerusalem was therefore important. And 'because it was across the Pai Marire border, the mission had to be founded there. There was a significance.'[40] Once Meri was up there, the Catholic mission stayed on.

By June 1883, when Suzanne left for the Whanganui River, she was forty-eight. She had been in Hawke's Bay for twelve busy, happy years. But the pace of her life was telling on her. In 1881 she had already written to Poupinel how 'old age, a premature old age, is dragging me towards the grave'. She said that her 'last prayer would be for the Maori mission'.[41] She was ill again with what she thought may have been angina and Dr Spencer apparently gave her about six months to live. Medical opinion always considered the swampy flats of Hawke's Bay bad for her. She was now living out at Pakipaki partly because the new superior at Meanee, Father Sauzeau, had objected to a woman being there. Sauzeau also disliked Soulas, so Suzanne may have been a pawn in the contest. It was an appropriate time to move on, although her friends at Pakipaki never thought so. They missed her and her healing, and wrote asking her to come back or, if that was not possible, at least to send medicines.

The settlers learnt of her departure only a week beforehand. The *Daily Telegraph* of 15 June hinted at their loss by bigheartedly emphasising Whanganui's gain: 'Sister Mary Joseph will also be extremely useful to the natives of that part of the country on account of her experience and ability in medicinal practice.' They just had time to organise a hasty farewell, when Airini Karauria, among others, presented her with gifts. Airini was descended from or closely related to several important chiefs: Karauria, Tiakitai, Te Moananui, Tareha and Renata Kawepo. She was also married to an Irishman, G. P. Donnelly, so could represent both cultures. But her gift was on behalf of Maori, and hers was the one the *Daily Telegraph* of 22 June 1883 emphasised:

> Amongst other tokens of esteem presented to Sister Mary Joseph on the eve of her departure from this district is a handsome silver cup, bearing the following inscription, which speaks for itself:– 'To Sister Mary Joseph from Airini Donnelly, in remembrance of many kindnesses to her and her people. Napier, June 21, 1883.' On the other side of the cup a similar inscription appears in Maori. ['He tohu aroha maharatanga mo te nui o ona arohatanga ki au me aku Iwi.']

The *Hawke's Bay Herald* of 15 June spelt out clearly what she had
contributed to the area:

> This announcement will be received with heart-felt sorrow by everyone who
> knows Sister Joseph, and who does not? Her genuine sympathy with, and
> practical kindness to, those in trouble have made her name a household word
> in this district. The manifestation of her practical Christianity has never been
> hampered by questions as to creed or belief; merely to be in trouble is sufficient
> claim on her kindly offices. Roman Catholics and Protestants alike will be
> sorry to lose her, and would only be too glad if those in authority could see
> their way to leave her in her present ample sphere of usefulness.

She left. She took the train south, then crossed the Manawatu Gorge by
the narrow, winding coach-road, and travelled from Palmerston North by
train again to Wanganui. Wanganui township would draw her down the
river many times over the years to come. Suzanne liked company and
dealing with people. In July 1883, in spite of New Zealand's depression,
Wanganui was 'a lively town supported by flourishing rural districts and
a vigorous coastal export trade'.[42] At the same moment as she arrived, the
travelling correspondent for the *Auckland Weekly News* was observing
all the bustle, the crowds flocking in for the weekly livestock sale, the
buggies, the horses, 'the seven coasting steamers discharging and
reloading at the wharf'. The freezing industry was getting under way in
Wellington, and Wanganui was supplying it. Inadvertently, in settler
terms, she was going to do her bit for the opening up and colonising of the
river 'by removing the fear'.[43]

Redwood timed an 'episcopal visitation of this district' to be in
Wanganui to farewell her as she boarded the waka at Upokongaro on 4
July. A whole fleet of canoes laden with goods to set up the mission was
waiting to go. Redwood wanted to get on his way back to Wellington, so
Soulas was obliged to set off although some of their boxes had not yet
arrived from Pakipaki. Suzanne had 'to wash and wear' her clothes for
some weeks. Men of status had come down the river to take the party
up to Hiruharama: Werahiko, Poma, Keremeneta, Reone, Wi Pauro,
Materoa and others. It was midwinter and the *Wanganui Chronicle*
reported fine weather with southerly winds. It would be very cold on the
river. They could be starting in mornings wrapped in thick river mist
which would slowly lift to reveal the cliffs, the bush, the hills and long
stretches of water.

She was not the only passenger on the three-day trip. In fact, officially
she was only the companion, supposedly temporary, for two young Sisters

Hiruharama (Jerusalem) on the Whanganui River in the early 1880s, looking down from the site of the church of St Joseph.

Poutini of Ngati Hau.

Taiwhati, who is reported to have asked for a priest to come to Hiruharama.

Ranana, 1885. Alfred Burton photograph showing Te Keepa's meeting-house from near where the Church of the Sacred Heart now stands. 258 MONZ

Neri Metera of Ngati Ruaka, Ranana.

In 1880 a community of the Australian Sisters
of St Joseph of Nazareth came to Wanganui.
Mother Hyacinth is standing. Sister Teresa
(left) went to Hiruharama with Suzanne.

Wanganui in 1881, a well-established town and port.

The government schoolhouse at Hiruharama,
known as Keepa's house, where the sisters
and Suzanne lived and taught for the first
years in Hiruharama.

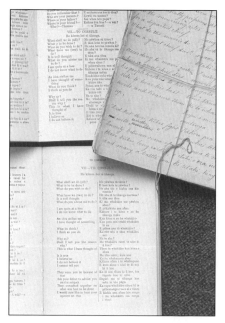

*New and Complete Manual of Maori
Conversation and a Complete Vocabulary*,
1885. Sample manuscript pages on the right;
on the left, a page of Suzanne's edition.

The church of Hato Hohepa (St Joseph) was built at Hiruharama in 1885.   MAW

The first sisters of the Third Order Regular of Mary in New Zealand: Mother Mary Joseph (right) and her ABC, (from left) Sisters Bridget, Anne and Carmel.

Suzanne and Sister Magdalen, late 1888 or mid-1889, on the collecting tour to raise funds to build a new church and convent.

In the late 1880s, the Salvation Army extended its mission from Wanganui upriver to Hiruharama. The front page of its magazine *War Cry* on 9 November 1889 featured their arrival. The Catholic presbytery stands forlornly alone on the knoll where the church had been burnt down.

The rebuilt church and presbytery at Hiruharama, with the convent behind.   MAW

Building timbers are stacked behind Fathers Soulas and Broussard.   MAW

Father Christophe Soulas or
Pa Hoani Papita. His fellow
priests sometimes called him
the Patriarch of Jerusalem.
MAW

The Catholics withstood the
Salvation Army, fighting like with
like by founding a band.
Te Manihera Keremeneta (Rure),
in the uniform of the Catholic band.

Looking across the river from Hiruharama to Kauaeroa. The river mist like a furled scarf lies
along the slopes of Morikau in the background.   ANNE NOBLE, 1982

of St Joseph from Wanganui, who had agreed to take on the school and mission, along with Soulas, for a trial period. In a letter to Moreau, Soulas referred to Sister Teresa as the superior and Sister Mary Joseph as her 'aid'.[44] She was going to help them learn Maori and, as she did for Soulas, smooth the cultural transition. Her position was ambiguous from the start. The message in Hawke's Bay had been different. In the newspaper account her departure seemed definitive and her role more managerial: 'Sister Mary Joseph has received instructions to remove from Meanee to the Wanganui district where she will take charge of two other sisters appointed to labor among the Maoris in a wild tract of country sixty miles up the Wanganui river.' The newspaper was not to know that a layperson could not be in charge of two religious.

Send up that parcel : Tukuna atu tena takai [45]

Before Sister Mary Joseph left Meanee, Father Soulas had sent from Wanganui a long letter with suggestions and instructions for her.

> Dear Sister,
> You will be pleased to learn that the gospel seed has born fruit during my absence. The Maoris tell me that they have at least three hundred now attending the Catholic prayers. In a big meeting down at Ranana, a pa which is completely Protestant, there were only fifteen Maoris lately turning up to sing those droning psalms that you know of, while everybody else turned up to the Catholic prayers. May God be blessed!
>
> All the big prayer-books have run out; they are in demand everywhere. So instead of one hundred, bring three hundred of them.
>
> As soon as your parcels are ready, send them.
>
> I was thinking about your dispensary, and here's what I've decided. First of all, as regards your bags of herbs and other things like rosemary, sage, etc., the best thing to do is to bring everything, even what's at Pakipaki, because you won't be going back this year . . .
>
> As for jars, bottles . . . best to bring all your bottled remedies, and also bring empty bottles, the ones you dispense your medicines in, because here you won't find any little bottles in the pa.
>
> Here's my plan. I'll set it out for you so you can see what you have to do . . .

In Soulas's plan, Suzanne might eventually go back to Pakipaki with a couple of other sisters, if they became available, to restart a school and medical dispensary there. Or else, come February next, she might go up to the Waikato with a postulant to do the same. Then again, she might die:

It's settled that we will have three Sisters available in a fortnight when the bishop comes. You'll be admitted into the Convent here, but not as a postulant since there won't be any recovery. You'll be there as a help to the Sisters or as a friend if you like, or even a boarder. In any case, you'll not have any work imposed on you. . . .

I'll change paper; the other would strain your eyes . . .

On different paper, he wrote on. For someone contemplating dying, she had a lot of packing to do:

What should you bring? That's a serious question. God alone could give you a right answer to that one. For my part, I think you must bring everything . . . so, cauldrons, pots, distilling apparatus, evaporator . . . bottles, jars, drugs, herbs . . . in short, everything you have got. . . .

Pack everything carefully lest something get lost. You know old boxes are for sale at Neal and Close's . . . Ask Fr Reignier if Joseph can help you. When it comes to making boxes, Cyprien knows how to do it better . . .

Pack everything of mine except for the following; in general anything to do with the horse, except you can bring the spur, the one at Pakipaki, and my best whip; it's in the corner of the wardrobe or near the *washing-stand*. Bring my new horse blanket, too, for the nights; it's in my bedroom, and then you can bring back my old one from Pakipaki and put it in my bedroom at Meanee. Let Brother Basile know about this.

It'd be a good idea to go to Pakipaki and take from there what belongs to you – blankets, sheets, linen, clothes . . . you can leave the cooking pots, but bring the knife for opening *tins*, also your little harmonium which is out there already. Bring slates, school books, and everything you'll need for the school . . . and board games and my alphabet letters . . . All our books at Pakipaki, also the ones at Meanee [he lists them], even the big dictionary of great men, they're all to take the road to Wanganui. Don't forget my papers. There are some of them in the right hand drawer at Pakipaki, the others, including your will, are in Father Séon's box at Meanee, the others on my table. Don't forget my cassocks and other things in the cupboard above Fr Michel's bedroom; the key is on my mantlepiece behind the homeopathy box. However, leave some rosary beads, crosses, statuettes, and holy medals at Meanee and Pakipaki, but pack up most of them . . . [46]

With the packing of her boxes, Suzanne's life changed direction. How much did she think of dying when she was sorting and parcelling? Once he had her up at Hiruharama and it looked as if she were going to survive, Soulas would not have wanted her to leave and would presumably do anything and everything to keep her: for her French companionship, her well-informed intelligence, her rapport with Maori and familiarity with the language, her medical knowledge (his interest in medicine and concern about illness had a touch of the morbid), her domestic skills, her

Hi Marjorie,
    Drew took me to a second
hand bookshop that they go to so he
asked Annie the lady who owns it
about your request. She immediately
went and found this book for you.

        love
        David
          x

maturity and life experience. Reignier may have realised this, since he sent his regards, not to 'Sister', but to 'Rev. Mother Doctor' Mary Joseph, in a mid-July letter to his old colleague Moreau.[47]

The river here is very deep, swift, and strong :
E hohonu ana te awa i konei, e kaha ana te ia, e tino tere ana nga wai [48]

It seemed a well-planned and well-supported team moving up the river. Soulas, the young and active priest, was going to be joined later by the experienced seventy-year-old Father Moreau, who had agreed to help get the river mission going again. And middle-aged Sister Mary Joseph, the lay sister, would help the two young sisters, Teresa and Aloysius. The superior of the Wanganui Sisters of St Joseph, Mother Hyacinth, was going up for a week just to help them settle in. Yardin, when he first met these sisters in 1880, thought them 'very, very young and *shy, very much*'.[49] There would be three French and three Australians.

What was special and significant about the Sisters of St Joseph in the story of Mother Aubert was the origin and development of their congregation. Unusually for the times, it was Australian – practically local. Mary MacKillop and Father Julian Tenison Woods had started the Sisters of St Joseph in the colony of South Australia back in 1866. 'They set an indigenous social movement in train, took on the education of the poor in Australia, . . . built and travelled with a 19th-century ferocity that makes you gasp – all that alpaca in an Adelaide summer.'[50] They had a democratic, egalitarian, active and centralised concept of what the sisters would be and do. Mary MacKillop met intense opposition from diocesan bishops, who kept on trying to manipulate and control. To safeguard the special nature of their work, she succeeded in gaining a Decree of Praise for the congregation in 1874, making it more independent of the bishops.[51] She also edged her sisters away from Father Woods, whose charisma and vanity had their dangers for a common-sense world view.

But the sisters who came to Wanganui in 1880 were a Bathurst group who had separated from the original congregation in 1876. They remained under diocesan control with the name of the Sisters of St Joseph of Nazareth. They also kept links with Woods and still considered him as founder. Soulas could register the fact that out in the antipodes a priest had already been the founding father of an indigenous female congregation and had exercised a strong psychological and mystical influence over some of its members. In the tradition of the Wanganui sisters, Woods' role as founder of the Sisters of St Joseph was enlarged while Mary MacKillop's founding role was played down.[52] Woods continued as adviser and wrote to the sisters in New Zealand with the manner of a spiritual director.

The little Wanganui community was diocesan but its origins were not quite the norm for New Zealand. Mary MacKillop was Scottish–Australian; Julian Woods was English; the congregation was Australian. Its presence could have set Soulas thinking fast. And inklings of this might be nudging into Suzanne's consciousness. After all, what was going to happen to her in the rest of her life, with a nebulous status of maybe Third Order Regular, maybe not? Her stop-gap phase was over. Now the Maori mission was launched again, she would probably welcome having her role regularised. And why not as *R. Mère Docteur Marie Joseph*, as Reignier shrewdly divined?

Sister Aloysius later recalled the trip. They spent the first night at Atene. The sisters sat up all night huddled in a whare after chasing out some pigs who snuffled and rooted outside during the night; 'the cold was intense. . . . The early morning saw us on our way again; sometimes we used to get out of the canoe and walk for awhile; I remember having to climb very high hills. Mother Aubert used to keep us alive with her merry laugh.'[53] Passengers walked while the canoes were poled through the rapids. The track was sometimes on one side of the river, sometimes on the other, and often beside a sheer drop. In the bush the water lay and formed thick mud to clog their boots and hems. The women may not have known it, but the men paddling and poling the laden canoes were being as kind as they could: 'My father [Wi Pauro Marino] was one of them . . . To save the sisters, they get in the river and pull the canoe up, the sisters on it . . .'[54] Three days of bush tracks, overhanging ferns, papa cliffs, eel weirs, rapids and still reaches, then past Moutoa and round a wide curve of the river – Hiruharama at last.

The Australian sisters remembered a warm welcoming party and 'a sort of banquet' waiting. The women then 'made haste to reach [their] own house, a little higher up'. It was the long wooden government schoolhouse. Suzanne, who had just been sent from Ars a framed collection of tiny mementos of the curé, used to say he had described this house to her in prophecy all those years before, and she was startled on arrival to recognise it there in front of her. It was only ten years old, and adequate if a bit spartan. Soulas and Father Moreau were in a house down at the pa at first but came up for meals served by the women in the little parlour.

The schoolhouse was home, school and church. Children and adults came to school. Discipline was handled down at the pa, not in school. With the parallel sentences in English and Maori from Colenso's 1872 *Willie's First English Book*, Meri taught the students by day and the sisters by night. People came to morning prayers, to Mass, to prayer and instruction every evening at five; on Sundays to Vespers and Benediction. They were following regularly a spiritual routine that would normally be found only in a religious community. Meri made candlesticks for the October nightly Benediction out of hollowed potatoes wrapped in red paper. To Sister Aloysius it seemed to take a long time to recite the rosary and celebrate Benediction in Maori. She also recalled that, when Soulas was away, a Maori catechist conducted the service and preached a sermon which Meri used to say was very good.

Suzanne obviously did not die. Father Moreau died instead, and the sisters were left with Soulas as confessor as well as superior, not the kindly old man that Redwood had carefully appointed for them. Suzanne was only half-way through her long life. She had her share of illness after this, but it was a normal share. The change of climate may have suited her, as predicted. Instead of dying, she started gathering in the women who would still be with her when she finally did die, forty-three years later.

Suzanne began recruiting women now because she was soon appointed to set up and lead a branch of the Marist Third Order Regular of Mary. The Sisters of St Joseph stayed just over a year at Hiruharama before withdrawing. The decision to go was not initially their own. Sisters Teresa and Aloysius had not been there long before it was suggested that the Third Order Regular of Mary, well used to small Pacific Island missions, would be better suited to isolated Maori mission work. In fact both congregations were active and open, but the French congregation was the one whose *pionnières* Suzanne had wanted to join in the 1850s and to which she had affiliated herself in 1870. Now in the 1880s their congregation had been constituted officially. Its Marist connection made it attractive. Having a community of the Third Order Regular of Mary at Hiruharama was a way in which Suzanne could become a nun again, still within the Marist fold.

The two congregations had different priorities in their work. The

Sisters of St Joseph saw themselves principally as teachers, whereas Suzanne's gifts and interests ranged widely. She could never confine herself mainly to teaching. She was all for going out and about – on foot, on horseback, by canoe – on pastoral and medical visits around the various pa. Soulas wrote to Poupinel in July 1884 describing how she had cured the son of a Turakina chief who then, in appreciation, converted to Catholicism.[55] Suzanne's activity was good for the mission. In such an isolated outpost, Soulas's plans to combine teaching and nursing in the new mission, as the Marist women were doing in the Pacific, made good sense. Redwood wrote later to the Marist superior general in France that to train English-speaking Sisters of the Third Order in New Zealand would be useful also for English-speaking Pacific missions such as Fiji.[56]

There is no record of major differences between the women, although the Sisters of St Joseph remembered Suzanne wanting them to recite the rosary instead of the Little Office of Mary. In Suzanne's recollections, the sisters had been given strict instructions to keep to their Rule, and this meant that she as a secular had to keep her distance at first and take meals all on her own in the tiny scullery. Father Moreau stopped this.[57] The evidence points more to discord between Father Soulas and Father Kirk, the Wanganui parish priest who saw the community as 'his' sisters. Concerned letters were soon going between the Wanganui convent, the Wanganui presbytery, Hiruharama, and the bishop in Wellington.[58] Redwood wrote supportively to Sister Teresa telling her nobody had the right to open letters she sent to the bishop.[59] A letter from Mother Hyacinth shows her puzzled and rightly wanting to know what any objections to the sisters might be.

When everything is taken into account, it is most likely that Father Soulas envisaged a prospering mission base supported by a female congregation primarily under his leadership and secondarily under that of the sister who had been working with him for four years. He knew Suzanne's worth, and he set about making his vision real. There was nothing amiss with the Sisters of St Joseph. In essence, they made way tactfully in 1884 so that the energy and vitality and skills and passion and vision of Suzanne Aubert – the whole gift of her calling – could be channelled through religious life.

In May 1884, Redwood authorised Soulas to receive postulants to follow the Rule of the Third Order Regular of Mary and appointed Sister Mary Joseph as interim superior. Back in June 1883, it was clear that

Soulas had already been thinking instead of a new women's order for the Maori mission.[60] He came back to this theme and in July 1884 Redwood tersely set him right. His letters to Soulas were becoming quite blunt. 'I never for one moment contemplated the foundation of a *new* order. . . . What I intended was that the same order that already exists in France and in the Islands be set up in New Zealand . . . I did not intend, and I do not intend to sanction the foundation of a *new* order.'[61]

Suzanne had not lived a convent life for a long time, and here she was all of a sudden, at forty-nine, a potential mother superior looking for women twenty to thirty years younger as companions. Some would say later on that Suzanne never really could live the true congregational life of a Sister of Compassion. Her independence and need to be on the move had set deep in her nature. The mother superior never quite replaced the roving missioner. But at Hiruharama she could still be both, and the early sisters remembered the first years as idyllic whenever she was there.

Ellen O'Rourke had emigrated from Ireland in 1879 to Hawke's Bay where she met Suzanne, who cared for and cured her invalid sister. Ellen would help Suzanne teach catechism to Maori people at Meanee. She was educated, knew some French and quickly picked up Maori. In August 1884, Ellen came to Jerusalem as a postulant. She became Sister Anne, calm and 'in the early days keensighted enough to keep a balance between the authority of Father Soulas SM and Mother Aubert'.[62] Entering with Ellen was Eliza Brownlie, who was born close to Wanganui, at Turakina. The daughter of a Scottish–Irish farming family, she became Sister Bridget – the only sister Suzanne called by a pet name. She was the 'Dear Biddie' with the suntanned face who lived much of her life at Hiruharama. Suzanne's letters to her from Rome thirty years later tell of her affection and nostalgia for these early days. Tall, shy and quiet, the Irish-born Susan Gallagher was the third, Sister Carmel. Suzanne saw Anne, Bridget and Carmel as the ABC of the congregation, or as the three posts which held up the porch of her wharepuni, the new institute founded upriver.[63]

Before the two Sisters of St Joseph went back down the river, perhaps it was they who unwittingly set Suzanne onto her major contribution to Maori-language learning and Maori publishing history in New Zealand. Suzanne was teaching Maori to Teresa and Aloysius. She had already written the Maori–French phrase-book for Soulas. Other French priests who came would use the increasingly battered manuscript until it was last seen at the Wanganui Presbytery with Father Ginisty, around 1915.[64]

At this earlier time, with the Australian sisters, she would be working between English and Maori. Presumably what she was doing with them inspired someone to think of publication.

Protestant missionaries and ex-missionaries had been publishing Maori grammars, dictionaries and phrase-books. Colenso's *Willie's First English Book* was stocking the Native Schools. Richard Taylor, too, had produced a book covering botanical, zoological, geographical and some cultural word-lists. These books were being revised. Suzanne herself had been working on a major English–Maori dictionary since the late 1870s. A heavy leatherbound volume is filled in her neat writing with 17,000 English entries with many of the Maori equivalents already alongside. It remained unfinished, however.

She now set to in 1883 and wrote a Maori–English phrase-book on a whole variety of subjects which people of two cultures might meet and converse about. As she put it on the title page of the 1885 printed book, it was a *New and complete manual of Maori conversation containing phrases and dialogues on a variety of useful and interesting topics, together with a few general rules of grammar and a comprehensive vocabulary.*[65] She pointed out that she had 'endeavoured to make this little book useful to Maoris, as well as Europeans'. No doubt Soulas could see fund-raising potential for the mission, and Redwood quickly lent his support. He liaised with the printers down in Wellington, Lyon and Blair. In May 1884, he wrote that the manuscript was safely with them. When the school was closed for a time while local Maori were required to attend the Native Land Court, Suzanne went down to stay at Wanganui to correct the proofs, leaving Teresa and Aloysius on their own.

To raise sales potential, she wrote to Sir George Grey for permission to adapt material from his 1855 English and Maori *Polynesian Mythology and Ancient Traditional History of the New Zealand Race*. The 1867 edition of Taylor's work had included a short extract in Maori from this work. She explained to Grey: 'The aim of this publication is to facilitate among the Maori people the work of the Sisters of the Third Order of Mary that Monsignor Redwood has just charged me with founding at Hiruharama.'[66] Grey fished back in his memory for the nun he had met in the 1860s and scribbled in the margin an accurate, and even understated, image from those days: 'a poor but hard-working nun'. Presumably he was already planning another edition, or did her May 1884 letter prompt him to bring out his own second edition in 1885? Grey represented

Hinemoa in her hot pool 'trembling all over, partly from the cold . . . and partly also, perhaps, from modesty'. Suzanne, with missionary weighting, put it the other way round: 'She was ashamed, and therefore she shivered, and sat in the hot springs to warm herself; but love was stronger than shame.' The sentence closes in vintage Aubert fashion. Suzanne nearly always ended on a positive, optimistic note.

Previous publications in Maori had been overwhelmingly religious and the few early phrase-books were minimal. The conversation section of Leonard Williams's *First Lessons in the Maori Language with a Short Vocabulary*, first published in 1862, had only eight pages of practical phrases. More to the point, the few books that had been produced were predictably utilitarian and colonising. Even an 1879 edition of Kemp's *The First Step to Maori Conversation: a Grammar and Phrase Book of the New Zealand Language*, first published in 1848, gave English and Maori equivalents for a few phrases 'of everyday importance to settlers and traders'. It was still a pared-down survival kit for 'Load my ship with spars' type of trade contacts and, of course, land buying:

Conversation about Land.

My friends,	*e oku hoa.*
I am desirous of buying some land,	*e hia-hia ana au ki te hoko whenua.*
Where?	*i whea?*
How much do you want?	*kia pewhea koia?*
A large piece,	*kia nui.*
A small piece,	*kia iti.*
Who are the owners of the soil?	*kowai nga putake o te whenua?*
We are,	*ko matou.*
Do you consent?	*e whaka-ae ana kotou?*
We are glad of that,	*e koa ana matou ki tena.*
I wish to have the fern cleared off,	*e mea ana nu kia para te rarauhe.*
What will you pay?	*he aha te utu?*
Two shillings a day,	*kia rua hereni mo te rangi kotahi.*
The roots must be removed,	*me tango nga paiaka.*
And the stones must be rolled on one side	*ko nga kowhata me hurihuri ki tahaki.*
We cannot agree for that,	*kaore matou e pai ke tena.*
We agree.	*ka whaka-ae matou.* [67]

These few books were being revised and reprinted again and again.

Most Maori language was being acquired orally, of course, especially in areas of traditional culture. Suzanne, however, documented the language where it could interface with, or overlap, the settler world. She launched into something quite different from anything before, a book just like any Spaniard would take to Italy, like any French traveller would take to Germany. She was writing to get over the cultural border. Her book idealistically assumed a lively populace of Pakeha and Maori who would be wanting to communicate, to gossip ('He gets his living by sponging on others : Tona ora he pinono'), to travel in company ('It is very slippery; take care not to fall : Ka nui te maniani. Kia tupato koe, kei hinga a ki raro'), to weather storms together ('Let us shelter ourselves : Me noho tatou i tetahi wahi maru'), to share an accommodation house, to discuss health, sea travel, trade, earthquakes, politics, the situation in Austria or France. In her manuscript she crossed out 'The Americans have sunk an English ironclad with 150 men on board'. Since that may have been seen as detrimental to the image of Empire, she wrote carefully over the top some wishful Franco-Prussian war retribution: 'The French have sunk a German ironclad . . .' Perhaps she steered herself away from that, too, because in print it became the French sinking the Americans.

Whole sections covered how to express shades of feeling, needs, evaluation. This was totally new in New Zealand Maori publishing. Parts of it must surely have been utopian at the time, but if that was the way she envisaged a bicultural society of New Zealand, it must have come from a solid core of respect which she only occasionally coated with mission-language references to 'the poor Maoris'.[68] Several sections reveal the woman. The fun that people spoke of comes through. Playing – ball, football, top, whip, swing, marbles, kite, doll, cricket, to play, to slide – takes up a good part of the section 'On Education'. Horse-racing, an area where Pakeha and Maori interacted from early on, starts off 'On Plays and Amusements': 'You shall ride on my horse : Tera koe e haere i runga i taku hoiho. They are racing : E oma whakataetae ratiu. Do not waste your money : Kaua e maumauria ou moni'. But the twenty-five entries in this section are mainly for children: 'Come and play with us : Haere mai ki te takaro i a matou. Hullo, children, are you romping about? : E tamariki ma, kei te toa koutou?'

The book had less the language of the traditional culture than the neologisms or borrowings of European influence – the Maori equivalents of 'coffee pot', 'bananas', 'lemonade'. It was the language of contact; that was the kind of woman Suzanne was. She did not flinch from including a few remarks on the contemporary drinking problems of Maori, remarks which now seem judgemental. Yet when the book came out again, under the Maori editorship of Apirana Ngata, those sentences remained exactly as they were.

In 1894 Whitcombe and Tombs bought out Lyon and Blair.[69] In 1901 a second edition was printed with the title *Complete Manual of Maori Conversation and Grammar, with Vocabulary*. Suzanne knew nothing about this.[70] The initials of her name as author had disappeared and 'A. T. Ngata, M.A., LL.B. (Barrister-at-Law)' was acknowledged as editor.

Ngata had probably been approached to prepare another edition. In his student years in the 1890s, Ngata, with Reweti Morgan, had been working on Maori education and health, in close association with James Pope of the Department of Education. They were also helping distribute around Maori settlements copies of Pope's book *The Health of the Maori* or *Te Ora mo te Maori*.[71] Pope was Inspector for Native Schools for twenty-four years from 1880. He was improving the materials sent to schools, which included English periodicals passed on to Maori adults after being used in class.[72] These could lie behind Suzanne's section giving phrases on international politics. She had sent Pope a copy of her work in 1885. He had written back in October that it would be 'an extremely useful book' and that he would return 'the marked proofs'.[73] Could he have referred Ngata fifteen years later to Whitcombe and Tombs? Some time between 1894 and 1901 someone rode roughshod over the discreetly identified S.A. If it was Pope, it seems out of character.[74] And the book did not go on the government-provided Native Schools booklist.[75]

Ngata certainly enlarged and improved the grammar section. In her introduction, Suzanne made it clear that she was giving only a 'few general rules of grammar', almost as an afterthought. She did acknowledge Leonard Williams's book in this section. Whitcombe and Tombs must have had educational sales in mind, because the grammar section was greatly enlarged. Ngata supplied more detail, gave examples and elaborated on difficult points.[76] For instance, she had not mentioned that Maori adjectives come after the noun – as a French speaker, this system came naturally to her. Ngata explained it. He then wrote a much briefer introduction, and the new edition was launched. The main body of text was a straight reprint of her work, without acknowledgement.

Her book, with Ngata's mana as a worthwhile 'imprimatur', sold thousands of copies. It was reprinted again and again, with just a few editorial revisions. A 1948 letter from Whitcombe and Tombs stated that it took all their time to keep it in print, and it was reprinting again right then.[77] It seems to have been used extensively up to this time in the denominational schools like Te Aute and St Stephen's which educated generations of Maori.[78] It helped Maori to learn English; it helped Maori to learn written Maori; it helped English to learn Maori. 'Quaint' as it now seems in many parts, it is still in print[79] and may have helped Maori to learn Maori. Modern opinion is that it was multi-purpose: 'Aubert's contribution was to provide a useable source of colloquial, idiomatic Maori for those learning Maori and to a certain extent for those learning English [her original dual intention], not as the main learning tool but as something to extend it. Many people, of course, used the book to give them enough to work on then went out to use it, not worrying about any formal learning.'[80]

But the publishing history of her book is also an example of the rewriting of history. Although Ngata did not claim to have written the text, by the 1964 edition the original concept was firmly described as Ngata's: 'The book was originally prepared under the guidance of the late Sir Apirana Ngata, the notable Maori scholar, who edited the text.' Bibliographies, however, assign it to Suzanne Aubert. The Maori of this book has always been regarded as good.[81]

In 1906 William Bird, the inspector then in charge of Maori education, confirmed his apparently separatist opinion that the department was 'educating Maori boys and girls for the Maori people only and not to mingle with Europeans and compete with Europeans in trade and commerce'.[82] In the Aubert–Ngata book people are definitely mingling. As for competition in trade and commerce, Suzanne had sections on farming, fishing, market and trade. In 'On New Zealand' she gave a long extract from a newspaper report detailing all the produce Maori were selling in Auckland at the time of their commercial triumph in the 1850s. But competition was not the overriding theme. Her section 'On work' has 'If we work together we can succeed : Mehemea ka mahi tahi taua tera ano e taea.'[83]

CHAPTER TEN

Hiruharama – the church
1885-1889

How happy I am : Katahi te hari o toku ngakau[1]

Eighteen eighty-five must have been one of the happiest years in Suzanne's life. The sisters always said these first few years on the Whanganui were a period of great happiness for them.[2] For her it had nothing to do with the publication of the *Manual* and everything to do with her feet firmly treading once more the path of religious life – living with, even leading, a group of hard-working and pleasant young women in a thriving mission station. There was lots of tramping around, horse-riding and doctoring to satisfy her, and soul-inspiring religious interest coming from the marae.

Alfred Burton, the photographer, came to Jerusalem in May 1885. The spirituality in the area struck him: 'The religious zeal of the people is a fact that came under our notice, for in several of the villages where we "put up" the bell regularly summoned them to morning and evening prayers, conducted by one of themselves.'[3] Hiruharama catechists at this time included Materoa and Reone; down at Ranana was Neri Metera. Burton was impressed with 'the perfect beat kept by everyone in the congregation, and the musical cadence in the responses'. The sisters went down to the whare runanga in the evenings to join in prayers – the rosary, hymns and the 'Sub Tuum'.

Burton and his travelling companion, Edward Payton, stayed two nights in the presbytery. Both were impressed with Suzanne's medical expertise when Burton sprained a leg trying to get a particular camera angle. Payton said she was 'a very accomplished physician', while Burton used an older term for doctor: 'Sister Mary Joseph at once exercised her widely-known skill as a leech.' They both enjoyed another of her skills, story-telling. 'Sister Mary Joseph is most un-nunlike, being very chatty, and in every way a most kind and sensible "sister superior". She told us of all her experiences on first coming to New Zealand', especially how her 'half-caste' pupils helped her learn English and 'taught her all the slang and bad language they could'.[4] Suzanne's friendly face, quick laughter and unaffected conversation come out, fresh and alive, from their writing.

Every morning, in the early light, Suzanne was out in her garden between morning prayers and Mass. If the weather was bad, she wore a waterproof cape, lined with the ever-useful red flannel. She imported seeds from France and grew a wide variety of vegetables, including *topinambours*, or Jerusalem artichokes, which figure in many of her recipes. The young novices were energetic and keen, with a sane dose of settler irreverence. One time, one of them swooped short little Suzanne into the washing basket with the bundle fresh from the line. Another time, on a day of snow which had its own novelty, she copped a snowball as she walked by; she shot one back. Later, in the hectic Wellington years, the sisters looked back a bit wistfully to this time.

In February 1885, Bishop Redwood wrote to her: 'Your photo in your religious habit came to me today . . . How well it suits you, you look quite rejuvenated. May you live to see many good New Zealand girls dressed in that habit.'[5] In 1885 there were six sisters. Suzanne was head of a new household, building up a home. Their lifestyle was sparsely simple. They drank kopuka 'tea', tawa berry 'coffee' and akitea 'cocoa'. She was often writing down handy household hints. Their boots, soaked and glued by the Whanganui mud, had to be dealt with all the time. After washing them, you could blacken them again with iron acetate from 'soaking old nails or other old iron in beer', or else use beaten egg with the last application blackened with soot. You then softened them with turpentine and waterproofed them with yet another recipe which combined tallow, lard, new beeswax and olive oil dissolved together over the fire. All ready to head down the bush tracks again. They needed comfortable boots. Over the years, Sister Anne lived with the Metera family in Ranana during the week, while she taught at the school. She used to walk up to Hiruharama every weekend. She had to cross the Mangoihe creek by stepping along a wire, holding a higher wire for support.

Payton wrote about the 'small Catholic nunnery, where some half-dozen nuns are taught the Maori language and customs before being sent in to the world on their holy mission'. Every religious congregation has its Constitutions. The first manuscript draft of the Constitutions up at

Hiruharama stated: 'The Sisters are instituted exclusively firstly to work in the Maori mission, secondly for poor European villages where there are no means of having other Sisters.' So intense was this mission aim for Suzanne that she overlooked, or may not have initially known, that the first aim in canon law has to be one's personal salvation. Above all, she and Soulas were setting up an active congregation, active also in the sense of going out beyond the convent. She even wrote instructions to be sociable into the Constitutions: 'When [the sisters] go through the pa they will stop and say a few words to the Maoris they meet.'[6]

There was to be no division into choir and lay sisters as in many other orders. They all lived and worked on the same level. This was how it was with the Sisters of St Charles back in Lyon, also with Mary MacKillop's sisters in Australia. There was to be no item of luxury in the convent – no carpet, for instance. 'Cleanliness and simplicity must be the sole adornment.' But Suzanne had a writer's pen and kept adding, describing, animating, making a large, chatty document out of the draft Constitutions whereas these would normally be written in sparer, more ecclesiastical language. It might be the bare minimum but in her pages she set up a home: 'The tables can be covered with oil cloth, the windows can have little curtains and blinds, the doors can be provided with a bootscraper outside and a doormat inside.'[7] Clogs were kept behind the door. The mud was always a problem.

Because of the damage to her system from the ammonia accident in 1866, Suzanne had a very plain diet. She also had the streak of asceticism that ran through the Curé d'Ars, Father Séon and her brother Camille. The sisters would never be pampered. 'They will eat neither sweets nor pastry delicacies nor custards or fancy puddings, these things being good only for pandering to one's sense of taste at the expense of religious restraint.' But she added as usual a positive note: 'However, they can have from time to time *scorns* or *buns* with their cup of tea.'[8]

At Meanee in the 1870s, neighbour Mary Brandon – whose children watched to see Suzanne's red flannel petticoat whisk through the fence wires near their house on her herb-gathering expeditions – would see her returning and had 'tea and hot scones ready for her'. For this Suzanne 'was very grateful, because it was often very cold in the early mornings'.[9] Later, in spite of the stark lifestyle the Sisters of Compassion were known to have, she sometimes said that New Zealanders did not have the same spirit of penance she had known in Europe. But she knew how to work to the strengths of people and when to ease up.

So the sisters went out and about, in their little capes in the cold weather, carrying an umbrella if need be – for Suzanne such an essential item that she wrote it into the Constitutions – and a bag, sometimes a kete, with their scissors, pocket knife and handwork. As with all congregations, their day was mapped out for them. They were to get up at five o'clock. This would become earlier still, at twenty to five, probably after the orphans and babies came. Two hours in those days were set aside for learning Maori, science and medicine. Just as she made allowances for Pakeha scones, Suzanne also knew when to be flexible to meet Maori culture. The sisters always went to Maori prayers in the evening. 'Since Maori prayers can often run on into tea time and recreation, these will be variable to fit in with Maori prayer time.'[10] Finally, after a long day in the school, in the pa or on the move, at a set half-past nine the 'candles will be blown out and the Sisters in bed'.[11] The night would be very dark and very quiet at Hiruharama, though there could be a morepork, or a dog or two disturbed down at the pa.

The Maori mission was growing apace. Young priests were starting to come again from France, partly as a result of internal church–state tension, partly from the years of publicity and pressure from Suzanne, Redwood and Soulas. Father Melu had arrived in March 1884, Father Leprêtre next in March 1885, and Father Cognet in January 1886. Each one arrived eager, ready for the adventure of the river and the bush, all set to learn Maori.

The work was expanding. With Soulas, and sometimes on their own, they were going further up the river, to the Raetihi area, south around Turakina, further down the coast to revive the old mission area of Otaki, across into the Wairarapa, back to Pakipaki and Wairoa to keep Catholicism alive there, west into Taranaki to Okato and elsewhere. Horses, bush, risky river crossings and long hui discussions into the night with Raumati and other Maori prophets filled out their letters. In fact, they did not stay long at Hiruharama but went in turn to the new mission stations being opened or reopened. As time went by, after the first flush of pleasure at their arrival, they tended to find it better for themselves, as well as for the expansion of the mission, to move out. Soulas was not at all easy to live with.

Claude Cognet was perhaps the most enthusiastic and also the most naive. His letters spoke in superlatives. Soulas, with men from Ngati Hau, was waiting for him at Wanganui, to take him up the river on the canoe trip that never failed to impress every new traveller. Sister Mary Joseph was down there too, he wrote, 'the most illustrious of the missionaries of New Zealand'.[12] Everything he saw he touched with optimism. Cognet, now Pa Koneta, wrote to his family in May 1886 how happy he was: God was treating him like a 'spoiled child'.[13] He was in charge of the mission while Soulas and Leprêtre were away and Sister Mary Joseph was helping him with his Maori. He too came from Lyon, and his square face and frame resembled her brother's a little. They both had positive personalities, and both peopled their letters with names and happenings.

Later in the year, about September, Soulas sent Cognet to live in Ranana, which still had Protestant connections then and was under the strong influence of Te Rangihiwinui, also known as Te Keepa or Major Kemp.[14] But there, 'with this good people where I count only friends', Cognet lived in the house of Neri Metera, in a room 'alike in all ways to a European hotel room'. Even the rains continuing heavily through spring did not dampen Cognet. 'After a month of almost constant rain', he wrote back home, 'we are entering a summer which promises a magnificent harvest. The climate of New Zealand is one of the finest in the world. Plague, cholera, pox, rabies and the great many other ugly diseases have not appeared yet on these shores. Protestantism is the only serious disease.'[15] He conceded that even this was not life-threatening. 'Nobody molests us and we are completely free to go where and do what we wish.'[16]

Once, lost in the dark on a new track from Murimotu to Pipiriki, his horse rightly baulked on the edge of a sheer drop above Mangoihe. The ridge dropped away on either side as well. Cognet knew that some Maori were camping out nearby: 'I grabbed my whistle and like Roland at Roncevaux, I sent my desperate call, praying to the Holy Virgin to carry the cry of her child to its destination.' The voice of Tamakehu, the catechist he knew well, came up the hill: 'Stay right where you are or else you've had it. I'll show you the way.' A light came, showed the steep zigzag descent and a trembling Cognet was welcomed by Tamakehu and Reweti at the Maori camp up on the other side. They took care of him with fire, food, hot tea, a quickly erected bivouac with fern bed, and lots of cheerful talk to take his mind off the 'awful nightmare': 'I spent a wonderful night.'[17] The sisters, Suzanne especially, also rode in this wild country.

In January 1886, Redwood 'appointed Sister Mary Joseph Aubert Superior of the Third Order Regular of Mary in New Zealand for three years, subject to a further appointment by election with the Bishop's approval'.[18] First she had to make her three vows, and could not really be superior until a year after this. She insisted on one condition: she was never to be sent out of New Zealand, as she had made a vow long before to consecrate herself to the Maori and never return to France. Redwood agreed. It was wise for her to stipulate this, as the larger congregation was French and had active missions in the Pacific Islands. It was not impossible, though a little unlikely, for her to be shifted around. Once Redwood accepted this condition, nothing would have stopped her from going ahead. On 23 January 1886 she made her three vows of poverty, chastity and obedience.

Cognet arrived the same month. With him on the ship was Sister Marie du Saint Sacrement. She was French, of course, and had been sent out after Soulas and Redwood had asked for a professed sister as a novice mistress for the growing congregation. Redwood had written to the vicar general of the Marists that 'some French Sisters are needed to inspire these colonial girls, who are by nature self-centred and lack the spirit of sacrifice, along with apostolic zeal and the spirit of devotion and self-abnegation. Give us the spark, and we will set alight the sacred fire here.'[19] Presumably he was flattering French pride to gain his staff. Or did he, a New Zealander himself, never have scones with his tea?

But he redeemed himself, from a New Zealand if not a French perspective, by asking also not for simple peasant girls to be sent but women with some cultivation, that 'veneer without which the Tertiaries would be despised by an aristocratic people as New Zealanders are. Who out of the young Colonial women would want to join an order which does not have a certain tone and a certain profile? Recruiting and the future depend on the fortunate impression which will be created at the outset.'[20] A calling to religious life would always be on its spiritual merits, but this concern about creating a 'fortunate impression' to attract young women to the new congregation was partly why Suzanne turned a blind eye from time to time when her French credentials acquired a fresh 'veneer'.

Marie du Saint Sacrement had been hoping to join other French women working in the Pacific Islands. Suddenly she had been asked to go to a chilly, remote, bush-clad valley in an English-speaking country, to form women for religious life. Soulas had tried to make the mission French-speaking, and wanted the novices to learn to speak French. Sister Carmel partly succeeded, but learning Maori was their priority. The idea of speaking French was dropped when no more sisters came from France and New Zealanders were all around. The multilingual Suzanne would have been the obvious choice for novice mistress, but she was decidedly the superior. She was never very good at delegating, and the newly arrived Sister Marie du Saint Sacrement may have felt hampered. She was also lonely.[21] When Father Joly, the Marist Visitor, came to Hiruharama, he took her away with him, and she went to work in the Island missions as planned.

This left the new congregation without a novice mistress. Soulas tended to step in and fulfil much of this function. The sisters stoically accepted him but were never as happy when Suzanne was not there. Soulas, like Pompallier before him, could not overcome his need to be all things everywhere. He could not easily delegate, either, and was quick to become suspicious; in spite of his energy, planning and single-minded championing of the Maori mission, he kept on putting its smooth running in jeopardy by his thin-skinned reactions. Redwood's letters were polite, supportive of the mission, but increasingly curt. Other priests, in their Pakeha parishes, shrugged their shoulders at Soulas's tenseness and tantrums. The danger was that any disengagement or disapproval would reflect badly on the Maori mission in general, and that Suzanne would come under the same cloud that was growing above Soulas in diocesan and Marist circles. Father Joly's report of August 1886 foreshadowed this. He praised the Hiruharama mission but there was a faint coolness as he removed Sister Marie du Saint Sacrement.

Soulas was a man of many projects. One he now launched with zest was the promoting of Sister Mary Joseph Aubert. As always, he recognised the calibre of the person he was working with. So had Father Reignier, so had Poupinel, so had Redwood. But they saw her as 'a good, devout, hard-working woman', the invaluable aide, the *bonne soeur*. Soulas saw something else: a powerful leader, an achiever, one who, in both religion and management, could stride along skylines. He pushed her to meet her potential – which she did, eventually going across the horizon, far beyond him. But there was always the risk that, as her strong-stemmed poppy began to grow above others in the field, the priests irritated by Soulas might flail at her as well. Being associated with Soulas, with his difficult personality, could compound her indiscretion of being an achieving woman.

Already, in April 1885, Soulas had sung her praises to a colleague in

France, and the letter had been published in the Marist Annals.[22] Then, in June 1885, he wrote a long letter of thanks to a society of *dames* who had sent him a gift, perhaps money, perhaps vessels or vestments for the new church being built. He needed still more money for churches and a new convent. He painted for them the inadequacy of having the schoolhouse doubling as a convent. The low roof meant the little beds upstairs were almost at floor level; the wind whistled through the rafters.

He backgrounded all that Mother Mary Joseph, their 'sister, Mademoiselle Suzanne Aubert, of Lyon', had done for Maori Catholicism in New Zealand. She had been the 'one and only missionary to the Maori' for so many years. Her nursing, her high reputation among the chiefs, her baptising of the children, her travelling were all included. 'My letter would have to be as big as a book to be able to tell all the aspects of heroism which won for Mother Mary Joseph the admiration and confidence of everyone.' Soulas described the distress among the Hawke's Bay settlers, Protestant and Catholic, at her departure, how she had left to help him found a school in the middle of impenetrable mountains and forest, how she was 'the real mainspring of that enterprise'. He continued the story of how she had agreed to help the Sisters of St Joseph even when it was thought she was dying.

Then, with a sudden Soulas leap out of the prosaic, he pitched head-long, this time not into vituperation, but into the whirlpool of myth-making:

> How beautiful in the eyes of the angels must be this humble Sister, who made herself so small, in spite of her family and her extraordinary knowledge. She, who could speak six living languages, who had been sought after in the highest society, who enjoyed such a high reputation, who had refused the charge of a hospital with the position of resident doctor, made herself the servant of two poor Sisters, who were a thousand feet beneath her in every way, and yet did not seem to have any idea of the greatness there was in an act which involved such abandonment of self. If this is not heroism, then the word should be removed from the dictionary.[23]

Soulas had a personal and mission agenda to advertise and it was good publicity material. But Suzanne, who was obviously already chatting her way into slightly inflated credentials, dropping pebbles into ponds, needed to take care. This could get people's backs up.

Soulas did not stop at heroism. He hinted at sanctity. In 1887 he more than hinted at it in a twenty-three-page letter he wrote to the Marist superior general all about the Maori mission. 'It goes without saying that anything concerning Mother M. Joseph must be kept secret until her death. It's only for your sake, as you are the Father of the Society to which she belongs, and also in order not to lose memories which are so edifying, in case I die before she does, that I'm writing you these lines about her. Keep them carefully, because one day perhaps the Church will ask you to have such an extraordinary life written.' He was obsessed with death, anyway, going so far as ordering coffin timbers to have ready at Jerusalem in case he or any of the sisters should die. Such a preoccupation ran through Breton Catholicism and was personified in their 'grim reaper' figure, the *ankou*.[24] In the fastnesses of the Whanganui, Soulas often fell victim to morbid anxieties.

He proceeded to pass on the stories she must have told him: the predictions of the Curé d'Ars; how Antoine Pompallier was also at Ars in 1858; how the death of the curé gave her the cover to disguise her departure; how a woman possessed by the devil had predicted her long voyage; how four years before they went upriver she had described a dream to him in which she clearly saw the schoolhouse at Hiruharama in every detail; how a Maori prophet from Taupo had come to her in a vision. On his twenty-second page, he began to draw his conclusions:

> It was Sister Mary Joseph who made the Bishop open his eyes and see how a priest was needed for the Maoris and who got His Grace to promise that he would write to the Society to ask for a missionary. Without the precious help of this dear Sister, I would never have succeeded. I would probably have died and the Maoris would never have had any priests. And if I hadn't succeeded, the Bishop of Auckland would never have felt obliged to do something for the Maoris in his diocese. So Sister Mary Joseph has certainly been the cause of the revival of the mission to the Maoris and of all the good which will be done in the future. . . .
>
> Keep these scribbled notes as one day they could be useful. I'm not in too much of a hurry to canonize people who are still alive but I can't help admiring what is admirable. I have never come across anyone who represents for me the idea of a saint as much as Sister Mary Joseph.[25]

It was the double bind of Catholicism, combining the requirement of absolute humility with the goal of sanctity which was held out to everyone as recognition of excellence. And, just as in secular life, the goal of accomplishment and 'coming first' could be pushed and punished at the same time. Such paeans of praise made Suzanne vulnerable. Life could get a little intense up there at Hiruharama with Breton *ankou* or Maori taipo haunting the night and coffin timbers drying in wait for sainthood.

Oh! how beautiful it is! : Koia ano te pai![26]

In 1885 Ngati Hau, with Soulas, Father Melu and then Father Leprêtre, Suzanne and the novices, built a beautiful church on an equally beautiful site. To any traveller rounding the bend in the river just below Hiruharama it would be the instant focal point of the panorama unfurled. The swirl of the river across the base of the canvas was matched by the curves of the hills overlapping one another against the sky. The houses spaced themselves out in groups above the river, just below the central knoll where the clean-lined spire of the simple church went skyward. The picture had the intensity of focus of an Italian painting of the crucifixion with the cluster of figures at the foot of the cross. It was a very soul-satisfying scene for any missioner.

The land right at Hiruharama had been cleared of virgin bush for some time. Both contemporary letters and the 'Reminiscences' tell how Ngati Hau families, men, women and children, camped a few miles away in the bush and worked for three months with Soulas, felling trees, pit-sawing them and hauling the sawn boards to the site. The women carried the shingles in sacks on their backs. The people donated the price of their woolclip to buy dressed timber and building materials in Wanganui and transported them upriver, load after load, by waka. People from the other kainga on the river, Protestant as well, lent canoes and manpower for the job. The sisters helped carry the piles up from the river to where the foundations were marked out. In her 'Aide-mémoire', Suzanne noted: '10 April 1885. The Sisters dig the holes for the foundations. Father Soulas sets the first pile in place.' In fact, Suzanne said that she had turned the first sod; the sisters did dig the holes, but not to the full depth. The local men finished them and proceeded with Soulas and the Wanganui firm of Barnett, Battle and Hackett to build their church.

It was designed by Thomas Turnbull, Wellington's foremost architect at the time.[27] An illusion of stained glass came from transfers which Suzanne had ordered from France and Sister Anne applied to the windows. The women worked 'early and late' to cross-stitch an intricate carpet from patterns and wool again ordered from France. Blue and beige framed a mass of crimson roses. And there was a harmonium, of course. There is no mention of a building fund in the diocesan records. In fact, a letter from Redwood suggests strongly that Soulas did not wait for diocesan approval before building. The costs were met partly by Ngati

Hau, by possible donations from France and, it is believed, by Suzanne herself. Certainly billed to her account in France were cannon balls used by Ngati Hau in the opening celebrations.[28] They called it the Church of St Joseph, Hiruharama. No saint could have been better chosen as patron. He brought together the bush-clad, tree-sawing and timber-building frontier of men, Pakeha and Maori, and the growing world of settled families. Meri would have been trotting out the Hohepa in her name.

There were going to be no half-measures for this opening. The bishop with his mitre and crozier would be present to bless the church at Christmas, 1885. Suzanne wrote eleven foolscap pages describing the festivities. Between five and six hundred people came. There had been a panic: on 19 December word had come through that Redwood might not make it. After all, Christmas was a major church event in Wellington as well. Ngati Hau were 'indignant and griefstricken'. Soulas shot down the river to 'obtain the presence' of His Lordship. At half past three on the morning of 24 December rifle shots and the pealing church bell announced the arrival of Redwood, Sauzeau, Soulas, Melu and canoemen – weary, as the *Yeoman* put it, from 'not making any stoppages by the way but journeying all night' to get there in time. The sleepers scrambled out of their dreams and went down to the river. Some created an instant arch of greenery, others covered the dust of the track with branches of leaves, others reloaded their rifles for the welcoming volleys. Soulas and the catechists in their ceremonial cloaks greeted Redwood, and the old chief Poutini gave the speech of welcome. Young people sang and performed dances.

Redwood, tall, handsome, fit, eloquent and still only in his mid-forties, did not let them down. Everything went perfectly. Suzanne described the preparation for the hangi. About eighty people received communion at Mass the next morning, Christmas Day, the day of the opening. At nine o'clock Redwood blessed the church, celebrated Mass and ceremonially gave the sisters their new habit. This was his seal on the foundation of the Third Order Regular of Mary in New Zealand. Suzanne mentioned how Françoise Perroton of Lyon had sown the seeds of this congregation so long ago, in 1845.

At the back of the big marquee was a long table, decorated with greenery and 'cracking under the weight of the food', for the bishop, clergy and sisters. The local people and their other guests ate, in five successive sittings to cope with the numbers, at two long mats occupying the rest of the tent. Suzanne listed what she called a 'banquet worthy of Gargantua', which included six thousand birds preserved in fat and one thousand loaves of bread. She added that the magnificent feast was going to cost them at least six months of deprivation and want, but it was important culturally for them, they wanted it, and were pleased with its success. They had prepared everything themselves. She had to describe for her French readers the unfamiliar five-tiered combined Christmas and 'christening cake' for the church. All iced, it rose three feet high – Redwood's version said five feet – in five layers. It was decorated with frilly paper and topped with a cross of red flowers. 'On the first layer was outlined in bold sugary letters the inscription "Wanganui 1885", on the second "Kirihimete 25" (Christmas 25). On the third "Hiruharama" (Jerusalem) and finally on the fourth "Ranana" (London), the name of the place where it had been cooked. It would have done a first-class Paris pastrycook proud.'[29]

Poutini spoke, Redwood replied, and the Protestant chief from Ranana, standing to the left of Poutini, gave, as Suzanne put it, 'three hipi! hipi! hipi! hurrah!' From Hawke's Bay had come Raniera, the catechist who had sustained Catholicism during the years without a priest. He also spoke.[30] Vespers were sung in Maori, then the Benediction in Latin, followed by confirmations, marriages and baptisms. In the evening everyone joined in the Maori prayers and the rosary. Zeal, as well as appetite, was replete. In the farewell speeches the next day, the oratory of Hoani Takarangi Metekingi stood out. Then the ceremonies ended with Ngati Hau distributing to all their departing guests gifts of money, food and livestock, all of which Suzanne described, down to the pigs grunting as they were dragged by the hind legs from their mud-holes. 'Nobody was forgotten and everyone went away joyful and contented.' Before leaving, Mr Battle proudly took a photograph of the church he had helped build.

I shall perform the journey on foot : E haere a waewae ahau
These are good boots : He putu pai ano enei[31]

Less than three years later, on 20 November 1888, the church was a heap of ashes – torched in the middle of the afternoon while most of Hiruharama was over the other side of the river shearing. Soulas and all the sisters except two were away, up at the recently bought farm. Everything went up in the November wind – church, vestments, vessels, harmonium. Even the presbytery was alight but people, seeing the blaze, had crossed the river in time to save it. Sister Anne and Sister Helen received burns getting furniture and other items out of the presbytery. The people planted a felled bluegum on the charred knoll and draped it with black crepe. Mourners came from Kauaeroa, Ranana, Pipiriki and all around for a tangi.

There were planned bush fires and accidental blazes all over New Zealand through the 1880s.[32] The *Wanganui Chronicle* even used the image in regular advertising: 'Another large fire, and one which it will take the combined efforts of all the other bootmakers to quench, is now raging at R. Hannah and Co.'s. They are firing their cheap boots and shoes all over the district . . .' But the burning of St Joseph's, Hiruharama, was apparently the first arson attack on a New Zealand church. There had been quarrelling, with racist undertones, between Ngati Hau men working on a contract for bush-felling and one Jimmy McDonald, who was perhaps the camp cook. As the newspaper put it, the 'fire is supposed to have been the work of an incendiary, and a white man has been arrested, on a warrant, on suspicion. Constable Bell proceeded yesterday to the village in a canoe to make inquiries.'

On 21 December McDonald was brought before the resident magistrate at Wanganui, 'on remand, charged with having set fire to the Catholic Church at Jerusalem. Several witnesses were examined for the prosecution . . . His Worship said that in his opinion there was not sufficient evidence to send the case before a jury and he would dismiss the information. In his opinion, the police were thoroughly justified in the action they had taken, as there was strong evidence against the accused. McDonnell [McDonald] was then discharged.'[33]

The story has it that no Maori was called on for evidence. So the Hiruharama people took it upon themselves to assess the whole affair. They had a tradition of discussion and independent appraisal.[34] A couple of years before, in 1886, the Marist Visitor, Father Joly, had been unsettled to find such a judicial air. He had expected gifts and monetary contributions as well as welcoming speeches, and was surprised to get only speeches. He compared Ngati Hau unfavourably with the natives of the Society of Mary's Pacific missions. In his speech to Ngati Hau he spoke of the interest that the superiors and His Holiness the Pope had in them. A speaker rose to thank him but added that he would have a much better understanding of this interest if either the superiors or the Pope – or both – were to send out some money. Joly expected someone to

protest at 'such impertinence' but nobody did.[35] Someone should have
done Joly's homework for him. Ngati Hau at that time were crippled
financially, along with many other Maori, by the costs of attending Land
Court hearings and defending claims.[36] They had just spent perhaps all
they had on the building and consecrating of the church for the Marist
mission, as Suzanne had made clear. Now, in 1889, both at the tangi over
the fire and when the arson charge was dismissed, they made their
judgement. Materoa said: 'The Pakeha burned it down. Let the Pakeha
build another.'[37]

Suzanne had already left to start collecting for another. She was almost
a month on the road by the time the charge was dismissed. Soulas had
been devastated, and in his initial newspaper report pointed out that the
church was insured for only half its worth. In 1887 he had already been
writing about their hopes of collecting money to build a convent and now,
with the emotional pull of the fire, a collecting tour could cover both.
Father Garin's Nelson church had been accidentally burnt in 1881 and
people had contributed generously.[38] Soulas had Suzanne on the road
within four days of the fire, but she would already have been waterproof-
ing her boots in readiness. On 1 December 1888, the *Yeoman* started off
the appeal:

> The loss sustained by the Roman Catholic Up-river Mission has been very con-
> siderable, and in order to raise funds to relieve them to some extent, Sister
> Mary Josephine is now in town soliciting subscriptions. As to the work carried
> on by this lady and her small band of assistants we can bear testimony. Among
> the natives their labours have been productive of much good, and we trust that
> all creeds without distinction will assist them in their labour of love by giving
> something to help them rebuild their church and so encourage them in the
> good work they have undertaken.

The obvious place to go was Hawke's Bay, where her last memories
were the warm farewell, the chalice and a red velvet purse of £60. She
went down the river by canoe, on to Wellington by train for diocesan
permission to collect, and up to Napier. Did Suzanne breathe a little sigh
of relief to be independent and on the road again? She had done some
travelling back and forth when Ngati Hau were based at Wanganui for
Land Court hearings, and when she was organising the printing of her
Maori phrase-book. But she had just spent five and a half years being
responsible for a fledgling community of young women, supervised
closely by overly keen Father Soulas. This was probably the most

constraint on her movements and independence since the mid-1860s. In a sense she was 'going home' to revisit her friendly lay Hawke's Bay past.

She was not alone. With the short, square-framed, fifty-four-year-old, firm-walking Suzanne was Sister Magdalen, born Violet Savage on the West Coast. She was still young, serious, taller and willowy. She was a true New Zealander, with no French accent, but she looked good in the French-style habit and goffered cap. Recruiting was always on the agenda, and she made a fitting advertisement for prospective postulants.

Father Patterson gave them a warm welcome in Palmerston North, then sent them and their 'portman' on through the gorge and up into Hawke's Bay. In their portmanteau were the publicity leaflets and printed lists for their collecting – and clean caps. Suzanne was always fussy about the caps and spent many gale-whipped days meticulously goffering the frills. Suzanne noted each day's activities in a tiny diary. '5th Dec: . . . we were well received at Pakipaki. Slept at Moroney's.' This may have been the time Mrs Moroney of the boarding-house at Pakipaki answered the door to a nun dressed all in grey, then it dawned on her that this was in fact a dark habit dredged in grey dust. It was Suzanne. She also spent Christmas at Pakipaki, meeting up with familiar people. But she was not wasting time merely socialising: 'Sunday, 13th January, 1889: Spent today quietly. Visit a few friends so as to get the talk over not to encroach on work days.'

She expected to collect easily in familiar territory. But things had changed. For one, Father Reignier had just died, in October 1888. '6th Dec. Went to Meanee, visited F. Reignier's grave'. Hawke's Bay was in the grip of depression, it was right on Christmas, with other calls on people's wallets, and, as she admitted later, 'Nobody was interested in the Maoris.' Reality was embarrassing to the former indispensable 'sister'. She gathered in only £267 12s, even from visits to the wealthy squattocracy. Around Napier and Hastings she was feeling slightly dejected. 'Tuesday, 15th January, 1889: Visit offices, do very little. . . . Friday, 18th January, 1889: Go through town. Raining. Go up convent. Mend. Saturday, 19th January, 1889: Go to Shamrock. Do nothing. Go to Meanee.' She was writing in English in this diary and there was confusion with French. The 'do very little' and 'do nothing' really meant the financial result of the day: 'make very little', 'make nothing'.

It was on this collecting tour, however, that Suzanne Aubert really went public for the first time. And the stories about her en route began to gather. The Shamrock was one of many hotels she visited and she said she was usually treated with courtesy. But at one Napier hotel some people were watching her as she asked men to contribute. They passed the story down their family: 'Three of them did so, and the fourth one spat in her face. She simply wiped her face and said, "Thank you, you have given me something for myself." By this time one of the others had knocked him down.'[39] What she meant in her reply was that the money was going to Jesus and the spit she kept for herself.

Begging was new and difficult for her then, but later on in Wellington it became a daily part of the work of her order, the Sisters of Compassion, with their begging prams almost an icon. New sisters found it gruelling to have to go through the streets and into hotels. So in the *Directory*, their training manual, Suzanne wrote a section on 'Begging'. The analogies were tightly linked to the figure of Jesus: 'If we meet rebuffs, He met them first, and still meets them. If we are insulted and refused, He was so first, and is so yet.' She taught them to respond in the same way as she had.[40]

She did not get rebuffs from only the odd down-and-out. When she lived in Hawke's Bay, she had had a free pass for the private railway which she used to take to Pakipaki. Now, in 1889, she tried for another: 'Monday, 28th January, 1889. Visit Ormond. Ask railway pass. Told might as well go to the moon.' J. D. Ormond, Member of the House of Representatives, was known to be irritable. He may not have been at liberty just then to give passes, though Wellington City Council later gave her free passes on the trams, and so did Hatrick's on the Whanganui river-boats. But she needed to give Ormond the chance. The theme of the opportunity for redemption that the rich and powerful had through giving was important in her religion. Giving was not just passing across money; she was also 'challenging them to look into their inner depth as human beings'.[41]

The two women set out to walk around the sheep stations and, even though the immediate revenues were not great, the results down the years were important. On this collecting tour Suzanne dusted off all the public relations skills she had enjoyed trying out in Auckland in the late 1860s. Not only did some of the families of the Hawke's Bay squatter hierarchy become benefactors – for example, the Anglican Nairn family, who earned a mention in the diary: 'We received the best and kind reception' – but through their wider kinship groups down in Wellington she started to build up an infrastructure of financial, legal and political influence and advice. The Johnston family, for instance, would figure in her story from then on. Their extended family included Graces, Rollestons, Percevals, Hislops, all of whom linked into the 'charitable scene'. Some of her later popularity among the gentry and their town cousins was earned on foot on her collecting tour, even if those who responded to later appeals for the poor were, in 1889, less interested in the Maori mission.

They covered a wide circuit of sheepruns. Diary entries named runs and runholders: Chambers, Nelson, McCarthy, Tiffen, Coleman, Donnelly, Broughton, Lowry, Maraekakaho, Walker, Whitmore, Thomas, Poukawa, Hamlin, Buchanan, Johnston (of Tamumu), Nairn, Hunter, Crosse, Ormond, Harding, Herbert. The list was a who's who of Hawke's Bay. It was a long, dusty route that she and Sister Magdalen took, sometimes by cart but often on foot. Suzanne sometimes strode ahead and a 'footsore' sister trailed a bit behind.[42]

> Wednesday, 13th February, 1889: We walked from Nairn to Hunters, round Blackhead. We had a fearful storm of wind and rain. We lost our way, paddled in the mud across the bullocks. We met Revd Simcock at Hunters, he was very kind.
> Thursday, 14th February, 1889: Mr Hunter send us with his spring cart to Porangahau.

This story, fleshed out, along with other episodes from the trip, went into Suzanne's repertoire as a raconteur. There were several narrow escapes from wild cattle in her wanderings over the years. The men at Hunter's warned them not to try their luck again with wild bullocks. Twice later, they turned back when cattle barred their track. The friendly evening with Hunter and Rev. Simcox was also an opportunity for linking into a kinship group, as Paul Hunter's sister in Wellington, Mrs Moorhouse, became a supporter in later years.

The trip then changed direction, going south. 'Wednesday, 20th February, 1889: We went straight through to Wellington.' From Wellington, they took a boat to Greymouth. They were crossing into the brand-new Christchurch diocese, separated from Wellington in 1887. Suzanne needed the approval of John Joseph Grimes, Catholic Bishop of Christchurch, to collect in it. He was at Greymouth at the time, so she headed straight there. He gave permission, but only if she did not double up with Father Ginaty, who was collecting at the same time. His project was the Christchurch Mount Magdala Institute, established for the 'rescue' and rehabilitation of prostitutes.

New Zealand was on the threshold of a 'bricks and mortar' phase of welfare development.[43] Both Ginaty and Suzanne were energetic publicists and both would be working in different women's social welfare areas – both insisting on a non-denominational basis, both with support across the denominational lines.[44] Here they were together on the West Coast, and entries recorded them advancing and retreating as diplomatically as possible in parish after parish so as not to cramp the other's style. Each parish priest struggled to deploy the pair of them as strategically as possible.

Suzanne's twin goals were to raise money for the Maori mission and to publicise the congregation, especially among young women. Her convictions and personality were so strong that, on her way, she also laid down the foundations of her future work by inspiring and motivating the people she met. She could not have done what she was to do throughout the coming years without the solid underlying support of all her helpers. Perhaps she unconsciously realised this as, down in the Catholic heartland, she recorded name after name. Through March, April and early May, the West Coasters file through the diary: mine managers and influential later benefactors such as Kennedy, Burke, Whelan; families of future sisters like the McCormacks; other religious sisters. Mother Clare Moloney of the Sisters of Mercy became a real friend. Then there were lots of local women – mothers and daughters. But the miners and 'blokes' in general were recorded as well. Men pitching in to help were always 'St Joseph' to her:

> 9th April: Went down and round Waimangaroa with Mrs Sullivan. We slept at Mrs Frank. We had a grand view of the incline with the trucks going up and down.
>
> 10th April: Mrs Sullivan gave us a letter for her mother at Ch-Ch. We went by train to Ngakawao. Took lodgings at Mrs Howard, very kind. Went round a few tents. Mr McKenny partner of Mr Brandon send for us and volunteered to go round and collect for us. Most kind.
>
> 11th April: Very wet day. We stay at Mrs Howard. Mr McKenny goes round for us. I write letters.

She was becoming much happier. Everyone was being 'kind'. And she could close the door just a little on the memories of 1870s Hawke's Bay and open another in her heart to the Irish-descended parishioners of the West Coast. She wrote breezily home from Denniston in April:

> My dear Sister Bridgit,
> I see by Sister Carmel's letter that while we are hunting for money in the bush

of the West Coast you are hunting for tawas at Jerusalem [for their 'coffee']. I wish I had as heavy a bag as you have and we would trot away pretty quick up the Wanganui River. [Though] we do not go fast we go pretty steadily so far. We could have done worst. You may transplant the cabbages where the carrots, the artichocks or the beets were, or even where the onions were. If we were nearer we would help you with pleasure to eat the melons and vegetables. We see very little of them in our travellings. . . .

See that the box where the carpet is be well closed and well supplied with camphor. Let all that belongs to the carpet be well packed in it. Else it would come to grief. Do not forget that there are clogs in the new house in a box behind the door. If no salicilic acid has been put in the quince wine, remind Father of it. A tablespoonful for a cask. How is the vinegar?

I remain with best love, dear Sister

Your affectionate Mother

Sr Mary Joseph[45]

In mid-May they crossed the Alps, sharing the coach with a woman and a parrot. Suzanne admired the 'wild mountains' she had never seen before, slept at the Bealey, thought Porters Pass 'dreadful', and at Christchurch found that Bishop Grimes had withdrawn leave for collecting. Back they went on the *Penguin* to Wellington, to pass two and a half months in winter tramping the streets of the capital and outlying districts, even up to Kaitoke. So warm and homey had been her experience on the West Coast that the diary entries for Wellington were spartan by comparison: '4 July: [Went about.] Bought a sausage. Lasted 6 meals. We took meanwhile our lunches in Mrs Sharpe garden.' The city might not have the networking of the rural communities but all these entries of midwinter, minimal outdoor meals also suggest that Suzanne was giving herself and Sister Magdalen a dose of Curé d'Ars austerity, almost welcoming the symbolic 'no room in the inn' to balance the emotional cocoon of the warm reception on the West Coast.[46]

This did not mean that she was at all depressed. Even when meeting a refusal, she was jotting down what would make for a good story to tell later: '7 August. Went around Newtown. Parrot in big house saying "dreadful, dreadful" in shaking her head as the Mrs. refused.' The entry continued: 'Saw poor paralysed Italian woman', which showed her mind filing away the plight of the incurable people she had seen. Inadvertently, it became also a reconnoitring trip, and she returned to Jerusalem to assess over the next years where she had sensed need. She had seen the condition of women and children in the 1880s depression, and had given a commitment to one desperate Hawke's Bay widow to take some of her children as soon as possible. Ironically for Ngati Hau, the trip would eventually lead their Meri back into the world that had started to encroach on her Maori mission life in 1870s Hawke's Bay – the world of Pakeha New Zealand and its needs. And it would bring another major turning-point in her life.

She went down south again for spring, first through Marlborough and Nelson. There were recorded 'sightings'. A Mrs Sugden remembered seeing the little nun tramping around 'in men's Blucher boots, half way up the calf'.[47] One of Suzanne's handy tips for boot care could account for wearing men's larger boots: 'To make boots impermeable to the cold, all that is required is to wrap the feet in an old newspaper. You will be sure of having warm feet all day. The folds of the newspaper will not hurt your feet at all. On the contrary, they will be very comfortable.'

Joseph Ward (not the future Prime Minister but one of Nelson-Marlborough's English Catholic subset and a brother-in-law of Arch-bishop Redwood) tucked a pen-portrait into his journal:

> 1889 Sept. 8th Sunday: Good drop of rain last night. Fine growing morning. To Mass not Benedn. Saw two nuns from near Wanganui 'Jerusalem' up Wanganui River. Church burnt down – a Maori one – They're begging the means to rebuild. Sister Mary Joseph an elderly lady – French – strong short broad; dark brown eyes. Very intelligent look – been for years principally among the Maoris, is skilled in medicines made from herbs. The other young; was at school in Nelson with Edith [his daughter]. Violet Savage. I gave a couple of pounds – sorry I could give no more.[48]

Then it was back to the mines on the West Coast for more friendship and infectious helpfulness:

> 4th November: Drove to Kirwin. Canvassed the Progress. Slept at Mrs Kirwin's. Mrs Costigan comes in the evening and proposes to escort us to Inkerman.
> 5th November: Left at 6 a.m. with Mrs Linch. Mrs Costigan overtook us on the road. Went round the Drake, the Happy Valley and the Scotia and reached Inkerman in the evening. Slept at Mrs Boyle's. All the people very kind. McCullum, 16 children.
> 6th November: Walked to the Globe. Missed the shift and went to sleep at Mrs Costigan. Had tea at Mrs Kennedy.

She did not give in. Next day, she walked the four miles uphill again to the Globe mine, to catch the shift.

Women and girls were not left anonymous; on page after page she recorded their names, along with what they did. In the male world of the mines of Westland, these women emerge from the diary pages at ease, at home, and capably working in together to help Suzanne. The two nuns are handed from Mrs Kirwin to Mrs Lynch to Mrs Costigan to Mrs Boyle to Mrs Kennedy. On it went. Suzanne listed families offering money, a bed for the night, a meal, a lift, a hand with the collecting; getting children to show the way, arranging the next contact:

> 16 October: Mr and Mrs Hinnegan escorted us to Mr Blanchfield and Miss Blanchfield finished to escort us to Maori Creek. Very steep hills and bad tracks. We slept at Mr North's. Very kind.
> 17 October: Went around Maori Creek with Miss North. . . . Master North drove us to Marsden. Sleep at Mrs Russell's. Very kind.
> 19 October: Slept at the convent where we were most welcomed. Saw the Fathers. Very kind. Left for No Town, walked up there. Slept at Mr Gillen.
> 20 October: Very stormy, kept in doors.
> 21 October: Went up and down hills with Miss Gillen.
> 22 October: Went up to Red Jack with Miss Gillen and Miss Lavery [Devery].

The Gillin-Devery family could go under the microscope as a sample, one of many.[49] Patrick Gillin was thirty-seven years old, a Catholic from Belfast and a successful Otago gold prospector, when in 1868 he married eighteen-year-old Sarah Devery, born in County Offaly, Ireland. The marriage was apparently arranged and it worked. Fifteen children were born between 1869 and 1894. The family were involved in many business ventures around No Town, Red Jacks and Kamaka, and known also for their kindness to swagmen and clergymen alike. Once, Sarah Gillin nursed for days a Chinese miner ill in his hut with pneumonia while Patrick kept his fire going day and night.[50] Suzanne felt at home in this sort of atmosphere. She held strongly to an ideal of the helpful, tolerant, practical pioneer family. It was what she wanted to believe and somehow she made sure she met up with her beliefs.

The trip was drawing to a close: 'Friday November 15: Left for Lyell. Slept at Mr Fennel's. November 16: Went up to the Alpine with Miss Ryan. Came down the incline being hardly able to walk.' Could the tireless walker be slowing down? On 20 November they arrived back in Nelson. 'November 21st: We were half dead, and did nothing except going to the Editor of the "Colonist" – he was very kind and gave us a grand "local".' Her definition of half dead was more active than others' might be. A full report of over six hundred words appeared in *The Colonist* of 22 November 1889. Here is the future Mother Aubert, the strategist, skilfully at work. The article happened to put most emphasis on the school in the work of the mission. It was no coincidence. Nelson had given the lead to free and secular education in New Zealand, back in the days of New Munster, Domett and Stafford. She knew this from the Auckland schooling rows of the late 1860s. So she angled the article to get the best reception:

> There is no school within 50 miles of Jerusalem, and even now there are 40 boys and one girl being trained as best they may be under disadvantageous circumstances. Sister Mary informs us that the school is conducted on a broad basis, no religious teaching is imparted during the ordinary school hours. . . . The school is open to all, free of charge, and has proved of much advantage. It is surely needless to commend the mission of the self-sacrificing Sisters.

Suzanne returned to Jerusalem in December, with a total collection of just over £1000. Over the next two years, the new church rose and sent a spire skywards again. A little behind, a two-storeyed convent added its comforting shape – not a squared block to deaden the delicacy of the scene and loom over the marae, but a wooden farmhouse, inviting gabled and lean-to additions over the years. As with the first church, Suzanne's French inheritances would help provide the money for the convent additions.

She came back with more than money. She had with her two very young West Coast girls, Katie Hartnett and Annie McQuilkin, who were the first to join the congregation as a result of her recruiting. She had written to Katie in October and among more serious matters had posed this question: 'Now I cannot promise you lollies in Jerusalem. How will potatoes do instead? No lollies, no pudding, no tea. Will not that be dreadful? How can a vocation stand it? I leave you to ponder over such a question and when you write to me again you will tell what you think.'[51] Katie and Annie took up the challenge and she met them at the steamer in Wellington. They reached Jerusalem together on 12 December.

Others would come fairly quickly. Sister Angela remembered the hint of fun she got in her Hokitika convent school:

> We children had heard at school that some visiting sisters were expected, whom we called 'The Maori Sisters'. Our Sisters corrected us for saying this, and told us the expected guests were Marist Sisters who worked for the Maoris . . . I got a good view of the newcomers, and my first thought was: 'They are Maoris, after all! The first one is, and the other is half caste at least.' They were well tanned by the Hawke's Bay sun and wind, as it was only ten days since they had left there. Besides to my mind, Mother Joseph walked like a Maori woman, with a swaying motion, and she had broad shoulders just like one.

As I settled this in my own mind, I was overcome with the conviction that God willed me to join them – not at once, but later on.

The two sisters and Father Martin were laughing as they came in, evidently at something that Mother Joseph was saying, for she entered first, and looking back over her shoulder, she seemed to be making an apt rejoinder, or saying something witty that amused them all. So there was no halo or anything strikingly spiritual about the new arrivals to account for the impression they created in the onlooker.[52]

Suzanne stopped looking to France for nuns. Her most suitable fellow workers were obviously going to come from New Zealand. In fact, after her collecting tour she probably felt that New Zealand was home now, not really a foreign mission field any more.

CHAPTER ELEVEN

Hiruharama – the medicines
1890-1894

This farm is mine : Naku tenei pamu
We are planting fruit trees : Kei te whakato rakau hua matou[1]

Suzanne was away from Hiruharama for a year. She spent just over a week in Wanganui township between 28 May and 5 June 1889 and the diary entries are non-committal: 'Went to Wanganui . . . Not much . . . Went about . . . Not much . . . Not much . . . Kept quiet . . . Went to Mr Provost . . . Went about . . . Went back to Wellington'. There is no indication that she went upriver in this time. Why not? She had been away since November 1888 and nothing would be more understandable than to go back home and check on how things were. Did she not want to have the progress of her collecting trip halted by the needs of those left behind? She may have been praying and trusting but meanwhile keeping her face turned resolutely south. Trials and hardship were meant to be part of religious life.

The year proved eventful for the community at Hiruharama. Down in Ranana, Waretini died and there was a big tangi. For Ngati Hau at Hiruharama, there was the death of Poutini, the old chief who had headed the welcome at the opening of the church. His son, Neri Poutini, was a strong Catholic. At harvest time the sisters could hardly keep up with the ripening fruit and vegetables. The cucumbers were ballooning in size. The women boiled down eighty pounds of beeswax from the hive to make candles. Suzanne's household instructions sent from down south would be timely.

Father Soulas, too, was keeping her informed and seeking her advice. He was very busy. In spite of Materoa's statement that the Pakeha were to rebuild the church, it was still of course Ngati Hau's land and their church, and Soulas was planning its rebuilding with them. Materoa was, in fact, encouraging everyone to pitch in: Te Rangi agreed to approach his people; Pine wanted the *Tuhua*'s first trip upriver after Suzanne's return to bring the timber for the church. Rawiri said that, for them to have a true idea of the results of the collection, Suzanne needed to go straight to the pa from the boat, not to the presbytery first, 'for fear', Soulas wrote, 'that I'll take from you part of the collection. When you've said how much you've got, then they'll see.' Rawiri was astute and recognised Soulas's obsessiveness about money, but may not have realised Soulas and Suzanne were in regular communication. 'Try not', Soulas added, 'to tell even Sister Magdalen the true total'.[2]

While Suzanne was away, Soulas was literally keeping the home fires burning. In December the spiralling smoke from his bush clearing darkened the skyline along with all the other fires covering New Zealand. In May 1888 they had bought a block of land to farm from Alexander Annabell and Walter Abram; rather, Suzanne's money had paid for it but it was registered in Soulas's name. As he explained to Father Martin, the Superior General of the Society of Mary in France, the farm was in his name because 'supposing she preceded me to her tomb, I would not have to pay death duties . . . after her death'.[3] He added that he also managed the property at that point, 'with authority to dip into the purse of our generous Sister till it's empty (which is going to happen soon)'. Suzanne must have reconsidered this decision, because in 1892 the deeds were transferred 'with difficulty' into her name, with a mortgage to Harriet Broughton.[4]

The hillside slopes of the farm rose steeply behind Hiruharama to a high plateau running north towards Pipiriki. From the tops could be seen Ruapehu's broken crags to the north-east and Taranaki's cone neatly outlined westward across the ranges. Only fifty acres had been cleared when they took it over, and Soulas set to and cleared a block of 550 acres. But he had been having arguments about money with the three men felling the bush. They had fallen behind on the contracted acreage. 'I've finally got rid of our contractors without going to court. Thanks be to God and St Joseph too!' His fires got out of control at one point, accidentally singeing fruit trees they had already planted and burning a larger area than intended. But the fire had saved them from paying for more bushfelling; it was a blessing in disguise. 'God perhaps allowed us not to have the whole area felled so that we wouldn't be dragged into too much expense, may His name be praised! As a result of this mishap, we probably won't have to borrow much as there's a difference of £200 less. In the meantime I've bought cattle and cows at two, three, four pounds.'[5]

The contractors leaving with some of their money withheld was in his view part of God's plan.

The farm was to fund the mission, which otherwise depended mainly on what came from the Propagation of the Faith, and this was subject always to Archbishop Redwood's allocation. Soulas felt that Propagation's money was intended solely for mission to indigenous people; Redwood did not always agree. In isolated Maori districts the missioners did not have the steadier income of money given to parishes by their settler families. In fact, Soulas told Father Martin that even getting agreement to buy stock from local Maori at what he thought a reasonable price was a bit like 'running from Caiaphas to Pilate, from Pilate to Caiaphas'. So, in setting up their farm, Suzanne and Soulas would have had in mind the calm and the independence of the fields of Meanee where the busy farmer brothers worked to support the mission: Brother Basile riding with his newborn, motherless lambs across the front of his saddle, Brothers Athanase and Joseph in the garden, Brother Cyprien among the rows of grapevines. Except in times of Hawke's Bay flood, it was a pleasant scene to remember.

There was an interest in orcharding around Wanganui, and Suzanne and Soulas were friends with the French Provost family, who had an orchard at Mosstown between Wanganui and Fordell. Their son, Eugène, who was about seven at this time, remembered Suzanne in her 'big blue dress and a flax hat' and the way she laughed: 'She'd throw her head back and laugh!' His mother first saw Suzanne after Mass in Wanganui, sitting on the ground by the roadside and talking with the Maori women resting at the edge of the gutter. Land Court sittings kept many Maori clustered waiting in Wanganui. When Suzanne was told that French women were there, she jumped up and crossed the road to switch languages and greet them.[6]

Like Soulas, the Provosts had originally come from Brittany. Provost made and bottled wine for Soulas. His advertisement for cider, sold through 'Mr Siddle, of Ridgway-street, his agent', featured in the *Wanganui Chronicle*. In December 1889 it recommended 'a visit to his plantation, which is full of interest to all having a taste for orchard culture'. He advertised in the Wellington papers also. Suzanne's diary note in early June 'Went to Mr Provost' probably meant business, though she regularly called there as a friend. It was largely through him that the orders were placed for the cherry trees, chestnuts and other fruit trees that would gradually cover the slopes of the farm. Soulas wrote later to Provost discussing fruit-drying equipment as prunes would be cheaper to freight down the river than fresh plums.

In Hawke's Bay in January her diary records a visit to Friedrich Sturm, the orchardist who gave New Zealand Sturmer apples. In one of her collections of recipes and hints, slotted between 'Perfumed sachets' and 'Floating Island' are her careful notes in French of his recommendations:

Fruit trees (Sturm)

The walnut is extremely hardy. Planted at gaps of 25 or 30 feet it should yield returns after 10 years. The crops could easily be exported. The chestnut is sensitive only to late frosts and that only as regards the blossom. After 15 to 20 years it should yield 50 bushels per tree. It would be better planted half-way up the slope rather than on the hilltops. Spaced at 30 feet, sheep would graze underneath without harm and without damaging the trees, even when they are young. If you saw that sheep as they ran were knocking some sideways, all you need to do is put a bit of manuka brushwood at their feet.

The olive is the best investment of all. It can be planted on hilltops. After 10 years it should yield 20 to 30 gallons of oil per tree. After 7 years it should already be paying. Each of the above trees pays better than a sheep of the best breed. And trees planted at gaps of 25 to 30 feet do not hinder the sheep from grazing. The olive grows very well from a slip three feet or more in length. The three trees above, when grown together, should after 10 years give good returns. Any of them at 7 years old should pay better than anything else.[7]

She was channelling the advice back to Soulas, because in March he wrote to her asking, 'How many olive trees should there be?'

Over the next few years Maori and Pakeha helpers dug hole after hole at these recommended intervals and the sisters came after to plant and refill, bracing themselves on the steeper parts of the tumbling hillsides, their blue habits smudged by the blackened tree stumps. Between the rows of young trees, Brother Stanislaus McMullen ran sheep. He had come to help Father Soulas, but an exchange was arranged: the sisters cooked and kept house for the priest down at Hiruharama while for years the brother lived and worked up at the farm. To get to the farm from Hiruharama, you walked three miles up a punishingly steep track. Over the years, the sisters often trudged it daily, in hot dusty summer, in slithery boggy winter. Wild boars and cattle cracked the undergrowth in the bush alongside the track; moreporks hooted by night.

Thousands of fruit and nut trees went into the paddocks of Suzanne's farm. A cashbook records the figures for 1893 alone: 'chestnuts 1164, filbert 60, walnuts 548, quinces 600, cherries 248, plums 60, apples 227, pears 30, gooseberries 147'.[8] As the Whanganui River turned into a transport and tourist artery in the 1890s, punnets of cherries were readily bought by the passengers on the riverboats. The total of cherry trees rose to over a thousand and 'the Cherry Farm', though no longer owned by Suzanne or the sisters after 1907, carried on in the lives of local Maori for generations. They speak with nostalgia: 'We used to live up there, really we weren't allowed out of Ranana but when it was cherry time, everybody went to Jerusalem.' With kerosene tins either side of the saddle, they would ride right beneath a certain tree – 'we knew the good one!' – and pick straight from horseback. 'The quality was better than South Island cherries.' 'Sometimes I go back there, when I'm in Jerusalem, I go straight up to the cherry farm, go down the hill, sit down there, and look at the trees and think of the sisters and just pray for them'.[9] Chestnuts, too, became a staple in their diet, with various ways of cooking them, but mainly boiled. Rure would feed the kids in the 1930s: 'He used to take all the kids up to his farm. He used to cook up chestnuts for us kids at school. He'd put the billy on and cook us some kai.'[10]

While Suzanne was away, Sister Anne was acting as superior. Her letters suggest she was leading carefully and capably enough, but a page in Soulas's handwriting added to the early draft of the Constitutions was all about the danger of the oldest in religion being left in charge if she were 'an ignorant sister lacking in judgement and savoir-faire' and how he wanted none of 'these brainless women' in the Third Order, 'ignorant and full of self-pride'.[11] He had obviously clashed with Sister Anne at some stage. The 'Reminiscences' noted that he 'generally countermanded every single one of Mother Aubert's instructions to the Sister who was Superior in her absence. Both Sr Anne and Sr Bridget had experience of this.'[12]

Sister Anne had to cope with more than one crisis. Soulas's letters to Suzanne at this time have running through them the theme that it was the work of the devil which had brought about the burning of the church and which continued to threaten the mission. It would be hard to keep confident and level-headed in this atmosphere. Sister Anne described a 'terrible thunderstorm' which did not help the sisters, 'the lightning & thunder comming at the same instant & the smell of brimstone about the place was sufficating'.[13]

Sister Helen, one of the two sisters who had battled the fire to save the presbytery and its contents, was having trouble following the pattern of life set out in the Constitutions; she 'did not seem inclined to comply with the rule in any point whatever', wrote Sister Anne, and in January she ended up having a kind of nervous breakdown. One night she had slipped out of the old schoolhouse which was still the convent then and crossed the river by canoe to Kauaeroa, where with Rure and Werahiko's help they traced her the next day and brought her back. Sister Anne's letter to Suzanne of 1 February described how it seemed as though Sister Helen was being physically assaulted by the devil, with crashings and bangings in the room overhead. The sisters nursed her and cared for her until she left on the mail boat on 2 February 1889. She later married and kept in touch over the years.

Two weeks later, she was followed by another sister, Veronica. In December, Soulas had written: 'Everything's going fine. As for big miss high and mighty, I've set her straight with eight days of silence and all the dishwashing for having too much to say while we were away.'[14] But Sister Anne's 15 February letter to Suzanne said: 'you must know about Sr Veronica, she is going away by the mail boat tomorrow. She has behaved herself very well, especially this last week since Father went away, so we are only three now . . .'[15] The discreet clue 'since Father went away' is one of several hints that Father Soulas kept close control over the sisters whenever Suzanne was absent, which would be quite often over the years.

Obedience was an essential part of religious life, and Sister Anne had obviously reported Sister Veronica's attitude, but Soulas sometimes pushed obedience too far. Later on, when Sister Prisca walked the long track up from Ranana as usual, crossing the wire over the Mangoihe creek, she was sent packing by Soulas, who claimed she had come at the wrong time. He would not allow her even a rest or a drink before she turned back to Ranana. On the other hand, Sister Anne had reported that, in Helen's case, 'since Father has come home her mind seem[ed] to take a better turn'.

On the question of control, Soulas's fellow priests knew where to touch this susceptible man on the raw. In January he was at the Marist retreat in Wellington with colleagues who had met in the meantime and talked with Sister Mary Joseph. He wrote to her: 'I've heard talk that you were wearing the trousers, excuse the expression you know what it means, and that consequently you were leading me by the nose . . .'[16] Soulas recognised her abilities, and, far from repressing them, he actively encouraged them. But the comment implies that some people thought she was overstepping the mark in her confident approach and dealings. This is the first documented indication of clerical reaction against her abilities since Bishop Croke's opposition in 1871. It would not surface overtly under Redwood's benign attitude towards her, until his vicar general, Thomas O'Shea, and Bishop Henry Cleary in Auckland tried to tighten up from 1912. But even in 1895, when her public profile was much higher than in 1889, one priest at least was bristling. Father Maillard wrote to Father Cognet referring to 'Mother Mary Joseph, at the very least lady governor, if not queen of New Zealand, with as much power over the hearts of the ministers as over that of Father Soulas . . .'[17]

Other trials came to test the community in Hiruharama in 1889. In August, down in Wellington, Suzanne made an entry in her diary: 'Went Hanson St, Adelaide Rd etc. Salvationists offered me a war cry'. She was referring to the magazine of the Salvation Army, called the *War Cry*. The Salvationists had reached Jerusalem in March, and were threatening the equanimity of the Catholics up there. Poor Father Soulas in Hiruharama and Father Cognet in Ranana! They thought they had safely re-established a strong Catholic Maori mission in this isolated area, one that was flourishing in comparison with the stonier soil of Hawke's Bay. And now the Salvation Army had paddled and poled its way upriver to breach the walls of Jerusalem.

As the *War Cry* reported it, 'God in a wonderful manner opened up this river for us, and we succeeded in planting the yellow, red and blue in Jerusalem.'[18] In September, in spite of opposition, the 'flag still waves triumphantly, reminding all of the blood that cleanses from all sin'. The poignancy, the irony, was that there was then no proud Catholic church and spire on the knoll to symbolise that faith. The Salvation Army by coincidence was almost occupying a vacuum. Rev. Richard Taylor might have seen symbolic justice, if his Anglican timbers really had been dismantled by newly zealous Catholics after Father Lampila's triumph in the 1850s.

The Salvation Army had come to New Zealand in the mid-1880s with an active sense of mission. Newspaper accounts show some early opposition and some fines for obstructing the thoroughfare, but at the turn of the century André Siegfried was struck by the absence of raillery at its public gatherings and its general acceptance in New Zealand. The Salvation Army was also well launched on its social welfare work, and Siegfried saw this as a clear reason for its success: 'it is charitable and democratic. Its service of help is very well organised, and it does excellent work among the poor. Besides this, the people feel at home with it. It has no stylish and aristocratic hierarchy; poor and rich are equal in its eyes.'[19]

Salvation Army captain Ernest Holdaway had been in Wanganui in 1886 and was back there in 1889. He was very tall, very handsome, very keen and put a lot of intelligent effort into learning Maori. In January 1889, Maori were gathered in Wanganui for weeks on end to attend a Land Court sitting. They were attracted to Holdaway's meetings and Tamatea Aurunui of Ngati Hau invited 'Horowe' and Wiri Grey to visit his pa at Hiruharama. They based their mission in the long attic room of his gabled house and soon had a brass band formed from converts.[20]

Staunch Catholics from Hiruharama first asked Holdaway and his people to leave. The *War Cry* said they 'threatened to spike our drum'. Soulas wrote back to France in August that one old Catholic warrior told Aurunui that 'scattered to the four winds will go army, barracks, music and musicians'.[21] Down at Ranana there was equally keen interest in the army, but Father Cognet's August letter also promised a rallying of the defence 'to throw to the eels and trout of the Wanganui trombones, cornets and drums'.[22]

It did not come to that. Suzanne returned with her collection money and the church finally rose again, and the convent alongside. Chalice, linen, vestments and statues were once more donated from France, and Catholic presence and faith were secure enough until the next major challenge, from Ratana.[23] The Salvation Army stayed on until its own governing body in 1894 rearranged the organisation of its Maori mission and specialist work in remote districts declined.

In engaging with the Salvation Army, Suzanne, Soulas and Cognet decided to fight like with like. Soulas wrote to Redwood for permission to set the catechism to music. Suzanne, at one stage on her trip, had been given £200 for her own purposes. Her 'own purposes' were always mission purposes. She bought band instruments, which Maori players mainly paid off over the years in sheep. Under cornet player and bandmaster Christophe Soulas, the 'nine cornets, four clarionets, four horns, one trombone, two baritones, one euphonium, two bassoons, and two drums' of the Catholic mission played on. They would later combine with Ranana players and Te Rangihiwinui's Putiki band to form the successful Taitoko band.

Have you taken any medicine? : Kahore ano koe i kai rongoa?
Take it morning, noon and night :
Kainga i te ata, i te awatea, i te ahiahi[24]

At Hokitika on the West Coast in March, Suzanne had taken time to make up one of her medicines to give to the rheumatic miners at Rimu and Woodstock who had talked to her of the aches and pains from their waterlogged life. A local chemist let her use his dispensary. Suzanne was still very much the doctor, the nurse, the chemist. When she lived in Hawke's Bay, she would work on her experiments with the encouragement of Dr Spencer and a chemist, Alexander Eccles, and she developed a range of remedies using indigenous plants. They were intended for Maori and she always called them rongoa. The 1883 *Brett's Colonists' Guide* noted the work being done in that district but pointed out that the field of local medicine was still largely unexplored:

> A scientific analysis of the properties of New Zealand vegetable products is a tempting field of research still open to the analytic chemist. Except the koromiko (*veronica*), which is being regularly compounded by a Napier chemist as a diarrhoea mixture, none of the native plants have yet been systematically utilised in medical practice, although some are known to possess valuable properties.[25]

Over the next decade, Suzanne set out to change that.

In the 1870s and early 1880s, her rongoa were dispensed freely from the 'red shed' at Meanee. But through the 1880s a project to market them to a wider public, for the benefit of the mission, was slowly taking shape. From the early 1880s, after Soulas arrived, there is evidence that testimonies of satisfied users were being gathered. And when Soulas sent her instructions for what to bring to Hiruharama from Pakipaki and Meanee, he repeated in three different sections of the letter the need to bring everything 'to manufacture your medicines, so cauldrons, pots, distiller, evaporator, bottles, jars, drugs, herbs . . . in a word everything you have'.[26] There is no suggestion that he had commercial manufacture in mind but the constant theme leaves room for conjecture.

By 1886, three years after she arrived at Hiruharama, there was definitely talk of commercialisation. Soulas and Cognet had approached a chemist in Lyon named Larochette, according to his letterhead a *pharmacien de 1re classe*, who had previously worked in Paris hospitals. He wrote back to Suzanne offering to manufacture a product with profits shared equally, and 'you could in this way render aid to your cherished

Maori mission by increasing its monetary resources'.[27] Could she send him a sample to be analysed in France? He would report back whether there were grounds for hope. A sample of Karana, one of her medicines, was sent and the report was favourable; it was 'superior to quinine in the treatment of atonic stomach ailments'.[28]

In August 1887 Suzanne's ever-obliging brother Camille, now parish priest at Cuinzier, wrote to the Society of Mary on her behalf to support a request to manufacture the medicines in France under the society's auspices.[29] Soulas also wrote an enthusiastic twelve-page letter to his superior general in France: the Larochette project could make 15,000 francs as annual net profit; Larochette would like to label it the 'Elixir of the Marist Fathers of Oceania'; there were well-known precedents for this in other religious orders; after Suzanne's death, then his death as her heir, the society would inherit, provided that profits still went to the Maori mission and the society's apostolic schools; Abbé Camille Aubert was acting for her in France. Could they please give their approval?

Perhaps the Marists would have been reluctant anyway, but the rest of Soulas's letter must surely have raised eyebrows. He did not stop at Suzanne's medicines. He also wrote page after page describing his own 'inventions' – 'two inventions in one day!' 'It was last night,' he said, 'when Mother Mary Joseph was talking about a substance known to be good at preventing seasickness, with just one or two days' dose, that an old idea flashed into my head. My poor brain gave me no rest until I had worked through this idea and finally I have discovered a way to execute it.'[30] He too, it seemed, had an answer for seasickness. In that sleepless night, he said, he had designed a type of bed which would never sway but always keep its equilibrium. He wanted to patent this and, with all the seasick-prone passengers on the steamers plying the seas, it would bring great revenues. If Suzanne's project ever stood a chance with the Marists, the feverish pages of this and Soulas's other scientific ideas for fundraising would have had them backing right off.

Soulas was an enthusiastic amateur in science and medicine. This was not unusual. Missionary after missionary dealt with medical problems and from their ranks came valuable observation of their environment. Father Woods, the co-founder of the Australian Sisters of St Joseph, was known for his scientific writings. In the early draft of the Constitutions, Soulas and Suzanne put aside two hours of science and Maori study each day for the sisters. Yet in their memories of Father Soulas's science the sisters indicated they felt they were gently humouring a decidedly eccentric whim. The word 'experiments' was firmly in inverted commas and he 'spent a lot of money in importing apparatus, which never seemed to arrive quite complete!' 'He was almost a genius in some ways, but he badly needed a practical Superior over him.'[31]

The Marists in France declined to give their approval. 'We cannot lend our name for commercial joint ventures of this kind however worthy might be the aim', wrote Father Martin to Suzanne's brother. 'It would be completely contrary to our custom and spirit. It will not be difficult to find some other organisation equally fit to promote and launch the product.'[32] On 31 August 1891, after registering trademarks on 6 August, Suzanne signed a contract with Dunedin-based Kempthorne and Prosser, who had already begun enthusiastically to advertise her remedies. In her home town of Wanganui, for example, under 'Public Notices' and 'Business Notices' in the *Wanganui Chronicle* of 27 August 1891, Suzanne's medicine, Natanata, was advertised for sale alongside the column extolling the American (non-religious) Mother Seigel's Syrup, and Sander & Sons' Eucalypti Extract.

Natanata was recommended for 'Diarrhoea, Vomiting and general sickness', which were 'frequent complaints with females'. As 'a purely vegetable preparation . . . it is a splendid medicine for infants', 'highly recommended to ladies during pregnancy', to be used 'for all female ailments, and the many troubles attending weakly children'. It 'should be in every household'. Sister Mary Joseph Aubert 'has been most fortunate in the experiments she has made with New Zealand vegetation, in discovering a most valuable remedy'. Paramo and Karana featured in other columns of the same issue, Paramo for 'Liver Complaint' and Karana for when 'the digestive organs are out of order':

> How often does a man, too, in meeting an old acquaintance have a merry evening and suffer terrible from the effects the next day.
> SISTER MARY JOSEPH AUBERT, in her researches amongst the plants of New Zealand, has discovered there is a very valuable remedy for these complaints in our own vegetation, and, after experimenting for a number of years, has now brought forward the medicine called KARANA.

In this way, the needs covered ranged from those of tired heavy-breeding women, with their babies at their skirts in isolated homesteads or village cottages, to hard-drinking pioneer blokes, 'old people, who had ruined their constitutions by the abuse of intoxicating drink and who were debilitated and suffering after turning over a new leaf'.

This was the beginning of an ambitious publicity campaign which would transform Suzanne from Mother Mary Joseph to the widely known Mother Aubert, the 'New Zealand Vegetatist: her Remedies are the very best'. By 5 January 1892, Marupa was being advertised for its properties in protecting against the terror of the new illness, influenza, which was 'raging with direful effects in Sydney, Adelaide and Melbourne'. Following the custom of the times, recommendations stacked up, in her case from 'VICE-REGAL AND THESPAIN [thespian] TESTI-MONY' and 'THE CHURCH, THE [S]TATE AND THE STAGE' – which meant Archbishop Redwood and Bishop Grimes for the church, recent governor Lord Onslow for the state, and the highly regarded actors Myra Kemble and Walter Bentley for the stage. Onslow, who had been anxious for the health of his family and avoided living in Wellington whenever possible because of its poor sanitation, was reported later to have 'got a rap over the knuckles from a British medical journal' for supporting a patent medicine.[33]

By 13 April 1892, the Wellington *Evening Post* recorded that the 'demand during the past month shows that they are now fully established as the chief proprietary medicine of New Zealand'. Ten thousand bottles were sold in the first three months in Wellington alone. New Zealand flocked to take its own medicine. By late 1892 a competitor discreetly tried to enter the field: from Patea a chemist, A. Gower, launched 'MA-URU (Prepared only from the growths on New Zealand)', with the help of veteran missionary Rev. J. Hammond.

The advertising would cause a small controversy among Wellington theatre-goers in 1892. The 'Wellington Wing Whispers' correspondent to the *Otago Witness* explained to Dunedin readers that the 'drop scene of our Opera House is an advertisement sheet, the centre space being occupied by a pretty landscape, upon which "Mother Mary Aubert's Remedies" are set forth, and clustered around this are a goodly number of well-displayed advertisements of local industries.' The contract for this was for three years in all but the orchestra had already had twelve months of it and was rebelling at scene changes being constantly jarred by what the *Evening Post* called 'an incongruous invitation to buy coal and tooth brushes, basinettes and photographs, firewood and baby-linen . . . every evening the "drop" has been hissed by the pit'.[34]

Permission had been granted by Archbishop Redwood 'in the hope that such vegetable medicines may become more publicly known, and assist the good cause in which the Rev. Mother works'.[35] By St Patrick's Day 1892, the approval of the Catholic newspaper, the *New Zealand Tablet*, had also made its way into the advertisement for Marupa in the *Wanganui Chronicle*:

> The religious orders continue to maintain their reputation as benefactors of Society in temporal as well as spiritual matters. A new proof of this is furnished in the remedies which have been discovered by Sister Mary Joseph Aubert of [the] Order of *Notre Dame des Missions* [*sic*]. . . . It is to the credit of the Catholic Church in the colony that one of its missionary Sisters has distinguished herself in this way, probably conferring on the world a benefit, little, if anything, inferior to that conferred, for example by the Jesuit Fathers who discovered the curative properties of the Peruvian bark. Not only suffering humanity but science itself owes a debt to this lady, who has made it acquainted with properties of natural products, hitherto unsuspected, and has enriched the pharmacopoeia. We have further in the matter an instance of how religious devotion is calculated to quicken the faculties and to develop the best qualities of human nature. Sister Mary Joseph is to be warmly commended for her discoveries . . .[36]

The advertisements constantly informed the public that her medicines were purely vegetable in origin, 'in no way hurtful in . . . action'. No 'worthless quackery' was being introduced. 'Mother Mary Joseph Aubert . . . has not unduly sought to pry into the secrets of nature; but she has by long and careful study discovered that certain New Zealand herbs and plants have health-giving properties of an extremely high order'.[37] The theme of 'trustworthy' was important to settlers. Most households were immigrant still. Wrenched from extended family knowledge of childcare and medical lore, often far away from available doctors and unable to pay for them, they relied greatly on patent medicines. Yet from the 1880s the accusation of quackery and charlatanism was hanging over the purveyors of patent medicines, and their customers were accused of gullibility.[38] Many of the medicines, even those for children, were known to contain large quantities of narcotics – especially opium and laudanum – and a fear of addiction was growing.[39]

Mother Aubert's purely vegetable medicines came as a relief; buyers could feel they were handling 'safe' products, both for themselves and for their children. They could also feel they were helping in 'good works', not dubious personal gain, and meanwhile the handy bottle of patent medicine was there on the shelf. The *Weekly Herald* of 15 August 1891 recorded a child's prayer: ' "Dear Lord", she lisped, "make me pure," then

Looking north from the hills above Hiruharama towards the orchard of cherries, chestnuts, walnuts and other fruit trees, c.1940.

Looking from the top of the farm behind Hiruharama in 1967, towards the remains of the orchard. The river runs hidden behind the spur in the middle distance.

The drying house at the farm, built with shutters for ventilation. The sisters stayed in the shed behind where the medicine was boiled down in large vats. Photo c.1915, after Suzanne had sold the farm.

A Sister of Charity, from Suzanne's model congregation in France, dispenses medicine.
BIBLIOTHÈQUE NATIONALE, PARIS

Brother Stanislaus, Thomas McMullen, who worked on the farm.   MAW

After the court case with Kempthorne and Prosser's, the medicines sold through Sharland's carried the assurance, under an uncompromisingly severe likeness, of Suzanne's personal supervision.

Fruit candi

Fruit candi   a delicious fruit candi may be made by adding chopped raisins and figues, or dried cherries or any firm preserve to a syrup made by stewing 2 lb of sugar with the juice of two lemons, or with a cup of vinegar flavoured with essence of lemons.

Other receipt.

Stir in a half cup of cold water three cups of dark brown sugar, a little gum arabic or one white of egg, boil slowly, stirring constantly. Skim the dark foam off, taste it by a few drops thrown in a cup of cold water. When nearly done add a pinch of soda and a teaspoon of butter — When almost done drop in any fruits, dip out separately for five minutes, taking up syrup with each. Lay on a buttered dish.

To clean tripe.

Tripe   *to clean*   *Guts*   Wash it first in cold water; then dip it in boiling water till you can scrape it. Then lay it flat on a table, scrape it with a spoon and boil it till soft. Then pull it out and throw it in cold water.

Guts

Put them in lukewarm water the inside out and scrape them with a spoon.

To make boots Waterproof

Boots   *Waterproof*

½ lb tallow or mutton suet
4 oz of lard
2 oz new bees wax
2 oz olive oil
dissolve over the fire, mixing well and apply to the leather.

Extract from Suzanne's household hints and recipes.

Hiruharama, c.1895. The 'orphans' have joined the community. The new gabled addition to the convent is complete, smoke curls up from the chimney and long lines of washing stretch out to the right of the presbytery.

In 1898 a reassuring photograph of the children was publicised. Suzanne (centre back) holds Francis, the godchild of Archbishop Francis Redwood. Kate Young stands beside her on the right. John McMahon is in the middle row, at far right: he is looking away from the camera and the enlarged side of his face is visible.

Grace Neill, Assistant Inspector of Hospitals and Charitable Institutions.

Jessie Williamson, in 1898.

This representation of a French Hospice for Foundling Children on the corner of an imaginary Hell St shows a baby being deposited in a *tour*, the cylinder-like turnstile used to hand over babies and guard anonymity. The sister stands ready to turn the *tour* to the inside. BIBLIOTHÈQUE NATIONALE, PARIS

A smiling Suzanne (centre), Sister Baptista and the family at Hiruharama in 1902. John McMahon and Rewi Crichton are seated on the right in the second row. NZ HERALD

1918 letter from 'Grandma' to Joe Kenny, who had been wounded in France.

19/2/. No. 22406 — Private J.J. Kenny. — Grey Towers
Hosp. — Hornchuch — Essex — London.

My Dear Boy, I cannot tell you how pleased I was to get your nice affectionate letter of 3d inst. which I received only three days ago. I thank God that you are still alive and are a good faithful boy to God and Country. You did not forget grandma and I can assure you that Grandma dearly loves her boys and that she prays for each of them every day with all her heart. I have no doubt that you have had many narrow escapes, but I did not hear of what has happened to you. Evidently you must have been wounded as you are in hospital. I wish I was near you, but you have better than me watching over you. You have God, the Blessed Virgin and your glorious Patron S.t Joseph. You have always also by you your guardian Angel to protect and defend you. Have courage you will get through. Going to confession and Holy Communion will strengthened you and comfort you. I fully understand that you get depressed some times, but try to be as brave in hospital as you were at the front. Offer all your pains to God and He will reward them all.

Joe's cousin Charlie Kenny was also a 'Jerusalem Old Boy'.

Photograph of Suzanne used for the specially issued travel document in lieu of a passport, Rome, 1919.

she hesitated, and went on with added fervour a moment later, "make me absolutely pure, like Sister Aubert's medicines." '

The newspaper columns also reassured the country that, in spite of economic depression, every day saw 'the resources of this grand country gradually opened up in some respect, great or small', such as 'the discovery that certain herbs in the New Zealand flora have health giving and curative properties of the highest order. We allude to the AUBERT REMEDIES, for which we have to thank that grand woman, Mother Mary Joseph Aubert, who, from the depths of the "forest primeval" has culled the plants from which are extracted MARUPA, NATANATA, PARAMO and KARANA.'[40]

So the attribute of 'local' was added to that of 'trustworthy'. 'Support local industry', as headlined in the Wanganui *Yeoman* on 4 July 1891, was becoming an important theme. The country had a new, Liberal govern- ment proposing changes in social justice and social welfare and it was becoming aware and proud of nationhood. That is what Governor Onslow emphasised in his testimonial; her labours were certainly 'of great value for the relief of human miseries' but they also appeared to him 'capable of furthering colonial industry'.[41] Premier John Ballance, who led the Liberals to victory in January 1891, came from Wanganui. His base was hers also: the bush society of the southern half of the North Island. His 1892 Budget spelt out that 'the only safe policy for the colony is one of self-reliance – one which fosters colonial enterprise'.[42] The marketing of Suzanne's medicines drew on three intertwined qualities of the nationalistic image the Liberals were building up of New Zealand: caring, innovative and independent. Her agents billed themselves as 'Kempthorne, Prosser & Co.'s New Zealand Drug Company, Limited' and concert programmes edged with advertisements were headed 'Mother Mary Joseph Aubert's New Zealand remedies'.

The newspapers did not greatly emphasise the Maoriness of her rongoa, though. The closest they got was an article, not an advertisement, in the *New Zealand Times* of 18 September 1891, referring to her 'study of certain medicinal plants, known no doubt to the Maoris. . . . There is among [them] considerable knowledge of the healing qualities of various plants. That knowledge, in competent hands, ought to prove exceedingly valuable to mankind, and profitable to the Colony.' In fact, very little was known of traditional Maori medicinal practice in day-to-day life. Early explorers like Cook and Banks had found the Maori very healthy, and

Banks wrote that 'such health . . . must make physicians almost useless:
indeed I am inclind to think their knowledge of Physick is but small'.[43]
Father Servant, one of the earliest men to live among Maori and to discuss
their lifestyle with dispassionate observation, thought that '[a]lthough
New Zealand harbours many plants with medical virtues the natives have
a very limited knowledge of herbs'.[44] He listed a few, then referred to
the custom of summoning the tohunga. Anthropologists consider that
tohunga 'had some knowledge of the therapeutic value of plants, but the
accepted theory of disease limited experimentation'.[45]

Cook and other observers noticed the use of herbs by women in
steam treatments and external application but most writers, including
Colenso and Best, thought that Maori traditionally did not take medicine
internally. With only gourds and wooden receptacles as containers, it
would not have been easy to make medicines which needed boiling. Yet
by the mid-nineteenth century the list of native medicinal plants known
to be used by Maori was full enough to suggest that it could not have been
developed in less than half a century. Since the missionaries for their part
still seemed generally to be treating Maori with European remedies or
placebos, much of the knowledge was undoubtedly there in Maori life
all along.[46]

When she came to New Zealand, Suzanne quickly applied her knowledge of chemistry and botany to experimenting with medicines. It is not
certain that she was using native plants in Auckland but it is very likely.
From 1862 she was largely in the company of Maori women, and she had
Peata, a woman of mana who, she said, 'taught her everything', and the
other Maori novices and pupils to advise her. From early in her time in
Hawke's Bay she was regularly seen with Maori women, gathering roots,
barks, leaves and plants across the hills and swamps. Women could be
recognised as tohunga makutu in their areas of specialised knowledge
and gifts, and healing was one of these.[47] Suzanne's rongoa were the
culmination of years of shared expertise.

Her handwritten notes list several Maori plant names under many
different headings: 'Venereal disease', 'Internal Compl', 'Skin diseases',
'Cuts, ulcers, wounds', 'dissentery', 'Scrofula', 'Itch', 'Dartres', 'Stimulant',
'rhumatic', 'Purgatives', 'Bitters', 'Blister', 'Colds', 'Coughs', 'Perfumes,
Mosquito etc', 'Tooth ache', 'Dyes', 'Aromatic', 'Demulcent', 'Asthma',
'Antifebrifuge', 'Tonics', 'Astringent', 'Emetiques', 'Sea sickness' (fern
root being listed for her old enemy).[48] She also had a list headed: 'To

try'. *Brett's Colonists' Guide* in 1883 had a five-page section on 'Maori Pharmacopoeia' and the application of plants it suggests tallies with her fuller lists.

Exactly what plants went into Suzanne's medicines, and in what proportions, is no longer known. She tended to guard the recipes zealously with a certain dramatic secrecy. Some details were at one stage in two exercise-books, red and black, in a tin box. The sisters helping her with all the manual work of preparation were never initiated into the whole process. At a particular stage of evaporation, Suzanne would have to be called, even in the middle of the night, and she would complete the work herself. Ultimately the recipes disappeared – lost, or more likely, as in the traditional stories, destroyed by Suzanne. She had largely stopped making medicine by the turn of the century, for several reasons.

One was that the publicity got out of hand and was too worldly. When she went to Wellington, her customers recognised her. Kempthorne and Prosser supplied a 'handsome bromide enlargement' of a photograph of 'the Rev. Lady' to chemist shops. People were 'so eager to interview the old lady that she was simply bewildered. Even in her passage along the streets persons thronged upon her'.[49] She was not yet sixty, but already she was the very visible and public old woman, Mother Aubert.

Part of Suzanne's nature would presumably have liked this – she certainly enjoyed her popularity in Auckland in 1869 and 1870 – but the other part would have scented the real danger to religious life. The same woman wrote and profoundly believed: 'Let us not try to be known, let us not seek for publicity, let us be known only by the good which we are called on to do. Let us remain very small in the conviction of our nothingness, for it is only when the heart is empty that God fills it.'[50] Medical skill was meant to be a means to mission. Under the heading 'Concerning Medicine', her draft Constitutions laid down: 'The Sisters will study medicine with care, not from any desire for recognition but from a pure spirit of charity for the suffering members of Jesus Christ, and as a powerful means of gaining, through the tending of the body, the healing of the souls of their patients.'[51]

Another was that the sheer work involved was enormous and must have taken her away from other mission activities. The sisters were still planting fruit trees during these years when they walked the hills, picking and gathering; stripping and sorting bark and leaves. They were once seen up to their armpits in water, collecting from the river's edge. Suzanne had built up at the farm a two-storeyed house without inner partitions and with shutters allowing air to circulate to dry the vegetation. The sisters stayed in an earthen-floored shed next to it, rolling out their bedding on a long worktable each night, and sleeping amid the boiling, evaporating mixtures in their bricked-in vats. An attempt to ease the work was made. Robert Hannah wrote from Wellington that he had enquired about importing a 'bark machine' at her request. Father Soulas had drawn designs for an intricate automatic stirring device which may or may not ever have been made, which may or may not ever have worked. There is mention in the documents of some 'apparatus being broken'.

When the liquid had evaporated sufficiently, the concentrate was poured into demijohns, each with a label attached coded according to its type. They were hauled by sledge the three miles down the steep hill to Jerusalem. The sisters trudged down the rough track alongside, guiding the horse. Then down the river went the jars on Hatrick's river boats to Wanganui, where Kempthorne and Prosser took delivery of them, paying £10 per liquid gallon. They made up the medicines and bottled them.

There was also the danger that the rate of bushfelling would threaten production. It became more difficult for Suzanne to get certain species she needed. But it was the sheer demand for the medicines, prompted by the exuberant advertising and the public who had been 'so universally satisfied', which overwhelmed Kempthorne and Prosser's and Suzanne's capacity to keep going.[52] The operation became too big too fast. Kempthorne and Prosser even had agents in New South Wales and Victoria, and Orlando Kempthorne had plans for further afield. At the beginning of August 1891, an article referred to 'this lady's face beaming with smiles'. By 16 August 1892, 'Cook & Gray, Accountants, Wellington' had certified 38,472 bottles sold.[53] In the photo alongside this announcement, in spite of the freshly goffered frills softening her square little face, Suzanne looks a bit worn and harassed.

Suddenly the contents of some bottles of Marupa and Paramo began fermenting, and complaints came in. Suzanne could not understand why. Her friend Martin Kennedy, whom she had met on the West Coast in 1889, suggested she approach the Colonial Secretary, Sir Patrick Buckley, to arrange for samples of the medicine as prepared by her to be analysed in the government laboratory and compared with sample bottles from Kempthorne and Prosser. In May 1893, the report of the Colonial Analyst, William Skey, went back to Buckley's office and to her. The bottled mixtures were much weaker than her samples and therefore prone to fermentation.[54] A court case in February 1894 found for Sister Mary Joseph against Orlando I. Kempthorne, who was required to pay her £210 damages with costs according to scale. The cost of advertisements appearing 'in 47 papers daily' had led Kempthorne to reduce orders for the actual medicine and instead to dilute what he had in stock.

The case was initiated by her lawyer Charles Skerrett, who had power of attorney from her, without her instructing him to do so. As well as protecting her reputation, it may have been a way to free her from a contract and an enterprise which could have been fast diverting and draining her energies. Suzanne could not easily delegate, and she did not have enough sisters to cope. It was not like writing the prayer-book or the manual of Maori conversation, which would have needed a burst of concentrated energy over a year at most. The medicines would be a continuing responsibility. Suzanne was an intensely spiritual person whose whole day was directed to faith, in active form. A busy commercial venture was not the best expression of this for a tiny, foundling congregation, even with the best of mission intentions. From now on, she spoke of Providence as her bank, and she relied on the providential support of many different people, which would bring both spiritual value and heart-warming human bonding.

On 21 March 1894 she was released from the contract with Kempthorne and Prosser. She was sensitive to the good name of herself, the congregation, and the mission. She made her apologies to her public in a broadsheet titled 'Fair Play', as she launched a small range of the rongoa at reduced prices. She prepared and bottled these herself, marketing them through Sharland's. She continued this for a while, with help from Louis Pascal, a French friend in Palmerston North, and from supporters in Wellington.

But her growing involvement with the medical world in Wellington after the turn of the century led her away from patent medicines. By 1908 the Quackery Prevention Act had, at least officially, tightened up on them. The British Medical Association and its New Zealand associates would have nothing to do with the purveyors of patent medicines. One doctor referred to her disparagingly as 'Mother Seigel', the ever-present American medicine-maker in the newspaper columns. Suzanne, fiercely proud of her integrity in medicine and wanting to be associated with professionalism, was stung. 'New Zealand's vegetatist' stopped making her medicines.

There is, too, the big question of her relationship with Maori who felt they were sharing their taonga with someone they respected. The interference with the medicines, the court case, the unwelcome publicity, could have had a sense of defilement for both them and her. It is significant that, in a river version of the disappearance of the recipes, she returned them to the waters of the Whanganui.

Maori had been involved all along: Ngati Hau and Ngati Ruaka, and possibly other hapu further afield, helped gather the plant stocks needed. People from the river remember their grandparents' and great-grand-parents' talk. Tamakehu, Rure, Neri Metera were named among those who used to 'help nga none ki te kimikimi i nga rakau e mahi, make up medicines for healing. There were quite a few of them; I know Tamakehu was one of them. I heard my grandmother saying that they used to get up and go on their horses and help nga none, to help them get the medicines together and sell them.'[55]

Because of her skill in medicine, did Maori give Meri the status of a spiritually powerful and mystically gifted healer? Hori Paamu Tinirau and Tanginoa Tapa, two learned kaumatua from Ranana and Parikino who were 'strong on the Supreme Being', Io, 'held her in high admiration because of her healing'. They did not talk about bottling and preparation, but about the cure used and its effect. They seemed to relate to her as a developer of Maori medicine, even though she was not Maori. When they got together, they used to speak about her as a 'healer'. Tinirau 'was an intellectual himself' and his respect for Mother Aubert was for her cures, for what she did, for what she knew.[56]

In Hawke's Bay in the early to mid-1880s, Paora Kaiwhata of Moteo, Ngarati of Pakipaki and Renata Kawepo of Omahu had sent her notes in gratitude for her healing. The notes could have been partly solicited as testimonials, since the medicines project had already been conceived by then, but nevertheless their statements stand. In 1893 Hoani Tokotoko of Te Karaka asked her to come and see him before he died, 'you who have saved the life of so many who were already shrouded in death'. And in 1894 a Pakeha farmer wrote:

> I beg to tender you my heartfelt thanks for what you have done for my family. When, a few years ago, I was listening to some Maoris speaking about 'Mary' I enquired, 'Who is Mary?' I got the answer – 'The woman who is raising the dead to life.' I little dreamt that I should have the pleasure to know you, and to be indebted to you for such unexpected cures . . .[57]

Yet the general feeling among Maori and from the documentation is that Mother Aubert was regarded not so much as a mystical healer but as a skilful doctor who used, respected and added to the knowledge of the vegetation they knew, and brought to her cures and to her nursing all the power of her own faith and prayer. Her gift was to combine good medicine, common sense, laughter, friendship and love in a holistic view of life and health where intense spirituality was all around. The same Tinirau taught his mokopuna a prayer: 'Te Ariki i mua, te Ariki i muri, te Ariki i runga, te Ariki i raro, te Ariki i roto i ahau; Manaki tia ahau, i ahau e haere nei i te huarahi'. The Lord in front of me, behind, above, below, within me; Guide and protect me wherever I go.[58]

CHAPTER TWELVE

Hiruharama – the children
1891-1898

Childhood : Tamarikitanga

Who is that child? : Ko wai tena tamaiti?

I do not know, he is a new-comer : Aua hoki, he tauhou ano ia[1]

Straight under the heading *Des Enfants* in her draft Constitutions, Suzanne wrote in her clear, beautiful handwriting: *Les Soeurs aimeront les enfants dont elles sont chargées.* There it was, her very first and essential requirement for childcare, spelt out with all her confidence that it would be fulfilled: 'The Sisters shall love the children who are in their care.'[2] The four pages of guidance that follow applied at that time mainly to the teaching and care of the Maori children in the school, but her philosophy was exactly the same for all the other children who came to live with them in the 1890s. At the same time as the sisters and Suzanne were planting fruit trees, hunting for leaves and bark, stirring and carting medicines, teaching school and religion, nursing and doctoring by horseback, training new women joining the community, helping to build, rebuild and extend the church and convent, and keeping house for the presbytery, they were also bringing up a large family of babies and children.

By mid-decade, when the main tree-planting was finishing, the sisters' dark blue clothes might have had about them the strong whiff of toddler ammonia, the acid odour of baby spills, as much as the pungent scents of bush burn, bracken or bitter medicine extract. Suzanne's sewing skills had adapted for her community 'the most sensible habit in New Zealand – a hardwearing woollen skirt, and a separate cotton top, detachable sleeves. The skirt worked just on five strong hooks and eyes.'[3] The women would need every washable fibre of this outfit as they changed, cuddled and fed child after child, as they strung up line after line of nappies, sheets and baby clothes in the years to come. Suzanne's exercise-books filled up with more 'Hints for Household Management'. One, labelled in French 'precious recipe', might have been useful for their habits. You could replace soap for washing dark materials with spinach water or an infusion of ivy leaves.

Every bit of caring for people, Suzanne directed, was to be done with love, where the loving itself was also to be a perpetual exercise in learning to live fully. 'Love is the life of the heart, and like the pendulum of a clock which sets in motion all the other parts, love gives to the soul all the movement it has. . . . It is by loving that we learn to love.'[4] She kept stressing that discipline was to be formative, not soul-quenching:

> Never show the child anything dark, fearful, cruel: it would make a bad impression. Never give signs of impatience or severity: it would freeze its little heart. Be firm, but kind. Do not overlook its little caprices, for a child – even under three months old – can already have a temper and self-will. Do not give way to it, and you will train it to behave.[5]

'The Sisters shall love the children' was followed immediately in the manuscript of the Constitutions by 'They are expressly forbidden to hit them'. She gave the same message in the *Directory*, later printed as the training manual for the sisters:

> – You have to be patient with others.
> – With everybody?
> – With everybody and everything.
> – But when we are tired and extremely sleepy, and when we have to pacify a capricious child, who will scream all the louder, as if to provoke us, can we not give him a slap?
> – Slap your own temper, and be patient with the child whom your impatience will not calm. You know it is Jesus. Surely you will not slap Him. Be patient.[6]

Whenever she was away from Jerusalem, especially after the turn of the century, she would be writing letters back to Sister Bridget, swapping news but also answering queries and discussing clothing, toys, fruit bottling, feeding, illnesses, schooling. In these letters she would reaffirm that discipline was to be loving. 'My dear Sisters', she once wrote, 'I am so tired that I must come to a close. But not before sending you all fond love. Do all for God, be very obedient for His Sake. Be very patient with the children. Beating, shaking, stamping does them no good. It only impresses them that the aunties have a very bad temper and that they can follow their exemples.' Ruby Taylor remembered how Suzanne put this into practice:

> [On being] told that I had been naughty, she very gently took my best pinny off me & put it on me inside out, & I was heartbroken; it was worse than if she had given me a good hiding. I have always remembered her gentle ways for

she would not allow us to receive corporal punishment & like the above incident, if we were naughty, if there [were] cakes or sweets given out, the naughty ones were not given any – & I am sure there were times when we deserved a good hiding.[7]

In this growing family she was forming from 1891, in this rambling, scrambling home that was not quite an institution, Suzanne was 'Grandma' to the kids and the sisters were their 'Aunties'. Albert McFadden, who came to Jerusalem in 1895 at the age of three weeks, remembered as an old man: 'When we were there we did not call the Sisters "Sister". We were taught to call them "Auntie". I remember well Auntie Bridget, Auntie Dolores, Auntie Prisca, Auntie Carmel and Auntie Veronica.'[8] Suzanne was 'Grandma' for the rest of her life. In 1924, the eighty-nine-year-old woman signed her letter to thirteen-year-old Stanley Laird as 'Your devoted old "Grandma", Sr M. Joseph Aubert'. But she lost no authority as matriarch in staying Grandma. Thelma Howard was fifteen when Suzanne died and remembered that 'Mother liked us to call her "Grandma" and "Grandma" we did. But when she said "Do it," we did it!'[9]

Usually, the children coming into her family had no knowledge of any other relatives. Their parents were mostly not married to each other and sometimes they would be handed over anonymously as babies. In the language of the times, they were foundlings. One baby was, in fact, found in a basket by the captain on one of Hatrick's riverboats, carefully dressed and with a label attached, 'To Mother Aubert, Jerusalem'. In Suzanne's strong belief in the Holy Family of Nazareth, each of these children was the representative of Jesus:

> The Foundling is the child of God. It is the little brother or sister of the Divine Infant, for Whom 'there was no place in the inn' of Bethlehem. For us, the Foundling is His representative; it is poor and despised; there is no room for it – not even in a mother's arms! For one reason or another, she is obliged to part with it . . .[10]

Each child would have Jesus's mother, Mary, as their mother figure and Joseph as father. But the sisters, as Grandma and Aunties, were also giving the children a human family circle and were making sure they would be able to relate to them and depend on them as relatives:

> [T]he Sisters must identify themselves with the children, sharing their joys and their sadness. They must always have for them an affectionate smile and a kind, cheerful word, a smile being for infancy what a warm ray of the sun is for young plants.

As the children grow up, prepare them to face the world, its illusions, its dangers, its storms. Make them feel that they will always have in the Sisters real and devoted friends, in whom they can trust and confide. Help them in everything you can. Keep yourselves acquainted with all that concerns them. Act always as a mother to them, whether they are in the Home or out of it in the cold world.[11]

Merweh Madson said she looked on the sisters 'as my parents'. She remembered how Sister Isidore 'always had the time to listen while we told her of our grievances. . . . I loved her so much.'[12] John McMahon said of Sister Chanel: 'She was another Mother of mine and was always trying to make my life at Buckle St [in Wellington, where they later shifted] as near home life as possible. I could bring my school mates in and was allowed to go to their places.'[13]

The first children Suzanne took were not newborn babies. In 1891, Alfred and Lily Bignold, aged six and four, came from Wellington. And from Hawke's Bay came the three McKay children. In 1889, Suzanne had promised their widowed mother to take some of them as soon as she could, to help her cope. Edith, aged eight, George, five, and Mary, three, came up the river in December 1891. Their mother died in 1896 and before that they had already been legally transferred to Suzanne's care until they came of age.

These five were the first of many Pakeha children, and a few Maori, to live with the sisters and to join the local Maori children in their school. Girls and boys sat on separate sides of the classroom, as was standard practice, but Maori and Pakeha sat together. Suzanne was firm about this: 'You may keep the girls away from the boys, but not the Maoris from the pakehas. You would injure the school and offend the parents.'[14]

The 'orphans' would play with the children from the marae, sliding with them down the muddy slope in their bare feet, going eeling, watching with fascination the thousands of little whitebait being meticulously turned to dry brittle in the sun. Hohi Albert, born at the turn of the century, could remember as a little girl playing with the orphans and felt 'the sharing was too deep' for any real cultural unease.[15] Their prayers before school were all in Maori. Rewi Crichton, who was Pakeha in spite of the Maori name his mother had given him, remembered that invitations to 'big feasts or kai with the Mother and the Sisters were one of the many highlights. We all sat crosslegged around a central big mat loaded with food; flax and feathered mats kept us warm on an earthen floor. We ate with our hands, taking the food from large dishes and pans.'[16] They went out in the canoes to catch geese and other wildfowl. They remembered the chanting with the rhythm of the paddles.

John McMahon wrote about the monthly four-mile walk down to Ranana that he remembered making as a little boy on what was called 'Ranana Sunday'. Sister Prisca lived there. As John said: 'Week after week and year after year Sister Prisca tramped the lonely and dangerous sheep tracks from Ranana to Jerusalem in order to get to a weekly Mass and Holy Communion and join her Community if only for one day a week.' But once a month they went down to Ranana instead:

> As we reached the last hill top behind the wool-shed, we could see the Church and school building that was also Sister Prisca's humble one-roomed cottage. These things soon faded from our minds for now we could see Sister standing by her lonely shack, grand old Ned [Neri Metera], the Haami and Pauro families all up from the lower Pa to welcome us. And what a welcome awaited us. As we passed through the entrance gate, not one all carved and arched, as you would find in Rotorua, but a typical Maori gate thrown wide open, hanging on wire or flax hinges with a sheep skin or two thrown over it. But our eyes rested on none of these things. We saw only its open welcome, and those who stood awaiting our arrival. How pleased Sister Prisca was to see us all. Of course we youngsters were the first to reach her, for once inside the gate, nothing could hold us back.
>
> Then old Ned would come along; always a gentleman, he would stand back until Sister had spoken to us all. Time went all too quick for me to describe how we spent the day. All I know is, that Sister Prisca saw that we were all happy, and had plenty to eat and drink. While we enjoyed ourselves outside, Sister's loneliness all passed away, for she was now with the Sisters from Jerusalem, having a good korero.[17]

With the first children had come Kate Young, the fifteen-year-old daughter of a Protestant family Suzanne had known well in Hawke's Bay – Margaret Young was the midwife Suzanne had helped there. The 'Reminiscences' record that Kate's parents allowed her to go to the sisters at Jerusalem, 'thinking it would advance her education, though there was no boarding school there'.[18] But it is far more likely that, at fifteen, she went mainly to help with the children. Kate had a special link with Suzanne. As a little girl she had been raced to 'the Sister at the Mission', her right arm severely burnt after playing with matches and a candle. Suzanne treated it and fought with the doctors at Napier hospital to save it from amputation. Kate remembered the sister picking her up and holding her close while she prayed to the Virgin Mary to save the arm for her. Treated and splinted by Suzanne, the arm healed, though it became contracted as Kate grew without Suzanne there to insist on massage and exercises. Kate stayed to help at Jerusalem until 1900.

The cost of supporting all the children was a concern. Both the Marist priests and the sisters of the little congregation were already over-stretched financially on their Maori mission, with limited funding from the Propagation of the Faith. Housing, feeding, clothing and rearing up to forty-seven Pakeha children – the number the family eventually grew to – could never come from that budget. Suzanne was again putting her private money into the settlement at Jerusalem. When her much-loved and ever-helpful brother Camille died in 1890, he left her some money. Her mother died in 1894 and Suzanne came into the greater part of her inheritance, including the property at rue Montagny in Tarare. But the initial profit from the medicines had gone mainly into equipment and the two-storeyed house and shed up at the farm. There was not enough for the children. She began negotiations with the government for support from the industrial schools system, which dealt with 'neglected' children.

By the 1890s, New Zealanders were stepping out of the spare, tough life of settlement and mission into a society which already had in miniature the features of most other Western nations: centralised government, steamers, railways, telegraph, education, mines, farms and cities. And in miniature form, even though the Liberals tried to facilitate access to the land, New Zealand was experiencing the social problems of an industrial-ising and urbanising society. When Suzanne travelled in 1889 through the centre of New Zealand, from Napier to Christchurch, she had seen the difficulties many families were facing in both town and country.

Especially affected were mothers who were widows or whose husbands were often absent on seasonal work – shearing, bushfelling, fencing – or itinerant work such as gumdigging and goldmining. Sometimes they never came back and in the 1880s and 1890s the lure of Australia took a tide of men from depressed New Zealand. Whether at home or away, the men often had regular drinking binges which absorbed what family money there was. The loneliness of the immigrant family, without wider familial support in a land that might provide opportunity but was no utopia, took its toll on men, women and children.

People who came to New Zealand were generally not moneyed and they had a strong hope to 'better themselves'. Most had brought a horror of the hovering possibility of the workhouse, as in the English poor law system.[19] But New Zealand, too, had harshly defined, minimal government 'charitable aid' at the time and private charities in an infant society could depend only on the temporary energy of a few people. Dependent women had reason to be afraid. Becoming pauperised carried all its stigma of being what you somehow deserved. If the new country was meant to provide opportunity, then you were considered less than energetic and resourceful if you did not prosper. A strong current of thought – shared by Robert Stout, Premier from 1884 to 1887, and Dr Duncan MacGregor, who for twenty years from 1886 was Inspector-General of Hospitals and Charitable Institutions – held that the poor comprised a pollutant in society and that a Darwinian struggle for the survival of the fittest logically classified them as unfit, a 'residuum' of humanity.[20]

Suzanne could never think like that. She knew there were 'real rogues' among the people she met, 'as misery [destitution] is such a bad adviser, especially for young people who are repelled everywhere', but redeeming their inherent worth, as equal representatives of Jesus, was her goal:

> We must not pay attention to any poor man or woman because of their exterior; often they have neither the appearance nor the countenance of reasonable persons, being so coarse and rude. But, reverse the medal, and you will see by the light of faith that the Son of God, Who has willed to be poor, is represented by that poor creature. Rescue these wrecks of life, these poor spars tossed about by the storm, broken on the reefs of human misery.
>
> We have no right to believe we are the friends of Jesus Christ if we are not anxious about the souls whom He has redeemed at the price of the shedding of His Blood.[21]

There was generally widespread reproof of parents considered feckless and neglectful of their offspring. Children could even be charged with the 'offence' of being neglected. This could be carried to absurd lengths, as the ironic tone and exclamation mark of the *Wanganui Chronicle*'s report on 14 December 1888 indicates: 'At Dunedin the other day an illegitimate child a month old, whose mother had died in the Benevolent Institution, was brought up at the R. M. Court and gravely charged "with having no lawful and visible means of support"!'

But the inherent rights of childhood were gradually being recognised, and working in Suzanne's favour in the 1890s was MacGregor's belief in state support for children, 'whom he considered educable and still worthy of investment'.[22] The alternatives the government funded after the

Industrial Schools Act of 1882 were 'boarding out' in individual homes, and residential care in recognised private and state industrial schools. (The name 'industrial' indicated manual training.) Suzanne proposed that the Hiruharama community be recognised as one of these. Archbishop Redwood reported back to her in March 1893 that 'Mr Ballance, the Minister, is very favourably disposed towards your work and is willing to assist as far as the present law will permit him.'[23]

However, the government did not plan to recognise any more institutions at the time. William Habens, both Secretary of Education and Inspector-General of Schools, proposed a way around the legalities, to assist her. The magistrate could commit children to the industrial schools in Nelson or Upper Hutt, and their names would be on the school roll, but in fact the children would be with Suzanne and the money for their maintenance would come to her. And this is just what Judge Charles Kettle in Wanganui did. From 1893 until 1906, the 'Mission Home, Wanganui (Mother Aubert's)' was receiving annual funding for between three and eight children from the industrial schools rolls.[24]

Then, in 1895, four years after the first of her children arrived, Suzanne started to take in newborn babies. It was a watershed year for her, and the decision was supremely important for the congregation. It was her later determination to keep caring for babies born out of wedlock, in the way she thought best met their needs and the needs of their mothers at the time, which brought her into conflict with church authorities. In March, a local doctor, Patrick Connolly, met her at the quay in Wanganui as she was leaving on the riverboat. Knowing she would not refuse, he handed her a newborn baby he had delivered. It was nameless. Suzanne took the little boy and called him Joseph for St Joseph, and March for the month he was born. Joseph March, the first of the babies, went up the river into the special care of Sister Dolores.

After him, other babies came fast, sometimes brought by Suzanne returning from a trip to Wellington. Rewi Crichton was brought by train from Auckland. Francis Chamberlain came a special way in June 1897. Suzanne had been in Wellington and saw a distraught woman with something in her arms heading quickly at dusk towards the rocks near Oriental Bay. Suzanne hurried after her, catching up with her just in time. She had been planning to drown herself and the baby in the winter dark of the wild coastline. She was 'a waitress in a boarding-house for gentlemen on the Terrace'.[25] Her baby had been placed with a foster-mother whose fees she found hard to meet. She fell behind in payment and the woman had appeared in the dining-room at dinner time that night. In front of all the boarders, she thrust the baby at her, saying very publicly: 'Take your child if you can't pay for it. I won't keep it any longer for you.' The mother gave the baby boy to Suzanne's care. Suzanne then approached Archbishop Redwood, who baptised the baby himself on 15 June. He also stood godfather to him, giving him his own name, Francis. Nothing could have been more soul-satisfying for Suzanne, who now had the full blessing of the archbishop. This made the congregation's work with illegitimate children more acceptable and official.

By the 1890s there was widespread opinion that the country was being 'overrun with bastards'. The generation born of the prolific immigrants of the 1870s had reached employable and reproducing age. The country had slipped into recession and girls were being sent out often to sweatshop jobs as poorly paid seamstresses or as domestic servants in homes, hotels or boarding-houses. If they could not live at home they were especially vulnerable, and many were becoming pregnant.

There was also an element of 'wild colonial youth' in this boisterous generation growing up away from some of the social strictures of Britain, and their elders and politicians shook their heads over the 'larrikinism' and flirting, and wondered about imposing curfews.[26] But even if some girls may have kicked over the traces as much as the men, they were also susceptible to pressure and seduction by employers.[27] And it was the young women who would bear the shame, which was still very strong in a small society where you could not easily be anonymous. Their sense of shame was leading to insanitary abortions, concealed pregnancies and solitary childbirth, deaths from exhaustion and infection, suicide and infanticide.[28] Any number of inquest cases tell their stories.[29]

Eighteen ninety-five, the year Suzanne started caring for newborn babies, is significant because illegitimate babies, baby farming and infanticide were featuring strongly in the press then. On 12 August Minnie Dean was hanged, convicted of killing a baby in her care, and under suspicion of the deaths of six other unaccounted-for children. Labelled a 'baby farmer', she was the only woman ever to be hanged by law in New Zealand. There were certainly many unscrupulous baby farmers, a term introduced in Britain in the 1860s to designate the women, and sometimes men, who were the paid childcare workers of the nineteenth century. The atmosphere of shame and concealment led to a

lot of horrific abuse. But in the same period, while inquest juries were surprisingly lenient on clear cases of infanticide, baby farmers became
scapegoats for the birth and childcare problems of society as a whole.[30]

In New Zealand there was very little monitoring of the people whom
mothers paid to take in babies until January 1894, when the Infant Life
Protection Act 1893 first came into force. This required caregivers to
be registered, to provide details of the children and submit to regular
inspections of their homes and charges. Minnie Dean was caught in this
tightening-up. At her sentencing, the *Southland Times* wrote: 'How many
poor children are done to death, or at the best miserably ill-treated by
these harpies can never be known.' Yet, the community having flushed its
collective guilts through the expiatory channel of Minnie Dean, the paper
could carry on and admit a truth: 'The fault unmistakably lies with society
which, tolerant of any amount of immorality in man, has no sympathy or
pardon for the woman, but for one fault condemns her irretrievably.'[31]
Minnie Dean's defence lawyer, Alf Hanlon, had made this point too.
Unless the child born out of wedlock was sent away, the mother could not
hold up her head again. When a woman took a child to nurse, she really
had to hide the names from enquiry.

The subsequent Infant Life Protection Act of 1896 meant the mother's
identity had to be registered. She was also usually expected to breastfeed
the baby for six weeks at least before handing it over to government-
funded care. This requirement was sensible from a health perspective, but
it meant the woman could not possibly hide the fact of her childbirth.
There were hardly any places in institutions for newborn babies, and yet
a woman could not get a job with a baby in her care. The possibility of
suicide and infanticide was stronger than ever. Suzanne always dealt with
the here-and-now: she took the newborn babies when 'respectable' homes
were reluctant to do so.

A growing wave of public opinion also wanted to remove the stigma
from the child and to share the mother's blame with the father, who was
so far unscathed. Suzanne thought that the fear of having his name
publicised could lead to the father urging abortion on the woman. She
believed in protecting everyone from stigma where possible – fathers too.
She 'did not care to disclose the names of married men, because it might
injure them, or break up their homes', her statement at a later inquest
maintained. This protection of the family unit came probably from her
background in the bourgeoisie as much as from her religious dedication

to the concept of the Family of Nazareth. 'Single men, as a rule', she added, '"put their hats on, and went away," and the unfortunate girls never heard from them again.'[32] The nineteenth century still saw a debonair quality in the heterosexual adventures of the roving, unattached male, but the female was damned by a double standard. Any lapse by a woman was labelled as immoral.[33]

Suzanne's immediate concerns were saving the life of mother and child, and providing a chance for the mother's 'rehabilitation'. She believed very strongly that, given the climate of public blame, the mother had the right to guard her identity as a secret. She set out to create a caring environment for the child and to make sure there was the chance for the mother and child later to be reunited. Suzanne refused to reveal the identity of the mothers who handed over their babies. Her 'open' register of babies did not usually have their birth names. She kept another register privately, with the mother's particulars. The mother could visit the child, and also reclaim it later.

Suzanne was, of course, going against government regulations which required inspection of registers. Although she had many sympathisers, her home was unlikely, therefore, to be recognised or be eligible for state funding for the 'foundlings', as distinct from the other 'neglected' children. Up at Jerusalem she and the sisters just had to manage. At first they had the babies sleeping in their own dormitory by night, and with them in the kitchen by day, lined up on their potties if need be. Children were everywhere. One of the tourists who were now coming up 'the Rhine of New Zealand' was R. P. Collins, a building contractor from Wellington. He saw the crowded conditions and at his own expense built a large extension in 1897, adding another gable, which almost doubled the size of the convent. But almost immediately that was full. By July 1898, there were forty-seven children, thirty-two under four and sixteen not yet walking. Suzanne tried a different tack with the government, petitioning Parliament on 27 July for a building subsidy.

In the numbered points of Petition No. 83, presented by W. Symes, the member for Taranaki, she summarised her philosophy:

13 They [the babies] belong to every part of the Colony and to every denomination. In fact the number of those not belonging to Roman Catholic parents is by far the larger.

14 We make no distinction of Creed.

15 We keep the strictest secrecy about what we know of the parents, in order

to help the unfortunate mothers to regain a respectable place in society. And I am happy to say that so far the result has been most satisfactory. Girls who would have had only the option between the harbour and the street are now decent wives and useful members of society.

16 For mercy and secrecy have always proved to be the most powerful means of rescue in such cases.

17 Mercy without secrecy often becomes cruelty and misses altogether its aim.

18 We look upon the little ones as being our own and we consider our task over only after they are respectably settled in the world . . .[34]

Her handwritten notes for this petition, with their crossings-out and amendments, show even more the way she was thinking. She considered that 'the Infant Life Protection Act . . . though very good in its meaning, fails in [a] great many cases to attain the desired end'. It was failing because:

> The young woman who has for a moment forgotten herself under the pinch of poverty and a delusive promise of marriage, will, if she has preserved any self respect, rather hide and starve than expose her misfortune to publicity by appealing publicly for an assistance which labels her and her outcast infant. And it will not be long before she is driven to some desperate action if a merciful hand is not discreetly held out to her. . . . The rich is able to cover his fault, the poor cannot cloak his and he sinks deeper and deeper.[35]

Suzanne was an intelligent and independent thinker, and aware of the reasons for the stance the government took. That did not affect her own determination, which was fuelled by her spiritual beliefs right from her childhood in France. The children were to find in the sisters 'mothers, to whom they owe not only material life, but moral life, Christian life, that is to say, a happy life in spite of all'.[36] Then there was the commitment to saving the souls of children. Throughout the nineteenth century there was a very high mortality rate among illegitimate, abandoned or foundling children in France, and a constant suspicion of infanticide. Devout people tried to save these souls. In Catholic theology the child was paramount and its right to survive in childbirth, for example, took precedence over the mother's. For a baby to die unbaptised meant that in the afterlife it went to limbo instead of heaven. To avoid this, anyone, even a layperson, had the right and responsibility to baptise a baby who seemed at the point of death. Father Reignier's baptism registers of the 1870s show Suzanne doing this in Hawke's Bay.

Suzanne's mother and grandmother had both worked in an *oeuvre*, one of the charitable organisations of the bourgeoisie, aiding the mothers and protecting their anonymity, helping them to survive. The principle of the sanctity of life meant that suicide was a sin. The sisters remembered Suzanne telling them that her mother, Clarice Aubert, 'aimed first of all at restoring their self-respect and with a view to this, she exerted every effort to maintain secrecy'. The phrases would recur again and again: 'begin life again with no fear of any slur on her good name'; 'make a respectable marriage'; 'lead an honoured life thenceforth'. Clarice said that the best way to prevent a 'second fall' was to ensure secrecy about the first. She disapproved of institutions for unmarried mothers, because a girl's good name was 'irretrievably lost if she was placed in one'.[37] Suzanne walked firmly down the same track.

The problem of foundling babies and abandoned children was acute in nineteenth-century France, partly because of the large number of impoverished young women now in factories. By 1866, almost one and a half million women were working in industry, about thirty percent of the total workforce.[38] From 1837 to 1846, about a third of all births in Paris were illegitimate. At one period, as many as a quarter of all newborn babies and half of all illegitimate babies in Paris were abandoned each year, left at the state *hospice*. Lyon too was a major industrial city, with women working at the silk looms. The charitable church-run factories, under attack in the 1848 revolution, were set up partly to give a supervised work situation which would guard the chastity of girl workers. These factories were all around the areas in which Suzanne grew up.

Paternity suits were forbidden by the French civil code of the time. Seduction was not punishable. Men were not required to support their illegitimate children. A high percentage of births were to servant girls, yet they had no redress against employers who got them pregnant. And the sentences for infanticide seemed to be tougher on the women than in New Zealand.[39] The state had to take responsibility for abandoned children. France was in advance of other countries in doing this, but the system was flawed, partly because of the magnitude of the task. Facilities for the continuing care of children were skeletal. Infant mortality fell more slowly in France than in other countries. In the mid-1850s, the death rate for foundling and other children in the state's care was fifty-six percent.[40]

The main method of receiving the children was traditional but always controversial. Cylinder-like turnstiles called *tours* were built into the walls of foundling *hospices*. You could place the baby in the half-circle on the street side, quickly ring a bell and disappear. The half-circle would be turned to the inside and the baby taken in. Your identity would never be known unless you left details or clues pinned to the child. Bourgeois Catholics on the whole supported this, as they believed it preserved the honour of both the woman and her family and therefore lessened the risk of abortion, suicide and infanticide. Other Catholics like Alphonse Lamartine supported the *tour* as an example of Christian charity. He was restating the argument of St Vincent de Paul, that this would protect the children from infanticide and give the mothers a chance to redeem themselves. This was a strongly held opinion in Lyon, and Suzanne's often-repeated belief.[41]

But opponents, often social purists, thought the *tours* encouraged promiscuity and casual abandonment. In 1849 a commission investigated the whole system.[42] By the late 1850s many *tours* were closed down and, without this screen, a woman's 'lapse' suddenly became much more public. Suzanne was a young woman actively working in social welfare at this time, with a mother and grandmother following the subject keenly and worrying about the probability of renewed suicide and infanticide.

Suzanne was also influenced by her own family experience, which must have welled up for her in the 1890s. While New Zealand government thinking favoured children being fostered or 'boarded out', she disliked the system intensely (though she accepted it reluctantly once children were about twelve, when most were going out to work anyway). Her reactions to 'boarding out' and 'baby farmers' were instinctive and strong:

> The poor little illegitimate children are often entrusted to mercenary nurses, terrible 'makers of Angels'. They have their own children, they have their own work, and they neglect the poor little ones whom they consider as a means of livelihood, as a speculation. They only half feed them, and they neglect much more the care of their soul and of their education, as they themselves are so much the more incapable of forming the heart and the mind of the children, and they tolerate immorality; so that those poor little creatures are at a school of spiritual and corporal misery, and seem to be vowed to a miserable life in all respects here and hereafter. [43]

She would talk about her brother Camille's experience. Their mother had been ill since the birth of Louis, the disabled child. When Camille was born in 1840, he was put into the care of a rural wet-nurse. This was not at all uncommon in France at the time, though Camille was with a private wet-nurse, not one of the state-funded *nourrices*.[44] Most of the babies abandoned at the *hospices*, which were way-stations rather than institutional homes, were sent out to the country to wet-nurses or foster mothers. The state system did not have a good reputation. Fostering was the cheapest option and the responsibility at this time was diffused far down the social scale. The children suffered and the mortality rate was high. Her little brother was absent from Suzanne's life for his first four years, as Clarice Aubert remained ill, Suzanne said, until her miraculous recovery at Fourvière in 1845. Camille 'had been reared in such simple surroundings and on such plain fare, that every day [now] was a feast day to him'.[45] She must have felt some lingering concern about why her little brother had been left so long in this way, why he could not have had care closer to home, why his milieu had been so spartan when their own family was bourgeois. Fostering was anathema to her: the system seemed to rub out the soul of the child.

All her French experience of foundling babies and their care went into Suzanne's 1898 petition to the government in New Zealand. The petition clearly outlined her philosophy and was received by the Public Petitions Committee with respect. On 29 July, 'having found the object and methods to be most worthy', it recommended the petition to 'the favourable consideration of the Government'.[46] The Premier, Richard Seddon, wrote to Suzanne in Wellington, where she was staying with friends, the Lynch family, that 'the matter will receive consideration'.[47]

The Lynches were neighbours of the Seddons in Molesworth St, and Seddon's daughter, Elizabeth, remembered Mother Aubert coming more than once before breakfast to bail up her father over some issue, and entertaining the children while she waited for him to emerge.[48] Suzanne admired 'his efforts to assist the working-man and the poor. "We got on very well together", she would say'. Suzanne must have been aware of a new emphasis on accessibility after the Liberals took office. William Pember Reeves described this as 'a privilege that the colonists in a democratic country like this have of writing to and of enjoying the closest communication possible with those who are intrusted with the government of the country'.[49] Suzanne Aubert availed herself of this privilege to the full.[50]

And the net of benefactors, the first strands knotted on the collecting tour of 1889, was also being strengthened in its weave. Suzanne, always willing to provide an opportunity to 'do good', once climbed steep Tinakori Hill to visit Sarah Rhodes at her Wadestown home, The Grange. Sarah was genuinely not at home and wrote to Suzanne as soon as possible afterwards, on 25 July 1898:

You have my fullest sympathy in all your good works – particularly the Foundling Home at Jerusalem – towards the maintenance of which kindly accep[t] the enclosed small cheque as a donation.

I have a profound respect for all good Catholics – but as I am a member of the English Church I am not in a position to offer any advice to one of your great experience . . .[51]

Suzanne's 'great experience' was not enough, however, to deal with what was happening at Jerusalem in her absence at that time. Babies were dying. Five 'puny and delicate' new ones had come on 12 July, 'three of whom were noticed to be unwell on the way to the institution'. By 27 July six children had died from some undiagnosed infection which the various doctors now involved – Anderson, Connolly, Wait and Christie – thought could have been measles but might have been connected with 'the cow's milk being affected by the herbage on which the cattle feed at this time of the year'. (In *Brett's Colonists' Guide*, widely used in New Zealand at the time, there was no mention of scalding the cow's milk given to babies in order to sterilise it.) The resulting inquests were held down in Wanganui and reported fully in the *Wanganui Herald*, the *Wanganui Chronicle* and the *Yeoman*. The frail figures of Arthur Lucas, Thomas Keily, Annie Hoare, Miriam Boon, Sylvia Davis, Mary Pettit, and later Frances Stanley, were laid out in the newspaper columns, along with the story of their brief time at Jerusalem.

At the inquests Mother Mary Joseph was called to account for the secrecy which surrounded the identity of the children in her care, and her opposition to government supervision was strongly questioned. A deputation had already gone to Parliament protesting against public money being spent on 'the provision of facilities for covering up the consequences of vice'.[52] And a defender of secular policies in a newspaper column was not convinced that 'the cause of public morality can be furthered by such large power of "hushing up" cases being entrusted to two irresponsible persons like Mother Aubert and Father Soulas'. Clearly, tax-payers' money would not now be going up the Whanganui River without considerable scrutiny. 'Already', the columnist continued, 'we have committed the error of granting aids to certain religious institutions such as the Magdala Home at Christchurch, and it is only right that this pernicious principle should be nipped in the bud.'[53]

Suzanne gave a strong defence of her policies. She never 'had any objection to the inspection of food, clothing and buildings, but objected to the inspection of the register in which the full names appear. . . . [She] objected to the mother's name being disclosed because in her experience it blasted her for life. . . . She left it to the mother to disclose or not as she pleased.'[54] Public reaction was generally supportive of 'the self-devoted woman who mothers so many unfortunates'.[55] F. M. Spurdle would write to Seddon from Wanganui in January 1899 of 'the Mother's care and the benefits of home-life and training' that Suzanne was giving to these 'infant waifs', and urged the Premier not to interrupt her methods as 'a certain amount of secrecy is necessary in many cases'.[56]

Suzanne's defence of anonymity held other risks for her, which seem not to have been aired in the papers of the time. Later, however, Archbishop O'Shea would worry that this 'secrecy' would only fuel rumours – more common in other colonies, though whispered in New Zealand – of priests' babies, nuns' babies, hustled away illegitimate babies of rich people – and little corpses in lime pits.[57]

Most sensible people could at least respect Suzanne's reasoning, though, and she had the support of intelligent and influential women in Wanganui. Jessie Williamson, president of the Wanganui Women's Political League, was one. The two women probably knew each other already, as Jessie's husband was a chemist who stocked Suzanne's rongoa. The secular champion of women's rights and the devout Catholic nun were well suited in personality.

Jessie Williamson had four daughters and still found the energy to be an active altruist and advocate for social change. She was an important member of the National Council of Women and was 'noted for her enthusiasm, and shrewd common sense'. She was remarked on for her 'merry face, amusing sallies and fluent Irish tongue'; everyone 'brightened up visibly when Mrs Williamson began to speak'.[58] She gave evidence at one of the inquests. She visited the Jerusalem home once a month, she testified, as honorary inspector appointed by the Education Department to oversee the eight older children then funded by the industrial schools system. Her defence of Suzanne and the sisters was whole-hearted. 'Could not speak too highly of the way the Home was managed. The children's bedding was good, as was everything else. Saw the children at lesson and at play. Had every opportunity of forming a good opinion.'[59]

Suzanne knew how to issue a timely and effective press release. When the crisis was on the wane but still fresh in the public's mind, the *Wanganui Chronicle* of 18 August 1898 carried her message:

Mother Mary Joseph Aubert begs to return her most sincere thanks to the people of Wanganui for the sympathy they have shown her in her trouble. She is happy to report that only one baby is still now in a bad state of health at the Home. The others are fast recovering. Mother Mary Joseph desires to express special thanks to Mr Hatrick for his kind offers; to the members of the jury for their sympathetic and gratifying rider; to Mr John Duncan for the gift of £5 and two cases of oranges; to Mr Hatrick for a case of oranges and a half cwt of lollies; to Mrs Kitchen for a perambulator and a cradle; and to Mesdames Mitford, Mayes, Austin, Connolly, Duncan, Bowen, Kitchen, Ellis, Hartshorn, and Williamson for clothes for the babies.

The Mesdames of Wanganui would rally for the babies as the Dames de Saint-Nizier had done in her youth.

By no coincidence, surely, 18 August was also the date of the annual meeting of the Wanganui Women's Political League, and the next day's *Wanganui Chronicle* carried their resolution, proposed by Mrs Williamson and seconded by Mrs Wright: 'Recognising the value of the work carried on at Jerusalem, on the Wanganui River, by Mother Mary Joseph Aubert, the Wanganui Women's Political League respectfully urges the Government to grant her the monetary aid she is petitioning for, providing', they added, 'that, to guard against possible future contingencies, the Institution is brought under State Supervision.'

Jessie Williamson wrote to Suzanne on 22 August, almost apologising for the final clause:

Dear Mother Mary,
Just a word to explain the newspaper report I send you. I, being in the Chair, could not bring forward business on my own account, and I asked Mrs. Bullock if she would do it at our Meeting. She did not atten[d] through illness, but wrote the Resolution which you will see in the paper, and forwarded it to me at our Meeting with a letter asking me or someone else to propose it for her.

Of course, knowing your objections to 'State Supervision' I would neither have mentioned such a thing, nor have put it in if I could have kept it out, but as you will see, I could not. I sent it, this morning, to the Premier.

I shall be sending you a sack of clothes next week, so don't be puzzling this time over where they have come from.

I hope your babies are all well now.
With much love,
Yours sincerely . . .[60]

On the whole the members of the league would have wanted state supervision. They also supported boarding-out as being in general more humane and natural than institutions. Jessie Williamson would also argue elsewhere that 'men should be forced to acknowledge their role' in illegitimate births.[61] But the warmth in Jessie's letter shows that the women were largely giving a vote of confidence and trust in Suzanne personally and acknowledging, as they said, the 'value of the work'. The inquest jury had also recommended supervision, along with praising her work.

Christie, one of the doctors, had noted: 'It is unfortunate that the institution is so far from medical aid. I advise that it be put under supervision.'[62] The medical aspect of care was important. Suzanne, the expert, had been away in Wellington for a long time mounting the petition to Parliament. Institutionalised care of babies, with bottle feeding instead of breast milk, was known to increase greatly the risk of mortality. Infections and epidemics could quickly bring death to babies like these, living in close quarters. The Jerusalem babies often arrived already ailing, sometimes starving, sometimes infected with venereal disease. Jerusalem was not the place for tiny sickly babies. After the inquests she was recommended to take in no new babies for the time being.

Suzanne wanted to restore a positive image of her babies and children after all this. She wasted no time in providing the right publicity. On 20 August, the Wanganui *Yeoman* announced:

> We have been shown a photograph of a number of the children at the Foundling Home at Jerusalem, and the healthy and contented appearance of the unfortunates speaks volumes for the care and attention bestowed upon them by Mother Mary Joseph Aubert and her competent assistants. The picture is on view in Messrs H. I. Jones and Sons' windows.

At some stage in 1898, either then or in preparation for the petition, the photograph had been taken by the well-known Wanganui photographer A. Martin. Mother Aubert is there, holding little Francis Chamberlain, the archbishop's protégé. Kate Young is there, too, and perhaps one of her sisters, but no 'competent assistants', no religious sisters in their habits and goffered coifs. Why not? Perhaps Suzanne was playing down the sectarian element, bound to be controversial, as she went about seeking secular finance and good will. H. I. Jones and Sons, Booksellers and Publishing Agents, had mounted the photograph. Suzanne herself may have stepped into the offices of the *Yeoman* to show them the photograph before it was displayed. If not, she would have arranged promptly for this to be done.

It was another clear-sighted woman, Grace Neill, who now found a solution to the secrecy versus supervision impasse. In that crucial year of 1895, Dr Duncan MacGregor requested a female inspector to handle 'the numerous and delicate questions affecting women which have to be dealt with in connection with our system of charitable aid, and our hospitals and asylums'.[63] Grace Neill was appointed. She was a brilliant, enterprising, hard-working woman, a trained nurse, a widow on a small salary raising a son on her own. She was 'omnicompetent', even writing MacGregor's annual report on occasion. The less capable women she once labelled as 'brazen-faced beggars of the female sex'[64] might not have got from her the compassion Suzanne felt, but the two would respect each other.

Their acquaintance began with a misunderstanding. Grace went unannounced up to Jerusalem in mid-October and was promptly sent packing by a sister suspicious of 'supervision'. Suzanne was away, back down in Wellington. On her 'Lunacy and Hospitals' letterhead paper, as 'Asst Inspector Hospitals & Charitable Institutions', Grace wrote stiffly but neutrally to her on 18 October from Chavanne's Hotel in Wanganui:

Dear Madam,
According to instructions received, I visited Jerusalem last Friday in order to make a report upon the orphanage there to the Hon. W. C. Walker, Minister in Charge of Charitable Institutions.
Unfortunately you were absent, and during your absence and without your permission, the Sister in charge could not allow me to go through the institution and I had to leave Jerusalem next day with my errand unfulfilled.
I must return to Wellington today, and regret much that I have had no opportunity of meeting you.
I remain, Madam, yrs faithfully . . .[65]

Suzanne sent an answer post-haste, also speeding another apology to William Walker, the minister. The two women may already have met or communicated after Grace's return.

Dear Madam,
In reply to your courteous letter of 18th Oct / 98 re your visit to Jerusalem and especially more so after having heard from you today the particulars of that unfortunate visit, allow me to express to you my deep regret for my having been absent at the time and to apologise to you, as head of the Institution, for what has happened. Had I been there, two minutes of explanation would have prevented the sad and thorough misunderstanding which must very much hurt your feelings and which I assure you grieves me at heart.

Hoping that on your next visit I shall have the pleasure to welcome you there myself. I remain
dear Madam
Yours sincerely . . .[66]

With the air cleared instantly and satisfactorily, Grace Neill set out to help Suzanne on the same day. She was a person to resolve problems: 'Could you make it convenient to see me here tomorrow (Saturday) before 1 p.m.? Or on Monday at any time? On reconsidering the matter – looking more carefully into the Act, I am inclined to change my opinion as to the advisability of registration in your case . . .'[67]

By the following day, 22 October, Grace had outlined three options. Suzanne could register, receive payment and be subject to supervision under the Commissioner of Police – this meant open records, of course. Or she could ask to be exempted from registration, though Grace felt this was unlikely to be granted. Third, she could 'remain unregistered, and therefore unable legally to take money for children placed in the Home, but to request the Minister in charge of Charitable Institutions to allow an officer of his Department to visit Jerusalem at uncertain intervals, in order to inspect the Home as to sanitation, food, clothing, and general well-being of the children, and make report to him thereupon'.[68] Suzanne could send a voluntary return accounting for the children, but being required to identify them only by the initials corresponding with the names in her 'private book'.

Regular, helpful contact with a department inspector would keep the reputation of the foundling home above suspicion and both women knew that Suzanne would be unlikely to get government money without supervision. This was a turning-point, after which Suzanne began to refer firmly to Providence as her bank. Her letter went to Walker the next day, accepting the third alternative – although she carefully made no reference to initials of children, only numbers. Joseph Ward wrote to her on 31 October. He marked his letter 'Private' as he often did when he wrote to fellow Catholics, as he was sensitive about being thought partisan. He had seen Walker, who 'was of [the] opinion that if you came under No. 3 there would be no trouble. He assured me that it was not contemplated to exercise control over the institution or to interfere in a meddlesome way with the good work you have in hand . . .'[69] The voluntary inspector appointed in January was, not unexpectedly, Jessie Williamson. Everyone was satisfied and nobody was 'meddlesome'. Jessie carried on actively working for the rights of children; in 1906 she was lobbying with Kate Sheppard and Ada Wells for a new government department 'headed by a capable woman, to look after waifs and strays'.[70]

So the sisters took in no new babies up the river but carried on feeding, changing, and chasing the many scallywags they had. One priest said they were 'a lot of little hangmen up there'; he was possibly overwhelmed by the little bodies bumping down the wooden stairs and rattling their tin cans in the orchard below the convent. Suzanne's injunctions to the sisters against raising their hands to the children in anger were probably directed as much at herself. The reality was never totally holy. John McMahon reminded the sisters of how he had been clipped over the ear by Suzanne with a volume of *Lives of the Saints* when she caught him at the telephone in the Wellington Buckle St home. He had been plotting the death of the scruffy dog that she loved and nobody else, it seems, could bear. She once up-ended and spanked Rewi Crichton with her slipper. He wrote to her when she was very old to ask her, tongue in cheek, if he could have the slipper as a memento, a sort of 'relic': 'Please remember me to the other dear Sisters . . . I remember the many charitable and motherly deliberations – for we were indeed wild, but you can rest assured, dear Mother, they have not failed in producing their desired effect. . . . You won't forget that slipper I asked for? I shall never forget that slipper.'[71]

All the children had work to do. Albert McFadden recalled: 'I used to take a pack horse up to the farm to get the milk.[72] There were square cans with each can perhaps holding five or six gallons of milk; these were tied, one on each side of the horse's saddle. My pack horse who was named Takuwhero [or Takuiro] would not let a person walk behind him and consequently you had to lead him. If you tried to get behind he would rear up on his hind legs, lay back his ears, buck and try to jump on you. . . . One of my small duties was to beat kerosene tins to frighten the birds away from the many cherry trees which grew around the settlement when the fruit was ripe. . . . I still remember the black cherries and the sweetheart cherry. We used to go down to Hatrick's boat which used to stop at Jerusalem, to sell cherries in small flax baskets made by the Maoris, for one shilling a punnet.'[73]

Rewi, too, remembered the scary trip on the lonely track to and from the farm with wild pigs confronting the packhorse, the 'deafening chorus of locusts buzzing in the trees around', and the joy of arrival with 'the hearth fire cakes in the earth floor kitchen of the Farm House as a reward':

> It was a relief
> I quivered like a leaf
> to see the open gate.
> And, there the farm; the journey's end; what comfort there.
> The warmth of love, of care and kindness, was home once more.
> To the kitchen to fare
> We churned cream so rare
> It had an earthen floor,
> while there so close, through all the while, the King was there
> just behind the door.[74]
> I remember it well, right next that kitchen bare.
>
> The hum of bees just over there, their hives.
> I think the honey we shared,
> and I am sure the potatoes in the shed
> must have thought we never cared
> as we scampered over their bed
> but I remember it was warm in there,
> no doubt we didn't care.
>
> Don't you remember?
> There, the old store near,
> and the barn quite new – on the crest of the hill.
> We were sheltered there,
> twice or more,
> why, I remember the sack-cloth beds,
> as arranged above the floor.
> Then off to the garden, astride the horse, over the hills,
> the hothouse too, all white in the midst,
> and still far, far away
> the cherry tree tops called us from play
> to work. Do you remember?[75]

Rewi also remembered what Suzanne in her sixties looked like to them:

> For some unknown reason I and another boy of my own age were very fond of Mother. We sought her company and clung to her commodious blue skirt or gown whenever she was around. A gift of sweets often rewarded singing duets, in which she joined to our joy and merriment.
>
>   This surging emotional dynamism in our midst made us all more or less oblivious of an eye defect that burned with a firey light in a face almost round, broad and flat but with a mouth perpetually gay with a kind and loving or forgiving smile. The cast nor eye did not trouble us, but kept us in childish

awe. Above all this there flowed from a big heart much bigger than her almost masculine frame, a warmth of maternal love that won our lasting love and affection.[76]

He and several other 'orphans' fought in the First World War. The sisters tried to find where they were and sent letters. Suzanne would do the same from Rome. In February 1918 she wrote to 'No. 22406 Private J. J. Kenny' in Grey Towers Hospital in Essex. 'My dear boy,' she wrote, 'I cannot tell you how pleased I was to get your nice affectionate letter of 3d inst. which I received only three days ago. I thank God that you are still alive. . . . You do not forget grandma and I can assure you that grandma dearly loves her boys and that she prays for each of them every day with all her heart. . . . My poor boy, if you are sent back before you are quite well, you may be sure that the Sisters will befriend you, that you will always be their little Joe and grandma's little Joe however big you may be now.'[77]

CHAPTER THIRTEEN

Wellington – the Daughters of Our Lady of Compassion 1899-1904

The wind has changed : Kua rere ke te hau
Where is your mother going? : E anga ana to whaea kohea?
– To Wellington : – Ko Poneke[1]

In the early 1870s, Suzanne had dismissed Wellington. The new capital was 'horrible, so awfully windy you can't stick your nose out of doors'.[2] But in January 1899 she went to live and work there and, except for one break, was based there for the rest of her life. When the *Yeoman* promoted the August 1898 photograph display of the 'healthy and contented' foundling children at Jerusalem, the newspaper also recorded elsewhere: 'it is stated that the Roman Catholic Church has in contemplation the establishment in Wellington of a branch of a sisterhood which devotes itself exclusively to visiting the sick, succouring the needy, and housing the needy poor'.

Priests and doctors in Wellington were asking for help. The emphasis of the Sisters of Mercy there had been primarily on teaching. They coped as best they could with cases of distress, but there was no other female congregation in the city of Wellington. Suzanne was by now well known for her work in nursing and medicine and with disadvantaged children. She was at ease in the company of Pakeha and Maori, Catholic and non-Catholic. She had wider experience than any other religious sister in New Zealand at the time. She was the one that Drs Grace, Cahill, Martin and Mackin were asking to bring sisters to Wellington.

For her part, Suzanne had been frequently indicating interest in wider social welfare work. In 1895 she had told the Irish activist Michael Davitt, who was touring Australia and New Zealand, that the 'aim of our institution is works of charity in their widest acceptance'.[3] In the same period an article in the Melbourne *Advocate*, originating possibly from the agent for her medicines there, had said that, as soon as 'the aid of charitable people' made it possible, Mother Mary Joseph Aubert would be erecting a special building to receive 'all those incurables who because of their deformities, or of the disgusting nature of their sores, or of the slight [unlikely] chance of ameliorating their condition, are refused admittance elsewhere'.[4] In those days, incurable cancers of the mouth and throat, for example, resulted in extreme disfigurement and you had to be strong-stomached to nurse sufferers. At Jerusalem she had already been nursing a few old 'incurable' Maori women for years. The statement in the *Yeoman* must surely have been referring to her sisters, and the source was possibly Suzanne herself. Two Wellington girls who later joined the congregation remembered 'there had been talk for months before of Mother Joseph bringing her Sisters to Wellington'.[5]

Suzanne had been told not to take in new babies or children at Jerusalem for the time being. But she was not used to marking time. She arrived in Wellington to set up work at Buckle St, on the edge of the Basin Reserve, late in the evening of Friday, 6 January 1899. It was Epiphany. Tramping up with her from the waterfront Tory St station were Sister Magdalen Savage, her companion on the collecting tour ten years before, Sister Agnes Brownlie and Sister Marcelle Small.

Delays in Wanganui over Christmas and New Year and extra costs for the children had emptied Suzanne's purse. But somehow she wanted this. She would have expected, would even have made sure, that for such a momentous new venture some stoic trial needed to be endured, some feat of asceticism or act of mortification accomplished, for them to be worthy of the task. She once told her sisters to 'remember that you cannot be good without having to offer up the daily sacrifices which are inherent in our lives. We cannot drive to heaven. The road is narrow and we have to tread it on foot, regardless of the thorns and stones. No sacrifice – no reward – no heaven.'[6] So, with only half a crown, they arrived at nine o'clock, unannounced, without welcome and lacking the key to their unfurnished rented cottage. Her friend, Miss Christie, crowded all four women for the night into one little bedroom of her boarding-house nearby.

Also close by was St Joseph's, the local church which was then an out-station of St Mary of the Angels in the central city. On Sunday, Father Ainsworth as curate rallied the parish of Te Aro to help the sisters, and a cooked leg of mutton, Mrs O'Dea's Sunday joint, was one of the Epiphany gifts that were ferried across the doorstep of the bare cottage. At the same time, and with justification, Father Devoy bridled that he had not been told either by Archbishop Redwood or by Mother Mary

Joseph just when the sisters were coming into his parish.

The dramatic streak in Suzanne's nature would have allowed for both reactions. First, the people's warm and immediate bringing of gifts would create a positive, symbolic precedent to serve as a point of reference hereafter. As well, perhaps an equally symbolic notice was being served, a hint that Mother Aubert, with a rather quirky and sparky independence, was quite likely to take venturesome initiatives without too much consultation. Her own sisters knew and accommodated this trait in her character. Sister Angela has a rueful tone in the 'Reminiscences' when she explains a journey Suzanne made to Napier: 'She was thoroughly consistent in always having as an object of her journeys charity towards God or towards man. She was almost equally consistent in hiding from her right hand what her left was doing!'[7]

The *New Zealand Times* of 9 January 1899 announced their arrival:

> On Friday last the Rev. Mother Mary Joseph Aubert, accompanied by three sisters of her Order, arrived in Wellington. The Order is known by the name of 'The Sisters of Our Lady of Compassion'. The sisters are at present occupying a small cottage next to St Joseph's Church, Buckle-street. The sphere of the ladies' labour is entirely among the poor and the afflicted. They will be constantly occupied in finding out the poor of the city and in doing all in their power to alleviate their distress. They also attend to the sick and work for those who cannot afford to pay for a nurse, but for their own support they depend entirely on the voluntary offerings of friends and sympathisers. The 'Sisters of Compassion' will no doubt find ample scope for their zeal among the distressed and afflicted of the city. The headquarters of the Order is at Jerusalem on the Wanganui River, where a foundling home is established for orphans and poor children. The efforts of the good sisters in Wellington will doubtless be productive of much good among the poor.

There was no mention here of Maori mission work. The focus of the article (or press release) was held firmly on social welfare. The sisters had served their apprenticeship in this with the foundling home up the river.

There was another indication of change. The clear gazetting of the name 'The Sisters of Our Lady of Compassion' turned over a leaf in Suzanne's Marist history. The New Zealand Sisters of the Third Order Regular of Mary disappeared from sight as the fresh page of the Daughters of Our Lady of Compassion was smoothed down.[8] Alice Brett remembered Archbishop Redwood coming to preach a welcoming sermon on the Sunday night at St Joseph's. He described the Magi following the star to Bethlehem, then brought closer to home his Epiphany theme. He 'spoke of his "own Sisters", who had just come to the parish. He said: "They are my own. *I gave them their name*. They have followed the star of their vocation, and it has brought them here . . .".'[9]

They had, in fact, already spent six years as his 'own Sisters', a purely diocesan congregation no longer connected to the Society of Mary. In September 1892, they had become the Daughters of Our Lady of Compassion, the name he had selected for them to reflect the compassionate nature of their fledgling work for 'all suffering'. Suzanne's interpretation of the French *Filles de Notre Dame de Compassion*, however, was more as subordinate 'handmaids of Our Lady', with the emphasis on work and service, but Redwood opted for the familial tone of 'daughters'. He brought them securely within the family circle of Nazareth, and the homelike theme suited the community's philosophy.

Just as the 1884 handover of the Maori mission from the Sisters of St Joseph to the Third Order Regular of Mary is unclear in the documentation, so is the changeover to the Daughters of Our Lady of Compassion. There is a vagueness in Marist and archdiocesan records which suggests feelings rather than hard facts: apprehension, puzzlement, a slight disapproval, a distancing. The little Third Order Regular of Mary at Hiruharama had been Marist in affiliation, diocesan but technically linked (as were its sister diocesan communities in Oceania) to the recently formed congregation at Saint Brieuc in France. This was led by the founding sister, Madame des Groues. The title of *Madame* for the superior was in the tradition of the old orders. Suzanne implied in later years that Madame des Groues had not been keen on the New Zealand branch; apart from the risk of the congregation spreading itself too thinly, however, there was no reason for this. Madame des Groues could only benefit from having a pool of English-speaking sisters available for the Islands.

The mission priests at Hiruharama were also Marist and French. There was no theoretical reason why the Marist connection could not have continued for the women as well. But there were practical reasons why it did not. The Whanganui River mission became marginalised in the society. Maori mission tended to do so anyway, as growing Catholic New Zealand pulled up the tidier patchwork of Pakeha parishes over the frontier missions. Maori missioners, well into the twentieth century, would sense from their colleagues in parishes that they were considered peripheral, abnormal and even on occasion financially dispensable.[10] Soulas's Hiruharama station was already exceptional in being totally Maori; most priests now had more Pakeha than Maori to care for.

But in the 1880s and 1890s the personality of Father Soulas aggravated any expected frontier isolation. He was dedicated to Maori mission and he fought, argued and quibbled in its defence for years. He knew that Maori people, with their own priorities and money difficulties as they grappled with the Land Court, for instance, would be unlikely to supplement a priest's or a community of sisters' income in the way Irish parishioners were long used to doing. The Propagation of the Faith's vote of money to the Maori mission was tiny for New Zealand budgets; it was geared to the simpler societies of the Pacific Islands.[11] And Archbishop Redwood, like other bishops, did not always use it on indigenous mission. It could be used partly for his travel to and from Europe, for instance.

Yet Soulas kept losing his sense of proportion and went beyond concern over general and valid issues to become personal and paranoic. He worried and engaged in nitpicking over money with what his fellow Frenchmen labelled as a Breton fixation. He quarrelled, with the threatened touchiness of the senior in the field, with probably every man in the new wave of priests coming to Hiruharama with their innocent illusions – then disillusions. One by one they went away again, and the more personal reasons for their shift were usually camouflaged or subsumed by the call of extending or reviving mission elsewhere. Even though he was sharing regularly in retreats, and representing Maori mission, Soulas, in both his heart and his actions, began to be alone and to be left alone. He later neglected to send in his mission reports to the Society of Mary; his financial accounting tended to be a mystery.

There was also the underlying feeling that Soulas would rather hold the community of sisters in reserve, not quite fully integrating them in the Third Order Regular of Mary, so as to retain the possibility of an indigenous order. Father Woods, as co-founder of the Australian Congregation of the Sisters of St Joseph, with a branch of his own since 1880 in Wanganui, provided a model. Redwood had had to correct Soulas tersely in 1884: 'I have not for a single moment entertained the idea of founding a *new* order . . . I have no intention of approving a new order.'[12] But Soulas persisted in thinking of them as *his* sisters and Father Forestier alluded to 'Father Soulas's Sisters' when he sent a donation in 1889 from the superior general in France for the rebuilding of the burnt church at

Jerusalem. Soulas noted to Suzanne that this implied 'a slight suggestion of schism' but that the Marists must not have been wanting 'to demolish our Sisters since they publish our foundation'.[13]

The Society of Mary was nevertheless holding back. Even before the fire, Suzanne had been preparing a collecting tour for a convent but, as Cognet reported, she was waiting for 'a *definitive* answer' as an assurance that would enable the sisters to 'develop in peace under the Society's wing. . . . When this response comes, she'll be on her way without delay.'[14] All this hesitation made Suzanne discuss a fall-back alternative with the archbishop on 29 November 1889, at the end of her collecting tour: 'Saw His Grace, who promised diocesanship'.[15] They were already diocesan under the Third Order, so this entry in her diary must refer to independent diocesanship, should they be separated from the Society of Mary.

Father Leterrier arrived in New Zealand in late 1889 to be provincial of the newly established separate Marist Province of New Zealand. In February 1890 he wrote back to Father Martin, the superior general in France, and revealed his own ambivalence about what still seem to be Father Soulas's sisters:

> I've strongly advised Father Soulas to be content for his new foundation with the approval of the Archbishop, who willingly recognises the precious services that these Tertiaries can give to the Maori mission and willingly consents to approve them as a diocesan community. I don't know the reasons blocking their affiliation to the tertiaries of Lyon but they can, it seems to me, carry on their good work without this affiliation.[16]

Despite the vows the sisters took, and the appointment and later confirmation of Suzanne as superior, it would seem that full integration had not been made.

In 1891 Father Joly, the Marist Visitor based in Sydney, was again inspecting the New Zealand stations. He had already had mixed feelings about Hiruharama in 1886, and this time the marginalisation of Soulas was clearer still. He wrote to Martin:

> As a result of a conversation with Father Leterrier about Father Soulas and the difficulties he and I have with this priest because of his fixed ideas, his way of treating his colleagues and his community of Sisters of the Third Order – in brief because it is impossible to come to any practical or useful decision with him apart from his own ideas – it has been agreed that I will not go up to Jerusalem.[17]

Leterrier is equally curt in an August 1891 reference to 'Father Soulas, staying put in Jerusalem where he is totally absorbed in his farm and his convent'.[18] By February 1892 Leterrier, while acknowledging Soulas's stalwart pioneering of the Maori mission, was exasperated:

> I don't know what he's getting up to with his farm and other transactions [the medicines, for instance], where he's trying to cloak himself in far too much mystery. To avoid any more control, even the most innocuous kind, he's just sent [Father Maillard] packing without any authorisation.[19]

The sisters became increasingly scapegoated in Leterrier's eyes for the way Soulas bore grudges, and for his rigidity and toughness towards the younger priests when they needed a colleague and mentor. In March 1892, Leterrier wrote to Martin that Soulas should have been 'giving them direction as well as the Sisters, & not sending them away and shutting himself up in this foundation with its highly unlikely chances of success'. What was Soulas thinking of, asked Leterrier, taking on projects like 'an orphanage for children, a hospital for old people'? What was he up to 'putting everything to the account and in the name of Sister Marie Joseph'? This did not go down well with Leterrier, 'especially seeing that everything was handled between those two a bit too secretively'. He thought the projects would be a drain on the mission, not a support.

The affair needed settling: 'It has been agreed on between the Archbishop and myself that next month we will take advantage of our visit for the opening of the new church to bring out into the open, if it is possible, the whole position and management of the church and convent.'[20] In the event, the opening of the church was postponed. But Leterrier, as head of the Society of Mary in New Zealand, decided that the spirit of the Jerusalem community was entirely different. The sisters would not be part of the wider Marist family.

Suzanne felt that her roots went deep into Marist soil, from her childhood onwards. All accounts report that she was devastated by the decision. The January 1894 minutes of the Marist General Council in Lyon record that, through Father Cognet as intermediary while he was in Lyon, she tried to negotiate a union of the Daughters of Our Lady of Compassion with the Society of Mary 'by bonds purely spiritual', a 'sharing in the spiritual goods of the Society'.[21] The council decided to consult Soulas for his opinion, and nothing came of it.

Yet there would always be a bond with the Marists. The link might not be official but it came from historical association, affection and a high degree of shared spiritual heritage. The closeness of the Wellington sisters in Buckle St to St Joseph's church, and to the Marist college of St Patrick's where the sisters ran the infirmary, reinforced the ties; so did the continuity of the Sisters of Compassion along with the Marist mission at Hiruharama. The 1898 Visitor regretted the 1892 decision. He was sorry the 'Jerusalem sisters aren't joined to our Third Order, because in terms of devotion, denial of self and zeal, they would not easily be matched by many others'.[22]

Suzanne was seldom a passive victim of circumstance. Her planning might often be *ad hoc* but she usually had plans in hand. Where did she stand in this process of ambivalence then final decision-making? In spite of her regrets, she certainly was ready for the eventuality. Redwood's March 1892 letter to her, at the same time as Leterrier was sending his to France, indicated this. 'As to the name to be given to your nascent Congregation', he wrote, 'I am somewhat perplexed to find one. Perhaps you will suggest the one you think most suitable.'[23] In the end he chose the name but she may well have guided his thinking.

One of Suzanne's qualities was the ability to sum up a setting, a situation, a society of people. It could be that, while genuinely wanting to be part of the Marist family of missionary women in the Pacific, she also sensed that the nature of the developing country called for something homegrown, or tailored to fit. She did not contemplate that her sisters, who were nearly all New Zealand-born, would work in the close-knit world of Pakeha Catholic education, with its tendency sometimes to lose sight of the local milieu because of its telescopic focus back to Ireland. The majority culture, admittedly, had its educational telescope fixed on England, but her point was that Catholics needed to understand and reach other New Zealanders. She was itching to make her mission 'to care with compassion for the sufferings' of Maori and Pakeha, 'all creeds and none', with regard for the way they thought and felt. She had the intuition and also the intellectual and spiritual skills to design a sisterhood to suit.

In essence Suzanne was feeling the unspoken wrench that settler people felt at many times: there was no going back, yet how did you keep your own centuries-old birthright and treasures intact and still let yourselves and your children open up to the whakapapa and taonga of the new? Redwood, with his Marist background, French education, English birth and New Zealand settler childhood, could possibly understand the competing tugs, and he seemed to be waiting to see what happened, letting history take its course. He must have sensed that

Suzanne understood and cared about New Zealanders because he tended to give her a surprisingly free rein where others might have tried to curb her enthusiasms. He was letting the creative spirit of the community develop, what is called the charism of a congregation – its spiritual energising force that propels it in its own special direction and defines it as different from another.

It is clear from the flow of Suzanne's first writing of the Constitutions – which is where a congregation's creative impetus is formulated into a practical blueprint – that the vision was emerging out of the setting. Her draft is vibrant with time and place. Redwood had advised back in 1884: 'A rule which will grow up out of *custom* and local circumstances is far more likely to be a success than rules drawn up *a priori*, and consequently more theoretical than practical.'[24] Imported congregations often brought from Europe their Constitutions and routines intact, with the result, for instance, that northern hemisphere building plans drawn to face south for the sun sometimes took concrete form in New Zealand turned to the dark and the cold Antarctic gales. But Suzanne, admittedly strongly French in so many attitudes, and her sisters, with their Irish heritage, were from the outset making adaptability and sensitivity to contemporary local needs part of their charism. Even though some of the exuberance was predictably brought into canonical line in later years, the women's spirituality had by then channelled its course safely down to bedrock.

So Suzanne firmly called Archbishop Redwood the founder of the Daughters of Our Lady of Compassion, perhaps diplomatically removing the possibility from Soulas and also adding to the credibility of the new congregation. It was canonically recognised on 14 September 1892 as a diocesan congregation with simple annual vows at first, changing to five-yearly vows by the turn of the century. Suzanne was appointed first superior on 14 October.

None of the sisters left at this point, even though they had lost the more secure and prestigious link with the Society of Mary which would have reassured their families. Apart from Pompallier's shortlived Sisters of the Holy Family in Auckland and a small group of Maori sisters in Northland,[25] this 1892 congregation was the only Catholic one to originate within New Zealand. It was egalitarian in concept: there was no division into choir sisters and lay or manual sisters. It was also an active congregation, not enclosed or semi-enclosed. A dowry of £50 was desirable, but no woman was denied entry if she or her family could not meet this requirement.

The aims of the congregation, as Suzanne saw them, were simple. 'The Sisters have been instituted solely for the Maori and for the poor and they must flee from everything which would tend to attract them towards the rich as something which takes them out of their vocation. [This] would only serve to withdraw from them the necessary grace which God will give them to be able to persevere in their holy state as long as they remain faithful to their vocation to the most neglected, the poorest and most ignorant members of the people.' Such people held within them the kernel of the Family of Nazareth, and the sisters were to keep this always in mind:

> They will remember often that under this rough and sometimes even repulsive skin is a soul redeemed at the cost of the blood of Jesus Christ who promised to recognise as done to himself whatever would be done to the least of his people. They will count themselves fortunate to lead a pure and hidden life, the most like the life of the Holy Family. Which is what Our Lord did. He made himself poor and obedient. He was in the eyes of the Jews simply a craftsman son of a craftsman. The Holy Virgin carried out under the gaze of those around her the ordinary tasks of the women of the people. With the work of his hands, Saint Joseph earned his living and that of the Holy Family.[26]

Suzanne kept a hard-working, hand-working Family of Nazareth as the firm benchmark for her sisters.

The settlement at Hiruharama had obviously not been seen by the Marist administrators as flowing smoothly in the mainstream; it had revealed for them signs of dangerous eddies and whirlpools. Suzanne had her own adventurous liking for new and daring challenges where she could put her faith to the test. She saw any figurative shooting of rapids as the quintessence of both mission zeal and personal salvation. So, although the community was quite orthodox in a religious sense, there was another, unconventional aspect to it which unsettled many of the clergy. This had to do with the manual work that Soulas, Suzanne and the sisters had added to the teaching and nursing of the Maori of the river. They were also bush farming, orchard planting, trading with tourists, making and marketing medicines, and raising lots of children, probably without testing any of these compounding and increasingly public activities against the norm for the Third Order Regular of Mary – indigenous mission teaching and nursing. They could be seen as different from the spirit of the Society of Mary.

Suzanne had an unflagging work ethic that was integral to her faith. She copied out once the example of a French congregation where the sisters kept a human chain moving bricks all night on one project. Mission was essentially active to her, and even praying was to be simple and, as she would often say, 'on the go'. Contemplation and communion with God were in no sense omitted. She scheduled her days around the rhythm of religious life. But it was rhythm and movement, not stillness. The sisters prayed as they walked and as they worked. The nature and level of the work, however, disquieted visiting priests.

At this stage of her thinking, Suzanne felt that the example of hard work showed an integrity and commitment which would galvanise hard-working pioneers to support her and respect her creed. She explained this to Michael Davitt. As Mother Aubert, taking up 'her needle and spade', she also featured in the Melbourne *Advocate*: 'The Protestants around us need to see workers. If we are gratefully to accept the alms that charity thinks well to bestow on us, we must know how to gain our living and that of the members of Christ with whom we have charged ourselves. Let us reckon first on God, and afterwards on our own arms.'[27] Their arms and their legs and their backs, in fact – because the sisters worked as hard as many of these settlers who had combined road and rail navvying with bush clearing and breaking in farms. Brother Stanislaus looked after the sheep and cattle at the farm but Sister Carmel and Sister Martha joined him for years in cutting scrub and tending the huge orchard.

They still slept on a table, as the floor was earthen and Suzanne also thought floor-level draughts were unhealthy. They would roll up their bedding in the early morning and take their lunch in tucker-bag pockets out to the paddocks, saying their morning prayers on the way. Meditation was done at work. They returned only in the evening. Everyone helped when required – tree planting, fruit picking, haymaking, potato grubbing, bushfire fighting. If the sisters' work had been confined to conventional convent sewing and laundering, it would probably not have caused comment, no matter how much they might have slaved over their needles and tubs, as Suzanne and the Sisters of Mercy had done in the 1860s. It was the outdoor pioneering that raised eyebrows.

This view of Suzanne's sisters never quite disappeared, and young women right through the twentieth century would be warned off joining the congregation because 'they work too hard', 'the life's too tough'. Once, in the mid-1890s, Redwood had to respond to complaints from the clergy that 'there was no real religious life for the Sisters, they were only station-hands'; they were 'working like men'. He came upriver to investigate, unannounced and alone, and went on up to the farm. He was welcomed warmly and served a meal in the earthen-floored combination kitchen, living-room and bunk-room. The sisters went outside and ate their meal, sharing the few remaining tin plates and serving one another from a saucepan on the ground in the middle. Redwood went to the window and watched them. They were all young, laughing, healthy and happy, and their spirit of faith seemed fine. 'He went away well-satisfied, and there was no more talk of closing down.'[28]

To Sister Martha, Suzanne had the knack of making work fun:

> Our work in those days was very hard. . . . She taught in the schools, she worked at any duty in the house or garden, and could tend the sick perfectly. I saw her race in a piece of digging – and win! I saw her race in a piece of sewing – and win! I saw her continue the game of throwing snowballs – and of course, she won![29]

Perhaps the younger women let her win. It is just as likely, though, that she was racing and winning on her own merits.

As the century drew to a close, the Sisters of Compassion in Wellington began to be recognised as they walked along the streets. The medals of their new order shone on the short capes of the habits which, nostalgically and practically, were unchanged from the French Third Order original. But they did not abandon Jerusalem and Ranana. The nine women firmly stretched their energies and resources between the river and the city. The rebuilt church, the combined and extended convent, school and orphanage, the simple presbytery which nestled into the church and looked like two boatsheds linked with a verandah, all kept their rhythm of life basically unchanged. The angelus rang its steady reminder to prayer, Rure and the other catechists spoke the Maori for the Mass, the harmonium played, the children learnt in school and the orphans scampered up and down the track to the pa. With the winter mud, the poverty and the hard work, it was no idyll, but it was home. Anne, Bridget and Carmel stayed there, with Martha and any novices who entered. With Brother Stanislaus and Soulas, they carried on running the farm, which Sister Magdalen once recalled wistfully: 'I see it all up there lying bathed in the quiet sunshine of a Sunday evening.'[30]

The others went to Wellington with Suzanne, who would come back to visit as regularly as she could. Suzanne would always feel the pull of the road, the river, the rail. In August 1899, an anxious and exasperated letter went up to Jerusalem:

Dear Sisters
There is one thing we would like to know; that is, the whereabouts of Mother. The last letter we received told us to expect her last Thursday night, so Sr Marcelle and myself went down to the foot of the street and watched the trams untill half past eleven; Friday night the same but there was nothing but disappointment. Saturday we came to the conclusion she had either not left Jerusalem, or else that she had stopped on the way. Any information will be most gladly received, we will look out for Mother tomorrow, or else a letter.[31]

Suzanne was sixty-five years old in 1900 when a French traveller met her on the river. Gaston de Ségur thought he had never seen, in all the countries he had visited, such a graceful river as the Whanganui, except perhaps the Rio-Cobre in Jamaica. It was nonsense to have the 'virginal Wanganui coupled with the old German Rhine'. Suzanne boarded the riverboat at Hiruharama, sat beside him on deck and struck up a conversation – in English, of course. He detected her accent first, they discovered they were both French, and switched languages to chat happily the rest of the way. De Ségur was so struck with this encounter that he wrote a lengthy account of it in the book he published of his travels. He made a mistake with her name, though, calling her Marie-Xavier instead of Marie Joseph:

While the puffing *Ohura* slips among the ferns and the age-old rocks of the Wanganui, we forget everything, both the charm of the landscape and the crowd of admiring tourists, to enjoy the pleasure of this encounter that chance has arranged for us. The nun tells me how, when she was very young, she left her country, sent as a missionary to the other end of the world. She tells me about the mishaps of the voyage by sailing ship which lasted three months; then the hardships and countless difficulties of her task at the outset. She had to learn English first, Maori next [probably the reverse], in order to explain the Bible and the catechism to the natives; half-castes took on the responsibility of teaching her, and these rascals taught her all the swearwords and slang they had in their repertoire. Now the main obstacles have been overcome: Catholic influence, she adds with a beaming smile, is gradually spreading among the untamed natives of the *King-Country*.

When the steamer draws alongside the quay at Wanganui, where its passengers quickly scatter through the pretty white town, three people still linger together for some time at the quayside which is being engulfed by the invading dusk. We are Sister Marie-Xavier, my comrade R***, whom I have introduced to her, and myself. The charm of the little exiled nun has worked its effect over him as well as over me, and his rough, tanned colonial face softens as he listens to her. But the hour to part has sounded its note. Shaking for a final time the hands held out to me, I bid farewell to the sister from the convent at Hiruharama, farewell to my comrade in adventure; we all three take our leave of one another, to resume our route towards the separate goals that destiny has marked out for each of us . . .[32]

Suzanne emerges from this entirely true to form: ready to strike up a conversation, ever the raconteur trotting out the same stories she had told Burton and Payton fifteen years before, unselfconsciously promoting Catholic mission, which was now establishing itself north of Raetihi, showing herself as still proudly a missionary to the Maori. De Ségur was so entranced with his time canoeing with Maori guides north of Pipiriki that she may not have complicated matters by discussing the Pakeha orphans and destitute city-dwellers of the capital, where she was choosing to send sisters instead of to Raetihi.

The two men linger at the wharf, loath to part from the little old nun, and finally leave on a spiritual note, conscious that all must follow paths in life with their own individual destinations. Suzanne's own life was now as 'Mother Aubert', adopted by Wellingtonians and cheerfully anglicised into Mother 'Orbit'. After leaving de Ségur and spending the night in Wanganui, she took the train back to the capital to carry on down that path.

> *Is the post gone? : Kua riro pea te meera?*
> *Is the post come? : Kua tae mai ranei te meera?*[33]

Half the sisters were now in Wellington; half still in Jerusalem. Joseph Ward introduced penny postage at the start of 1901, and the sisters' letters begin.[34] Suzanne's days of writing mostly in French were over. Her English was very good, but had occasional quirks of spelling and idiom. By the beginning of 1901, the Wellington community was two years old, up and running before the wind:

My dear Sisters
I have received your kind wishes and we heartily reciprocate them. Let the past pass away with the dying century and let us all begin a new era of true religious life and self sacrifice. The field is large but the labourers are few, and what labourers are we?
  I see that you thouroughly enjoy yourselves. We have no time for that sort of work here. However, I took the Sisters to the 'flag station' on Boxing Day. The

wind was blowing [a] hurricane and it was the greatest fun. We went up in 55 minutes, set up there for about one hour, warmed our frozen teeth with bananas, and came down in 35 minutes, the skirts of our habits acting as sails. We were back for diner.

Happy New Year to you all from all. Many people here inquire about you. Good bye and God bless you.

Your affec. Mother in J.C.

M. Mary Joseph Aubert[35]

The annual Boxing Day picnic would be the only day off work the sisters ever had.

Suzanne always believed that reflective Mary and practical Martha should 'walk hand in hand' and in nearly all the letters over the years – usually written in 'only two words hurriedly', 'on the go', 'between two trains', 'on the trot' – the hand clasp was firm. 'God bless you all dear Sisters', she wrote typically to 'Sister Bridget & Co'. 'We send you Sisterly love. Prepare to spend the Month of May in a Saintly manner to amend for the past and secure the future. Receive fervently Holy Communion on the feast of the Patronage.

'Put the milk separator up stairs. We may have a chance to dispose of it if there is no longer use for it.'[36]

Her letters were brisk and bossy but rarely boring:

Wellington 8th May 1904

Dear Sisters,

I have a lot of letters here about miscellaneous things, so I shall answer them in one and everyone will know what to do.

First I fail to see any harm in having ferns about the altar and statues, but be careful about making a mess with water or mud. It would never do.

2d. Have the Litanies of the Blessed Virgin and three Memorares on the eight of each month till Decembre.

3 Father Devoy told me to tell the Sisters to take no notice of Father Perthuis' fads about Litanies and Hymns and I quite agree with him. If he is offended let him be on that point.[37]

4 Hitting and pocking the children and being rude and rough with them must be completely stopped. Let it be one of the special practices in honour of our Blessed Mother during this month and a preparation for the month of the Sacred Heart meek and humble. I send you in the box a splendid spiritual reading book on patience which I hope will be of use to you.

5 I will send you two boxes this week. One with things for the brother to sell to the Maoris and the other with things for the Sisters and for the children; as the children have enough of winter clothes I will keep here part of what I had cut for them.

6 About the bad knee, let the sufferer avoid scrubbing the flour, but I do not think that going about would hurt.

7 As your letters generally cross mine on the road, write on Sundays, post on Mondays, and I will answer on Wednesdays or Thursdays, so there will be more order and less loss of time waiting for answers.

8 The grand question of milk and food – If there is no milk to drink at dinner it does not matter, let it be water as we always have in Wellington.

I have been disturbed I cannot finish this just now. I will write again by next boat the bill of fare.

In a hurry, dear Sisters. God bless you all.

With much love

Your old mother in J.C.

M Mary Joseph [38]

'Miscellaneous things' were crowding into her life from all sides. But she was responsible for most of the crowding. The first emphasis of their work in Wellington, and what the priests and doctors had mainly requested, was home nursing of the 'sick poor'. They started this immediately by day and night, in the network of little streets and alleys around Te Aro. 'Yesterday at diner time', Suzanne told Sister Bridget, 'we went unexpectedly in an house in which we found a man, his wife and five children. The table was laid and the meal consisted of half a loaf of bread, a scrap of butter and *one* onion. There was neither mattras nor blankets and the poor wife had been and was still ill. We meet terrible cases . . .'[39]

To increase their skills in nursing, she enrolled the sisters in classes run by the St John Ambulance, which formed an Ambulance Corps and a Nursing Guild for women in Wellington in January 1900.[40] The 'lady superintendent' was Jessie Sexton, a trained nurse who later became a Sister of Compassion. Suzanne kept each new intake of women studying. In 1905 eight sisters were 'hard at work studying for the St. John Ambulance'. Sister Anthony shared the lighter side with the Jerusalem sisters: 'The Sisters went to an inspection of the St John's Ambulance; the Inspector happened to have a very long neck, and Sr Salome of course made great fun of him, and said his neck wanted a big knot tied in it. And in punishment for her nonsense she had a stiff neck the next morning and it is not quite better yet. She has taken a firm resolution to let people with long necks alone for the future.'[41]

New Zealand persisted in the idea that the 'deserving poor' must surely be only a few irreproachable widows. There was scant government financial relief. It was to help families who sat down to bread and one onion that Suzanne and her women first went out begging. They began with baskets given by Mrs Kennedy, but these proved heavy to carry. Suzanne marched into Edwin Arnold's caneware shop and asked him to make large wicker hampers on wheels, hybrids of a wheelbarrow and a pram. She would, she told him confidently, pay him when she could. Edwin Arnold, a JP and non-Catholic, agreed, fell in behind and supported Suzanne keenly ever after. The prams had noisy wheels. That proved to be an advantage. People heard them coming along the street and had time to get ready their leftover food and any other gifts they had.

The intention of Mother Aubert's prams quickly caught on among the people. Only eight months after arriving in Wellington, the sisters and their prams were already a respected institution. Two sisters set out on their errand on 13 August 1899.

> Father Devoy telephoned for us to go to the Victoria Hall to get the scraps, so in high jubilation, we peramed it up, Sr Marcelle and I. When we arrived we saw a cart, loaded with ferns, ginger beer and other harmless looking liquour, milk, a basket of pieces of cake. We passed the cart very discreetly but one of my men saw us and called us by name. I went and they gave me some milk and the basket of cake, which I emptied into the peram. They told me to go into the Hall and see if there was anything more for us.

The sisters found to their embarrassment that they had been given not only their own share but the Mercy Convent's by mistake. 'Sr Marcelle heard one of the men saying, "Jingo, they have got all," and the other answered, "I'm not sorry, it has gone into good hands."'[42] Suzanne's sisters would have benefited from the enthusiasm new arrivals attract, but the descriptions 'one of my men' and 'called us by name' show that the sisters were known and liked. This tended to remain so. 'The Sisters of Compassion', explained a St Patrick's old boy, 'were the ones who smiled at you in the street and said hullo.'[43]

Nevertheless, most sisters, unlike Suzanne, were used to the anonymity of the country and cringed at the exposure. Begging was simply not a New Zealand custom. Even Suzanne recognised that they could not do it in Wanganui. She always wore her goffered cap well back from her face, which she fronted expectantly to the world. The sisters in the photographs, from the time they arrived in Wellington, seem to be edging their goffers further and further forward, as if the blinkered look helped them through the humiliating embarrassment of begging.

In her talks to them (which were called 'conferences', from the French word for lectures), Suzanne had to keep extolling the spiritual as well as charitable gains from the begging. On one occasion she emphasised the get-up-and-go qualities of the 'strong women' of the gospel. Sister Agnes wrote down in her exercise-book what Suzanne told them:

> They must have been laughed at many a time. When people saw them tramping after Our Lord, they must have said: 'Look at those crazy women. They are mad. Why don't they stay at home and live quietly with their families?' But the Holy Women took no notice. . . . Now our life is like that of the Holy Women. We have to do their work. Our Lord did not shut Himself up in a cloister when He came on earth. He led an active life . . . We have to live an active life serving Our Lord in the person of His Poor and afflicted, but there is nothing in such a life to prevent attaining the highest contemplation. On the contrary, it is the life which of all others will lead quickest and surest to union with God.[44]

The sisters came to accept this combination of the 'pure and hidden' life of Mary of Nazareth or Mary of Bethany with the bustling publicity of the Martha figure trundling the pram down Lambton Quay. The latter could have its thrills and spills, as Sister Veronica explained:

> Now I must tell you about a great expidition that took place yesterday of which Sr Salome was the center of attraction, having gone out on the afternoon round with Sr Camillus and the prams being very much loaded. In crossing Lambton Quay, a colision took place between a motor byke and Sr Salome's pram. Well, to give you Sr Salome's words when they arrived home: 'Mother I was going in front. I heard a crash, I looked behind, and saw the pram smashed & the man sitin on top of it.' His byke was partly smashed, his head and face were cut, but as yet we have not heard the extent of his injury. Sr was not hurt although she got a great shock. There was enough pudding and kai on the road to feed the crowd that gathered round.[45]

Suzanne took advantage of her known virtue of begging and soon struck up a good relationship with the mayor and staff of the Wellington City Council. 'I am always begging', she wrote to Mayor J. G. Aitken in 1904, 'but it is for the poor in whom you take such a kind interest.'[46] She happily asked for and got free advertising on trams for her fundraising socials, a free pass on the trams and free use for some years of the Town Hall and organ for fundraising concerts. She would write back 'begging to thank' them for their generosity.

The St John Ambulance Nursing Guild, set up in 1900, promised an alternative supply of district nurses. Even before then the sisters were finding that many people were chronically ill and needed more constant nursing. Suzanne already had a long-cherished idea of a home or hospice for 'incurables', and promptly got the unanimous vote of her community in support. There was a property for sale nearby, and she consulted Redwood. His telegram of 16 June 1899 replied: 'Buy on your own responsibility'. She did, mortgaging the new property and remortgaging the Jerusalem farm. The sisters took possession in September, and on 21 December the *New Zealand Tablet* published Suzanne's press release bringing to the attention of 'generous readers' the costs of a 'large addition to our place for the reception of those poor incurables whom hospitals will not keep and the charitable homes will not admit'. It was, she said, 'an humble beginning', and Suzanne would have several more of these to share with 'the generosity of charitable souls' in the future.

St Joseph's Home for Incurables opened in late January 1900, its eleven beds covered in bright sateen and print patchwork sewn by the sisters and 'sewing bee' helpers. There were two wards, one for men and one for women. By July a bequest enabled Suzanne to buy two adjoining cottages and these, linked together, became 'the O'Meara Wing', which trebled the number of patients they could receive. A wide balcony ran the length of the north side. Here the fitter old men gathered in the sun and played cards.

The home was the first of its kind in New Zealand. Several doctors took an interest in the work and gave their services free, both in attending patients and in increasing the sisters' medical and nursing skills. The sisters were always busy, and the nursing was often unpleasant, but in her letters Sister Veronica, like most of them, looked on the bright side:

> The Home is as full as can be of patients. The last one we received last night, an old woman bedridden came by the late train and the beautiful scent that came with her both from sore legs and other causes was marvelous. The first thing was to give her a bath and so on. The remainder of her toilet was completed this morning. She is a nice old body for all that; but the poor old Maori is the pick of all he is such a nice old chap, talks very good English, every one likes him, of course as you know he is blind and paralized so he cannot move out of bed.[47]

An *Evening Post* article on 23 October 1903, under the heading 'Care of the Poor', surveyed their work. 'The mission of the Sisters', it said, 'is one of mercy, of aid to the sick, the distressed, the unfortunate, to lift humanity from the slough of the world, no matter how they got there.' The last clause was the crux of the matter. Demographic change meant that the rigid division into 'deserving' and 'undeserving' poor, which withheld help from so many, was no longer valid in New Zealand. The number of men over the age of sixty-five increased by fifty percent between 1896 and 1901, whereas the population as a whole grew by only ten percent.[48] The ratio among those over sixty-five was roughly sixty males to forty females. Until the First World War, there were only marginally more married men than bachelors in New Zealand.[49] For many, there was no family back-up, no custodial care, in their old age. The country was filling up with 'cantankerous old codgers', many with a life behind them of hard work, but also of transience and drink. When they could not survive independently in even the neatest or barest bush whare, where did these old men go to die? Most charitable organisations avoided them in favour of salvageable children and genteel widows.

The labour market for the old colonial 'jack of all trades' was drying up and, even if he was not yet quite 'incurably' aged or ill, he was very often without work. This made him all the more 'undeserving'. A Wellington magistrate, W. M. Haselden, questioned the toughness on vagrancy in 1900: 'It's not right to send men to gaol who have committed no offence, except that of being helpless and unable to take care of themselves.'[50] It began to dawn on some that the 'undeserving poor' were 'not so readily identified as hardliners supposed'.[51] The 1898 old age pension was an attempt at redress but it had many strings attached.

Jobs were meant to exist in the legendary rural wonderland, but many of the men the sisters began helping were coming instead to the city for casual and seasonal work on the wharves. Much of their time was spent unemployed. So from 1901 St Joseph's began to have its day clientele as well, men once described in a *New Zealand Times* article as 'Wellington's Workless, Wet and Weary Wandering Willies'.[52] They came for the hot soup, served in large pannikins from the slide window of the kitchen. Soup kitchens had been run in Auckland and elsewhere at times of need, but Suzanne was well used to them from her French background: the *soupe populaire* had a strong tradition in several of the Lyon parishes. The 'eighty or ninety men a day' at Buckle St must have occasionally jostled and grumped, because Sister Agnes wrote down Suzanne's directions from her talks: 'When those poor "soup men" are impatient at the slide, do not flare out, and say "Let them wait!" Remember it is Our dear Lord, or St Joseph who is there.'[53]

So many areas of need were becoming apparent all around. But government charitable aid remained minimal except for children. The relatively few and spasmodically resourced voluntary charities, mainly linked to churches, also tended to choose orphans, rather than cripples, drunkards and the diseased. But Suzanne chose the lot, or as near as she could manage. In France it was not uncommon to have a largish institution run, for example, by the Sisters of Charity and incorporating the old with the young, the sick and crippled with the fit who lacked family.[54] Suzanne dreamed of a central, holistic solution like this where she and her faith would be available to all.

It also made financial sense to have a multi-branched welfare enterprise because, whatever the subset whose need she brought to the attention of Wellingtonians, the proceeds of their charity usually went to more than one. She once wrote to the town clerk, for instance, asking for free use of the Town Hall for a concert in aid of the 'sick and incurable children and foundlings . . . and also . . . adult incurables'.[55] Children were the main drawcard to open the purse-strings. But the old bachelor blokes, washed up like gnarled driftwood reminders of the proud forests they once felled, could benefit from the wave of generosity. And Father Pertuis, a tired old priest now very deaf and slipping into his second childhood, could sit at his window in a big chair and watch the children playing in the crèche yard.

By 1903 St Joseph's Home at Buckle St had as resident patients not only men and women who were terminally ill but also helpless children who were crippled and disabled. For non-residents, it offered soup morning and evening, and distributed food and clothing parcels. It ran a crèche full of lively children. In October 1903 an *Evening Post* journalist toured the home with its 'blue-robed, active women' as the 'staff of sixteen gentle nurses' and its 'masterful little woman who acts as councillor and guide to the institution'. The crèche or 'daylight home for babies' was about to open its doors. It was the first in New Zealand:

> It will be open from 7 o'clock in the morning until 5 o'clock in the evening, and during those hours babes under the age of three years whose parents find themselves hampered with the care of them, and are prevented from earning a livelihood, will be received and delivered back again. During the intervening hours the Sisters will act as mothers to the children, provide for their wants, and soothe their fears or pains. . . . Each child on being received from its mother will be cleanly and newly clothed, fed at the proper time, and 'changed' before the mother calls to receive it again in the evening.

A week's notice was needed before a child was accepted, 'to enable enquiries to be made' about meeting the criterion of poverty. The only charge was 'for milk – amounting to a few pence'. Suzanne's volunteer 'ladies' sewed away at clothes she cut out at the weekly sewing bee, so that tired parents could pick up their children, dressed once more in their own clean clothes and nappies, which had been kept aside while they spent the day in crèche-provided ones. As a little girl, Sister of Mercy Veronica O'Brien, lived just over the way from the Buckle St home. She remembered regularly helping in the late afternoon to dress the children back into their own clothes. The crèche took in up to thirty-four children.

The extra washing coming from this determination to help the parents was added to the sisters' workload. Heavy sodden linen, pegs and flapping lines were their daily lot, whether from the spills and incontinence of the sick old or healthy young. Suzanne wrote to Sister Carmel one wintry July day in 1905: 'We have receive[d] lately 4 more men, and several children at the Creche. The washing every day is terrible, and the drying is as bad. We have had very stormy weather.'[56]

Suzanne was punctiliously clear that everyone knew that any help the sisters gave was available to all. 'No questions are asked – any religion or any sect is served.' Another catchcry became 'All creeds or none'. Into the Constitutions went:

> The liberty of conscience of the patients ought to be respected and the visits of Protestant ministers to their co-religionists tolerated. . . . If the patient in danger is a non-Catholic the Sisters can let him send for his minister.[57]

This was done. Rev. W. Ballachey, for instance, who was Anglican chaplain at the public hospital, held services in the wards. Such openness was not common, and Suzanne would get into trouble with bishops later. At the time, though, multi-denominational Wellington visibly relaxed into a spirit of good will to match that of 'its' sisters.[58] As the *Evening Post* said on 23 October 1903, the home 'exists wholly by the efforts of the Sisterhood and the gifts of the people of the city'.

Notwithstanding that, it was mission all along for missionary Suzanne – but by example, not compulsion. The Constitutions continued:

> Whatever may be the religion of the patient in danger, the Sisters can and must try their best to help him die a happy death. If he is a Catholic they can use every means in their power. If he is not a Catholic, they have always the resource of prayer. They can also suggest to him gently sentiments of love of God, of contrition, of resignation to the Holy Will of God.

Though often unspoken, mission permeated her daily routine. In 1904 Suzanne wrote to the sisters at Jerusalem about an 'edifying' conversion.

But she was rarely capable of pontificating, and in her letter salvation beat its rhythm with an unconsciously comic echo of 'Solomon Grundy':

> We had a great consolation last week. A bigotted protestant woman suffering from cancer of the stomach was admitted into the Home about a month ago. A fourthnight ago she begged of her own accord to be admitted in the church. She was baptised on Wednesday, went to confession on thursday, received her first communion and extreme unction on friday, spent the night in prayer – died on Saturday and was buried today [Sunday]. Half an hour before her death she wrote on the slate: 'How merciful God has been to me a sinner.' It was most edifying.[59]

By 1906, so much had happened. Properties had been bought, with mortgages and overdrafts dependent on the city's generosity. New sisters were joining in numbers boosted by added exposure and popularity in the capital. By then, the sisters were also poised for the new adventure of the huge institution being built out at Island Bay. At Epiphany 1906 they probably had no idea of the complications this would bring in the next few years. They celebrated their anniversary, eating the same simple food as they ate on arriving in 1899, and bringing the Hiruharama community to them in spirit. Suzanne wrote to Sister Carmel on 7 January: 'Yesterday was the anniversary of the foundation of Wellington. We kept it in the evening with Maori songs, cheese and dripping. How those seven years have fled! Where shall we be next year? Where God wishes.'[60]

CHAPTER FOURTEEN

Wellington – Buckle St and Island Bay
1904-1906

What I desire is to show my love :
Ko taku e minaminatia ai ko taku aroha ano
I wish to find out what I can do for you :
E rapu tonu ana ahau ki tetahi mahi maku hei painga mou[1]

In the photograph taken of Suzanne and the orphans at Jerusalem in 1898, little John McMahon, just behind Rewi Crichton on the right, is eyeing something or someone alongside the camera. His face tilts in observation with a hint of quizzical appraisal and the slant of his cheek shows up his disability. John was born with one side of his body noticeably bigger than the other. In 1904 he developed an infection which was slowly poisoning his system. The children were still living up in Jerusalem then and he was taken down to Wanganui hospital for treatment. Poultices and lancing were unsuccessful in halting the spread of the infection and the doctors telegraphed to Suzanne in Wellington for permission to amputate his arm at the shoulder to save his life.

Suzanne's reaction to the telegram was immediate. She took the next train for Wanganui and, fired up with determination, marched into the hospital, past the other patients' beds to John's in the far corner. John was very weak with a high fever, and thirsty, too, because liquids had been withheld as part of his treatment. He was only ten, dangerously ill and very lonely. 'But now', he remembered, 'all was different. Here was someone who was not only a friend, but a mother to me. Mother had travelled three hundred miles from Wellington to fight my battles. My temperature must have dropped many points. Her first words to me were: "How are you, my boy?"'

Suzanne asked the nurse to get John's clothes. The nurse said she would go and ask the ward sister, 'but this round about method was no good to Mother, for she was now getting angry':

'Will you get that boy's clothes at once,' was Mother's next request. The tone of the 'Will you' was enough for the nurse who produced my clothes from the locker. Mother and the nurse were pulling on my clothes the best way they could as I could give very little help, when in comes the Medical Superintendent and operating doctors all ready for the job! I think Mother summed up from their visit that they intended to operate irrespective of what she had to say. It was not many minutes before they found out that Mother had a say, and a mighty big say at that!

After some heated exchange of words with the Medical Superintendent, Mother helped me to my feet, and said she was taking me home. My poisoned arm was tied up somehow around my neck, and Mother steadied me by the other. Then the procession started down the ward to the entrance where she had a cab waiting to take us to the Station. The patients all looked on in amazement and with expressions of pleasure on their faces, as I had their sympathy. All the way down the ward, Mother and the doctor were going it hammer and tongs over the removal. There was a halt at the entrance door. From a few words I could gather, the doctor seemed to be placing the responsibility she was taking before her. Mother was quite prepared to take all the responsibility and said so, in very definite terms. I do not know whether the Medical Superintendent started to get officious or said something to stir Mother's anger, but the last I heard was Mother telling him to take his own medicine, and she would take her boy.[2]

From Wanganui, just before they took the train to Wellington, she scribbled a note back to Sister Carmel in Jerusalem: 'I am taking John to Wellington today, to save his arm from the knife. Pray hard. High interests are at [stake].'[3] John only just survived, after months and months at Buckle St of doctors' attention and the sisters' nursing and prayers for him. Suzanne's high-handed action had carried a distinct element of risk. So why, apart from her known preference not to amputate where possible, had she got so upset and whisked John away? What were the high interests at stake?

The sisters recalled that Suzanne had imputed to the doctors a cavalier willingness to amputate in John's case because he was disabled anyway. And this, rightly or wrongly interpreted, brought from her an almost visceral reaction of anger and protectiveness over his rights. John was intelligent, would go on to have a good education and a steady government position as an adult, and his disadvantage was slight compared with others. But it still set him visibly apart from the norm.

John was the first of the physically disabled children Suzanne would care for. She called them 'incurables', which was the current term and the one she was used to in France. Nobody else in New Zealand was specialising in the care and education of the crippled and socially ostracised children usually found cooped in a back room or cared for in the cramped kitchen of their struggling parents – children with spina bifida, Down's syndrome, hydrocephalic enlarged heads, with severe harelips and cleft palates, cerebral palsy, shrivelled or distorted limbs. And from her work with illegitimate babies she knew that the almost untreated syphilis and gonorrhea of the times were resulting in babies born blind, deaf and paralysed.

The forces propelling Suzanne were rarely impersonal and theoretical. To illustrate her concerns, she would share with the sisters her memories of past experiences. The way she felt about her youngest brother's experience of four years with a peasant wet-nurse had coloured her views on boarding out babies. And the short life of her brother Louis gave her a special relationship with disabled children. The votive painting at Fourvière clearly shows Louis's enlarged head. For Clarice there was the shock of her little daughter's crippling accident, compounded by the birth of a disabled child, and both followed closely by her own illness. Perhaps all this made her unable to cope with her last baby, unable to keep Camille near her. The sketched outlines of Clarice's experience lie behind the crowded and vivid canvas of her daughter's life.

Suzanne fought for John McMahon also from the depths of her own psyche. Inside the fiery, authoritative, articulate woman storming into the ward at Wanganui was the hurt of the little girl who had nearly died in the frozen pond of St-Symphorien-de-Lay. Suzanne remembered years of struggling to recover from crippled arms and legs, from blind eyes where for a while only the whites were visible. She remembered people recoiling at the sight of her; she remembered feeling a freak. She remembered, too, her mother reinforcing the ugly truth of her lost prettiness, out of a misguided wish to harden her to the reactions of others. She said her aunt Zoé had been horrified when she overheard Clarice doing this and convinced her not to.[4]

If Suzanne's memories were accurate, she had spent long periods at spas and shrines in the company of other disabled and crippled people. She remained always with the cast in her eye signalling her out, as Yardin had noted back in 1860. She once wrote that she was *assez laide*, 'ugly enough', to travel alone without the protection of a companion.[5] Under the bravado of these words, there would have been layers of the unexpressed, repressed hurt of a girl born into a bourgeois world where appearances mattered.

Suzanne once went to a private meeting in Wellington for people, mainly doctors, working in health. The meeting was arranged by Dr William Chapple, a member of Parliament who, like Dr Duncan MacGregor, was an exponent of eugenic selection. They were to hear Joseph McCabe, a visiting lecturer promoting eugenics and the elimination of the 'unfit'. The ideology of 'social purity' was a strong, almost nationalistic force building up at this time, influencing the women's movements as well.[6] At the close of the meeting Suzanne stood up. She protested against the proposal to form a committee to further these views, because, she said, 'if those views had been in force when I was two years old, *I would not be here*. I was a *monster!*'[7] She meant 'a curiosity, a freak'. She said it with droll humour and was greeted with laughter and a flurry of questions. But the popular Mother Aubert, by identifying herself with people with disabilities, was deflecting the focus back to a concept of human respect and possible rehabilitation.

She did this constantly. Dr Fred Bowerbank had only just arrived in New Zealand and set up practice in Wellington when Suzanne called to see him in mid-1907. With her usual assumption that it would be a welcome privilege for all to help, she invited him to be honorary visiting physician at the home she had recently started at Island Bay 'for babies born with congenital deformities and also for little "unwanteds". . . . She said they had no money', Bowerbank recalled, 'and it was possible to start only in a small way. . . . She told me there was a desperate need for such a Home, as there was no institution for the care of these tragic cases, and we finally arranged that I should visit the Home of Compassion once a week, or more often if necessary.'[8]

Much more than her personal experience was fuelling her, of course. Her faith that Jesus was equally in everyone sent her gathering in the incurables. In her instructions to the sisters working with these people, she wrote:

> Let us take care of them to honour Jesus Who became as it were struck with leprosy, an object of horror, in order to cure us of the leprosy of sin. In honour of Jesus raising the dead to life, giving sight to the blind, hearing to the deaf, speech to the dumb, and motion to the paralytics. . . .
>
> In the Eucharist Jesus may be styled the Divine Incurable; incurable of His mercy and love; and it is by this incurable affliction with which, so to say, mercy and love make Him suffer, that He cures what would be incurable diseases of our souls.[9]

She was always emphatic that any person's outward disability which might repel the caregiver was more than matched by inward disabilities in everyone, and that Jesus cared for all people regardless. In the days when many disfigurements of birth or disease were not treated or treatable, these were supportive words. Bowerbank found the nuns 'always cheerful and full of humour' as they nursed their little patients, 'the majority being cases with marked congenital brain deformities such as hydrocephalics and the like. These were obviously incurable and, although the expectation of life was usually not more than a few weeks or a few months, the nurses treated them as if they were normal.'

The guidance Suzanne gave still held good years later. Dr Elsie Gibbons, as children's registrar at the Home of Compassion from the late 1940s, observed it in practice over forty years:

> It was said that the best nursing in Wellington was at the Home of Compassion. So if you had cases that required expert nursing, you got better nursing at the Home of Compassion than anywhere else. It's because of the nuns. Those nuns were indoctrinated in their training and they are very compassionate. That compassion is built into that whole organisation. Irrespective of a person's status, he is treated as individual and so the amount of institutionalisation and depersonalisation that went on in the Home of Compassion was minimalised. I formed the impression that Mother Aubert had a great deal to do with it. . . . It permeated the whole of their houses, this warmth and this compassion. And I was always struck many times by the extreme kindness of these women to the handicapped and unfortunate people, not just one of them but the lot of them.[10]

Suzanne had been planning a hospital for incurables for a long time. There was talk of it in her interview in 1895 with Michael Davitt. Incurables of all types were on the whole unable to earn and were typically stigmatised among the poor. The Sisters of Compassion, when they worked outside the Maori mission, worked only for the poor. 'Incurable' meant for Suzanne both terminally ill adults and crippled or congenitally disabled children. Both found a home initially in Buckle St. She was right when she told Bowerbank the country had no real institution for incurables. Even the terminally ill were generally being ignored by authorities as much as possible:

> Advanced cancer and tuberculosis cases accelerated a shift in the nature of indoor relief. Sufferers from both diseases were unwelcome in nineteenth century medical institutions. Branded by their lack of potential for heroic medical intervention, these patients were rejected by the hospitals, which increasingly saw themselves as places of cure. The State was urged to provide 'homes for incurables', but successive governments were unwilling to provide

for such unproductive material. . . . However, the benevolent asylums were equally reluctant to provide for 'incurables', arguing that this was the role of the hospitals.[11]

Suzanne pressed steadily for support for both types of incurables. But it was under the umbrella of the children that she launched her biggest drive so far. The truth was that children were more emotively marketable. Bowerbank considered that 'Wellington Hospital, for a capital city, was still lagging behind in facilities for the treatment of sick and injured children. Certainly an up-to-date fever hospital was opened in 1910, but there was only a single ward for sick children, and no facilities whatever, for the cases which Mother Mary wished to treat.'[12]

As she brought the rights and needs of these people to the attention of Wellington, Suzanne had to tread a fine line, running the risk that visitors, even if they came with compassion, would derive a kind of side-show fascination. A reporter for the *New Zealand Times* was shown all the facilities that the five buildings clustered around Buckle St offered in 1906, and gave what seems a fairly honest and straightforward contemporary reaction:

> The Home for Incurable Children was next visited. Poor little ones – infantile paralysis and imbecility are the troubles here. One girl was in bed, she is the victim of a burning accident, bright and intelligent-looking, but hopelessly incurable. 'Some days she can walk on crutches, but she is not well today,' said the Sister. 'We have had her for eleven years. She was at the Home at Wanganui and has been transferred here for medical treatment.' Of all the sad sights on God's earth this is surely the saddest. Pretty-faced children, deformed beyond description, look up at the Sister; some come to be petted and spoken to. One curly, tow-headed four-year-old boy laughs, and offers half an orange. I bend down to shake his little hand and the Sister explained: 'All his left side is paralysed, and his arm is useless.' These are the happy ones, they play and laugh. By the fire several little idiot girls sit in chairs, their weird old faces and claw-like hands grieve the very soul of the onlooker. They croon and chatter in a most pitiable fashion. The Sister says brightly: 'Oh, I haven't shown you our baby. She is eleven months old, and was skin and bone when we got her.' The infant lies like a log in its cradle. Sister appears to love it, but the visitor looks with horror – there is no life or happiness in the stolid, staring eyes.[13]

Through reports like these, Suzanne was able to shock, alert and rally Wellington to help. By 1905 she was publicising the large home she was planning out at Island Bay, the newly developing suburb to the south. As always, it was made quite clear that the facilities would be without charge and open to all in need, regardless of their denomination, if they had any. The registers of Buckle St from 1900 show cancer sufferer and Irish Roman Catholic Tom Dawson followed by John Winter, English and Anglican, paralysed and disfigured by psoriasis. Patients who were Wesleyan, Salvation Army, Presbyterian or Baptist joined the predominant Catholics and Anglicans. Among the children, Dudley Burns, admitted 'blind, deaf and paralysed' at age ten, was Anglican, as was two-year-old Della Smith, with 'rickets etc.'. Ada McCormick, an epileptic girl of thirteen, was Presbyterian. It was part of Suzanne's nature to be interested in everyone. She also had an uncanny intuition, a shrewd judgement which enabled her to tap settlers' antipathy towards old world divisions and to turn this positively, uniting the various sections of society behind her projects.

But it was the missionary in her that made her insist that her work 'must all be for the salvation of souls, not the sanctification of good Catholics'.[14] She used this argument whenever she had to refuse offers of funding from fellow Catholics if they required that she restrict her services to Catholics. Martin Kennedy, then a director of the Bank of New Zealand, was one influential adviser and long-time supporter who tried to do this. She used to visit him often, catching him at his home before breakfast to ask his advice on financial questions, just as she did with Seddon and other busy public men. They would sometimes argue issues heatedly. Kennedy's daughters remembered him saying to her: 'What's the use of your coming to me for advice when you have your mind made up already?'[15] But their relationship was close, going back to her 1889 collecting trip in Westland, where he then lived. She valued his knowledge and cautioning, and would always benefit from his recommendation of Charles Skerrett as her lawyer – the future Chief Justice proved a wise choice.

At this point in Suzanne's life, as she moved more than ever into large-scale planning and canvassed the circuit of business, local government, national politics, medicine and law, she found echoes of the world of her father in the capitalist climate of 1850s Lyon. She said that Charles Skerrett, both physically and in character, reminded her reassuringly of her father. The confidence of the Liberal government, the atmosphere among the self-made men who had not lost touch with their background, the bustle of the capital, all were reminiscent of the Lyon she had known just before leaving. She, too, had an eager optimism and assurance, and a keen nose for the whiff of fun in the midst of busyness. She was confident, at ease, undeterred.

Her habit might be patched and her boots dusty, but Mother Aubert marched the streets of Wellington, up and down steps and in and out of influential offices. Weather-browned, wrinkled and without her false teeth, she would go down the road with her own steady rhythm that people noticed. 'She walked with a special sort of gait', they would say. She explained that she had been taught it by a Scots settler as a way of covering great distances while conserving your energy. The little, square, unstayed woman in the wind-billowed skirts might be lost in her own meditation, because she prayed constantly as she walked, but she was recognisable. She was becoming a point of reference: 'there goes Mother Aubert'. She was becoming an institution herself, an icon, an assurance of care. And her short and pithy prayer style, her devotions 'on the trot', as she would say, meant that she could snap immediately into recognition, a greeting, a smile, an overture – and action. The relationship between Suzanne and Wellington was dynamic.

Lyon in the late 1850s had exploded with private and civic rebuilding on a grand scale. Father Rocher's letters to Poupinel in Sydney had described this with amazement. Religious institutions were rebuilding ambitiously at the time the twenty-five-year-old Suzanne had left France. The building she now envisaged for Island Bay was also large for New Zealand and 'very French', travellers said. She conceived it at a time when New Zealand's response to social welfare concerns was well into a secondary stage. An imposing 'bricks and mortar' approach reassured citizens that their nation was past the simple colonial phase. Big institutions, preferably visible on hillsides, helped to open contributing purses.

This was happening all around the country, and Suzanne's design for Island Bay was one of the more ambitious. When tenders were called, blunt Martin Kennedy did not hide the fact that he was impressed. 'I congratulate you, in which Mrs K. joins, in being able to accept a tender for such a large amount of your new building, Island Bay. You are a millionaire.'[16] Like her, he saw the workings of Providence: 'It is surely God's work or you could not make such progress.' She sent a drawing of the plans to Bishop Lenihan in Auckland and he wrote back in December 1905: 'I like the appearance of the building very much; it will look magnificent when it is finished. Do tell me the secret of your success.

I want money so badly up here, and I must learn your means of getting on so well.'[17]

The secret of her success was a policy indefensible in business terms. She planned and proceeded with no money to speak of. Yet on a site of thirty acres, she had a building designed 'three hundred and fifty feet in length by one hundred and forty in depth, [to] accommodate three hundred children. It does not include the laundry and other necessary accessory buildings.'[18] These would come later. Archbishop Redwood would refer to Suzanne's 'holy audacity of faith'. He gave her, despite the agitated concerns of his diocesan council, an amazingly free rein in her activities. Some priests felt that, as far as Suzanne was concerned, 'he came, he saw, he concurred'.[19] His brief note to her on 12 August 1905 must have been written confirmation after much discussion, but its approval was untrammelled by cautionary guidelines:

> Dear Reverend Mother,
> I am very glad to hear that you wish to transfer to Island Bay, Wellington, the institution for foundlings and neglected children now at Jerusalem, Wanganui River. I thoroughly approve of this design and impart to it my best blessing.
>   Yours faithfully
>   Francis Redwood S.M.
>   Abp of Wellington[20]

A month later, on 8 September, he was being supportive in a practical way:

> I have heard with much pleasure that it is your intention to found a hospital at Island Bay for poor, sick, & incurable children. I feel sure that such a much-needed work of charity [will] meet with generous public support, and I trust that with the blessing of God it will be in the near future an unqualified success.
>   To emphasise my appreciation of your undertaking I ask you to accept the enclosed contribution of £10 . . .[21]

Suzanne could lobby expertly, picking off sectors with ease. It was not for nothing that an entry in her *New and Complete Manual of Maori Conversation* read: 'I wish to be near Government House, or Parliament House : E pirangi ahau kia noho tata ki te Whare o te Kawanatanga ranei o te Paramete ranei'.[22] She now armed herself with letters of unqualified support for her plans from twenty-eight doctors practising in the Wellington region. She had the medical professionals in hand.

She also knew how to get good journalistic coverage to inform and activate the public. She was known to use the spectre of newspaper exposure as leverage with the government. Once, she was waiting outside the office of Joseph Ward, then Minister of Public Health, to demand action over the case of a woman with tuberculosis who had come to Buckle St. Tuberculosis patients were not meant to be with others, yet the government had no alternative measures ready. The issue was becoming politically hot. Ward may have been avoiding her, 'not available'. She waited – and waited. Finally she heard the secretary go into the inner office and say softly: 'Mother Aubert is here and she is getting angry.' Suzanne took her cue and called out: 'Mother Aubert is not *getting* angry. She *is* angry! And what is more, if something is not done for that woman immediately, she will take a cab to the *Evening Post* and have it published in tonight's paper!'[23] Other arrangements for the sick woman were quickly made.

Suzanne was well aware of the value of publicity. The collecting prams, steered by the young sisters and rattling and banging their way around the streets, were a daily advertisement. When the shift to Island Bay finally took place, it was done partly on foot – a strategically cumbersome procession of prams, carts and embarrassed postulants stopping the traffic and turning the heads of passengers in the passing trams. She had a pretext to halt it for a long time outside the rugby grounds, until the game ended. The spectators leaving were to see and take note.

She also had documented approval from financial experts – even if Martin Kennedy's recommendation on 2 March 1906 has a slightly bemused tone:

> Dear Mother Joseph,
> Re your letter intimating that you propose accepting a tender for part of your Home at Island Bay, to cost not more than £13,000:
> — That you have in hand £3,000, and promises certain for another £3,000, that you expect £2,000 from the sale of your Wanganui property, and to collect a further £2,000 while the building is in progress.
> — Considering what you have done these last few years, and your own personality, in the realizations of your hopes in the forecast of your finances, I am of [the] opinion you are justified in accepting the tender you have indicated, more particularly as several of the promises you have were given on the understanding that you were commencing the building forthwith.
> — The manner in which your charity has been conducted since your arrival in Wellington has met with general approval from the entire Community, and I feel sure you will have general financial support in any movement you initiate for providing funds for the proposed Contract.[24]

Kennedy was saying in essence that the force of her personality and her track record in Wellington would compensate for what were hardly more than promises and high hopes and, on that financial basis, she was justified in continuing. Suzanne's own catchcry would be: 'Providence is my bank'.

So Archbishop Redwood, even if he shared the diocesan council's growing doubts, would have had trouble going against this strongly flowing tide of professional, public and financial lay approval. He had not been a prickly figure in her regard, like Bishop Croke long ago or his own vicar general, Thomas O'Shea, to come. Sixty-seven-year-old Francis Redwood had been bishop now for thirty-two years and was a mellow figure of the capital's establishment. He handed over his money with the rest of them.

Redwood, as she recalled it, even encouraged Suzanne to participate in the Plunket Society and the Society for the Protection of Women and Children, and to associate with members of the Charitable Aid Board. This was most unusual for a woman religious at that time. While her presence there, as a woman with expertise in medicine and social work, was valid, she could also represent Roman Catholic charity among the secular and non-Catholics. 'You go! You can do it', she remembered him saying, 'we [the clergy] can't. It will do good. You can show them Catholic principles without seeming to do it. You can teach them the difference between mere philanthropy and true Christian charity.'[25]

Annie McVicar, justice of the peace and member of the hospital board, looked back at Suzanne's contribution at meetings of the Society for the Protection of Women and Children: 'She never spoke unless her opinion was asked, and when she gave it, it was in a few words but very much to the point. She had such knowledge and such wide experience of human nature, that she taught us many things. I had many reforms in view, I was eager to get things done, and she would say – laying her hand on my sleeve – "You will do well if you get the half of that in twenty years", and she would laugh quietly at me. She was so wise, she seemed to know all about every problem that came before us! Well, the twenty years have gone, and some of the things I wanted have been done, but only about half, as she foresaw.'[26] In 1908, Suzanne was at the inaugural dinner of the newly formed Trained Nurses' Association. Dr Agnes Bennett gave a speech and in it dubbed seventy-three-year-old Mother Aubert 'The Grand Old Woman of Wellington'.

And then there were the potential benefactors, whom Suzanne also lobbied energetically – or rather, to whom she took her Christian mission, because that was how she saw it. Getting the rich to share with the poor would bring them happiness and increase their chances of a better afterlife. Her Catholic theology believed that good works as well as faith played a part in people's salvation. Suzanne often said she had been impressed since she came to New Zealand with the spontaneous generosity and unselfishness of its settlers and would think: 'if only that is done with a supernatural motive, if only it is inspired by *charity*, those people will be *saved*'.[27] Charity was love for God expressed in service of others. The concept of charity came from the soul and was to be distinguished from secular philanthropy. Suzanne was conservative in some ways and had been reared in the pious tradition of the symbiotic interdependence of rich and poor.[28] The poor needed help from the rich; the rich needed the poor to accept their help, to assure their own salvation.

The sharing of wealth was a topical subject in Liberal New Zealand with the breaking up of extensive old land holdings. The *Yeoman* of 21 January 1899, for instance, ran a full editorial on 'The Duties of Wealth'. The rich had a duty to share with those who had helped them amass their fortunes, or else class conflict or 'perhaps a revolution of the whole social system' could be the consequence. The paper spoke of the liberality and philanthropy of American millionaires with their endowments. Although it hoped that New Zealand would never have millionaires, 'as the making of a millionaire is the crushing to the earth of large numbers of helpless toilers', it thought that wealthy people in New Zealand could do more than they were doing at present.

Studies of the Liberals show that, for them, 'class interests' were not to stand in the way of the interests of the community as a whole. 'Liberals usually accepted that social divisions existed. What concerned them was the character of the relationship between those divisions and society as a whole.' They were talking about moral attitudes: they did not want 'a selfish preoccupation with the interests of one's own section'.[29] So it was considered patriotic to want something for the good of the whole community; this was the government's 'forward and progressive policy'. Ballance's 'self-reliance' Budget of 1892 had already handed local 'capitalists' the challenge of 'fulfilling all the duties of a colonist' and investing in 'the progress and destiny of New Zealand'.[30]

Suzanne understood and applied the philosophy and the psychology of the Liberal heyday. She simply added to these her religious dimension. She expected to find in people an inherently spiritual yearning to share. Back in Napier in 1889 there had been John Ormond's grumpy refusal of a train pass. Yet Ormond's wife could have given her an example more in line with her own intuition. Hannah Ormond kept a diary for many years, and one 1882 entry foreshadowed Suzanne's interpretation of the 'duties of wealth'. Hannah would have liked more chances to be generous with her money even if simply by sharing meals, but her irritable husband was blocking her. 'I think I am doing', she wrote, 'a good action. I chafe at having so little power to do anything for anybody with all our riches – Glad to have had a chance put before me & already I see it must be stopped somehow.' Her husband, she continued, had 'no breath of charity or pity only pure selfishness – & no consideration for my feelings'.[31]

Hannah undoubtedly knew her Gospel text: how difficult it was for rich people to enter the kingdom of heaven, more difficult than for a camel to pass through the eye of a needle. Mother Aubert would offer them many chances, by giving and by working, to squeeze their way through. In 1909 she went back to Otatara in Hawke's Bay to help nurse her long-ago acquaintance, Airini Karauria Donnelly, on her deathbed. Airini was by then probably one of the wealthiest people in New Zealand with huge landholdings clouded by years of legal and personal controversy. It is possible that Suzanne was there not just as the consummate nurse, skilled as well in Maori ways. She could also, by the mere fact of her presence, have been holding out to Airini the possibility of spiritual gains by sharing her heritage with the poor.

Suzanne made it clear to her sisters that taking the message of the needs of the poor to the rich was an exacting part of their apostolate. How to do it without falling prey to sycophancy and snobbishness? André Siegfried, a French socialist touring the country just after the turn of the century to observe the progressive social policies of the Liberals, had identified snobbishness in the New Zealand psychology:

> Snobbishness, like imperialism, has found at the Antipodes a soil peculiarly favourable to its development. . . . In the political arena, there is a strong opposition to wealth; in Parliament, wealth is a subject for inflammatory speeches; and yet in everyday life it is given a consideration which would be quite natural anywhere else, but which seems paradoxical in these new democracies.[32]

Suzanne did have a *soupçon* of Lyon rising-capitalist snobbishness in her make-up. And the stories of her noble background were circulated to galvanise the more snobbish New Zealanders. The observation that 'she courted them' is a fair comment on Suzanne's link with the influential.[33]

In principle, however, and mostly in practice, she was on her guard with the wealthy. In the 'Letter to the Novices' she wrote, by then from long experience, on the subject of 'begging in the houses of the rich':

— Can we extend our devotedness to the rich?

We owe to the poor our love and care, and we must be their servants; but we owe to the rich the honour of charity. On reading the Gospel, one would be led to believe that they have a poor chance of salvation. Our Saviour's language in their regard is severe. Let us be their apostles. By begging our bread from them, by carrying to them the wailings of the unfortunate, by recalling with gentle instance to them the great law of charity and the responsibilities of fortune, let us induce them to give alms to the poor out of their wealth, their intelligence and their heart, in the name of Our Father Who is in heaven; and the moment they will do so, the proud selfishness which fastens them to the earth will thaw like ice in sunshine, and the good they will do to others will render them better, and put them on the good road, the way of the blessed.

— Then begging in the houses of the rich is an apostolate?

It is an apostolate which has its good side, but is also fraught with many drawbacks, even dangers, and must be undertaken with the utmost precaution. It occasions much waste of time, it dissipates the heart. We have to wait for the gentleman, compliment the lady, honour both, praise the children, say many useless words in drawing-rooms, to get money. We are exposed to boast of what we are doing, and what we are not doing, to hear words of flattery, apt to swell us, like a frog, with vanity, fill our heads with twaddle and the spirit of the world. Begging from door to door broken food or cast-off clothes is less dangerous.[34]

Her mission was to make the act of giving an expression of faith. She argued that no one, not even an atheist, is averse to a blessing and in her lively letters of thanks over the years she would always include a blessing, implying that as a matter of course the donor had a higher motive in mind than mere philanthropy. And this would help lead to a true act of charity the next time the person gave. 'Once alms are given for the love of God', she would say, 'the door is open for His grace to enter even souls who are in sin, were it only at the moment of death!'[35]

So Mother Aubert's thanks routinely called down a blessing on the giver, whether the gift was cash:

My dear Mrs Riddiford,

How kind of you to have thought of us in your lovely Longwood, and to have sent us the handsome Christmas gift of £3,000 which went so far . . . You do not know what a terrible beggar you so graciously invited to call on you when so hardly pressed, but I will try to behave decently. Meantime, I will heartily pray for you and for your dear babies. . . . God bless them.[36]

or a cow:

Dear Mr Abbott,
The valuable little cow you so very generously sent us arrived safely on Thursday night. The Sister in charge of our dairy told me that the new arrival 'possesses every quality a good cow ought to have'! . . . I heard of the weary tramp through the rain you and your brother had on Thursday morning in order to put the animal on the train, and I can only hope and pray that Our Divine Lord will repay you with His own heavenly interest for every step you took. May He bless you and your brother and your families every day more and more for all your generous charity to us, extending over such a long series of years, that you must have laid up a great store in the heavenly treasure-house.[37]

or the free services of a doctor. In 1924 eighty-nine-year-old Suzanne sent a shakily written letter to Dr Agnes Bennett, who was going overseas to study developments in medical treatment. It ended:

May I take the liberty to give you a most affectionate kiss at the last minute as the seal of my deep gratitude for your untiring kindness and invaluable services to our poor, suffering inmates, for which may God bless and reward you as He alone can do it.[38]

Benefactors great and small are woven into the history of Suzanne and the Sisters of Compassion. Five stories speak for many others:

— Sir Joseph Ward was a devout Catholic and a steady supporter of Suzanne. In his will, the only bequest outside his family was for £1000 to the Sisters of Compassion. He was also a natty dresser and was distressed once to find that his best dinner suit had gone that morning by mistake with a bundle of clothes to the Home of Compassion. Only a hasty telephone call from Premier House saved it from gracing a thankful and penniless fellow citizen.[39]

— Mother Aubert goes into the office of a businessman. 'Take a chair', he says to her, gesturing from his desk. 'Thank you very much', says Mother Aubert, and takes the chair home with her, undoubtedly blessing him as she goes.[40]

— Alexander Turnbull had no love for the 'begging sisters' and suddenly decided they were not to call at his house. He thought they had taken something. Mother Aubert went and accosted him in his office. 'They took nothing but what was given to them. My sisters are not thieves', she said. She then turned the tables: 'I will not let my sisters go to your house again.' Almost immediately, she placed an order for £100 worth of goods with his firm – the cradles and little iron bedframes for the new home. He was astonished and mortified. He arranged for all the tea samples to be saved for the sisters and made up the quantity to a half-chest each month. The sisters did not go back to his house; they went to his warehouse instead. The firm stayed a benefactor ever after.[41]

— Mother Aubert, coming up Tory St with the begging pram, is approached by a little boy of about four years old. 'Do you take pennies?' he asks hopefully. 'Yes', she says, and he rises on tiptoe to put a penny or two in the pram, then slips away. Mother Aubert thinks the gift a blessed one.[42]

— Mother Aubert dozes off, sitting tired on the steps of St Mary of the Angels church in Boulcott St. She wakes, gets up and walks on her way. Pat Lawlor, the altar boy, finds a pile of coins beside where she has been, presumably gifts from people passing by the sleeping old woman.[43]

In 1906 Our Lady's Home of Compassion rose on the edge of the first ripple of hill to the east of the Island Bay valley. Behind the building, a scarp shot up to the ridge running high and narrow along to Cook Strait. A wind grittily served notice of future company on the day the foundation stone was laid by Archbishop Redwood. The public had been invited and Redwood asked the collectors to go around the crowd, starting off with £20 from himself. Thomas Hislop, the mayor, praised the work of Mother Aubert and said that in 'preparing for that new building the Mother had made persistent requests to the Corporation to help her, and what that body had been able to do in improving the road to the site, it had done'.[44] Campbell and Burke, the construction firm, had agreed to stop and start according to finance coming in. The theme of the newspaper coverage was the need for 'the generous co-operation of the public' for a project 'inspired by a compassion which cares nothing for creed'. The Town Hall concert of 11 July 1906 followed that theme, and New Zealand's leading musicians donated their talents. Tenor E. J. Hill's song was a new composition by his brother, Alfred Hill, to the words of a Banjo Patterson poem. Cyril Towsey, 'the best accompanist in New Zealand then', was organist and pianist.[45]

Not much is recorded in the letters between Wellington and Jerusalem about the building of the new institute. Suzanne's letter to Sister Bridget on 4 January 1907 tells why:

Your letter arrived this morning just after Rure had left. . . . I do not think you need a long letter when you are so soon to see a living gazette whose editor declared before he left that he would have enough to say for at least a fourtnight when he reaches his destination.[46]

The 'living gazette' was Te Manihera Keremeneta, or Rure as he was known to most in Jerusalem. Rure's wife had died in 1903. Over the time of the building of the Island Bay home, he was often in Wellington helping Suzanne.

Rure's whakapapa traces him back to Turi of the waka *Aotea*. He was perhaps the most strikingly devout of the Catholic community at Hiruharama. His parents had been there in Father Lampila's time. Rure was baptised when Father Soulas, Suzanne and the Sisters of St Joseph arrived at Hiruharama in July 1883. He was confirmed at the opening of the church in December 1885. His devotion never seemed to waver. Photos show him as strikingly handsome, well-knit, upright. He once said later in life that he would have liked to be a priest himself. It was Rure who set a benchmark for stability of faith, ascetic piety, hard work and loyalty both to his Maori values and to the Pakeha religious who had come to live alongside him. He loved and respected Meri.

Rure wrote letters to his parents and relayed news in person. His 'gazette' leaves only a whisper through the record. 'I know that Rure is sending you the News; as for me I have not time to breath[e]. Several novices are bad with influenza which does not mend matter', wrote Suzanne.[47] Another time Sister Veronica wrote: 'Rure is grubbing up the firs [she meant furze or gorse] at the home. He says when he goes home, he will have enough to talk about for a year. He wants to come back here for a year to clear the ground.'[48] 'I suppose Rure gave you all the news about the furnishing tea etc.'[49]

Rure would have found out, even just by sensing them, the enormous stresses of the gamble Suzanne had taken. Mother, wrote Sister Veronica, was 'of course very worried and tired as she has a lot of anxiety and plenty of trot[t]ing to do; the new building at Island Bay is going up rapidly and the bills for it are also coming in rapidly'.[50] Rure was the main link with the river community. Some of the sisters missed it keenly, as Sister Veronica let Sister Bridget know: 'You said in your last letter it was no good writing anything about the Maoris as it did not interest us but it is just the thing that does interest us.'[51] Through 1906 and 1907 Rure was a mainstay for Suzanne and the sisters, and he quietly knew it. This is clear by reading between the lines of another of Suzanne's letters upriver:

> I thought that Rure was going home tomorrow, and at the last minute I hear
> he is not. It is not me who keeps [him] here though he is useful. But he likes
> to be here longer. I will talk to him again, so that he goes this week at least
> for some time to look after his parents' potatoes. Then if he likes to come back
> he will be welcome.[52]

'The Home is opened at last', was Sister Veronica's announcement
to the river community on 30 April 1907, 'and it is a beautiful building.
The Sisters are not living here yet, but we come in and out as there is
heaps to be done here. I suppose you have Rure's "letter" before this,
describing the opening.'[53] So Rure's voice relating in Maori to Ngati Hau
and the Hiruharama sisters the story of the crowded opening of Meri's
Home of Compassion is the vivid, unheard korero behind Sister
Veronica's account. It would have reminded them of their own magnificent opening ceremonies in 1885 for the church they had built with
Suzanne.

Meanwhile Sister Veronica carried on writing from her own viewpoint:

> However, I shall just tell you a little about things. Mother and the Sisters were
> out here most of last week, filling beds, pillows, and getting things straight for
> Sunday. It was a very busy, excitable week both at Buckle St and the Bay. To
> make a long story short, Sunday morning arrived at last, and we found
> ourselves making beds, cots, three rows in each of the four big wards down
> stairs, and two rows in surgical, infectious, suspicious and convalescent wards
> up stairs.

Even the beds themselves carried the surely near-saturation fundraising
message:

> A few of the beds were completely made to let people see what they would be
> like, more had only a quilt, more only the sheet, and the greater number only
> the mattress. Each bed had a label of different discriptions varying as to the
> amount of clothing on each. Some of them were of this discription: 'I am so
> cold. Who will pity me?' 'Dear kind lady, clothe me' and so on.

Then the ceremony began:

> There were several flags flying from the towers and one from the hill. At
> about half past one the members of the committee arrived, also two or three
> police in uniform. Then the crowd began to gather. His Grace arrived about
> half past two accompanied by Father Lewis, Devoy, O'Shea, Kimbell,
> Moloney – the other clergy were Revd Hills, Venning, Herring, Ainsworth,
> Bartley, Gilbert and Graham. The ceremony was commenced about 2:30 p.m.
> when His Grace blessed the place. The procession was headed by a number of
> small boys in surplices, the one foremost carrying the crucifix. Next came His

Grace, blessing each room as he passed, then a number of clergy in surplices followed, and then the crowd. I forgot to say in front of all was Rure making room right and left for the procession, which being ended the speaches commenced. A platform was errected in front of the main entrance for that purpose. . . . I cannot tell you what was said for I did not hear any of the speaches. The crowd was so great it was impossible to get near.

It did not matter that Sister Veronica could not hear Redwood, or Acting Premier William Hall-Jones, or Mayor Hislop, or Hon. James Carroll, the Minister of Native Affairs, or Mr Wilford MHR, or Judge McArthur, or Edwin Arnold replying on behalf of Suzanne. Their speeches were reported in the newspapers anyway, following the general theme 'Where all creeds meet'. Sister Veronica summed up the essence that all the people standing like her, with sore feet, would have got: 'they all spoke very well of Mother and the work, and the new Home and I don't know what not. There were a number of aristocrats present, also about a dozen Doctors. At all posts were to be met collectors . . .'[54]

A form of collective canonisation has been envisaged for the humble spirituality of Lyon's various nineteenth-century religious figures.[55] The way Wellington pitched in and made possible what Suzanne projected as realisable also has an echo of some collective sanctity at work. On opening day, well over two thousand Wellingtonians swarmed over the flat promenade roof of their Home of Compassion with a proprietorial happiness. Mother Aubert was becoming public property.[56] The combination of her and the people who helped her made for synergy. Hall-Jones told the crowd that 'it was by the little streams trickling down that great rivers were made; and they, by the aggregate of their offerings, could assist the good Mother to carry on her good work with even better results'.[57]

McArthur said the secret of Mother Aubert's success was in the word 'love'. 'We might, like Rockefeller, endow universities; or, like Baroness Burdett-Coutts, give money to churches; or lavish money all over the world like Carnegie; but if we lacked love it would avail us nothing. Love included patience, sympathy, kindness, it rejoiced in sincerity.'[58] When Suzanne wrote her book of Maori conversation, she brought together the two ideas of showing your love and doing something for another. 'What I desire is to show my love : Ko taku e minaminatia ai ko taku aroha ano' is followed by, 'I wish to find out what I can do for you : E rapu tonu ana ahau ki tetahi mahi maku hei painga mou'.[59] Both expressions have a tentativeness about them. They do not imply a top-heavy, one-way condescension, but a dialogue between equals. This was what was now being communicated between Mother Aubert and the people, the people and Mother Aubert. Working together with her would have helped disparate groups find again in their new world a sense of cultural wholeness within a co-operative community.[60]

CHAPTER FIFTEEN

Wellington – the Home of Compassion
1906-1907

It is getting cloudy : Kei te puta mai te paroro
The rain is pouring down in sheets :
Kei te ringihia te kai a te ua, ehara i te hanga![1]

'This is a splendid house. To go from one end of the hall to the other you fancy you are going down some big avenue. The walls are of lovely white plaster', wrote Sister Baptista at the start of a letter in early August 1907. Suzanne would not have been pleased to know she was openly praising the building itself. When some of the clergy had said how proud she must have been of it all, Suzanne replied that, if pride ever came into it, she wished it would fall down. The service of God was meant to be a matter for humility.

But the Home of Compassion came closer to crumbling than Suzanne would have wished, and sooner than she would ever have imagined. Sister Baptista's confident start was just reassurance. She went straight on to bring Sister Bridget up to date with the tougher facts about the 'lovely white plaster' walls:

> but it is such a pity after all the expence to see how they have been spoiled with the rain coming in everywhere. The repairs have not begun yet so Mother thinks that the house will not be opened this year. . . . Mother is well, though I always think she looks so tired and worried and ill. It is no wonder if you could only see the state of this house. She goes down to Buckle Street almost every day, sometimes stays overnight and when she comes up, as a rule [she] has a big load of bread or potatoes etc as heavy as one of us could manage.[2]

Suzanne was humping sacks of potatoes, heavier than a woman in her seventies should be carrying, out of her heartache over the new building. The laden footslogging up and down the Berhampore hill out to Island Bay was partly a penitential pilgrimage, an act of self-denial, self-chastisement, to try to right whatever had gone wrong. Sister Baptista recognised that. A month before, in early July, Suzanne had written to the sisters in

Jerusalem: 'Pray hard that God arranges everything for us. I do not know yet the whole extant of the wrongs of the new building, but what I know is really dreadful. And what about the cost?'[3]

What could possibly have gone wrong in two months, between the gladness of the official opening and these despairing letters? The defects and consequent damage had revealed themselves in the first heavy storm after the opening ceremonies. They had also revealed human error. The architect was James O'Dea. Like so many others, he had already generously given his services free. When Suzanne had acquired extra property at Buckle St, he had helped to alter and link up the cottages. In recognition, she wanted him to have the Island Bay project. With enthusiasm, she brought him her preliminary design ideas for Island Bay and he and his draughtsman proceeded from there. She did not know that O'Dea's knowledge and training fell far short of what was required for such a large building project. It turned out that he also had a drinking problem.

Miscalculations meant the girders were inadequate. One had already sagged from the weight of the crowd filling the home on opening day. As well, they were hollow and carried water which percolated down from defective asphalting on the flat roof. The weakest girder buckled badly. Rain was pouring down several walls, leaving on the freshly plastered walls trailing loops of water stain that are clearly seen in the photographs of the time. Through June, July and August, other architects' reports came in, from John Swan, Crichton and McKay, and Frederick Clere, who firmly and perhaps pointedly added to his signature his position as 'Architect to the District of Wellington Hospital Board etc. etc.' They all agreed: not enough damp courses, coke breeze concrete wrongly carried through parapet walls, girders 'on the light side', 'deficient in strength', 'not strong enough for the purpose to which they are applied'. They concurred, too, in what was needed, and slowly work got under way. After months of expensive repairs, the large wards of the Home of Compassion were neatly punctuated with the cool, clean lines of columns added to bear the weight.[4]

In the midst of this mess, Suzanne did not want to go open-handed to the public again. They had done enough, and she wanted the matter to be handled as discreetly as possible. As Mother Mary Joseph she was humbled; as 'the grand old woman of Wellington' she was humiliated. She was also trying to play down the publicity for the sake of O'Dea and his family, and for the building contractors, who had merely followed specifications. Inevitably, though, the news got into the papers and passed along the streets. Suzanne used to say how grateful she was when Chief Justice Sir Robert Stout and his wife stopped her in Willis St one day. 'Mother Aubert' had been keeping her head down. They spoke with her for a while, and told her how they felt for her and the trial she was going through. The best thing just then, she said, was that 'they did not offer me money. I was glad they did not. [They] understood so well all that had occurred. I did not have to make any explanation, they understood it all.'[5] Robert Stout was a former Premier; Anna Stout was a leading figure in advancing the position and condition of women. It did not matter that they approached human need out of a secular moral socialism and Mother Aubert from Christian mission. The Stouts were benefactors and their sons were later surgeons at the home but it was the friendly comfort that counted then.

A Redemptorist priest, Father Vaughan, commented to Redwood during the construction of the home that Mother Aubert was 'an extraordinary woman' to start such a work at her age. 'Why?' asked Redwood. 'She has extraordinary faith,' answered Vaughan. Redwood then said to his guests around the dinner table: 'Mine is greater – to allow her to do it!'[6] But the combined extraordinary faiths of archbishop and nun could not hide the possibility that Suzanne had taken on more than she could cope with, the huge building project out at Island Bay coming on top of all her other responsibilities. Never mind what extra energy might have come from religious zeal; in human terms she had overloaded herself. Back in the late 1860s, a stubborn young Sister Marie Joseph had worked herself into the ground to try to save the Nazareth Institute, and had gone with broken health to Hawke's Bay. Now an elderly Mother Aubert was pushing herself beyond her limits.

Before the opening of the Home of Compassion in April 1907, she was very ill. In early February she had collapsed and the doctors thought it was a heart attack. Her sisters wondered if it might have been a stroke, as she 'suffered some loss of power'.[7] But Emmeline Crombie, who would later enter the congregation, told Sister Bridget in Jerusalem what Sister Claver had said to her: 'it was a break down of the nerves with poor Mother; she was completely overdone & do you wonder at it, Sister?' The doctors were saying she needed 'complete rest & no excitement or worry'.[8] Suzanne was not very good at dispensing complete rest to herself.

On 18 February she wrote up to Jerusalem:

> I have just received your affectionate letter. I regret very much that you have
> been so alarmed. Kahore he take [Don't let it worry you]. I am much better
> and I hope, according to the Doctors, promise to be as well as ever in very few
> days. So do not be anxious but pray for me and also to St Joseph to send a few
> thousands as I want them badly to fix the accounts for the Bay.[9]

She had tried too hard to keep the momentum of the building going.
The original building programme, for instance, was to be for one wing
only, but she had authorised excavations for the other wing. Martin
Kennedy wrote to her tersely: 'you are better not to incur any more debts
by extending the foundations of the other wing. . . . It's very well to have
everything up to style if one has the funds; when looking to borrow on
weak securities it is often better not to incur the obligations.'[10] Sisters
recalled week after week of constant prayer and novenas made to St
Joseph as guardian and protector of the Holy Family. He was also, of
course, a carpenter.

By 7 April, not long before the opening, Suzanne was still a fair way
from recovery: 'Dear Mother is able to get up a little in the day time and
sit in the sun; that is the Dr's orders; but Mother has stretched it to cutting
out clothes, sorting, sewing and so on. She is still very weak after being so
long in bed and [it takes] very little to tire her. She gave us our reading
today for the first time since she took ill.'[11] At the opening a convalescent
and somewhat reduced Suzanne welcomed to the home the public who
probably did not know she was ill and who innocently left behind them
girders sagging from their enthusiastic weight. On the day, she was
photographed with Sister Agnes behind the first table they had in Buckle
St, made from a horse manure box which they had scrubbed and scrubbed
clean. This table represented their humble beginnings in Wellington and
meant a great deal to her. In the photo her hand is pressed on it as if she
is steadying herself.

It was this weakened Suzanne who was faced with repairs, and changes
to the building to make it more in line with hospital practice, which cost
almost as much as the original quote. In late August she let some of her
worry spill out in a letter to Sister Bridget: 'We are very much upsetted
between the building at the Bay, the social, illness and the exam for nurses,
and the preparation for the reception of novices. I do not know where to
turn.'[12] Suzanne's illness revealed a few potential cracks in the strength of
the congregation as well. Even though it did not have the same pool of

potential recruits as those congregations which ran secondary schools, it was growing steadily now. But Suzanne was far older than any of the others. She had for so long seen her sisters as young women that the fact that her original companions were now mature women in their forties was escaping her. Suzanne had not started to delegate responsibility – she would always find that hard to do. She was mother superior, secretary and treasurer.

While she was occupied with the planning and building at Island Bay, the women who were the Sisters of Compassion were actually managing complex organisations for a good part on their own. Up the river, they taught two schools, brought up their children in the orphanage, ran (with help) a farm and huge orchard, were the local district nurses – even midwives, occasionally, although Suzanne cautioned against taking over Maori custom in this. They trained the novices of the congregation, and were still missionaries to the Maori.

Down in Wellington, they ran a hospice for terminally ill patients, had hot food always available for the hungry, made up food and clothing parcels to hand out to families. They nursed, reared and cared for children with special needs, and dealt with a crèche crowded every day with thirty or more infants. They ran the infirmary at St Patrick's College, just through the back fence at Buckle St, and this often landed them with epidemics of sick boys among the fifty or so boarders. They trained for St John Ambulance and Red Cross certificates, handled collecting rounds, sorted, sewed, laundered, planned food distribution, cooked. They visited people in their homes and took part in the local parish. Somehow they still kept on an even keel their life and routine as religious.

So how, through these overloaded years, did these women relate to their sometimes bossy old French superior? Occasionally quaking, some-times muttering an inner comment, perhaps not questioning her quite enough out of religious obedience, they dealt her overall affection and respect neatly balanced. A great part of their own energies and capabilities came from Suzanne's influence, anyway. Insofar as she was the person who set the tone for the congregation, she made sure they did not lose the flavour and pith of their own natures. She was not squashing their individual personalities. She drummed humility into them, but also made sure they kept their self-esteem, because if they did not, God would: 'God deals with us', she said, 'as if He had a better opinion of us than we have of ourselves.'[13] They knew that any religious had to harness her character into the team she had decided to join. The long novitiate would train her to quell tendencies to break step or do anything to disturb the steady pull. Suzanne and the early sisters had not spent years among horses for nothing. Sisters of Compassion might be teamed together to work productively, but in the process their spirits, with few exceptions, were not themselves crushed.

This was the opinion of Dr Elsie Gibbons, who knew some of them much later in their lives. Sister Clotilde, she said, 'knew Mother Aubert well and she never lost her individuality and she never lost her personality. She was a vigorous woman who had her own opinions. I remember going down to see her one day and she was reading Jung. She said, "He's splendid." She had a really first-class mind.' And, 'Sister Isidore thought for herself. She was quite a strong woman. She wouldn't have taken any nonsense. Her mind moved quite fast and she wasn't put down.' In her view it had a lot to do with the training. 'Somehow or other, the Sisters of Compassion succeeded in not depersonalising their nuns. . . . I can only think that it was in the way that the novitiate was run. And I was often asked to see the novices, of course [as a woman doctor], and they were very kind to these women, because it's quite hard to be a novice, I think. And the novice mistresses were carefully selected.'[14]

It was Suzanne's spirit which lay behind this training. Sister Lawrence wrote notes from the novices' retreat in 1911 at which Suzanne told them to give their wills 'as much scope as possible' in the paradox of the religious life she laid out for them: the freeing of the will through its submission.

> Now you must say to your will: 'Now, little will of mine, I must bring you into subjection. If not, you will tyrannize over me and drag me down with you. I will give you as much scope as possible.' In going to God, never deplore having strong passions. They may become a source of great merit by their force. If we choose, they will take us to God. So never grieve over having strong passions. We must always have a pure intention.[15]

In Rome in 1915, Suzanne gathered together the essence of the conferences and other talks she had given novices over the years and wrote her 'Letter to the Novices'. This document went into the sisters' *Directory*, the manual that still guides their lives. Her spiritual philosophy of moulding yet empowering her sisters to take confident action is threaded through it:

> — What is the Novitiate?

It is an initiative, . . . The Novitiate is a school and a training-ground, wherein the Novice strives to learn and know all her energies, as regards the supreme business of her salvation, to absorb her mind, heart and will in their essential function, namely, the knowledge, love, and service of God.

— Is the Novitiate of great importance?

The Novitiate is of such importance that nothing can supply its place or make up for its deficiency. The Novice is detained therein in order to be spoken about herself, to bend her to self-denial and obedience, to concentrate her energies, to co-ordinate her efforts, to supernaturalize her views before she acts, to see Jesus always and everywhere . . .

— What is the hidden power that energises all the Novitiate?

It is the prospect of the service of Jesus in the poor. . . .

— How must we obey?

Obey with your heart and at the same time with your will. In all honesty make your Superiors' will your will, so that your submission, far from paralysing your faculties, as a sheep-like docility would do, will keep them always in full exercise, and your personality will thereby be strengthened. We ought to will so quickly what God wills that one could not tell who willed it first, He or we.[16]

Yet from 1906, the sisters nevertheless felt the tight reins of an ageing Suzanne. No cloak of spiritual stoicism could have hidden completely how harassed she must have been. They felt the curb of her tiredness and stress as she tugged at them with increasing impatience and occasional flares of anger. The doctors told them this was part of her illness and recovery, and to let it ride. Father Creagh, a Redemptorist priest who knew Suzanne well, explained it away as 'only a mannerism'; it was 'due to her French temperament' and to her 'hatred of insincerity and sham of any kind'. 'There was nothing in it', he said. 'I got it once, but I took no notice of it.'[17] Gentle Sister Bridget, one of Suzanne's first three companions and the one she could call Biddie, copped the occasional broadside over these highly strung months, but took it in her stride. It was right in the middle of the frantic lead-up to the opening, and while Suzanne was ill, that this letter went up to Jerusalem. It began without the usual 'Dear Sr Bridget':

Sr Bridgit

You can make 6 pillow cases for the presbytery. As for the broken panes of glass they shall have to wait until somebody in Jerusalem can put them in.

I have sent an order to Mr Hatrick for stores.

My dear child [Bridget was forty-seven by then], allow me to tell you that I thought it rather cool that you wait till the middle of April to write to me that you wanted 20 shirts, 20 p. of trowsers. As if we had nothing else to do but go straight to a shop to buy them or sit down and the all of us sew for Jerusalem for two or three weeks. You might have fitted some before this and sen[t] me word a month ago at least. You have good will but not much mind of management. You will have to wait now. We cannot do impossibilities . . .

But Suzanne ends typically, warming the letter. She shows Bridget that the load of exasperation is shared; there are other pressures as well:

The college is full of sick boys. We are going to have a jolly time of it again. Now God bless you all. Let us pray hard for one another. The Sisters are fairly well except Hilda who has managed to sprain her ankle again.
Your affectionate Mother in J.C.
M. Mary Joseph[18]

Suzanne on the whole flashed out only at the deed or misdeed. She did not hold grudges against the person. Once the storm had passed, the sunshine came out. Nearly thirty years later, John McMahon remembered this. As a boy at Buckle St, he once had to lie low, keeping out of Grandma's way when she was stomping after him, uprooted manuka saplings in her hand. They were her rare specimens, not the common tea-tree as he thought when he pulled them up to chase and switch a girl who was teasing him. Some time later, Suzanne came across him hard at work cleaning the long forms the children sat on. She asked him: 'What are you doing?' Expecting her temper still to be hot, he nervously told her he was 'helping Auntie Marcelle to do the ward'. 'That is good', she replied and walked off down the path to the gate. John said he was 'simply petrified' when she spoke to him and he was sure she could see it. She 'had at that moment buried the hatchet and so gave me another life. I am sure she was laughing to herself going down the path, as her shoulders were shaking.'[19]

Neither would she mind when she realised someone had checkmated her with skilful but fair ingenuity. Martin Moloney, the city council clerk of works, had got the parish men to shift an old morgue as a shed for the Buckle St sisters. Suzanne arrived on the scene too late to stop it. She was angrily 'walking up and down', he said, 'with an umbrella in her hand which she grasped in the middle of it and not by the handle'. He went up to her and she said: 'I wanted that shed for Island Bay.' He answered: 'All right, Mother, we'll shift it to Island Bay for you whenever you say the word.' She burst out laughing. It had just been solidly built in, fixed alongside another back shed. She said nothing more about it.[20]

The sisters' life was hard. They lived, like their patients, on 'what came in'. Suzanne was heard to say that New Zealand girls did not have the same spirit of penance as she had known in France. But she also often held that her sisters' lifestyle was so rigorous anyway that there was no real need for extra penances. Her postulants and novices, for instance, were sent down to rummage on the very public auction floor of the fruit and vegetable market. They would emerge from the rank pile of rotting, reject pumpkins, stained yellow, spotted with seed and clutching the one good pumpkin there might still be left. A proud young Wellington woman caught doing this by people who had known her previously in secular life would need few other exercises in humility and penance. Or else she might have walked home scarlet-faced in the company of Mother Aubert who once was carrying a clean chamber-pot (one offering) filled with strawberry jam (another offering). This would scrape off another layer of pride.

Along with almost every Christian of the time, Suzanne believed that you had a better chance of attaining a goal if you denied yourself some comfort or pleasure. Her personal model was extreme: Jean Vianney, the ascetic Curé of Ars. Sister Clotilde, looking back, wrote that she and her fellow novices had 'wished Mother had chosen a saint who was less penitential than St Vianney!'[21] Suzanne denied herself often. She would trudge purposely down the unevenly ridged and rutted middle of the track from the farm instead of the smoother clay of the edge. Or she would stand cutting out clothes far into the night, would hump the heavy potatoes.

Now and then she offered up her sisters' self-denial as well. Sister Veronica was pretty sure this was what happened to her once in 1904. She was with Suzanne on a tour to introduce their Constitutions to the bishops of Dunedin, Christchurch and Auckland. Their endorsement was needed, to add to Redwood's, before Rome approved them. It was an important step in the congregation's development. They were in Christchurch for a week and Sister Veronica was hoping to see her own two Hartnett sisters in Lyttelton. She had not seen them for eleven years. But Suzanne stalled so long that they had to go straight to the boat without the Hartnett sisters being reunited, even briefly. Veronica knew that in these delaying tactics she was a sacrifice. She did not see her sisters for another eight years.

Sister Veronica was not passively meek and mild. She was capable of judiciously observing the older woman, understanding her motivations, not being bitter, yet still noting Suzanne's own come-uppance. Because she went on to share the rest of the story. The two women proceeded up north to Auckland. Suzanne chose not to go by sea from New Plymouth but unusually took the riverboat right up the Whanganui to Taumarunui and on by train. It was freezing mid-winter with snow on the hills. Suzanne refused offers of rugs. She kept the two of them up in the bows of the boat, standing and saying their prayers in the sharp cold air of the gorges. 'They read *The Imitation of Christ* as spiritual reading, and Sister Veronica felt like throwing the book in the river! She was conscious only of the cold.' She saw more self-denial in the cause. In Auckland, however, the tables were turned on Suzanne. She found out from her old friends, the Outhwaites, that a French naval ship had just left port. On board was a midshipman who was a relative of hers. The delay on the river had wrenched from her the chance of meeting him. Suzanne was crushed with disappointment while Sister Veronica 'was tempted to reflect on retributive justice'.[22]

Sister Veronica had entered the congregation quite young, at the age of sixteen. So she could easily have been two-dimensional, receiving the imprint of religious life so early that her own personality might not have fully developed. But a woman like that could not have analysed her superior with such acuity and humanity. Veronica was, in fact, clear-sighted, intelligently practical and even, like Suzanne herself, a bit tough. She was also perhaps the strongest upholder of Suzanne's tradition among the Maori, and was an excellent speaker of Maori. When Veronica was later brought from the river to Island Bay, Ngati Hau and Ngati Ruaka sent a petition packed with signatures asking for her to come back to them. They felt her absence keenly when she finally went from their lives to be superior of the congregation. Veronica was by no means squashed by her long association with Suzanne.

There was another dimension to the congregation that was being especially tested at this time. Suzanne had long ago accepted a very active religious vocation. She spoke of how she revered the strong mysticism of the contemplative Carmelite nun, St Teresa d'Avila, but that model was to be 'more admirable than imitable'. 'God gives His Spirit to His Saints', she explained, 'according to times and circumstances. Perhaps, had she lived in our times, instead of going to Carmel, Theresa of Avila – with her ardent and manly nature – would have been a daughter of Our Lady of Compassion, or of St Vincent de Paul.'[23] Suzanne's model of life-work was the active congregation founded by St Vincent de Paul, the Sisters of Charity. People were 'made for action', she wrote, 'just as the bird is for flight'.[24] Now she was pushing this concept of the active sister to new limits of definition as she tried to squeeze into twenty-four hours everything the women needed to do.

Her solution was always to combine the practical and spiritual. It was as though the two extremes were not kept far apart on a flat plane but instead met as though wrapped around a cylinder and joined. The sisters did not work, then pray; they worked *and* prayed. Suzanne once saw Sister Agnes scrubbing clothes at the tub, saying her prayers with her face turned slightly in the direction of the chapel. Suzanne took Agnes's face in her hands and brought it back to the tub. God was there, and there for the time being was her chapel.

With typically vivid and practical imagery, she once wrote to a new sister a clear explanation of this 'chapel of the tub'. The novices routinely started their life in the community with a long haul in the laundry:

> While you are at the laundry you can do as much for your Divine Spouse, as if you were in any other office, for the merit of our actions is not measured on their greatness, but on the degree of love with which we perform them.
>
> Purify more and more your intention while you are washing the clothes of suffering Jesus, and ask Him to make your soul spotless in His eyes, and to render you as supple in His hands, as the clothes you are washing are in your own hands. Allow yourself thankfully to go through the process of being soaped, steeped, rubbed, scrubbed, boiled, rinsed, hanged up, dried, mangled, or starched and ironed, put on the shelf ready for use, till wanted. It will be a splendid preparation for Holy Profession. If God gives me time and help, I will send to the Novices a little explanation of the above process of spiritual laundry work.[25]

In her explanations, Suzanne would use metaphors like this, or parable-like stories. They could be quaint or whimsical but never risible in the startling clarity of their message translated into the language of women.

She taught them that the contemplative path was not to be theirs. 'In some orders', she said on Retreat Sunday, 27 May 1906, 'they are forbidden to look up at all. They go about with their eyes always cast down. Now, would it do for us to go about with our eyes cast down? Certainly not! How in the world would we manage to see our patients or do our work? We certainly have to look a bit higher than the floor to see the cobwebs and dust that need to be brushed down. So you see, dear Sisters, that what would be good for the contemplative is not at all good for those engaged in active works of charity.'[26]

On 25 February 1906, she spoke to the sisters at the beginning of Lent. Sister Agnes took notes in an exercise-book. Suzanne told them:

It is not in reciting long prayers, or staying hours in the Chapel with long beads dangling in our hands and neglecting our duty. – No! On the contrary, it is far more pleasing to God to offer up our work with a pure intention. . . . Sometimes when we feel inclined to give a grumpy answer, and things go wrong with us, offer it up as a prayer, and a little act of Love of God. He does not want prayers that take us from our work and make us neglect our duty. Do you not think it would be much easier for me to stay a couple of hours in the Chapel (I do not want to set myself up as a model), instead of being on the trot all day long. But then I offer it up to Our Lord and say: 'I must do your work, my Lord, then take it all as a prayer.' [27]

Suzanne Aubert practised her own form of mysticism, even in her constant activity. The novices watched her once as they helped carry away the good potatoes she was sorting out of a dank, blighted and sprouting mass. Working away silently for two hours, she seemed to them to be totally lost in contemplation. It was often the same when she went through Wellington 'on the trot'. 'I throw no slur on prayer', were the words Sister Agnes copied down. 'Our whole life should be one long prayer. That is the true spirit of our Order, the spirit of a simple, loving faith, seeing God in everything, seeing His representatives in every one, doing His will in all we do. You must love Him with all your heart; and more than your heart, though that sounds too much, yet by His grace you will be able to love Him much more than your poor human heart could do by itself. If we can live like this, we shall always be united to God.' [28]

Suzanne trained the women to do every action, however exhausting and distasteful, as an act of prayer, and to pass, for instance, the night hours on the ward as if they were a series of devotions as meaningful spiritually as the communal recitation of the Divine Office, the formal Prayer of the Church, might be to an enclosed order. Their *Directory* specifically shows them how. For a few women, the unremitting physical work, and perhaps the lack of opportunity to withdraw into themselves for a while, did prove too much. The majority, however, thrived on the days and nights of tough work. They lived their fulfilling blend of spirituality and practicality.

So both the women and Suzanne were psychologically better equipped than most to deal with hardship and setbacks. Everything that happened in 1907, bad though it seemed to be in the middle of her illness and the winter damage out at Island Bay, was to be seen as part of what she called God's 'now', and within it were the seeds of future good:

The present moment, the *now*, contains all the love of the good God, all sanctity, our life and all eternity. What God wills, what He promises now, is precisely what is necessary for our salvation, for our sanctification. That trial of now, God has willed or permitted through love for us. Prayer gains for us now and always the courage and strength for all our duties, for every sacrifice, for every heroism.[29]

CHAPTER SIXTEEN

Wellington and Hiruharama
1904-1907

What is the reason of your grief? : Na te aha i rikarika ai tou ngakau[1]

Other trials had been part of the congregation's 'now' even before 1907. First, the farm at Hiruharama was not proving profitable, was too hard to run, and Suzanne needed the money for the new developments in Wellington. It went on the market in 1904 but proved difficult to sell. It was not sold until 1908 and even then there were more negotiations over stock and farm implements. Many letters to Bridget and also to Carmel, who worked with Brother Stanislaus, trace the last years of Suzanne's farm:

> I spoke to Hatrick about the wool. I am going to write to the Brother about it. The steamer will take it down on any day when there is a little water in the river . . .
>
> I wonder if the wool could be stored in a corner of the Nursery? If the 15 bales cannot be sent in a lot it might in two. It is bound to the Bank . . .
>
> There is absolutely not a cent left. The farm must pay its interests and other expenses, land tax, road board, repairs, insurances, etc. . . .
>
> You may expect at any time some gentlemen from Wellington to look at the farm. If they ask about the price, tell them that you do not know what I am asking for it, but that you were told it was worth £7 an acre and more on account of the fruit trees. Treat those gentlemen well, two of them are Catholics . . .
>
> I know nothing yet about the farm. It is of desperation . . .
>
> If anybody went up to look at it, let the Brother and you show it to best advantage. Land sells at high price now, and the orchard is unique of its kind in New Zealand . . .
>
> There will be a big loss on the wool this year [1905], on account of the bales having got wet on board of the steamer, if not before. Many of them had to be opened and got dried in a special house. It is for want of not having done what I recommended, that is to ask Kenny [the riverboat captain] the day

before, if he could take them. Again an expensive breach of obedience . . .

You did well with the cattle and other things. I do not know if the Brother is going back [he was ill and had been sent to Wellington to be nursed at Buckle St] and when he is going, if he does. I wish the farm was sold. It is such a drag and a worry. Island Bay is giving me a lot of anxiety . . .

I got the letters with the scanty news, but I suppose there are not many. I hope that you will soon recover from these nasty kicks. I received two letters about the farm; how I wish it was gone. Tell the Sisters to pray hard. There is plenty of difficulties here also. God help us all. . . . I have so much to do outside that I am hardly a few hours at home. Still it must be done. . . .

God bless you. Love to all from all.[2]

Finally the farm sold. The two-storeyed, shuttered house, the cherries, walnuts, chestnuts, filberts and all the rest went out of the sisters' hands. No longer did the orphans have to take their turn with the sisters to lead the milk horse up and down the steep track, the bad-tempered horse that might have been what gave Sister Carmel the 'nasty kicks' Suzanne had mentioned. But Suzanne still had a foothold on river land, with thirty-five acres down by the banks near the convent.

The greater trial, however, was Father Soulas, the priest who was a constant presence in the community from 1883 to 1904. Suzanne and the sisters and novices who had been upriver before 1904 were the ones directly affected. Indirectly the whole congregation suffered. Sister Agnes ended her notes on 19 March 1906 with Suzanne's words: 'let us . . . stand together as one in Unity and Charity. The winds of trials & afflictions may rage around us on every side, but they cannot harm us, for where Union and Charity exist, and the foundation is strong, all is Secure.'[3] Dealing with the 'trials and affliction' of Father Soulas had all been so discreet, so understated, that not all of the sisters knew how much unity and charity had been needed. None of the sisters knew all the pressures that had come on Suzanne; she did not know fully for a long time how they, too, had been treated.

Christophe Soulas, as he aged, realised he would never be the head of a united Catholic Maori mission working independently across each diocese. That had been his hope in the early 1880s.[4] It had faded as the immediacy of needs led to *ad hoc* solutions within the dioceses. Auckland had brought in the Mill Hill fathers in the mid-1880s and Maori mission had revived north of Taupo in a slightly different way from the Marist tradition further south.[5] Hiruharama was the only wholly Maori Marist centre but its very isolation cut Soulas off. And his crotchety, quirky personality finally exhausted the patience of those parish priests who might have respected his dedication to Maori mission. It especially alienated his fellow missioners. The long-bearded 'patriarch' became more and more marooned upriver.

In 1898 the Marist Visitor, Father Augustin Aubry, explained at some length the case of Father Soulas in his report to the superior general in Lyon, Father Martin: 'A lot has been spoken about and against Father Soulas. His colleagues on the Maori mission do not profess to be overly fond of him. And yet it is the most Maori of all the mission stations.'[6] There was grumbling, Aubry wrote, that the purely Maori mission work was being neglected in favour of the sisters' works, especially the orphanage. The priests were wanting to block the Propagation of the Faith's already meagre grant to the mission because of this. Aubry defended the sisters. Their other work, funded by the government and by Suzanne, was over and above their busy Maori work, he pointed out. The latter was just like the Marist sisters' work in the Pacific which earned its grant from the Propagation of the Faith.

Aubry had continued: 'There are lots of other stories bandied about against Father Soulas; but there is so much that is invented or dreamed up that you give up trying to find out what element there may be of serious fact in them. What is really lacking here as elsewhere, are regular and sufficiently long visits from the Father Provincial.' Among some of the stories would have been examples of Soulas's excitable, almost pathological paranoia, especially where money was concerned. Yardin had warned Poupinel and Redwood of it soon after Soulas arrived in New Zealand. 'Father Soulas's language is sanctimonious, but his words and actions turn to violence.'[7]

This touchiness got him offside with many people. A relatively mild example comes from government Native Schools files. Soulas went to see Education Secretary John Hislop back in January 1884 about the Hiruharama school, which he had revived six months before with the help of Suzanne and the Sisters of St Joseph. It had previously been a government school and he was hoping funding might be available. He jumped to the conclusion that Hislop was refusing outright any chance of financial help. He wrote a huffy letter to him straight after his visit, ending it: 'Not to expose myself to a probable refusal, I beg to be excused, at least for the present, if I do not forward to the Minister of Education the application you advised me to send.' Hislop wrote back that Soulas had misunderstood the fact that he was simply requesting an application and explanation of the case in writing before he could take it to the minister for a decision. Then comes on the file a memo to Hislop from James Pope, Inspector of Native Schools:

> I should think it is very important that the Reverend Father Soulas should be made to clearly understand that in your conversation with him (every word of which I heard) you did not give him the smallest reason to suppose that an application for aid to his Whanganui school would be refused.
>
>   It is not at all desirable that the Catholics should have another instance of 'Government persecution' to add to their present stock.
>
>   I would suggest that it might be advantageous to mention that in certain cases the Government *does* subsidize small schools that are not strictly under its control.[8]

Year after year Soulas would quarrel with people. Father Reignier at Meanee had probably been the first target in 1880. Sister Anne, who was in charge at Jerusalem when Suzanne was away, was the 'swell-head', the 'dumb-brain' he fumed about.[9] Sister Anne, like the priests, would not have felt 'overly fond' of Soulas. When ideas were sparking between French Suzanne and French Soulas, the Irish or New Zealand-born women must sometimes have felt excluded, not only by language. Intellectual and cultural condescension would also have come into it.

Father Cognet was attacked over the prayer-book revision. Even in Lyon, the priest who managed the Marist missions felt he had to deny a charge. In April 1902 he wrote to Soulas: 'Rest assured that we want neither your death nor that of your schools.'[10] Other priests, workmen, and Ngati Hau men like Keepa and Tamatea Aurunui, all had their turn. Keepa bested Soulas by reclaiming the original schoolhouse, and then applied to the government, unsuccessfully, to reopen a secular school. Tamatea Aurunui was the principal Salvationist convert at Hiruharama. He had a run-in early in 1893 with 'Hoani Papita and Tanirau' – Soulas and Brother Stanislaus. Both parties filed complaints with the Department of Justice, Tamatea's 'charge being that of sheep stealing against Hoani Papita, he having removed my mark'. He added significantly: 'I am not doing this to spite Meri.'[11]

It was inevitable that Suzanne's turn to feel the edge of Soulas's suspicion and anger would come. The burning intensity of his admiration for her was bound to collapse inwards at some stage into a black hole of brooding. It came at a predictable time. Suzanne left the river at the beginning of 1899. Already, she had had to wrest from Soulas the legal title to the farm bought just before the collecting tour with her own family money. It had been put in his name, according to his explanation, to avoid death duties, because he thought she might die soon, and certainly before him. He had also persuaded her to give him power of attorney for the farm when she shifted to Wellington, and she met the full force of his wrath in 1902 when she cancelled this.

Sister Anne had let Suzanne know of some money arrangements she disagreed with. Suzanne came up to Wanganui and the pair quietly withdrew the balance from an account to which Anne was co-signatory with Soulas. Suzanne then stopped the power of attorney and sold the farm's wool herself. But, with the uncanny accuracy of the naturally suspicious, he must have been alerted, because almost immediately and unexpectedly he came down to Wanganui to sell the wool in person. Usually it was done through a wool firm. She had not had time to write and explain to him her decision. His fury was intense. 'On his return home, Father Soulas wrote a dreadful letter to Mother Aubert' with the threat of dividing the sisterhood.[12]

Suzanne then came to Jerusalem 'probably to make the peace'. Soulas had been upstairs in the convent watching the arrival of the riverboat, going from window to window to see her coming up the track. He came down and locked the doors of the convent against her. He 'slammed' the front door in her face was how she put it in 1922, when she first referred to the incident again. Suzanne probably spent the night in the old whare where sick old Maori women had previously lived. Sister Rosalie remembered Suzanne coming into the convent in the very early morning. She assembled the community. 'She was deadly white, and trembled a little. She refused to take anything to eat, and she spoke for some minutes to the Sisters very impressively on union and charity, and obedience, until the steamer whistled. Then she left to catch it and went back direct to Wellington.'[13]

Soulas had pitched over-enthusiastically into the projects of the orchard and farm, and the commercialisation of the medicines. It is not recorded how he felt when that excitement came to a halt, but presumably more than a little flat. Suzanne was increasingly the one in the limelight, anyway.[14] In fact, it was partly because his fellow mission priests considered he was too absorbed in these projects and the orphanage with its Pakeha children that they resented him so. They had already been making digs at him for a long time. His letter to her in 1889 telling her they had suggested that she was the one 'wearing the trousers' and that she was leading him 'by the nose' is echoed in Father Maillard's letter to Cognet in 1895, with his neatly sarcastic reference to 'Mother Mary Joseph who is at the very least lady governor of New Zealand if not queen and who has as much power over the heart of the Ministers as over that of F. Soulas'.[15]

Suzanne had a great deal of influence in Soulas's life. Part of his acceptance among Maori came from his partnership with Meri, veteran missioner with thirty years of affinity with Maori custom, and expert in medicine. Getting his English a bit tangled in an 1889 letter to the parish priest of Wanganui, he acknowledged her primacy in medicine: 'in her staying at Jerusalem I don't practise medicine. I send any one to her so much that the Maoris thinking that I do so by ignorance have very little confidence in my medical knowledge'.[16] Part of his acceptance among Pakeha would also have come from association with the friendly and admired Sister Mary Joseph, all the more so as she grew into the well-known Mother Aubert.

Part of his standing in the Catholic world was going to come, he hoped, from being considered the 'Father Founder' of the first New Zealand congregation. And a good deal of satisfying activity was generated for him when the two of them combined their considerable intelligence and energies in creating mission school and church, publishing a Maori language manual, planting a commercial orchard 'in the back of nowhere', manufacturing popular local medicine, setting up an orphanage. So when Mother Aubert went south he must have felt lonely, increasingly bereft. He would also have been acutely aware of the busy life she was leading in the capital, surrounded often by influential figures, where he had no part. Once she was in Wellington, there was no reference to a 'founder' back up-country.

The sisters did not follow all that passed between Soulas and Suzanne, whether agreement or disagreement, simply because it was said in French. But Sister Anne and Sister Carmel knew enough to recognise that in the raised voices Soulas was sometimes insulting Suzanne. Sister Anne asked her why she put up with it, and Suzanne's answer was: 'If ever you hear me say a word against him, I authorize you to call me to myself. You know he is the only one for the Maoris.' Suzanne had pinned her spiritual hopes on Soulas as the Maori missioner to replace the old hero-missioners. In the manuscript of her Constitutions she spoke of being on the Maori mission as a 'privilege'. Other priests were going to stations where Maori mission was a declining part of their work. Soulas was the one who stayed with the Maori – another pointer that God accepted him as he was.[17]

There was probably more to it than Suzanne's incontestable dedication to Maori mission. She was the figure behind him, giving him a lot of his substance. But in him she had found someone who also dared to be different. With his intense and extreme personality, he was prepared to give things a go, to try incautious adventure. Backed by his faith in her, she could lead and create. He was even pushing her to do so. It could have been heady stuff, but within Suzanne was a core of spirituality that seems to have kept her grounded in simplicity, common sense and the humility she kept seeking while never doubting her own abilities.

She was loyal to Soulas on a third count, on the spiritual plane. Sister Anne was under the impression that Suzanne had made some sort of vow of obedience to him; Suzanne later admitted this. Since way back in 1879 he would have been her only steady confessor, therefore privy to her desires, doubts, dislikes, regrets and remorse. He 'must have known her great humility and fear of spoiling the work of God by her defects', thought Anne, and 'he played on this'. He would test her out.[18] Both Sister Anne and Sister Bridget said several times that

> no sooner was Mother's back turned – she had hardly boarded the steamer – when Father Soulas countermanded all her arrangements, often went directly against them. When Mother was asked what were the Sisters to do in such circumstances, she answered that they must obey the priest. Asked by Sister Anne why she said this, she replied that she feared for the Sisters' obedience. They could only obey one – if there were two Superiors, they might obey neither, and in any case, their conscience would not be clear.[19]

Suzanne was mistaken in letting Soulas, even implicitly, have that much entrée into her isolated community of sisters. She knew from long experience that he was a man of volatile temper. He was now lonelier than ever, perhaps more unpredictable. His letters to the Marists in France no longer have the ebullient reportage of the 1880s and 1890s. In his own words, 'circumstances do not let me reply to your kindly overtures with a smiling face – it is with a furrowed brow that I put pen to paper to give you sign of life'.[20] They are depressed letters churning over financial hardships, real and imagined.[21]

Suzanne was the superior and in her absence another *sister* clearly should have held the reins as acting or local superior, not the priest. The Constitutions, as was normal, left the direction of matters of conscience to the priest; the direction of conduct and management of the rest was the domain of the superior. Suzanne already had experience in the 1860s of an intrusive Pompallier.[22] And yet, just as Suzanne defended Bishop Pompallier to Poupinel early in 1866 because he was championing her Maori mission, she was also conceding to Soulas on similar grounds.

If Suzanne did say what Anne remembered, she was giving a confused message to the women, even though with the best of spiritual intentions. Some of them were young and impressionable, because the novices were still going to Hiruharama after the turn of the century. Only if Soulas was acknowledged as founder could he have any valid claim as superior, but Suzanne, and Redwood himself, held that the archbishop was founder. It was an ambiguous, even contradictory, message, but it had one clear line – they were being told primarily to obey Soulas. He would be actual superior; the sister as local superior would be nominal.

On 2 November 1903, Father Olier wrote his report to the Marist head-quarters in Lyon after his official visit through the missions. The problem with Soulas, he thought, was that 'he has set himself up as *Farmer*, *Postmaster* and above all *Founder of Nuns*. With all these goings-on how do you expect him to cope with a mission?'[23] The allusion to '*Postmaster*' was partly just referring to the fact that the congregation ran the local post office, but also, probably, a veiled statement of the reality; as the sisters said, 'all letters passed through his hands'. He opened all incoming mail to the congregation and controlled all outgoing. Towards the end of 1902, 'a young Sister recently transferred from Wellington and then in charge of the post office in Jerusalem, was obliged to write [to Suzanne] an appalling letter, under dictation from Fr Soulas! She was distracted all night, but next morning she managed to open the mail bag, take out the letter (which, of course, had been closed under the father superior's eye), steam it open, and add a postscript: 'Dear Mother, I wrote the above under dictation, but my sentiments are the exact opposite of what is written there, etc.'[24]

On 3 November, in a confidential letter to Lyon which he felt needed to be sent separately, Olier expanded on his official report. Over six long pages, and quoting from Soulas's letters that Suzanne had shown him in Wellington, Olier traced the sorry story. He implies that Soulas was the force behind the separation of the sisters from the Third Order Regular of Mary. 'So he clings to being considered founder and to hold absolute authority over the new order to the degree that he has made Sister Aubert take a vow to obey him in all things. She told me this herself and so did Bishop Redwood who has dispensed her from it.'

To the '*Farmer, Postmaster* and . . . *Founder of Nuns*' of the report Olier now significantly added '*master of novices*'. Soulas was 'the sole master of novices, and . . . he had appointed a mistress only as a matter of form; so much so that when I asked to see her, I was told that she had been in Wellington for a long time'. Olier disapproved that, 'as superior and master of novices', Soulas ate at the convent with the sisters; that he required a sister to sleep every night at the presbytery on the ground that he could be taken ill during the night; that he was teaching the novices to swim.

Olier had told him to stop all this, and Soulas had written one of his screed-like letters to Suzanne in Wellington, hauling her over the coals on a whole range of topics. Olier copied out quotes from it. On and on Soulas had gone, winding himself up. 'What is more, I *demand* an explanation', he wrote to her, 'of this crazy thing you've done if he [Olier] hasn't lied to me. How could you be so *stupid* to say to him, after I've repeatedly told you I would make *them* pay you back, "The convent is all mine, I paid for it, I am not asking to be reimbursed because the father and the brother are working for me at the farm."? Did you say that or did he lie? If you really did, you're in your right place in a *house for incurables*, but you ought to be there as a patient, and, better still, out at *Porirua* . . .'[25] After quoting this, Olier had to add '(*maison de fous*)', madhouse, to explain back in France the force of Soulas's '*Porirua*'.

Soulas's letter continued as a diatribe of scoldings and list of instructions that Suzanne *had* to carry out. He had also sent her a model of a will for her to make out immediately, with a list of wild conditions – nothing to be left for public or religious purposes, no property to be rented to Catholics but only to Protestants for private, not charitable ends, and so on. In writing this, Soulas had shown that even his entire religious vocation could be turned inside out when he was in the manic heat of his rage. How many other letters like these went up the chimney in flames when Suzanne burnt most of her private records in 1913? Father Olier quoted what she said to him in 1903: 'That one, according to Mother Aubert, is a fairly mild letter compared to others that he has written whenever the good sister dared to resist him or disobey him. All his colleagues on the Maori mission have received similar diatribes and even worse ones that they have kept. His Grace himself has not been spared.'

St Joseph's, Buckle St, where the sisters cared for the old, the terminally ill and disabled, and by day ran a soup kitchen and crèche.

The men at Buckle St.

'Wellington's Workless, Wet and Weary Wandering Willies' at the soup kitchen in Buckle St.

The women at Buckle St.

Sisters Baptista and de Sales with the begging pram.

Suzanne's letter to Hiruharama to welcome the twentieth century.

Suzanne and the sisters at Buckle St, c.1905. From back, left to right, Sister Philomena (novice), Sisters Francis, Gabriel, Anthony; de Sales, Camillus, Veronica, Patrick, Elizabeth, Vianney; Marcelle, Mother Aubert, Agnes; Claver, Chanel and John McMahon.

Vicar General Father Lewis, Mother Aubert,
Archbishop Redwood and Archdeacon Devoy
at the blessing of the foundation stone for the
Home of Compassion, Island Bay, March 1906.

The crowd at the opening of the Home of Compassion in April 1907.   ZAK, HOC A

A convalescent Suzanne sits with Elizabeth
O'Connor in her garden, 1907.

Sister Agnes and a weary Suzanne on the Home of Compassion opening day, with the first table they had had in Buckle St. Made from a manure box, for Suzanne it symbolised simplicity and poverty.

Te Manihera Keremeneta (Rure) with his parents. He was a mainstay of support during the building of the Home of Compassion, and on opening day led the procession of dignitaries.

Clinical ward for boys at the Home of Compassion. Women's sewing bees stitched the quilts for the children's beds. The water stains are clear on the walls, and the central pillars have been added for strengthening.

ZAK, HOC A

Suzanne walking the long corridor of the Home of Compassion.   ZAK, HOC A

The reservoir working bee behind
the Home of Compassion which ran
through October–November, 1907.

ZAK, HOC A

The Governor, Lord Plunket, visits the workers building the culvert. Suzanne is to
the right of the group.

ZAK, HOC A

The Trades and Labour Council and university students. Suzanne sits on the steep hillside in front of her blokes whom she would code name 'St Joseph'. ZAK, HOC A

The opening of the Jubilee Ward in 1912. Among the guests were Vicar General Thomas O'Shea, at centre back, Eileen Ward (daughter of Sir Joseph Ward), second to his left, Mrs T. G. Macarthy, one of Suzanne's major fundraisers and benefactors, at front left with Suzanne. Governor Islington is in the centre, with Archbishop Redwood and Lady Ward on his left. The wind blew a flurry of dust, but Suzanne and Mrs Macarthy talked on. ZAK, HOC A

In the newspaper write-up of the fundraising committee's teaparty, there was a distinct emphasis on the fashion details of the committee members.

Lady Plunket persuaded Suzanne to have this formal portrait taken in 1910.

In Marist archives there is a seething twelve-page letter from Soulas to the superior general in France, Father Martin. It was written on 7 November 1903, just after Olier's visit. As in most of his letters he defends the rights of the Maori mission. But the main theme is personal. Among other things Soulas referred to what Olier had said to him: '"You have *tyrannised* Mother Aubert, you have tyrannised the Sisters, yes, tyrannised is the word. So leave them in peace, these poor Sisters; they are the cause of all your troubles".' Soulas compared English trial law with the way he was now being treated and pre-judged by his superiors and colleagues. He wanted his father general to suspend sentence and leave the status quo for a few months till he could prove his innocence.[26]

What judgement, what sentence, what innocence? Olier had by now 'proposed to Mother Aubert to withdraw her novitiate from Jerusalem where it is very badly placed in the opinion of everyone, and to sell or lease the farm. She would have already done this, she told me, if Father Soulas had not formally opposed it.' The fact was that any action by the Marists or Suzanne was too late. Soulas had already crossed the boundaries certainly of propriety and possibly of sanity. Clear documentation comes ten years later, in notes of a letter Suzanne was writing to Bishop Verdon:

> I shall only mention one fact that can give a vista of what the pen refuses to write. He would get the Sisters to uncover themselves [she meant bare their shoulders] and administer to them himself the disciple [discipline] etc. He always enjoined on them complete secrecy on his doings and specially recommended [ordered] that I should be kept in the dark of what was going on. I had however my own suspicions but when I ventured to ask on three different occasions from men in authority amongst them, their answers proved [to] me that they did not believe me and things went on worst and worst until a retreat was given to us in Wellington by a Redemptorist father during which retreat the R. Father discovered and reported the terrible state of affairs.[27]

The discipline was not in itself anything unusual. It was made of short lengths of cord and was in standard use among religious as a form of penance or to quell rebellious or worldly thoughts. Self-flagellation was commonplace among the corporal penances used to mortify the spirit. Pious people, even some laypeople, practised these penances regularly.[28] Mother Cecilia Maher of the Sisters of Mercy had been known, before she came to Auckland, to administer the discipline to herself 'very vigorously' in the middle of the night; it was a 'sound as if men were threshing'.[29] Another important religious in New Zealand history, Euphrasie Barbier – Mother Mary of the Heart of Jesus – was so excessive in her penances, starving herself, wearing chains and a hair shirt, and using the discipline constantly, that her directors tried to get her to desist.

Indeed, the unusual thing about Suzanne Aubert is that there is no reference to her practising pious corporal penances at all. Some congregations of active sisters banned them, because the women needed all their physical strength for their work. The Sisters of St Charles in Lyon were one example. Any punishment Suzanne meted out to herself was in sheer hard work. She would speak against 'pious practices' and wrote in her first draft Constitutions: 'The Sisters, needing their strength to fulfil the often painfully hard duties of their vocation, and faced with the sufferings of real deprivation, will have no corporal penance as a matter of form, neither fasting nor discipline. Individual corporal penances will be granted only rarely and only by the Mother Superior, without whose permission no Sister may practise any . . .'[30]

This was her intention; but in the various manuscript versions lines have crossed out her handwriting where she set aside the discipline, and annotations have been added in the handwriting of Soulas, allowing the sisters to practise corporal penance with the approval of the confessor, and forbidding them to speak of any corporal mortifications. The later Constitutions permit the taking of the discipline on Fridays while reciting briefly David's psalm of repentance, the 'Miserere'.

In the practice of the discipline in Catholic religious life, it was absolutely a matter of self-application, in privacy. When Soulas prescribed and, worse, administered the discipline to others, he stepped far outside the bounds of Marist or any other definition of ascetic penance.[31] He was also giving the discipline to women. The unspoken subtext was crystal clear. It was in the realm of scandal. As confessor and effective leader of the community, he had forbidden them to speak of it. In November, Olier's and Suzanne's suspicions were clearly aroused. But, not knowing the story yet, Suzanne wrote to the sisters straight away:

> Do not loose courage, pray hard and God will arrange everything [she meant put everything right]. The clouds are too dark that something brighter is not behind. The storm will blow off and peace will be restored. Let us embrasse [embrace] the cross laid on our shoulders, Our Lord's one was much heavier and it is but right that we should have ours to follow Him. I would have gone up, but I cannot at present. We are in trouble here too so let us shake hands at the foot of the Cross. I hope that Father will come to Wanganui next Wednesday where I shall meet him and all those misunderstandings will be cleared.

We pray much for you, though I do not let the Community know the bad news I get from up there. My heart is with you all, do not be discouraged. Trust in God and in Our Blessed Mother. They will have pity of us. The devil is hard at work, but his power is limited, and let us hope that he will have the worst of it.[32]

It was not a question of clearing a misunderstanding, however. The next step was to free the women to speak, to arrange quickly an opportunity where a visiting confessor or spiritual director could help them get the problem out of confessional secrecy. This came in the retreats in early December, first in Jerusalem then in Wellington, led by Father O'Donnell, a visiting Redemptorist priest from Australia.[33] Knowledge of what had happened was kept within a small circle of diocesan, Marist and Sisters of Compassion superiors. Nothing seems to have been put officially in writing. In an effort to limit the damage, the sisters involved 'took a vow of silence before an Ecclesiastical Enquiry', probably and humanely just Redwood himself, as archbishop and founder. They were to have no further contact with Soulas.[34] He was immediately transferred to Okato in Taranaki, where he continued his work with the Maori mission. But this discretion or secrecy, though well-intentioned and something they themselves must surely have wanted in that era, would unwittingly have also compounded their emotional scars and left them feeling somehow guilty.[35]

Suzanne, however, wrote a letter to Carmel at this time, giving permission to write to the priest whose retreat had rescued them:

> About Father O'Donnell's message to you by the brother: it was very kind, but it is a little difficult in practice. First, you never know in what hands a letter may fall. 2nd. Any letter that you write to Father O'Donnell will be opened and read by his own Superior before he gets it. 3rd. The greatest caution must be taken not to write anything that may lead anyone to surmise things that ought to be buried in oblivion for ever, etc. etc.
>
> However, taking into consideration the exceptional past and present state of affairs, I give the Sisters permission to write to him on the strict condition that the subject of the letter will be really of a *serious* and *important* nature without any gossiping or triffling subjects of direction. And in speaking on strictly important matters, it must be done in a concise manner, as well as in a most prudent one. And the Sisters must not speak amongst themselves of what they write or of the answer to it. On those conditions, the Sisters may write to Father O'D. but the permission extends only till the time of the next Retreat. And may God derive His glory from it.[36]

There were hardly any leaks. Suzanne found out more from her sisters only when Soulas, as a very old man, came to the Home of Compassion in 1922 and sought reconciliation with the women.[37]

The congregation had been affected, all the same. Any hint of scandal would rock the foundations of their work, which spread beyond the confines of Catholicism. Bigoted anti-Catholics would pick at a weak point if they could. Any hint of the harsh way Soulas had treated the sisters would have been devastating.

Some of the clergy and diocesan authorities, for instance, disapproved of Suzanne's running a home for foundlings. They said, as she quoted them in 1913, 'that the Holy See objected to it, because it gave occasion to dissidents to say that Nuns were keeping Homes to shield the children of priests and nuns'.[38]

In the silencing, some of the trust and communication with this group of sisters was lost. In 1913 Suzanne jotted her thoughts into her notebook. It was a time of personal distress, and her disjointed and crossed-out notes, different from her usual articulate expression, show her pain:

> I felt it my duty to enforce as far as I could the separation of the [future] Novices and young Sisters from the Sisters who had been at Jerusalem so that they should not be exposed to hear of what the professed had been recommanded to bury if possible the remembrance of for ever.
>
> This has won for me the reputation of being an unbearable tyrant. Again unbecoming liberties [illegible] to religious has caused me to enforce regulations about the parlor and correspondance which has been the source of bitter complaints between some Marist fathers and Sisters. The old motto [as enforced by Soulas], do not let Mother know, is still in favour which renders administration extremely difficult . . .[39]

As if all this were not enough, Soulas did not quietly and penitently remove himself from her story. From Okato he continued to write letters trying to square the finances. He presented her with bills, tried rightly or wrongly to reclaim tools and implements, and threatened to take her to court.[40] Again, the public reputation and work of Mother Aubert were at stake. Cryptic references to 'F.S.', 'C.S.' and 'Okato' were used after the ecclesiastical ban discouraged contact. Suzanne wrote to Sister Carmel in 1904: 'There is trouble again about somebody at Okato, pray hard that things may be peacefully settled. It is very threatening.'[41]

On 30 May, she was writing to Carmel:

> Somebody who claimed £193 a while ago [which she paid], now asks £82 more. As money he had got for special purposes and which, he says, he employed for Jerusalem.

All the money of our Social and what we can get round the year, will barely meet his demand, and where is the money for the interests to come from? and all the other expenses? It will be a year of privations and hard struggle, and I hope that the Sisters will do all in their power to save expenses instead of looking out to try to have more comforts. For it is a struggle for life or death. . . . May God grant to the Sisters the true spirit of Holy Poverty, and Obedience, which they have vowed, and understand the value of self-sacrifice. . . . Pray for your old mother, who needs it badly.[42]

CHAPTER SEVENTEEN

Wellington – the children
1907-1910

This is a grand piece of work : He hanga pai rawa atu te hanga nei[1]

Suzanne did not believe in staying disheartened. Discouragement or unhappiness, she told the sisters often, was a species of pride and she spoke 'vigorously' against both. 'She was fond of saying: "If the devil can't make you sin, he will try to make you discouraged, knowing that discourage-ment is fruitful ground for venial sin! . . . If we were well persuaded of our own nothingness, instead of being discouraged, we would *thank* God we did not do worse!"'[2] In 1907, after the initial shock when the new building at Island Bay was declared unsafe, she would have thanked God that they had not done worse, and then got on with the job.

She liked work. She also needed it, almost craved it as a statement of being and as religious sustenance. 'A laggard is a bad soldier,' she wrote, 'he is often made prisoner. Let us not be slack in the service of God, else the devil will take advantage of us.'[3] In work she saw the apotheosis of the active sister serving God in the people around her; in work she realised her constant form of meditation; in work she served her penance; in work she met as many different people as she could. Her nature was outgoing anyway. And with her concept of God as being so firmly all around, she was open and eager for contacts. If she ever admitted, as she once wrote in October 1907 to Sister Bridget, that she was 'dead bit [beat] with work', she was stating a fact, not complaining.

She revered those who worked actively. She had taught the sisters about the 'strong women' of the gospel who struck out on the road to work with Jesus. Women supported her constantly with their regular sewing bees and contribution networks like Mrs Clarke's 'butter circle'. But her respect for the work of men was just as great. It went beyond a neutral regard. It was a fondness, a love for the large calloused hands

which sawed the stack of firewood miraculously topped up just when
needed, shifted the sheds, toted the coal, levelled the section, carted
cement. This recognition warmed with affection must have been balm to
the men.[4] Even if married, many had had no mother figure in their lives
since their arrival in New Zealand. Many had no family.

'In the world', Suzanne wrote, 'a man is received in accordance with
the clothes he wears; and he is shown out according to the spirit he
has manifested.'[5] If the sisters said 'God bless you' to every drunk who
lurched with a shilling in the direction of the collecting pram, they
honoured all the more those who helped in a practical way. Every man
who helped with his hands was code-named 'St Joseph'. Suzanne had
enormous reverence, tenderness and respect for Joseph of Nazareth. She
may always have had this, but it must also have developed in response to
the milling numbers of blokes, with family or without, moving around
the mainly rural New Zealand in which she had matured. So the sisters
relied on St Joseph and always laid by his little statuette a reminder of
the items they needed. A very small potato, all that was left, was put
there once in October 1909. A ton of undersize potatoes sent by mistake
to Government House was delivered forthwith. The sisters thanked
St Joseph and sighed as they scraped the tiny potatoes during their
recreation time.

The sisters knew they had 'to look after St Joseph' always, to help *him*
look after their needs. In later years, two sons of the Abbott and Murphy
families once walked from Pauatahanui all the way to Island Bay to bring
a couple of milking cows as a gift. Suzanne had prepared a meal for them.
When she heard they had left without realising this, she set off across the
paddock in pursuit. Sister Salome went on ahead to retrieve them from
Kent Terrace, two miles or so already into their way home, and persuaded
them back 'to please Mother'. The cups of tea and dinners Suzanne always
insisted on offering to carters were quite openly to help them keep away
from the malted nourishment of the pubs. But the foremost theme was
the supportiveness of the Family of Nazareth. Joseph had been chosen
as ultimately dependable; Joseph had helped bring up Jesus, had been
his steady male role-model. She made this quite clear in her *Directory*:

> The Church has gone to take out of his obscure workshop at Nazareth, St
> Joseph, the just man, chaste, devoted, laborious, modest, obedient, and poor;
> and She presents him to us, saying: 'Here is the Protector of the Universal
> Church!' And who, better than he, could be so? He who has been the

Protector whom God the Father, Himself, has given to Jesus and Mary! The only man who has had the happiness to provide bread to fortify His Body, and a roof to shelter His Head, for a God, poor, Who was going to save us.[6]

Suzanne also kept in mind the other male paradigm, more the Joseph of Arimathea figure – the business man, the influential man, the contributor rather than the doer. She had written in her draft Constitutions: 'It would be prudent and advisable to secure the assistance of a man of honour and experience in business, to help the Institute by his advice in the administration of temporal affairs especially law suits, transactions etc.'[7] Sister Angela remembered her once explaining why she consulted laypeople over money issues: 'A theologian will see the *moral* side only. He will tell me what I may do without *sin*. But many things that are not sin to do may well scandalize business people who act from a sense of honour.'[8] Over the years she built up a wide circle of helpers: her businessmen, mortgage guarantors like Catholic Martin Kennedy and Presbyterian Robert Hannah, her lawyers like Charles Skerrett, her politicians like Sir Joseph Ward, her co-workers in social welfare like Rabbi Herman Van Staveren, her doctors, her benefactors, her benign archbishop.

In October and November 1907, she gathered them up, together with her more customary manual workers, added in the mayor and the governor, and set them all to work as St Joseph-who-toiled-with-his-hands in a triumphant exercise of co-operative carting. It was the famous season of the working bees to help Mother Aubert get the materials on site for a water reservoir. Hundreds and hundreds of Wellington men and boys – and quite a few women – shifted the heavy gravel, sand and cement up the steep hill behind the new Home of Compassion.

Like all well-told feats of prowess, there are at least three versions of how they got going. The simplest is that Father Ainsworth, from the parish church next to the Buckle St home, had a relative, William Ainsworth, who was a military orderly at Government House and who told the governor, Lord Plunket, of the need for the reservoir. Suzanne's official version was written down in 1923. The sisters were first going to carry all the materials up themselves, she said. After all, they 'had no money!' Then:

I chanced to go to Government House and in the course of conversation, mentioned the project to Lady Plunkett. 'You are?!' she exclaimed, 'Are you serious?' 'Quite so.' 'Well then,' said she, 'you will begin in company with the Governor and a party from Government House! What day are you beginning?' And right enough, on the appointed day, His Excellency, with his Aides-de-camp, arrived, suitably attired for hard work![9]

Then there is the version of Anna Aramburu, whose French Basque mother shared a warm friendship with *la bonne mère Marie Joseph*. It was a different account, told to her closer to the event but also coming straight from Suzanne:

> Lord and Lady Plunket were no strangers to the Home of Compassion and Lady Plunket was a regular visitor. One day, as she and Mother Aubert sat chatting, Lady Plunket noticed a kind of endless chain of Sisters, coming over the hill, carrying what looked like sugar bags full of something on their backs. 'What are the Sisters carrying, Mother,' she asked. Came the answer, 'Sand, my Lady, for the construction of our Reservoir. To keep down the cost.' 'Well, did you ever,' said Lady Plunket, looking very serious. Then she brightened visibly. 'I'll tell the *Ex* [His Excellency] about that. We must do something about it.'[10]

A mix of all three probably happened, though Lady Plunket could not then have been a regular visitor at the unfinished, unoccupied Home of Compassion. The novices of the time remembered Suzanne entering the old ironing-room at Buckle St with a broad smile instead of the expected worry lines. They were all to go to Island Bay to carry shingle. She had just been with Lady Plunket, who was going to come out and see. There was certainly very little 'chance' involved in Suzanne's 'mentioning the project' at Government House, or very little coincidence, either, in the marshalled sisters parading their sugar bags outside the windows at the Home of Compassion.

Her public knew this. They did not mind. As the *Evening Post* put it: 'She is the apostle of optimism. She does not worry about whether people will help her sufficiently to realise her dreams for good; she knows they will. She has unbounded faith in Providence, but does not wait for the blessings to come showering down; she looks around for the watering-can.'[11] Mother Aubert watered the vice-regal garden and harvested her crop of blessings:

> Dear Reverend Mother,
> I told His Excellency your great work of carting sand up a hill and all the staff, as well as His Excellency, said nothing would give them so much pleasure as to put in an afternoon's real work for you – and I am to ask what afternoon would suit, as they are anxious to help. . . .
> Yours sincerely,
> Victoria Plunket.[12]

The *New Zealand Times*, the *Evening Post* and the *Free Lance* kept up a running commentary over the next few weeks. Reporters went out to note and stayed to help. Mother Aubert kept popping into offices, stoking the press with the latest enthusiastic update. St Patrick's boys began the work. They were really the first of the working-bee men; they had already been going to help. The governor's party pitched in on the same day:

> Without bothering to get under-rate permits from the General Labourers' Union the Governor and Lady Plunket did some navvying work yesterday . . . . His Excellency toiled in a white sweater, and Lady Plunket was attired in a large apron, lent to her by one of the sisters of Our Lady's Home of Compassion at Island Bay. . . . Church (represented by the Rev. Father Keogh, rector of St. Patrick's College) and State perspired together. Lord Plunket and Father Keogh got them each a grip of a box, and made two trips up the hill. Then Lord Plunket went one better. He shouldered a sack and went alone.[13]

Father Keogh followed suit. Over a hundred boys were also working. One sized up the white-sweatered work rate of the Governor of the Dominion and the portly, black-garbed effort of his own rector and reckoned that he and his mates had each carried far more.

Wellington College thought it could do its bit, too. 'Mr Firth, principal of Wellington College and the eighty-one boys who were with him . . . set to with such tremendous vigour that they had "piles of shingle, as if by magic" in their place. Mr Firth himself throughout the afternoon carried two bags of shingle per journey up the hill.'[14] Joseph Firth was a strong man and six feet five inches tall. He could double the others' effort with ease.

'No age or class is exempt', said the press, so the ages got younger. About seventy boys from the Marist Brothers' school came out twice on their holiday. Then came two parties of children, one 'consisting of friends of Master Pat Ward' – 'little Pat Ward . . . journeyed up and down with a tin bucket'.[15] Master Ward's father, the Prime Minister, sent £10 towards the work. As Postmaster General and Minister of Telegraphs, he may also have encouraged contributions from these departments. On 22 November, 'an army of letter-carriers invaded the premises, and appropriately enough, the work found for them was the carrying of posts for a fence away up the reservoir. . . . Later on, a contingent from the Post and Telegraph Department, under Captain Morris, took a turn at posting, and toiled until the whole of the day's mail had reached its destination.'[16]

The Legislative Council was represented by the Hon. R. A. Loughnan, and the medical profession had a couple of volunteers, Dr Pollen and

Dr Milsom. Then there was the city council. 'His Worship the Mayor, with the perspiration of toil bathing his alabaster brow, stood one recent day on the beetling cliffs of Island Bay, and heaved sand.' The 'Mayoress, who is always to the fore when there is a good work to be done, helped too'. Two hundred and twenty men, including off-duty tramway men, 'every available Corporation employee' giving their half-holiday, and 'fifty men pupils of the Wellington gymnasium', formed a chain passing the bags hand over hand up the hill. 'The Mayor led the party'. 'The City Engineer with his staff of engineers worked the gang' and 'altogether about 30 tons were shifted during the afternoon'.[17]

A parallel line of women, including Mrs Hislop, the wife of the mayor, passed the empty bags down their chain. On 17 November, Suzanne wrote to Sister Bridget: 'We are still very busy at Island Bay. People are coming to help nearly every day. Yesterday afternoon we had a very large party of workers, nearly 400 men and women for three hours; they shifted about 1200 tons of shingle up the hill [her figures were way out]. The Maire and his wife w[ere] at the head of them. They all looked contented and happy. Rure is delighted about the work. It gives us plenty [of] work also to attend on the people. We hope the Home will be finished sometime in January.'[18]

Women had also helped the week before. The *Evening Post* headed up a column on 'Lady Navvies' and reported: 'About thirty ladies manfully tackled the heap. An old man stood there with a long-handled shovel, and t[i]pped gravel into the bags, which were tilted up on to tender shoulders. The way was long, the sun was hot, the rough path was steep in places; the roses on many a cheek became still rosier, but it was a healthy glow . . . . Lady Ward, Miss Eileen Ward, and Miss Rubi Seddon were among the porters. Or were they portresses?'[19]

Alongside the Prime Minister's wife and daughter and the Seddon family were the 'Tireless Sisters':

> Two Sisters, in their dark-blue robes, plodded steadily up and down the hill, never faltering. Their conveyance was a box [set] upon two planks. One behind the other they strode up the slope, each time with an appreciable load. They scarcely paused . . . Their industry was an inspiration for all to see; it was a symbol of the Sisters' tirelessness in the cause of good; the comfort of others. . . . The work is there to do; they do it, and are very cheerful; that is all.[20]

Sister Bridget up in Jerusalem had a shrewd idea who the sisters might be: 'Little Mary wrote to us yesterday. She sent a peice cut out of a paper entitled Lady navvies; it did amuse us, mother, we were wondering wheather the two sisters spoken of were Carmel & Martha.'[21] These two, the Hiruharama farming sisters, had just come down with the children to live in Wellington. They were well used to carrying heavy loads on steep hillsides. In fact, while the helpers came mainly on Wednesdays or Saturdays (half-holidays), the sisters carried on carting in between.

About one hundred men from the Trades and Labour Council, organised by Allan Orr and W. H. Westbrooke of the Drivers' Union, had efficiently taken part. They arranged with William Hall-Jones, the Minister of Public Works, for the use of 'a cart-load of picks and shovels and pipes'. They made a culvert and built a road to the site so that horses could carry up the barrels of cement. 'Thirty-five men from the Corporation's works in Sydney Street joined in.' A 'party of Victoria College students, who would otherwise have found a life devoid of examinations very dull', gave a hand.

A photo shows this combined group stopped on the steep slopes to boil the billy. A couple of boaters mark out two 'chaps' from the university ranks; cloth caps and slouch hats prevail. Women juggle trays of tea mugs against the gusts of wind. Down at the front is a clearly happy Suzanne, sitting there with her foot angled to brace herself against the hill, surrounded by all her St Josephs. Suzanne was always as non-political as possible, but that day the Trades and Labour Council used her own tactic of lobbying and advertising through the news columns: 'The road constructed so rapidly on Saturday afternoon has, by the request of the road-makers, been named Union Road.'[22]

The decision to help a Catholic congregation had not been reached without argument among the unions. They were non-sectarian. They finally reasoned that they could help Suzanne 'because her charity was for all, and she made no distinction of race and creed'. Time and time again in her story this catch-cry recurs. It was the sowing of a theme that most New Zealanders were wanting to nurture as a concept of themselves – regardless of the denominational furrow they were in, regardless of what their ministers and priests might be preaching to them on Sundays. Thomas Cholmondeley had already remarked on this back in 1854 in *Ultima Thule*:

> What then is the religious condition of the ordinary colonist? He finds himself struggling in a new country, not as he struggled in the old – in the midst of a town or village community trained and minded like himself. No; English, Irish, Welsh and Scotch are flung together. What is the consequence? They

compare thoughts, ways, actions and words; they discuss systems; exchange customs; sift, weigh and balance their arguments and positions one with another. From an old church catechism, down to some new method of planting potatoes, nothing escapes. [23]

In 1880, a member of the Religious Tract Society visited New Zealand and was taken aback by the sight of Protestants and Catholics rubbing shoulders in Wellington: 'One can't help feeling that the spirit of tolerance is somewhat carried to excess when one finds Protestants patronizing the Roman Catholic bazaar. One admires their love more than their wisdom, their heart more than their head.' [24] In 1907, Suzanne and her townspeople were still letting love and heart win out.

Sunday might have become a day off in more ways than one. For some the strict Sunday observance – which André Siegfried had noted with amazement – allowed them a break from this process of adaptation. It let them withdraw, and breathe from the pews the 'faith of their fathers', with its familiar, reassuring whiff of their own ethnic and cultural background. On Sundays the Irish, the Scots and the Welsh could perhaps be away from reminders of the England that had subjugated them. Yet, for others, the denomination they belonged to was a practical matter – the nearest church. And it could also be the very reverse of clannish observance. The second generation of a family often had members ranging over Baptist, Brethren, Christadelphian, Roman Catholic, Anglican, Methodist, Presbyterian in a proudly fluid freedom of choice that they claimed in their new society. On Sundays they could demonstrate this.

The clergy sometimes co-operated in the process of adjustment. The earliest Catholic priest in Wellington, Franciscan Father O'Reily, regularly used to walk up and down the steep steps and paths between Willis St and Mount St, talking theology happily with Thomas McKenzie, an elder from St John's Presbyterian Church. He once took the service for that congregation when their minister was away, giving them their normal Presbyterian order of service. [25] A generation later, Archbishop Redwood and Rabbi Van Staveren promenaded and conversed along the pavements of The Terrace. [26]

Now, when sectarian lines were tightening noticeably, Suzanne was still in that mould. She kept intact the absolute wholeness of her own faith while helping to forge a nationally identifiable theology: the 'diffusion of friendliness'. [27] Many other people were doing the same – with race as well as religion. Even if part of their individual selves might be fettered by old prejudice, even if they were often indifferent to Maori or susceptible to cries of 'the yellow peril', they were nevertheless trying to assemble a collective *alter ego*. With the emotional equivalent of number eight wire, binder twine and bits of four by two, they were building their shelter where they could all gather as soon as they felt the warning spits from sectarian or ethnic stormclouds. This shelter was their reassuring shared 'identity' as the tolerant, egalitarian New Zealand public.

Thirteen years later, Suzanne used the image of shelter to make this point. Anti-English feelings were running high in 1920 as Ireland struggled to break free. All Catholic families and religious communities were affected. Sister Louise wrote in her journal what Suzanne told them on 17 December 1920. As usual, Suzanne taught by telling a story:

> Mother came into Buckle St. today and gave us a little lecture on detachment from country or national feeling. Before she went to Rome, the people of New Zealand were like one great family, Protestant and Catholic. Years ago, Mother was travelling on foot in the back blocks, on some of her usual errands – which we know were those of charity. Night was coming on, and the village to which she was journeying was miles away. She met a man in a cart who told her that the only place of shelter was a cottage near, but she need expect no hospitality *there* as the people were Presbyterians and, judging from her dress, she was a Catholic and a Religious; they would not let her in. Mother went to the door and a poor woman came out and insisted on Mother coming in and staying the night. She gave up her only bedroom for the use of her guest.
>
> Mother told this little anecdote as an instance of the friendly, charitable feeling which used to exist between all creeds and classes in N.Z. Now, of course, things were different, and Religious must be very careful to take no part in politics, and to be without a country, as it were, for Christ's sake. Christ died for all, and shed His Blood equally for the sinner as for the saint, and not for one nation only but for all nations. And so we must work for all, regardless of creed or nationality.[28]

Suzanne kept reinforcing this. After the working bee, Orr told her of the unionists' discussions and their decision, and remembered her reply: 'You may be a Catholic, you may be a Protestant, you may go to Church every Sunday and carry big books under your arm – prayer-books and hymn-books – *but if you have not the love of God and your neighbour in your heart, you are not a child of God.*'[29] On 23 November 1907, the *Free Lance* brought together the themes of work, tolerance and co-operation. It called her 'the wonderful old lady for whom everybody is glad to work. . . . It is because Wellington people know that anything done at the request of Mother Mary is done for humanity that they do it.' The people knew, too, that she identified with them, even down to the work itself. 'She is always busy with mind and hands, and always happy. . . . With all her years, she considered she was equal to a burden yesterday. Surreptitiously she marched with a bag up the incline. Near the top a man sighted her and rushed to relieve her. She clung to the pack, and the knight errant had almost to tug it away by main force.'

Jane had a son : Kua whanau te tamaiti a Heni
We shall have him baptised tomorrow : Ka iriiria ia e tatou apopo[30]

At Island Bay Suzanne now set about reconstructing her work with babies and children. The old people still remained at Buckle St but there were children already running around at Island Bay in 1907 – the Jerusalem family. The orphanage upriver was emptied of its last charges and, in two eventful train trips down, the children hit the capital. Rewi Crichton remembered the boat drawing away from Hiruharama and the people on the banks calling out 'Au revoir, au revoir'. Was he as an old man really remembering French or could it have been 'Haere ra'? At Buckle St first, they took a while to adjust. On 11 August Sister Baptista wrote to Sister Bridget: 'They are quite used to the trams etc. now; we are up on the hill and if the boys see any one going along the street they say look at that man going down the Pah; they seem to think they are in Jerusalem yet.'[31]

The Hiruharama community went back to being solely a Maori mission. The few sisters left up there, busy as they were with the school, missed the clatter and clutter of their young family. The orphanage dormitory had been an extension of their convent. Their home, after school hours, was now silent. 'I suppose you feel like poor lone widies [widows] at times', Veronica wrote to them, 'but still it must be nice, no farm, no children but the Maori [ones]. What a nice little thing Mary Teresa is (Rure's niece). Still I suppose you miss the children.'[32] They did. And looked for letters, at first in vain. Suzanne added a footnote to Baptista's 11 August letter. It was in her bossy mode, her 'stop all this stuff and nonsense; we are working for God' vein:

> I all earnestly advise you, dear Sisters, to work for God alone and never for the
> sake or the love of men who are so forgetful and ungrateful, for we never
> heard yet from the Angels!! (over whom you are, according to Kopa's letter,
> shedding floods of tears) a word of love or sorrow for Jerusalem or any one
> there. However, to teach them a leçon I will get one of them to write a letter

of thanks. If we never look for gratitude we shall never be deceived. Three of the boys are in bed with the measles, I expect them all to get them.

The publicity for the new institution had initially given more emphasis to the incurable children. Requests for help flooded in and, because she now had the facilities, Suzanne at first took in children with mental as well as physical disabilities. It was traumatic nursing for the sisters, who slept near their charges. In one instance, the steady thump, thump of two children banging their heads against the wall and cot through the night was unnerving. Suzanne never flinched from her dedication to 'incurable' children and sometimes confronted doctors who were wishing to try out new treatments. She had a horror of these people being merely the impersonal objects of experimentation. Her work continued to be supported by the public, and Lady Plunket paid for a large room to be used as a gymnasium for these children.

The sisters' work with 'foundlings' had been in abeyance since the late 1890s, except for the task of continuing to raise their existing large family. Diocesan opinion continued, on the whole, to be against any work with illegitimate children, unless the mother was also identified and involved. Suzanne would have played down this aspect of her project until the institution was safely, concretely in place. Even as she was planning it she admitted to Bridget that a lobby of doctors would help protect her from clerical opposition: 'I am very busy trying to get the Doctors here to back us for our Foundling Home here, for we must prepare for a hot time. However His Grace has sanctioned the work by writting. It is a blessing.'[33] Twenty-two doctors had lent their support and Redwood had written approving the transfer to Island Bay of 'the institution for foundling & neglected children now at Jerusalem'. He had also approved the foundation of 'a hospital at Island Bay for poor, sick & incurable children'.[34] His choice of words left room for her to go ahead with new foundling work. It was also general enough to allow diocesan opinion to oppose this work when babies were pouring in once more.

In 1908 unemployment rose. Dr Thomas Valintine had replaced Dr Duncan MacGregor as Inspector-General of Hospitals and Charitable Institutions, and was also Chief Health Officer. He identified 1908 to 1909 as 'a year of difficulty'.[35] Pregnant women and girls would have been afraid of losing their jobs; the fathers of their children would have been hard-pressed to help. Suzanne wrote to Bridget: 'Applications for babies are showering down. We will soon have to refuse them for want of room.'[36] George Joseph Whitford arrived on 26 November 1908, the same day he was born. 'His mother 17 years old', Suzanne wrote in her register, 'is a poor servant girl leaving [living] with her mother (a grass widow) poor herself'.

Violet Knox, born in Hawera, came at 'about a fourtnight old . . . . She was brought down by a woman, Mrs Steward.' The woman was very likely Frances Stewart, 'a prominent social activist' who 'saw herself first and foremost as a mother' with 'a keen interest in anything concerning children'.[37] She was the first woman member of a hospital board in New Zealand and worked strongly for improved nursing. In 1908 she became a keen supporter of Truby King's theories of infant care. This entry seems to indicate that the women's network in Wanganui was still operating in conjunction with Mother Aubert.

Not all the babies were illegitimate. In one case, the 'mother was deserted by her husband (a drunkard)'. Another entry in 1909 reads: 'The father died before baby was born. Mrs Ball has three more children the eldest of whom is only 6 years. Mrs Ball lives at Petone and goes out working. Phil [the baby] belongs to the Methodist Church. 21 April 1910: His mother married again and took him away.' Fathers occasionally brought the child or took responsibility: 'Both parents are Catholic. The father, a single man, acknowledges the child. The mother is willing to do what she can for the baby, when she is able.' A domestic servant from Dunedin and an 'N.Z. Artillery' man 'intend to marry. The father says that he will do what he can'. But usually the mother is alone. The entries name the fathers. Often they had 'cleared away' or were 'shifting from place to place'.

Suzanne wrote down the parents' intentions. One baby girl's mother was 'a waitress and the Father a Carpenter. The Mother is Church of England and is in hopes to claim her later. Miss McHugh agrees to give 5/- a week.' A domestic servant mother 'intends to take the child when bigger. The Mother thinks she can give bye and bye 2/6 a week'. A note is added to this entry: 'Returned: He was taken away to Sydney by his mother on the 22 October 1909'. Another: 'The mother thinks she can give 7/6 a week. Jeremia was returned to his mother on the 17th of May 1909'. There was no charge in spite of the mention of money. Many babies just arrived. Parents gave support for their babies only if they could. Those parents registering plans for the future were the ones likely to want to contribute.

She also carefully noted their wishes about baptism: 'The mother is Church of England, the father is Catholic. The child is to be baptised Catholic.' Or: 'The mother is Church of England and is getting the child baptised by the Church of England parson.' She was punctilious even to record a preference for no initial baptism: 'The mother is a Methodist who does not believe in baptism.' She carried through their wishes. The Presbyterian minister Rev. Shirer, for instance, was sometimes asked to come to the Home of Compassion to baptise Presbyterian children. As with the old people at Buckle St, the sisters' Catholic mission was to be through example, not compulsion. When a mother expressed a wish for her baby to be baptised Catholic, she herself was asked to write her wish in the register and sign it. Suzanne, of course, was a Catholic missionary through and through. Her babies were souls to keep out of limbo – that place, neither heaven nor hell, where the souls of those who had not done evil during their life could go when they were not baptised as Christians. Babies especially, as 'innocents', came into this category. If an unbaptised baby was in danger of death, then Suzanne could baptise it provisionally anyway. But not before.

What comes through with intense clarity from the plain language of the register is Suzanne's awareness of poverty, her non-punitive stance, the channels she left for a mother to reunite with her child, her sensitivity over religious feelings and the question of baptism. The parents were not just ciphers of sin; they were individual people who had been damaged by error of judgement. For their sake and their child's, Suzanne would be there to help them remake their lives, not squander them further in infanticide, suicide or prostitution. In reality, there were not many reported cases of women in New Zealand committing suicide in these years. In 1908 fourteen women were recorded as killing themselves, in 1909 twenty-two, in 1910 fourteen again.[38] Not all of these would be unmarried mothers. Cases of infanticide also were declining after the Infant Life Protection Act 1907, which required notification of birth within seventy-two hours. None of this would matter to Suzanne. The religious implications of suicide and infanticide were so great that even the chance of saving one soul would warrant her response.

The woman who got the working bees under way would be a valuable acquaintance for Suzanne in all aspects of children's welfare. Lady Victoria Alexandrina Hamilton-Temple-Blackwood, married to Lord Plunket, had appropriate credentials and the *New Zealand Official*

Year-book of 1909 lists them: 'Issue: Three sons (Honourables Terence, Brinsley, and Denis), five daughters (Honourables Helen, Eileen, Moira, Joyce, and Ethne)' – eight children born in fifteen years of marriage. She was actively interested in children and in 1907, with the publicity given by her patronage and participation, she boosted the beginnings of the Royal New Zealand Society for the Health of Women and Children. Its more usual name, Plunket, was in essence hers, not her husband's. In charity circles, she was energetic and articulate. On 21 March 1908, after the fête at the Home of Compassion, the *Free Lance* gave the governor a back-handed compliment:

> He looked immaculate in his dress and when the time came for him to say his piece he went right through without making a mistake. But then, the Governor has been in very favourable circumstances for learning the art of speechmaking lately. Her Excellency, Lady Plunket, has blossomed out so wonderfully as a public speaker that Lord Plunket cannot but profit from her eloquence.

Suzanne would need people like her, of high profile and public support, because the sisters' experience with foundling children would be much harder now than when they had started in the mid-1890s. When epidemics and infant illnesses were decimating the large families of the 1870s and 1880s, Suzanne and others like Archdeacon Leonard Williams, who had their circuit around the Hawke's Bay settlements, sometimes recorded a mother's intense grief. But death was an ongoing part of life, and babies were no exception. The parents met with consolation. Infant death was the shared experience of most families.

After the turn of the century there were subtle and important changes. Babies became an area of prime concern. A survey of all Australian colonies and most European countries from 1898 to 1908 had New Zealand 'conspicuous as showing the lowest death-rate', both in infant and overall mortality.[39] New Zealand's growing pride in nationhood came into play. Yet, in the Index of Mortality in New Zealand for 1908, deaths for children under one year of age were still 74.24 in every thousand, compared with 2.80 for between one and nineteen years, and 49.61 for sixty years and upwards.[40] The chance of death dropped phenomenally after the child reached one year of age. By far the main killers were birth, and illness in infancy. This situation needed attention.

Families were getting much smaller and more child-focused. Parents, and the state, did not expect these children to die; infant death was no longer admissible. Death, in fact, began to be divorced from normal family life. The Sunday visits to the cemetery to tend family graves largely stopped in the early twentieth century.[41] Lower infant mortality was a worldwide trend, along with smaller families. In a time of nationalism tinged with imperial and eugenist jingoism, New Zealand babies began to be seen as rarer commodities, prized stock of the Empire which needed to be reared safely through that risky first year. If they did not make it, they were 'lost to the Dominion by death', as the *Year-book* put it. The 'preservation of infant life' became a national duty. In 1904 Premier Richard Seddon had already published a memorandum on this in the press and talked of 'saving these valuable lives'.[42]

The rise of Truby King coincided with and reflected this trend. In 1909 he 'linked the care of babies to the health of the family, the nation, and the Empire'.[43] Childrearing became an issue of responsibility, and infant death took on a coating of culpability.[44] Suzanne would benefit from the developments of childrearing science but would now feel much more the pressure of social expectation and control. She would also meet some disapproval because her institution was protecting the mothers who, by not keeping and breastfeeding their babies, were 'neglecting' their primary function of motherhood.

The Plunket Society was founded, Truby King said, to spread scientific ways of feeding and training children so that 'the main supplies of population for our asylums, hospitals, benevolent institutions, gaols, and slums would be cut off at sources'.[45] Suzanne's institution came too perilously near some of these categories for people like King. He visited the Home of Compassion in 1910 and judged it too spartan. He was still considered something of a faddist then by Wellington doctors, but in 1916 the Home of Compassion became the first institution in Wellington to adopt his system.

Suzanne was specialising in the newborn babies, who were most susceptible to death, according to the national averages. Hers were even more vulnerable than the average. They were born in poverty, and their mothers had sometimes concealed their pregnancies and the births. They often came with a history of poor nutrition, again resulting from poverty and concealment. Many were already weakened by inherited tubercular and venereal diseases. On 17 April 1909, the day it was born, one baby arrived, the daughter of a domestic servant and a sailor. The entry added: 'The baby is recommended by Dr Bowerbank who thinks it will not live, but if it lives will be blind.' The baby died one week later. Suzanne was putting these babies together, upwards of a hundred in one institution, where an epidemic could easily cut back their fragile numbers. Government policy was still firmly in favour of fostering out, partly because of this risk. Sensitive to records of infant deaths, other institutions tended not to take such tiny babies and to transfer sick infants to the hospitals. The deaths would not be in their books.

Epidemics had swept the country in 1907 and Wellington had suffered severely. In fact, the *Free Lance* had used the analogy of contagion in describing the Island Bay working bees: 'Influenza and measles notwithstanding, no more violent epidemic has raged in Wellington than the present outbreak of energy.'[46] The *Year-book*'s table showing the comparative rates of infant mortality for 1907 and 1908, together with the mean rates over five years, gave Wellington the highest rate of death among children under one year: 9.35 to every hundred births.[47] Measles and whooping-cough had struck in 1907, scarlet fever and typhoid in 1908; influenza came and went. Suzanne wrote to Bridget in July 1908: 'We are quite upsetted to day by a second death among the children, caused by scarlatina. Tell Sister Magdalen it is the little girl from Reefton.'[48] But diarrhoea or gastro-enteritis was the major cause of infant death and, in her *New and Complete Manual of Maori Conversation*, 'The baby suffers very much from diarrhoea : Ka nui te torohi o te tamaiti' had been an important bilingual message. It was commonly called summer diarrhoea, but at the Home of Compassion the babies were affected mostly in spring and autumn.

So Suzanne had started her work again at a time when it was most needed, but also at a time of greatest risk to her credibility. She was also much more in the public eye than when she was taking in her babies upriver. She would need more than ever her backers like Lady Plunket and the doctors. Most of the babies lived, and thrived. But many died. In 1909 and 1910, when the rate of infant survival was improving in the country overall, death tolled from the pages of her register.

The sisters tried to improve the bottle-feeding, considered a main factor in infant diarrhoea.[49] Suzanne calculated the quantity needed for each of the babies. She worked late at night, and with failing sight transcribed and converted French metric calculations into imperial. She did not delegate or ask for help. She was the expert; the sisters were *young*. The sisters thought that for a month at least the infants were being undernourished. One sister 'remembered how she often woke up at night to see the light in Mother's office burning, and to say to herself: "There she is, gaining more merit by starving the children than I do by trying to feed them!"'[50] The appropriate formula in artificial feeding of children began to be hotly discussed internationally at this time – and in Suzanne's community of sisters as well.

Suzanne was an anachronism in any new religion of health which saw death as ultimate defeat. Even as a skilled nurse fighting to save lives, she still had her belief that in death the soul was liberated and united with God. The soul was what was permanent. In 1907 Francis, the boy who had been baptised as a baby by Archbishop Redwood, had been killed. Touching a wire trailing in the wet grass after a storm, he was electrocuted and died instantaneously. Suzanne was frantic about his soul. The children had been clearly told not to go near the wire. He had died in the very act of disobedience; how could his soul have a chance? She raced to Redwood, who had given the boy his own name. He rounded on her with, 'Who are you to dare to limit the mercy of God?', then comforted her with several reasons to reassure her that Francis's soul was safe.

Her reaction had been the instinctive 'I told him not to' which any parent recognises. It was as much a way to block her human shock and grief. But the story indicates how Suzanne's belief that the soul was paramount and that babies who had died could continue on as 'assets' in heaven would need to be juggled with the public perception that babies must not die. She would have to balance this with strong assertions that her institution, the only one taking in illegitimate children under the age of two years, was by this very fact saving many from death.

In January 1910, when Suzanne was away in Auckland, Mrs Ella Dick, the district agent of the Education Department, inspected the Home of Compassion. It was not funded by the government and was not considered a private institution either, because it did not charge. Nor was it a foster home. So it came under no ordinary government agency. Ella Dick considered that it should be taken over by the government, because it had been funded largely by public money. She was strongly in favour of individual foster homes. Ella Dick had exceeded her rights, Suzanne felt. When she was defending her work to the clergy, she would point out that public and specifically non-sectarian money was funding it. Conversely, when the government argued that it was public money, she was quick to point out that the sisters' 'patrimonial money' and hers had been invested in the farm and was now, after its sale, transferred to Island Bay.

Government opinion was 'not favourably disposed towards the rearing of infants in institutions', the Minister of Education wrote to Suzanne, 'nor to any system which enables parents to relieve themselves from the responsibility of caring for their children'.[51] Mother Aubert, however, had affection, respect and firm backing from so many people of note and from the public that the anomaly of her institution was formalised with a warrant of exemption. But the bass note of anxiety continued to resonate in both government and diocesan circles. The diocesan council began to watch Suzanne with alarm. With the venture she was planning in Auckland, this could only increase.

CHAPTER EIGHTEEN

Auckland – the children
1910-1912

Do you hear the thunder? : Ka rongo koe ki te whatitiri?
We may have a storm : Tera pea ka tutakina tatou e te tupuhi[1]

In 1910 Wellington decided that it would celebrate in style the fiftieth anniversary of Mother Aubert's arrival in New Zealand. Bishop Pompallier and 1860 seemed a long time ago and Pakeha New Zealanders were realising they had a history. Suzanne's story brought this home to them. In the newspaper she was reported:

> 'We were just four girls,' she said simply, 'and I am the only one alive.' . . . It was a party of twenty-seven, including the clergy, and Mother Aubert, still working vigorously, is the only survivor. One, two, three . . . up to twenty-six, she has sadly had the messages of her pioneer associates' deaths, but her courage for her work never falters.[2]

Her story was a shape they would like and keep as they cut the pattern of their history: 'She has been toiling in New Zealand for fifty years . . . and she has not been sitting in an armchair, merely directing operations. She has been simultaneously a field-marshal and a soldier in the fighting line. . . . Mother Aubert is the youngest old lady in New Zealand, and we hope that her youthfulness will be long spared.' She had 'kept a sunniness that is a cure for cynicism and pessimism'.

On 2 December in the Town Hall they were 'giving the old lady a big shevoo', as the Irish pub men outside the Royal Oak said. A name-studded committee, headed by Mrs T. G. Macarthy, had been organising the fund-raisers through the capital and beyond. A carnival and sports meet in Newtown Park, a children's flower pageant and 'Fight between St George and the Dragon' at the Town Hall, a 'Grand Fancy Dress Skating Carnival under the distinguished patronage of their Excellencies Lord and Lady Islington' all added the fun of the fair to the staider list of donations.

Rabbi Herman Van Staveren presided on the night.[3] The programme was full. The Prime Minister's Catholic daughter and the Rabbi's Jewish daughters also sang and recited. In his speech reported in the *New Zealand Times*, Lord Islington, Plunket's successor as governor, compared Suzanne to General Booth of the Salvation Army in England. Her impact on the society of the time was similar. 'This public testimony to the Reverend Mother', he said, 'was representative of all classes, all creeds and denominations. . . . Since 1860, a period almost synchronising with the country's development, she had labored tirelessly with no discrimination of creed.'

Dr A. W. Izard replied on her behalf.[4] He called her the 'Grand Old Lady', no longer just of Wellington, as Dr Agnes Bennett had said, but 'of New Zealand – her parish in the walk of humanity. The Rev. Mother, he said, wished him to say that she was very fully conscious of the share that the people themselves had taken in her work by their co-operation and practical sympathy.' The cheque for £2000 they had given her would go to a new ward for convalescent children at the Home of Compassion, the Jubilee Ward.

A tired Mother Aubert went home that evening with Sister Angela, sat down, rummaged in her large pockets – and could not find the cheque. The panic was shortlived; the cheque was found. The sisters continued the jubilee with their own celebration over the New Year, the true anniversary of when the *Général Teste* had sailed into Auckland's sunsplashed harbour. They decorated the tables with gold mottoes in French, Latin and Maori. Sister Lawrence recorded Suzanne's reply to the novices' address to her: 'Mother in her own very quaint way responded and said that although they spoke of her heroism in leaving France 50 years ago, that it was much easier to leave home such a long distance away, than do as they were – and their friends at the very door.'[5] In the Town Hall Suzanne had shared the credit of her achievements with the people of Wellington. Now she was reinforcing the novices too, downplaying her life-story in comparison with what they were giving up then and there.

The Jubilee Ward was built. Its opening in 1912, as well as the annual socials and concerts where New Zealand's top musicians gave their talents freely, the gala fêtes and other events, kept Mother Aubert and Wellington – dignitaries, charitable wealthy, and simple citizens – buoyed in their mutual esteem. On 26 February 1913, Suzanne wrote a letter to her friend in Auckland, Isa Outhwaite. It was a private letter to a layperson and the fun of being known, even lionised a bit, slipped through:

> You have been very busy with the Society for the protection of animals; so have I been for the protection of women and children. There was a large garden party at the Premier's residence. There were hundreds of babies and women. And sports to make money. Now fancy your fool of [an] old friend competing with the Cabinet Ministers and the Bank Managers to knock the pipe out of Aunt Sally's mouth, and winning 3 prizes too. Oh! the roars of laughter at the defeat of the Ministers! I choose for prizes lovely boxes of cigarettes which I offered to the Bank Managers to favorably clear their brains on the cloudy question of (my) overdrafts: reiterated roars. Then there was nail driving etc., etc., ending by fortune telling, quite enough to bring on my head 'toutes foudres du Vatican' [all of the Vatican's thunderbolts].
>
> I knew every body and every body knew me. We had three jolly hours, and made plenty money, but I hear an ominous rumbling report in the sky. Where shall I find shelter, after eloping (as was recorded) with an ex-Lord Mayor and M.H.R. [Member of the House of Representatives] in his motor.[6]

Suzanne was right to sense the rumbling thunderstorm of church disapproval looming over her head. She would need the shelter of her ever-handy umbrella. Way back in 1870, Bishop Croke had served her notice that religious sisters were meant docilely to reflect the wishes of the clergy. Apart from that episode, however, she had lived a life of open frontiers which she could cross with relative impunity. After the Nazareth Institute was disbanded in Auckland, the fifteen-year interruption in her official religious career meant that she was fifty years old before she was once again in a habit, fifty-seven by the time the Daughters of Our Lady of Compassion was formed. What was more, Archbishop Redwood liked and respected her. His view of her was confidently wide-angled, and he could see where Catholicism might benefit from her creative energy and popularity.

So it was not until she was an old woman of seventy-five that, as leader of a congregation, she ran into the stiff headwinds of the Catholic hierarchy. Other strong women of independent initiative in nineteenth-century congregations had done this when much younger. Mary MacKillop in Australia was the closest example. She was still a young woman in the 1860s when she was being harried by a succession of diocesan bishops. Boxed into the corners of their separate Australian colonies and mainly looking out to Ireland, they could not accept her wider all-Australian plans for the education and care of the poor. Further afield, Euphrasie Barbier, whose community had been formed in France initially to staff the Marist missions in New Zealand and Oceania, had fought her case with a steely strength belying her frail appearance. Mary Potter's nursing sisters, the Little Company of Mary, came to New Zealand in 1914. Mary Potter too had needed to battle against English bishops for the survival of her community's ideals.

From 1910 circumstances were beginning to coincide to strengthen the camp of those hostile to Suzanne Aubert. They would try to get her to toe the line, the straighter line that Rome had gradually been drawing. The Vatican had realised that anticlericalism and indifference were undermining the frame of Catholic Europe, and that mingling with other faiths in the new colonies could also dilute the integrity of Catholicism. To preserve the unbroken tradition, Catholic faithful were to stand further apart from the rest.

The Catholic school system had been maintained in New Zealand even after the 1877 Education Act brought most education under state and secular management. By now the network was firmly linked up across the parishes. Parents had to educate their children through these schools. If they were not exempted for reasons such as distance, the sacraments were withheld. Catholics' socialising was also being brought more within the parish circle. In the United States and Australia there were areas where Catholic settlers had concentrated together in sizeable numbers, and it was quite natural to know mainly fellow Catholics. But in New Zealand Catholics were scattered fairly evenly across the population. A separate identity would be both more noticeable and less natural, especially in rural areas and small towns. This was clear to Suzanne.

In 1908 Pius X issued the _Ne Temere_ decree, which formalised the church's disapproval of marriage between a Catholic and a non-Catholic. Any marriage ceremony involving a Catholic had to be conducted by the local Catholic priest or bishop. If the marriage had been performed without dispensation in the bride or groom's Anglican, Presbyterian or Methodist church, for instance, the marriage was invalid from a Catholic viewpoint. And the corollary was that any children could be regarded as illegitimate in the eyes of the church.

When the impact of this filtered through in New Zealand newspapers, the controversy sharpened the debate over state legitimacy and supremacy versus church hegemony. It also helped whet the knives of the more bigoted anti-Catholics. Over the years there was room for argument on both sides at even the simplest level. The catechism spelt out the meaning of the decree clearly to the Ngati Hau children from Hiruharama. Later, in 1920, Sister Lawrence thought that the archbishop 'might like to know that our Maori children are taking a great interest in the Ne Temere. I am afraid at times their attitude is rather military for they suggested to the Sister who teaches them that they should go to the various Pahs along the river and fight all the Protestant children'.[7] She put a damper on their zeal.

Rome was also shifting its attitude towards foundling homes. Anti-clerical opposition in France had peaked just after the turn of the century. The work of many Catholic congregations had had to close down. The church had to be very careful to keep its reputation beyond reproach. It did not want accusations that foundling homes harboured either the by-blows of the wealthy or the hidden children of priests or nuns. Or that such institutions were in any way speeding the babies to heaven. It would be easier for the church if Suzanne dealt only with identified Catholic mothers and their babies.

The bishop of each diocese in the Catholic world had to apply directives or recommendations coming from Rome. It depended on the individual man whether the process was tactful or dogmatic: he had considerable local power. In Wellington, Redwood was fairly open-minded and conciliatory.[8] He gave enough rein to his clergy and religious. He once said: 'I have a great body of priests and I trust them'.[9] But Redwood was getting old. He had been bishop since 1874, archbishop since 1887. Administering the diocese was probably beginning to pall. He travelled a lot. He was nicknamed by some clergy the 'Archbishop of Tours', a pun on the French town of that name.[10]

By 1910 the work was devolving more onto Father Thomas O'Shea, vicar general since 1907. His background was strongly Irish, but he was among the first priests to have received all their training in New Zealand. He had come as a young Marist priest of thirty-one to head the parish of Te Aro with its church right next door to the Sisters of Compassion's cottages in Buckle St. He rose quickly to prominence. He was a hard-working man, friendly with the laity and dedicated to the Catholic school system. Children over the years remembered his short, close-knit, trim-bearded figure with affection.[11] He would mingle with them on frequent visits, get down to their level and talk to them. Redwood had seemed to them more distant, even snobbish.

O'Shea believed in systems and order. He fitted the mould that Cardinal Paul Cullen had cast in Ireland for all the leaders of the clergy serving the Irish diaspora.[12] He did not deal easily with difference. Priests, sisters and parishioners were all to conform. Likewise, Maori were to integrate into European patterns of life and religion. Father Delachienne of the Marist Maori mission was, like Suzanne, being rather unconventional. He was actively encouraging and taking part in large, well-attended hui at Pukekaraka, the church community and marae at Otaki. O'Shea later wrote disparagingly of the hui as 'useless big meetings, which made a great show, but from which absolutely no benefit of a religious or practical nature resulted'.[13] Delachienne's colleague, Father Melu, had protested in careful English: 'Are not the meetings central to the civil or religious life of the Maoris? Have we not ourselves our conferences and congresses?'[14] O'Shea summarily transferred Delach, as he was known, from Otaki. Catholic kaumatua emphasised in a petition to the Marists that the reason for Delach's success and bond with them was his ability to assimilate 'te tuturu o te maoritanga', the quintessence of Maoritanga.[15] But O'Shea's vision was blinkered. Maoritanga was irrelevant. He just wanted the Marists to report Delach and Melu to head-quarters in France for 'conspiring' against ecclesiastical authority.

It was unlikely that O'Shea would ever let Suzanne be. Like Delach, she would have to be brought to heel. O'Shea's own close observation would have confirmed this. As parish priest next door to the original Buckle St community, he would be aware of the sisters' hard work there, and equally conscious of extra strains on them from Suzanne's new project at Island Bay. Her constant comings and goings would be unseemly, in his view. Neither was he likely to allow that her convictions, and the policy and methods she had developed, were admissible, even if arguable. He undoubtedly found her innate tactical skills frustrating and goading. She had always been mindful of religious obedience and hierarchy and had cleared all her new ventures with Redwood, but she was very careful to prepare a strong position in advance. Unconsciously, O'Shea was probably trying to outmanoeuvre her. And he could do this through her vulnerable work with foundlings.

Along with many others – Catholics, Protestants and free-thinkers – he did not agree with her that anonymity could serve a good purpose, that society would continue to punish and pull the mothers down unless they were protected in some way. But his opposition to her work may not have been coming primarily from an ethical stance. He seemed to be attempting to regulate and control the independent, innovative woman. To be fair to O'Shea, Suzanne's determined championing of this work probably did not come wholly from her social philosophy or deep religious beliefs either. She was a strong woman of God staking out boundaries of initiative and defending them against encroachment.

Jules Michelet, the nineteenth-century historian recording and influencing public opinion in France when Suzanne was a child, wrote that womankind would be a *puissance de mal*, a force for evil; that women would wield the power of *une sorcière*, a witch, if ever they came out from the private sphere.[16] Mother Aubert was a woman emerging from the private sphere. To the mostly conservative clergy, she might carry this indefinable aura of threat. Paradoxically, Suzanne had to take sanctuary in the loved persona that Wellington people had co-opted and made an icon, the persona that was her own person, anyway – the tolerant mingler, the defender of the poor and the handicapped and the powerless mothers, the woman who did not check you out for religious affiliation before she helped you. The high regard of the general public gave her protection.

By 1910, Suzanne seemed to be in a safer position strategically. She had just set up a new foundation in Auckland. The Daughters of Our Lady of Compassion had expanded into another diocese. This was an important move, necessary for the development of any new congregation, and especially for the kind that Suzanne seems to have had in mind for her sisterhood – a papal congregation. Whereas some congregations were formed loosely in diocesan communities, each one under the control of the local bishop, others opted for central control with the communities all linked back to a mother house. Some of these congregations were answerable not to the local bishops but directly to the Vatican as papal congregations. This gave them considerable independence within the diocese, although ultimately the more direct links with Rome tended to tame congregations and make them more conservative anyway. Mary MacKillop, Euphrasie Barbier, Mary Potter and others had managed to gain for their congregations the Decree of Praise, the first step towards full papal recognition which acknowledged, legitimised and protected the vision each had of her own congregation's constitution and goals. Suzanne might have the support of wider Wellington, but only recognition from Rome could give her ecclesiastical protection.

By 1909 the English version of the Constitutions of the congregation had been completed and formalised. The framework of administration followed that of a papal congregation. Sister Angela recorded that this was 'the cause of a good deal of criticism of Mother in clerical circles. Many thought her "an ambitious old woman", for, as they phrased it, "she has made herself Superior General of a merely diocesan congregation". She was aware of this adverse view, and it hurt her a good deal though she mentioned it only to one or two Sisters, telling them that the government of the Institute had to be laid out on the right lines from the first.'[17]

A congregation had to be strongly established before it could receive a Decree of Praise. Its strength was usually gauged by the numbers of people joining and the spread of its work through branch houses in other dioceses. For several years, Suzanne had been either making tentative overtures to the other dioceses, or receiving signs of interest from their bishops – Verdon in Dunedin, Grimes in Christchurch and Lenihan in Auckland.[18] This was normal procedure, and to be expected of a confidently growing local congregation. Redwood had already cleared the path for expansion on 4 July 1907: 'I am glad to learn that there is hope of your making a foundation of your Sisterhood in the Auckland diocese', he wrote to her, 'and I have much pleasure in recommending your Sisters warmly to His Lordship the Bishop of Auckland on whom it depends to approve of a foundation of your order in that diocese.'[19]

The congregation was growing steadily, in fact, but not fast enough to service all of Suzanne's multiplying areas of interest. In 1905 Bishop George Lenihan had already invited her to work on the Auckland Maori mission. She did not have enough staff then. But five years later, in 1910, when Lenihan invited her to Auckland to set up a foundation for babies in need, she moved smartly. By then it was a political move as well as expanding the work she was dedicated to. O'Shea was now vicar general in Wellington and the change of climate was noticeable. Bishop Lenihan in Auckland had seemed well disposed towards her.[20] He would hold a certain balance of power, would probably neutralise, she hoped, some of O'Shea's growing asperity.

Lenihan had invited the congregation at a time when the other denominations around him were expanding their commitment to children in this increasingly child-oriented age. The Baptists were developing orphanages in Ponsonby and Remuera, the Presbyterians in Meadowbank.[21] By 1909 the Anglican orphanage in Parnell had opened large new buildings in Papatoetoe. The Sisters of Mercy had always run a large orphanage, but nobody was really taking in babies. The Presbyterian home, for instance, and the Wesley home which opened in 1913, took no children under three.

As well as strength there was vulnerability in the move to Auckland. There was not quite enough money or a sufficient workforce. The sisters eyed a higher, sharper peak of 'All for God', as Suzanne was always reminding them, and bent to the climb. It was yet a further stage of poverty for the sake of mission. Novices shared each other's veils, swapping them hurriedly at the changeover between two Sunday Masses because there were not enough available. Any leftover cold tea from yesterday was to be topped up with today's water. French Suzanne and the New Zealand sisters would never have the same idea of what constituted a cup of tea. Sister Lawrence said she did not mind how many dead flies went by mistake into the cake crumb pudding, 'as long as she could get plenty – she was always starving'. The laundry fire for the huge amounts of washing – from upwards of a hundred babies – was often stoked with left-over donated bread along with gorse roots and dried cow dung which the sisters gathered from the Island Bay hillsides.[22]

There was also a risk that the overworked sisters might lose their all-important unity of spirit in the rush to establish a new foundation so far away. Already some Buckle St sisters felt that their elderly incurable patients were playing second fiddle to the foundlings and incurable children at Island Bay; that their cottages, now badly in need of repair, were being overlooked while resources went to the larger, more visible institution. Suzanne would exhort the sisters to keep their unity of spirit, perhaps without looking hard enough at what she herself could do to promote this. When she went to Auckland, she had not set up the Wellington communities to function efficiently in her absence. She handled the money still. She was responsible for the admissions of babies.

Not only were the sisters in the two Wellington communities reduced in staff and resources, they were hamstrung administratively. Their letters chased after Suzanne. She wrote once to Sister Bridget on 5 March 1911: 'I received your letter of January, but with most of my other letters, it had to run after me on the Main Trunk Line. From Auckland it came with me again to Wellington, then went up again to Auckland, and finally back to Wellington again, under such pressure of business and circumstances that I did not find time to answer.'[23] They noticed that decisions she would have approved willingly had she been there suddenly seemed the wrong decisions when made in her absence.[24] Occasionally doctors diplomatically helped them by taking the initiative. Dr Kington Fyffe once restocked the Island Bay dispensary. Suzanne arrived back from Auckland to find this, muttered but meekly paid the bill. She was careful to reorder what he had stocked from then on.

The foundation in Auckland was absorbing Suzanne's time, attention and money. It was also calling her emotionally. The sisters noticed and understood that Suzanne was excited about the move back to Auckland:

> Until it was mooted no one had suspected how dear the place was to her. She really loved that city, where she had come in her youth, full of enthusiasm and ardour to win souls for Christ. All that she suffered there only served to deepen the strength of her attachment to it. There was something quite unusual, quite out of keeping with her natural character – or, should one say, her spirit of detachment in her barely suppressed eagerness in making preparations, selecting Sisters, and planning for the new establishment.[25]

The sisters may not have recognised the other exciting and energising thrust, the importance of the foundation to the progress of the congregation itself.

A fiftieth jubilee would normally top off a lifetime's achievement. But there was no sense of retirement for Suzanne. From 1910, when she was seventy-five, she was often travelling alone between Auckland and Wellington, sitting up in the train overnight to save money, refusing to use Martin Kennedy's regular cheque to obtain more comfortable accommodation. He had tried to earmark it for that. Suzanne liked trains as much as she hated ships. 'What a fine thing railways are : Katahi te mea pai ko te rerewe' was her recommendation in both languages. A shakiness in her usual neat handwriting occasionally signals a letter written on a train. 'Just a few hurried lines', 'between two trains', 'just two words', 'I just drop these few lines at the Post Office at the last minute', 'just two lines in a hurry', 'a few words to catch the mail . . .' beat out the regular rhythm of her train travel. In February 1910 she wrote: 'My poor life will be spent chiefly on the Main Trunk Line'; the sisters, too, said that at this time she 'lived in the train'.[26] And her *Directory* makes it clear she lived her religion in the train: 'Let us offer our journeys on the railroad in order to honour the speed with which Jesus daily and constantly descends from heaven to earth in obedience to the priest's word at Consecration.'[27]

The first small group of four sisters went up with Suzanne to Auckland in January 1910. Sister Anthony and Sister Salome kept a 'Pioneers' Diary' – on brown paper, as the community had no writing paper. Before going to the station, they had called on Archbishop Redwood in Hill St for his blessing: 'He remarked on our smart appearance, even the old Lady's too.' As the train chuffed its way into the wilds of the North Island, the excitement of a new venture was registered in the diary. 'The darkness is with us', wrote Sister Anthony, 'so we have resolved to say our Evening Prayer, and try to sleep, but it seems hopeless, as just when you are getting off, the train whistles, or stops. We have tried various positions; one even tried sitting on the floor! Sr. Salome had her head out of the window, and discovered by her cap when she awoke, it had been raining!'[28]

In Auckland Bishop Lenihan gave them a warm welcome: 'When we were coming away, he gave us his blessing, called Mother "his dear old friend", and said we would be very happy together. We then came to our new Home, and found Father Wright and Mr Little [a member of the St Vincent de Paul Society, who had rented the house for them] waiting to see if they could help us in any way. The house was full of emptiness.'[29] It was not, really. It was full of mosquitoes which came to greet them in the night as they slept in a row on the hard floorboards. For the next few days Suzanne's hands were swollen with bites.

Within a short time the house in Hobson St was rapidly filling also with babies. By March they had fifteen and more coming. As Suzanne wrote, there was 'plenty music with the babies'.[30] By April even Suzanne had to admit the house was full: 'The applications are showering in, but we refuse them all, whether they come from Priest, Magistrate, Police or People. The other night we had three after half past eight. You could not imagine such things unless you see them.'[31] Already, because they turned away no one in need, they had the inevitable dilemma confronting them. A sick baby had been brought in, and died within two hours. They had their first inquest on their hands. On 3 May, Suzanne was writing to Sister Chanel: 'We have two babies very bad. I am afraid they will die. A death would mean an inquest etc. etc. God help us.'[32] The babies did not die, but in the spring months of October and November Suzanne and the sisters in Auckland were confronting epidemics: 'Just a few hurried lines for we are having extra work with measles and quarantine in the House.' And: 'Just two lines. All my time has been taken up to the last minute. The House is full of sickness. One of the babies is dying with meningitus.'[33]

The house in Hobson St could be only a temporary measure. It was not big enough, and because it was rented it could not be altered. For £4000, with deposit money advanced by friends and loans arranged, Suzanne bought a large property in Mt Eden. It had belonged to Josiah Firth, an influential businessman in the province of Auckland before he went bankrupt. 'Firth's Castle' had been his dream house. Its stone tower, and wooden façades (from when his money ran out), rose among four and a half acres of lawns, trees and shrubs. The Auckland sisters wrote back to commiserate with the Island Bay women in their bleak southerly gales. And they suffered in turn in the sweaty, mosquitoed summers.

Up to forty children soon filled their new home, which they named St Vincent's. It reinforced the link with the seventeenth-century French saint, Vincent de Paul. He had founded Suzanne's loved Sisters of Charity and had championed the needs of foundling children. The children were all under school age, except for three who walked each day to Newmarket School. Some were orphans; most came as illegitimate babies.[34] The home was across the road from the Mater Misericordiae Hospital run by the Sisters of Mercy. Compared with the 1860s, relations now were sisterly and harmonious. Sisters from both houses crossed the road sometimes to share Mass when there was none in their own house.

St Vincent's was bought and opened in the interregnum between two bishops. Bishop Lenihan had died unexpectedly in February 1910, just a month after the sisters arrived in Auckland. The new bishop would be Henry Cleary, consecrated early in 1911. It was evident that the sisters' work would be better for a permanent home, but there would always be those, Cleary foremost among them, who believed that Suzanne had moved extra swiftly to consolidate herself in the interregnum. That was probably true. The changeover of bishops historically could spell trouble as the new man asserted himself. There had been nothing formal in writing to confirm the new foundation before Lenihan died. Suzanne would have wanted to secure her own property in Auckland as a lever to convince the new bishop to continue what Lenihan had started. After all, it had been her lack of 'inalienable' property that had defeated her when Bishop Croke arrived in Auckland so many years before. In 1910 priests and laypeople were urging and helping her to settle on the Firth property. She did not act unilaterally. But her action must have seemed like a challenge. Cleary would never believe the evidence that Lenihan had asked for her in the first place.[35]

Instead of Suzanne having a counterfoil to O'Shea in Bishop Lenihan, now she could see forces marshalling on two fronts. O'Shea would have an ally in Bishop Cleary, an Irishman who had come from twelve years in Dunedin as editor of the *Tablet*. He was following in the footsteps of its previous editor, Bishop Moran, the bearer for so many years of the flag of Catholic argumentation and Irish identity in the sectarian south. Moran had been strongly opposed to Redwood and the French Marists. Suzanne was French and seen by the Irish Cleary as a protégée of Redwood. She was also too independent, too unconventional, too visible. Henry Cleary was an intense, brilliant man skilled in philosophy and dialectic. As his priests found out to their cost, he was 'good at winning arguments'.[36]

The two protagonists sized each other up almost immediately, while Cleary was still on his way to Auckland. Sister Chanel's diary for Sunday, 8 January 1911 recorded:

> His Lordship the new Bishop arrived in Wellington, Bishop Cleary of Auckland. He stayed at His Grace the Archbishop Redwood.
> Monday, Mother called on him and received his blessing.
> Tuesday, [he] won all our hearts by a very gracious act; he paid and sent Mother a first class ticket also a sleeping berth for the Auckland train.
> Mother left for Auckland, Tuesday morning.[37]

Cleary's action would not have won Suzanne's heart. Behind the genuine generosity another message was clear to her. He would have been told that she was adamant about not using Martin Kennedy's money on her own travel comfort. Her personal hallmark was poverty and simplicity in the extreme. Cleary's very first action was to present her with a *fait accompli* – a prepaid ticket for a first-class overnight berth, not money that she could divert as she wished. As a religious and the mother of the congregation, she was to travel with discretion and decorum, not hobnob with any old passenger. Her little old body was not to be seen crumpled, collapsed and nodding gap-mouthed in sleep with all the others on the hard carriage seats. Mother Aubert was already getting a hint to conform. But Sister Chanel's diary is clear. Suzanne squared her fists. Knowing probably from Monday of the intended ticket, she had left by the morning train. And Sister Angela records that she went second class.[38]

The choice to work with illegitimate babies would never be easy. The whole question of shame and blame, of responsibility and payment, seemed to have no answer. The task would be harder for Suzanne in Auckland than in Wellington, where she had been known for a long time. There the public had come to trust her through the medicines, through her work with the city's old and poor, with the incurable children and the crèche. They could then accept the stance she took over foundling children. In Auckland she did not have a long association behind her.

As she went about setting up St Vincent's, letters argued back and forth in the newspapers. George MacMurray's opinion was fairly orthodox: 'Mother Aubert's Home is very unlikely to minimise child murder, but the separating of mother and infant in the first six months of the child's life prevents the maternal love for the child to be developed, and throws away the mightiest factor in the salvation of the girl – whilst screening the sin gives impunity and encouragement to men who are prone to immorality.' But 'Compos Mentis' wrote in support of Mother Aubert: 'There is an element of refined cruelty to send a helpless infant and a single woman-mother forth into a pitiless world to fight the battle of life.' M. Redford agreed: 'Under present conditions, a girl's downfall is public property, and the girl loses her self-respect and drifts. Each individual life is full of mistakes, but the individuals do not shout their errors from the housetop. The girls must receive some consideration, and I would screen every weak sister all in my power. I trust that every broadminded, right-thinking person will encourage that noble woman Mother Aubert in her great work.' And Thomas Gresham pointed out that 'Mother Aubert's system in no way contemplates the [long-term] separation of a mother from her child.'[39]

MacMurray's comment about child murder underlined the fact that, in spite of the Liberals' tightening of Infant Life Protection Acts between 1893 and 1907, there was still infanticide. In 1911, *Truth* reported that twenty-nine percent of all infant deaths came under 'Mysterious "Other Causes"':

> Within the past week or two in the city of Wellington alone, there have been found two miniature mites of humanity who came from God knows where, and who were thrown out as one might throw out a shovelful of refuse, one a newly-born infant . . . and the other a child anything up to ten days old, who had, according to medical testimony, BEEN DELIBERATELY SUFFOCATED AND MURDERED.[40]

Suzanne was known to have consulted *Truth*; she also had John Jeffares, the farmer and workman at the Home of Compassion, tell her anything relevant from its pages. From her own experience, she wrote in 1910 to the Education Department an impassioned defence of her work. On 'Statistics of Births and Deaths' she wrote: 'The statistics of death are most misleading, because the Registrar-General has never had, and never will have, the returns of the sea, of the rivers, of the ponds, of the ditches, of the lonely roadsides, of the sewers.'[41] She fought to retain for women anything that would be an alternative to infanticide.

The tide of government and public opinion was flowing more and more strongly towards fostering illegitimate children in individual homes. It was the trend overseas, and it made sense: there was far less danger of epidemics. But foster homes did not generally take very small babies: the risk of them dying was statistically still too great. Religious orphanages could be choosy, as well. The North Canterbury Charitable Aid Board claimed in 1913 that Christchurch religious organisations 'would not touch' the illegitimate children who numbered nearly half of the board's children in care at the time.[42] And, in any case, they did not take them as babies. So how could a mother, lacking enough money to pay for foster care from birth, hide her shame, begin a new life, yet still keep in touch with her child? Suzanne knew that she could provide this missing link in caring.

In Auckland she was helped by some priests and laypeople who were working among young people in need. A friend, Caroline Hawkes, brought cases to her attention. On 12 July 1911, she wrote to Suzanne:

My dear little Mother,

Dean Hackett was here today about a very sad case of two respectable girls . . . they belong to two most respectable families though poor and it would mean ruin to them if the disgrace of the girls were known . . . One man used to dine with Father Hackett and he treated him like a brother. He is only come out from Ireland and used to go to Holy Communion every month and the scoundrel has left the poor girl without any means and cleared back to Ireland. The Dean said that if he could have got hold of him he thinks he would have shot him. The other poor girl's case is nearly similar. . . . So the Dean told me to tell you could you take the two little children when they were *four weeks* old so that the girls could go home as they will be supposed to be on a visit. . . . The poor girls are in a dreadful state of mind and he wants to be able to tell them there is a shelter for the little babies. . . .

I hope you are well and for goodness sake do not work yourself to death. Now I must stop.

With all my best love and plenty of it . . .[43]

In Auckland as in Wellington, Suzanne had marched with open eyes into an area of social welfare fraught with the likelihood of higher mortality. The special schools section of the Education Department kept a watching brief from 2 December 1909, when an *Auckland Star* clipping, introducing the work of the sisters, began the file on 'St Vincent's Home, Auckland'. The department's disapproval of Mother Aubert's approach runs clearly through the pages and the mortality figures from Island Bay are noted. The alternatives of boarding out and the mother 'taking responsibility' are strongly promoted.[44]

Sarah Jackson was the District Inspector for Institutions, appointed under the Infant Life Protection Act. Her first report was cut and dried: 'I am sorry to find that Mother Aubert proposes a Home for Foundlings. Unless this Institution be carefully watched, it will do more harm than good . . .'[45] Sarah Jackson noted in her reports the babies who died or were ill. In 1911 there was an epidemic of influenza; in November 1912, twenty were 'convalescent after chicken-pox'. But her opinion of the management grows from a cryptic 'Good, as far as it goes' to 'The Sisters do the best they can, under a bad system' (which may be referring to Suzanne's continuing as manager while she was going to and fro between Auckland and Wellington) to 'Improving', 'Good', and 'The nuns are now doing very well with the babies'.[46] As inspector, she was aware of the delicacy of this type of child, as she had written in her 1911 report on another institution: 'In considering death rate at Door of Hope it must be remembered that babies are received here who on account of ill health are refused admissions elsewhere.' Suzanne had visited the Door of Hope in 1910 and found their approach the most like hers.

Only people licensed as foster-parents under the Infant Life Protection Act could 'in consideration of any payment or reward' keep a child away from parents or guardians for longer than seven days. Private charitable institutions had to have an exemption from this section (41), which was aimed at preventing babyfarming. In 1910 Suzanne applied for a renewal of the Island Bay exemption, and for a new exemption for St Vincent's in Auckland. Her case seemed strong, as she did not charge for care but received money only if it was offered. The Education Department, however, was again insisting that full particulars of the mother and child be released. George Fowlds, the Minister of Education, made it clear that he was 'not favourably disposed towards the rearing of infants in Institutions, norby any system which enables parents to relieve themselves from the responsibility of caring for their children'.[47]

Suzanne stood firm. Her lawyer, Charles Skerrett, replied to Edward Gibbes, Secretary for Education: 'MMJA [Mother Mary Joseph Aubert] will not submit to [the required open record-book] because it would be against the interests of the mothers of illegitimate children that may be received in the Home. Such informations, for humane reasons, and having regard to the effect it is likely to have on the future lives of the Mothers, the R[everend] M[other] will not consent to disclose.' Through Skerrett, she then went on the attack:

> I have on her behalf the honour to apply that you will hear counsel and witnesses on her behalf before witnessing her application for exemption in the case of [St Vincent's Home for Foundlings] and before cancelling as you threaten to do the existing warrant of Exemption in respect of the [Home of Compassion at Island Bay]. I have the honour to apply that you will fix a date for the purpose of hearing Counsel and Witnesses.
>
> The Institutions which MMJA has established have been the work and care of her whole life and the efficient conduct and progress of these Institutions are as dear to her as anything can be to a human being. The spirit of philanthropy and charity which has activated the R. M. in the establishment and maintenance of these Institutions cannot for a moment be doubted. It will therefore be seen how important the Rev. M. regards the questions raised by your letter of 4 May.[48]

Between May and July 1910, the battle raged. The department was also requiring 'two qualified nurses with special training in the care of children, together with a sufficient number of assistants to provide (including qualified nurses and assistants) one woman for every four infants under twelve months old'. The requirement for nurses was totally justifiable in view of the deaths in 1909. Gibbes' reply to Skerrett had not failed to point this out. The rate would always be high, anyway, because the little incurables frequently did not live, but the seven deaths in 1907 and the fourteen in 1910 were a more acceptable bracket around the horrific figure of forty-six in the epidemic strike of 1909. This had sent a shudder through the government, the church hierarchy and the community of sisters alike.

Suzanne would have loved to comply with this ideal condition. Having her sisters as qualified and registered nurses was a goal to this woman who had always wanted to be a 'proper' nurse herself, if not a doctor. It would be all the more satisfying now that nursing was being established as a highly regarded profession. From the beginning the sisters had followed courses with the St John Ambulance and Red Cross. The doctors coming to Buckle St and the Home of Compassion had already been giving free training and lectures. She would keep pushing for trained sisters. But in 1910 she simply did not have any. Two of the more experienced trained nurses in the region, Eva Webber and Jessie Sexton, were about to join her congregation, but they were not there yet.

The doctors rallied to her defence to convince the department that the deaths were not caused by unskilful care on the part of her sisters. Kington Fyffe argued strongly in a letter of support that the babies who died had weakened constitutions on entry. In early June Fyffe and Elliott led the Wellington division of the British Medical Association in a meeting with Gibbes to discuss the issue. They suggested that the honorary medical staff of the home would train the sisters, who would then sit an examination by government-appointed examiners.

By late June, a resolution was being reached. The register to be kept 'shall not be open to inspection, provided that the Manager shall give the names of inmates resident in the Home when asked to do so by an authorized officer of the Education Department; and further, shall give the names of the parents and other details that he may require to the Minister of Education at his express request'.[49] Suzanne annotated her copy: 'Such a register has always been kept and I am prepared to comply with the remainder of the condition.'

With the nursing, one member of the medical staff of each institution would be responsible for its medical conduct for at least a month, the responsibility being rotated among the doctors. The requirement for a patient–staff ratio had meanwhile gone. Training and lectures would be given to the sisters. The Hospitals Department would 'endeavour to arrange for more complete courses in training and nursing to be taken by attendants of the Home in public institutions'. Suzanne was delighted and immediately wrote her reply: 'I would be thankful if the Hospitals Department would arrange, in accordance with our conversation last Saturday, to have two of my Sisters at a time receive a complete course of training and nursing at the Wellington Hospital'.[50] The certificates of exemption were issued and all seemed fine. And resolving the controversy had miraculously opened up a clear path to real nursing.

The medical superintendent required two conditions for the sisters' hospital training. Hester Maclean, who had by then replaced Grace Neill in the Department of Hospitals and Charitable Aid, discussed them with

Suzanne. The first was that the sisters live at the hospital, as other trainee nurses did. This was impossible then for a community of religious, and the condition was waived. The second was that they change into the usual nursing uniform each day on arrival at the hospital. Henry Hardwick-Smith, the superintendent, felt that uniformity with the other trainee nurses would protect them from prejudice. As probationers, they were all bound to make mistakes of some sort. Suzanne agreed to this condition.

O'Shea, the vicar general, did not agree. He was not too pleased with Suzanne anyway. The government had also offered free training at St Helen's obstetric hospitals in Wellington and Auckland for two sisters. But Suzanne had replied firmly to Education Minister Fowlds: 'As we do not intend to ever attend obstetrical cases, I consider a course of training at St Helen's Hospital as of no use to us.'[51] O'Shea, Cleary, even Lenihan and the Society of St Vincent de Paul in Auckland, had been wanting her to care for pregnant Catholic girls during the birth, and for them and their babies afterwards. This was the standard approach of other denominations, too. At the time the only Catholic maternity home for 'fallen women' was Mount Magdala in Christchurch. Again, Suzanne knew this was not her field. She felt strongly that girls who had made that first mistake were often branded for life by their suspiciously long six-month absence in these institutions, where they also toiled away at exhausting laundry work.[52] In saying no to the government, Suzanne was also saying no to the bishops.

But the Sisters of Compassion were still a diocesan congregation. Redwood had the power to refuse permission for them to train in nurses' uniform. He did.[53] In this way Suzanne's sisters were blocked from the full training offered freely by the government. It would be years before they found another way to reach state recognition and registration as nurses. At a time when solutions were being worked out in the co-operative spirit that Suzanne liked, and just when the way seemed clear, the hierarchy of the church closed the door.

CHAPTER NINETEEN

Rome
1913-1918

I am alone : Ko ahau anake[1]

By the end of 1912, Sister Angela was secretary of the congregation. She had worked in city offices before entering the community, and she kept minutes beautifully. Not that any had really been written before 1912, but in that year the running of the institute was abruptly brought into line. Her very first minutes recorded what happened at the extraordinary general chapter of 6 November 1912.[2] Chapters in religious congregations are the major assemblies for both spiritual self-assessment and decision-making. They are held every four to six years and are attended by appointed and elected representatives. The sisters' 1909 Constitutions provided for chapters, but Suzanne had not so far, apparently, called any formal assembly.[3] This extraordinary general chapter was specially 'convoked by the Very Reverend Dean O'Shea, Vicar General, who presided in person'. Change was on his agenda.

On 21 September 1912, Archbishop Redwood had asked Dean Patrick Smyth, rector of the Marist Seminary, to make in his name a 'thorough Canonical Visitation of the Sisters of Our Lady of Compassion'. Smyth was to speak with the sisters individually. This was normal and required. It gave each sister an outlet for any criticism or suggestions which would be handed on anonymously to the higher superior. 'The scope and extent of your questionings are left to your sagacity and prudence', wrote Redwood. 'When you have finished the visitation, you will draw up in writing a report upon it for the Vicar General of the Archdiocese.' Redwood also instructed that 'this visitation be made as early as your convenience will permit'.[4] This would be convenient also for the archbishop, with his long-time association with Suzanne. He was about to sail away to Rome, and the visitation would be made while he was overseas.[5] He would not be expecting it to be easy; O'Shea would deal with the matter.[6]

Smyth's report back to O'Shea on 22 October was framed very firmly, but also positively and humanely. He began by stating that he 'found a good religious and self-sacrificing spirit right through the community'. The twelve pages of analysis and recommendation had as conclusion:

> *In fine*, I wish to state that the sisters, whilst they have made known their little grievances, and have found fault with the administration of the Institution and have considered their Rev. Mother somewhat austere and at times unapproachable, yet one and all have given expression to their deep respect and sincere love for her person, their devotedness to her, and their gratitude for all that she has done for the Community and the works of the Institute.
>
> The work is most meritorious. May God prosper it and reward the noble Rev. Mother and her truly self-sacrificing children of our Lady of Compassion.[7]

O'Shea wasted no time in calling the chapter. He came on 6 November, not with the text of Smyth's report, which Suzanne and the sisters probably never saw, but with his own prepared letter and copies of it ready to distribute to each local superior. There was to be no chance of misunderstanding or avoidance. It was a businesslike letter, without the warm tone running through Smyth's report. O'Shea formally read it out to the assembled chapter. The theme throughout was: 'the reforms and changes hereinafter specified shall be carried out as soon as possible'.[8]

There would be improvements in the sisters' clothing and food, including the longed-for afternoon cups of tea. On the spiritual level, more time was to be devoted to study and conventional religious instruction, especially in the novitiate. More time was also to be allowed for the normal and traditional religious exercises like visits to the 'Blessed Sacrament, Mass, the Office and the Rosary'. Sister Angela later detailed how most of the sisters' spiritual 'free time' had been inevitably eroded. Saying the rosary in common could combine with laundry work but not so much with childcare. The 'Sisters were only together when bathing or feeding the infants. . . . Phrases of the prayer mingled with interjections to infants pulling each other's hair . . . simply led to questioning one's conscience as to whether one was "saying prayers for purgatory or heaven!"'[9]

At best, these innovations would ease the physical and spiritual life of exhausted sisters. O'Shea had been parish priest at St Joseph's, next door to the Buckle St community. He knew how hard the sisters worked and how overstretched their resources were with the addition of the homes at Auckland and Island Bay. At worst, the changes could sterilise the special spirit of the congregation, the potentially energising mélange of spiritual and practical which infused their daily routine at even the most prosaic level. In fact, the sisters would quite soon come back to Suzanne's teaching of spirituality.[10]

O'Shea read on, detailing the required changes in the running of the congregation. The local superiors and novice mistress 'should exercise the authority' of their office and 'must not be constantly applying to the Rev. Mother for permissions which they can give themselves'. Suzanne was to hold regular meetings with her assistants. A 'competent Econome' should keep proper accounts in each house. These measures were well overdue in the Institute of the Daughters of Our Lady of Compassion, until now led by Suzanne as superior, secretary and treasurer in one. She did have more education, more life experience and a wider and shrewder vision than her sisters, but many were resourceful women and had a lot to offer. O'Shea and Smyth 'found amongst them a majority of good souls, and even some rather fine characters'.[11] Suzanne knew this better than they, but it was more than time for her to acknowledge it.

The changes were clearly representing the wishes of some of the sisters. Suzanne wrote later to Redwood that some of the changes were gradually happening anyway. Two days later, O'Shea wrote confidently to Redwood: 'Rev. Mother was not at all pleased with many of them, but I was firm. And I know her good sense will make her see after a while that the reforms made will serve to strengthen the Institute and relieve her of a lot of anxiety.'[12] Nevertheless, the particular spirit of the congregation might again be compromised. Smyth had commented that the previous first assistant, Sister Bridget, was away upriver at Jerusalem while the present one, Sister Carmel, was kept milking the cows and working in the garden. It was a legitimate point: Suzanne was not consulting her four elected assistants nearly enough. But it overlooked the fact that all fifty of the Sisters of Compassion, from Suzanne to the newest postulant, worked physically in whatever was their own equivalent of tending the garden. There was no separate echelon of administration. That was part of their essence.

With his next decrees, however, O'Shea trespassed over Suzanne's psychological and spiritual boundaries. Any 'considerable expenditure' was now to be 'placed before the Ecclesiastical Authorities whose advice and wishes must be strictly observed'. The deeds of all properties were to be in the names of at least three trustees, among them sisters – but he did not spell out then that one trustee would automatically be the archbishop, according to Article 82 of the decree of the 1899 Council of Wellington. The local bishop (in Wellington's case, an archbishop) was canonically the first superior of any diocesan congregation.

Next, the sisters were to fade from the streets of the city: 'The perambulators at present used by the Sisters at Buckle St must be done away with immediately.' Instead, a horse and cart would be driven by 'a male patient'. The pushing had been heavy and a cart would be much more practical. But Suzanne's perambulating women, out in the weather and available to the people at walking, talking speed, had been a visible daily sign of Catholic care and, important for her, of Catholic integration in the life of the city. She saw this as part of mission. In addition, Suzanne thought walking would cure almost all ills. The thrice-daily excursion with the 'perambes', she held, accounted for 'the exceptional health the Sisters enjoyed'. It was a strong argument.[13] Pius X was at the time recommending more physical exercise for religious in their convents.

O'Shea read out still more changes. Many were valid – about safeguarding sisters' dowries 'if any', leaving a Book of Customs to follow when the superior was not there, carrying out property repairs. But when the word 'foundling' was spoken, he sprang the lock on Suzanne's emotions. The works undertaken by the order seemed 'too numerous' and O'Shea decreed that 'the Foundling work should be discontinued', 'the Foundlings done away with'. The Holy See did 'not approve of nuns having Foundling Homes'. The sisters would have more time for the 'visiting of the poor & sick in the City parishes'. This would mean Catholic parishioners. Suzanne's sisters were to stay far more within denominational limits, reduced from their public role as ecumenical ambassadors of Christian love.

Suzanne sat through all the reading – perhaps, as often, sitting slightly forward in her chair with her hands spread palm-down on the lap of her habit. Then she reacted. The minutes record the scene:

> Immediately the President [O'Shea] finished reading his letter, the Superior rose & protested against the expulsion of the Foundlings, saying the Foundlings are to us the representatives of the Divine Infant, His little brothers & Sisters; how can we turn them out? They have souls as well as the

others; they are as dear to God, He gave His Son to die for them too. What will become of them, who will take them if we are to turn them out? It is in our Rule, approved by His Grace; it has been in our Rule since the beginning that we are to care for them, & much more to that effect.

O'Shea remained unmoved and the argument continued:

The President remarked that 'Rome does not approve'. The Superior answered that Rome objects to religious caring for infants in the very first period of life, and that we do not take them until they are a month old. There are Institutes for Foundlings in Rome itself! The President observed that older Institutes were permitted to continue their works but that new ones would not be approved. The Foundlings must go. The Superior hoped that the day that sounded the Requiem of the Foundlings would sound her own too.

The President was emphatic that Rome did not approve the work & we must obey. He then handed copies of his letter to the Local Superiors & instructed them to have it read to their subjects, & a copy also to the Secretary for the Records of the Chapter. He instructed the Council to see that its provisions were carried out as soon as possible.

The President then said the customary prayers & the Chapter was terminated.[14]

Sisters Carmel, Bridget, Claver, Chanel, Anthony and Agnes had watched Suzanne jump to her feet and engage in battle with the archdiocesan administrator. Sister Angela witnessed rather than watched; she was probably using her shorthand skills to grasp the moment for the record, Suzanne's heat matching the coolness of her neat, formalistic opponent.

The chapter was over. But a new council had been elected and it now sat immediately, still 'under the Presidency of the Vicar-General'. Many of the straightforward policy changes were set in place. O'Shea brought up another matter next: Jerusalem. There was 'no Community life there, consequently no religious life, a state of things that could not be allowed to continue. It was for the Council to decide whether or not the Sisters should be withdrawn.' Smyth had been concerned to find up there that the sisters rode 'alone on horseback to visit Maoris and to go to their school' – 'Sisters should never go out alone', he added. But had O'Shea not done enough in one day without moving against Jerusalem as well? In his words there was no mention of the sisters' long association with Ngati Hau and Ngati Ruaka. The man who would later not be able to understand Father Delach's absorption of Maori values into Catholic life at Otaki would not understand the bond Suzanne also had.

Once more she fought back:

The Superior General spoke eloquently of the many reasons for the Institute continuing its work at Jerusalem as long as possible. Those reasons are chiefly the Foundress left her home and came to New Zealand fifty-three years ago for the Maories not for the Whites. The Institute was founded for the Maories, it was its first work . . .[15]

Angela wrote on for twelve more lines, following the rest of Suzanne's argument. O'Shea came back with his ultimatum: 'The Sisters must have more Community life or they must close the House.'

By and large the sisters had welcomed the visitation. It pointed out defects in the direction and management of the congregation and its houses. Suzanne acceded to changes. But the purpose was not merely to improve the conditions of the sisters and the way the congregation functioned. The diocesan authorities were seeing Suzanne's protests in terms of a power struggle: 'The real objection of Sister Mary Joseph Aubert here as elsewhere', Redwood would write to Rome, 'is that her absolute authority to do as she wishes, without consulting her Sisters or the ecclesiastical authority, has been brought into question.'[16] They intended to harness Suzanne once and for all – even if, as she saw it, they let this New Zealand congregation founder in the process. A woman of her age could not fight back indefinitely.[17] Breaking her hold would be done symbolically by ending three associations she held dear. First, she was to stop work with foundling children. Second, work with non-Catholics would be greatly reduced. Third, the sisters' turangawaewae link up the river could be severed.

The very notion of religious life meant the harnessing of personality and self-will to spiritual aims. It also meant, in practical terms, being harnessed to ecclesiastical authority. In this second area Suzanne's independence had been unusual. All of the measures against her now were defensible according to current trends. O'Shea was simply implementing church policy. He was being direct with Suzanne. Objections to her work and leadership were stated then and there, in an open if insensitive way. With so much coming at once, however, Suzanne felt there would be still more. Her intuition may have been right. O'Shea's antagonism was now deep-set enough for him to choose to believe that she received 'a very large sum annually from very wealthy people in this Dominion, as hush money, to look after the results of vice in high places. It is well known they are not the children of the poor.'[18] The accounts about the babies and the entries in the registers do not justify this assertion.

The trauma of the visitation, the November chapter and all the events which followed would serve as a catalyst in the long run, would eventually be a cathartic experience from which the women emerged stronger, more united and clear-sighted. But from that meeting, for over a year, feelings were raw and susceptible. Sister Bridget, Suzanne's Jerusalem companion since 1884, was now no longer on the council. After the meeting, Suzanne met her at the bottom of the stairs and exclaimed, 'Oh, Biddy, you are sent away – they have turned us both out!' Neither had been turned out. But Suzanne, perhaps more than Bridget, felt that way.

Suzanne's vulnerability shows in sixteen pages of disjointed notes in a little notebook, the draft of a letter to Bishop Verdon in Dunedin. They are dated 6 January 1913, Epiphany and the 'fourteenth anniversary of our foundation here'.[19] She felt 'so miserable and out of place'. She saw herself 'in the impossibility of doing any good and in the hourly danger of doing harm'. But how, she questioned, could everything be deemed bad when they had done so much in so few years? It had seemed guided by God: 'Whose work is it? Surely not mine.'

Suzanne's drafts are usually clear, confident, with few changes. Here line after line of crossings-out, insertions and amendments track her distress, even though one tart passage shows her still deftly counter-attacking: 'The new members of the administration under the direction of the Very Rev. Vicar General are endeavouring to repair the faults of my management [or: redress the grievance of my mismanagement] so conspicuously prejudicial to the Sisters' health that since our foundation in 1884 we have not buried a Sister yet.' There was pain in this defiance, though, because Suzanne knew then that the novice mistress, Sister Marcelle, was dying of tuberculosis. She died one week later. Suzanne loved her and relied on her. When she had been told that Marcelle would not recover, Suzanne stood still for a long time by the window of her room, silently crying. She said, 'I have not cried like this since I heard of the death of my father.'

To Verdon she forced out the pain of her feelings: 'My relations with the Sisters are unbearably strained.' It was in these pages that the story of Soulas's treatment of the sisters came out, to explain why she had resolutely kept the Buckle St sisters who had been up at Jerusalem then and the newer Island Bay community as separate as possible. Smyth and O'Shea had both criticised this enforced isolation.[20] Suzanne wrote that the whole process 'won for me the reputation of being an unbearable tyrant'.

This was not so, as Smyth's summary of the sisters' overall opinion shows, but just then she felt so alone. The jumbling within her emotionally, of the spirit of obedience and rebellion against it, of distrust combined with her more usual optimistic trust, comes in her last words: 'Now, My Lord, though the greatest sorrows and regrets of my life have been caused in the name of obedience, and though I feel such a distrust of men [or: in men], I wish to do God's Holy Will. Have pity of my weakness, help me.'

A major subject in her letter was the care of the illegitimate babies:

> I began to look after foundlings in Auckland in 1862. I have been fighting for them ever since against wind and tide under the most unfavourable conditions and now that we can harbour them . . . We must part in the name of Rome. Oh! . . . My Lord, pardon me. Where is St Vincent de Paul and his Sisters of Charity? If I were younger I would go and throw myself at the feet of the Holy Father in Rome and plead for the soul and life of the innocent victims of human frailty . . .

She dramatised a voice for the babies: 'There is no room for us on earth. Will there be one under ground or in the waves of the sea? – where so many have prematurely been heartlessly consigned before us? Won't you try to save us for His sake?'

Suzanne was not likely to give up meekly. On 28 April 1913, she sent a long letter to Redwood, who had just returned. 'I cannot believe', she wrote, 'that when Your Grace has left unlimited powers with your Very Rev. Vicar General, Your Grace intended the complete disorganisation of the Institute; and to refuse to acknowledge the several verbal and written authorisations of its works.' She outlined the times Redwood had supported her work, with foundlings in particular. Now it was being opposed on the grounds that it meant too much expense and work for the sisters, and the Holy See opposed it because 'it gave occasion to dissidents to say that Nuns were keeping Homes to shield the children of priests and nuns'. The institute had hardly any debt now, she said. The 'Divine Infant' himself had provided. 'As for sheltering children of priests and nuns', she continued, 'we have none, and if we had a few among our hundreds of others, what harm?'

She went straight on: 'When I undertook, at the Council, the defence of the foundlings, the V. R. Vicar General silenced me by saying "Sit down, whatever is said, it will be done". Surely Your Grace would not say the same.' This, she wrote, would serve only 'to destroy the confidence of the public in Catholic works, to dry the source of financial assistance'.

She tried a veiled threat: the papers might hear of this. 'I wish to keep away from Your Grace the sound of a music which would be most distressing to your ears.'

She also used the argument of public reaction as the reason for not handing over the deeds of the institute's properties. The monies for them had been given by people belonging to 'every denomination', mostly for 'the sake of the Foundlings'. The church's credibility and good faith were at stake. Her conscience rebelled, she said, when she was being ordered to hand over deeds at the same time as stop work with babies. Even though O'Shea had told her she could not appeal against his decision, she would anyway. 'I am not conscious that I ever desobeyed you before', she ended her letter to Redwood. 'I have no mind to do it in the future, but I think honestly that it is my duty to plead for the Foundlings and for justice. Happen what may to me. I humbly apologise if I have given any displeasure to Your Grace, and I crave for Your blessing, may be on a bad head [her draft has 'hot head'] but on a loyal and devoted heart.'[21]

Redwood did not intervene on her behalf. On 12 May he wrote one of his brief, carefully non-committal answers. He would not 'attempt to answer' by letter; he preferred to talk it over with her one day. Meanwhile, no baby 'would be admitted without the previous permission of the Ordinary [O'Shea], as I believe is the case at present'.[22] Did he really think a bland message like this would disarm her? In Auckland in 1871, when Bishop Croke expected to appropriate for other purposes the funds Suzanne had in hand for a native institute, she had stubbornly tramped the streets of Auckland, ill and exhausted, handing the money back to the various donors.[23] Redwood might not have heard this story. But he would have been expecting high-calibre resistance, and he avoided her on his return. It was said among the clergy that the diocesan councillors did not want him to meet her personally; 'she would talk His Grace over' just when they were trying 'to set things to rights'.[24] When he did come to the Home of Compassion, he did not see Suzanne at all, although she sent word that she would like to speak to him. Instead, he spent almost two hours solely with the new assistants. It seems a cowardly and hurtful action.

An even bleaker future, in Suzanne's eyes, soon stretched before the Sisters of Compassion. In May, O'Shea was appointed coadjutor archbishop, Redwood's assistant with the automatic right to succeed him as archbishop when he died. From that moment Suzanne would know that, as a diocesan congregation in Wellington, and probably also in Auckland under Cleary, they would lose most of their independence of initiative. On 22 May she wrote to Sister Bridget in Jerusalem: 'You must know that Father O'Shea is now Archbishop Coadjutor with right of succession. Things are very much laughed at here about the babies. Nothing will be decided before three or four weeks. Pray hard. The Institute has never been in such a pass. God bless you all. In haste.'[25]

As June and July went by, Suzanne made a decision. The only hope was to become a separate, papal congregation. Even though old, she would take her 'hot head' and her 'loyal and devoted heart' to Rome to fight for her foundlings and for the independence of her institute. The precarious solidarity at that time in the community, so tightly instructed by O'Shea, meant that she could not confide in the sisters. Constitutionally, they owed obedience to him. Emotionally, they were all torn.

She quietly travelled up to Takapau in Hawke's Bay to discuss the affair with her benefactor and friend, Sydney Johnston, and came away with a £50 cheque for her boat fare.[26] She consulted with five priests, who gave her a letter of recommendation.[27] This was also a political move on their part. They were secular, diocesan priests who were then strongly opposing the Marist O'Shea's appointment as coadjutor archbishop.[28]

Edwin Arnold, who made the prams for her, and Dr Kington Fyffe were also privy to her plans. Fyffe wrote for her a warm defence of her work with the babies: 'if your work was done away with there would be a blank left which could not be filled – I unhesitatingly say that it would be a *crime*, because your Institution is the only one of its kind in the colony which is open and free to any class and any religion. I am not a member of your Communion but of the Church of England and on this ground, as well as upon the medical basis, I am proud to be able to bear testimony on behalf of the noble work you have beg[u]n and carried out in this colony.'[29]

Meanwhile, Suzanne was stalling for time over the trust deeds, which were still in her name alone.[30] Her sole ownership of publicly funded properties was highly irregular. She had tried in 1911 to reassure Bishop Cleary that there would be 'no trouble about it at the time of my death, as everything will be going into the hands of trustees belonging to the Institute for the benefit of the different works established . . . in order that the intentions of the benefactors should be carried out'.[31] The bishops argued, with reason, that her will could be contested by her next of kin. But Suzanne kept her name alone on the deeds as her trump card to ensure that the original purpose would not be deflected or usurped. If she signed them over, any trustees from among the sisters would also be joined by the local bishop. Control of the properties and of their use would effectively be lost.

Her lawyer, Charles Skerrett, drafted a letter which she sent to O'Shea on 11 February. It suggested that she should wait until Redwood returned before signing the transfer of the property. O'Shea's answer was predictable. His letter of 5 February had not been a 'request' but 'his decision . . . and from it there is no appeal in the proper sense of the term. For the decision of the Vicar General in the present circumstances is the decision of the Archbishop, since His Grace and his Vicar General constitute one and the same tribunal. . . . Consequently the decision that was given last year must be obeyed. When you have done this and not before, you can have recourse to the Holy See and ask it to review my decision.'[32] She was to obey 'this command' within twenty-one days.

On Skerrett's advice and her own inclination, she did not obey. Skerrett's carefully worded memoranda of 19 December 1912 and 18 July 1913 reviewed both canon and secular law and concluded that the bishops could suppress the works of the congregation but not the congregation itself, nor treat its property as church property. He also considered that Redwood's lack of consultation with her was unethical. Skerrett concluded: 'I trust that I may be permitted to express the wish that you will be successful in your effort to frustrate the attempt to divert to other purposes the moneys which have been contributed for distinct and definite purposes.'[33]

Skerrett also helped her prepare her own statement, in which she reiterated: 'I feel bound to emphatically state that these subscriptions were given and received upon the faith that these institutions were undenominational and conducted upon an undenominational basis.' In it she acknowledged she was under religious obedience. 'Nevertheless I desire it to be understood that if I am called upon to obey I shall do so only because of the solemn obligation of my vow and under the compulsion of that obligation.'[34] Along with other crucial lay support, Skerrett's documents went with her to Rome. In one letter to him in October 1916, she told him: 'you have been my best and wisest friend in all my difficulties'.[35]

In July Suzanne went back up to Jerusalem. There on that winter

Sunday morning, for whatever reason, she burnt her private correspondence with its family record, as she would also do in Wellington. It was
then that Sister Rosalie caught the smell of burning wool and found
Suzanne standing by the fireplace built of river stones, with her skirt
alight. Early next morning Suzanne boarded the riverboat in the same
habit, with a new panel hurriedly sewn in. She would have looked back at
Hiruharama as the boat rounded the bend on the way down to Moutoa
Island – the familiar and loved cluster of houses around the two marae,
and the church, convent and presbytery on the rise above them. She knew
there would be a long trip to Rome before she could come again. In fact,
it was the last time she saw Hiruharama.

> *To go on board a steamboat : Ke kupu mo te eke kaipuke tima*
> *I have only a carpet bag : He putea anake taku*[36]

Suzanne had a simple list of a few clothes to take, written in a mix of
French and English, as were so many of her recipes and household hints.
Alongside the bottom of the list, down by '1 *tablier neuf* [new apron],
1 cape *neuf*, 1 *voile neuf*, a whole habit, 4 p red stockings, 3 p black new
stockings, 6 p ditto old, 1 old habit . . . 12 collars, 4 caps', come the words
'*Sac* Isa' – Isa's bag.[37]

Isa was Louisa Outhwaite, Suzanne's friend from the 1860s in
Auckland. The Outhwaite home had been her haven when Bishop Croke
put an end to her work. Once Suzanne was regularly going to Auckland
again, the friendship with the three remaining Outhwaites – Isa, Victorine
and Charlie – had been renewed. In the time of distress before her
departure, Suzanne was living mainly in the Auckland community. Once
more, this family came to her aid. Through the kaleidoscope of Suzanne's
correspondence with Isa, her candid friendship with laypeople is glimpsed
in vibrant changing colours. Her affection, warmth and humour, her good
and bad moods, her astuteness and determination, her devotion and piety,
her homesickness, are all there. Suzanne would always be desperate for
mail. She wrote to Isa soon after arriving in Rome: 'My heart lipped
[leaped] with joy when I received you[r] dear letter, I could have jumped
summer salts, for you are the only friend who does not seem to have
forgotten me in New Zealand.'[38]

Isa's bag went with Suzanne everywhere: 'You remember the black
work bag you kindly gave me when I left, well, it does all the campagne

with me, like the Napsack of the soldiers, carrying my over all and my provisions of all sorts. The dear old bag! it will be a fine keepsake. It brings you constantly before my mind.'[39] Suzanne had chosen the right word. Isa's support and friendship remained constant. When Suzanne left, she had Isa handle her mail. It was Isa who took her to the wharf on 1 August 1913 and saw her safely on board the *Niagara*; it was Isa who broke the news to the sisters in Mt Eden; it was Isa who saw them struggling to come to terms with it.

Suzanne had gone without telling them. But she wrote them letter after letter as soon as she was away. If they had known she was going without diocesan permission, they might have been conscience-bound to tell their ultimate superior, the archbishop. Suzanne did send a letter by the pilot boat to Redwood, too late for him to order her back, but as soon as she safely could. The 'strain of the last ten months' was sending her to Rome, 'trusting in God and in His supreme Representative on earth'. She asked for Redwood's blessing. 'I only stand for the works you have established and sanctioned and which must be dear to your heart.'[40]

Suzanne, the poor sailor, endured the sea voyage to Vancouver. But among the passengers were lay friends from Wanganui. She had company and support. Even though she was a seasoned train traveller, she found the long stretch across Canada tiring. At Sainte Anne de Beaupré on the St Lawrence River, she suddenly found again her world of over fifty years before – the world of piety, relics, shrines, pilgrimages and miracles. It had been largely missing in her missionary life in a mainly Protestant culture. She was deeply moved by the devotion of the pilgrims at Sainte Anne de Beaupré. It was the first of many shrines she would visit while away.

In England, she promptly set about strengthening her case. 'You would have been pleased', she wrote to Isa, 'to hear of the exceeding kindness of our three last Governors whom I met in London, Lords Ranfurly, Plunket and Islington. They rivalised in graciousness . . . The Ladies paid me all sorts of delicate attentions, and I grew conscious that the shorter the stay the better for me.' While she was there, she visited 'several of Dr Barna[r]do's Homes, and other such places to see how they were conducted and with what results'.[41]

The three former governors supplied Suzanne with letters of support. She had 'devoted her whole energy and life to the benefit of her fellow creatures. Whilst I occupied the position of Governor of this Dominion', wrote Islington, 'I had the privilege of being brought into contact with her.'[42] Ranfurly thought the same: 'I knew Mother Aubert well as a worker in the interest of child welfare. . . . I can personally testify to Mother Aubert's great energy and her determined efforts in the interests of the mothers and children.'[43]

Suzanne had crossed to Ireland, then back to England, to catch up with Plunket. Her work was 'magnificent', he wrote: 'The work carried out by this Lady is, in my opinion, one of the finest charities in that dominion and she is respected and beloved, and her name honoured, by all classes and creeds in New Zealand.' He gave her the endorsement she wanted: 'Probably the most useful part of her work is the reception of illegitimate babies on behalf of their unfortunate mothers, and the method [by which] she carries out this delicate task has helped very many young women to regain their lost characters and to successfully start life again.' He wrote more in the same vein, then concluded:

> I consider it an honour to be permitted to testify my admiration for the Home of Compassion and my respect for the indomitable energy and noble self-sacrifice of Mother M. J. Aubert, and I know that this is the general feeling amongst the public and the Press in New Zealand.[44]

These statements were in a way defining for the Sisters of Compassion what is termed the charism. This 'admiration', 'respect', and 'general feeling' for the spirit of the Home of Compassion and Mother Aubert could testify to the purpose of charism, which was 'to make the Church visible and credible as the holy People of God'.[45]

Suzanne also found support among New Zealanders in London, reporting happily back to Isa: 'The High Commissioner was very nice. I met Mr Douglas McLean at his office. He and his Mrs. were well, and contemplated spending part of the winter in Rome. I met friends every-where.'[46] Former Prime Minister Thomas Mackenzie's letter as High Commissioner for New Zealand joined the former governors' in her growing dossier for Rome. She had obviously impressed on each man that the work for the babies was to be emphasised, because that was at stake. Her 'philanthropic efforts especially in connection with her Foundling Hospital', wrote Mackenzie, 'have, I am sure, in recent years met with the support of all right thinking people. I should be glad to learn that Mother Aubert's further endeavours on behalf of humanity are crowned with success.'[47]

She will be cordially received : Ka rahiria mariretia ia e matou[48]

More than fifty years before, Suzanne had made a vow that, if only she were helped to leave France, she would not return. That was her sacrifice. Now she had to be persuaded to cross it, and she went as quickly as possible 'to avoid french soil'.[49] A crowded Rome, packed with pilgrims for the jubilee of Constantine, looked suspiciously at the shabby little old woman. She was dressed as a religious but she was on her own. Convent after convent was full, or else said it was. Propaganda Fide finally found her accommodation at the convent of Our Lady of Sion.

Suzanne had every intention of completing her business and returning to New Zealand as soon as possible. With the help of contacts among the Sulpicians, especially Monsignor Ercole, she arranged her first meeting with Monsignor Laurenti, the secretary of Propaganda Fide. With him was Monsignor Pecorari, who handled affairs connected with New Zealand. None of them knew then that a bulging file would build up over the years before the *'vieille soeur des Antipodes',* the old Sister from the Antipodes, as she called herself, would say goodbye to Rome.

Suzanne did not, of course, have the necessary letters of support from the ordinaries (the local bishops). Redwood had been taken aback by her departure. A prompt letter to his fellow Marist in Rome, Father Copéré, shows this: 'I find her proceeding a very strange one. She is 77 years of age and, perhaps, her mind is somewhat affected. . . . My purpose is to put you on your guard, so that nothing may be settled by Propaganda, or by any other Sacred Congregation, before the whole matter has been referred to the Archbishop of Wellington, whom she has not consulted about her voyage, and whose permission she has neither sought nor obtained.'[50]

But Laurenti, Pecorari and Cardinal Gotti, Prefect of Propaganda, read her explanations, memoranda, letters of introduction, and copies of previous correspondence over the years with Redwood and others. She had brought copies of anything relevant in support. She would spend the next six years writing, copying and translating. In October 1913, she wrote optimistically to Isa:

> My business is now at the Propaganda where they excuse me for having gone without permission. I had to translate everything in french and an explanation is going to be asked from Wellington. But they are well disposed here for the foundlings and so far there is fair hope to save them. I have seen twice Our Holy Father in company with some pilgrims. I have got His blessing

for you, dearest, also for Victorine, for Charly, for my Sisters [and the] babies. I am to have a private audience.[51]

Suzanne said that she pleaded the cause of the babies with Pius X and he blessed her for having come and told her it was 'the work of God'.[52] She said that Cardinal Gotti was 'favourable to the cause of the children, but communications were to be exchanged with New Zealand before anything could be finally settled'. 'Propaganda is very kind. I implicitly trust in it after God.'[53] Gotti would be a worthwhile ally, and one who could appreciate Suzanne's personality and sense of vocation. He was her own age, and extremely intelligent and capable. He was known for his ascetic lifestyle, his dedication to hard work, and his devotion to serving and expanding missions.[54] In 1903 he had been considered as a likely successor to Pope Leo XIII. As Prefect of Propaganda Fide he promoted the granting of Decrees of Praise to missionary congregations such as the Maryknoll and Mill Hill fathers. He would not be likely to dismiss her case out of hand, despite Redwood's initial request for Propaganda 'kindly to be firm and strict with her' and send her straight home.

She told Isa of her audience with Pope Pius X: 'I pleaded for my babies, but nothing has been decided yet. The whole matter has been sent to N.Z. to know what their Graces have to say, and I have been recommended meantime to hold my tongue and say nothing. So my lips are sealed for the present. I meet with much kindness.' She was hopeful but also realistic. 'Dairie,' she asked Isa, 'write to me and let me know plainly what is going on, good or bad, I wish to know the plain honest truth. Nothing is worst than uncertainty, and besides, I have to prepare my batteries for I expect a hard struggle.'[55]

The hard struggle would come over the properties. If she signed over the trust deeds, she predicted that the work for the babies would be 'undermined', suppressed, altered to incorporate Catholic maternity work, or the number of admissions restricted 'to a few favoured Catholics', in this way going 'against the known and formal wishes of the benefactors'.[56] If she did not sign, she would not receive the required 'letters of praise' from the two New Zealand dioceses. The document she laid before Propaganda stated her position then:

> I now humbly beg the Holy See to examine the cause of the foundlings, and to allow me to place the management of the Institute properties, which are all in my name, in the hands of the Archbishop and reputable laymen, charging

them to watch over the work for foundlings, in order that it may be continued on the same footing as it was prior to November, 1912, and that the donations of benefactors shall be employed in accordance with their intentions.[57]

She explained more to Skerrett on 15 July 1914: 'I expect that the next news will be that I have been put out of office . . . then I would have no power or voice at all, and the only means left to me of protesting, in order to secure the future, would be the holding of the deeds of the properties.' Significantly, she felt encouraged by Propaganda, which 'has, so far, given me no command (in which case I would be bound to obey). It leaves me a certain amount of latitude. Our Holy Father, who cannot personally interfere, shows me sympathy and bids me to have courage. I need it.'[58]

Suzanne stayed in Rome for six years. The progress of her case slowed at times almost to a halt, documents being lost at one stage on a shelf at the Congregation of Religious. She sensed she needed to wait to see the process out, even if, as she wrote to the Whitakers, her bookseller friends from Lambton Quay: 'I do not stay here for my own enjoyment. I miss home very much.'[59] O'Shea recognised her strength of purpose: 'she appears to have no intention of returning, unless she gets her own way. However, nobody would wish her back except for the fact that the title of the lands etc. ought to be put in proper order.'[60]

By 4 April 1915, she was explaining to Isa: 'My own affairs are on the "Stand Still" untill a letter from Bishop Cleary arrives; then it will be resumed to be finished when?' She wrote: 'Our Holy Father very graciously gave me words of great encouragement lately, but all is not finished yet, but I am in gre[a]t hopes. Only they are such slow coaches here.' The thread ran through her letters. The 'network of red tapes here is something awful'. It was the 'land of taihoa'. 'Had Our Lord been judged in Rome, He would have been living still!'[61] Suzanne, in her loneliness, learnt to wait as best she could:

> I have plenty of writing to do, and when my head and eyes akes to much, I fly on a round of the city. I visit churches, Institutions, catacombs, old ruins. I talk with God and the departed. Very little with the living. Still I have a faithful visiteur who comes, not through the door, but through the wi[n]dow to keep me compagnie. You guess, a dear old grey pussy cat, who rubs himself against my legs, looks at me, says Miew, and coils himself at my feet to sleep. You would love him.[62]

Isa was an animal lover like Suzanne herself.

Bracketed between her arrival and departure lay the years of world war. The war would disrupt communications and lose letter after letter for her. It would also bring extreme privation to her life in Italy, once that country too declared war on Germany. Her homegoing would be blocked and her days filled with nursing war-wounded and caring for refugees. She cut back further on food to buy the liberal paper, *Il Messagero*, and scan its columns for reports of New Zealand soldiers in battle. Standing at the newspaper kiosk, lost in its pages, she was unaware that this would scandalise the clergy. A religious should be seen reading only the conservative Vatican-approved papers – which would not have the reportage she craved. A passing monsignor told her off.

On 19 June 1915, her eightieth birthday, Suzanne wrote to Sister Dolores up the river at Jerusalem: 'Our Maori contingent was greatly admired and was highly praised in the papers the other week. How much I would like to meet some of them. I am sure we would have a good "tangi". Most of them are in the Dardanelles. God have mercy on them, especially on their poor souls. Pray hard for them.' And she added a message, sending her love: 'Ma te Atua koutou e manahaki. Kia ora. Waimarie. Na te koutou hoa aroha, Na Meri Hopeha.'[63]

Good news was so scarce, she said. Once Italy was in the war, there was no coloured clothing around her any more; everyone was in mourning. A touch of jingoism and hyperbole crept in from her reading: 'The galantry of our troopers is much exalted also: the papers spoke yesterday of a N.Z. boy who killed 200 germans with his own hand. Isn't he a wonderful lad!! May he be spared himself. Many people are speaking of visiting our marvellous Island after the war. It is becoming more and more celebrated every day. Maui must be very proud of his fishing and of his sons, who are really very good.' In July 1916 she was worrying for her boys: 'We have intense heat, no rain at all. How welcome a bit of Wellington brise [breeze] would be! I heard that seven of our foundlings are at the front, how many more will go, and how many will return?'[64]

She wanted to be part of it all, too. She had already tried in October 1914: 'I wanted to go to the front with the Red Cross with the allies, but Propaganda will not allow me to go, though everything was arranged.'[65] At the end of 1916, she was still wistful: 'I heard, this morning, that Bishop Cleary and Bishop Clune are visiting the Australian soldiers at the front. I wish I was there also. Though I can walk a long distance it is now at a slow pace. Our body does not keep young for ever.'[66]

Suzanne did work actively through the war. She had started with the huge earthquake in January 1915, centred on the Abruzzi town of Avezzano. Rome was 'like an immense hospital where trains and automobiles are following one another, loaded with wounded, mangled bodies and half demented refugies'. 'The authorities at first declined to enroll me, thinking that, owing to my age, I could not work. At last a grand doctor took me on trial on his staff, and the next day I heard from him: "You work like a horse, we have plenty work for you".' The nursing renewed her energy and she enjoyed the company of the surgeons. 'With some I carry on double duty very pleasantly, they teaching me Italian and I teaching them French, as we work away on minced limbs and perforated bodies.'

She spoke of 'stolid eyes' from shock, of rats gnawing to stumps the hands and feet of people trapped under rubble, of flesh minced with 'bones, gravel, cement and dirt'. She collected her food in a billy from a soup kitchen, and nursed from six in the morning to eight in the evening, dressing wounds first, then massaging injuries in the afternoon. The massage, she explained to Sister Claver, was why her handwriting was 'awfully shaky', but 'I thank God to be able to be on my feet from morning till night, running as quickly as the young Nurses'. 'When I am hard at it', she wrote to Isa, 'I feel quite young again and never feel tired until it is over. Oh, Isa dear, work is a great blessing. I appreciate it more than ever.' The hard work kept her 'out of the madhouse'.[67]

With Propaganda's approval, she enrolled in the Italian Red Cross, confidently wearing her New Zealand St John Ambulance medal as though it were the medal of a registered nurse. When the convoys of war-wounded came in, she carried on through the 'stifling heat', 'the fleas and moskitoes', the threat of cholera. She recalled how at eighteen she had nursed cholera victims, and thought she could 'volunteer again at eighty'. Later, her doctoring spirit was enthused by rehabilitation work: 'The education of the disabled soldiers is very successful. What a boon it will be for many noble men who otherwise would have had the perspective of a most miserable life. The methods are very interesting. Are you doing anything in that line in New Zealand? I suppose you will.'[68]

As poverty and hunger hit the people of Rome, her nursing moved also into the slums. 'I am doing more of private nursing in wretched hovels and under circumstances that bafle description. Oh! the scenes of witness I never saw before, I never dreamt of. It is heart rending. We often exchange our thoughts by silent looks. What a language the eyes can speak, especially when they express the feelings of the heart, of a crushed, agonising heart.'[69] She caught lice along with her patients, and the kindly Sisters of Sion began to look a little askance at their boarder.

Suzanne busily 'Martha-ed' through her days in city hospitals and slum homes. But, with her characteristic blend of Saint-Nizier activity and Fourvière devotion, she also brought the reflectiveness of Mary of Bethany to her life in Rome. Her spirit soaked up the reverent atmosphere in the churches, whether everyday simplicity or feast-day ceremony. Her musician's heart responded to the Gregorian chant, whose revival Pius X was strongly encouraging. She wrote to Edwin Arnold: 'I never heard such melody as I heard in a catacombe thirty feet underground. It will ring in my ears till my last day. It was the yearly High Mass in the Crypte of St Cecilia.'[70]

Before she began her nursing again, she had been in as many churches as she could, praying for the sisters and the congregation, for her case, for her friends. She enrolled them at shrines under the protection of each saint. With a pilgrim's enthusiasm she wrote to Isa soon after arriving: 'Since I've been here I've visited 228 churches; I'm told I've still got 137 to go. I find that hard to believe. I cannot imagine where they are.' By February 1914 she had found most of them. 'I have visited 325 churches or holy places in Rome, and every where a loving mention of your names was made.'[71]

During 1914, Suzanne went to the shrines at Genezzano, Assisi, Campocavallo and Loreto, where the simple house of the Family of Nazareth was believed to be. Gabrielle Périer, her cousin from Tarare, had recently died, leaving her some money, and she gained permission from Propaganda to go on these pilgrimages, funding them with Gabrielle's bequest. With folded handkerchief, she surreptitiously wiped the walls of the house at Loreto, so that she could bring back motes of dust. She just managed to save the precious handkerchief from the eagerly laundering hands of her sisters on her return to New Zealand. Other mementoes of relics grew into a collection. 'I send you a leaf of box', she wrote to Isa, 'which has touched the very spot on which stood the ca[u]ldron of boiling oil in which St Jean was plunged. It is only a small memorial of a wonderful miracle. Wherever I go, I try to bring back a little keepsake. If you saw my indescribable miscellaneous collection you would laugh at me I know.'[72]

The figure of the Bambino, the baby Jesus at the Franciscan shrine of

Ara Coeli, became her symbol for the work with the babies. Soon after she arrived, she wrote to Isa: 'I go every day to pray at the shrine of the Bambino. I send you a picture that has touched Him. You know that he was carved by a monk in a piece of olive tree from the garden of Getsemani and painted miraculously at night by Saint Luc.'[73] To Sister Carmel, who had not been well, she wrote: 'I have great hope that the Divine Bambino will win the case. He does so many wonderful things in Rome. I love to visit Him every day. We have long talks together, and I will have a very special one for you. His Custodian, a dear old Franciscan Father, has said Masses at His altar for my intentions, and he has always such encouraging words and fatherly smiles.'[74]

In Rome, Suzanne's bond with the Curé of Ars became stronger than ever. Her belief in his influence on her life-story and on the history of the Sisters of Compassion seemed more than vindicated. The 'statue of the saintly Curé of Ars', she told Carmel, 'is on our Holy Father's working table. A Monsignor was telling me the other day in speaking of the Bambino and of the Holy Curé: "You have in them very powerful advocates".'[75]

Suzanne said she helped with the growing dossier of the canonisation process, then well under way. She told Sister Angela: 'Somebody was telling me the other week: "I did not know you were on such good terms with the Curé d'Ars; your affairs will go well".'[76] Pius X had been actively promoting his cause, and Suzanne wrote to Sister Claver in July 1915 that the last recommendation of the Pope to her before he died was 'to place our affairs in the hands of the Holy Curé d'Ars'.[77] Suzanne's link with the curé worked well for her case. Jean Vianney, beatified but not yet canonised, was placed among the patron saints of her congregation. A Redemptorist priest wrote to her in 1919: 'don't forget that the Blessed Curé has his spiritual guns and submarines ready to fight your battles and help your order to do its work properly, for was it not he that decided your vocation?'[78]

The expression of her faith might have been simple and direct in her life out in New Zealand, but Suzanne would always be intensely moved by the beauty of liturgy. She wrote a pages-long letter describing Holy Week in Rome. She found especially powerful the effect of the Maundy Thursday Mass in San Giovanni in Laterano:

> Holy Communion was almost constantly given to a crowd of people of every nationality, who like the ocean waves, were coming, rising and retiring with a

murmure of prayer and a wonderful regularity. The atmosphere was one of mingled awe and love. The Divine Presence was penetrating you in a manner unknown at any other Altar. I never felt anything like it. No wonder. Above that Altar was solemnly exposed a very large piece (about four or five feet long) of the table on which Our Lord instituted the Holy Eucharist, and gave His Own Divine Body and Blood, as food to His Apostles. It was as if receiving Holy Communion from the Hand of Our Lord Himself. To try to express the feelings of one's own heart would be a useless and almost a sacrilegeous attempt. . . . The depth of the emotion nearly takes your breath away: your very self seems ebbing in the embrace of Jesus. I cannot find words to speak of it any longer.[79]

As the war gradually brought many religious into the haven of their mother houses, Suzanne had to find new accommodation:

I have just now a very hard time. The Rev Mother of the Convent where I lodge gave me notice to leave a fourthnight ago. Since that, I have knocked in vain at 52 convent doors. They all answered, We have no room, and I am not permitted to live in any private family. It is a bad note in Rome. I am worried more than I can tell, and my old legs stiffly protest against running from morning till night all over Rome for a shelter.

Propaganda has always been kind to me, and I hope that they will take the matter in hand and find a corner for me somewhere. The running and the worry make me dizzy.[80]

Father Pietro Fumasoni-Biondi, a canon attached to the staff of Propaganda Fide, arranged an exemption for her to live the rest of her time in Rome in the attic of his father and mother's home, where he and his younger sister were also living at the time. Suzanne told Sister Claver she 'was treated as one of the family' from the first. Suzanne coached Fumasoni-Biondi in English, and also convinced him that his sister, Agata, was right to marry instead of entering religious life. In December 1916, Suzanne wrote to Isa: 'The venerable Canon in whose house I live has been made Archbishop and Apostolic Delegate in India. . . . He is only forty four years of age and is likely on the way to a Cardinalate. He is an old college mate of the present Pope. He is a kindly, saintly man with a dignified appearance.'[81]

She was right about his future. Fumasoni-Biondi became a cardinal in 1933 and Prefect of the Sacred College of Propaganda, where he had first met Suzanne. He also became Cardinal Protector of the Sisters of Compassion.[82] Over the years, first Suzanne's then the sisters' letters to him and his family kept the friendship warm. Fumasoni-Biondi's father, Filippo, wrote to her once: 'I have always had for you unlimited esteem

With space now available at the Home of Compassion, Suzanne once more worked with babies.
ZAK, HOC A

'Nursing Staff' at the Home of Compassion, c.1908. Suzanne wanted her sisters to be state-recognised trained nurses. Suzanne sits forward in her chair, with her hands typically spread in her lap. Sister Angela, later her secretary, is on the far left of the middle row. ZAK, HOC A

St Vincent's Home in Mt Eden, Auckland, in 1910.

Bishop George Lenihan.

Young girls on the front steps of St Vincent's.

Henry Cleary,
Bishop of Auckland
ACDA

Vicar General
Thomas O'Shea.　　MAW

O'Shea's consecration as
Coadjutor Archbishop in
1913: from left, Bishop
Verdon of Dunedin, O'Shea,
Archbishop Redwood, Bishop
Cleary of Auckland.
MAW

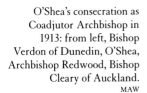

The sisters share Christmas dinner at Hiruharama in 1916.

The sisters
continued to ride
horses, despite
objections.

With Ngati Ruaka
at Ranana, the
sisters farewell
World War One
soldiers, 1917.
Neri Metera stands
in the centre; his
wife, Taho Miriama,
is third from left,
back row.

Sister Clotilde, the trained nurse who helped Suzanne in the negotiations to begin state nursing training.

Mother Aubert, aged ninety: 'She was a tiny little woman, a plain woman. She had a very strong face – a strong wide jaw – and determined looking, but when she smiled, her whole face lit up, the face smiled.'

Hester Maclean, as Director of Nursing, supported Suzanne's nursing project.

Suzanne's coffin leaves the Home of Compassion on 4 October 1926. Rure (left rear) helps carry it to the hearse. *NZ FREE LANCE*

Sister Carmel leads the waiting sisters. *NZ FREE LANCE*

Harry Ashworth (seen here with Father Devoy blessing the new collection van) was altar boy at her funeral.

Outside St Mary of the Angels after Suzanne's Requiem Mass.

The sisters at Karori Cemetery walk down the path lined by boys from St Patrick's College. The pallbearers walk alongside, with Rure at the back.

Suzanne wrote shortly before she died: 'Rivers do not return to their own source.'
The Whanganui flows down to the sea.   ANNE NOBLE, 1980

and have been attracted by your qualities of character. . . . All of us in the house thank you for that rich lesson given to us how to live united with God, and for that lesson in economy which is the secret of a long life. You must excuse me for wanting to speak these truths, but you must accept them because they have given an example to us and were handed on to others. Your stay in Rome was wonderful.'[83] Agata's daughter remembers hearing how the family loved Suzanne but how she insisted on living her simple, solitary, ascetic life, declining to join in any comforts and living on what seemed a diet mainly of *cipolle*, onions.

The waiting and working for the Decree of Praise did seem to her like a series of trials. Her case had appeared to be progressing steadily under Pius X, but he died on 20 August 1914. The changeover to the papacy of Benedict XV would have slowed the process. Then Cardinal Gotti died, in March 1916. Cardinal Serafini succeeded him as Prefect of Propaganda. Yet the wait was in essence a blessing – or, as she would have put it, a 'God sent'. Suzanne in Rome – living with her simplicity and extreme poverty, working long hours of physical labour, writing into the night with her astute mind, handling her case with diplomatic aplomb, worshipping at shrine after shrine and making at each a 'visit of supplication' for the future of her work, praying as she went – was herself the strongest argument which finally gained for her congregation its Decree of Praise.

Serafini, in a long memorandum to Cardinal Falconio, Prefect of the Sacred Congregation of Religious, referred to 'this good Sister, more than eighty years old, . . . waiting here and praying fervently – *pregando fervidamente*'.[84] Respect in the covering summaries grew into support. For some, the support warmed into affection touching on veneration. In 1919 Sulpician Monsignor Ercole told her: 'When I think of the six years that you spent in Rome, during which your goodness enkindled my spirit, and your energy renewed mine, it seems to me I lived in a beautiful dream.'[85]

Going to Rome was also in the long run a blessing for the community of sisters back in New Zealand, though they did not think so in the first shock of her leaving. When she went, she thought she had left affairs in order for them. But she tried to block diocesan control by having Skerrett handle her bank account and Isa Outhwaite her correspondence, otherwise the diocesan superior would have the right to read all mail. The sisters were for a while penniless until they, Skerrett and O'Shea sorted out another system. Sister Angela remembered early on taking a pile of bills and the empty cash-box to the Sanctuary and leaving them on the steps while she 'asked Our Lord to do something about the matter'.[86]

Yet the long wait, with its many reinforcing letters, was enough for them to understand what was at stake, to comprehend and trust Suzanne's action. In the same way, Suzanne once more trusted them. She would send 'motherly love to all the Sisters' and enclose individual letters. When new caps, sewn for her by Sister Martha, arrived safely in their careful packaging, Suzanne wrote that they brought 'such a perfume of Home'.[87]

Six years were also enough to allow the senior sisters to develop from apprentices to true managers, unimpeded by Suzanne. Sister Claver might have seemed an unlikely woman to be left in charge. She never did project the conventional strong qualities of leadership. But her homely spirit was a respite. Her letters point to a courteous, facilitating atmosphere that worked towards resolutions wherever possible without compromising lightly on the congregation's ideals.

So affairs were never at a stand-still with the Sisters of Compassion. They rebuilt the crèche, improved the routine of childrearing and standardised it under the Plunket system – the first institution in Wellington to do so. They obtained government inspection and advice for the schools up the river. The report on Sister Damien at Ranana reads: 'Very Good indeed. Very modern methods are used, the children are alert & intelligent and the results are admirable.'[88] The minutes show they arranged for Sister Damien to train for a Teachers' D Certificate.[89] The help of the public continued. Suzanne knew that the institute was surviving safely when she heard how the men of Island Bay had arranged a big working bee to gather firewood for the sisters. Allan Orr and the union men carried on helping. All was well, she felt, if St Joseph was still at work for them.

The sisters held safe and nurtured what they knew now was also *their* vision for their congregation and its work. They carried on being strong women. Father Vibaud protested to O'Shea from Jerusalem: 'The Sisters believe and they often told me that they are in charge of the mission as well as the priest. Sr Veronica told me that were I a gentleman I would do nothing without letting the Sisters know as it was done in the past.'[90]

Even though they received hardly any postulants through these years, a lack which would affect their work for a generation to come, they carried on.[91] No woman left the Daughters of Our Lady of Compassion in all this time, in spite of encouragement from some clergy to do so. Sister Clotilde once stressed: 'We just didn't [fizzle out], & though conditions were hard and we had nothing but alms to live on, *none of us left*.'[92] The theology of weathering tests and trials to bring you nearer to the glory of God strengthened the sisters, even if they did not all subscribe to it with the same gritty keenness as Suzanne. On 7 June 1915 she wrote to Angela: 'Now let us put our shoulders together to pull in the right direction. . . . The greater the efforts of the Opposition will be, the better for us, because God will stand Himself for the defence of His work.'[93]

Suzanne once gave Sister Claver a message for the sisters: 'Keep stirring on straight to God in spite of the difficulties.'[94] She meant 'steering', but 'stirring on' suited the hard work the women put in. As time went by, their constancy and energy, and what a former Marist provincial, Dean Pierre Regnault, called their 'deep, lively faith', gained respect. He wrote to Sister Claver from Waimate on 25 August 1916: 'So holy is the work you are doing that God will not abandon you. He may send you crosses as proof of His love, but He will help you to plant your Institute deep in the soil of the garden of the Church.'[95] When he wrote this, the sisters were facing perhaps their toughest time. Bishop Cleary had just closed down St Vincent's home in Auckland.

Henry Cleary never gave Suzanne his support for the Decree of Praise, even though she had needed it. Such a small congregation of fifty women would not normally be considered; as well, she had only the fluctuating support of one diocesan leader, Archbishop Redwood. At the outset, Redwood had sent to Rome seventeen pages of background detail, well-argued criticisms of her management, and doubts about the aims of the institute.[96] By December 1914, when he was again in Rome, he had reconsidered, and wrote his request to the Pope to grant the Decree of Praise. He included the work for illegitimate children.[97] Rome had already given its approval for this in April, 'not only for the present, but also in the future'.

When Suzanne went to Rome, she had at first been hopeful that Cleary would send a letter of recommendation. Pecorari at Propaganda finally sent a cable in March 1915: 'anxiously expecting laudative letter for Compassionist Sisters'.[98] Instead, Cleary's opposition grew into a personal campaign against her, which had as much to do with his own ill health as with the issue at stake. On doctors' orders he was to do no work for three months in late 1915. Isa reported that hundreds of letters were piling up for his attention. Suzanne wrote to Sister Clotilde on 20 February 1916: 'Pray much for poor Bishop Cleary. He must suffer a good deal from his inaction. I am glad that his displeasure is more against your humble servant than against the Institute.'[99] Suzanne would usually find a positive way of viewing things: 'As for the Most Rev. Coadjutor and Bishop C., they are instruments in the hands of God', she reassured Angela, 'to show by their opposition that the Institute is His work. Let us pray hard for them and have patience. They will not be able to resist the Quadruple Bambino, Pius X, Bl. Vianney, and St Joseph.'[100]

Cleary's nerves were always taut, but he later strained them further as a chaplain in the front-line trenches over the harsh winter of 1916-17. This brought him almost to the point of physical and emotional break-down.[101] Adding to the stresses on him would be the growing antipathy in Auckland between Catholics and Protestants. Later in the war, this was fuelled on the one side by Catholic rallying to support Ireland's bid for liberty, especially after the Easter Rising of 1916. On the other side, the formation of the extremist Protestant Political Association fanned anti-Catholic feelings. Cleary's opposition to Suzanne's work being open to other denominations was partially formed out of this growing antagonism.

Cleary still wanted St Vincent's home to handle maternity work for unmarried Catholic women, to counterbalance the Salvation Army and Anglican alternatives. Suzanne disliked the inevitable branding of the women, and did not want to take the work on. If Cleary was a trustee, he could possibly force the issue. An impasse developed over both the property titles and the maternity work. It was an 'unpleasant situation', as Cleary wrote to Isa Outhwaite, which 'must either mend or end'.[102]

The first papal delegate to be responsible for Australasia, Bonaventura Cerretti, arrived in New Zealand early in 1916. He had the Aubert case as a high priority. Propaganda Fide had briefed him on the *benemerita Suora*, this 'worthy Sister', and told him that it had 'warmly recommended' the work with babies.[103] Suzanne had met him in Rome. 'Humanly speaking, the last hope rests on the Papal delegate', she wrote to Isa. 'He is well-informed of the position and he is a clever and honourable man in his dealings. He is held here in great consideration: he speaks english fluently and is of easy access. I am sure that you would be delighted with him.'[104]

Cerretti visited the Home of Compassion on the second morning after his arrival in Wellington. 'Where do you think he said his second Mass in New Zealand?' wrote Sister Claver on 22 January 1916. 'He bestowed on our little Order the great honour of saying Mass in our little Chapel at Island Bay! . . . He told us he had seen you in Rome, and had spoken to you on two or three occasions. He gave us every encouragement for the future of our Order. He said nothing can keep back from us now the approval of our Order, the Decree of Praise, except the final arrangements of properties and monies, according to Canon Law. . . . [He] spoke a few encouraging words to us all, saying amongst other things, you all look very happy.'[105] Cerretti heard both sides of the story in New Zealand. Firmly in Suzanne's camp was Isa, who was going to 'contrive', she said, to communicate with his secretary, to clarify the affair from a laywoman's viewpoint.

Bishop Cleary came to Rome on 7 June 1916 and attended a meeting with Laurenti and Pecorari, of Propaganda Fide, and Suzanne. There were some heated moments. Cleary went back to the Irish College, where he was staying, and next day wrote a letter to Father Mahoney, his vicar general in Auckland. Suzanne would do nothing without first receiving the Decree of Praise, he said. This condition was a 'moral impossibility' which he was sure Rome would not accept.[106] In the meantime he had decided that St Vincent's home was to be closed down 'without further negotiation or delay'.

For her part, Suzanne returned to her attic and promptly wrote to Cardinal Falconio, the Prefect of the Congregation of Religious. As long as the institute and its works 'are not recognized by Rome', she said, 'they are exposed, at any time, to be the helpless and unhappy victims of the unwise speculations or prejudices of some Ordinary in our faraway land, as a sad experience [h]as proved in the respective cases of Bishop Pompallier, Bishop Croke and Bishop Cleary'.[107]

The sisters were stunned when the closure was announced. If they stayed on in the home, 'no priest would conduct any religious service, and . . . the Blessed Sacrament would be removed'.[108] They would be unable to make collections in the diocese. Effectively, as religious, they were expelled from Auckland. The clergy thought the Sisters of Mercy could take over the work meanwhile.[109] If ownership of the property was sorted out, it could in the future be a useful annexe to the Mater Hospital over the road. The Sisters of Mercy refused, saying they did not have enough staff. They helped the Sisters of Compassion place 'the wee children' who were concerning Sister Claver.

The doors in the home were shut; no children played any more in the tower or through the grounds. The Sisters of Compassion returned to Wellington, taking a few of the children with them. In Rome, Suzanne heard of the attempt to carry on the work under diocesan control, and cabled to William Fallon, her lawyer in Auckland: 'Close Home; put secular in charge' – 'so you see', wrote Mahoney to Cleary, 'she still has her bristles up'.[110] Suzanne shot the same instruction to Sister Claver. A 'secular guardian' was to live downstairs. The caretaker was to be lay, with no allegiance owing to the bishop.[111]

In theory, Suzanne was now in a very weak position. A congregation seeking a Decree of Praise should have expanded into other dioceses. Her sisters were now in only one. But the action rebounded against Cleary. He had acted while the affair was under investigation in Rome. As Suzanne wrote to Sister Claver in October, 'Propaganda *certainly did not approve the suppression of the Home.*'[112] Now that the sisters were no longer in Auckland, the long-awaited approval from Cleary was suddenly superfluous. Suzanne began to see his action as 'a blessing in disguise'.

In January 1917, Propaganda sent a cable to Archbishop Redwood: 'Delay measures against Compassionist Sisters'.[113] He, too, reacted. He told Cardinal Serafini, Prefect of Propaganda, that any measures against the sisters had occurred in another diocese. He was still waiting for Suzanne to transfer the properties to a diocesan trust, and had been waiting for three years. He wanted her now to comply unconditionally. She 'must not place any conditions or clauses in the Deed of Trust that are contrary to the wishes of the Archbishop'. In the meantime, he revoked his petition asking for the Decree of Praise for the Sisters of Compassion. On the ground that the sisters had no security if Suzanne's property could be contested by next of kin, he proceeded against them: 'I deem it prudent until directed to the contrary by Your Eminence to refuse permission to the Institute from this date to receive any more subjects or postulants.'[114]

Cleary had delayed the transfer of deeds by refusing to have Redwood's name as co-trustee on the deeds of the Auckland property. Both names had been on the draft drawn up by Skerrett long before. Redwood too was retrenching. Propaganda decided to finish the affair. It was undertaking the 'moral impossibility' that Cleary had dismissed. Not only was it proceeding with the award of the Decree of Praise before the deeds were signed, it also advised Suzanne now to have neither diocesan leader as trustee.[115]

And so it happened. On 1 April 1917 the Decree of Praise was granted by Pope Benedict XV to the Daughters of Our Lady of Compassion, the only Catholic congregation born and growing to maturity in New

Zealand. Cardinal Aidan Gasquet, who became the congregation's first Protector, told Suzanne that the discussion and voting in the council of the Congregation of Religious had been unusually short. The decision was unanimous.

After the Decree of Praise was gained, the signature of Suzanne Aubert went on the deeds of transfer. She as superior general, Sister Angela as secretary general and Sister Veronica as treasurer were now the trustees. These three women – Suzanne Aubert, Johanna Moller and Margaret Hartnett – featured alone on the deeds: there was no bishop, no 'reputable layman'. The congregation's aims which Suzanne had fought to retain were also protected in the wording of the deeds. The thirty-five acres at Jerusalem which she had bought with her family money remained her own property, willed to the congregation solely for the use of the Maori mission, nothing else.

On 2 February 1917, Suzanne had written to Sister Claver, preparing her for the imminent decree: 'If we obtain "the Decree", let us receive it with a deep feeling of our unworthyness and of loving gratitude to God, for mercifully choosing us, *misérables* creatures, to do His work. Be modest in the success, no boasting: we should spare the feelings of those whose opinion was unfavorable to us.'[116] She wrote to Redwood on 12 May 1917: 'I hope that you received the telegram that I had the honour to address to you to tell you that the Good God at last permitted that we receive the Decree of Praise. I am including a copy of this in this letter, thanking you from the depth of my heart for the recommendations which Your Grace kindly gave us. On my side I have kept my promise and I have signed the act of cession of goods under the direction of His Eminence Cardinal Gasquet, our Cardinal Protector. Thanks be to God I am no longer a proprietor but I am and I shall always be the respectful and devoted daughter of Your Grace.'[117]

Nothing with Suzanne could be resolved without some drama. Cleary was once more in Rome in June 1917 and asked to see the signed deeds at Propaganda. He exploded with anger over the woman he was beginning to codename the *'santa donna'*.[118] He noticed that the Jerusalem acres remained her private property. He was concerned that the deeds had not been registered yet. And, most important, he pointed out that the wording had Suzanne promising to transfer the deeds 'when called upon', not immediately. He alerted Propaganda, Gasquet and Redwood. Letters passed to and from Ireland, Italy, England and New Zealand. Cleary said he would be quite prepared if necessary to come back to Rome from New Zealand to pursue the matter.[119] He also still wanted his name on the Auckland property deeds.

Gasquet sifted out the essentials. The deeds were to be annotated and the transfer made. They were to be sent to be registered in New Zealand immediately. But the Jerusalem land was firmly Suzanne's, safeguarded for the Maori mission. Introducing the bishops' names into the title deeds was 'absolutely unacceptable'. Restricting admission to baptised Catholic babies only was also unacceptable. There was to be no question of suspending Suzanne's Decree of Praise, as Cleary had wanted. 'It is unthinkable to punish in such a way a person who has always shown and still shows such deference and obedience to the Holy See.' The congregation was now under the protection of Rome.[120] Suzanne signed the immediate transfer, which was registered in New Zealand in January 1918. She wrote to inform Cardinal Tonti, Prefect of the Congregation of Religious. She was 'happy to be in law and in deed as poor as a church mouse'.[121]

The wording of the Decree of Praise held safe all the works Suzanne had started. It also gave her wide scope for new directions in health care. And it protected her unswerving resolution that the work of the Sisters of Compassion would be 'without distinction of sex or religion'. After years of effort and hardship, Mother Aubert had gained what she had come to Rome for. Back in August 1913, she and Isa had envisaged a brief, urgent trip. Just after she left, Isa wrote her a message: 'Now, dear Sister mine, may God bless your goings and comings, and permit your safe return to your many, many children in this, your adopted land.'[122] It was a message that would wait for six years to come true. It was now time to go home.

CHAPTER TWENTY

Wellington – the hospital
1919-1926

Your mother is growing very old :
Ko to whaea kei te haere ake ki te ruruhitanga
The night is near : Ka tata te po[1]

Suzanne was old. Eighty-two, eighty-three, eighty-four – the years were
going by in Rome. She was 'stiffening up' and becoming more 'shaky'.[2]
Her frame was bending. The small but broad-shouldered woman was
thin from hardship. Instead of the usual square gaze, a narrower face
looks out from the photo on her travel documents. Cataracts were
clouding her eyes. She was knocked over twice in the street. One time a
cart ran right over her and she lay unconscious till she struggled up again.
Bishop Cleary wrote about this with concern. A quickly quenched fire
in the house had also seared an eye and permanently injured it. She was
ill at one stage with what she called 'a mild touch of the pest' – the 'plague'
of the 1918 influenza.

Suzanne was chafing to go home. 'I generally wake up at about 1 a.m.',
she wrote to Sister Anthony, 'and I fly in spirit to dear old New Zealand.
I roam through the chapel, the infirmary, and the Homes. I try to guess
what is going on there.' But leaving Rome was not easy. In September
1917 she wrote to Sister Claver: 'I will try my best, by hook or crook, to go
back as soon as I can possibly do so, by any way available.'[3] There was a
chance of travelling with the new Apostolic Delegate, Bartolomeo
Cattaneo. That fell through. Years later he apologised to the sisters: he had
not wanted to be encumbered with an old, old woman. By May 1919, she
was writing to her friend Nancy Johnston in London:

> I am still in the impossibility to leave Italy. Whenever I ask for a ticket, I am
> told: 'Wait till peace is restored', and peace never comes. . . . Our Cardinal
> Protector told me the other day: 'As you cannot swim, stay patiently where
> you are.' Everyone says: 'There are no passenger boats available for New
> Zealand.' Now, my dear Miss Johnston, do you think that the difficulties

are really as unsurmountable as they are represented? Old age is steadily increasing them. Several American and Australian people are here in the same predicament, but it is a poor consolation. Meantime, it is of no use to lament . . .[4]

She was not going to budge without her important documents. Suzanne trusted her legal mind: it was her family birthright and she husbanded it. She had proved in Rome the effectiveness of being able to produce in evidence the necessary document, the essential letter, the proof of a signature – whether it had been Redwood's approving early Constitutions, or Bishop Lenihan's inviting the sisters to Auckland, or the governors' supporting her work. Papers were now being confiscated at borders. She dreaded the hackneyed scenario: the spy dressed as an elderly nun. When sent separately, documents were also disappearing. She copied and recopied, and posted packets to Sister Claver: 'I will keep sending you, as they are ready, duplicates of all documents worth keeping in case that anything happened to the originals which I keep with me. All that translation and writing is a heavy tax on my old shoulders, but I do not grudge the work for the Institute.'[5]

Once again, the delay had its advantages. By 1917 Rome had finalised the Code of Canon Law. While she was still there, Suzanne redrafted her Constitutions with the latest advice and guidance so that they were as correct and up to date as any. This strengthened the canonical standing of the Decree of Praise. The amount of writing Suzanne had to do in Rome was enormous. Every letter or document that was relevant to her case had to be translated into French for the Sacred Congregations. This did not finish when the Decree of Praise was granted. 'I am crushed with work', she told Sister Claver, 'and I have, in spite of all, to begin the translation of our revised Constitutions which cannot be completed before the publication of the New *Canonical Code*, sometime in August.'[6] Yet by being on the spot in Rome, able to talk persuasively and convincingly in both French and English, able to handle Italian competently, and translating everything as she went, Suzanne could weave a net of ecclesiastical support and contacts just as she had done among the lay-people of New Zealand.

She was also writing a less formal document for the sisters. Her hands were rheumaticky and her eyesight very weak, yet her clear script flowed on as she wrote four of the five parts that make up the *Directory of the Daughters of Our Lady of Compassion*. This was finally printed in

Wellington in 1922, with Redwood's assistance. Suzanne defined a directory as 'a collection of theological, moral and ascetical observations which teach the members of an Institute the best manner to fulfil their duties and to practise the virtue of their state or calling'.[7] For the new canonical format of the Constitutions she had had to cull many fuller and more homely directions from her previous versions. These were revised and became the first section of the directory. Then she wrote the 'Letter to the Novices' based on the spiritual ideas in her conferences. Its first title was 'Mother Joseph to her Chicks' – the pet name she had called the novices ever since 1890 when de Lostalot, the French consul in Wellington, had teased her for 'chicken-stealing' her first very young recruits.

The sisters had no written record of Suzanne's teaching apart from notes they had taken. But, while she was in Rome, most were still quietly following her way. The visitation in 1912 had criticised the training in the novitiate as 'inadequate' and 'not on orthodox lines'. Sister Clotilde was a novice at the time and remembered: 'we were introduced to more formal methods of meditative prayer . . . However, after experimenting in more mathematical methods of prayer, it is true to say that all finally returned to Mother's simple methods. We read the three great books of Crib, Calvary and the Tabernacle with the eyes of faith, which Mother later wrote of in the Letter to the Novices.'[8] The 'three great books' referred to her way of weaving the life of Christ into their own.

The printed 'Letter to the Novices' reads quaintly in parts. It has suffered from a double translation. The style is an amalgam of Suzanne's original idiosyncratic English in a natural, spoken style, a second version in French, and a further translation back into English by Redwood.[9] Some of the content could be daunting to anyone unfamiliar with the lifestyle and spiritual context of pre-Vatican II religious. But this is balanced by a piquant humour and a directness which bring the pages to life. Human nature is understood. Faith could be simple and down to earth without losing, for her, the attractiveness of transcendency. This shows even in the very last sentence: 'May this scribble help you somewhat on the way to heaven!'[10]

The 'Letter' is framed like a catechism in questions and answers, but progresses conversationally. The wards become a stage with all the people taking part: the sisters, the orphans, the incurable children, the old women and men:

— But when a crotchety old woman, in an awful temper, throws at our head her cup or her pillow, can we not give her a good shaking?

Give a good shaking to her pillow, try to catch the cup and let it not be broken, and smilingly replacing the pillow, say gently: 'Thank you, Grannie,' and Grannie will first look at you to see that you are not making fun of her, then she will calm down, and Our Lady of Compassion will give you a look of love, and your heart will be happy. Patience will have gained a double victory.

— Listen to me, please: the other day a half-rotten old man, a surly old grizzly bear, called me every bad name his tongue could utter, was insufferably insulting. It was really too bad after all I had done for him. How could I endure it?

My dear Sister, how hard you are to please! You did not understand the man's language. He showed you the greatest consideration, and thanked you after the manner Our Lord Himself was thanked. You ought to have been proud and grateful, you ought to have interpreted every epithet as a compliment, and welcomed each remark as a dainty little button-hole posy. . . .

— I do my best to put everything in order, and I have hardly finished when So-and-So comes and turns everything topsy-turvy. Would that not provoke an Angel?

The Angels never lose their patience. Imitate them. Keep your temper, or else you will add confusion to disorder.[11]

Suzanne could lose patience. When she felt strongly about issues, she could lose her temper, 'slap her hands on her thighs' and 'stamp her feet'.[12] She knew that goodness had to be worked on constantly, crafted gently. The 'Letter' let the novice know that it is natural to have rebellious thoughts. It vented and acknowledged her feelings, and did not make her feel guilty. It helped her on her spiritual journey while letting her still be her own woman.[13]

Suzanne sat quietly in churches during the deserted midday hours in Rome and worked away at the latter sections, writing them in little Italian exercise-books. The 'Life of Union and Practice of the Hours' was written for her 'hens', the professed sisters.[14] The theme was similar. The sisters, as Clotilde explained, 'must live in the Presence of God in their various occupations, not by frequent visits [to the Blessed Sacrament], or long periods in the Chapel. . . . Each hour of the day and each duty was specified, each with the three intentions, Nativity, Passion, & Eucharist, so that every Sister could take a subject that suited her [state] of soul.'[15]

Suzanne sent this to the sisters and, with a diffidence that was almost shyness, suggested they try it:

I beg of you, dear Sisters, to pray for your poor old mother who loves you dearly, and who has sent you a Xmas box which has taken her a long time to write and has been approved and recommended by high authorities, among whom is our Cardinal Protector, who kindly encouraged me all along. Try, dear Sisters. One hour a day of special intention is not a hard and difficult task. It will not give you additional work, though, if you are faithful to it, you will soon advance steadily and surely on the path of perfection to which we are obliged to tend . . .[16]

Suzanne was buoyed by the encouragement she was getting. 'His Eminence Cardinal Gasquet is taking a very keen interest in our Directory [which] has [now] to be submitted to the approbation of the [Sacred] Congregations'.[17] Gasquet was the sisters' well-chosen Cardinal Protector. He was English, but of French background, a church historian and a Benedictine. Suzanne's religious apprenticeship in New Zealand had been unusual and minimal, compared with the norm. A strong Benedictine influence remained from her girlhood schooling. Gasquet would understand this, as well as her fusion of French and Anglo-Celtic cultures. Suzanne had a high regard for him. She allotted him four attributes in a blend she valued: 'He is a saintly and powerful [Cardinal Protector], shrewd one too, and so kindly disposed as well.'[18]

Suzanne's 'shrewd' men 'in high places' encouraged the writing partly because they saw how frail she was growing. It would help her come to terms with slowing down. She admitted this:

Dearest Sisters, I am with you in mind, though I am bodily separated from you by the wide ocean. I have been told to throw a bridge over it by writing for you and by prayer intermixed with charity. Well, I am trying to do so. The mixture suits me best, as I am not allowed to do now a full 12 hours day service in the hospitals and ambulances. They are afraid it would be too much for me at my age. I must be contented with being a stop-gap here and there.[19]

The men liked what Suzanne was writing. Their respect for her intellect and spiritual integrity grew. She said they suggested to her the subject of the fourth part, the 'Spiritual Tonic'. Lepidi, the Vatican Censor, wrote his imprimatur on both the French and English versions and also urged her, she said, to follow the 'Letter to the Novices' with one for the professed sisters. Later, in New Zealand, Dean Pierre Regnault borrowed both these documents:

Were I to follow my inclinations and yield to a strong temptation, you would not see either of these two manuscripts for at least six months or till I would have time to take copious notes. It is supernatural life made practical for and brought within the reach of the most uninitiated. . . . Both manuscripts have been a revelation to me, and whilst reading them I often said to myself:

'Why was not supernatural life brought within our reach, in that simple way, when I was a novice or scholastic?'[20]

The sisters in New Zealand were meanwhile adjusting to being a papal congregation without their superior general. More than two years would go by after they gained the Decree of Praise before Suzanne came back. The clergy's reception of the news of the decree had been mixed. Warmth had been matched with taciturnity. Sister Angela wrote in September 1918:

Sister Claver and I called on His Grace Archb[ishop] O'Shea Saturday the 31st of August, and asked him if the Sisters could take their perpetual vows, as according to our new rule. . . . Mother, he hum[m]ed and hawed and said at last: They had better not, as he had received no word from Rome about our Order. This is not the first time that we have felt there is something kept from us, and if you know of anything don't you think it is best for us to know, for it upsets us very much when His Grace makes us feel that we are far from secure. I don't mean to say: he says that in words, but we take from his manner. So, if there is anything you know could you not tell us.[21]

Sister Claver, one of Suzanne's first 'chicks', had always a 'childlike love' for her, as Clotilde explained, 'even though there was much about [Suzanne's] views and aims that she could not understand'. The more subdued Claver whom later sisters remember may have given all the energy she had over the years of skilful mediation. The long haul would have drawn all her strength and left her drained. Clotilde remembered that it was Sister Angela who bolstered Claver through the six years: 'It was at this time that Sr Angela's understanding of Mother, and the strength of her loyalty and faith in her, shone to a brilliant degree. . . . Sr Angela was a very firm and strong anchor that did major work in steadying the rocking Institute in hard and anxious years. It was as if the little ship were being buffeted by storm waves on every side.'[22] Yet, when a young girl from Taranaki, Mollie Conaglen, visited the home in these years, to her 'it never appeared that they were under stress and strain. . . . They all seemed to be so happy. There was a happy atmosphere, a lovely atmosphere in the home.'[23]

The sisters were as busy as ever. The influenza epidemic struck and killed in Wellington at the end of the war. The Sisters of Compassion, most of whom had St John Ambulance certificates, joined in the work organised by the Vigilance Committee in Island Bay. Sister Clotilde, as a trained nurse working under Dr Fyffe's instructions, was given considerable medical responsibilities in Island Bay and Berhampore.

O'Shea authorised the sisters to go out alone during this time. Peter Fraser was member of Parliament for the area and also a city councillor. He worked closely with the sisters. Cars and drivers were put at their disposal and Clotilde was assigned a motorcycle. The unconventional image of the sisters on horseback up the river was matched in the steep streets of Wellington by a nun speeding around in a sidecar.

The Marists offered St Patrick's College to the Department of Health as a hospital for the emergency, and asked for it to be staffed by the Sisters of Compassion. Hester Maclean was in charge of nursing. She agreed, provided that either Clotilde or Genevieve, the trained nurses she knew, was matron. Genevieve took charge at first. The boys were sent home and their dormitories were filled with the sick. The sisters themselves then fell ill. Sister Natalie, looking after sick toddlers in the Island Bay nursery, died. The way Wellington looked to its sisters and valued their nursing, 'free and across all creeds', only made Suzanne more determined for them to be trained as nurses and recognised by the state.[24]

I am going home : E hoki ana ahau ki toku kainga[25]

In Rome Suzanne was still having trouble finding a way to return to New Zealand. She had been more than fifty years away from France and had lost her French citizenship. She had not been naturalised as a New Zealander. She could not easily get a passport or visa from either country. Finally, a lengthy rescue operation to bring Mother Aubert home got under way. It involved the sisters, several members of the Johnston family, Sir Joseph Ward, Sir Thomas Mackenzie, Cardinal Gasquet, the French and British embassies in Rome, and many bit players. In May 1918, Ward was on his way to London, where he and Prime Minister William Massey, heading the wartime coalition government, were part of the Imperial War Cabinet.[26] His wife had alerted him to Suzanne's difficulties and he went armed with a memorandum from the sisters. From his office in the Savoy Hotel, he wrote to Suzanne saying he was

> glad to hear that . . . your splendid work in New Zealand has been approved by the High Authorities of the Church, and I quite understand your desire to return to the Dominion. I have made representations on your behalf and I am enclosing herewith an open letter, which you can show to the Embassy in Rome . . . On your arrival in England you should call at the office of the High

Commissioner, Sir Thomas Mackenzie, when arrangements will be made for your passage out to New Zealand by the first available steamer . . .'[27]

His letter 'To All Whom it May Concern' assessed her as 'known and respected throughout the length and breadth of New Zealand for her valuable work . . . It will be greatly esteemed if every aid is given to this lady . . .' Suzanne wrote home happily: 'Sir Joseph Ward is not leaving a stone unturned to ease everything for me.' 'The kind recom[m]endation of Sir Joseph has had a magic effect, thanks be to God.'[28]

Still there were delays. Suzanne's 'bulky lot of papers and documents concerning our Institute' could not travel through France with her. By 1919 it was Nancy Johnston in London who became Suzanne's delegate to the New Zealand High Commission: 'If the Hon. Sir Thomas McKenzie could kindly allow me to have them addressed to him, through the English Embassy . . . Dear Friend, may I ask you to approach the High Commissioner on my behalf?' In August 1919 Nancy had the way clear. 'Thanks be to God and to you', Suzanne wrote to her. 'I have at last my passport and I am in hopes to leave Rome within a week's time . . . P.S. The parcels directed to the High Commissioner are leaving today.'[29] Suzanne's dossiers went to London in the British diplomatic bags. She despatched them gratefully. With a specially issued travel document in lieu of an official passport, New Zealand's *ambassadrice extraordinaire* finally left Rome. But not before one last appointment: 'I had a parting private audience with Our Holy Father. He was so exceedingly kind and gave me such an abundance of blessings for ourselves, and for all our friends and benefactors of all creeds.'[30]

Suzanne stopped in France on the way to London. She had been persuaded to feel freed from her vow never to return. In Paris she visited the Mother House of the Sisters of Charity in the Rue du Bac, which she said she remembered from the 1850s. She still hankered after the medical traditions of this congregation. The Sister of Charity was for her the archetype of the active nursing religious sister.

She even visited Lyon. Father Raffin, the Superior General of the Society of Mary, had been friendly and supportive in the lead-up to the Decree of Praise. Suzanne responded readily. When Raffin was in Rome during her stay, they seemed to have discussed and resolved what had led the Marists in 1892 to exclude the sisters on the Whanganui River from the new Third Order Regular of Mary. When he returned to Lyon, they exchanged letters. Suzanne was one of the few left who could still remember from her Lyon childhood far back into Marist history, to 'Fathers Colin, Cholleton, Poupinel, Forest, Séon, Petitjean, Yardin, and so many others of saintly memory. All this is very old, but the memory of the heart does not age.'[31] Whereas so many people now were associating Suzanne primarily with the social welfare projects, Raffin was aware of her part in Marist Maori mission history. He put this first when he wrote to Dean Holley, the head of the Marist Province in New Zealand. She 'has well and truly earned [the Decree of Praise] through her devotion and zeal for the Maoris and for the abandoned orphans'.[32]

Suzanne had felt very alone in 1913 and 1914. So, when Redwood came to Rome at the end of 1914 and once more put his support behind her, she never forgot it. Raffin wrote that, when he congratulated her on the decree, she thanked him then added that it was to 'Bishop Redwood, after God, that she was indebted for this favour'.[33] Suzanne and Raffin were getting on well. She did not let the diplomatic opportunity slip by and suggested he encourage his clergy in New Zealand to ease up on her: 'Very Reverend Father, dare I ask you please to let the members of your Society in our country know that you desire that in the future genuinely friendly relations should exist between your Society and our little Institute, which, by the Decree of Praise, is recognised as a Congregation depending on the Holy See? For my part, I am ready to do everything in my power to promote this good understanding . . .'[34]

In Lyon Suzanne stayed, at Raffin's invitation, with the Sisters of the Third Order Regular of Mary. She went to Fourvière, bypassing at first the great new basilica and heading for the sanctuary of her youth, now tucked alongside. She saw there for the first time the votive painting of her mother's recovery in 1845. Suzanne stood in the sanctuary and looked at her whole family, up there on the wall – all dead now except her. In the picture, the theme of family and the theme of women reveal much of what made Suzanne the person she was.

She went once more to Ars, where the wave of 1850s religious fervour had washed her in the direction of the Pacific. In 1925, the same year that the Curé d'Ars finally became St Jean Vianney, Suzanne turned ninety. For her birthday, Wellingtonians gave her £200. For once the money did not go straight into her works at home. Some went to France so that the Daughters of Our Lady of Compassion could record their part in the curé's story, his part in theirs. The inscription curves around the marble wall of the basilica in Ars.[35] Suzanne would tell visitors about the curé, about his prophecies for her, and how he was appointed a patron saint for the congregation even before he was formally canonised.

On 15 September 1919, a tired and travel-stained Suzanne was met at the station in London by Father Alan Perceval, one of the Johnstons. Soon after, the *Ruahine* arrived in port from New Zealand and off stepped Suzanne's companion of the collecting tour long ago, Sister Magdalen. She had taken leave from the congregation in the early 1900s to train as a nurse, and did not readjust to religious life. She was now Nurse Violet Savage. The sisters had sent her over to England because they were worried that the sea voyage might affect Suzanne's failing health. She 'loved Mother', explained Angela, 'and could be relied upon to take good care of her. Mother loved her too and would yield to her influence more readily than to that of any of her Sisters, whom she was apt to treat as children'.[36]

With Violet Savage came a new-sewn outfit. Suzanne, who badly needed it, was spruced up. In a fresh habit, cap and veil, the now presentable Superior General of the Sisters of Compassion once more made her calls – on the Islingtons, the Johnstons, Cardinal Bourne, Barnardo Institutes. She had asked the Pope for special blessings on former governors Plunket, Islington and Ranfurly, High Commissioner Mackenzie and, in Wellington, Dr Fyffe. They had all written letters of support for her in 1913. She said Islington was delighted: 'I want somebody's blessing', he told her.[37]

Suzanne was nettled by the thought that a hardy pilgrim like her needed help. Nancy Johnston remembered:

> The Nurse whom the Nuns sent . . . to look after M. Aubert caused the latter a good deal of annoyance, as Mother A. was not used to having a watch dog. Also the poor Nurse wasn't used to London traffic, & we were told by Mother A. of the trials of being clutched at just when she was going to cross the road, & 'she do grab the veil nearly off my head!' On one occasion when Mother A. came to tea with us, she arrived well ahead of the escort who panted along later.[38]

Out on the street one day, Suzanne was suddenly recognised by some Wellington soldiers still in London. They clustered around, shaking her hand and talking, then escorted her across the street. She said goodbye to them: 'Now take care of yourselves, and God bless you.' The policeman on point duty asked them who 'the little old woman was'. They told him she was 'from New Zealand and there was nobody like her'.[39]

Finally Suzanne boarded the *Bremen* in December 1919 and headed home. Cardinal Gasquet went to Plymouth to see her off. With Suzanne, the botanist and gardener, went some giant strawberry plants she had sought out in France. The High Commission helped her with import clearance. And a letter went from Sir Thomas Mackenzie to the captain: 'The Reverend Mother Aubert . . . has acquired . . . a new strain of strawberry plant upon which she places high value, and she fears unless special care is taken of it, it may perish during the voyage. The object of this letter is to ask you if you would be so good as to give instructions for reasonable precautions . . .'[40] The crew watered the strawberries with enthusiasm. In New Zealand they cropped at no bigger than normal size.

Nancy Johnston was travelling on the same ship. It was 'a very crowded voyage', she remembered. 'Going through the children's saloon one day I saw the fantastic sight of Mrs Seddon (Dick's wife), skirts held high, dancing a horn-pipe (or some such), M. Aubert roaring with laughter and clapping her hands to keep time with the music provided by a steward upon his mouth organ.'[41]

But there was none of this vivacity on 28 January 1920 when Suzanne landed. She had become very ill two days out from Wellington. Two of her grown-up Jerusalem boys were at the wharf to pick up their Grandma. John Heappey now owned a taxi. He and John McMahon swept a very weak Suzanne out of an officer's care and carried her to the car. The sisters quietly postponed their celebrations. They were 'shocked to see her so aged and looking so ill'. Suzanne 'crept upstairs to the Chapel, noticing the decorations as she went'.[42] She knelt at the altar-rail without moving for so long that one by one the other women, except Claver, slipped away to their duties.

Suzanne nearly died. In the years she had left she was weakening physically all the time – slight heart attacks, a stroke that partly paralysed her left side, a painful cataract operation that went wrong. When she recovered from her first illness, she started to go out walking again. She thought she could pick up her old routine through the streets and the government and business offices of Wellington, and for a while she did. Once she walked with novices from Island Bay to pick walnuts and walnut leaves from a Thorndon garden. She wanted to make medical infusions for Tim Herlihy, a sick neighbour down the road. Another time she insisted on struggling straight up the hill behind the Island Bay home to check a high point on the ridge, a possible site for a statue. The climb was another trial of faith. She found it harder coming down. She would not be carried. She 'simply sat on the ground and slid down'. Suzanne moved very slowly now; she needed a helping arm alongside.

Out in the garden, Suzanne would lean on a small spade and direct Sister Carmel where to plant the French seeds she had ordered from Vilmorin, Andrieux & Cie. Suzanne 'was always insistent on the importance of vegetables . . . Sister Carmel seemed to be able to grow anything and everything Mother wanted'. The community ate endives, globe artichokes, garlic, new varieties of tomato, beets and salad greens. French delphiniums grew tall and blue among the flowers. Around the property Suzanne and Carmel kept adding to the plantings of New Zealand trees and shrubs – ngaio, karaka, koromiko to buffer the southerly winds.[43]

Then Suzanne could not manage to go out any more. She stayed in her spartan upstairs room, writing or working with her secretary, Angela. She became the Mother Aubert that visitors came to see and journalists reverently reported on:

> The sunshine picked out the high-lights on the bare polished floor. A small fire glowed in a grate in one corner of the room. By the window, seated in a deep chair, was the frail figure of Mother Mary Aubert, Christian, philanthropist, and foundress of the Order of 'Daughters of Our Lady of Compassion'.
>
> Papers and books lay on the table before her; she has recently been engaged in some translation work. Her active mind is alert, although her frail body, worn with an excess of zeal, a long life of labour for others, is now confined to a chair.
>
> 'I cannot work now – only this hand can write,' and she lifted the thin, trembling right hand from the folds of her dark blue habit.
>
> 'But you still direct,' I suggested. 'They know what you would have done.'[44]

Nelle Scanlan saw that ninety-year-old Suzanne, appointed by Rome as superior general for life, was in charge: 'She is still controlling the destiny of the organisation she has brought into being. Still planning for its future expansion in which she will bear no part.'[45]

Mollie Conaglen had meanwhile entered the Home of Compassion in March 1923, and took the name Sister Eustace. She remembered Suzanne as approachable, lovable and 'very much in charge':

> She was a tiny little woman, a plain woman. She had a very strong face – a strong wide jaw – and determined looking, but when she smiled, her whole face lit up, the whole face smiled. She looked up at me so sweetly and I thought she was lovely. She was really quite old when I entered. Even then, she was very much in charge, in command. One morning she called me over

and she said in quite a stern voice: 'Eustacia, come over here to me at once!'
I wondered what on earth I'd done. And she said: 'I cannot see your face.'
When the goffers were first worn, they were full, you know, full out. Well,
they gradually goffered them till they had them goffered right in. 'I can only
see your nose,' she said. And she put her two hands in between the goffers
and splayed them out and brushed them back across my head.[46]

When Suzanne pushed back and fanned out the novice's goffers, she was
making a point. She did not like the image of the downcast nun. She liked
faces to be up, seeing the world and being seen.

Harry Ashworth was one of the children there at the time.[47] He
thought of Island Bay as his home, the sisters as his family. He helped
Sister Bridget milk the cows by hand in the early morning. Sister Carmel
taught him the Latin he needed to be altar boy. His memory was of
Suzanne as she weakened. 'She walked with sticks.' But he, too, remembered her still alert. She would 'blow her trumpet' at him if he nodded off
while serving as altar boy. 'I'd be that tired getting up early in the
morning. I'd be serving the Mass with the priest, and I'd half-pie doze off
. . . When one of the kids did anything wrong she'd tell them straight.'[48]

Other sisters touched their brushes to the impressionistic portrait of
Suzanne at this time: 'Tiny, only about five foot; that magnificent smile,
very alive, alert, vivacious, whole face lit up'; 'extremely direct'; 'not
moody, never went into silences, could get very cross, but moody, no'. 'She
was hard on her Sisters and expected an almighty lot but they loved her.
She was fair.' 'She got on well with men. She would give a warmer
welcome to our fathers than to our mothers.' She always had work on
hand. Even when she was very old, she would 'unravel wool', sitting there,
no longer able to draft, cut out, sew or knit. And 'every night she would
be kneeling at the altar rail in the chapel, not down the back but kneeling'.
'It cannot be said that Mother did not listen and she wouldn't take advice,
that she did not trust her Sisters.' There were sisters whose 'brains she
picked'. 'She trusted Clotilde.' 'When Sister Clotilde came, an educated
person, she took all she could from her and she listened to her, and she
did as she was asked to do by her.' Sisters Angela and Cecilia, too.[49]

As well as the pleasure in waiting for Suzanne's return, there must
have been apprehension. 'When the nuns were waiting for Mother to
come home, they were nervous. "Sister Claver said she would have to
get up a sycamore tree!"'[50] She did not have to, nor did Suzanne have
to pause beneath the branches and call her down. When Suzanne saw

some of the changes in the running of the institute that had been made while she was away, she gave her opinion: 'rat-holes', she muttered as she passed by the practical partitioning in the children's ward. The minutes record a few incidents when Sister Claver or others bravely made a stand. But Suzanne, too, had been nervous about the homecoming. The traumatic months after the visitation before she left for Rome in 1913 had been her last memory. O'Shea's actions may have come partly from the initiative of some senior sisters. They had definitely supported him then; some were philosophically still inclined to. Shortly before Suzanne died, she said to Claver that 'they told me when I was leaving that I might meet more difficulties in New Zealand. I came home, and there were no difficulties.'[51]

Well, it is only what we expected :
Ko ta matou ano tena i mahara ai o mua iho[52]

Suzanne stepped back into leadership on 22 February 1920 at the first general council meeting. She was still weak, but was swinging back into action. Once more the minutes recorded it:

> She spoke at length of the necessity of observing holy Poverty because of the many buildings that were needed immediately – the Home for Incurables seemed the most pressing. Then there was a place for the Boys between the years of seven & twelve. Rome had allowed us to keep Boys until twelve – this was unusual as seven or at most eight was the limit for Sisters, but they had granted it themselves.[53] . . . She had obtained authorisation for all those buildings.

She went on to discuss a separate novitiate, a separate building for older boys, and 'there was another work which had been spoken of in Rome, for which she had obtained permission as it was needed, & would be needed more in the future in order to keep in touch with our girls, that was to have a place for them where they could come if they were out of work, or ill, & it could be a place of reunion for them. She thought it would be better to have it at Buckle St.'[54]

She also discussed Jerusalem. There had been a 'crying irregularity', she said, in the council elections when Veronica was brought down to Wellington as treasurer. 'Had I been here', the minutes report her saying, 'I certainly would have sided Sr Veronica being left in the Missions, as it seems to be the Will of God to leave her there. She understands the

Maoris & they like her. There is no one to take her place with them.'[55] A petition in Maori had gone to O'Shea from the people of Hiruharama and Ranana to have Veronica reinstalled. At this time O'Shea had been proposing a new Catholic mission area based on Kaiwhaiki on the lower Whanganui.[56] He wanted the Sisters of Compassion to staff it. They were in favour but their numbers were too few. When Suzanne returned, she would not send just anybody, as the minutes explained: 'She said it would need five Sisters to begin with, of whom one at least must speak Maori well & understand the Maori ways.'[57]

Sister Angela said of Suzanne: 'Notwithstanding her love for the poor and her sympathies with the trials and troubles of the working class, the notion of delegated authority – whatever her theories on the subject – never appealed to her in practice.'[58] But no longer would Suzanne's word carry almost automatically.[59] The sisters must have quailed at the prospect of more excessive holy poverty for the sake of more building. Her plans to start extensive alterations were several times opposed by the council: 'The First Asst. objected to all available funds being sunk in repairs so as to leave nothing for the upkeep of the Home which had not enough income to meet expenditure.'[60] And once more Suzanne was confronted by O'Shea.[61] He wrote a long letter on the subject to Redwood, again in Rome:

> I am very sorry to have to say that Rev Mother Mary Joseph Aubert, who recently returned from Rome, has already begun to give trouble again. However we have sufficient powers from the Holy See to deal with her. . . . And as she is a most difficult woman to deal with, in order to strengthen our hands, I have revoked the permission, given to the Sisters while she was in Rome, to go into the different parishes and make collections. . . . We must be very firm, otherwise things will become a hopeless muddle. She has the old woman's craze for building at present . . . and so squandering money.[62]

O'Shea referred to the infant mortality in 1908 and 1909 and worried about it in the sectarian climate of 1920: 'In the present wave of bigotry in N.Z. and with the P.P.A. [Protestant Political Association] watching for the least scandal, we can not afford to take any risks in these things.' He was more than justified in feeling concerned about the PPA.[63] The minutes in fact record Suzanne having to reassure the sisters over 'certain threats of Mr Howard Elliott concerning "A Convent at Island Bay" and their possible meaning'.[64] This was the worst period in New Zealand history for religious intolerance. But by 1920, in Britain, Australia and New Zealand, statistics were showing that the old illnesses were no longer killing babies as they once did. O'Shea would have opposed whatever Suzanne did, as long as she persisted in her independence.

Suzanne kept developing and revising plans through the next years as part of a wider scheme, her last big project: a training hospital for nurses where her sisters would gain their state registration. Everything she did in her remaining life has to be measured against this priority. Buckle St patients were transferred to Island Bay not just because the older buildings were now substandard, but because she wanted to increase the number of beds at Island Bay to meet the requirements for a training hospital. Nor did she want the sisters detailed out to sick-visiting.[65] Her reluctance to staff a new mission at Kaiwhaiki may not have resulted just from the lack of fluent Maori speakers in the congregation.[66] She was wanting to concentrate her work. The same argument would apply to her decision not to proceed with developing new property in the Buckle St area which the sisters had acquired in her absence. It also applied to the decision to sell the Auckland home, which had been rented since Bishop Cleary closed the work down in 1916.

Suzanne said she had received advice in Rome to concentrate the work and not to spread too quickly into potentially disparate new communities before a strong unifying spirit had been built up in one main location. This was another argument for her own training hospital. If sisters went elsewhere, for instance to Australia, to train in Catholic hospitals, they could return with their spirit as Sisters of Compassion weakened. The spiritual argument was also a practical one. She needed as many women as she could get, working and nursing on site during their training, in order to maintain and extend her work. The large nursing communities of the Sisters of Charity lay behind her concept.

Suzanne was talking about this quite openly from the beginning. In August 1920 the architect's and city engineer's report said the Island Bay building could not stand the alterations she wanted. Suzanne's disappointment comes through in the minutes: 'She began by saying that we had been building castles in the air, we had been speculating on beginning the training of our Sisters next year – when it would be begun, she did not know! Mr Morton, the City Engineer (to whom she was very thankful) will not allow the building on the roof . . .'[67]

In her planning Suzanne came up against Coadjutor Archbishop O'Shea's opposition. He seemed to fear that she was in competition with the first Catholic hospital being planned for Wellington. It was to be established by the Sydney branch of the Little Company of Mary, known then as the 'Lewisham Sisters' after the Sydney suburb where their original hospital was. O'Shea had been impressed with their care when he was a patient in their Christchurch hospital, opened in 1914. He was keen to have one of their hospitals in Wellington and had been planning for it since the early 1920s. The first Lewisham Sisters arrived in January 1926. All along, the timing was parallel to Suzanne's project.

But Suzanne's wish for trained sisters went way back to before 1910, when Hester Maclean had offered state training and the archdiocese had vetoed it. Suzanne's only chance, as she saw it, was her own training hospital. This would be catering for different patients from the paying and mainly Catholic clients of Lewisham Hospital, later renamed Calvary Hospital. Suzanne's would be serving free of charge her usual people, the poor and needy 'of all denominations and none'. In a way, setting up a hospital like this would also represent her stand against the growing sectarianism, would continue her mission among the general public. In a way, too, as O'Shea kept renewing his ban on public collections, he was attempting to efface the sisters' presence from this wider domain. But the more they were kept from collecting, the more public donations and bequests kept arriving. Suzanne put it down to Providence.

Suzanne had spent years working with doctors in Rome hospitals; she had given herself the mantle of medicine from an early age; since 1900 her sisters had been the only ones in institutional nursing in Wellington. Her project to build a hospital was entirely understandable. She wanted desperately to have it in place before she died, because she was the one who had the network of government contacts and the driving force to make it happen. She poured her failing energies into this dream until the last moment. It was a race against time.

From the start, offsetting diocesan disapproval, she had the backing of lay and medical officialdom. On 11 April 1922, Suzanne had written a long letter to the Minister of Health, C. J. Parr, asking for the Home of Compassion to be recognised as a training hospital:

> In order to ensure the efficiency and permanence of the Institution, it is absolutely necessary to train its Sisters for the present and the future. We, therefore, humbly beg you, Sir, for your benevolent consideration of our petition to be allowed to give our own Sisters only (that is to say, only the members of our Institute) the hospital training without which it is impossible to carry on efficiently or extend our own special work.[68]

, Hester Maclean, as Director of Nursing, conveyed Parr's regrets and refusal to Suzanne. But Hester did not stop there. Her own chief interest in her work was 'especially the training schools for nurses'.[69] She had even offered Karitane training to the sisters while Suzanne was in Rome. Just as Grace Neill had done years before over the babies, Hester Maclean took the initiative. With Clotilde and Suzanne she had already devised an interim scheme which would edge the Sisters of Compassion closer to their goal. She put this formally now:

> I would suggest that you should proceed with the scheme for training a limited number of your Sisters, giving them the same training by lectures and practical nursing as is required under the Nurses Registration Act. Their progress and knowledge could be tested by examination conducted by medical practitioners and trained nurses and certificates of success awarded. Registration is a mark of qualification needed for nurses competing with others in the outside world, but is scarcely needed for those who will be working under the conditions of the members of your Sisterhood, and there is no reason why they should not become equally efficient nurses as those who are required to pass the State Examination.[70]

Sister Clotilde as matron began giving regular lectures. Doctors came free of charge to give lectures more formally than before. There was now an 'Honorary Medical Staff': Drs Whyte, Corkill, Lynch, Hardwick-Smith, Shirer, Roche-Kelly, Rhind, and several others. Unofficial exams, similar to the national ones, were set and marked on a volunteer basis by Edith Sealy, former matron of Otaki hospital, helped by Cecilia McKenny. Like the working bees, it was once more a case of people wanting something and making it happen.

Dr Thomas Valintine, the Director-General of Health, supported the experiment and helped work out details. He came often to visit Suzanne. She would send in her annual report to the department. She said she did not want her women passing the exam other than on their own merit. She wanted her sisters to be 'expert'. Valintine reassured her: 'I am glad to see that the arrangements are so satisfactory with regard to the training of the nurses. You may be quite sure that none of your probationers will pass their examination through favour, but will be treated as probationers in other hospitals with every fairness and consideration.'[71] Passing the three-hour 1924 paper was definitely on merit only: two sisters failed. Jessie Bicknell, who had succeeded Hester Maclean in 1923 as Director of Nursing, broke the news: 'I regret to state that Sisters M. Augustine and Mary Margaret were unsuccessful in their examination, all the others

passed, Sister Mary Paul coming first.'[72] There was a flash of Aubert
displeasure in Suzanne's response: 'I am very much pleased that none
were passed through favour, but simply on their personal merit which
evidently is not great.'

Typically with Suzanne, her next words turned to diplomatic
overtures:

> I and Sister Clotilde have been keenly interested in the perusal of the
> examination papers which you so graciously condescended to send me. I hope
> that the examination next year will show a steady progress, justifying the
> much appreciated condescention of the Department of Health towards us.
>
> I would be delighted if, at any time, you could renew at the Home of
> Compassion our old acquaintance.
>
> I am Dear Miss Bicknell
> gratefully and affectionately yours
> S. M. Joseph Aubert, sup. gen.[73]

Suzanne's networking often developed into friendship. Jessie Bicknell was
a thoroughly professional advocate of nursing as a career. She had been
matron of the hospital ship *Maheno* in the First World War, and this
would surely have set Suzanne talking of nursing back in Crimean war
days. Jessie also had a 'keen sense of right and wrong and a dry sense of
humour' which would appeal to Suzanne.[74] She made friends with the
sisters. She would visit, send Christmas presents and flowers from her
own garden.

By late 1924, Suzanne was weakening fast. At the same time, she was
stepping up her efforts for the training hospital.[75] By now mostly with
'Nurse Webber' (Sister Clotilde) as her delegate in visits, she kept up
her pressure on the department, in her letters retreating merely to sally
forth again:

> Dear Doctor,
> Kindly excuse me for troubling you again, but what could I do without you?
> We wish to have our Home registered as a Hospital, to enable us to take a few
> acute medical cases. . . . If you grant the necessary permission to establish us as
> a small Hospital we would be happy to offer our humble services to the
> authorities of the General Hospital to relieve them of any poor (acute) cases
> when their accommodation is overtaxed. [76]

By 1925 she was optimistically heading up her annual report: 'REV.
MOTHER AUBERT'S HOME OF COMPASSION TRAINING SCHOOL'. She was
discussing her schemes with her council. 'The Superior General spoke of
the need for a free Operating Theatre and outlined the scheme to convert

the big drying shed into a school, and the present schoolroom into a dormitory for the healthy boys, leaving space then to clear Ward VII for a Theatre Block.'[77] With departmental inspection and advice, she finally began the changes which would create a theatre and surgical ward, essential for a training hospital. At the end of 1925, she was over ninety years old. Greater urgency had crept into her tone: 'May I request you kindly to give this matter your consideration and send your Inspector out as soon as you can conveniently do so, as it is so important for us to have the work concluded as soon as possible.'[78]

Doctors willingly paced and measured the wards, and worked out where the theatre and side ward would go. Jessie Bicknell had 'a certificate for sanitary plumbing' and worked out plumbing improvements. Plans were approved; alterations were done; for days on end holes for steam ducts were bored noisily through brick and masonry walls near Suzanne in her room. A team of volunteer men helped once again. By March 1926, the work was done and the hospital was ready. Suzanne had ordered a Pietà, a statue of Our Lady of Compassion. Redwood had agreed to bless the statue and the 'surgical section exclusively reserved for the poor'. The Minister of Health would open the new theatre. It would be like the old days. Only it did not turn out like that.

Invitations had already gone out. The Governor-General and his wife had to decline with regret as they would be out of town. Then a newspaper article wrote about the opening and mentioned the admission of acute medical cases.[79] Redwood reacted at this point. He wrote to Suzanne on 1 March 1926: 'I was told by you that it was proposed to erect merely an operating room where the patients in the Home could be operated upon by the Doctors gratuitously. I have no intention of approving your design to turn the Home into a Hospital such as you describe. Consequently I absolutely decline to have anything to do with the proposed ceremony, and I am amazed at the deception to which I have been subjected.'[80] He made himself even more clear a month later: 'Incurability, certain or nearly so, is alone the essential condition for the reception of adult patients. Your Institution is a Home for Incurables not a hospital for poor patients.'[81]

The ceremony was cancelled. The hospital project was in abeyance. Redwood and Suzanne had been on their old friendly terms, so this break was unexpected and traumatic for her. Redwood's reaction was ill advised and he later apologised, but not before Suzanne had died. The wording of the Decree of Praise had in fact given her wide scope for medical work in hospitals. Listed first among the aims was 'to work for the relief of the sick and of those suffering from incurable disease, without distinction of sex or religion, in the hospitals and institutions established for this purpose'.[82]

As far back as 13 April 1921, she had detailed for Redwood the nursing training necessary to achieve this aim and what it might entail in extending or modifying the building. It was a long, friendly, clear letter in which she shared with him her proposed blueprint for future work. She referred specifically to 'a surgical Hospital for training Nurses, with annexes complete'. With almost breathless energy, she wrote of:

> rendering possible the training of the Sisters as certificated Nurses, by erecting two surgical Wards (for the poor only), which, being connected with the Wards of our Incurable Children and Adults, would give a sufficient number of patients to justify the recognition of the Government and the condescension [she meant 'kindly co-operation'] of the doctors who are willing to give lectures and demonstrations to enable the Sisters to pass successfully the examinations for a first-class certificate. It is becoming more and more necessary that most of our Sisters should be certificated to be able to carry on satisfactorily our works. We sadly feel the need of it.[83]

Redwood had replied to this letter and mentioned the surgical ward, the training of the sisters, the hospital and operating theatre. But a typed letter of 12 May 1921, signed by Redwood though bearing the hallmark of O'Shea, cautioned the 'Reverend Mother General':

> Some of the new proposals, such as the surgical ward for instance & the Convalescent Home, will receive our approbation only after the most careful consideration. . . . We may say here, that we have no confidence whatever in the statement that the Government or even the Medical profession are favourably inclined to them. . . . Plans & specifications of new building & of structural changes to present buildings, must in every case be submitted to us & to our Diocesan Building Committee, for our approval in writing . . .[84]

O'Shea probably hoped that, once Suzanne had died and the force of her personality had gone, such a large scheme would not eventuate as a popular counterpoint to the other hospital which he himself was promoting – or, at least, not for a good while. It must have been hard for O'Shea, for years the meticulous administrator working back home for an imposing archbishop often absent overseas. When O'Shea finally went to Rome in 1922, he was apparently greeted with coolness in hierarchical circles which had warmed to Suzanne. He was hurt, Sister Angela was told, and when he returned he would have nothing to do with Suzanne.[85] He refused the sisters' request to come and see her when she was dying.[86]

Suzanne also indulged in some game-play. The minutes, for instance, record her carefully using the word 'Ordinary', the correct term under canon law rather than 'Bishop', more than perhaps she needed to in New Zealand: 'She would write to the Ordinary first & ask him if June would be convenient for him. She called him the Ordinary (she explained) because that was the custom in Rome, the term was no disrespect, – it had a consecrated usage.'[87]

The final changes to the building were nearly all internal and theoretically did not need approval from Rome. As the project edged towards completion, she was vague about specific details to Redwood when he visited. In principle he knew about it; he may not have been fully updated.[88] She was tending to talk just about the 'theatre', to play down the extent of the modifications. His letter is clear: 'I wish to draw your attention to this all important point: no building, or important structural change, in your Institutions, must be undertaken without the previous approval of the Ordinary, that is, of the Metropolitan or his Coadjutor, Archbishop O'Shea, and the plans of such buildings or changes must be submitted to the Building Board of the Archdiocese.'[89] Suzanne had taken a gamble. She would not have wanted to be stopped at this stage by either man. She had been hoping for an amicable *fait accompli*, her vision both blessed by public approval and consecrated by her church.

Suzanne's hospital did come into being a few years after she died. A month after her funeral, Redwood relented. He wrote to the council: 'Patients suffering from incurable disease, providing they are poor and cannot pay anywhere else, may be operated upon at the Home of Compassion, for such diseases as cancer, etc. A few cases for operation, sufficient to provide for the completion of the training of the Sisters, may be admitted, always provided they are of the very poor, who cannot pay elsewhere.'[90] The sisters at first sat the same exams as the state nurses but obtained a temporary certificate, equivalent to state registration, for use in their hospital alone. By 1931, with the help of Thomas Valintine, Jessie Bicknell and Judge Blair, a partner in the law firm with Skerrett, the home was finally recognised by the government as an A-grade training hospital.[91] Sister Eustace was one of the first sisters to gain state registration. When she read their names in the newspaper, she felt like 'turning a somersault'.[92]

Suzanne had her 'expert', 'efficient' nurses. Sisters of Compassion went on to top New Zealand in nursing exams. The matron and nurses were respected by the doctors, Dr C. T. Collins among them. The hospital had a reputation for 'devotion to nursing': in the evening 'you'd find the same nurse on who was on in the morning. It made looking after a patient very simple. Obviously it was very tiring for the nurses but it made nursing here absolutely perfect.' 'They were so accurate, the whole presentation. . . . My job was to get other doctors to come here. I was never turned down by any doctor in Wellington, whatever his religion was. . . . I almost had a queue of people wanting to work here. . . . There was never a point of inviting Catholic doctors. . . . I can remember times when on the whole ward there wasn't a Catholic patient.' The reputation was not just because of excellence and continuity in nursing: 'There was a spirit in the place. You got it when you walked in the front door. You might feel tired and weary but you felt relaxed once you walked in. The whole atmosphere of the place was really quite special. You felt as if you'd come home.'[93]

. . . I will go to the funeral : . . . Ka haere ahau ki te nehunga[94]

Suzanne died on 1 October 1926. The months leading up to her death had been painful. In her last ascetic feat of self-denial, maybe to put right the anguish of the hospital débâcle, she had made the doctor promise to give her no pain relief. She wanted to die. She lay there, pleading in French to God or Jean Vianney to take her away. Archbishop Redwood came to see her as soon as he arrived back from Australia. They had known each other a long time – since 1874, when the confident and optimistic new bishop had met the equally confident and optimistic Sister Mary Joseph at Meanee. Sir James Carroll had called earlier on, but she was seeing nobody. 'She will see me', Carroll said. He bent down beside her narrow, low iron bed and took his parting with a long-held hongi.[95]

Wiki Pauro Marino wrote from Ranana. She said that Meri was the living link with parents now gone. Neri Metera had died not long before, in July 1924. Before that, Suzanne had been sending medical advice, and glasses for him to try.[96] Marked 'urgent', Suzanne's shaky writing had gone to Neri's daughter at Ranana, sending love and sympathy: 'Ka nui te mihi aroha a Meri ma nga none katoa ki te iwi a Ranana.'[97] Now, at Suzanne's dying, Wiki's letter was wistful: Meri would understand her feelings about this, and would realise too how much Wiki loved her:

E kui, tena koe i roto i nga mamae tanga ote ao. He aroha noaha ake, ituhiatu ai. E te mea ko koe te oranga ake onga matua. Heoi, ma te Atua koe ekukume ake kite mate kite ora. Kia ora koe. E hara ite tika nga mea tena, hei whakapiri noa atu i toku aroha kia koe.[98]

Valintine came often. Sister Eustace remembered him at the end: 'He asked to be at her deathbed when she was dying and when we were all kneeling around her praying, he came in and he had some kind of limp and had great difficulty, but he knelt down and kissed, kissed her on the brow, the reverence he had for her; . . . I wonder what it would have been that she could draw all these people.'[99]

The news of Suzanne's death made headlines. 'She was one of the greatest women in public effort and loving self-sacrifice New Zealand has known.'[100] It was broadcast on radio even in Australia.[101] A stream of people began to come out to Island Bay, thousands of them, queueing up the stairs to pay their respects. The Catholics among them touched her habit with their rosaries. Sister Baptista wrote to her sister: 'All ranks and denominations of people teamed in on Saturday, Sunday and Monday from early morning till late at night; the last night we had to leave the door open till midnight.'[102]

Her funeral was on 4 October, the morning when Wellington stopped for a woman of its own. Charles Skerrett was now Chief Justice, succeeding Sir Robert Stout. He postponed the Supreme Court sitting. Valintine memoed his staff at the Department of Health about Suzanne:

> I . . . would be glad if as many officers of the Department as possible could attend her Requiem Mass to be held at St. Mary of the [Angels], Boulcott Street, at nine o'clock tomorrow morning where I am proud to say special seats have been reserved for officers of the Department. I need not remind officers that it is not a question of creed with us, it is a question of the recognition of the services of a very splendid and devoted woman who by her life and example has left an example to us all.[103]

The newspapers reported that a hundred people from the Health Department were there.

The day of the funeral was bright and clear. In the photographs the children were lined up outside the Home of Compassion as a guard of honour. Girls' plaits shone and they squinted against the low morning sun as they looked up the road to see the hearse coming. Sister Carmel was in the front of the group of sisters waiting. The men who would carry Suzanne, Te Manihera Keremeneta and Tim Herlihy among them, lifted the leadlined coffin on their shoulders. Rure's hair was now grizzled grey.

His Pakeha fellow pall-bearer clasped him around the shoulder as they took the weight together. Father Mark Devoy, who had been constantly with Suzanne through her pain and dying, waited as they put the coffin into the hearse. From the garden that she had been planting in the gully alongside the home, the spiky tufts of the cabbage tree heads sent out shafts of light as they bent in the breeze – Suzanne's *brise* that had so often spun its grit against her walking figure. Small, square cars, threaded neatly like beads, followed the hearse as it set off along Dee St.

Those arriving early found the church already packed. 'It was very quiet in the church', wrote Eileen Duggan for the *New Zealand Times*. 'The sunlight . . . flecked the pure white of the pillars. . . . The whole church rose up as the members of her order filed in. . . . From the choir came the splendid swell of the mighty Gregorian chant. . . . The full Mass was sung, the fullest Mass of all for those who die in God. All that her creed had to offer of sight and sound was offered to her sleeping.' Other papers picked up the story: 'Within the church, and without, every creed, colour and generation the country knows was gathered. Many of them had come from afar at great sacrifice.'[104]

With the group of leading clergy assisting Archbishop Redwood was Dean Regnault. He was a French Marist and 'one of Mother Aubert's oldest friends'. The sub-deacon was Father Venning, who had come from Hiruharama. He was the first Maori missioner there who was not French. He bore the cross at the head of the procession, symbolising in a way the passing at Suzanne's death from the old French missioners to the new. Eileen Duggan reported Redwood's farewell: 'She realised the identity between Christ and the lowliest of her brethren . . . So when she composed the rule for the new Order she founded, a rule first approved by His Grace and afterwards by Rome, it was not surprising that it was [inspired by] this passage from the words of Christ: "Whatever you shall do for the lowliest of Mine it is done unto Me."'[105]

Named among those listening were Charles Skerrett, Sir Robert Stout, Sir Joseph Ward, Sir John Hosking, ex-mayor and member of Parliament Sir John Luke, Peter Fraser, Rabbi Van Staveren, former Presbyterian Moderator Rev. Kennedy Elliott. Unnamed were Suzanne's capable and enterprising women friends, among them the fund-raising volunteer Mrs Macarthy-Reid and Jessie Bicknell the public servant.

Outside, 'Willis St and the Quay were as silent as unpeopled lands, though thousands lined the route.'[106] The clear daylight picked out the plain cross on the coffin as it turned the tight corner of the steps of St Mary of the Angels. At the foot of the steps, the cross-bearer in his ornate dalmatic was flanked by the priests of the choir. The lace on their surplices swirled in the gusts of wind. The Hibernians lined the steps, and their feet walking alongside the hearse would be the only sound in the street crammed with people.

About ninety cars passed along Lambton Quay behind the hearse. Others had given up and after the Mass had driven the other way to the cemetery at Karori. Hundreds, blocked from the church, had already gone there. Harry Ashworth was chief altar boy at the funeral, and it was the traffic that stayed most in his memory: 'They stopped all the traffic in Wellington, from St Mary of the Angels to Karori, trams and all that were stopped.'[107] The *Evening Post* reported that cars 'were still emerging from the Karori Tunnel after the leading cars had entered the cemetery gates'.[108] A newspaper told how one curious bystander along the way asked, 'What religion was this woman?' 'The answer, sublime in its comprehensive succinctness,' wrote the reporter, 'came from a workman resting on his shovel by the roadside: "That is a question she would never have asked you or me!"'[109]

The path down through Karori cemetery was lined with boys from St Patrick's and the Marist Brothers' schools. The sisters walked down between them. Their shoes were nuggeted shiny in the sun, their hands tucked in their big sleeves. The large tassled ends of their blue girdles swung like long poi as they walked. The silvery medal of the Daughters of Our Lady of Compassion weighed down its light blue cord and cut a clear angle on their short capes. The *Benedictus* of the choir floated up the gorse-covered hill. There were birdcalls in the midday air. The sisters gathered around and watched as Rure and his companions lowered Suzanne into her grave. Then they said goodbye.

The *New Zealand Times* editor said goodbye in the language of journalism. He first referred to her spirit of 'Suffer the little children to come unto me', then continued:

> Here was the inspiration of all her strong powers – courage, initiative, organisation, discipline, practical sense, devotion to duty – which otherwise employed would have assured her a princely fortune, but employed as they were came to a great success in a noble field and left an example which will stir the hearts of men and women to warm, respectful veneration while human life endures on earth.

There is a memorial of this great woman in the Home of Compassion on the Island Bay hillside – a home most wonderful in view of its origin and development from nothing. Another and wider memorial lives on in the hearts of all who know the story of this wonderful old pioneer, and treasure their respect for noble natures and for the holy simplicity which throws the halo of great virtue over ordinary actions.[110]

One of Suzanne's 'orphan' girls, then aged sixteen, would remember Maori gathering at the graveside; they were 'very impressive with their farewell'. They 'called Mother Meri'.[111] Puarata Menehira, Puke Rangitauira, Tehukinga Potaka and Neri Poutini spoke for themselves and the people of Hiruharama. They sent their mother on her way to their parents and ancestors, those people who held the faith when she had lived up the Whanganui, caring for their bodily and spiritual well-being. She had been a mother also to the orphans and homeless. She was to go with their love. Taken in death, she would go to life:

> Mihi aroha ki to matou whaea atawhai kia Meri Hohepa. Haere e Meri, haere e kui. Haere ki ho matou matua me ho matou tupuna. Kinga tangata naana i pupuri te Whakapono i nga ra e noho ana koe i Wanganui ia matou e atawhai ana iho matou tinana meho matou Wairua. Haere ete Whaea ote Pani mete rawakore, haere ki to tatou Ariki. Naana nei i whakatakoto te huarahi e tae atu ai tatou kitona rangatiratanga i te rangi. [112]

The stars are shining : Kei te piata nga whetu[113]

Among her papers Suzanne had a devotional card of Our Lady of Fourvière. Usually the stars of Mary are depicted on a crown, or around her head. The Mary on Suzanne's card has stars around the hem of her skirt. True, she is shown, as often, removed from the earth: she is standing on puffs of cloud. Nevertheless, the potential for Mary's stars to touch land is there. She could be woman, and real, companionable and imitable. In Suzanne's faith, the spirituality of stars and the reality of earth could meet. She made the stars of Mary's hem shine at floor level alongside other women. 'Let us do our housework and cleaning in union with Mary,' she told them, 'who performed her household duties as any other woman, but with perfection.' Suzanne's Mary is not alone. The housework was also done in 'union with Joseph, who swept his workshop and kept it in order', in 'union with the Child Jesus, Who helped His Mother at home'.[114] Her Mary and Joseph and Jesus are seen at home in Jerusalem or Buckle St; they are family.

The words are universal: woman, man, child; kitchen, workshop, home; sky and land. But the context of life in New Zealand was not universal. It was also particular, different from anywhere else, and Suzanne was always able to grasp the reality of her context. There might be the pulpit record of religion, with its expressions of faith usually divorced from people's daily lives, with sermons which, like a subset of an empire theme, could have been preached anywhere in Ireland for the Catholics – or in England, Scotland, Wales for the rest.[115] But that was not all there was. The land and the mingling people were steadily having an effect. People began to sense 'the growth of a shared identity, shared with all comers, reasonably and by choice'.[116]

Suzanne's whole story indicates that she was aware of this from the outset, and preferred it. About two years before she died, she was developing or copying ideas in an exercise-book. She was writing in both French and English at once, it appears, the words eddying around each other as the sentences progress. Then in English come the words: 'Rivers do not return to their own source . . .'[117] Suzanne's French past would always be there, swelling the waters of her present, and its ripples would often be at the surface, but her river would flow on to a future of shared identity.

No state church developed in New Zealand. Churches did not have direct power. They were 'voluntary associations' only; their power was their 'appeal to individual conscience'.[118] The story of Suzanne and the people of New Zealand sends a shaft of light down into the often hidden world of ordinary people's spiritual history, showing consistently that there could be a willingness to co-operate, reasonably and by choice. Her people were choosing not to reflect the official stance of many ecclesiastics from overseas. The two main clerical bigots who stirred up dissension and disruption during and after the First World War, the Protestant Rev. Howard Elliott and Catholic Dr James Kelly, had both come recently to New Zealand. Suzanne had been here from 1860 and sensed more than they did a deep-down need in people for reasonable community and harmony.

In both setting and catching the mood of the people as she did, Suzanne could be a puzzle and a threat to those in authority. She was signalling change. Even her congregation's formation was exceptional within New Zealand Catholicism. It came not so much from the accepted doctrinal and theological reading of the times, or from close adherence to the norms of Catholic observance, as by translating into their daily lives the message of the Nazareth Family. The strength of their spirituality came from a local matrix. It was like a gem in the hand with different facets reflecting different lights, some from afar but some from nearby.

Suzanne made an original claim in the *Directory* that the first Christian theologian was a woman, Elizabeth, the mother of John the Baptist. When, according to St Luke's account, the pregnant Mary visited her, Elizabeth 'was the first human creature', said Suzanne, 'to recognise and adore, in the Son of Mary, the Son of God, even before His birth. She was the first theologian to formulate and the first evangelist to announce the divinity of Jesus Christ and the Maternity of Mary.'[119] Suzanne, too, may have been breaking new ground. Apart from the prophets of the syncretic Maori faiths with their blend of traditional and Christian themes,[120] she may have been the first to formulate a New Zealand expression of Christian spirituality. She was 'earthing the Gospel in local soil'.[121]

The fact that she was a woman is relevant. She did not have the more conformist power of the pulpit. She made a virtue out of necessity; she made a strength from her 'weakness'. A study of the nineteenth-century American preacher Sojourner Truth – woman, black and former slave – noted: 'Prohibited by church discipline to head established churches, these female prophets heeded the divine calling to preach and reached wide, heterogeneous audiences.'[122] Suzanne, too, reached wide. And by very public example she 'preached' a message of change. Hers was a prophetic voice. She was signalling much that surfaced later in Catholicism with the Vatican II changes of the 1960s: the harmonising of liturgy with different cultures and contexts, the ecumenical reaching-out to different faiths, the expression of some freedom of conscience, and acknowledgement of women's rights.

Suzanne was fairly conservative in her tenets and would not have felt she was pushing boundaries. In her actions, though, she was often doing so. It was this that may have disturbed many of the clergy and made them feel threatened, although they could react in the same way to independence among their fellow men as well. For whatever reason, after her death the memory of Suzanne began to be presented safely in pious, self-perpetuating and mostly unquestioned legend, or else was quietly effaced.

During the 1938 Auckland centennial celebrations marking the beginnings of Catholicism in New Zealand, Sister Clotilde noticed this happening and made a diary entry: 'In all the articles written of Bishop Pompallier and his companion missionaries, there was no mention of Mother Aubert, or the Order she founded. Also, in the well-illustrated and comprehensive programme arranged for the Centenary functions, the absence of any reference to her and her great work amongst the Maoris, and later amongst the poor and afflicted of both races, was very marked.' Some clergy over the years continued to edge women away from the New Zealand congregation.[123]

Yet nobody was more Catholic than Suzanne. She was not compromising her faith. Her story tells of nineteenth- and early twentieth-century Catholicism, its missionary surge, its symbols of piety, its international cohesiveness and power.[124] But she was also responding to the here-and-now of her context. Suzanne's faith breathed a matter-of-fact acceptance of her time and place through the week as well as on Sunday. The dynamics of people shaped it. Her congregation was not an 'external construct' but was grounded and local, not just by the accident of its foundation but in its whole spirituality. The sisters record with laughter how they have been seen as 'ordinary', how they are in fact ordinary. To be ordinary is to be 'not unusual'. Suzanne was creating a model of faith which was to be natural and at home, not unusual. She 'was imitable to some extent, not just admirable. It made sense in a new society.'[125]

Sister Clotilde once quietly accosted one of Suzanne's old opponents, Monsignor Cullen. His sister was being nursed at the Home of Compassion at the time. It was years after Suzanne's death but Clotilde wanted to restate her case: 'Mgr immediately told me that our Institute amazed him. He had never before seen such a lot of happy religious, and could hardly believe such a spirit existed – spontaneous and "bubbling up"! He had seen it from many angles while visiting his sick sister.' Clotilde records very clearly her long discussion with Cullen, who was still sceptical about Suzanne herself. Then she finishes up: 'We know *how* and *where* [the spirit] originated, and truth will come out in the long run – it always does.'[126]

Suzanne was the woman who marched through the yards at ram fairs, who scrambled up mining inclines, who bedded down in whare, wharepuni, Presbyterian cottage or Irish Catholic pub; whose 'heart leapt with joy' in London when she was greeted with 'Tena koe';[127] who wanted desperately to get back to New Zealand. Sir James Wilson, a Presbyterian friend, wrote to her in 1920: 'I often think of the time we first met on the little steamer that ran up and down the Whanganui river. I asked you if "you were never lonely", but you laughed at the idea and said: "that sometimes you went up the hill at the back of the house and shouted and laughed for joy".'[128]

The people filling the life of this woman, who never locked herself away from contact, came from many backgrounds. Some new settlers stayed more or less serene and secure – or bound – in their old religious or social beliefs. Others were changing. Most, by the very meaning of the word 'settler', were having a go at settling in together. Suzanne believed that Christ was in everyone. That meant in all her neighbours, no matter how different they were. She was continually spreading this belief out into the public domain. Her faith conveyed trusting tolerance and shared identity. What she gave, she received as well, in a spirit of liking and love, of hopeful common sense, of infectious goodness.

Joan Akapita of the Whanganui River pinpointed this. 'We're talking', she said, 'about goodness – understandable, achievable goodness.'[129] That is not far from Poupinel's assessment of thirty-year-old Suzanne when he met her early in 1866: 'I think she is a sensible person with a love of goodness.' At the age of eighty-eight, she signed a letter to Jerusalem. She was Sister Mary Joseph Aubert, 'with plenty love'.[130]

Epilogue

Accept this book : Tangohia tenei pukapuka
It is at your service : Kei tou ringaringa ano to mea[1]

There are three tellers of this story, just as there are for any other. I have chosen what to tell and how to tell it, and what to leave out. You have taken in and interpreted as it suits you, and let some of it go by. Suzanne – accessible and elusive, historical and legendary – also had a strong hand in the shaping of her story. There are as many triangles of authorship as there are readers. All of us bring the dynamics of our time, place, culture, beliefs and personality. Dispassionate objectivity is impossible; the story is never pasted down once and for all.

Stories, like scenes, have their different viewpoints, their different interpretations. The first view of Jerusalem as you round the bend in the road or river is breathtaking, especially if you have Christian iconography in your make-up. The church is right in the centre, delicately simple and comfortingly solid. The river, the houses, the hills and the sky serve to frame it. Its spire, with the figure niched below it of workman Hato Hohepa, is a welcoming beacon. But if your experience of religion is different, if Pakeha mission history strikes discordant notes, or even if isolated hill country is frightening, you could possibly sense a wall of hills, a spire snatching the attention from nature all around, a church looming above with the settlement in restless meekness below. You bring to Hiruharama whatever is influencing you.

There are other views as well as the one from the parallel road and river. Jerusalem looks quite different when seen from the hills around. Across the river a level ridge runs along to the bluff where the pa of Werahiko and Poma was in the days when Kauaeroa was peopled and Father Lampila had his mission there. Sometimes goose-white shapes stand at the edge of the bush, maybe descendants of the geese gathered by

Suzanne on her collecting tour, gone free in the wild. The graves of the
Moutoa dead are over there.

From the Kauaeroa side, the view is wide-angled. Across the bottom is
the silent push of water down the channel of the river. There are no rapids
at this point, only an even khaki or flax-green grosgrain band as a
strengthening baseline. Above it, the paddocks slant back on the left,
propped between the river and the line where the scrub starts. Pakeha
poplars make a stand; willows line the bank; oaks and walnuts cluster
nearer the houses; paradise ducks claim the wet hollows of the paddock.
Further up, the hills climb way back to the ridges of Suzanne's orchard,
where a few old chestnut and cherry trees, grown stiff and aching, still
manage to flower in spring. This is all to the left. The farming heights of
Morikau rise on the right to balance.

The church is down below, just left of centre. The base of its spire is
rounded and close to you over the water, the warm brown shingles
and light weatherboards touchable in the late afternoon sun. The convent
sits, comfortable alongside, with its hem of red corrugated-iron sheds –
Suzanne's cheeky flash of red. Father Soulas's statue of Mary is in the
garden between. Rure kept her dress fresh-painted through the years.

Central to the picture are the two marae, cradled within the arms of the
church and the river. Their land and houses surround them. Then, when
you look up, you suddenly take in what lies beyond. The valley of the
Motuihe creek, which you do not notice from the river or the road, lies
open, relaxing back to the sky. It seems a gentle valley with wide curves
among the hills and gorges of the river. Its breadth surprises you. You are
being let into an unexpected secret which delights.

In just such a way, Suzanne's vision of large-hearted spiritual neigh-
bourliness – call it arohanui – was an open vista. One by one, thousands
of New Zealanders drew alongside her, viewed it with pleasure, and
headed on in that direction. Sometimes they even helped show her the
way. Getting there across the gap would never seem hard to her. From
Rome she had told the sisters: 'I am with you in mind, though I am bodily
separated from you by the wide ocean.' To 'throw a bridge over it', she
wrote to them her directions for living together their clear and simple
faith. Bridging gaps was what Suzanne Aubert did best, and with an
inviting confidence she directed those around her to do just the same:
'Throw a plank across the stream for us to cross to the other side : Kahu-
papangia te awa ki te rakau kia whiti tatou ki tera taha.'[2]

Author's Note

In writing this book I have kept very consciously a wide perspective. I decided to do this early on in my reading when I became aware of the places Suzanne Aubert had been, the varied issues she dealt with, the thousands of people who filled her life. The book was obviously not going to give you as readers a tranquil stroll in the company of a cloistered nun. You were going to have to crowd in with all the characters elbowing their way into the pages, and perhaps even feel footsore occasionally as you covered the distances with her. To have a narrower focus and lesser momentum would be untrue to the very person the book was portraying.

I found myself wanting the original Marist story slotted safely in for its huge influence on her life; I wanted the Clercs de Saint Viateur and the Franciscans to be there for their revelatory experience contemporary to hers; I wanted the Sisters of Mercy in their own right, not seen merely as counterfoils to Suzanne's activities; I wanted Antoinette Deloncle's story to speak for those women in colonial New Zealand who were lost on the way; I wanted the Auckland depression of the 1860s explained so as to interpret the close of the Pompallier era; I wanted Leonard Williams's voice to give an East Coast setting for the subtly changing missionary angle of the 1870s – and so on through the book. I wanted the narrative to incorporate, as it were, the interweaving tales of different groups of pilgrims in order to portray more richly the landscape and the times they were passing through, and to throw into clearer relief the personal experience of the little woman out at the head of this particular pilgrimage. Because, again to be fair to the nature of the woman, any story about her would need to reflect the history of the people and the country she was actively and intensely committed to.

The story therefore became very full. Yet I find myself feeling apologetic to those whose families have in their heritage a 'Mother Aubert' tale which did not go into the book. In spite of the big cast list, there are still many characters offstage. For this reason, the people in the dedication are there also as representatives, each to head a long roll of named and unnamed contributors to the story of Suzanne Aubert.

Most of the primary source material for this book is in French, quite a lot of it as yet untranslated, and much of the quoted text you have been reading is in translation. The translations from French and Italian are mine except for a few where the original was not readily available, and for some of Philip Turner's excellent translations in his thesis, 'The Politics of Neutrality: the Catholic Mission and the Maori 1838–1870', in which the original French also appears for verification.

Existing translations, even good ones, may not always pick up the nuances of the context, the relevance to connected events or people, the implied references that can reveal themselves to someone reading across the range of material in the original language. However, the Sisters of Compassion are fortunate to have had for years the skilled voluntary help of Father Maurice Scully, whose understanding of the context has combined with his knowledge of French to enable an appreciable proportion of their archives to be made available to English readers. Material in translation is increasingly accessible in Marist archives as well, and a major project is under way to edit, publish and translate the early Marist mission correspondence from Oceania.

Any particularities of English spelling found in quotations appear as they were in the original document. Corrections or clarifications are within square brackets. Most of the Maori language in the text has come from older sources, which did not use the macron or long vowel marker, or from Suzanne Aubert's *New and Complete Manual of Maori Conversation*, where, although she did use macrons, they were combined with other diacritical marks that were not always consistently applied by her or the printer. For consistency, therefore, it was decided that Maori printed in the text, including the few quotations from my recent interviews, would be without vowel markers.

The areas covered in this book have been wide-ranging, and it is possible that, because my background is in language more than in history or religion, there are errors of fact or some further knowledge to be uncovered on certain points. I welcome any contributions which add to the understanding of Suzanne Aubert and her life work.

Acknowledgements

The Sisters of Compassion invited me to write this book and I have loved both the work and their company. In thanking Sister Catherine Hannan and the sisters of the General Council, I am thanking them all. I would like especially to thank Sister Bernadette Mary Wrack, who has given me the constant support both of her archival knowledge and of her friendship which I value highly.

The sisters have a long association with Ngati Hau and Ngati Ruaka of the Whanganui River. Throughout the researching and writing, I have appreciated the help they have given and the interest they have in this book which tells some of their own story. Their families knew Suzanne Aubert as Meri, and this is the name used in the Maori title they have chosen: *Te Ao o Meri*. To begin the book, they give Meri her voice in Maori and depict her there with them:

> Standing on the banks of the flowing Whanganui River,
> I can hear the trickling streams flowing towards
> the river and the sweet call of the shining cuckoo,
> and my gaze goes out to a mass of people gathering.

Both to those named in the Whanganui section of these acknowledgements, and to others unnamed, I give my heartfelt thanks. Kia ora koutou.

The book is considerably richer for the contribution of the Marist community, whose own story runs parallel throughout. I particularly thank Father Michael O'Meeghan, who has shared his knowledge with me and encouraged me all the way. My gratitude and thanks go to Brother Gerard Hogg, who willingly and efficiently helped me with archive research and allowed me to use the archives also as a quiet reading-room. My thanks also to Fathers Paul Bergin, Grahame Connolly, Noel Delaney, James Durning, Patrick Kinsella, Gaston Lessard (in Rome), Denis O'Hagan, Kevin Roach, Claude Rozier (in Lyon), Maurice Scully, Brian Wysocki, and Brother Adrian Kennedy.

The Stout Research Centre at Victoria University of Wellington is a vital national resource, especially for researchers and writers coming from outside academia. My grateful thanks go to Stout Centre directors John Thomson, Charlotte Macdonald and Allan Thomas, to Valerie Jacobs, and also to fellow residents Margaret Tennant, Jane Tolerton,

Brad Patterson, Adrienne Simpson, Bill Renwick and Janet McCallum, among others, for their friendly and helpful advice. I also have greatly appreciated valuable guidance on New Zealand history from Charlotte Macdonald and on French history from Susan Grogan, both from the history department of Victoria University.

A Claude McCarthy Fellowship from the New Zealand Universities Vice-Chancellors' Committee, an Award in History from the Historical Branch of the Department of Internal Affairs, and funding from the Sisters of Compassion, all enabled me to work fulltime on what turned out to be a big project. For this I am very grateful. I would like to thank the French Embassy in New Zealand for its interest, and for its help towards research in France and Rome through a grant from the Ministère des Affaires Etrangères. A Harriette Jenkins Award from the New Zealand Federation of University Women helped me carry out many valuable interviews. I also acknowledge with thanks a grant from the 1993 Suffrage Year Centennial Trust: Whakatu Wahine. In inviting me to contribute to his two collections of essays on historical contacts between New Zealand and France, John Dunmore helped set me on the road to this biography; I sincerely thank him for this.

My thanks to colleagues and friends at the Correspondence School for their invaluable help: Madeleine Waddington for our rewarding shared work on Mère Marie Joseph at the outset; Thoron Hollard and Marilyn Doak for unstinting warm encouragement and skilful volunteer 'project management' during the writing; Anthony Dreaver for first suggesting a 'Claude McCarthy Fellowship and a room at the Stout'; Alan Dodds and Maggie Friend for granting prolonged leave; also Noel Dowrick, Beverly Fairfax, Malcolm Geard, John Gwillim, Rob McEwen, Margaret Northcroft, and Darrel Surman.

My love and thanks to all my family and friends who have helped me right through this project – even to the extent of getting bogged knee-high in the winter mud of the cherry farm or braving the Whanganui rapids in the cause of research.

My thanks link up a wide circuit of people: Cardinal Thomas Williams and Archbishop Thomas White facilitated research in Wellington, Lyon and Rome; the French Ambassador, His Excellency Gabriel de Bellescize, and the Cultural Attaché, Jacques Costa, helped with research in France and Rome; Joan Akapita talked with me in her home in Ohakune all one afternoon and evening; in Flaxmere Piki Kenrick gave me the benefit of his knowledge of Pakipaki; Brother Robert Bonnafous in Rome not only responded to my letter with a bulky packet containing a treasure of documentation about Suzanne's fellow passengers but also followed this up with more help when I was in Rome; Ralph Gibson of the University of Lancaster sent me essential advice on accessing French civil and religious records; Erina Scanlon sat with me at her kitchen table in Wanganui and through her words took me straight to the angelus scene in the potato gardens at Ranana. These people are only some of the links in a long chain.

My research has taken me into a great many archives and libraries in Auckland, Wellington, Wanganui, Napier, Lyon, St Etienne, Tarare, Paris and Rome – and into correspondence with archives further afield. The references and bibliography indicate the major ones. I have not always known who the archivist helping me was. If names are omitted, I apologise.

In addition to those people already named, I here acknowledge and thank the following people within the main areas of their contribution, interest and support – and I commemorate some among them who are no longer alive:

France and Rome
Robin Anderson; Anthony Angelo; Marinette Aunier; Marie-Danielle Babou; M. Berthaud; Henri Bibost; Louise Buckingham; Marcella Ciatti; Marie-Hélène Clabaut; Georges Cuer; M.-L. Débias; Madeleine de Terris; C. Dieras; Joëlle Etèveneaux; James FitzPatrick; John Fleming; Gabriel Fouillant; Marie-Josephe France; John Gauci; Renée Grignon; Beverley Grounds; John Hanly; Elisabeth Hardouin-Fugier; Willi Henkel; Vicki Herbert; Carl Hoegerl; Henri Hours; Bertha Hurley; Philip Jebb; Desiree Jury; P. Landau; Howard Larsen; José Antonio Lezama; Odile Lolom; Antoine M'Buyi; André Maire; Josef Metzler; Christiane Mortelier; Rebecca Mulvey; George Naidenoff; Paul Nyaga; Joseph Payen; Solange Poulet; Bernard Prince; Jean Pupunat; Rhys Richards; M.-J. Rosier; Jacqueline Roubert; Maureen Skehan; Sr Geneviève, Soeurs Bénédictines de Pont de Beauvoisin; Denis Tranchard; Hernàn Arboleda Valencia; I. Vernus.

Auckland
Bruce Bolland; Roger Blackley; Rosalie Conder; Veronica Delany; Marcienne Kirk; Jack Lee; Errol Lee-Scarlett; Philippa McManus;

A. Meek; Sue Pirini; Anne Salmond; David Simmons; Ernest Simmons; Rory Sweetman; K. Verdich; Ian Waters.

Hawke's Bay
Joy Axford; Kathleen Browne; Zelma Dickson; Annette Fairweather; Yvonne Francis; Peter Gasson; Piki Kenrick; Peter Lineham; Irene Lister; Patrick Parsons; Frances Porter; Francis Rasmussen; Johnny Ropitini; Tarcisius Walsh; Norma Sinton.

Whanganui
Hohi Albert; Rollo Arnold; Sarah Ashby; Noel Bamber; Arthur Bates; Bruce Biggs; S. Boland; D. Buckley; Labouré Butler; Te Ma Butler; Mavis Donnelly; Patricia Charlton; Matthew Cosgriff; Jocelyn Cumming; Margaret Donaghy; Philippine Dunne; Ivan Emia; Marie Therese Foale; Lynley Fowler; Thelma Grabmair; Mark Gray; Genevieve Grieg; John Haami; David Hamer; Laurence Hay; Rita Hickey; Ada Hina; Bronwyn Labrum; Tricia Laing; Matiu Mareikura; Ted Matthews; Dorothea Meade; Joan Metge; Jan Moen; Anne Noble; Kay Noble; Claudia Orange; Joanna Paul; Lucy Pauro; Pestall Pauro; Peti Poumua; Hugh Price; Maurice Provost; Erina Pucher; Margaret Pugh; Chris Pugsley; Bill Robinson; Anna Maria Shortall; David Simmons; Morvin Simon; Hilary Stace; Ailsa Stewart; Diane Strevens; Veronica Sussmilch; Dovey Taiaroa; Chris Tapa; Eileen Tapa; Winiata Tapa; Ngati Tawhiri; Natalie Te Huia; Celia Thompson; Jim Traue; Weheora Wanihi; Teresa Warbrick; George Waretini; Pehi Waretini; John Waugh; David Young.

Wellington
Godfrey Ainsworth; Lucy Alcock; Harry Ashworth; Ross Bly; Justin Cargill; Cyril Collins; Eustace Conaglen; Bronwyn Dalley; Brian Davies; Michael Fitzgerald; Anne Galvin; Elsie Gibbons; Manuka Henare; Caroline Innes; Hugh Laracy; Jeanne Latimer; Peter Latimer; Tim Lovell-Smith; Winifred Moriarty; Veronica O'Brien; Patricia O'Connor; Brendan O'Gorman; Kathryn Patterson; David Retter; James Veitch; Patrick Velvin; James Walker; Sarah Williams.

Finally, I would like to express my pleasure and thanks to Bridget Williams, Andrew Mason and Madeleine Collinge, of Auckland University Press/Bridget Williams Books, and Robyn Sivewright, of Afineline, for their interest and thoroughness in the publication of this book.

Measurements

The imperial measurements used in this book with their metric equivalents.

Distance

1 inch	= 25.4 millimetres	
12 inches	= 1 foot	= 0.3048 metre
3 feet	= 1 yard	= 0.9144 metre
1760 yards	= 1 mile	= 1.609 kilometres

Area

1 acre	= 4840 square yards	= 0.405 hectare

Weight

1 ounce (oz)		= 0.065 gram
16 ounces	= 1 pound (lb)	= 0.4536 kilogram
1 ton		= 1.016 tonnes

Capacity

1 gallon	= 4.5 litres

Notes and references

Abbreviations

AAL — Archives de l'Archevêché de Lyon

ACPF — Archivio della Congregazione di Propaganda Fide

ADR — Archives Départmentales du Rhone, Lyon

AFFM — Archivio dei Fratri Franciscani Minori, Rome

AIM — Auckland Institute and Museum Library

AJHR — *Appendices to the Journal of the House of Representatives*

AMO — *Annales des Missions d'Océanie*

APF — *Annales de la Propagation de la Foi*

APL — Auckland Public Library

APM — Archivio Padri Maristi

ASMA — Auckland Sisters of Mercy Archives

ATL — Alexander Turnbull Library

AU — University of Auckland

CSV — Archives des Clercs de Saint Viateur

CU — University of Canterbury

DNZB — *Dictionary of New Zealand Biography*

HOC A — Home of Compassion Archives

ICR — Archives of the Irish College, Rome

MAW — Marist Archives, Wellington

NAA — National Archives, Auckland Regional Office

NAW — National Archives Head Office, Wellington

NZJH — *New Zealand Journal of History*

NZPD — *New Zealand Parliamentary Debates*

OPM — Archives, Oeuvres Pontificales Missionaires (formerly Oeuvre de la Propagation de la Foi)

OU — University of Otago

RL — Redwood Letterbook (in WAA)

RNDM — Archives des Religieuses de Notre Dame des Missions

SM — Society of Mary

SRC — Scritture originale riferite nei Congressi (in ACPF)

VL — Viard Letterbook (in WAA)

VUW — Victoria University of Wellington

WAA — Wellington Archdiocesan Archives

See also Bibliography: Archival Sources.

PROLOGUE

1 Suzanne Aubert, *New and Complete Manual of Maori Conversation*. Wellington, 1885, p.104. The quotations which begin each chapter are all taken from her book of conversational phrases. The writing of that book is discussed in Ch. 10.

2 E. Fisher, 'Wanganui River Settlements', typescript, 1969, p.7, Whanganui Regional Museum.

3 Miria Clarke, interview with Fr Paul Bergin.

4 Whitirina Taurerewa, interview with Fr Paul Bergin. Ivan Emia, interview with author.

5 Weheora Wallace [Wanihi], interview with author.

6 Erina Scanlon, interview with author.

7 Joan Akapita, interview with author. 'Katorika' is Catholic; 'Mihinare' (missionary) is Anglican.

CHAPTER ONE: *France – the mission, 1838–1859*

1 Aubert, *Manual*, p.100.

2 E. R. Simmons, *Pompallier, Prince of Bishops*. Auckland, 1984, pp.155–57, quotes Garavel, Journal of Events, 17 June 1859, POM 24A-1/2, ACDA.

3 Rocher to Poupinel, 16 Sept. 1859, OP 458.221, VM 211, APM.

4 Extracts from their letters in *Our Pioneer Sisters*, from Correspondence 1836–83, Missionary Sisters of the Society of Mary, typescript, Rome, 1973, v.1; full letters in OP VM, APM.

5 Rocher to Poupinel, 16 Nov. 1859, OP 458.221, VM 211, APM.

6 Ibid., 17 Feb. 1860.

7 Pompallier to Barnabò, 23 April 1860, POM 20-4/4, ACDA.

8 W. McDonald, Diary 1859–60, p.43, POM 28-3/1, ACDA.

9 Rocher to Poupinel, 18 May 1860, OP 458.221, VM 211, APM.

10 McDonald, p.43.

11 Yardin to missionaries in Oceania, 8 Sept. 1857, Letters to Missionaries, p.258ff, APM. Quoted in M.-C. de Mijolla, *Origins in Oceania: Missionary Sisters of the Society of Mary, 1845–1931*. Rome, 1984, p.29.

12 He preached suitable messages for each situation. He praised the Propagation of the Faith in Saint-Nizier, the church which had seen its beginnings. In the chapel at the shrine of Our Lady of Fourvière, he 'spoke most forcibly on the virtues of The Mother of God and her powerful intercession for poor Sinners'. In the cathedral he again spoke of the mission work of the Propagation of the Faith, the 'subject in aid of which he had been invited to preach by The Respectable President of the Propagation'. He dined with the members, and 'amused them by little anecdotes of his travels & labours'. McDonald, pp.44–45.

13 McDonald, p.45.

14 Aubert, *Manual*, p.17.

15 McDonald to Propagation of the Faith, 2 Feb. 1860, in *Annales de la Propagation de la Foi [APF]*, 1860, v.32, p.307. He was scribing Pompallier's account.

16 Ibid., p.309.

17 These organisations have similar names but are totally different. The first is a lay-originated and -directed missionary funding organisation (now called the Oeuvres Pontificales Missionnaires), based in Lyon where it had begun in 1822. The second is the Vatican congregation (since 1967 called the Congregation for the Evangelisation of People) which directed most missionary endeavour from 1622. The money came from the first; the instructions from the second.

18 For a good, succinct background to the Marist mission, see M. O'Meeghan, 'The French Connection', *NZ Historic Places*, 44, Nov. 1993, pp.4–9. Longer studies are R. Wiltgen, *The Founding of the Roman Catholic Church in Oceania 1825 to 1850*. Canberra, 1979; J. Hosie, *Challenge: the Marists in Colonial Australia*. Sydney, 1987; K. Roach, 'Venerable John Claude Colin and the Mission in New Zealand 1838–1848', doctoral thesis, Gregorian Univ., Rome, 1963; M. O'Meeghan, 'The French Marist Maori Mission', in J. Dunmore (ed.), *The French and the Maori*. Waikanae, 1992; E. Simmons, *Pompallier*; P. Turner, 'The Politics of Neutrality: the Catholic Mission and the Maori 1838–1870', MA thesis, AU, 1986; L. Keys, *The Life and Times of Bishop Pompallier*. Christchurch, 1957.

19 Quoted in E. Simmons, *Pompallier*, p.22.

20 Pompallier to Fransoni, 10 Sept. 1836, Doc. 402 in J. Coste and G. Lessard (eds), *Origines Maristes (1786–1836)*. Rome, 1960, v.1, p.917.

21 W. Colenso, *The Authentic and Genuine History of the Signing of the Treaty of Waitangi, New Zealand, February 5 and 6, 1840*. Wellington, 1890, p.15; quoted in Turner, p.31.

22 Comte to Colin, 25 April 1841; quoted in *Annales des Missions d'Océanie – correspondance des premiers missionnaires [AMO]*. Lyon, 1895, v.1, pp.538–39.

23 Turner, pp.33, 34.

24 Colenso, *The Signing of the Treaty of Waitangi*, p.13; quoted in Turner, p.38.

25 Rev. R. Taylor, Journal, 6 Feb. 1840, v.2, p.189, AIM; quoted in Turner, p.95.

26 C. Orange, *The Treaty of Waitangi*. Wellington, 1987, pp.52–53; Turner, pp.96–106; Keys, pp.126–27.

27 See Ross to D. Simmons, Notes on manuscript, 1979, Ms 1442, Ruth Ross Papers, Box 35, p.25, AIM, for discussion of schooner and Pompallier's 'grand seigneur' manner.

28 Roach, pp.595, 596.

29 Garin to Colin, 19 Jan. 1842, quoted in *AMO*, v.1, p.543.

30 N. Taylor (ed.), *The Journal of Ensign Best, 1837–1843*. Wellington, 1966, p.382, entry dated 5 Dec. 1842.

31 Forest to Epalle, 9 Nov. 1842, quoted in *AMO*, v.1, pp.545–56.

32 Ibid., p.556.
33 Petitjean to Colin, 18 May 1842, 669/12, APM; quoted in Turner, p.149.
34 Petitjean to Colin, 18 May 1842, Z 208, APM; quoted in Roach, pp.254–56.
35 Turner, p.28 and Appendix A.
36 Forest to Epalle, 9 Oct. 1845, Z 208, APM; quoted in Roach, pp.440, 441.
37 Since the British annexation, the English-language problem was a concern found also in the letters of the priests, who saw the islands of the tropical Pacific mission as more suitable for them than this increasingly Anglicised colony.
38 Colin to Fransoni, 15 May 1847, Acta 210, p.357v, ACPF; quoted in Roach, p.488.
39 Acta 210, p.211, ACPF; Roach, p.574.
40 E. Simmons, *Pompallier*, p.119.
41 Theodore Zeldin, *France 1848–1945*, v.2. Oxford, 1977, pp.1004–5.
42 Turner, p.193.
43 Pompallier to Bourand, 18 March 1852, POM 22-2, ACDA; quoted in Turner, p.192.
44 Petit to Pius IX, 14 Oct. 1852, Udienze, v.116, f.2459–60v, ACPF; quoted in E. Simmons, *Pompallier*, p.135.
45 E. Simmons, *Pompallier*, p.139.
46 Mother Cecilia Maher to Mother Catherine Maher, 3 May 1850, ASMA.
47 Ibid., shipboard, Oct./Nov. 1849, Letter 9, Oceanic Collection, ASMA.
48 Ibid., August 1850, ASMA.
49 Ibid., 12 May 1853.
50 Mother Cecilia Maher, 'Historical Summaries', [1877], p.115, ASMA; Mother Paula Ennis, 'A brief sketch of the Missionary Labours of the Sisters of Mercy, Auckland, New Zealand, 1850–1888', p.4, ASMA; Sister Borgia Tyrrell, 'Memoir of Mother Cecilia Maher', 1877, pp.9, 17, ASMA.

CHAPTER TWO: *France – childhood and family, 1835–1860*
1 Aubert, *Manual*, p.27.
2 A. Rochefort, 'Les Soeurs de Saint-Charles de Lyon et l'éducation féminine au 19e siècle (1802–1904)', thèse de maîtrise, Lyon II, 1989, pp.139–42.
3 J. Gadille (ed.), *Le Diocèse de Lyon*. Paris, 1983, pp.245–46.
4 Reignier to Rouzioux, from 'station de St-Joseph' [Pakowhai], 11 Jan. 1855, in *APF*, 1856, v.28, p.375.

5 Poupinel to Maîtrepierre, 3 April 1858, in APF, 1859, v.31, p.467: 'J'étais loin d'être véritablement *un homme*: je n'étais pas aguerri pour ces sortes de voyage.' His emphasis seems to be acknowledging the pioneer status of the hardened bloke.
6 Ibid., p.475.
7 De Mijolla, pp.39, 51–52.
8 Gadille (ed.), pp.217–18.
9 Registre de la Paroisse de Saint-Nizier, AAL. Every year the *Annuaires de Lyon* also listed many of the *oeuvres*, the charitable societies of the different parishes, mentioning committee members and work covered.
10 'Procès-verbal de l'Assemblée générale de l'Oeuvre des Incurables: Oeuvre des Dames de la Paroisse de Saint-Nizier, 1844–1867', I 584 C7, AAL.
11 Aubert, *Directory of the Daughters of Our Lady of Compassion*. Wellington, 1922, Part II, pp.41–42.
12 This was a group of lay sisters at the time, tertiaries. In the 1880s, they would become the Third Order Regular of Mary, later called Soeurs Missionaires de la Société de Marie – the 'SMSMs'. See de Mijolla for the development of this congregation.
13 Yardin to Poupinel, 18 Aug. 1860, VM 211, APM.
14 Sister Angela Moller, 'Reminiscences of Mother Mary Joseph Aubert, Foundress of the Sisters of Compassion', typescript, 1945, v.1, p.132, HOC A.
15 R. David and H. de Vries, *The French Legal System: an Introduction to Civil Law Systems*. New York, 1958, p.24.
16 Etats-civils: Tarare 1831–34, 1832 Mariages, f.19, 4846 4E, ADR.
17 Abbé Burlon to Dean Regnault, 25 Sept. 1921, writing what he had just been told by the widow of Suzanne's elder brother, Alphonse. Clarice had lived with them in her old age.
18 Etude Me Captier, Tarare 1832, Acte No. 547, Contrat de mariage 3E 16 604, ADR.
19 The place of the trousseau in social history is being studied. See Agnès Fine, 'A propos du trousseau: une culture féminine?', in Michelle Perrot (ed.), *Une histoire des femmes, est-elle possible?* Paris, 1984, pp.155–88.
20 Moller, 'Reminiscences', v.1, pp.10–11.
21 *Annuaire de la Ville de Lyon et du Département du Rhône*, 1840s–60s, ADR.

22 Recensements fiscaux, 1841–45; 1847 pour 1848, p.59, AML.

23 Suzanne's sister-in-law gave the age of 'just twelve'; but Sr Angela Moller notes in 'Reminiscences', v.1, p.36: 'Mother used to tell us barely 14'.

24 See A. Roger and A. Sorel, *Codes et Lois Usuelles*, 41 edn. Paris, 1909; R. David, *English Law and French Law: a Comparison in Substance*. London, 1980, pp.48, 57, 58, 61; David and de Vries, pp.22, 24, 86.

25 Registre de police: Tarare, 1818, no. 37, ADR.

26 Roger and Sorel, pp.33–35.

27 Justice de Paix: Tarare, 1818–19, 2270, No. 13, ADR.

28 Déclarations des mutations par décès: Tarare, 1826, 352 Q 12, p.129, ADR; Matrices cadastrales 1850–1910, A224, A225, A225 bis, Archives Communales de Tarare.

29 Aubert to Isa Outhwaite, 16 May 1914, CLE 125-4/9, p.5, ACDA.

30 G. Cholvy and Y.-M. Hilaire, *Histoire religieuse de la France contemporaine 1800/1880*. Toulouse, 1985, p.256.

31 Aubert, 'Aide-mémoire', ms, p.11, HOC A.

32 E. de Rolland and D. Clouzet, *Dictionnaire des Communes du Département du Rhône*. Lyon, 1903, v.2, p.546; *Annuaire de la Ville de Lyon et du Département du Rhône*, 1848.

33 F. Braudel, *The Identity of France*. London, 1988, v.1, p.251.

34 Fr C. Rozier, interview with author. See also M. Stewart-McDougall, *The Artisan Republic: Revolution, Reaction, and Resistance in Lyon, 1848–1851*. Montreal, 1984, p.17.

35 Stewart-McDougall, p.1.

CHAPTER THREE: *France – women and faith, 1789–1860*

1 Aubert, *Manual*, p.60.

2 Archives des Soeurs Bénédictines, Pont-de-Beauvoisin.

3 Moller, 'Reminiscences', v.4, pp.605–6.

4 Aubert to Sr Marie de la Merci, 11 Sept. 1917, 239/2, HOC A.

5 Sr Angela Moller finished writing the 'Reminiscences' in 1945. There are seven typescript volumes. In the later ones, the sisters' own experience could serve as a cross-check on the record. But the earlier sections are based largely on Suzanne's anecdotes and reflections and have to be questioned historically. Ruth Ross subjected these to sceptical scrutiny in the 1970s. Research to date is confirming some of what Suzanne said, and finding other parts quite probable, but continues to question some aspects.

6 R. Gibson, *A Social History of French Catholicism 1789–1914*. London, 1989, pp.126–27.

7 G. Cholvy, *La religion en France de la fin du XVIIIe à nos jours*. Paris, 1991, p.39.

8 Moller, 'Reminiscences', v.1, pp.135–36.

9 Liszt's last-known stay in Lyon was in 1845: see A. Sallès, *Liszt à Lyon (1826, 1836, 1837, 1844, 1845)*. Paris, 1911.

10 R. Ross, 'Comments on Vol. 1 of the Reminiscences of Mother Mary Joseph Aubert, Foundress of the Sisters of Compassion'. Auckland, 14 Jan. 1972, Env. 59, HOC A. This is a 51-page typescript of detailed and constructive criticism; see also Ross correspondence, MS 1442, Ruth Ross Papers, Box 32A, AIM.

11 See B. Holmes, 'When Memory Plays Us False', *New Scientist*, 23 July 1994, pp.32–34, for the effect of retelling in imprinting a memory of an unreal event.

12 See Gibson, *French Catholicism*, for a full and clear analysis of the whole subject.

13 From about the mid-eighteenth century, people's attitudes to the organised church had been changing. There had been growing Enlightenment scepticism among many of the educated. There was also an overall fall-off in religious observance which can be measured in various ways: for example, by less money left in wills as offerings for Masses said for the soul, or by lower attendance at Easter Mass. See Gibson, *French Catholicism*, pp.3–5; M. Vovelle, 'Du serment constitutionnel à l'ex-voto peint: un exemple d'histoire régressive', in J. Le Goff and R. Rémond (eds), *Histoire de la France religieuse*. Paris, 1991, v.3, pp.220–21.

14 Gibson, *French Catholicism*, pp.52–53.

15 An excellent analysis of this is given in O. Hufton, *Women and the Limits of Citizenship in the French Revolution*. Toronto, 1992. See pp.96–97: 'This is the woman in Revolution whose spectre will haunt the politicians of the nineteenth century and serve to confirm them in

their efforts to deny women the vote. Certainly, this woman has significance in the history of the Roman Catholic Church for it is her commitment to her religion which determines in the post-thermidorean period the re-emergence of the Catholic church on very particular terms, which included an express rejection of state attempts to control a priesthood and the form of public worship. Counter-revolutionary woman is therefore of consequence in the ongoing religious and political history of France.' An important treatment of this topic is found also in C. Marand-Fouquet, *La femme au temps de la Révolution*. Paris, 1989, pp.40–45, 143–58, 358–59, 373–75 esp.

16 For the implications of this, see Hufton; also Vovelle in Le Goff and Rémond (eds), v.3, pp.208–16.

17 R. Gibson, 'Le Catholicisme et les femmes en France au XIXe siècle', *Revue d'Histoire de l'Eglise de France*, 79, 202, 1993, p.68; T. Tackett, *Religion, Revolution, and Regional Culture in Eighteenth Century France: the Ecclesiastical Oath of 1791*. Princeton, 1986, pp.172–74.

18 Gadille (ed.), p.216; R. Bonnafous, *Louis Querbes et les Catéchistes de Saint-Viateur*. Paris, 1993, pp.19–20. Note that, in Lyon, only five out of fourteen parish priests took the oath: see Tackett, *Religion*, p.352. D. Kerr, 'Priests, Parishioners, and Politics: Cabuchet, the Colins, and the Oath to the Civil Constitution', *Forum Novum*, June 1994, pp.370–88, studies the experience of the family of the Marist founder, Jean-Claude Colin, during this period.

19 *Les Soeurs de Saint-Charles, Annales de la Congrégation, 1860–1874*. Lyon, 1915, p.51.

20 Gibson, *French Catholicism*, p.47.

21 Bonnafous, pp.44, 46, 55.

22 Moller, 'Reminiscences', v.1, p.379; also Fr M. Mulcahy, *Marist Messenger*, 1 March 1960.

23 Valnet to Aubert, 3 May 1891, Env. 1, HOC A.

24 Gadille (ed.), p.226.

25 Aubert, *Directory*, p.229.

26 Cholvy and Hilaire, pp.80, 158–59; P. Boutry, 'Le mouvement vers Rome et le renouveau missionnaire', in Le Goff and Rémond (eds), v.3, pp.426–37; Gadille

(ed.), pp.223–26.

27 Cholvy, p.55.

28 Cholvy and Hilaire, p.194.

29 For example, *Les Soeurs de Saint-Charles de Lyon*, pp.385–86.

30 11 Oct. 1858, AFA, APM; quoted in *Our Pioneer Sisters*, v.1, p.77.

31 Philippe Boutry, the foremost historian of the Curé d'Ars, refers to these more than 500 letters as revealing women's 'long apprenticeship in inferiority'; see P. Boutry, 'Réflexions sur la confession au XIXe siècle: Autour d'une lettre de Soeur Marie-Zoé au Curé d'Ars (1858)', in *Pratiques de la Confession: Des Pères du désert à Vatican II, Quinze études d'histoire*. Paris, 1983, p.237.

32 C. Moses, *French Feminism in the Nineteenth Century*. New York, 1984, p.34.

33 Aubert to parish priest of Ars, 20 Nov. 1919; printed in *Annales d'Ars*, June 1920, pp.25–28; Env. 39, HOC A.

34 Aubert to Isa Outhwaite, 7 July 1914, CLE 125-4/11, pp.3–4, ACDA.

35 Aubert to Nancy Rolleston, 7 Aug. 1922, Env. 6, HOC A.

36 *NZ Tablet*, 19 May 1925, p.21.

37 Hufton, p.108.

38 See C. Larkin, *A Certain Way: an Exploration of Marist Spirituality*. Rome, 1995, e.g. pp.40, 50, 79.

39 Garin to his parents, 17 April 1846, *AMO*, v.1, pp.200–1.

40 Abbé Burlon to Regnault, 25 Sept. 1921, p.5, Env. 1, HOC A. Note that Clarice's recovery, and others, were publicised in printed leaflets. These were finally banned in 1847 by Cardinal de Bonald, who disapproved of what he saw as a populist and sensationalising trend.

41 Paul Brac de la Perrière, quoted in E. Hardouin-Fugier, *Guide de Fourvière*, Commission de Fourvière, undated, p.63.

42 Moses, pp.17–20; Hufton, pp.121, 143.

43 M. Warner, *Alone of All Her Sex: the Myth and Cult of the Virgin Mary*. London, 1976, surveys the image of Mary in the church over the centuries.

44 Perroton to Eymard, 2 Aug. 1846, *Our Pioneer Sisters*, v.1, no.13; quoted in de Mijolla, p.40.

45 De Mijolla, p.23; Roger and Sorel, p.32, Titre IX, 'De la puissance paternelle'.

46 T. Zeldin, *France 1848–1945*, v.1. Oxford, 1973, pp.292–94, 298.

47 For a valuable discussion of this, see

Hufton, pp.131–40; also Gibson, *French Catholicism*, p.187.

48 C. Langlois, 'Féminisation du catholicisme', in Le Goff and Rémond (eds), v.3, pp.292–310, esp. pp.300–1.

49 See Gibson, 'Le Catholicisme et les femmes', p.66.

50 C. Langlois, 'Indicateurs du XIXe siècle. Pratique pascale et délais de baptême', in Le Goff and Rémond (eds), v.3, p.240.

51 Gibson, *French Catholicism*, p.209.

52 Abbé Burlon to Fr Regnault, 25 Sept. 1921, p.4, Env. 1, HOC A.

53 Archives des Soeurs Bénédictines, Pont-de-Beauvoisin.

54 Cholvy and Hilaire, p.139.

55 Langlois, 'Féminisation', in Le Goff and Rémond (eds), v.3, pp.304–7.

56 Moses, pp.18, 22.

57 Gibson, *French Catholicism*, p.46; Gibson, 'Le Catholicisme et les femmes', p.72; T. Zeldin, 'Conflict in Moralities', in T. Zeldin (ed.), *Conflicts in French Society: Anticlericalism, Education and Morals in the Nineteenth Century*. London, 1970, pp.14–35.

58 Zeldin, *France 1848–1945*, v.1, pp.285–92.

59 Moller, 'Reminiscences', v.1, p.72.

60 Gadille (ed.), pp.219, 227.

61 Registre de la Paroisse de Saint-Nizier, AAL; *Annuaires de la Ville de Lyon et du Département du Rhône*, 1840s–60s, e.g. 1845, p.222: Oeuvre de la Marmite, Providence de Saint-Nizier.

62 For instance, the sheltered workshops for young women, run by the church, were attacked by socialists as a conservative and ultimately unjust system which artificially depressed wages.

63 Rocher to Poupinel, 17 March 1860, OP 458.221, APM.

64 C. Langlois, *Le Catholicisme au féminin: les congrégations françaises à supérieure générale au XIXe siècle*. Paris, 1984, p.643.

65 Procès-verbal de l'Assemblée générale de l'Oeuvre des Incurables, 21 Dec. 1858, I 584 C7, AAL.

66 Langlois, *Le Catholicisme au féminin*, pp.627–30.

67 For a discussion of this, see Moses, pp.18–20; Langlois, *La Catholicisme au féminin*, p.643.

68 Gibson, *French Catholicism*, p.118.

69 Langlois, 'Institutions et modèles', in Le Goff and Rémond (eds), v.3, pp.400–5.

70 *Les Soeurs de Saint Charles de Lyon*, p.178.

71 Camille Aubert to Poupinel, 4 Dec. 1868, Env. 1, HOC A.

72 Moller, 'Reminiscences', v.1, p.163.

CHAPTER FOUR: *From France to New Zealand, 1860*

1 Aubert, *Manual*, p.84.

2 Archirel and Grange to Favre, 29 March 1861, NZ 34v, CSV.

3 Ibid.

4 McDonald, Diary 1859–60, endpapers.

5 K. Condon, *The Missionary College of All Hallows, 1842–1891*. Dublin, 1986, p.83.

6 Pompallier to All Hallows, 3 May 1860, POM 22-7/18, ACDA.

7 Ibid., 29 Aug. 1860, POM 22-7/19, ACDA.

8 Or possibly nine: there is some confusion in the documents.

9 Pompallier to Favre, 18 Aug. 1860, NZ 24, CSV.

10 Pompallier to Barnabò, 23 April 1860, POM 20-4/4, ACDA.

11 Bonnafous, p.117.

12 Grange to Favre, 25 July 1860, gén. H. Favre 3, CSV.

13 Favre, circular, 21 Aug. 1860, circ. P. Favre 27, CSV.

14 Fabre to Favre, 7 Aug. 1860, NZ 7, CSV.

15 Archirel to Favre, 28 Aug. 1860, NZ 28, CSV.

16 Pompallier to Favre, 18 Aug. 1860, NZ 24, CSV.

17 Archirel and Grange to Favre, 29 March 1861, NZ 34-3, CSV.

18 Ibid.

19 Dr L. Thiercelin, *Journal d'un baleinier: Voyages en Océanie*. Paris, 1866, v.1, p.20.

20 Archirel and Grange to Favre, 29 March 1861, NZ 34-3, CSV.

21 Ibid.

22 Moller, 'Reminiscences', v.1, p.168.

23 Aubert, 'Aide-mémoire', p.4.

24 Thiercelin, pp.22, 163.

25 Aubert, *Manual*, p.83.

26 P. Darmendaritz, Logbook; quoted in Keys, *Pompallier*, p.297.

27 Pompallier to Barnabò, 23 April 1860, POM 20-4/4, ACDA.

28 Guillot Frères to Pompallier, 9 April 1860, SRC Oceania, v.7, pp.1023–24, ACPF.

29 Moller, 'Reminiscences', v.1, p.170.

30 Archirel and Grange to Favre, 2 Jan. 1861, NZ 32, CSV.

31 Barsanti to Servo, 7 Dec. 1861, M126, 1861–67, p.350, AFFM.

32 Sr Philomena Dwyer, Diary, 13 and 17 Sept. 1850, ASMA.

33 E. Simmons, *DNZB*, v.1, p.350.

34 See A. Salmond, *Two Worlds: First Meetings Between Maori and Europeans 1642–1772*. Auckland, 1991, pp.185, 308, 309, 361; J. Dunmore, 'The First Contacts', in J. Dunmore (ed.), *The French and the Maori*. Waikanae, 1992, pp.13–14.

35 Robin to Favre, 9 Aug. 1860, H. Favre 13, CSV.

36 J.-B. Pompallier, *Etat succinct et précis de la Mission Catholique à la Nouvelle-Zélande, et spécialement dans le diocèse d'Auckland*. Paris, 1859; SRC Oceania, v.6, p.885, ACPF.

37 Archirel and Grange to Favre, 2 Jan. 1861, NZ 32, CSV.

38 Pompallier to All Hallows, 9 Jan. 1859, POM 22-7/17, ACDA; writing in English.

39 J.-B. Pompallier, 'Petite collection de mots maoris', in *Notes grammaticales sur la langue maorie ou néo-zélandaise*. Rome, 1860; SRC Oceania, v.6, p.919, ACPF.

40 W. Williams, Journal, 24 July 1840, in F. Porter (ed.), *Turanga Journals*, Wellington, 1974, p.119.

41 Pompallier to Fransoni, 4 Feb. 1848, SC IV, ACPF; quoted in Turner, p.46.

42 J.-B. Pompallier, 'Instructions pour les travaux de la mission', ms, [29 Jan 1841], p.21, POM 14-3, ACDA.

43 L. Keys, interview with Sr Angela Moller, Wellington, 4 May 1959, L. G. Keys Papers, WAA.

44 Aubert, *Directory*, p.28.

45 Felton Mathew to his wife, 30 Jan. 1840, quoted in Keys, *Pompallier*, p.121.

46 Pompallier to Gore Browne, Auckland, 15 Feb. 1859, GNZ 282.95 N5, APL.

47 Aubert to Sr de Sales, 16 June 1916, Env. 25, HOC A.

48 *Southern Cross*, 1–5 Jan. 1861.

CHAPTER FIVE: *Auckland – new mission recruits, 1861–1863*

1 Aubert, *Manual*, p.47.

2 Barsanti to Minister General, Propaganda Fide, 3 March 1861, SRC Oceania, v.7, p.110, ACPF.

3 *Southern Cross*, 4 Jan. 1861.

4 Jourdan to Minister General, Propaganda Fide, 26 Dec. 1861, SRC Oceania, v.7,

p.48v, ACPF.

5 Moller, 'Reminiscences', v.1, p.178.

6 Pompallier to Barnabò, 5 May 1861, SRC Oceania, v.7, p.125v, ACPF.

7 Pompallier, *Mission Catholique à la Nouvelle-Zélande*; SRC Oceania, v.6, p.880, ACPF.

8 See C. Macdonald, *A Woman of Good Character: Single Women as Immigrant Settlers in Nineteenth-century New Zealand*. Wellington, 1990, pp.157–64.

9 Viard to Yardin, 7 Jan. 1862, VL 3, p.214, WAA.

10 Pompallier to Propaganda Fide, Report for 1861, SRC Oceania, v.7, p.514, ACPF.

11 Tyrrell, p.11.

12 *Southern Cross*, 1 Jan. 1861, p.3; F. Porter, *Born to New Zealand*. Wellington, 1989, p.150.

13 Viard to Chataignier, 12 Aug. 1865, VL 4, p.167, WAA.

14 H. B. Morton, 'When Auckland Was Young – Life in the Early Sixties', from supplement to *NZ Herald*, 16, 23, 30 June, 7, 14, 21, 28 July 1923, 995.71 M88, APL.

15 Nuova Zelanda ed Indie Orientali, M 126, 1861–67, p.450/1, AFFM.

16 Viard to Yardin, 6 July 1861, VL 3, p.146, WAA.

17 These came later in the 1860s and would be members of the independent congregation of Sisters of the Mission, under Euphrasie Barbier (see Ch. 7).

18 Viard to Yardin, 7 Jan. 1862, VL 3, p.214, WAA.

19 Viard to Poupinel, 21 June 1862, VL 3, p.300, WAA.

20 Viard to Pompallier, 29 Aug. 1862, VL 3, p.322, WAA.

21 J.-B. Pompallier, 'Souvenirs de la Nouvelle-Zélande, et des travaux de l'Eglise pour elle', in *Mission Catholique à la Nouvelle-Zélande*; SRC Oceania, v.6, p.899, ACPF.

22 Pompallier to Maher, 14 Feb. 1862, ASMA.

23 Sr M. Veronica Delany, *Gracious Is the Time*. Auckland, 1952, p.62.

24 Archirel and Grange to Favre, 29 March 1861, NZ 34/1, CSV.

25 Ibid., 2 Jan. 1861, NZ 32/1, CSV.

26 Ibid., 29 March 1861, NZ 34/4, CSV.

27 *The New-Zealander*, 9 Feb. 1861.

28 W. Atkin of Tamaki, in ibid.

29 Pompallier to Propaganda Fide, Report for 1862, SRC Oceania, v.7, p.514, ACPF.

30 See J. Belich, *The New Zealand Wars*. Auckland, 1986, Ch. 4.

31 See Turner, 'The Politics of Neutrality'. For similarities in personality between Grey and Pompallier, see Belich, pp.122–25, and Porter, *Born to New Zealand*, pp.159–60.

32 Shortland to Pompallier, 13 April 1864, MA 4/6, p.308, NAW.

33 Pompallier to Propaganda Fide, Report for 1861.

34 See Belich, pp.102–14.

35 *Southern Cross*, 1 Jan. 1861.

36 Pompallier to Favre, 1 Aug. 1864, NZ 69/4, CSV.

37 Nuova Zelanda ed Indie Orientali, M126, 1861–67, pp.447/2–448/2, AFFM.

38 Ibid., p.448/2.

39 Turner, pp.224, 238.

40 H. Meade, *A Ride through the Disturbed Districts of New Zealand*. 1871, Ch. 11; quoted in Keys, *Pompallier*, p.339.

41 Nuova Zelanda ed Indie Orientali, M126, 1861–67, p.449/1, AFFM.

42 Ibid., p.348/2. See Turner, pp.192–93, and E. Simmons, *In Cruce Salus,* pp.65–66, for similar, modern assessments.

43 Galosi to Franciscans, 8 Jan. 1862, SRC Oceania, v.7, p.369v, ACPF.

44 Nuova Zelanda ed Indie Orientali, M126, 1861–67, p.361/2, AFFM.

45 Ibid., p.447/2.

46 Ibid., p.446/1.

47 Jourdan to Minister General, Propaganda Fide, 26 Dec. 1861, SRC Oceania, v.7, pp.49-49v, ACPF.

48 Tyrrell, p.17.

49 Viard to Barnabò, 2 Feb. 1863, SRC Oceania, v.7, p.771, ACPF.

50 Pompallier to Barnabò, 8 July 1862, SRC Oceania, v.7, pp.584–584v, ACPF.

51 *Taranaki Herald*, 13 Sept. 1862.

52 *Daily Southern Cross*, 22 Sept. 1862.

53 Maher to Mother Catherine in Carlow, 26 Sept. 1863, ASMA.

54 Tyrrell, p.17.

55 Aubert, 'Aide-mémoire', pp.7–8.

CHAPTER SIX: *Auckland – the Nazareth Institute, 1863–1869*

1 Aubert, *Manual*, p.33.

2 Moller, 'Reminiscences', v.1, p.189, from conversation with Nelly Boylan, 1935.

3 Pompallier to Peata, POM 22-2/38, p.45, ACDA.

4 Maher to Mother Frances Xavier Warde, 4 Aug. 1849, ASMA.

5 Pompallier to Epalle, 14 Jan. 1840, OOC 418.2, APM.

6 Viard, 'Memoirs', Part II, p.5. WAA.

7 Pompallier to Viard, 26 Jan. 1851, POM 22-2/36, p.43, ACDA.

8 Pompallier to Peata, POM 22-2/38, p.45, ACDA.

9 Pompallier to Viard, 24 April 1851, POM 22-2/70, p.80, ACDA.

10 Pompallier to J. McDonald, Nov. 1869, INT 1, 1-6/1, ACDA.

11 J. Lee, '*I have named it the Bay of Islands . . .*'. Auckland, 1983, p.225.

12 See C. Orange, *Treaty of Waitangi*; Turner, p.97.

13 See, for example, A. G. Bagnall and G. C. Petersen, *William Colenso, Printer, Missionary, Botanist, Explorer, Politician: His Life and Journeys*. Wellington, 1948, pp.50–51; Porter (ed.), *Turanga Journals*; J. Binney, *The Legacy of Guilt: a Life of Thomas Kendall*. Auckland, 1968; Turner, pp.152–53.

14 Pompallier (under name of Walter McDonald) to Propaganda Fide, 2 Feb. 1860, SRC Oceania, v.7, pp.987–97, ACPF; also *APF*, v.32, 1860, pp.307–13.

15 Moller, 'Reminiscences', v.1, p.195.

16 E. Jackson, *Delving into the Past of Auckland's Suburbs*. Auckland, 1976, p.25; D. Simmons, personal communication.

17 See Belich, pp.36–43.

18 Ibid., p.186.

19 Catholic spelling was *Meri*, compared with Protestant *Mere*.

20 *AJHR*, 1862, E-4, pp.15, 20.

21 F. D. Bell to Pompallier, 15 Nov. 1862, MA 4/5, p.276, NAW.

22 *AJHR*, 1863, E-9, pp.11–12.

23 *AJHR*, 1863, E-9A, pp.2–3.

24 *AJHR*, 1865, E-3B, p.1.

25 Viard to Pompallier, 19 April 1863, VL 4, p.7, WAA.

26 R. Ross to J. Dunmore, 13 Sept. 1974, Ms 1442, Box 34 F2, AIM. Bidois had been a crew member of the *Sancta Maria*. His son Peter (Pitua) Bidois married Mary Ann Borel, 'who had been educated in a convent in Auckland along with Adelaide Bidois, born 1854'.

27 *AJHR*, 1862, D-16A.

28 Aubert to Isa Outhwaite, 10 May 1915, CLE 125-4, p.16, ACDA.

29 Moller, 'Reminiscences', v.1, p.197.

30 *AJHR*, 1867, A-3, p.11.

31 Ibid.

32 *AJHR*, 1862, E-4, p.21.

33 Poupinel to Favre, 12 March 1866, OP 458.221, APM.

34 See Porter (ed.), *Turanga Journals*, p.51; H. W. Williams, *A Bibliography of Printed Maori to 1900*. Wellington, 1924.

35 See J. Mackey, *The Making of a State Education System: the Passing of the New Zealand Education Act, 1877*. London, 1967, p.101.

36 For settler and Maori education in Auckland province in 1860s, see *AJHR*, A and E series; T. Beaglehole, 'Maori Schools 1816–1880', VUW thesis, 1955; J. Barrington, 'Maori Education and Society 1867–1940', VUW thesis, 1965; J. Barrington and T. Beaglehole, *Maori Schools in a Changing Society*. Wellington, 1974; I. Cumming, *Glorious Enterprise: the History of the Auckland Education Board*. Christchurch, 1959; J. Lynch, 'The Struggle between Denominationalism and Secularism in Auckland Education 1840–1877', MA thesis, AU, 1958; W. Sutch, *Poverty and Progress in New Zealand*. Wellington, 1969; Mackey, *State Education System*; J. Mackey, 'Catholic Schools and the Denominational System in Auckland 1840–1868', MA thesis, AU, 1950.

37 R. Stone, *Makers of Fortune: a Colonial Business Community and Its Fall*. Auckland, 1973, p.8.

38 For instance, 'Pompallier accepts fifteen destitute boys', 28 April 1864, MA 3/2, 1864/939, NAW. See W. Swanson, Report of Destitute Children's Schools Committee of Auckland Provincial Council, 16 Feb. 1869, *AJHR*, 1869, A-5, p.40; also J. Elphick, 'Auckland 1870–1874: a Social Portrait', MA thesis, AU, 1974, pp.23–24.

39 *NZPD*, 1868, v.2, p.191; quoted in Barrington, 'Maori Education', p.8.

40 *AJHR*, 1869, A-5, p.41.

41 Elphick, pp.20–21.

42 Register 11 M, deed no. 32874, Deeds Index 2A, p.973, Deeds Office Auckland; cited in Ruth Ross Papers, Env. 58, HOC A.

43 *AJHR*, 1867, A-3, p.13; also *AJHR*, 1868, A-6, p.1.

44 Cumming, p.50.

45 H. Morton, 'When Auckland Was Young'.

46 Janvier, Procureur impérial to Governor, Nouméa, 12 July 1870, Ministère de la Marine et des Colonies, et Ministère de la Justice et des Cultes, Archives Nationales, France; in POM 45-2, ACDA.

47 *NZ Herald*, 19 Feb. 1868; *Evening News*, 18 Feb. 1868.

48 Vaile to Barnabò, 26 Nov. 1869, SRC Oceania, v.9, pp.1001–3, ACPF.

49 Commandant Commissaire Impérial to Ministre de la Marine et des Colonies, Papeete, 20 April 1870, Section Outre-Mer, C.106 H 23, p.2, AN; in POM 45-2, ACDA.

50 Pompallier to Stafford (Colonial Secretary), 3 Feb. 1868, IA1, 1868/439, NAW. In this letter, Pompallier discussed naturalisation for Boibieux, Suzanne and Lucie Pompallier and said his absence would be 'about seven months'. It is not clear why he was initiating this.

51 See POM 45-2, ACDA.

52 Yardin to Forest, 14 Aug. 1868, CF1/HD1 f.128, MAW.

53 Yardin to Forest, 8 Oct. 1868, CF1 f.24v, MAW.

54 Pompallier to Propaganda Fide, 21 Jan. 1869, SRC Oceania, v.9, p.51v, ACPF.

55 And irritated Yardin, who disputed the accuracy of a pamphlet accompanying the *Notice*, SRC Oceania, v.9, pp.62–63; text of *Notice*, SRC Oceania, v.9, p.912, ACPF.

56 Pompallier to Pius IX, 23 March 1869, SRC Oceania, v.9, p.166, ACPF.

57 Pompallier to J. McDonald, 27 Nov. 1869, INT 1, 1-6/1, p.3, ACDA.

58 J. King, for Memorialists, to Barnabò, 28 Aug. 1869, INT 1, 1-5/2, ACDA. A telling part of this Memorial is its reference to Propagation of the Faith money without mentioning Maori mission, as noted by Lilian Keys. See also E. Simmons, *In Cruce Salus*, pp.96–97.

59 See Mackey, *State Education System*, pp.102–3.

60 First Report of the Commission of Enquiry into the Condition and Nature of Trust Estates for Religious, Charitable, and Educational Purposes, *AJHR*, 1869, A-5, p.13.

61 Pompallier to J. McDonald, 27 Nov. 1868, POM 23/5, ACDA.

62 Galosi to Propagation of the Faith, 8 April 1868, H 31 HO1001, p.23a, OPM.

63 Boibieux and Grange to J. McDonald, 12 Feb. 1869, POM 23-4, ACDA.

64 Pompallier to J. McDonald, 1 May 1868, POM 23-5/4, ACDA.

65 Ibid, 26 Dec. 1868, POM 23-5/3, ACDA.

66 Aubert, Statement taken to Rome, Notebook 6, HOC A.

67 MA 4/11, pp.62–63, NAW.

68 Sr Maire [*sic*] Joseph to Pollen, 20 April 1869, AGG-A 1 1869/292, NAW.

69 [*NZ*] *Herald*, undated cutting, POM 23-4, ACDA.

70 *Auckland Free Press*, 19 May 1868, in McDonald's scrapbook, POM 42/7, p.48, ACDA.

71 *Daily Southern Cross*, 13 Jan. 1870, pp.1, 3; 21 Jan. 1870, p.3; 30 March 1870, pp.4–5.

72 *AJHR*, 1868, A-6, p.11.

73 [*NZ Herald?*], McDonald's scrapbook, POM 42/7, ACDA.

74 Viard to Barnabò, Wellington, 2 Feb. 1863, SRC Oceania, v.7, p.770v, ACPF; see also Lee receipt, POM 25-4/4, POM 8-4/15, ACDA.

75 Pompallier to J. McDonald, 27 Nov. 1869, INT 1, 1-6/1, p.4, ACDA.

76 *Daily Southern Cross*, 17 June 1870.

77 *NZ Herald*, 5 July 1870.

78 Aubert to Poupinel, 4 June 1870, Env. 2, HOC A; Moller, 'Reminiscences', v.1, p.285.

79 Ruth Ross conjectured that Aubert was the incendiary or knew who it was: R. Ross, Env. 59, p.36, HOC A. A more likely theory is that it was an insurance fire, as the Bennett brothers were in financial trouble; *Daily Southern Cross*, 6 July 1870, p.7.

80 *Daily Southern Cross*, 30 March 1870, pp.4–5. John Campbell is *not* the Auckland businessman and philanthropist John Logan Campbell.

81 Aubert to Poupinel, 20 Dec. 1869, Env. 2, HOC A.

82 Ibid.

83 See E. Simmons, *Pompallier*, p.187: 'The sooner he was out of it the better.'

84 Goold to Barnabò, 24 Feb. 1870, SRC Oceania, v.9, pp.1010–13, ACPF.

85 Aubert to Poupinel, 20 Dec. 1869, Env. 2, HOC A.

86 Ibid., 4 June 1870.

87 Ibid., 20 Dec. 1869.

88 See E. Simmons, *In Cruce Salus*, pp.98–99; *Pompallier*, pp.189–90; *Catholic Church in New Zealand*, p.50. He analyses the situation accurately, sums her up humanely and succinctly, but nevertheless singles her out.

89 Auckland extracts from Goold's diary, in P. Moran, *History of the Catholic Church in Australasia*. Sydney, no date, p.801.

90 Dwyer to Barnabò, 25 July 1869, SRC Oceania, v.9, pp.294–95v, ACPF.

91 Aubert to Poupinel, 23 Nov. 1869, Env. 2, HOC A; see also Sr M. Paula to M. Catherine, Auckland, 18 Nov. 1869, Mercy Archives and INT 1, 1-9/3, ACDA.

92 [Fr M. Watson], *The Society of Jesus in Australia*. c.1910 (no title page), based on excerpts from Dalton's diary.

93 J. King to Propagation of the Faith, 5 Sept. 1870, Paris file, 32, 205, OPM.

94 Pompallier to J. McDonald, 1 May 1868, POM 23/5-4, ACDA.

95 Poupinel to Yardin, 5 March 1866, OP 418, p.7, APM.

96 Moller, 'Reminiscences', v.1, p.226.

97 Petitjean to Favre, 26 Feb. 1868, Z 208, APM; also Env. 4, HOC A.

98 Poupinel to Favre, 19 June 1866, OP 418, APM (copy in Poupinel copybook, v.2, p.426).

99 Pompallier to Barnabò, 30 May 1866, SRC Oceania, v.8, p.517v, ACPF.

100 Aubert to Poupinel, 20 Dec. 1869, Env. 2, HOC A.

101 Ibid., 23 Nov. 1869.

102 Ibid., 4 June 1870, Env. 2, 3.

103 Minutes of Diocesan Commission, 25 Jan. 1870, INT 1, 1-4, p.22, ACDA.

104 Ibid., pp.23–25.

105 Aubert to Poupinel, 4 June 1870, Env. 2, HOC A.

106 Personal communications from Fr C. Rozier and Marinette Aunier, Lyon, 1993.

107 Sisters of Mercy archives, Wellington.

108 *Daily Southern Cross*, 11 Oct 1865, p.1.

109 Archives of New South Wales, 4/655, letter no. 69/2921; 3/3320, no. 880/89; 4/8149, p.47, 4/8150, p.106; 4/8152, p.154; 5/5883; 3/4658, p.263; Rydalmere Hospital, legal files, 19/11330.

110 Pompallier, 'Instructions pour les travaux des missions'.

111 J.-B. Pompallier, *Instruction sur la sagesse chrétienne*. Paris, 1859; SRC Oceania, v.6, p.890, ACPF; Leçon 4, parallel text in Maori and French.

CHAPTER SEVEN: *From Auckland to Meanee, 1869–1872*

1 Aubert, *Manual*, p.66.

2   Reignier to Yardin, 26 July 1869, Z 208, APM.

3   See E. Isichei, entry on Euphrasie Barbier, *DNZB*, v.2, p.25.

4   C. Aubert to Poupinel, 4 Dec. 1868, Env. 1, HOC A. For her reasons against returning to France, see also Reignier to Poupinel, 17 Jan. 1871, Z 208, APM.

5   Poupinel to Aubert, 1 Aug. 1871, Env. 3, HOC A; M. O'Meeghan, 'The Marist Family', *Bedean*, 1966; F. McKay, *The Marist Laity: Finding the Way Envisaged by Father Colin*. Rome, 1991, Ch. 1.

6   See, for example, Viard to Aubert, 22 Nov. 1871, Env. 3, HOC A.

7   Reignier to Yardin, 23 Nov. 1869, Z 208, APM.

8   Suzanne might have read the report of this in *Hawke's Bay Herald*, 4 May 1883.

9   D. Akenson, *Half the World from Home: Perspectives on the Irish in New Zealand, 1860–1950*, Wellington, 1990, p.164; also pp.161–63 for the Cullenite 'ecclesiastical empire' in Australia and New Zealand.

10 N. Vaney, 'The Dual Tradition. Irish Catholics and French Priests in New Zealand: the West Coast Experience, 1865–1910', MA thesis, CU, 1976, pp.167, 120.

11 P. O'Farrell, *Vanished Kingdoms: Irish in Australia and New Zealand*. Sydney, 1990, p.xxii. See also P. O'Farrell, *The Catholic Church and Community in Australia: a History*. Melbourne, 1977, pp.197–202, for the rise to dominance of these bishops.

12 M. Quinn to Kirby, 7 Sept. 1870, Kirby Papers, ICR; quoted in R. Sweetman, 'New Zealand Catholicism, War, Politics and the Irish Issue 1912–1922', PhD thesis, Cambridge Univ., 1990, p.10.

13 See Vaney, p.77, for Moran's founding of *NZ Tablet* in 1873 as part of this policy.

14 See H. Laracy, 'The Life and Context of Bishop Patrick Moran', MA thesis, VUW, 1964, p.36.

15 Vaney, p.1.

16 Croke to Kirby, 10 July 1871, Kirby Papers, ICR; quoted in Sweetman, 'New Zealand Catholicism', p.10.

17 Aubert to Yardin, from Auckland, 20 Jan. 1871, Env. 2, HOC A; 5–1, MAW.

18 *NZ Tablet*, 23 Aug. 1889, p.19; quoted in Laracy, 'Bishop Moran', p.121. Laracy's chapter headings are pertinent: 'Moran Against Otago', 'Moran Against New Zealand'. Suzanne's attitudes to a devel-oping New Zealand were positive.

19 See R. Sweetman, 'The Catholic Church in Nineteenth-century New Zealand', paper delivered at Canada–NZ Comparative Seminar, Univ. of Edinburgh, 19 May, 1985, p.4: 'The cleansing of the augean stables would surely commence in earnest!' Note that Croke commendably bought back the property at St Anne's.

20 He meant Mangonui. Note that Meeanee is the present-day spelling but at that time it was Meanee.

21 Reignier to Aubert, 13 Nov. 1870, Env. 3, HOC A.

22 Aubert to Yardin, 20 Jan. 1871, Env. 2, HOC A; 5–1, MAW.

23 Aubert, Statement for Propaganda Fide, HOC A.

24 Moller, 'Reminiscences', v.1, p.297.

25 M. M. Bernard Towers, 'Memoirs', ms, v.1, pp.25–26; v.2, p.130, v.3, p.4; ASMA.

26 Moller, 'Reminiscences', v.1, p.296.

27 G. Lennard, *Sir William Martin: the Life of the First Chief Justice of New Zealand*. Auckland, 1961, p.4.

28 *Daily Southern Cross*, 16 Feb. 1871.

29 Reignier to Poupinel, 14 March 1871, Z 208, APM.

30 Ibid.

31 Aubert to V. Outhwaite, 4 April 1871, CRO 6-5/1, ACDA.

32 Aubert to M. L. Outhwaite, 29 April 1871, CRO 6-5/2, ACDA.

33 For the background to the Meanee Catholic Mission, see K. Mooney, 'Meeanee Roman Catholic Mission, Hawke's Bay', typescript, MAW; and J. Mannix, 'Mission Residence and Properties, 1850–1971', typescript, Mount St Mary's archives, Greenmeadows.

34 O'Farrell, *Vanished Kingdoms*, p.154.

35 Aubert to M. L. Outhwaite, 29 April 1871, CRO 6-5/2, ACDA.

36 Reignier Ledger and Memorandum 1870–1890, Meanee, DNM 2/37, MAW.

37 Aubert to M. L. Outhwaite, undated, CRO 6-4/9, ACDA.

38 Sr Luigi Hawkins, St Joseph of the Sacred Heart, interviewed in 1932, HOC A.

39 She earned praise in newspapers for her choir results, and her harmonium has stayed in Hawke's Bay, passed down the women of the Harpham-Ridley-Hunt-Dickson family.

40 Aubert to M. L. Outhwaite, 11 Jan. 1872, CRO 6-5/4, ACDA.

41 Sr Marie de la Rédemption to Aubert, 13 (or 15) June 1872, Lettres diverses, v.7, pp.1–2, RNDM.

42 *Hawke's Bay Herald*, 7 Feb. 1872.

43 Especially after 1874. See Laracy, 'Bishop Moran', pp.142–44.

44 Aubert to M. L. Outhwaite, 10 Oct. 1872, CRO 6-5/7, ACDA.

45 Aubert, *Manual*, p.57.

46 This was how she signed herself as a witness at weddings: Marriage Registers, 1875–76, 208/20 PM Reignier (D), MAW. Note that 'Sister of Charity' as a generic term for nurse shows the importance of this congregation. A good overview is in R. Numbers and D. Amundsen, *Caring and Curing: Health and Medicine in the Western Religious Traditions*. New York, 1986, pp.135–36.

47 Pompallier to Alletag[?], 16 May 1851, POM 22-2, No. 80, p.90, ACDA.

48 Turner, pp.150–51.

49 Aubert to M. L. Outhwaite, 30 July 1872, CRO 6-5/3, ACDA; Lady Martin's book was *He Pukapuka Whakaatu Tikanga mo nga Rongoa mo nga Kai*. Auckland, 1869.

50 Brandon children, as told to a granddaughter, Margaret Lawrie: Lawrie to Fr Unverricht, 9 Sept. 1986, Acc 208/20, MAW.

51 Aubert, 'Household Remedies', HOC A.

52 Aubert to M. L. Outhwaite, 11 Nov. 1872, CRO 6-4/8, ACDA.

53 Elphick, p.56.

54 Memories of Mrs Dempsey, 10 Nov. 1931, HOC A.

55 See S. Eldred-Grigg, *Pleasures of the Flesh: Sex and Drugs in Colonial New Zealand 1840–1915*, Wellington, 1984, pp.112–15.

56 See MA 3/3 1423, 11 July 1871, NAW; Reignier to Poupinel, 28 April 1873, Z 208, APM.

57 Aubert to Poupinel, 29 May 1874, 9–1, APM.

58 Lopdell recollections, Env. 69, HOC A; also J. Broyer (Br Athanase) to Poupinel, 4 May 1877, Z 208, APM.

59 P. Anderson, Diary, 1876–77, All Saints' Church archives, Taradale; original in Mitchell Library, Sydney. Anderson was in Taradale from 1873 to 1877. My thanks to Irene Lister for this.

CHAPTER EIGHT: *Hawke's Bay – Maori and Pakeha, 1872–1879*

1 Aubert, *Manual*, p.104.

2 W. Williams, *Christianity Among the New Zealanders*. London, 1867, pp.335–36.

3 W. Williams to McLean, 5 Jan. 1872, Williams MS Papers 69:33, ATL.

4 New Zealand Telegraph, 6 items from telegrams involving Suzanne, McLean, Bishop Williams and Napier Gaol staff, 4 Jan. 1872, Donald McLean Papers 1832–1927, MS Papers 0032, 66, 67, ATL.

5 Aubert to McLean, 11 Jan. 1872, Donald McLean Papers, ATL.

6 Aubert to M. L. Outhwaite, 11 Jan. 1872, CRO 6-5/4, ACDA.

7 W. Williams to McLean, 26 Dec. 1871, 2 Jan. 1872, Williams MS Papers 69:33, ATL.

8 Ibid., 5 Jan 1872.

9 Ibid.

10 Aubert to Poupinel, 29 May 1874, Env. 3, HOC A.

11 P. Anderson, 'Reminiscences', ms, CY Reel 135, p.98, Mitchell Library; also in ATL.

12 Pompallier, 'Instructions pour les travaux de la mission'; quoted in M. O'Meeghan, 'Catholic Beginnings in New Zealand: an Overview', in *CBRF Journal*, 121, 1990, p.33. Pompallier's work is available in translation in a 1986 Massey research paper by K. Girdwood-Morgan.

13 W. L. Williams, Journal, v.7, 1872–73, pp.70, 75, 96, 246, MS Papers 2463, ATL.

14 Ibid., v.10, 1875, pp.114–15, MS Papers 2466, ATL.

15 Bagnall and Petersen, p.358.

16 W. Colenso, 'Certain Errors of the Church of Rome plainly shown from Holy Scripture . . .', Napier, 1898, pp.43–44, as quoted in M. Mulcahy, 'Catholic Missionary Activity in Hawke's Bay 1841–1861', typescript, 208/23-C, MAW.

17 M. Campbell, 'The Evolution of Hawke's Bay Landed Society, 1850–1914', PhD thesis, VUW, 1972, p.304. See Ch. 10, 'Religion', for a general discussion.

18 Aubert to M. L. Outhwaite, 11 Nov. 1872, CRO 6-4/8, ACDA.

19 Reignier to Poupinel, 9 Aug. 1878, Z61–410, APM.

20 Akenson, p.24.

21 This point is taken up in P. Lineham, 'How Institutionalized Was Protestant

Piety in Nineteenth-Century New Zealand?', *Journal of Religious History*, 13, 1985, pp.174–75: 'In New Zealand many services were commenced at the initiative of laity and, in the smaller towns and the countryside, Christians of all denominational backgrounds simply wanted services of some form to take place.' And: 'However, a feeling of distaste for denominational pedantry was characteristic of most New Zealand laity of all denominations. Ecclesiastical barriers were irrelevant when on every other day of the week colonists worked fairly co-operatively in establishing the community. [Among Anglicans] lay demands for greater co-operation surfaced at the General Synod in 1871.' See also W. H. Oliver, 'Christianity Among the New Zealanders', *Landfall*, 77, 1966, p.7, where he compares New Zealand with Australia, the US and Canada.

22 P. Anderson, 'Reminiscences', p.171.

23 Quoted in Laracy, 'Bishop Moran', p.78, from W. Parker, 'John Sheehan, native minister and colonial', MA thesis, AU, 1963, pp.6, 74.

24 See R. Arnold, *The Farthest Promised Land: English Villagers, New Zealand Immigrants of the 1870s*. Wellington, 1981, pp.127, 156, 165, 356.

25 J. Graham, 'Settler Society', in G. Rice (ed.), *Oxford History of New Zealand*, 2nd edn. Auckland, 1992, p.127; see also Laracy, 'Bishop Moran', p.79.

26 Moller, 'Reminiscences', v.1, p.291.

27 S. Nairn to her father, T. Wright, 4 March 1877, Nairn Papers, Folder 2, ATL; quoted in Campbell, p.242. New Zealand's high birth rate is discussed in Macdonald, Ch. 6.

28 W. L. Williams, Journal, v.7, 1872–73, p.86, MS Papers 2463, ATL.

29 Moller, 'Reminiscences', v.1, pp.343–46; Reignier to Poupinel, 11 Nov. 1876, Z 61–410, APM.

30 W. L. Williams, Journal, v.8, 1873–74, p.174, MS Papers 2464, ATL.

31 Reminiscences of John Dooney, Taradale, HOC A. (He was born in 1890, so he would be remembering what he had been told, not what he had seen.)

32 Aubert to Poupinel, 29 May 1874, Env. 3, HOC A.

33 Favre to Barnabò, 14 Jan. 1873, SRC Oceania, v.9, p.1370, ACPF.

34 Aubert to M. L. Outhwaite, 21 March 1875, CRO 6-5/8, ACDA.

35 Ibid. Note too Fr J. Joyce (19 Aug. 1981) recalled overhearing Redwood say: 'I have a great body of priests and I trust them', quoted in N. Simmons, 'Archbishop Francis Redwood, His Contribution to Catholicism in New Zealand', MA thesis, Massey Univ., 1981, p.36.

36 Aubert to M. L. Outhwaite, 21 March 1875, CRO 6-5/8, ACDA.

37 Kawepo to Aubert, from Omahu, 1 Aug. 1881; Kaiwhata to Aubert, from Moteo, June 1882, HOC A. For Kaiwhata and the background to the 1840s and 1850s, see P. Parsons, entry on Paora Kaiwhata, in *DNZB*, v.2, pp.252–53; also J. Grace, *Tuwharetoa*. Wellington, 1959; Bagnall and Petersen.

38 Mooney, pp.5–6, citing McLean, the surveyor Rochfort, *Hawke's Bay Herald*.

39 Yardin to Germain, 2 March 1876, Env. 2, HOC A.

40 Reignier to Favre, 13 July 1875, Env. 2, HOC A.

41 14 Dec. 1877, Env. 3, HOC A.

42 Aubert to Poupinel, 22 April 1877, Env. 3, HOC A.

43 Redwood to Favre and Poupinel, 2 July 1875; 8 Feb., 26 July, 15 Dec. 1876; 4 March, 14 Nov., 1877; 27 Feb. 1878, RL 1, WAA.

44 Redwood to Cardinal Franchi, Prefect of Propaganda, 1 July, 21 Oct. 1875, RL 1, WAA.

45 Redwood to Aubert, 26 Jan. 1877, 29 Jan. 1878; Poupinel to Aubert, 12 Jan. 1878, Env. 3, HOC A.

46 Redwood to Favre, 15 Dec. 1876, RL 1, p.62, WAA.

47 12 Jan. 1878, Env. 3, HOC A; one aspect was the Society of Mary's other commitments, e.g. to education in France. It was a 'multi-purpose' society. See J. Durning, 'History of the Maori Missions', typescript, p.17, MAW.

48 Aubert to Poupinel, 22 April 1877, Env. 3, HOC A.

49 Ibid, 14 Dec. 1877, Env. 3, HOC A.

50 J. Durning, personal communication, July 1993. Note that Fr Delachienne, wanting himself to produce a new prayer-book in the early 1900s, once wrote to the Marist Provincial about the 'poor, poor Maori of the prayer-book' (Suzanne's, and Cognet's to follow).

Durning thinks 'one *poor* is enough'.

51 P. Bergin, 'Hoani Papita to Paora: the Marist Missions of Hiruharama and Otaki, 1883–1914', MA thesis, AU, 1986, p.9.

52 9 Aug. and 12 Sept. 1878, Z61-410, APM.

53 14 Dec. 1877, Env. 3, HOC A.

54 Poupinel to Yardin, 2 Dec. 1878, PHL 3, No. 9, MAW.

CHAPTER NINE: *From Pakipaki to Hiruharama, 1879–1885*

1 Aubert, *Manual*, p.104.

2 29 Jan. 1879, Env. 3, HOC A; 13-1, MAW.

3 Ibid.

4 Redwood to Favre, 12 Jan. 1879, RL 1, p.341, WAA.

5 Aubert to Poupinel, 17 June 1879, Env. 3, HOC A.

6 20 June 1880, Env. 2, HOC A.

7 Yardin to Poupinel, 12 June 1880, Env. 2, pp.3–4, HOC A.

8 Aubert to Poupinel, 20 June 1880, Env. 2, HOC A.

9 Ibid.

10 Soulas to a confrère, July 1880, *AMO*, v. 5, p.69.

11 Yardin to Redwood, 6 May 1880, SM personnel box, WAA.

12 Aubert to Poupinel, 7 Nov. 1879, Env. 3, HOC A; 15-1, MAW.

13 See Aubert to Poupinel, 21 March 1881, Env. 2, HOC A; 25-1-6, MAW.

14 Reignier to Redwood, 18 May and 16 July 1880, SM personnel box, WAA.

15 Yardin to Poupinel, 14 Jan. 1880, Z 208, APM.

16 Soulas to Redwood, 19 June 1880, SM personnel box, WAA.

17 Aubert to [Poupinel?], undated draft, mid-1880s, Env. 4, HOC A.

18 Yardin to Redwood, Wellington, 25 July and 4 Sept. 1880, SM personnel box, WAA.

19 Yardin to Redwood, 4 Sept. 1880, ibid.

20 Soulas to Cognet, 18 April 1894, HD 5, p.155, MAW.

21 9 July 1880, PHL 3, No. 24, p.42, MAW.

22 Redwood to Favre, 22 April 1881, RL 1, p.485, WAA; see also Poupinel to Redwood, 2 Nov. 1881, SM personnel box, WAA.

23 Redwood to Favre, 23 Feb. 1883, RL 1, p.426, WAA.

24 Luck to Benoît, 23 July 1883, LUC 25-6/1, ACDA.

25 Soulas to Artignan, 24 April 1885, *AMO*, v.6, p.132.

26 Redwood to Favre, 23 Feb. 1883, RL 1, p.427, WAA.

27 J. Vibaud, 'The Society of Mary in the Wanganui–Taranaki', ms, c.1932, MAW, p.38, based on oral information.

28 Poupinel to Lagniet, 14 July 1865, in *APF*, Lyon, 1865, v. 37, p.215.

29 R. Taylor, Journal, 9 Oct. 1862, XII, p.36; quoted in Turner, p.210.

30 D. Young and B. Foster, *Faces of the River: New Zealand's Living Water*. Wellington, 1986, p.18.

31 At Ranana, September 1856, and at Parikino, October 1860. See Turner, pp.154, 177–181.

32 W. Baker, Journal: 'Whanganui River with Rev. Taylor, 1848 Oct–Nov', MS Micro 7/24, pp.1, 24, ATL.

33 Young and Foster, p.20.

34 A. Bates, personal communication, 28 April 1993; see also M. Smart and A. Bates, *The Wanganui Story*. Wanganui, 1972, Ch. 8.

35 Soulas to Poupinel, 17 March 1884, *AMSM*, v. 5, p.553.

36 See T. Barrett, 'Early Maori Schools', in *New Zealand Founders' Society, Whanganui Branch, Newsletter*, 28, Nov. 1965.

37 Native Schools Buildings and Sites: Hiruharama (Jerusalem, Wanganui) Native School, BAAA 1001/245e 44/4, NAA.

38 Report of the Maori Mission Committee, App. 22, Presbyterian General Assembly, 1883.

39 J. Akapita, interview with author.

40 Ibid.

41 21 March 1881, Env. 2B, HOC A.

42 R. Arnold, *New Zealand's Burning: the Settlers' World in the Mid-1880s*. Wellington, 1994, p.180.

43 A. Bates, personal communication, Wanganui, 28 April 1994.

44 3 July 1883, Acc. 210/4, MAW.

45 Aubert, *Manual*, p.114.

46 Soulas to Aubert, 11 [June 1883], Env. 4, HOC A.

47 16 July 1883, HD7, p.294, MAW.

48 Aubert, *Manual*, p.85.

49 Yardin to Redwood, 22 April 1880, SM personnel box, WAA.

50 M. Fraser, 'Two rebels of Australia's religious life', *Sydney Morning Herald*, 10 Sept. 1994.

51 See M. Foale, *The Josephite Story*. Sydney, 1989; P. Gardiner, *Mary MacKillop: an Extraordinary Australian*. Newtown, NSW, 1993.

52 D. Strevens, 'The Sisters of St Joseph of Nazareth, New Zealand', MTheol thesis, Melbourne College of Divinity, 1995.

53 Sr Aloysius, 'Reminiscences', typescript, Sisters of St Joseph of Nazareth archives, Wanganui.

54 H. Albert, interview with author.

55 17 March 1888, *AMSM*, v.5, p.553.

56 Redwood to Martin, 27 Jan. 1885, Env. 4, HOC A.

57 Moller, 'Reminiscences', v.2, p.7.

58 See Strevens, pp.55–57; also HD2, p.274, MAW; RL 2, p.28, WAA.

59 Redwood to Sr Teresa, 23 Aug. 1883, RL 1, p.388, WAA.

60 Soulas to Couloignier, 17 June 1883; cited in Bergin, p.18.

61 17 July 1884, RL 1, WAA; Env. 4, HOC A.

62 Sr Clotilde Webber, memo, Env. 88, HOC A.

63 Aubert to Brownlie, 9 July 1918, Env. 52, HOC A.

64 A. Venning to Aubert, Env. 5, HOC A.

65 For a fuller discussion of this book, its background and publishing history, see J. Munro, 'Suzanne Aubert and the Meeting of Language', in *NZ Language Teacher*, 22, 1996.

66 Aubert to Grey, 29 May 1884, GLNZ A16A, APL.

67 H. Kemp, *The First Step to Maori Conversation*. Wellington, 1879, p.33. This book also included reference to Grey's *Mythology*.

68 *Pauvre* has more endearment in its tone than English 'poor', in any case.

69 I. McLaren, 'Whitcombe's Story Books: a Trans-Tasman Survey', typescript, Melbourne, 1984, p.205.

70 H. Williams, *Bibliography of Printed Maori*, p.148, notes that Whitcombe & Tombs also took over the remaining stock of Tregear's *Maori–Polynesian Comparative Dictionary* from Lyon and Blair in 1897 and issued it with a new, undated title page.

71 See *AJHR*, 1892, E-2, Native Schools, pp.3–5, 14.

72 W. Renwick, entry on James Henry Pope, in *DNZB*, v.2, pp.394–95.

73 Pope to Aubert, 16 Oct. 1885, Env. 3, HOC A.

74 There seems to be no record of a contract or correspondence between Whitcombe & Tombs and Ngata, though there must have been. The Whitcombe & Tombs files contain their correspondence with William Bird, who prepared later editions: see Whitcombe & Tombs file 93, W. W. Bird, Hugh Price Collection, Wellington.

75 E.g. BAAA 1001/772c 44/5/2 pt 4, 773c 44/5/2 pt 7, 774a 44/5/2 pt 8, 782a 44/5/11, 1915–45, NAA. Correspondence and booklists do not mention the *Manual*.

76 My thanks to Jenny Jacobs of the Maori Language Commission for helping to analyse the differences.

77 To William Bird, 27 May 1948 (see n.74).

78 Barrington and Beaglehole, p.207.

79 As recently as 1979, 1984, and a 1999 Southern Reprints, Christchurch, edition.

80 D. Simmons, personal communication, 14 June 1993; also Bruce Biggs (personal communication, 25 June 1993): 'I have always had a copy of it and used it personally when I was first learning Maori.'

81 Ngata's direct reprint is proof enough. D. Simmons, 14 June 1993, and Biggs, 25 June 1993, support this from their experience.

82 Quoted in J. Barrington, 'History plays part in failure', *Evening Post*, 10 June 1993. (Bird later revised Aubert/Ngata's text.)

83 Aubert, *Manual*, p.126.

CHAPTER TEN: *Hiruharama – the church, 1885–1889*

1 Aubert, *Manual*, p.36.

2 Moller, 'Reminiscences', v.2, p.24.

3 A. Burton, *Through the King Country with the Camera: a Photographer's Diary*. Dunedin, 1885, entry for 9 May; A. Burton, *The Maori at Home*. Dunedin, 1886, p.10.

4 E. Payton, *Round about New Zealand*. London, 1888, p.255.

5 15 Feb. 1885, Env. 19, HOC A.

6 'Constitutions of Third Order of Mary. Enlarged and Revised by Mother Mary Joseph Aubert and Rev. Father Soulas',

ms, p.109, HOC A. She wrote them; he annotated them. Suzanne also had lengthy instructions, theoretical at that isolated stage, for going through Pakeha settlements. These aimed more at curtailing stops for gossiping: the sisters could go into shops but only to buy what they needed.

7   Constitutions, p.88.

8   Constitutions, p.119.

9   M. Lawrie to Unverricht, 9 Sept. 1986, Acc 208/20, MAW.

10 Constitutions, p.121.

11 The French reads poetically: 'les bougies seront soufflées et les Soeurs couchées'.

12 Cognet to Gay, 19 March 1886, *AMO*, No. 1, p.250.

13 18 May 1886, *AMO*, No. 3, p.266.

14 In addition to Anglican connections at this time, Ranana by the end of the 1880s would have Salvation Army and Ringatu interest, as well as Catholic. See J. Binney, *Redemption Songs: a Life of Te Kooti Arikirangi Te Turuki*. Auckland, 1995, pp.431–34.

15 Cognet to family, 1 Nov. 1886, HD5, pp.256–57, MAW.

16 Cognet to Rougier, 1 Aug. 1887, Jerusalem Mission file, p.8, n.3, APM.

17 Ibid., pp.2–3.

18 Redwood to Soulas, 21 Jan. 1886, RL 2, p.72, WAA.

19 Redwood to Martin, 27 Jan. 1885, Z 151, p.1, APM.

20 Ibid., p.4.

21 Redwood to Forestier, 26 Feb. 1887, Z 151, APM.

22 Soulas to d'Artignan, 24 April, 1885, *AMO*, No. 1, p.135.

23 Soulas to 'Chères Mesdames', 28 June 1885, 28, APM. His hyperbole led him to dismiss the Sisters of St Joseph without justification. He also called Suzanne 'a real heroine, another Mlle Perroton' in a letter to Bishop Lamaze, 17 June 1885, AET 720, APM.

24 Gibson, *French Catholicism*, pp.176–77.

25 Soulas to Martin, 10 Sept. 1887, Env. 4, pp.13, 22–23, HOC A.

26 Aubert, *Manual*, p.41.

27 Turnbull had designed two central Wellington churches (St Peter's Anglican church in 1879 and St John's Presbyterian church in 1885) at about the same time as the little Catholic church at Hiruharama. He would also design the General Assembly Library in 1899, among other important Wellington buildings. See C. Cochran, entry on Thomas Turnbull, in *DNZB*, v.2, p.553.

28 Forestier to Redwood, [1886], Z 151, APM. Her bill was 9 Nov. 1885, f.103.

29 Aubert to Society of Mary, [January 1886], Z 65610-1, p.5, APM.

30 *Yeoman*, 1 Jan. 1886, p.11.

31 Aubert, *Manual*, pp.73, 108.

32 See Arnold, *New Zealand's Burning*.

33 *Wanganui Chronicle*, 26 and 30 Nov., 22 Dec. 1888.

34 J. Akapita, interview with author. S. Katene, in 'The Administration of Maori Land in the Aotea District 1900–1927', MA thesis, VUW, 1990, points out (p.33) that Ngati Hau shared Aotea ancestry from the north and Kurahaupo from the south.

35 Joly to Dunand, 1 Sept. 1886, in *AMO*, No. 4, July 1887, p.445. Fr Martin had in fact sent £20, a sizable donation, from the Society of Mary for the building of the church.

36 See Katene, pp.51–52.

37 Moller, 'Reminiscences', v.2, p.71.

38 *NZ Tablet*, 29 April and 12 Aug. 1881.

39 Brandon family, in M. Lawrie to Unverricht, 9 Sept. 1986, Acc 208/20, MAW.

40 Two sisters and a collecting pram feature in a later Wellington 'spitting' incident witnessed by a member of Hugh Laracy's family. The response was very similar.

41 Sr Margaret Anne Mills, personal communication, 1994.

42 Shanley to Moller, 8 Nov. 1926, HOC A.

43 See J. Robinson, 'Of Diverse Persons, Men and Women and Whores: Women and Crime in Nineteenth Century Canterbury', MA thesis, CU, 1983; also M. Tennant, *Paupers and Providers: Charitable Aid in New Zealand*. Wellington, 1989, for studies of 'rescue' work among 'fallen women'.

44 M. O'Meeghan, *Held Firm by Faith: a History of the Diocese of Christchurch 1840–1987*. Christchurch, 1988, pp.151–56. At one stage Ginaty was advertising in the *Tablet* for funds for eight different projects.

45 Aubert to Sr Bridget, 5 April 1889, Env. 52, HOC A.

46 Sr Bernadette Wrack, personal communication, 1993.

towards women which makes it so hard for one of them who has erred to retrace her steps, and obtain employment in any respectable establishment'.

34 Aubert, Petition for assistance to enlarge the foundling home at Jerusalem, Wanganui River, presented July 1898 by W. Symes MHR to the Public Petitions Committee, Env. 9, HOC A.

35 Env. 9, HOC A.

36 Aubert, *Directory*, p.273.

37 Moller, 'Reminiscences', v.1, p.139–40.

38 Moses, p.27.

39 Ibid., pp.30–31.

40 Brochard, *La Vérité sur les enfants trouvés*, 1856, p.51; quoted in T. Zeldin, *France 1848–1945*, v.2. Oxford, 1977.

41 See K. Lynch, *Family, Class, and Ideology in Early Industrial France: Social Policy and the Working-Class Family 1825–1848*. Wisconsin, 1988, pp.124–25. Ch. 4, 'National and Local Policy on Foundlings and Abandoned Children', discusses the whole issue. The welfare system for foundlings in Lyon at this time was outlined in each *Annuaire*, under the heading 'Bienfaisance'. The Hôpital de la Charité received them.

42 *Travaux de la Commission des Enfants Trouvés, instituée le 22 août 1849, par arrêté du ministre de l'Intérieur, Tome I: Procès-verbaux des séances de la Commission – projet de loi; Tome II: Documents sur les Enfants trouvés*, Paris, 1850. This discusses the arguments, gives figures by *département*, etc.

43 Aubert, *Directory*, p.273.

44 See R. Fuchs, *Abandoned Children: Foundlings and Child Welfare in Nineteenth-Century France*. New York, 1984. Chs 5 and 6 discuss the *nourrice* system in detail, its poverty and the high chances of infant death.

45 Moller, 'Reminiscences', v.1, p.37.

46 Env. 9, HOC A.

47 29 July 1898, Env. 9, HOC A.

48 Moller, 'Reminiscences', v.2, p.227. As Elizabeth Gilmer, Seddon's daughter was later a Home of Compassion benefactor.

49 Quoted in Hamer, p.43.

50 Quite apart from the fame she gained through the medicines, Suzanne must have been getting better known in Wellington circles. Her lawyer, Charles Skerrett, would later succeed Robert Stout as Chief Justice, and she had almost

an entourage of advisers among both Catholic and non-Catholic business people. From 1895, when Father Maillard made his apt little crack about her 'having much power over the hearts of the ministers', there are documented dealings between her and the Premier, the Minister and Secretaries of Education and Justice, the Commissioner of Police and individual members of the House of Representatives.

51 Env. 9, HOC A.

52 Unattributed cutting, 13 Aug. 1898, Press Cuttings Book 1, HOC A.

53 Env. 9, HOC A.

54 *Wanganui Herald*, 8 Dec. 1898.

55 M. D. to Editor, *Wanganui Chronicle*, 11 Aug. 1898.

56 See O'Meeghan, *Held Firm by Faith*, pp.151–53, for the Magdala project.

57 See Sweetman, 'New Zealand Catholicism', pp.198–200. Also O'Shea to Redwood, 8 Nov. 1912, WAA; Aubert to Redwood, 28 April 1913, WAA.

58 Quoted in B. Labrum, entry on Jessie Williamson, *DNZB*, v.2, p.583. See also E. Sampson, remembering Williamson from 1902, in *Women Today*, 1, 6, Sept. 1937, p.130; quoted in J. Devaliant, *Kate Sheppard*. Auckland, 1992, p.160.

59 Unattributed cutting, 31 July 1899, Press Cuttings Book 1, HOC A.

60 Undated letter, Env. 9, HOC A.

61 B. Labrum, '"For the better discharge of our duties": Women's rights in Wanganui 1893–1903', in *Women's Studies Journal*, Nov. 1990, p.146. See also B. Labrum, 'Wanganui Women's Political League 1893–c.1902', in A. Else (ed.), *Women Together: a History of Women's Organisations in New Zealand*. Wellington, 1993.

62 *Yeoman*, 13 Aug. 1898.

63 Quoted in Tennant, *Paupers and Providers*, p.41.

64 *AJHR*, 1896, H-22, p.32. Tennant, *Paupers and Providers*, uses Neill's comment to head her chapter on women.

65 18 Oct. 1898, Env. 9, HOC A.

66 Ibid., 21 Oct. 1898.

67 Ibid.

68 Ibid., 22 Oct. 1898.

69 Ibid., 31 Oct. 1898.

70 Devaliant, p.189.

71 Crichton to Aubert, 31 May 1925, Env. 8, HOC A.

72 Suzanne once told the sisters that no child

was to make the trip twice in the same day and never in the dark – which presupposes both had happened before.

73 McFadden, 'My Memories', HOC A.

74 The 'King' was the Blessed Sacrament which Redwood had permitted them to keep up at the farm. To have it in a chapel rather than the church was a privilege sometimes granted to mission stations in primitive conditions.

75 Crichton to Moller, 22 May 1932, Env. 8, HOC A.

76 Crichton to Rafter, 14 May 1967, Env. 8, HOC A.

77 19 Feb. 1918, Book 11, HOC A.

CHAPTER THIRTEEN: *Wellington – the Daughters of Our Lady of Compassion, 1899–1904*

1 Aubert, *Manual*, pp.66, 51.

2 Aubert to Outhwaite, 31 Aug. [1872], CRO 6-5/6, ACDA.

3 M. Davitt, *Life and Progress in Australasia*. London, 1898, p.397. Suzanne had invited Davitt to Jerusalem. When he could not fit this in, she went to Napier to see him. Again, as with the 'secular', inclusive education angle emphasised in Nelson in 1888, she promoted her work fittingly to Davitt: 'I found her a wonderfully bright and cheerful little woman, full of enthusiasm in the cause of humanity, and very proud of being associated with the best Catholics in the world, the "Irish Nuns", in her mission of charity and religion.'

4 Quoted in Moller, 'Reminiscences', v.2, p.213.

5 Sr Vincent Casey and Sr Vianney Brett, in Moller, 'Reminiscences', v.3, p.5.

6 Aubert to Sr Carmel, 16 Oct. 1904, Env. 23, HOC A.

7 V.2, p.212.

8 The official name is the Institute of the Daughters of Our Lady of Compassion, but the congregation has usually been known as the Sisters of Compassion, sometimes the Sisters of Our Lady of Compassion.

9 Moller, 'Reminiscences', v.3, p.6.

10 See Durning, p.18: 'Father Venning's accession to the Maori Mission excited a certain amount of comment and he was regarded as something of a curio'; also p.30. See also Bergin, pp.iv, v.

11 See, for example, Pestre to Aubert, 11

Nov. 1898, Env. 3, HOC A.

12 Redwood to Soulas, 17 July 1884, Env. 4, HOC A.

13 14 March 1889, Env. 4, HOC A.

14 Cognet [to a Marist priest], 2 Feb. 1888, Jerusalem file, APM.

15 Ms Book 20, p.331, HOC A.

16 Leterrier to Martin, 9 Feb. 1890, Z 418, APM.

17 15 August 1891, Z 331, APM.

18 Leterrier to Martin, 12 Aug. 1891, Z 418, APM.

19 Ibid., 24 Feb. 1892.

20 Ibid., 24 March 1892.

21 Raffin, Minutes of Council, 11 and 12 Jan. 1894, 342.3, APM.

22 Aubry, Report 1898, Z 331, APM.

23 Redwood to Aubert, 29 March 1892, Env. 19, HOC A.

24 Redwood to Soulas, 26 July 1884, Env. 4, HOC A; also WAA.

25 See E. Simmons, *In Cruce Salus*, p.261. These were the Maori Sisters of Mary formed by Bishop Liston in 1937.

26 Constitutions of Third Order of Mary (red exercise-book, French ms, which appears to be the earliest document), under 'But de l'Ordre', HOC A. The Daughters of Our Lady of Compassion Constitutions were simplified but not radically altered from those of the Hiruharama Third Order Regular of Mary.

27 Quoted in Moller, 'Reminiscences', v.2, pp.212–13.

28 Ibid., p.205.

29 Sr Martha (Charlotte Hinnegan) in 'Biographical Notes of Our Early Sisters', Part II, Env. 88, HOC A.

30 30 Jan. 1905, Env. 23, HOC A.

31 Sr Magdalen to Jerusalem, 13 Aug. 1899, Env. 23, HOC A.

32 G. de Ségur, *Une Saison en Nouvelle-Zélande*. Paris, 1901, pp.278–79. My thanks to David Hamer for bringing my attention to the passage in this book in the ATL. De Ségur used the word *religieuse*, which covers all members of an order or congregation. 'Nun' is the loose English equivalent. Suzanne hardly ever referred to herself as such, because officially it is restricted to a member of an old order.

33 Aubert, *Manual*, p.115.

34 See M. Bassett, *Sir Joseph Ward: a Political Biography*. Auckland, 1993, pp.111–12. Ward, a good Catholic, perhaps deserves

28 Env. 88, HOC A.
29 Quoted in Moller, 'Reminiscences', v.3, pp.215–16.
30 Aubert, *Manual*, p.105.
31 Env. 23, HOC A.
32 29 Aug. 1907, Env. 23, HOC A.
33 17 Aug. 1906, Env. 23, HOC A.
34 12 Aug. and 8 Sept. 1905, Env. 19, HOC A.
35 Tennant, *Paupers and Providers,* p.185.
36 Aubert to Sr Bridget, postscript dated 15 Dec. 1908 to letter of 11 Dec. 1908, Env. 23, HOC A.
37 B. Labrum, entry on Frances Ann Stewart, *DNZB*, v.2, p.480.
38 *AJHR*, 1909, H-31, p.14; 1910, H-31, p.20; 1911, H-31, p.23.
39 *New Zealand Official Year-book 1909.* Wellington, 1910, p.264.
40 Ibid., p.265
41 See E. Olssen, 'Towards a New Society', in G. Rice (ed.), *Oxford History of New Zealand*, 2nd edn. Auckland, 1992, p.258.
42 Quoted in J. Drummond, *The Life and Work of Richard John Seddon.* Christchurch, 1906, p.341.
43 This theme is analysed in E. Olssen, 'Truby King and the Plunket Society', *NZJH*, 15, 1, April 1981.
44 See P. Mein Smith, 'Truby King in Australia', *NZJH*, 22, 1, April 1988, for an analysis of this.
45 Truby King, *Feeding and Care of Baby.* London, 1913, pp.151–52; quoted in Olssen, 'Towards a New Society', p.264.
46 *Free Lance*, 23 Nov. 1907.
47 *New Zealand Official Year-book 1908.* Wellington, 1909, p.270.
48 28 July 1908, Env. 23, HOC A.
49 See Mein Smith for the growing controversy over types of artificial feeding.
50 Moller, 'Reminiscences', v.4, p.519.
51 G. Fowlds to Aubert, 16 May 1910, Env. 18, HOC A.

CHAPTER EIGHTEEN: *Auckland – the children, 1910–1912*
1 Aubert, *Manual*, p.50.
2 Undated, unattributed cutting, Press Cuttings Book 1, p.37, HOC A. Sr Angela's 'Reminiscences' suggest that this extract dates from the opening of the Jubilee Ward, built with the money from these birthday celebrations. Suzanne would have told a similar account then.
3 Van Staveren and his family figure now and then in Suzanne's story. For the rabbi's contribution to Wellington, see S. Levine, *A Standard for the People: the 150th Anniversary of the Wellington Hebrew Congregation, 1843–1993.* Wellington, 1995.
4 It was customary then for a man to reply in public on behalf of a woman. Suzanne had two further reasons: religious sisters did not normally participate in a public forum, and her accent was still very French. Izard, though, was allocating to her pastoral responsibilities for the whole country.
5 Sr Lawrence, Diary, p.13, Env. 88, HOC A.
6 CLE-125, ACDA.
7 Sr Lawrence to O'Shea, 2 Sept. 1920, WAA 14; also Env. 61, HOC A.
8 An example is his handling of the Ratana influence among Maori Catholics, and the issue of transfer of priests. See N. Simmons, pp.34–35.
9 Memories of Fr J. Joyce, 19 Aug. 1981; quoted in N. Simmons, p.36.
10 R. Sweetman, 'New Zealand Catholicism', p.220.
11 E.g. P. Lawlor, *The Demanding God: Some Boyhood Recollections.* Wellington, 1972, pp.147–48.
12 See Akenson, p.164.
13 O'Shea to Marist Provincial, 12 Feb. 1917, MM7, p.45, MAW.
14 Melu to Smyth (Marist Provincial), 'Notes on the Otaki Maori Station', c. Dec. 1914, MM7, pp.50–53, MAW; quoted in Bergin, p.125.
15 A. Te Ara-o-Rehua, T. Tonihi, and A. Te Hiwi, 'Petihana ki te tino tumuaki o nga pirihi o te Ropu o Hata Maria', 29 June 1914, Z 65 610, APM; quoted in Bergin, p.127.
16 Quoted in Perrot (ed.), p.8.
17 Moller, 'Reminiscences', v.4, pp.455–56.
18 E.g. Aubert to Lenihan, 31 March 1905, LEN 39-4/2, ACDA.
19 Env. 13, HOC A.
20 The Sisters of Mercy in Gisborne had experienced a different side of Lenihan. See M. Kirk, 'The Story of the Foundation of the Sisters of Mercy in Gisborne, 1894–1904', research essay, 1994, ASMA.
21 The Presbyterians, like Suzanne, would admit children of all races and creeds but stipulated that 'their religious training was to be in accordance with the

doctrine and discipline of the Presbyterian Church of New Zealand'. See G. Seed, 'The Churches and Residential Care of Children in Auckland', MA thesis, AU, 1967, p.49.

22 Moller, 'Reminiscences', v.4, e.g. p.268.

23 Env. 23, HOC A.

24 Moller, 'Reminiscences', v.4, pp.459–60.

25 Ibid., p.345.

26 Ibid., p.376.

27 Aubert, *Directory*, p.127.

28 'Pioneers' Diary', Env. 21, HOC A.

29 Ibid.

30 Aubert to Sr Chanel, 3 May 1910, Env. 21, HOC A.

31 Ibid., 24 April 1910.

32 Ibid., 3 May 1910.

33 Ibid., 20 and 26 Oct. 1910.

34 Sr Damien, Reminiscences, Env. 18, HOC A.

35 E. Simmons, *In Cruce Salus*, p.220.

36 N. Simmons, p.187.

37 Pp.42–43, Env. 21, HOC A.

38 Moller, 'Reminiscences', v.4, p.447.

39 Unattributed cuttings, mostly from *Auckland Star*, August 1911, HOC A.

40 Quoted in Eldred-Grigg, p.148.

41 Undated, Env. 18, HOC A.

42 Quoted in Tennant, *Paupers and Providers*, p.133.

43 Env. 15, HOC A.

44 Education Dept, Special Schools (St Vincent's Home, Auckland 1910–16), CW, W1043, 40/6/43, NAW.

45 Ibid.

46 Report on Institutions: Infant Life Protection, 1911–13, BAAA 1960/1a, NA.

47 Fowlds to Aubert, 16 May 1910, Env. 18, HOC A.

48 Skerrett to Gibbes, 26 May 1910, ms copy by Aubert, Env. 18, HOC A.

49 Fowlds to O'Shea, 24 June 1910, Env. 18, HOC A.

50 Aubert to Fowlds, 4 July 1910, Env. 18, HOC A.

51 Ibid.

52 See Moller, 'Reminiscences', v.5, p.115, where, among objections to maternity work, are: '. . . c) The necessity of making girls work who do not want to work, and the obligation of placing the refuge under the "Factory Act", which would be a cause of great inconvenience; d) The invincible repugnance of the majority of girls to remain secluded for six months, and thereby render their fall notorious. Infanticide would appear to them much to be preferred.' In 1911, Father Holbrook in Auckland had to acknowledge that 'several girls escaped on their trip from here to there [Mount Magdala] within the last couple of years' (Holbrook to Cleary, memorandum, 27 June 1911, CLE 125-1/6, f.3, ACDA).

53 Moller, 'Reminiscences', v.4, p.402

CHAPTER NINETEEN: *Rome, 1913–1918*

1 Aubert, *Manual*, p.80.

2 Sister Angela described this chapter 'an "Extraordinary" one in every sense of the term': 'Reminiscences', v.4, p.550. See pp.545–60 for her account of the visitation and chapter meeting.

3 See Constitutions of the Institute of Our Lady of Compassion, or Constitutions as from 1905 to 1909, ms in Suzanne's handwriting, Ch. X, HOC A. There had been elections: e.g. in the Register of Professed Sisters, v.1, Sr Bridget was 'elected third assistant by secret scrutiny' on 5 Aug. 1896, 'reelected 2d assistant by secret scrutiny at the unanimity of voices [votes]' on 23 Aug. 1902, and again in Aug. 1908.

4 Redwood to Smyth, 21 Sept. 1912, WD1, p.121, MAW.

5 Suzanne must have realised this. A similar evasiveness by Redwood when he was in Europe in 1914 earned her judgement: 'He has thrown everything on the shoulders of the Little Man he has left over there, so that matters are growing more complicated, through that very convenient way of washing one's hands.' Aubert to Isa Outhwaite, 7 July 1914, CLE 125-4, ACDA.

6 See, too, O'Shea to Smyth, 13 Feb. 1913, WD1, pp.91–92, MAW: Redwood 'will be only too glad to save himself the bother of the business by taking refuge in the legal technicalities in as far as they prevent a reopening of a matter already decided by the Vicar General'.

7 Smyth to O'Shea, 22 Oct. 1912, MIS 1, pp.187, 197–98, MAW.

8 Minutes of General Chapter, 6 Nov. 1912; Minutes of General Council, 6 Nov. 1912–21 June 1921, p.3; also Env. 20, HOC A.

9 Moller, 'Reminiscences', v.5, p.24, HOC A.

10 Memoir by Sister Clotilde of her conversation with Mgr Cullen, HOC A. The

letters written in 1904–06, Env. 23, HOC A.

3   Pp.8–9, Env. 88, HOC A.

4   Poupinel to Redwood, 10 April [1883?], SM box, 1880s, WAA: 'F. Soulas has laid out for us a mission plan for the Maoris: an independent apostolic prefecture which would have under its jurisdiction all the Maoris of the two dioceses where they live.' Poupinel approved this plan but, because of the situation in France, the Marists could not staff it.

5   For the background to this, see Bergin.

6   15 April 1898, Z 331, APM.

7   Yardin to Redwood, 4 Sept. 1880, SM box, 1880s, WAA. The French wording was 'ses paroles et ses actions tournent à la violence'.

8   Soulas to Hislop, 9 Jan. 1884; Hislop to Soulas, 11 Jan. 1884; Pope to Hislop, 11 Jan. 1884, BAAA 1001 245e 84/20, NAA.

9   Soulas's handwriting adds a page to the French manuscript of the Constitutions of the Third Order of Mary, seemingly the earliest version. On p.41 he argues against letting the acting superior be one of these '*têtes sans cervelles*', '*ces orgueilleuses ignorantes*' or a '*soeur ignorante qui manque de jugement*'.

10 Régis to Soulas, 11 Aug. 1902, Env. 3, HOC A.

11 Tamatea Aurunui to Morpeth, 2 Jan. 1893; Haseldean to Aubert, 16 Feb. 1893; Tamatea Aurunui to Hon. W. Cadman, 19 July 1893; Haseldean to Soulas, 4 Aug. 1893. PAR 4, pp.227–30, MAW.

12 It is a moot point whether the precedent of Father Woods effectively splitting the Australian Sisters of St Joseph would have any bearing. However, it was Woods' community that was so close.

13 Moller, 'Reminiscences', v.3, pp.51–52.

14 Literally, if the drop scene at the Wellington Opera House is remembered.

15 Maillard to Cognet, 1895, HD5, pp.171–72, MAW.

16 Soulas to Kirk, 16 Oct. 1889, PAR 4, p.267, MAW.

17 The people of Ngati Ruaka acknowledge his dedication to them and respect for Maori tradition and custom (personal communication, Pestal Pauro, Ranana, 7 Oct. 1995). In documentation, kaumatua took an important role in the opening of the Tawhitinui and Ranana churches, for instance. At Okato, where Soulas was transferred in 1904, records show he was really the only Catholic priest to keep working with the Maori. See, for instance, PCM O2, 25 March 1908, MAW.

18 As a very old man Soulas came to stay at the Home of Compassion at the request of his superiors, and against the will of the sisters. 'Dean Regnault (an ex-Provincial of the Society of Mary), who knew a great deal about affairs at Jerusalem under Fr Soulas, remarked that he considered it an exercise of *heroic charity* on the part of the older Sisters who had been with him there, to agree to the admission of Fr Soulas as an inmate of the Home of Compassion! And he said this with the greatest emphasis.' Sr Angela records how once more Suzanne seemed to bow before some authority or hold Soulas had, how again he influenced her dealings. The sisters finally asked for him to go and it was at this stage that they told her more fully of his treatment of them. He went to Hastings, where he died shortly before Suzanne. See Moller, 'Reminiscences', v.6, pp.321–24, 345–46; also SM Provincial Council Minutes, 27 June 1922, 16 Jan. and 31 Jan. 1923, PCM O2, MAW.

19 Recollections of Sr Anne, c.1940, Env. 88, HOC A.

20 Soulas to [?], 10 Feb. 1902, Jerusalem file, APM.

21 Soulas to Martin, 15 May 1900, Jerusalem file, APM. There are valid points, like the extra expense in building at Jerusalem because of the cost of transporting materials up the river; and the absence of any European families as steady contributing parishioners. The tiny allocation to the sisters from the Propagation of the Faith vote was a steady theme in his distress (see letter dated 10 Feb. 1902, above). It was true that the Jerusalem sisters lived an extremely frugal life.

22 Whether or not it was a major reason, Euphrasie Barbier, Mother Mary of the Heart of Jesus, is said to have used the instance of Auckland in the mid-1860s as an argument for the semi-enclosure of her Sisters of Our Lady of the Missions in New Zealand and the Pacific. See C. Couturier, *Unswerving Journey: the Life of Mother Mary of the Heart of Jesus, Foundress of the Congregation of Our Lady*

of the Missions, trans. R Sheed. Toulouse, 1965/66, pp.73–74.

23 Olier to Martin, 2 Nov. 1903, OP 418, APM.

24 Moller, 'Reminiscences', v.3, pp.52–53. Poignantly, one of the examples given of Soulas's power even as an old man was when he coerced Suzanne, very old and ill herself, to write letters to Sr Clotilde while Clotilde was at the deathbed of her Anglican father, trying to get her to convert the dying man to Catholicism. See Moller, 'Reminiscences', v.7, pp.13–14.

25 Olier to Martin, 3 Nov. 1903, OP 418, APM.

26 Soulas to Martin, 7 Nov. 1903, Jerusalem file, p.5, APM.

27 Ms Book 16, HOC A.

28 O'Farrell, Vanished Kingdoms, cites the case of Matt Talbot in Ireland, a reformed drunkard. When he died in 1925, he was found to have chains embedded in his flesh, with the skin grown over.

29 Sr M. Catherine Maher to Sr M. Paula Ennis, 28 June 1880, ASMA.

30 Constitutions of Third Order of Mary, French ms, pp.48, 49; 'Original Rule 1892 Third Order. Also Sisters of Compassion', p.25, HOC A.

31 By the time Soulas took his religious vows in France, the definitive Marist Constitutions of 1872 were in effect. These imposed no bodily penances, and stressed caution and guidance from a spiritual director in any personal choice to practise them. Interior mortification was recommended as preferable. See Constitutions of the Society of Mary, Latin text in conformity with the text approved by the general chapter of 1872, with English translation. Rome, 1992, Article VII, p.25; also Autour de la règle 1. Rome, 1991, pp.220–21.

32 Nov. 1903, Env. 23, HOC A.

33 O'Donnell was one of a team of five Ballarat Redemptorists, conducting retreats and parish missions around the country. All religious during retreats usually had read out to them the text of Pope Leo XIII's directives to religious communities, reformulated in 1890. In Wellington it had become widely available only in 1900, when it was printed in English as an appendix to the Decrees of New Zealand Bishops, 1899

Provincial Synod: Acta et Decreta Concilii Provincialis Primi Wellingtonensis, 1899, pp.95–98. The sisters most likely were hearing for the first time their rights as individuals to freedom in their choice of confessor and spiritual director, and heard the emphasis on making known in this way any abuse of authority from superiors. They were probably given extra encouragement to speak out. O'Donnell gave the retreat first to the sisters in Jerusalem. Sister Angela's 'blue notebook' records: 'Fr Soulas advised Sisters to reply to all questions, but to give no information for which they were not asked!' HOC A.

34 Aubert to Sr Bridget, 31 March 1904: 'I will answer F. Maillard. Watch closely. You know that we are forbidden to correspond in any way with Okato. I hope that nobody will place me in the sad necessity of reporting. We are obliged to obey His Grace before God and before the Church.' Env. 23, HOC A.

35 Even Olier's words, if Soulas recorded him correctly – 'They are the cause of all your troubles' – carried with them something of the backfiring, the automatic gun recoil of blame that echoes down women's history.

36 Undated, 1904, Env. 23, HOC A.

37 Sister Damien wrote a note in January 1968. It summarised what she, as a sister who had not been in the congregation at the time, knew of the story: 'Anyone reading the letter Sr A. has at the end of Bk I, from Fr S. to Mother at Meanee, telling her what she is to bring with her to Jerusalem, would know what he was like. In 1904 or 1905, I forget which, I was at Kaponga and went over to Opunake to stay the weekend with the McReynolds. At dinner time on Sunday, Father Soulas came in – he had been saying Mass for the Maoris. He talked the whole of dinner about a marvellous aeroplane he had designed, so I saw how queer he was. At Jerusalem he had the idea that he was the Founder and had to train the Sisters. Unfortunately, he made them all promise never to tell anyone, even Mother, and as they had no one else for confession, they were afraid. So I got little – it was too soon after his time. I was told about the discipline, but never heard the details, and thought they went into his parlour.

The only one alive who could tell would be Sr Patrick – she must know. Mother Zita was in office for so long that she probably knows. And Raphael probably managed to hear it. I was told that a strap hung on the kitchen wall. Fr S. sat at the head of the table, Mother & the Sisters all round. Every now and again he would tell a Sister to stand up and hold out her hand, and tell another to get the strap and give her so many cuts.

'I'm sure Mother would not be spared, when he would go to the length of making the Sisters lock her out of the house, when she came off the boat. All about that is in Sr Angela's book ['Reminiscences']. I did not hear about the cure for round shoulders, but quite believe it. Someone should get everything from Sr Patrick before it is too late – all the others are gone. It must have been after Mother came back from Rome that they had the private meeting at the Bay of all the old Sisters, and he apologised to them for all he had done and all had to promise never to talk about it.' Env. 88, HOC A.

38 Aubert to Redwood, 18 April 1913, 242/6, p.3, WAA.
39 Ms Book 16, p.12, HOC A.
40 See an undated letter to Sr Bridget, 1904: 'Pray hard and get the Sisters to pray, without entering into particulars. But there is trouble again about C.S. He claims £300 at once and threatens to put a claim of £1000 through the Supreme Court if he does not get satisfaction. If I hand that money we are completely ruined. If we go to court it will be a dreadful scandal. God alone can settle the matter. It is dreadful.' Env. 23, HOC A.
41 Undated, Env. 23, HOC A.
42 Env. 23, HOC A.

CHAPTER SEVENTEEN: *Wellington – the children, 1907–1910*

1 Aubert, *Manual*, p.42.
2 Moller, 'Reminiscences', v.3, p.184.
3 Aubert, *Directory*, p.335.
4 There are stories of men planting a quick kiss on old Mother Aubert, whether it was Dr Fyffe and Dr Valintine, or the non-Catholic who hopped off his coal cart to thank her in the street for nursing his mother years before.
5 Env. 105, HOC A.

6 Aubert, *Directory*, p.393.
7 French ms, p.24, HOC A.
8 Moller, 'Reminiscences', v.4, p.530.
9 Aubert to Goulter, 20 Jan. 1923, Env. 26, HOC A.
10 Reminiscences of Anna Gross, Env. 88, HOC A.
11 Undated cutting, Press Cuttings Book 1, HOC A.
12 Undated letter, Env. 14, HOC A.
13 Undated cutting, *Evening Post*, Press Cuttings Book 1, p.21, HOC A.
14 Ibid., p.25.
15 Ibid., p.22.
16 *Evening Post*, 22 Nov. 1907, Press Cuttings Book 1, p.23, HOC A.
17 *Free Lance*, 23 Nov. 1907, ibid.
18 Env. 23, HOC A.
19 Press Cuttings Book 1, p.24, HOC A.
20 Ibid.
21 Sr Bridget to Aubert, 10 Nov. 1907, Env. 6, HOC A.
22 Press Cuttings Book 1, p.25, HOC A.
23 Quoted in D. McEldowney, 'Ultima Thule to Little Bethel', *Landfall*, 77, March 1966, p.51.
24 A. Butler, *Glimpses of Maori Land*. London, 1886, p.77, quoted in O. O'Sullivan, *Apostle in Aotearoa: a Biography of Jeremiah Purcell O'Reily O.F.M.Cap., Wellington's first Catholic pastor*. Auckland, 1977.
25 See O'Sullivan, p.56, for the background to this story.
26 Redwood also attended 'the most important Christian ecumenical event of the nineteenth century' (Braybrooke, p.28, see below), the 1893 World's Parliament of Religions in Chicago, where Jews, Muslims, Hindus and other religions were also represented. Redwood was quoted in the published record of proceedings: 'Many affirmed that evidence of God's activity could be seen in all religions. "In all religions," said the Roman Catholic Archbishop Redwood of New Zealand, "there is a vast element of truth" (p.441).' Quoted in M. Braybrooke, *Pilgrimage of Hope: One Hundred Years of Global Interfaith Dialogue*. New York, 1992, p.36 (p.441 is in J. H. Barrows (ed.), *The World's Parliament of Religions*. Chicago, 1893).
27 Noted as a characteristic of New Zealand religion by H. Miller, quoted in *Landfall*, 77, p.3.

Directory printed in 1922 formalised Rome's approval of the congregation's own method of spiritual formation and renewal.

11 O'Shea to Redwood, 8 Nov. 1912, WAA.

12 Ibid.

13 Aubert, 'Copy of what I left at Propaganda, Notes in reply to Circular Letter of the Vicar General', 6 Nov. 1912, para. 10, HOC A; Moller, 'Reminiscences', v.5, p.22.

14 Minutes, 6 Nov. 1912, pp.5, 6, HOC A.

15 Ibid., p.8. See, too, Aubert, 'Case for the Defence', point 10, ms in French, Ms Book 5, pp.38–39, HOC A. The criticism was: 'The Sisters ought to be withdrawn from the Maori Mission. They have no community life there. They are on their own and there is too much work in the Institute. They could be of assistance elsewhere.' Her response was: 'The Sisters were founded in the first place for the Maori Mission. That is in our rules and in the formula of our vows. How do the Sisters live in the other Missions? This poor Maori Mission seems to have been and still seems to be the scapegoat.'

16 Redwood to Cardinal Gotti, 3 Jan. 1914, file 'Wellington: Suore di N. Signora della Compassione' 160, 295/914, f.8, ACPF. The language of aggression, significantly, comes in O'Shea's letters rather than Suzanne's, e.g. O'Shea to Smyth, 22 March 1913, WD1, p.94, MAW: 'Mother Joseph has capitulated at last.' And, again to Smyth, 23 April 1914, WD1, p.93, MAW: 'So, your report has been vindicated and we have triumphed all along the line, "Deo Gratias"'. Suzanne's language was that of defending, not attacking: 'Be on your guard'. When Bishop Lenihan and Father Tickell were in opposition to the Sisters of Mercy in Gisborne in 1904, Tickell used still stronger terminology in a letter to Lenihan, 29 July 1904: 'My Lord, these wretched, misguided women dare to defy your authority and consequently, the authority of the Church. There is therefore no help for it, the community must be extinguished, flattened, killed so to speak, unless the Sisters submit.' ACDA, quoted in Kirk.

17 See Aubert, 'Case for the Defence', Ms Book 2, p.48, HOC A. In the report on personnel, she wrote: 'The number of Postulants has diminished very much during the last two years, because of the rumours circulating that we have no stability, that we are not approved, that our life is too hard, that when the old woman dies everything will go to pieces, and they had better enter other Convents . . .' Sisters' memories corroborate this.

18 O'Shea to Redwood, 8 Nov. 1912, WAA.

19 Ms Book 16, HOC A.

20 Suzanne wrote in her defence to Rome that both 'the Vicar General and the Very Reverend Visitor' knew of the reasons for this. See Ms Book 2, p.21; also Moller, 'Reminiscences', v.5, p.20. O'Shea's 8 Nov. 1912 letter to Redwood has: 'Of course there are a few cranks in every Order and some in this one are the result partly of the Wanganui River training.'

21 28 April 1913, WAA.

22 Redwood to Aubert, 12 May 1913, Env. 20, HOC A. Regarding the admission of babies during this time, the women of the St Vincent de Paul Society would wait at O'Shea's office with requests. If there was to be no admission, they would ask him to nominate another institution (there was none). He got their point.

23 In a deposition to the Sacred Congregation of Religious, she recounted the story of Pompallier's debts and Croke's arbitrary action to explain a certain 'lack of confidence in the R.R. Bishops, her Superiors': 'Trust cannot be commanded. The poor Sister, although filled with deep respect for the episcopacy, cannot help reading the future in a past the memory of which haunts and tortures her.' Undated ms [1916], Env. 62, HOC A.

24 Moller, 'Reminiscences', v.4, p.595.

25 Env. 23, HOC A.

26 Aubert to Nancy Johnston, 20 Dec. 1921, Rolleston letters, copies in HOC A.

27 Frs Lane, McKenna, Power, Macmanus, Walsh, July 1913, Env. 20, HOC A. In Auckland, Father Tigar was also a confidant.

28 This is extensively documented. It is treated in a letter about Suzanne, but separately from her case, from Copéré to Redwood, 6 Nov. 1913, WD1, pp.132–33, MAW.

29 Fyffe to Aubert, 17 July 1913, Env. 20, HOC A.

30 E.g. Aubert to O'Shea, 18 Feb. 1913, Env. 20, HOC A: 'I feel it to be my right

to delay signing the transfer of the properties until His Grace the Archbishop is able to deal personally with the matter.'

31 Aubert to Cleary, 26 June 1911, CLE 125-5, ACDA.

32 O'Shea to Aubert, 3 March 1913, Env. 20, HOC A.

33 Memorandum, 18 July 1913, Env. 30, HOC A.

34 Statement by Mother Mary Joseph Aubert, undated, pp.2–3, 5, Env. 30, HOC A.

35 Aubert to Skerrett, 8 Oct. 1916, Letterbook 14, HOC A.

36 Aubert, *Manual*, pp.79, 81.

37 This list was found in the pages of a book. Suzanne told the sisters that, when Redwood was walking with her to Propaganda in Rome, he glimpsed her red stockings. He asked her why she was not wearing black. She answered that red was much cheaper. He told her that she 'must not wear the red ones, not even for the sake of Holy Poverty'. Moller, 'Reminiscences', v.5, p.106.

38 Undated, CLE 125-4, ACDA.

39 Ibid., 4 April 1915.

40 Aubert to Redwood, 1[?] Aug. 1913, WAA.

41 3 Feb. 1914, CLE 125-4, ACDA.

42 13 Sept. 1913, Env. 20, HOC A.

43 10 Sept. 1913, Env. 20, HOC A.

44 10 Sept. 1913, Env. 20, HOC A.

45 K. Rahner and H. Vorgrimler, *Concise Theological Dictionary*. Freiburg, 1965, p.72.

46 3 Feb. 1914, CLE 125-4, ACDA.

47 10 Sept. 1913, Env. 20, HOC A.

48 Aubert, *Manual*, p.59.

49 Aubert to Outhwaite, 27 Oct. 1913, CLE 125-4, ACDA.

50 12 Aug. 1913, 160, 2089/913, ACPF. Copéré was SM representative in dealings with the Holy See.

51 27 Oct. 1913, CLE 125-4, ACDA.

52 Aubert, record of her trip and experiences in Rome, Ms Book 9; Moller, 'Reminiscences', v.4, pp.14–15, HOC A.

53 Aubert to Sr Angela, 28 March 1915, Env. 22, HOC A.

54 R. Aubert (ed.), *Dictionnaire d'Histoire et de Géographie ecclésiastiques*. Paris, 1984, v. 20, pp.918–21. Like Suzanne, Gotti was 'un bourreau de travail' (a workaholic).

55 Undated, CLE 125-4, ACDA.

56 Aubert to Sacred Congregation for Religious, undated ms [1916], Env. 62, HOC A.

57 Aubert, 'Foundation of the Institute', ms, HOC A.

58 Letterbook 12, HOC A.

59 14 Feb. 1914, Env. 65, HOC A.

60 To Copéré, 24 July 1914, 160, 1832/914, ACPF.

61 Letters to Outhwaite, CLE 125-4, ACDA; memories of Mère M. Madeleine, ms, HOC A.

62 Aubert to Outhwaite, undated, CLE 125-4, ACDA.

63 Maori from Putiki, Wanganui itself and Parikino had joined at the outset. Ranana and Hiruharama men sailed later, in Feb. 1918. See C. Pugsley, *Te Hokowhitu a Tu: the Maori Pioneer Battalion in the First World War*. Auckland 1995, p.64 for a photograph of these men; also pp.36–41 for the Maori killed, wounded or missing on Gallipoli. Many were from Hawke's Bay, from families Suzanne would have known.

64 Aubert to Outhwaite, 16 May 1916, 20 Oct. 1914, 14 Dec. 1916, 18 July 1916, CLE 125-4, ACDA.

65 Ibid., 20 Oct. 1914.

66 Ibid., 14 Dec. 1916.

67 Ibid., 20 Jan., 22 Feb., 4 April 1915; to Sr Angela, 13 March 1915, Env. 22, HOC A; to 'Sr Claver & Co', 2 March 1915, Env. 24, HOC A.

68 Aubert to Outhwaite, 18 July 1916, CLE 125-4, ACDA.

69 Ibid., 16 May 1916.

70 25 Nov. 1913, Env. 27, HOC A.

71 Aubert to Outhwaite, 3 Feb. 1914, CLE 125-4, ACDA.

72 Ibid., 10 May 1915.

73 Ibid., 27 Oct. 1913.

74 To Sr Carmel, 23 Feb. 1914, Env. 23, HOC A.

75 Ibid.

76 20 March 1914, Env. 22, HOC A.

77 Env. 24, HOC A.

78 Balzar to Aubert, 1 Nov. 1919, Env. 32, HOC A; Moller, 'Reminiscences', v.6, p.121.

79 Aubert to Outhwaite, 16 May 1914, CLE 125-4, ACDA.

80 Ibid., 9 Oct. [1915].

81 Ibid., 14 Dec. 1916.

82 Battandier, *Annuaire pontifical catholique*.

Paris, 1913–48; *Annuario pontificio*, Rome, 1925–62.

83   11 Jan. 1921, Env. 40, HOC A.
84   28 Dec. 1915, 160, 289/916, ACPF.
85   12 Oct. 1919, Env. 32, HOC A; Moller, 'Reminiscences', v.6, p.120.
86   Ibid., v.5, p.36.
87   7 Jan. 1916, Env. 22, HOC A.
88   Native Schools Attendance Returns, BAAA 1001/23a, NAA.
89   Minutes of General Council, 6 Jan. 1918, HOC A.
90   13 Nov. 1913, WAA.
91   See Moller, 'Reminiscences', v.5, p.254.
92   Undated ms, HOC A.
93   Env. 22, HOC A.
94   10 July 1918, Env. 24, HOC A.
95   Quoted in Moller, 'Reminiscences', v.5, p.255.
96   Redwood to Cardinal Gotti, 3 Jan. 1914, 160, 295/914, ACPF.
97   Ibid., 12 Dec. 1914, 160, 2096/914, ACPF.
98   Env. 62, HOC A.
99   Env. 25, HOC A.
100   7 Jan. 1916, Env. 22, HOC A.
101   Cleary's illness was well documented, as was his tendency to let differences become extremely personal. Another example was his long battle with Kelly, extremist editor of the *Tablet*. Joseph Croke Derby was one of several priests in his diocese also to suffer under Cleary. 'There was to be no challenge to his power base'; 'He became obsessive over several issues and brought all the force of his intellect and dialectical skills to bear on destroying the opposition.' R. Sweetman, personal communication, 2 Nov. 1993. See also R. Sweetman, 'New Zealand Catholicism', p.188. Sweetman's forthcoming book, *Bishop in the Dock*, on Bishop Liston's sedition trial, also backgrounds this period, as does Akenson, pp.180–82.
102   4 April 1916, CLE 125-2, ACDA.
103   'Instruzioni generali e particolari della S.C. di Propaganda per Mgr Delegato Apostolico d'Australia', 18 Nov. 1914, 161, 1935/914, ACPF.
104   4 Jan. 1916, CLE 125-4, ACDA.
105   Quoted in Moller, 'Reminiscences', v.5, p.216.
106   8 June 1916, CLE 125-2/5, ACDA.
107   Undated, ASCR, Env. 62, HOC A.
108   Mahoney to Cleary, 16 Aug. 1916, CLE 115/1, ACDA.
109   Mahoney to Mother Alacoque McDermott, 14 Aug. 1916, ASMA. In Mahoney's letters to Cleary, one could possibly detect some solidarity for the Sisters of Compassion in the reaction of the Sisters of Mercy.
110   13 Sept. 1916, CLE 115/1, ACDA.
111   20 Aug. 1916, Env. 24, HOC A.
112   4 Oct. 1916, Env. 24, HOC A.
113   Env. 61, HOC A.
114   21 Jan. 1917, WAA.
115   Serafino, Voto del Consultore, 10 Dec. 1916, 160, 1461/16, p.4, ACPF; Env. 62, HOC A. Also Aubert to Skerrett, Oct. 1916; quoted in Moller, 'Reminiscences', v.5, pp.308–9.
116   Env. 24, HOC A.
117   Original in French, Ms Book 3, p.15, HOC A.
118   Cleary to O'Riordan, 20 July and 1 Aug. 1917, 22/119, 31/128, IRC.
119   Cleary to Gasquet, Bagenalstown, Ireland, 12 Aug. 1917, Gasquet Papers, Downside Abbey archives.
120   Gasquet to Tonti, undated, Env. 62, HOC A.
121   21 Jan. 1918, Env. 62, HOC A.
122   21 Aug. 1913, Env. 15, HOC A.

CHAPTER TWENTY: *Wellington – the hospital, 1919–1926*

1   Aubert, *Manual*, pp.55, 54.
2   Raffin to Holley, 4 April 1918, GHL 2/30, MAW.
3   Env. 24, HOC A.
4   Despite the reference to hostilities continuing, the letter is dated 1919. Aubert to Nancy Johnston, 26 May 1919, Nancy Rolleston Papers, copies in HOC A.
5   9 Sept 1917, Env. 24, HOC A.
6   15 July 1917, Env. 24, HOC A. The Code of Canon Law was formally promulgated on Pentecost, 27 May 1917, to be effective from Pentecost, 19 May 1918.
7   Quoted in Moller, 'Reminiscences', v.7, p.179.
8   Sr Clotilde Webber to Fr M. Mulcahy, 'Reminiscences of M. Aubert's teaching Noviciate, 1910–1913, Island Bay', undated ms, Env. 88, HOC A.
9   Suzanne wrote it first in English, of course, as it was for the sisters, and in her own style: e.g. 'He welcomed in his way the weary travellers, lending them his breath as a heater and his straw as a bed – all that he had, dear old ox.' 'Dear old ox'

then went into French as 'pauvre chère bête'. Redwood translated the passage back: 'the ox . . . welcomed them in his way, and proffered his breath for warmth, and his straw for bed – all that he had, poor dear beast.' And her '. . . where they can feel at home in their rags, because lovable Poverty is Lady of the House . . . If the rich want to enter, they must first become poor in spirit, and humble, and have a card of introduction from the poor' becomes Redwood's '. . . to feel themselves at ease in their rags, since lovely Poverty is the hostess of the palace . . . If the rich enter, it is only by having become poor in spirit, after self-humiliation'. Suzanne's original English was more immediate and idiomatic. See Moller, 'Reminiscences', v.6, pp.313–14.

10 Aubert, *Directory*, p.77.

11 Ibid, pp.74–75.

12 Fr Bernard Hehir, 'Personal impressions', interview with Srs Melchior, Elizabeth, Monica, Rose, Adelma, Benedict, no date, 1976, HOC A. It is not clear who is speaking.

13 See Ch. 14. This was the 'indoctrination' that Dr Elsie Gibbons remarked on, which formed the spirit of the congregation in the novice while safeguarding her individual essence.

14 Parts of it reflect a Redemptorist influence gained partly from her devotional books on the teaching of St Alphonsus.

15 Sr Clotilde, 'Reminiscences'.

16 15 Oct. 1917, Mss 14B1, HOC A.

17 Aubert to Sr Claver, 22 Aug. 1917, Env. 24, HOC A.

18 To Sr Angela, 17 Sept. 1919. Gasquet thought well of Suzanne, too. When she died, he wrote to the sisters in his own hand: 'It was with deep sorrow that I heard of your great loss, at the death of your saintly Mother Aubert. I esteemed it a privilege to have known her and worked for her when she was in Rome. Not only I but many here in the Eternal City regarded her as a true Servant of God and I hope I may be spared to see at least the initial stages of the process of her Beatification. That she will most certainly be raised some day to the Altar I feel confident. Here we are beginning to get our recollections set down in order to be ready when the Official Examination shall have begun. I hope you in New

Zealand will collect everything about her and her many virtues whilst there are so many alive who knew her. I got a long account – taken from the newspapers you sent me – put into the *Catholic Universe*. It has been a great privilege to have known her. Anything that I can do to help you in your difficulties, if they still exist, I will gladly do.' Gasquet to Sr Cecilia Crombie, 10 Dec. 1926, Env. 51, HOC A.

19 22 Oct. 1917. Mss 14B1, HOC A.

20 Regnault to Sr Angela, 3 March 1921, HOC A.

21 Ms 14C2, HOC A.

22 Sr Clotilde, 'Reminiscences'.

23 Sr Eustace Conaglen, interview with author.

24 See 'Blue and White', St Patrick's College Jubilee issue, 1935; Moller, 'Reminiscences', v.6 pp.51–68.

25 Aubert, *Manual*, p.64.

26 See Bassett, p.239, for this period in London. Bassett, p.286, notes: 'It was announced in the press that Ward had left £1000 to the late Mother Mary Aubert of the Island Bay Home of Compassion which was to go to the institution. The rest was to be distributed among Ward's children.'

27 31 Aug. 1918, HOC A.

28 Suzanne to Sister Claver, 15 and 19 Sept. 1918, HOC A. Ward told some sisters in 1925 that Suzanne's 'stateless' situation had not been easy to solve. 'We had to make it a matter for the Government of New Zealand. We said it was true she was not a naturalised British subject, but she had lived so long among us and had worked so well for the country, that our Government would take as a compliment to themselves anything that was done for her'. Moller, 'Reminiscences', v.6, p.46.

29 Nancy Rolleston Papers, copies in HOC A. Pearl Dalziell and Fr Alan Perceval were also Johnston family members helping Suzanne. In a letter to Sr Claver, 31 Aug. 1919, Suzanne wrote: 'Miss Nancy Johnston called yesterday to see me. I was so pleased to see her. It is her who, through her influence in England, has finally extricated me from Rome. God bless her and her people; we can never pay our debt of gratitude to the Johnston family.' Suzanne was later asked by Nancy to be godmother to her

son; she had to be given ecclesiastical dispensation to do so.

30 Aubert to Sr Claver, 31 Aug. 1919, Env. 24, HOC A.

31 Aubert to Raffin, 21 Sept. 1917, Mss 14B, HOC A.

32 Raffin to Holley, 8 March 1918, GHL 2/29, MAW.

33 Ibid., 2 Feb. 1918, GHL 1/21, MAW.

34 Aubert to Raffin, 8 May 1917, Env. 34, HOC A. Dean Holley, the new Marist Provincial in New Zealand, told the sisters that Raffin did write. Moller, 'Reminscences', v.6, p.341.

35 From London, Suzanne sent to Ars an account of her link with the curé and of his prophecies to her. *Annales d'Ars*, June 1920.

36 Moller, 'Reminiscences', v.6, p.75. 'New Novices Names: . . . Magdalen "would not be given in the lifetime of the former Sister of that name for many reasons," not the least being that Mother loved to call her by that up to the time she died'. Minutes, 5 Feb. 1927, p.247.

37 Moller, 'Reminiscences', v.6, p.119.

38 To Barbara Harper, 11 June 1960, Rolleston Papers, copies in HOC A.

39 Guthrie to Sr Angela Moller, 'Reminiscences', v.6, p.114.

40 24 Nov. 1919, to A. Collyer, Env. 33, HOC A.

41 To Harper, 11 June 1960.

42 Moller, 'Reminiscences', v.6, p.132.

43 Ibid., pp.198–201.

44 Nelle Scanlan, in *NZ Free Lance*, 17 June 1925. Other journalists named included Eileen Duggan, Leo Fanning and Pat Lawlor.

45 Ibid.

46 Interview with author.

47 As a baby he played the infant Jesus in the manger for the Nativity scene at the Christmas Eve midnight Mass. Suzanne taught the sisters to see the child Jesus in each of the children of the Island Bay family. Having one of them as a real baby among the statuettes of the other Christmas figures was a tradition which continued for years. It was stopped by the archbishop in the 1950s.

48 Interview with author. It was hunger as well as early rising that caused the boy's tiredness: the custom then was to fast before Mass.

49 Hehir, 'Personal Impressions'.

50 Ibid. It is not clear who is speaking.

51 Env. 88, HOC A.

52 Aubert, *Manual*, p.43.

53 It would later be extended to fourteen, to fit in with the age at which many children finished New Zealand primary schooling then.

54 Minutes of General Council, 22 Feb. 1920, p.141, HOC A.

55 Ibid.

56 Following Cerretti's report, Cardinal Serafini had criticised the Maori mission work of the Wellington archdiocese in 1916. Archbishop O'Shea then visited the river settlements and proposed the Kaiwhaiki centre. The sisters' Maori mission work, which he had nearly closed down in 1912, was now considered valuable. But the reduction in the number of postulants over the previous seven years meant fewer sisters were available for new ventures.

57 Minutes of General Council, 29 Feb. 1920, p.143, HOC A.

58 Moller, 'Reminiscences', v.6, p.299.

59 E.g. when the sisters opposed her on an important 'concentration' proposal. See Claver to Redwood, 21 July, 9 Aug. and 30 Oct. 1923, WAA.

60 Minutes of General Council, 11 April 1920, p.149, HOC A.

61 O'Shea to Aubert, 3 April 1920, WAA. He revoked permissions to collect, required full accounting 'whenever he thinks well to exact it' and intended 'to use to the fullest extent the powers conferred upon us' to monitor Suzanne. Nothing was to be done without 'our written approval'.

62 8 April 1920, WAA.

63 R. Sweetman's forthcoming book, *Bishop in the Dock*, treats this subject. See also P. O'Connor, 'Sectarian Conflict in New Zealand 1911–1920', *Political Science*, 19, 1, July 1967, p.4.

64 Minutes of General Council, 11 Nov. 1920, p.165, HOC A. In 1920, Bishop Cleary picked up the general theme in a letter, referring to 'stories of secret burials, wholesale burials of massacred infants in lime-pits, etc., which were concocted and industriously circulated in Auckland in 1917–1918 – as usual, about unnamed convents – and which the police, after a searching investigation, officially declared to be utterly devoid

of foundation.' This did not apply to the sisters' home in Auckland. Cleary to Rev. W. J. Elliott, 6 Feb. 1920, CLE 89-2, ACDA.

65   See Minutes of General Council, 13 April 1921, p.172, HOC A.

66   See Aubert to O'Shea, 4 March 1921, Env. 61, HOC A, for fuller discussion of the Kaiwhaiki proposal.

67   Minutes of General Council, 9 Aug. 1920, p.160, HOC A.

68   13 April 1921, Hospital Training School Correspondence, 1910–59, HOC A.

69   Quoted by M. Burgess, entry on Hester Maclean, in C. Macdonald, M. Penfold and B. Williams (eds), *The Book of New Zealand Women: Ko Kui Ma Te Kaupapa*, Wellington, 1991, p.389.

70   Maclean to Aubert, 31 Aug. 1922, Hospital Training School Correspondence, 1910–59, HOC A.

71   Ibid., 26 May 1924.

72   Ibid., Bicknell to Aubert, 28 July 1924.

73   Ibid., 30 July 1924.

74   M. Burgess, entry on Jessie Bicknell, in C. Macdonald *et al*, p.87.

75   See Sr Clotilde Webber, 'Notes on Nursing Work', ms, 1932, HOC A: 'The usual objections were brought forward – why alter present arrangements, why the necessity to extend training & knowledge of nursing staff, both Dep. of Health & Gov. also B.M.A. were quite satisfied etc. etc. Mother ably pleaded change of officials, her own death, vacillating Governments, the venture of Inst into other countries, and above all her responsibility & right, not only to safeguard for the future those under her care, but also, after 60 years citizenship & work for the poor of N.Z. to expect & claim help & protection from the existing Gov. 'N.B. She approached the officials with quiet determination, a quaint humour, & humble but dignified demeanour. Nothing was too great a personal sacrifice, no rebuff too severe, where the possible safety of the poor of Christ, was in question.'

76   Aubert to Valintine, 29 Oct. 1924, Hospital Training School Correspondence, 1910–59, HOC A.

77   Minutes of General Council, 9 Oct. 1925, p.137, HOC A.

78   Aubert to Valintine, 28 Oct. 1925, Hospital Training School Correspondence,

1910–59, HOC A.

79   It also indicated that doctors might be remunerated for car expenses out to the home, seemingly against its 'free' philosophy.

80   1 March 1926, WAA.

81   6 April 1926, WAA.

82   Env. 62, HOC A.

83   Hospital Training School Correspondence, 1910–59, HOC A.

84   Env. 61, HOC A.

85   Moller, 'Reminiscences', v.6, pp.329–30.

86   Srs Cecilia, Alphonsus, Claver, Rose to O'Shea, 26 Aug. 1926, WAA; O'Shea to same, 26 Aug. 1926, WAA.

87   Minutes of General Council, 22 Feb. 1920, p.139, HOC A. In another instance, she had plausible reasons for not inviting O'Shea to the community's celebration of the canonisation of the Curé d'Ars. Moller, 'Reminiscences', v.7, p.125.

88   See, for instance, Minutes, 14 March 1926, p.162, HOC A: 'Questioned if she was going to write to the Archbishop, the Superior General said she would deal with that herself. It was not a matter for Council.'

89   6 April 1926, WAA.

90   8 Nov. 1926, WAA.

91   Blair drafted an all-important amendment to the Nurses and Midwives Registration Act 1925.

92   Interview with M. Graham and P. Crombie, 19 June 1991.

93   C. T. Collins, interview with author. This opinion is supported by interviews with L. J. Walker and Dr Elsie Gibbons, who describe how they came to work at the Home of Compassion (Sir Charles Burns arranged many contacts), and mention the shared doctors' discussions on Saturday mornings which were highly valued professionally.

94   Aubert, *Manual*, p.106.

95   Moller, 'Reminiscences', v.6, p.281.

96   8 May 1924, Env. 5, HOC A.

97   To Ani Haami, 14 July 1924, Env. 69, HOC A.

98   Pauro to Aubert, 1 Oct. 1926, Env. 69, HOC A. The sisters had been urgently called down to Wellington, and probably took her letter with them. She is writing the day Meri dies. Wiki's nephew, Pestal Pauro, remembers as a boy going with her to visit Rure, and the two old people would still talk about Meri. The text is:

'Dear Mother, I salute you in the midst of the sufferings of this world. It is my loving sympathy that urges me to write because you are the living link with our parents. May God bring you back from the gates of death to life. Long life to you. In these few words, I cannot give full expression of my loving concern for you. I remain your child, Wiki Pauro' (translation from M. Simon, *Hui Aranga 1946–1996: Te Aranga Ake*. Wanganui, 1995, p.vii).

99 Valintine actually had an artificial leg. His wish to kneel by Suzanne's bed was a sign of real love.

100 *Evening Post*, 2 Oct. 1926.

101 Sister Anastasia was Australian, and her sister told her of hearing it over the 'wireless'.

102 11 Oct. 1926, Env. 85, HOC A.

103 T. H. A. Valintine, 'To all Sectional Heads in Head Office, including the Acting Director, Division of Dental Hygiene and the Medical Officers of Health in Wellington', 4 Oct. 1926, HOC A.

104 *NZ Times*, 6 Oct. 1926.

105 *Dominion*, 6 Oct. 1926.

106 *NZ Times*, 6 Oct. 1926.

107 Interview with author.

108 *Evening Post*, 6 Oct. 1926.

109 *The Month*, 19 Oct. 1926.

110 *NZ Times*, 4 Oct. 1926.

111 Memories of Merweh Madson, 24 Oct. 1970, Env. 88, HOC A.

112 'This is the message of love to our mother, to Mary Joseph who has looked after us. Go, Meri. Farewell, you who are our elder. Go to our parents and ancestors, to the people who have gone before, who held the faith when you lived on the Whanganui and cared for our bodily and spiritual well-being. Go, mother of the orphans and homeless, go to our Lord. He may take you in death, yet you will go to life.' My thanks to Pestal Pauro and Ma Butler of Ranana for this translation; thanks also to Dovey Taiaroa.

113 Aubert, *Manual*, p.50.

114 Aubert, *Directory*, p.88.

115 See I. Breward, 'Religion and New Zealand Society', *NZJH*, 13, 2, Oct. 1979.

116 P. O'Farrell, *Vanished Kingdoms*, pp.xvii, xxii.

117 'Re novitiate', ms, p.5, HOC A.

118 Breward, p.143.

119 Aubert, *Directory*, p.419. See also pp.242–43: 'Let us imitate the Holy Women of the Gospel, they who provided for His needs and accompanied Him everywhere, in His travels, and to the foot of the cross. They never fled as the Apostles did, but they proved themselves, up to the end, the faithful companions of Jesus.... In spite of the love of St. John and the repentance of St. Peter, they were the first at the Sepulchre, and deserved to be the first to see Jesus Risen.'

120 See B. Elsmore, *Mana from Heaven: a Century of Maori Prophets in New Zealand*, Tauranga, 1989; also J. Binney, *Redemption Songs*.

121 Fr M. O'Meeghan to author, 20 Oct. 1995.

122 L. Bland and A. John (eds), 'Autobiography and Biography', in *Gender and History*, 2, 1, Oxford and Cambridge Ma, 1990, p.5.

123 Group interview, 20 Sisters of Compassion with author, Wellington, 13 Dec. 1994.

124 To some extent, once her community became a papal congregation, she had to take on more of Roman centralism than might have been preferable in local circumstances. Her letters symbolise this; using the accustomed phrase, she bowed to 'kissing the sacred purple'. Although still more open than many, the congregation became more conformist. Her successors could not do all that she did in the exuberance of pioneer independence. They were under local pressure to conform as well – e.g. within four months of Suzanne's death, the Minutes, p.249, record: 'Karitane Home Opening: The Vice-Superior said that His Grace had advised sending a polite note to the Karitane Committee, thanking them for their invitation and saying "our duties will not permit of our being present" adding these gatherings are not the place for Religious.' Sr Bernadette Wrack, the archivist, comments: 'Mother Aubert would probably have just gone!'

125 Fr J. Durning, interview with author. Also Durning to author, July 1993: 'Karl Adam, a German thinker, says there is no pure Catholicism, i.e. no pure 100% presentation of the faith Christ gave to the world anywhere. It is always modified by the culture of a people, conditioned

according to their own ways of thinking, sense of values etc. . . . So in each country, indeed in each generation there are differences, as far as Catholicism is concerned, that don't vitiate the message but record it more or less purely. . . . She would have been influenced by her long and wide contact with N.Z. style, its ideas, in general its culture.'

126 Env. 88, HOC A.

127 Aubert to Sr Claver, 17 Sept. 1919, Env. 24, HOC A.
128 20 Dec. 1920, Env. 44, HOC A.
129 Interview with author.
130 Aubert to Sr Veronica, 26 April 1923, Env. 25, HOC A.

EPILOGUE

1   Aubert, *Manual*, p.35.
2   Aubert, *Manual*, p.86.

Bibliography

Archival Sources

Correspondence, reports and other primary material from a number of archives have been the major source material for this book. The main archives have been abbreviated.

AAL Archives de l'Archevêché de Lyon: archdiocesan archives, Lyon, holding documents relating to Saint-Nizier.

ACDA Auckland Catholic Diocesan Archives: documents filed under the bishop of the time, e.g. POM (Pompallier), CLE (Cleary), INT (Interregnum).

ACPF Archivio della Congregazione di Propaganda Fide, Rome: correspondence and reports on mission affairs.

ADL Archives Départementales de la Loire, St Etienne: civil records for St-Symphorien-de-Lay.

ADR Archives Départementales du Rhône, Lyon: civil records for Lyon and Tarare.

AFFM Archivio dei Fratri Franciscani Minori, Rome.

AIM Auckland Institute and Museum Library: holds Ruth Ross Collection, and other Auckland material.

AML Archives Municipales de Lyon: municipal records for the city of Lyon.

AN Archives Nationales, Paris.

APL Auckland Public Library: early civic documents, directories, almanacs, the Sir George Grey Collection.

APM Archivio Padri Maristi, Rome: Marist Fathers Archive, holding documents from all Marist sources.

  Archives Communales de Tarare.

  Archives des Religieuses de Notre Dame des Missions (Sisters of Our Lady of the Missions), Rome.

  Archives des Soeurs Bénédictines, Pont de Beauvoisin.

  Archives of All Saints Church, Taradale.

  Archives of Downside Abbey, Bath: Benedictine archives holding Gasquet material.

  Archives of New South Wales.

  Archives of the Sisters of St Joseph of Nazareth, Wanganui.

ASMA Auckland Sisters of Mercy Archives.

ATL Alexander Turnbull Library, National Library of New Zealand, Wellington.

CSV Archives des Clercs de Saint Viateur, Rome.

HOC A Home of Compassion Archives, Wellington: records of the Daughters of Our Lady of Compassion. Documents are filed under a numbered envelope system.

IRC Archives of the Irish College, Rome.

  Marist Archives, Mount St Mary's, Greenmeadows: holds Hawke's Bay background material, also a collection of the *Annales de la Propagation de la Foi*.

MAW Marist Archives, Wellington: main repository of Marist material in New Zealand.

NAA National Archives, Auckland Regional Office.

NAW National Archives Head Office, Wellington.

OPM   Archives de la Propagation de la Foi (Oeuvres Pontificales Missionnaires), Lyon
        and Paris: correspondence and reports on mission funding and management –
        Océanie H 31 (Auckland); H 34 (Wellington).
        Salvation Army Archives, Wellington.
WAA   Wellington Archdiocesan Archives.
WCC   Wellington City Council Archives.
        Wellington Sisters of Mercy Archives.
        Whanganui Regional Museum.

Published Works

Akenson, D. *Half the World from Home: Perspectives on the Irish in New Zealand, 1860–
    1950.* Wellington, 1990.
Arnold, R. *The Farthest Promised Land: English Villagers, New Zealand Immigrants of the
    1870s.* Wellington, 1981.
Arnold, R. *New Zealand's Burning: the Settlers' World in the Mid–1880s.* Wellington, 1994.
Aubert, S. *Directory of the Daughters of Our Lady of Compassion.* Wellington, 1922.
Aubert, S. *New and Complete Manual of Maori Conversation.* Wellington, 1885.
Bagnall, A. G. and G. Petersen. *William Colenso, Printer, Missionary, Botanist, Explorer,
    Politician: His Life and Journeys.* Wellington, 1948.
Barrett, T. 'Early Maori Schools', *New Zealand Founders' Society, Whanganui Branch,
    Newsletter,* 28, Nov. 1965.
Barrington, J. and T. Beaglehole. *Maori Schools in a Changing Society.* Wellington, 1974.
Bassett, M. *Sir Joseph Ward: a Political Biography.* Auckland, 1993.
Belich, J. *The New Zealand Wars and the Victorian Interpretation of Racial Conflict.*
    Auckland, 1986.
Binney, J. *The Legacy of Guilt: a Life of Thomas Kendall.* Auckland, 1968.
Binney, J. *Redemption Songs: a Life of Te Kooti Arikirangi Te Turuki.* Auckland, 1995.
Bonnafous, R. *Louis Querbes et les Catéchistes de Saint-Viateur.* Paris, 1993.
Boutry, P. 'Le mouvement vers Rome et le renouveau missionaire', in J. Le Goff and
    R. Rémond (eds), *Histoire de la France Religieuse,* v.3. Paris, 1991.
Boutry, P. 'Réflexions sur la confession au XIXe siècle: Autour d'une lettre de Soeur Marie-
    Zoé au Curé d'Ars (1858)', in *Pratiques de la Confession: Des Pères du désert à Vatican II,
    Quinze études d'histoire.* Paris, 1983.
Bowerbank, F. *A Doctor's Story.* Wellington, 1958.
Bradwell, C. *Fight the Good Fight: the Story of the Salvation Army in New Zealand
    1883–1983.* Wellington, 1983.
Braudel, F. *The Identity of France,* v.1: *History and Environment.* London, 1988.
Breward, I. 'Religion and New Zealand Society', in *NZJH,* 13, 2, 1979.
Brooker, S., R. Cambie and R. Cooper. *New Zealand Medicinal Plants.* Auckland, 1987.
Burgess, M. Entry on Hester Maclean, in C. Macdonald, M. Penfold and B. Williams (eds),
    The Book of New Zealand Women: Ko Kui Ma te Kaupapa. Wellington, 1991.
Burton, A. *The Maori at Home.* Dunedin, 1886.
Burton, A. *Through the King Country with the Camera: a Photographer's Diary.* Dunedin,
    1885.
Cholvy, G. *La religion en France de la fin du XVIIIe à nos jours.* Paris, 1991.
Cholvy, G. and Y.-M. Hilaire. *Histoire religieuse de la France contemporaine 1800/1880.*
    Toulouse, 1985.
Cochran, C. Entry on Thomas Turnbull, *Dictionary of New Zealand Biography, Vol. 2,*

1870–1900. Wellington, 1993.

Colenso, W. *The Authentic and Genuine History of the Signing of the Treaty of Waitangi, New Zealand, February 5 and 6, 1840*. Wellington, 1890.

Condon, K. *The Missionary College of All Hallows 1842–1891*. Dublin, 1986.

Coney, S. 'Health Organisations', in A. Else (ed.), *Women Together: a History of Women's Organisations in New Zealand*. Wellington, 1993.

Coste, J. and G. Lessard (eds). *Origines Maristes (1786–1836)*, v.1. Rome 1960.

Couturier, C. *Unswerving Journey: the Life of Mother Mary of the Heart of Jesus, Foundress of the Congregation of Our Lady of the Missions*, trans. R. Sheed. Toulouse, 1965/66.

Cumming, I. *Glorious Enterprise: the History of the Auckland Education Board, 1857–1957*. Christchurch, 1959.

David, R. *English Law and French Law: a Comparison in Substance*. London, 1980.

David, R. and H. de Vries. *The French Legal System: an Introduction to Civil Law Systems*. New York, 1958.

Davitt, M. *Life and Progress in Australasia*. London, 1898.

de Mijolla, M.-C. *Origins in Oceania, Missionary Sisters of the Society of Mary 1845–1931*. Rome, 1984.

de Rolland, E. and D. Clouzet. *Dictionnaire des Communes du Département du Rhône*, v.2. Lyon, 1903.

de Ségur, G. *Une Saison en Nouvelle-Zélande*. Paris, 1901.

Delany, Sr M. Veronica. *Gracious Is the Time*. Auckland, 1952.

Devaliant, J. *Kate Sheppard*. Auckland, 1992.

Dictionary of New Zealand Biography. *Volume One, 1769–1869*, gen. ed. W. H. Oliver. *Volume Two, 1870–1900*, gen. ed. C. Orange. Wellington, 1990 and 1993.

Drummond, J. *The Life and Work of Richard John Seddon*. Christchurch, 1906.

Dunmore, J. 'The First Contacts', in J. Dunmore (ed.), *The French and the Maori*. Waikanae, 1992.

Eldred-Grigg, S. *Pleasures of the Flesh: Sex and Drugs in Colonial New Zealand 1840–1915*. Wellington, 1984.

Else, A. *Women Together: a History of Women's Organisations in New Zealand*. Wellington, 1993.

Elsmore, B. *Mana from Heaven: a Century of Maori Prophets in New Zealand*. Tauranga, 1989.

Fairburn, M. *The Ideal Society and Its Enemies: the Foundations of Modern New Zealand Society 1850–1900*. Auckland, 1989.

Farnham, J. 'A Stirring and Christian Solidarity: Women in the Church of Lyon, 1800–1850'. *Forum Novum*, Dec. 1989.

Fine, Agnès. 'A propos du trousseau: une culture féminine?', in Michelle Perrot (ed.), *Une histoire des femmes, est-elle possible?* Paris, 1984.

Foale, M. *The Josephite Story*. Sydney, 1989.

Fuchs, R. *Abandoned Children: Foundlings and Child Welfare in Nineteenth-Century France*. New York, 1984.

Gadille, J. 'La Reconstruction du diocèse après la Révolution (1803–1839)' and 'Les Catholiques lyonnais et la question sociale (1831–1871)', in J. Gadille (ed.), *Le Diocèse de Lyon*. Paris, 1983.

Gardiner, P. *Mary MacKillop: an Extraordinary Australian*. Newtown, NSW, 1993.

Gibson, R. *A Social History of French Catholicism 1789–1914*. London, 1989.

Gibson, R. 'Le Catholicisme et les femmes en France au XIXe siècle', *Revue d'Histoire de l'Eglise de France*, 79, 202, 1993.

Grace, J. *Tuwharetoa*. Wellington, 1959.

Graham, J. 'Settler Society', in G. Rice (ed.), *Oxford History of New Zealand*, 2nd edn. Auckland, 1992.

Grey, G. *Polynesian Mythology and Ancient Traditional History of the New Zealand Race*, 2nd edn. Auckland, 1855.

Hamer, D. *The New Zealand Liberals: the Years of Power, 1891–1912*. Auckland, 1988.

Hardouin-Fugier, E. *Guide de Fourvière*. Commission de Fourvière, Lyon, undated.

Hood, L. *Minnie Dean: Her Life & Crimes*. Auckland, 1994.

Hosie, J. *Challenge: the Marists in Colonial Australia*. Sydney, 1987.

Hosie, S. *Anonymous Apostle: the Life of Jean-Claude Colin, Marist*. New York, 1967.

Hufton, O. *Women and the Limits of Citizenship in the French Revolution*. Toronto, 1992.

Isichei, E. Entry on Euphrasie Barbier, *Dictionary of New Zealand Biography, Vol. 2, 1870–1900*. Wellington, 1993.

Jackson, E. *Delving into the Past of Auckland's Suburbs*. Auckland, 1976.

Kemp, H. *The First Step to Maori Conversation*. Wellington, 1879.

Kerr, D. 'Priests, Parishioners, and Politics: Cabuchet, the Colins, and the Oath to the Civil Constitution', *Forum Novum*, June 1994.

Keys, L. *The Life and Times of Bishop Pompallier*. Christchurch, 1957.

Kirk, A. 'Te Taua Whakaora', *Journal of the Whanganui Historical Society*, 6, 1, May 1975.

Labrum, B. '"For the better discharge of our duties": Women's rights in Wanganui 1893–1903, *Women's Studies Journal*, Nov. 1990.

Labrum, B. Entry on Frances Ann Stewart, *Dictionary of New Zealand Biography, Vol. 2, 1870–1900*. Wellington, 1993.

Labrum, B. 'Wanganui Women's Political League 1893–c.1902', in A. Else (ed.), *Women Together: A History of Women's Organisations in New Zealand*. Wellington, 1993.

Labrum, B. Entry on Jessie Williamson, *Dictionary of New Zealand Biography, Vol. 2, 1870–1900*, Wellington, 1993.

Langlois, C. 'Féminisation du Catholicisme', 'Indicateurs du XIXe siècle. Pratique pascale et délais de baptême' and 'Institutions et modèles', in J. Le Goff and R. Rémond (eds), *Histoire de la France Religieuse*, v.3. Paris, 1991.

Langlois, C. *Le Catholicisme au féminin: les congrégations françaises à supérieure générale au XIXe siècle*. Paris, 1984.

Laracy, H. 'Paranoid Popery: Bishop Moran and Catholic Education in New Zealand', *New Zealand Journal of History*, 10, 1976.

Larkin, C. *A Certain Way: an Exploration of Marist Spirituality*. Rome, 1995.

Lawlor, P. *The Demanding God: Some Boyhood Recollections*. Wellington, 1972.

Lee, J. *'I have named it the Bay of Islands . . .'*. Auckland, 1983.

Le Goff, J. and R. Rémond. *Histoire de la France religieuse, v.3: XVIIIe–XIXe siècle, Du roi Très Chrétien à la laïcité républicaine*. Paris, 1991.

Lennard, G. *Sir William Martin: the Life of the First Chief Justice of New Zealand*. Auckland, 1961.

Les Soeurs de Saint-Charles, Annales de la Congrégation, 1860–1874. Lyon, 1915.

Levine, S. *A Standard for the People: the 150th Anniversary of the Wellington Hebrew Congregation, 1843–1993*. Wellington, 1995.

Leys, T. (ed.). *Brett's Colonists' Guide and Cyclopedia of Useful Knowledge*. Auckland, 1883.

Lineham, P. 'How Institutionalized Was Protestant Piety in Nineteenth-Century New Zealand?', *Journal of Religious History*, 13, 1985.

Lynch, K. *Family, Class, and Ideology in Early Industrial France: Social Policy and the Working-Class Family 1825–1848*. Wisconsin, 1988.

Macdonald, C. *A Woman of Good Character: Single Women as Immigrant Settlers in Nineteenth-century New Zealand*. Wellington, 1990.

Macdonald, C., M. Penfold and B. Williams (eds). *The Book of New Zealand Women: Ko Kui Ma te Kaupapa*. Wellington, 1991.

McEldowney, D. 'Ultima Thule to Little Bethel', *Landfall*, 77, March 1966.

McKay, F. *The Marist Laity: Finding the Way Envisaged by Father Colin*. Rome, 1991.

Mackey, J. *The Making of a State Education System: the Passing of the New Zealand Education Act, 1877*. London, 1967.

Manson, C. and C. *Doctor Agnes Bennett*. London, 1960.

Marand-Fouquet, C. *La femme au temps de la Révolution*. Paris, 1989.

Martin, M. (Lady). *He Pukapuka Whakaatu Tikanga mo nga Rongoa mo nga Kai*. Auckland, 1869.

Matthews, E. 'Sarah Mary Gillin of Kamaka', in *Women of Westland and Their Families*. Westland Branch NCW, v.2, 1977.

Mein Smith, P. 'Truby King in Australia', *New Zealand Journal of History*, 22, 1, April 1988.

Metge, J. *The Maoris of New Zealand: Rautahi*. London, 1976.

Monfat, A. *Les Origines de la Foi Catholique dans la Nouvelle-Zélande*. Lyon, 1890.

Moran, P. *History of the Catholic Church in Australasia*. Sydney, no date.

Morton, H. B. 'When Auckland Was Young – Life in the Early Sixties', supplement to *New Zealand Herald*. June–July 1923.

Moses C. *French Feminism in the Nineteenth Century*. New York, 1984.

Munro, J. 'Suzanne Aubert and the Meeting of Language', *New Zealand Language Teacher*, 22, 1996.

Naidenoff, G. *Pauline Jaricot*. Paris, 1986.

New Zealand Official Year-book 1909. Wellington, 1910.

Numbers, R. and D. Amundsen. *Caring and Curing: Health and Medicine in the Western Religious Traditions*. New York, 1986.

O'Connor, P. 'Sectarian Conflict in New Zealand 1911–1920', *Political Science*, 19, 1, July 1967.

O'Farrell, P. *The Catholic Church and Community in Australia: a History*. Melbourne, 1977.

O'Farrell, P. *The Irish in Australia*. Sydney, 1986.

O'Farrell, P. *Vanished Kingdoms: Irish in Australia and New Zealand*. Sydney, 1990.

Oliver, W. H. 'Christianity Among the New Zealanders', *Landfall*, 77, 1966.

Olssen, E. 'Towards a New Society', in G. Rice (ed.), *Oxford History of New Zealand*, 2nd edn. Auckland, 1992.

Olssen, E. 'Truby King and the Plunket Society: an Analysis of a Prescriptive Ideology', *New Zealand Journal of History*, 15, 1, April 1981.

O'Meeghan, M. *Held Firm by Faith: a History of the Diocese of Christchurch 1840–1987*. Christchurch, 1988.

O'Meeghan, M. 'Catholic Beginnings in New Zealand: an Overview', *CBRF Journal*, 121, 1990.

O'Meeghan, M. 'The French Connection', *New Zealand Historic Places*, 44, Nov. 1993.

O'Meeghan, M. 'The French Marist Maori Mission', in J. Dunmore (ed.), *The French and the Maori*. Waikanae, 1992.

O'Meeghan, M. 'The Marist Family', reprint from *Bedean* magazine, Christchurch, 1966.

Orange, C. *The Treaty of Waitangi*. Wellington, 1987.

O'Sullivan, O. *Apostle in Aotearoa: a Biography of Jeremiah Purcell O'Reily O.F.M.Cap., Wellington's first Catholic pastor.* Auckland, 1977.

Parsons, P. Entry on Paora Kaiwhata, *Dictionary of New Zealand Biography, Vol. 2, 1870–1900.* Wellington, 1993.

Payton, E. *Round about New Zealand: Notes from a Journal of Three Years' Wanderings in the Antipodes.* London, 1888.

Perrot, Michelle (ed.). *Une histoire des femmes, est-elle possible?* Paris, 1984.

Phillips, J. *A Man's Country? The Image of the Pakeha Male: a History.* Auckland, 1987.

Polack, J. *Manners and Customs of the New Zealanders.* London, 1840.

Pompallier, J.-B. *Etat succinct et précis de la Mission Catholique à la Nouvelle-Zélande, et spécialement dans le diocèse d'Auckland.* Paris, 1859.

Pompallier, J.-B. *Instruction sur la sagesse chrétienne.* Paris, 1859.

Pompallier, J.-B. 'Petite collection de mots maoris', in *Notes grammaticales sur la langue maorie ou néo-zélandaise.* Rome, 1860.

Pompallier, J.-B. 'Souvenirs de la Nouvelle-Zélande, et des travaux de l'Eglise pour elle', in *Etat succinct et précis de la Mission Catholique à la Nouvelle-Zélande, et spécialement dans le diocèse d'Auckland.* Paris, 1859.

Porter, F. *Born to New Zealand: a Biography of Jane Maria Atkinson.* Wellington, 1989.

Porter, F. (ed.). *The Turanga Journals, 1840-1850: Letters and Journals of William and Jane Williams.* Wellington, 1974.

Porter, F. and C. Macdonald (eds). *'My hand will write what my heart dictates', the unsettled lives of women in nineteenth-century New Zealand as told to their sisters, family and friends.* Auckland, 1996.

Power, A. *Sisters of St Joseph of the Sacred Heart: New Zealand Story, 1883–1983.* Auckland, 1983.

Pugsley, C. *Te Hokowhitu a Tu: the Maori Pioneer Battalion in the First World War.* Auckland, 1995.

Renwick, W. Entry on James Henry Pope, *Dictionary of New Zealand Biography, Vol. 2, 1870–1900.* Wellington, 1993.

Riley, M. *Maori Healing and Herbal.* Wellington, 1994.

Roger, A. and A. Sorel. *Codes et Lois Usuelles*, 41 edn. Paris, 1909.

Sallès, A. *Liszt à Lyon (1826, 1836, 1837, 1844, 1845).* Paris, 1911.

Salmond, A. *Two Worlds: First Meetings Between Maori and Europeans 1642–1772.* Auckland, 1991.

Servant, C. *Customs and Habits of the New Zealanders, 1838-1842*, trans. J. Glasgow, ed. D. Simmons. Wellington, 1973.

Siegfried, A. *Democracy in New Zealand.* London, 1914.

Simmons, E. *A Brief History of the Catholic Church in New Zealand.* Auckland, 1978.

Simmons, E. *In Cruce Salus: a History of the Diocese of Auckland, 1848–1980.* Auckland, 1982.

Simmons, E. *Pompallier, Prince of Bishops.* Auckland, 1984.

Simmons, E. Entry on Jean-Baptiste François Pompallier, *Dictionary of New Zealand Biography, Vol. 1, 1769–1869.* Wellington, 1990.

Simon, M. (ed.). *Hui Aranga 1946-1996: Te Aranga Ake.* Wanganui, 1995.

Smart, M. and A. Bates. *The Wanganui Story.* Wanganui, 1972.

Stewart-McDougall, M. *The Artisan Republic: Revolution, Reaction, and Resistance in Lyon, 1848–1851.* Montreal, 1984.

Stone, R. *Makers of Fortune: a Colonial Business Community and Its Fall.* Auckland, 1973.

Sutch, W. *Poverty and Progress in New Zealand*. Wellington, 1969.

Sweetman, R. *Bishop in the Dock: the Sedition Trial of James Liston*. Auckland, forthcoming.

Sweetman, R. 'New Zealand Catholicism and the Irish Issue, 1914–1922', in W. Shiels and D. Wood (eds), *The Churches, Ireland and the Irish*. Oxford, 1989.

Tackett, T. *Religion, Revolution, and Regional Culture in Eighteenth Century France: the Ecclesiastical Oath of 1791*. Princeton, 1986.

Taylor, N. (ed.). *The Journal of Ensign Best, 1837–1843*. Wellington, 1966.

Taylor, R. *Te Ika a Maui or New Zealand and its Inhabitants*. London, 1855.

Tennant, M. *Paupers and Providers: Charitable Aid in New Zealand*. Wellington, 1989.

Tennant, M. Entry on Mary Joseph Aubert, *Dictionary of New Zealand Biography, Vol. 2, 1870–1900*. Wellington, 1993.

Thiercelin, Dr L. *Journal d'un baleinier: Voyages en Océanie*, v.1. Paris, 1866.

Thorpe, O. *Mary MacKillop*. Sydney, 1980.

Vovelle, M. 'Du serment constitutionnel a l'ex-voto peint: un exemple d'histoire régressive', in J. Le Goff and R. Rémond (eds), *Histoire de la France Religieuse*, v.3. Paris, 1991.

Waldersee, J. *A Grain of Mustard Seed: the Society for the Propagation of the Faith and Australia, 1837–1977*. Sydney, 1983.

Warner, M. *Alone of All Her Sex: the Myth and Cult of the Virgin Mary*. London, 1976.

Watson, Fr M. (presumed author). *The Society of Jesus in Australia*, c.1910 (no title page).

Webster, A. and P. Perry (eds). *The Religious Factor in New Zealand Society*. Palmerston North, 1989.

Williams, H. W. *A Bibliography of Printed Maori to 1900*. Wellington, 1924.

Williams, W. *A Dictionary of the New Zealand Language*, 3rd edn. London, 1871.

Williams, W. *Christianity among the New Zealanders*. London, 1867.

Wiltgen, R. *The Founding of the Roman Catholic Church in Oceania 1825 to 1850*. Canberra, 1979.

Wright-St Clair, R. *The Order of St John in New Zealand*. Wellington, 1977.

Young, D. and B. Foster. *Faces of the River: New Zealand's Living Water*, Wellington, 1986.

Zeldin, T. (ed.). *Conflicts in French Society: Anticlericalism, Education and Morals in the Nineteenth Century*. London, 1970.

Zeldin, T. *France 1848–1945*, v.1: *Ambition, Love and Politics*. Oxford, 1973; v.2: *Intellect, Taste and Anxiety*. Oxford, 1977.

Unpublished works

Aloysius, Sr. 'Reminiscences', typescript, Sisters of St Joseph of Nazareth archives, Wanganui.

Anderson, P. 'Reminiscences', ms, CY Reel 135, p.98, Mitchell Library, Sydney.

Anderson, R. '"The Hardened Frail Ones": Women and Crime in Auckland, 1845–1870', MA thesis, Univ. of Auckland, 1981.

Barrington, J. 'Maori Education and Society 1867–1940', Victoria Univ. thesis, 1965.

Beaglehole, T. 'Maori Schools 1816–1880', Victoria Univ. thesis, 1955.

Bergin, P. 'Hoani Papita to Paora: the Marist Missions of Hiruharama and Otaki, 1883–1914', MA thesis, Univ. of Auckland, 1986.

Campbell, M. 'The Evolution of Hawke's Bay Landed Society, 1850–1914', PhD thesis, Victoria Univ., 1972.

Dictionary of New Zealand Biography database files, for some information on Hawke's Bay and West Coast families named in diary of Suzanne's 1888–89 collecting tour.

Durning, J. 'History of the Maori Missions', typescript, MAW.

Elphick, J. 'Auckland 1870–1874: a Social Portrait', MA thesis, Univ. of Auckland, 1974.

Ennis, Mother Paula. 'A brief sketch of the Missionary Labours of the Sisters of Mercy, Auckland, New Zealand, 1850–1888', ASMA.

Fisher, Eric. 'Wanganui River Settlements', typescript, 1969,Whanganui Regional Museum.

Fleming, P. 'Eugenics in New Zealand 1900–1940', MA thesis, Massey Univ., 1981.

Girardet, E. 'La Véridique Histoire de St Symphorien, Bourg de route, et de la Ville de Lay sous la Révolution et l'Empire', typescript, St Symphorien de Lay, 1981.

Gray, J. 'Potions, Pills and Poisons: Quackery in New Zealand, circa 1900–1915', BA Hons paper, Univ. of Otago, 1980.

Katene, S. 'The Administration of Maori Land in the Aotea District 1900–1927', MA thesis, Victoria Univ., 1990.

Kirk, M. 'The Story of the Foundation of the Sisters of Mercy in Gisborne, 1894–1904', research essay, 1994, ASMA.

Laracy, H. 'The Life and Context of Bishop Patrick Moran', MA thesis, Victoria Univ., 1964.

Lynch, J. 'The Struggle between Denominationalism and Secularism in Auckland Education 1840–1877', MA thesis, Univ. of Auckland, 1958.

Mackey, J. 'Catholic Schools and the Denominational System in Auckland 1840–1868', MA thesis, Univ. of Auckland, 1950.

Mannix, J. 'Mission Residence and Properties, 1850–1971', typescript, Mount St Mary's archives, Greenmeadows.

McDonald, Walter. Diary 1859–60, POM 28-3/1, ACDA.

McFadden, A. 'My Memories of the time I was in Mother Mary Aubert's Home at Jerusalem and the Home of Compassion, Island Bay', 1971, HOC A.

McLaren, I. 'Whitcombe's Story Books: a Trans-Tasman Survey', typescript, Melbourne, 1984.

McMahon, J. 'John McMahon Remembers', 4 March 1934, Env. 8, HOC A.

Moller, Sr Angela. 'Reminiscences of Mother Mary Joseph Aubert, Foundress of the Sisters of Compassion', seven typescript volumes (a combination of biography and reminiscences), 1945, HOC A.

Mooney, K. 'Meeanee Roman Catholic Mission, Hawke's Bay', typescript, MAW.

Mulcahy, M. 'Catholic Missionary Activity in Hawke's Bay 1841–1861', typescript, 208/23-C, MAW.

Ormond, H. Diary 1882. MS 1741, Acc. 79-151/2, ATL.

Our Pioneer Sisters, excerpts from Correspondence 1836–83, Missionary Sisters of the Society of Mary, typescript, Rome, 1973.

Roach, K. 'Venerable John Claude Colin and the Mission in New Zealand 1838–1848', doctoral thesis, Gregorian University, Rome, 1963.

Robinson, J. 'Of Diverse Persons, Men and Women and Whores: Women and Crime in Nineteenth Century Canterbury', MA thesis, Univ. of Canterbury, 1983.

Roche, C. 'L'Enseignement médical à Lyon de 1821 à 1877', thèse Lyon MED, 1975.

Rochefort, A. 'Les Soeurs de Saint-Charles de Lyon et l'éducation féminine au 19e siècle (1802–1904)', thèse de maîtrise, Lyon II, 1989.

Ross, R. 'Comments on Vol. 1 of the Reminiscences of Mother Mary Joseph Aubert, Foundress of the Sisters of Compassion', Auckland, 14 Jan. 1972, Env. 59, HOC A.

Seed, G. 'The Churches and Residential Care of Children in Auckland', MA thesis, Univ.

of Auckland, 1967.

Simmons, N. 'Archbishop Francis Redwood, His Contribution to Catholicism in New Zealand', MA thesis, Massey Univ., 1981.

Strevens, D. 'The Sisters of St Joseph of Nazareth, New Zealand', MTheol thesis, Melbourne College of Divinity, 1995.

Sweetman, R. 'The Catholic Church in Nineteenth Century New Zealand', paper delivered at Canada–New Zealand Comparative Seminar, University of Edinburgh, 19 May, 1985.

Sweetman, R. 'New Zealand Catholicism, War, Politics and the Irish Issue 1912–1922', PhD thesis, Cambridge Univ., 1990.

Tennant, M. 'Women and Welfare: the Response of Three New Zealand Women to Social Problems of the Period 1890–1910', research paper, BA Hons, Massey Univ., 1974.

Turner, P. 'The Politics of Neutrality: the Catholic Mission and the Maori 1838–1870', MA thesis, Univ. of Auckland, 1986.

Tyrrell, Sister Borgia. 'Memoir of Mother Cecilia Maher', 1877, ASMA.

Vaney, N. 'The Dual Tradition. Irish Catholics and French Priests in New Zealand: the West Coast Experience, 1865–1910', MA thesis, Univ. of Canterbury, 1976.

Vibaud, J. 'The Society of Mary in the Wanganui–Taranaki', ms, c.1932, MAW.

Viard, P. J. 'Memoirs', WAA.

Webber, Sr Clotilde. 'Notes on Nursing Work', ms, 1932, HOC A.

Williams, W. L. Journal, v.7, 1872–73; v.8, 1873–74; v.10; MS Papers 2463, 2464, 2466, ATL.

Oral Sources

Notes made by Fr Maurice Mulcahy from conversations mainly in the 1960s, Env. 89, HOC A.

Fr P. Bergin. 'The Wanganui River Catholic Mission, 1929–69', oral history essay for MA, Univ. of Auckland, 1985. Bergin interviewed over 30 people of the river.

Sr Eustace Conaglen, interviewed by M. Graham and P. Crombie, Silverstream, 19 June 1991.

'Personal Impressions', Srs Adelma, Benedict, Elizabeth, Melchior, Monica, Rose, interviewed by Fr Bernard Hehir, Wellington, 1976, HOC A.

Interviews 1992–94 by Jessie Munro with:

Joan Akapita, Ohakune, 13 May 1993
Hohi (Sophie) Albert, Kaiwhaiki, 27 April 1993
Teira (Sarah) Ashby, Te Kuiti, 13 May 1993
Harry Ashworth, Trentham, 9 Sept. 1993
Kathleen Browne, Wellington, 6 June 1993
Patricia Charlton, Palmerston North, 29 April 1993
Cyril Collins, Wellington, 9 Nov. 1993
Sr Eustace Conaglen, Silverstream, 25 April 1992, 9 July 1992
Sr Philippine Dunne, Wanganui, 1 Aug. 1992
Fr James Durning, Wanganui, 15 May 1993
Ivan Emia, Flaxmere, 3 May 1993
Sr Anne Galvin, Wellington, 9 Nov. 1993
Elsie Gibbons, Eastbourne, 11 August 1993
John Haami, Wanganui, 18 May 1993
Ada Hina, Wanganui, 19 May 1993
Jeanne and Peter Latimer, Waikanae, 2 Nov. 1994

Sr Dorothea Meade, Wanganui, 1 Aug. 1992
Sr Winifred Moriarty, Wellington, 10 Nov. 1993
Sr Veronica O'Brien, Wellington, 21 Sept. 1993
Sr Brendan O'Gorman, Wellington, 19 Oct. 1993
Patrick Parsons, Taradale, 22 Jan. 1993
Lucy Pauro, Kaiwhaiki, 27 April 1993
Pestall Pauro, Wanganui, 28 April 1993
Solange Poulet, Pont de Beauvoisin, 15 Jan. 1994
Peti (Bessie) Poumua, Wanganui, 17 May 1993
Fr Claude Rozier, Lyon, 12 Jan. 1994
Erina Scanlon, Wanganui, 28 April 1993
Natalie Te Huia, Pipiriki, 14 May 1993
James Walker, Wellington, 29 Sept. 1993
George Waretini, Wanganui, 18 May 1993
Weheora Wanihi (Wallace), Hiruharama, 14 May 1993
and group interview with 20 Sisters of Compassion, Wellington, 13 Dec. 1994.

List of illustrations

France: between pages 40 and 41
Suzanne's parish church of Saint-Nizier today.
Pauline Jaricot, Saint-Nizier parishioner.
Suzanne's devotional card: 'Our Lady of Fourvière, pray for us'.
The sanctuary to Our Lady of Fourvière.
St-Symphorien-de-Lay.
Suzanne's family: father Louis Aubert; younger brother Camille; mother Clarice (probably); elder
   brother Alphonse.
Tarare in 1860.
Pilgrims cluster around the Curé d'Ars.
The Sisters of Charity at work.
Votive painting, Fourvière, 1865, probably showing Aubert family.
Further works of the Sisters of Charity.

Auckland and Hawke's Bay: between pages 104 and 105
Auckland in 1859.
Lucie Pompallier (Mother Mary Baptist).
Antoine Pompallier.
Bishop Jean-Baptiste François Pompallier.
Freeman's Bay, Auckland, 1863.
Bishop Thomas Croke.
Nazareth Institute, c.1866.
Suzanne, Peata and their pupils, probably 1869.
Father Victor Poupinel.
Father Euloge Reignier.
Father Antoine Séon.
Father François Yardin.
The presbytery and church at Meanee, 1870s.
The new presbytery, c.1880.
Brother Basile Montchalin.
The grape harvest, Meanee, 1880s.
Suzanne's pocket devotional books.
Bishop Francis Redwood.
The church at Pakipaki.
Urupene Puhara and his wife, Marata.

Hiruharama: between pages 152 and 153
Hiruharama on the Whanganui River, early 1880s.
Taiwhati.
Poutini.
Ranana, 1885.
Neri Metera.
Sisters of St Joseph, Wanganui.
Wanganui in 1881.
Government schoolhouse at Hiruharama.
Manuscript and printed pages from Suzanne Aubert's *New and Complete Manual of Maori
   Conversation*.
The church of Hato Hohepa (St Joseph) at Hiruharama, built 1885.
First sisters of the Third Order Regular of Mary in New Zealand.
Suzanne and Sister Magdalen on the collecting tour, late 1880s.
The Salvation Army arrives at Hiruharama, 1889.
Rebuilt church and presbytery at Hiruharama.
Building timbers stacked behind Fathers Soulas and Broussard.
Father Christophe Soulas.
Te Manihera Keremeneta in Catholic band uniform.
Hiruharama to Kauaeroa (1982).

Index

As many people named in this book are mentioned primarily in their connection with various religious orders and organisations, they are listed here under their order or organisation. For example, the individual Sisters of Compassion are listed under *Sisters of Compassion*; each woman's family name is bracketed after her name as a religious sister. Marist priests and brothers are listed in two groupings under *Society of Mary*, according to whether they feature within New Zealand (even temporarily as Visitors) or whether they were in correspondence from Europe; however, major Marist entries (O'Shea, Poupinel, Redwood, Reignier, Séon, Soulas, Viard, Yardin) are listed separately. For space reasons there are three further groupings: *Doctors and nurses helping Suzanne Aubert*; *French influences*; and *Wellington helpers and contributors*.